Demographic Diversity and Change in the Central American Isthmus

EDITED BY

Anne R. Pebley

Luis Rosero-Bixby

RAND

AUTHORS

Dolores Acevedo. The Lewin Group, 9302 Lee Highway, Suite 500, Fairfax, VA, 22031. Fax: (703) 218-5501, Email: doloresa@opr.princeton.edu.

José David Araya. Asociación Demográfica Salvadoreña, 25 Avenida Norte #583, San Salvador, El Salvador. Fax: (503) 225-0879.

Richard E. Bilsborrow. Carolina Population Center, University of North Carolina, 123 West Franklin Street, Chapel Hill, NC, 27516-3997. Fax: (919) 966-6638, Email: richard_bilsborrow@unc.edu.

José Mario Cáceres Henríquez. Asociación Demográfica Salvadoreña, 25 Avenida Norte #583, San Salvador, El Salvador. Fax: (503) 225-0879.

CELADE. Casilla 91, Santiago, Chile. Fax: (56-2) 2080196.

Isabella Danel. Womens's Health and Fertility Branch, Division of Reproductive Health, Centers for Disease Control and Prevention, MS K-34, 4770 Buford Highway NE, Atlanta, GA, 30341-3724. Fax: (770) 488-5965.

Erwin Rolando Díaz. Instituto Nacional de Estadística, Edificio América, 8a. Calle 9-55, Zona 1, Guatemala, Guatemala. Fax: (502) 232-4790

Laurence M. Grummer-Strawn. Maternal and Child Health Branch, Division of Nutrition, Centers for Disease Control and Prevention, 4770 Buford Highway, MS K25, Atlanta, GA, 30341-3724. Fax: (770) 488-4728.

José Miguel Guzmán. Adviser on Demographic Analysis, UNFPA Country Support Team, Office for Latin America and the Caribbean, Tomás de Figueroa 2451, Santiago, Chile. Fax: (56-2) 206-6105. Email: jmguzman@unfpacst.c1 - URL: http://www.unfpacst.c1

Peter H. Herlihy. Department of Geography, University of Kansas, 221 Lindley Hall, Lawrence, KS, 66045-2121. Fax: (785) 864-5276, Email: Herlihy@Falcon.cc.ukans.edu.

Albert I. Hermalin. Population Studies Center, University of Michigan, 1225 South University Ave., Ann Arbor, MI, 48104-2590. Fax: (313) 998-7415, Email: alberth@umich.edu.

Catherine Hoover-Castañeda. Doctoral Student, Department of Geography, University of Texas at Austin. Col. Loma Linda Norte, Calzada Los Alpes, #2333, Tegucigalpa, Honduras.

David Hubacher. Family Health International, PO Box 13950, Research Triangle Park, NC, 27709. Fax: (919) 544-7261, Email: dhubacher@fhi.org.

Elena Hurtado. Instituto de Nutrición para Centroamérica y Panamá (INCAP), Calzada Roosevelt 2-11, Zona 11. Apartado Postal 1188, Guatemala, Guatemala. Fax: (502) 4-736529.

Rodney Knight. International Population Fellow, 109 South Observatory, School of Public Health, University of Michigan, Ann Arbor, MI, 48109. Fax: (703) 875-4693, E-mail: knight@usaid.gov.

Uli Locher. Department of Sociology, McGill University, Stephen Leacock Building, 855 Sherbrooke Street West, Montreal, PQ, Canada H3A 2T7. Fax: (514) 398-3403, Email: IND6@MUSICB.MCGILL.CA.

W. George Lovell. Department of Geography, Queen's University, Kingston, Canada, K7L 3N6. Fax: (613) 545-6122.

Christopher H. Lutz. Plumsock Mesoamerican Studies, P.O. Box 38, Route 106, South Woodstock, VT, 05071.

Vincent McElhinny. Department of Political Science, University of Pittsburgh, PA, 15260. Fax: (412) 648-7277.

Ligia Moya de Madrigal. Caja Costarricense de Seguro Social, San José, Costa Rica. Fax: (506) 255-2549.

Harry Anthony Patrinos. World Bank, 1818 H Street, NW, Washington, DC, 20433, Fax: (202) 522-3233, E-mail: HPATRINOS@WORLDBANK.ORG.

Héctor Pérez. Centro de Investigaciones Históricas, Universidad de Costa Rica, Apartado 377-2050, San José, Costa Rica. Fax: (506) 234-6701, Email: hperez@cariari.ucr.ac.cr.

Marco Pinel. EFHS. Ministerio de Salud Pública, Honduras.

Ann P. Riley. Independent Consultant. Fax: (301) 270-8084, Email: ariley@capaccess.org.

Arodys Robles. Programa Centroamericano de Población, Universidad de Costa Rica, Apartado 833-2050, San José, Costa Rica. Fax: (506) 234-6701, Email: arodysr@cariari.ucr.ac.cr.

Luis Rosero-Bixby. Programa Centroamericano de Población / INISA, Universidad de Costa Rica, Apartado 833-2050, San José, Costa Rica. Fax: (506) 234-6701, Email: lrosero@cariari.ucr.ac.cr.

Juan Carlos Salguero. Asociación Demográfica Salvadoreña, 25 Avenida Norte #583, San Salvador, El Salvador. Fax: (503) 225-0879.

Renee Samara. The Alan Guttmacher Institute, 120 Wall Street, New York, NY 10005. Fax: (212) 248-1951.

Irma Sandoval Carvajal. IDESPO, Universidad Nacional Apdo. 86-3000, Heredia, Costa Rica. Fax: (506) 237-1104, Email: isandova@irazu.una.ac.cr.

Mitchell A. Seligson. Department of Political Science, University of Pittsburgh, 4N27 Forbes Quadrangle, Pittsburgh, PA, 15260. Fax: (412) 648-7277, Email: seligson+@pitt.edu.

Paul Stupp. Division of Reproductive Health, Centers for Disease Control and Prevention, MS K35, 4770 Buford Highway, NE, Atlanta, GA, 30341. Fax: (770) 488-5965, Email: pws2@ccddrh1.em.cdc.gov.

Margarita Suazo. Director of Evaluation, Asociación Hondureña de Planificación de Familia (ASHONPLAFA). Col. Alameda, Calle Principal. Apartado Postal 625, Tegucigalpa, Honduras.

Stanley Terrel. Child Survivor Advisor, U.S. Agency for International Development (USAID)/Honduras.

CONTENTS

PREFACE AND ACKNOWLEDGMENTS

The chapters in this volume were originally presented at the International Conference on the Population of the Central American Isthmus, organized by the Central American Population Program (PCP) at the University of Costa Rica in collaboration with colleagues at RAND. Both the papers at the conference and the subset that are included in this volume represent research in a broad range of disciplines including demography, public health, anthropology, history, sociology, human ecology, and economics. The conference played an important role in bringing together an international group of researchers working on related issues in the region. The objective of this volume is to provide, in one central location, a collection of recent research on demographic, social, and environmental issues in the Central American Isthmus for English-speaking readers, both those who are not familiar with the region and those who know it well. For Spanish-speakers, the same collection of papers has been independently published as *De los Mayas a la planificación familiar: Demografía del Istmo* (L. Rosero Bixby, A. Pebley, and A. Bermúdez Méndez, editors) by the Editorial de la Universidad de Costa Rica.

Neither the conference nor this volume would have been possible without the support of the Andrew W. Mellon Foundation. Both PCP and RAND have been fortunate to have the energetic encouragement and strong support of Carolyn Makinson at Mellon, on this and other Central America-related projects. The selection of papers and initial editorial work was carried out by Luis Rosero-Bixby and Alicia Bermúdez-Méndez and their colleagues at the University of Costa Rica. Papers originally written in Spanish were translated primarily by the authors or Loren Lewis at RAND. The English volume could not have been produced without Rachel Veerman, who maintained communication with authors throughout the western hemisphere, skillfully converted word processing, graphics, and map files created in innumerable software packages into compatible format, made original reproductions of many of the graphs and maps, proofread and double checked textual material, and coordinated all aspects of the production.

INTRODUCTION

ANNE R. PEBLEY

Many North Americans would be surprised to learn that neither Panama nor Belize are considered Central American countries, in the traditional sense, despite their obvious geographic location in the region (see Figure 1). The reasons provide tantalizing clues to the complex social and political history of the region, in its many incarnations. Since the Federation of Central America declared its independence from Mexico (itself newly independent from Spain) "Central America" has referred exclusively to Guatemala, El Salvador, Honduras, Nicaragua, and Costa Rica. The Federation lasted only until 1839, but the desire for some form of economic and political integration among these five nations has remained strong. The territories which now comprise these countries (plus Belize) share an even longer collective history as part of the Audiencia of Guatemala during the three hundred years of Spanish colonial rule, and in the case of Guatemala, El Salvador, and Honduras, many hundreds of years of settlement by the Maya and related societies in the preconquest period.

Despite their location, Panama and Belize have separate histories from other countries in the region and have only recently begun to be integrated economically and socially. At the time of independence in 1821, Panama chose union with Colombia and subsequently became independent from Colombia in only 1903, under the protection of the U.S. Navy (Pérez-Brignoli, 1989). Belize remained a British colony until 1981 and only in the past few years has Guatemala given up its claims to Belizean territory.

In this volume, we refer collectively to all seven countries located in the Isthmus as Central America, although the title of the book is more precise to avoid confusion.

For the most part, North Americans' views of Central America are refracted through the restrictive lens of recent U.S. foreign policy: the controversial Panama Canal Treaty, the Sandinista triumph in Nicaragua, guerrilla movements in Guatemala, the El Salvadorian civil war, the Iran-Contra Scandal associated with the U.S. support for Contras in Nicaragua, the capture and trial of Manuel Noriega, and revelations about U.S. support for violent Guatemala military regimes. There is no doubt that the U.S. and U.S. citizens have played a disproportionately large (and often malign) role in Central American history. Historical examples include the take-over of Nicaragua by the Tennessee adventurer William Walker in 1855, the building of the Panama Canal, the political activity of the United Fruit Company in several countries, the CIA-organized overthrow of the liberal Arbenz regime in Guatemala in 1954, and many, many others. Excellent accounts of this history are provided by Pérez-Brignoli (1989) and LeFeber (1993).

As the papers in this volume make clear, however, the Central American experience is important for North Americans and others to understand, for reasons unrelated to classic U.S. foreign policy interests. From a demographic perspective, Central American countries have experienced the decimation of indigenous populations and civilizations during and after the Spanish conquest, high fertility rates and dramatic fertility declines, rapid mortality declines and stubbornly high mortality rates, large intra-regional and international migration streams, and major refugee movements. Contrasts between neighboring countries in the region are often large and provide important lessons about the macrolevel as well as microlevel determinants of demographic behavior. For example, in the early 1960s, Costa Rica and Nicaragua both had very high fertility rates (an average of about 7 children per woman) but by the early 1990s, the Costa Rican fertility rate had fallen to 3, a level close to many industrialized countries. Nicaragua experienced a substantially less precipitous fertility decline; by the early 1990s, its total fertility rate was about 5 children per woman. Chapters by Guzmán, Hermalin et al., CELADE, and others in this volume show that the reasons behind these significant differences in demographic experience are complex and reward careful study.

Central Americans' experience with ethnic and cultural identity also provides considerable food for thought for scholars and others concerned with the meaning of ethnicity and the process of cultural change. Despite the ravages of the conquest and post-conquest eras, the indigenous population of Central America, and particularly in Guatemala and on the Atlantic coast of Nicaragua, has survived the past 400 years. In fact, high indigneous fertility rates in Guatemala combined with gradual improvements in health status and a reduction in political violence means the substantial majority of Guatemalans in the 21st century are likely to be indigenous (instead of the current 50% of the population). Yet with reduced repression and majority rather than minority status, the indigenous population may face a new set of problems related to maintaining its own distinct ethnicity (Rohter, 1997). There are also several other major ethnic groups in Central America including mestizos, creoles, garifuna, and those of European origin. Because of the unique history of each group, the choice between integration or retention of cultural distinctiveness is an important issue for each group. Several chapters in this volume provide a broad view of the history and current circumstances of different ethnic groups.

Cultural identity is also under threat in Central America because of the growing import of cultural influences from abroad, particularly from the United States. While U.S. citizens frequently fret about changes in U.S. society due to immigrants from Latin America, cultural exchange is a two way street. In fact, to this observer, the influence of the North American culture appears far more pervasive in Central America than the influence of Latin American culture in the U.S. The availability of cable television (including CNN, the Cartoon Network, and local U.S. channels), the ease of air travel, and the size of migrants streams between Central America and the U.S. have dramatically increased the adoption of North American ideas and values. The growing Protestant evangelical movement and the Mormon Church which have both made major inroads in traditionally Catholic Central American countries, have only accelerated the process of cultural change.

During the past several decades, Central American countries have also grappled with the complex issues of promoting economic growth and reducing poverty while avoiding environmental destruction. A history of extreme social stratification in many Central American countries has created large gaps in living standards between the majority of the population and the wealthy elites. However, rapid social and economic change is underway in all countries in the region. Changes include rapidly increasing ties to global markets, growth in industrial and formal sector employment, declining reliance on subsistence and plantation agriculture, and the development of a commercial capitalist class which is not closely tied to traditional landed elites.

High population densities, poor cultivation methods, poverty, and large inequalities in land distribution have led to overexploitation in agricultural land in many Central American countries. Like Brazil, Central America also contains some of the last remaining major tropical rainforest areas in the Western Hemisphere. Yet these forests are, in almost all cases, under siege from loggers, agribusiness concerns, and poor farmers trying to make a living. On the other hand, Costa Rica has set aside large areas as national parks and reserves and pioneered eco-tourism and other novel environmental strategies, in an attempt to preserve at least a part of it's natural environment. Other countries in the region have followed this example, although to date on a smaller scale. The Central American region will provide an important test case for whether appropriate solutions can be found and successfully implemented to restore depleted tropical soils and to preserve tropical forests and other fragile eco-systems, while improving the economic well-being of the population.

The chapters in this volume provide important and often novel insights into these and many other issues. My co-editor, Luis Rosero-Bixby, and I hope that this volume will stimulate readers to think about the complexities of the Central American region in new ways and will encourage future research by scholars both from the region and from other countries.

Finally, on a personal note, I want to express my admiration for and appreciation of the enormous efforts that Luis Rosero-Bixby and his colleagues put into organizing and hosting this conference, recruiting participants, selecting papers both for the conference and the volume, cajoling authors to finish their revisions, and providing continual support for the production of this English edition.

REFERENCES

LaFeber, Walter (1993) *Inevitable Revolutions: The United States in Central America.* New York: W.W. Norton and Co.

Pérez-Brignoli, Hector (1989) *A Brief History of Central America.* Berkeley: University of California Press.

Rohter, Larry (1997) "Maya Dress Tells a New Story, and It's Not Pretty" *New York Times*, June 13, 1997.

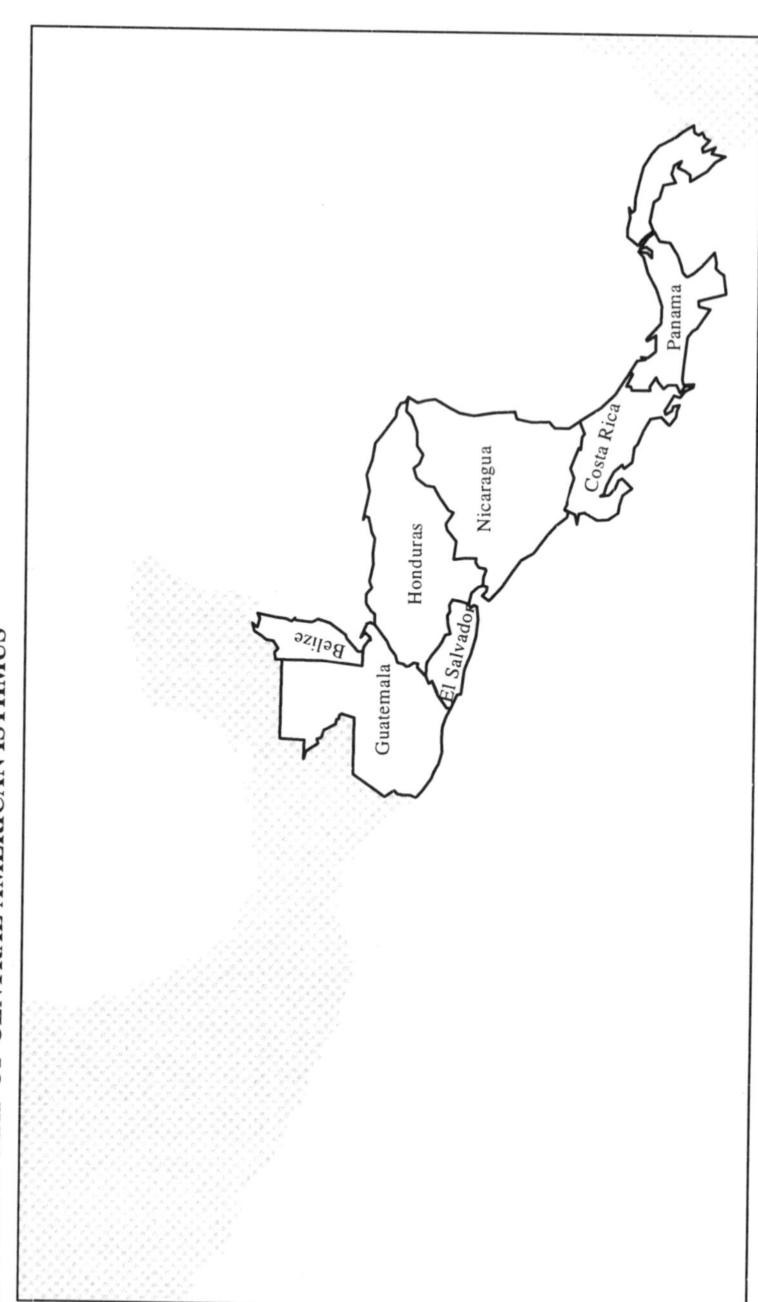

FIGURE 1. MAP OF CENTRAL AMERICAN ISTHMUS

Chapter One

THE DEMOGRAPHIC SITUATION OF CENTRAL AMERICA

LATIN AMERICAN DEMOGRAPHIC CENTRE (CELADE)

INTRODUCTION

In the second half of the 20th century, Central America has experienced dramatic demographic changes. Since 1950, the population of the region has multiplied rapidly, though at a pace that has been slowing. As a result of these trends, the relative importance of children, adolescents, adults and the elderly has been altered. In addition to the demographic importance of these changes, the changes in age structure have had direct repercussions on the overall composition of human needs and potential. These effects have been complemented by the migration of people throughout Central America, occupying new rural areas, increasing the density of others, swelling some urban locales and limiting the expansion of others. Migrations of great importance have crossed national boundaries and have occurred in a manner that is practically unprecedented in history. However, these changes have not taken place in a uniform manner. They have developed in heterogeneous ways, depending on national characteristics such as country, place of residence, social and ethnic groups and gender. This behavioral diversity cannot be attributed solely to demographic circumstances. Its determinants are more profound and must be sought in the economic, social, political and cultural heterogeneity native to the region.

Although experience to date offer us an indication of what will probably be the prevalent demographic situation in the final years of the 20th century, there are many uncertainties about the response of national societies. Certainly, numerous problems, many of which are already part of the everyday life of Central American countries, will have to be confronted. Other problems are related to demographic perspectives which must be understood to be able to explore the eventual effects they will have. However, population should not be perceived solely as a source of problems. It should also be clearly understood that the true potential of the region resides in its population. Adequate understanding of the population's potential is important to face the great challenge of constructing a tomorrow amidst the urgency of today. It is literally impossible to conceive of a productive transformation, or to advance toward greater human development, without the explicit consideration of the fact that the population provides the basis for achieving these objectives as well as being the ultimate beneficiaries of the process.

In this chapter, we will discuss different facets of demographic dynamics in Central America, with special emphasis on its rhythms, changes, and differentials. We conclude with notes that illustrate possible economic and social repercussions due to population change in the region. For practical reasons, Belize is not usually considered to be part of Central America, but rather part of the "Caribbean." However, to illustrate the demographic situation in that country, tables 9 and 10 which contain basic information on Belize are included at the end of this document.

BASIC INDICATORS OF DEMOGRAPHIC DYNAMICS

Around 1950, the population of the six Central American countries was slightly higher than 9 million people (Table 1). Of that total, a third lived in Guatemala, slightly more than a fifth in El Salvador, 15% in Honduras, 12% in Nicaragua, and the remaining 18% were almost evenly distributed between Costa Rica and Panama. In 1990, forty years later, the regional population had more than tripled to almost 29 million people. While the order of the countries by absolute population size remained constant during these 40 years, Honduras, Nicaragua and Costa Rica contributed most to the population increase. At the same time, El Salvador, Panama, and to a lesser degree Guatemala, experienced decreases in their relative importance in the Central American demographic picture.

The pace of the population growth in Central America has been among the highest in the world, reaching an annual mean rate increase of 29 per thousand (i.e., 2.9 %) between 1950 and 1990. However, as shown below, the increase was not constant during this time period. As a result of this accelerated growth, the *density* of the regional population rose from 18 to 58 inhabitants per square kilometer from 1950 to 1990. Within the region, El Salvador has experienced the highest demographic density of all the Central American countries, with a value close to 250 persons per square kilometer in 1990 (or more than four times the regional average). At the other extreme, Nicaragua and Panama have the lowest densities, with about 30 inhabitants per square kilometer in 1990.

To analyze the dynamic of demographic change, we examine changes in natural population growth and growth due to migration. With the exception of Panama, the countries in the region shared exceptionally high *birth rates* in 1950: the crude birth rates (CBRs) were 48 to 54 births per thousand inhabitants (Table 2).

A REGION IN THE PROCESS OF DEMOGRAPHIC TRANSITION

The above-mentioned indicators point towards movement from an initial situation of high birth and death rates, with particularly high levels of demographic growth, toward a situation in which there is a slow decline in the rate of increase, brought about by the decrease of birth rates as well as by the effects of emigration. Between 1950 and 1990, Central America began a demographic transition that is shown in a trend towards continuously declining rates of population growth. Certainly, as available information shows, the process has not been developing in the same way nor with the same impetus in all of the countries of variations in rates by social class and places of residence in each specific society. These variations are considered below. In any case, population projections indicate that during the last five years of the 20th century the average number of children per woman is expected to be substantially lower than prior to the 70s. Guatemala, which will maintain the slower rate of decrease observed in the 40 years prior to 1990, will continue to have the highest TFR with a value slightly lower than 5 in the year 2000. By 2000, we estimate that the average number of children per woman in El Salvador, Honduras and Nicaragua will vary between 4.2 and 4.5. In Panama and Costa Rica the TFR will be below 3 children, showing more profound change in reproductive behavior.

We use the *life expectancy at birth* (LEB) to examine the evolution of the mortality levels in the population. This indicator shows the average number of years of life that a newborn would live if he is exposed to age-specific mortality rates of a given time period or year. Around 1950, only Costa Rica and Panama demonstrated a LEB greater than 55. Forty years later, they are the only countries in the region where the LEB exceeds 70 years. In the remaining countries (except El Salvador) even greater total gains have been attained since 1950 than in Costa Rica and Panama: the LEB has increased by more than 20 years in four decades. Nonetheless, in 1990 the life expectancy at birth remained around 64 years. In other words, as in the case of birth rates, the intra-regional gap with regard to mortality existed since 1950.

There are two important observations to make about this intra-regional gap. First increases in LEB understandably become more difficult to achieve when they reach levels like those in Costa Rica and Panama since advances basically depend on the provision of health care for diseases that demand burdensome curative treatments and hospital care. Secondly, we should keep in mind that a large part of the gains attained by the other four countries in the region were obtained by combating infectious-contagious diseases through low-cost, preventive-type methods such as immunizations, the control of vector agents, and some types of environmental drainage.

Around the year 2000, according to population projections, the LEB of the population of Central America will reach 70 years of age. Although the intra-regional gap will remain, its size will lessen. As a result, while life expectancy for an average Costa Rican will be close to 76 and for a Panamanian 74, in all the other countries the LEB will be somewhat lower than the mean regional value. On the other hand, it is commonly known that in a "normal" population, the LEB is somewhat higher for women and Central America is no exception. This gender differential which in the 50s was 2 years, has been increasing as the overall length of life has increased. At the end of the century, the LEB for women in the entire region is expected to be 5 years higher than that for men. Finally, as will be shown in the case of fertility, mortality conditions differ considerably by social class and area of residence within countries, as discussed below.

Now that we have reviewed changes in the TFR and LEB since 1950, we can summarize the demographic transition process which has been taking place in this region during the past 40 years. In fact, both measures show a slow decrease of vital rates. Similarly, the existence of two distinct patterns in the region, mentioned previously, clearly emerges. The first pattern involves Costa Rica and Panama, which have experienced a decline in their reproductive rates that is considerably higher than the regional average. Both countries have also experienced significant gains in length of life. The second pattern involves El Salvador, Guatemala, Honduras and Nicaragua, which exhibit less rapid rates of TFR decrease at the same time that they are being left behind the other two countries in mortality decline. Although these two patterns may appear to be examples of the same transition to lower rates of natural increase, in fact they result from the unequal nature of the economic, social and cultural construction in the different nations which have been defined in the geographic context of Central American.

FROM VIGOROUS REJUVENATION ON TO GRADUAL AGING

If explanation of the determinants of population change means the exploration of relations between demographic, economic, social, political and cultural processes, then the evaluation of the repercussions of demographic dynamics would demand even more extensive analysis to identify causality lines. One less complex approximation consists of inferring the effects of the demographic transition by inspecting the changes in the age structure of the population.

A progressive movement, in the sense of changing the age structure, exercises a direct effect on the number of people in each age group. For example, changes may occur in the number of school-age, working-age or retirement-age people, as well as in the proportion of women who are of childbearing ages. It is important to note that substantial changes in the relative size of each group generally does not take place over short periods of time. Except for the effects of migration, most of the effects of demographic variables on the age structure are observed over relatively long periods of time. Part of the reason is demographic inertia (or momentum) which postpones the effects of changes in demographic rates on the age structure. For this reason, a decrease in fertility levels may have significant effects on the number of school-age children only after cohorts of reproductive-aged women begin to decrease in size, which may take one or two generations, depending on the rate and intensity of the decline. Note that even though the average number of children per woman decreases, the total number of children will continue to increase because the number of reproductive age women increases, as a consequence of previous high fertility. Similarly, the effects of a decrease in fertility on the size of the working-age population will begin to appear only after 15 or 20 years have passed.

In the Central American case, *the pre-school age population* (children 0 to 4 years of age), has been the age group most affected by the decrease in birth rate since the end of the 60s (Table 4). Although this age group had the least net growth between 1950 and 1990, the absolute number of preschoolers has tripled during this period, increasing from 1.6 to 4.7 million children. As expected, the changes in this age group parallel those in fertility rates during the period. Between 1950 and 1970, the proportion of the population in this age group increased within the whole region, but subsequently began a slow decline. Although the general pattern occurred in all Central American countries, the magnitude of change varied among countries. Thus in the 20 years prior to 1990, the decrease of the proportion of the population that was in preschool ages was visibly more marked in Costa Rica and Panama, where decrease in fertility has been more accentuated and sustained. Note that in the entire region, this decline in pre-school age children is still underway. While in 1950 preschoolers represented 17.8% of the total population, in 1990 they constituted 16.3% of that total. Toward the year 2000 however, this proportion will lessen even more and is expected to reach 14.8% of the total Central American population, with an absolute number of 5.6 million.

Simultaneously with this change, there has been larger growth in the *school-age population* (5 to 19). Between 1950 and 1990, this age group increased its numbers by a factor of 3.3, increasing from 3.3 to 11 million people. This change is a result of the large number of births that occurred before 1980, a period in which the decrease in fertility in some of the countries had just begun or was not yet evident. Between 1950 and 1990, for the region as a whole, school-age children increased from 36.3% to 38.0% of the population. Nonetheless, this proportion has begun to decrease especially in those countries where fertility decline began much earlier. For example in Costa Rica, school-age youth decreased from 40.6% to 32.5% in the 20 years prior to 1990. This rate of decrease will accelerate in the last decade of the century. In the region as a whole, it is estimated that the school-aged population will comprise more than 36% of the total population projected for the year 2000, when their number will rise to 13.7 million.

The *working-age population* (20 to 59) increased from 3.8 to 11.7 million people between 1950 and 1990, but its share of the population has shown little change: it increased from 40.4% to 41.4% during this 40 year period. However, halfway through that period (at about 1970) that proportion had decreased to 38.5%. In other words, while fertility remained constant and even increased, this age group tended to decrease proportionately, but when fertility began to decline, the working age population began to increase. This gradual increase in the proportion of the population in working ages implies two types of seemingly opposing economic and social effects: on one hand, it suggests a growing demand for employment; and on the other, it implies a gradual decrease in the dependency ratio in Central America. Both effects are shown by Central American data subsequent to 1970.

Finally, the *60+ population*, along with associated need for social security and health care services, grew considerably between 1950 and 1990. In this period, the absolute number of people 60 and over increased by a factor of 4 from 411,000 to 1.6 million people. Despite this substantial increase, the relative proportion of the population aged 60 and over increased only from 4.5% to 5.4% in the 40 year period. In Panama, which has traditionally had lower fertility, senior citizens comprise a greater proportion: about 7% of the population is 60 and over. In Costa Rica, where fertility levels have declined more recently, this proportion was 6.4% in 1990. This age group is also the one which will grow most rapidly in the future, reaching a total of 2.2 million people by the year 2000, equal to 6% of the total population projected for Central America in that year.

In summary, the population in Central America, which already had a young mean age in 1950 tended to become even younger well into the 60s. Subsequently, the gradual fertility decline has reversed this trend and a gradual aging process has begun. In other words, after a period of extension of the base of the population pyramid, a progressively thinning pyramid has emerged, generating simultaneously a slight increase in the middle and older ages. Nonetheless, we should note that the predominance of youth remains an important characteristic of the Central American population and will continue to be in the near future. In fact, in 1990 the population under 25 increased to 18.3 million people (or 63.5% of the population). This is an increase of 12.5 million young people since 1950. This young majority population places substantial demands on educational and health services and exerts pressure by entering the labor force and by participating in the decision making process, but also represents a considerable potential for revitalization. By the year 2000, this group will have increased by 4.5 million people and will be more than 60% of the total population.

INTENSE MOBILITY AND GROWING URBANIZATION

As with international migration, internal population mobility is an important element of the social, economic, political and cultural change in the Central American countries. Operating to reinforce or retard the consequences of natural growth, which already creates geographic differentials within countries, *internal migration* contributes substantial to intra-country differences in population distribution. However, its effects are not limited solely to differential population size, but also include geographic distribution of migrants' attributes. For this reason, internal migration is the most complex of demographic variables and difficult to describe and to explain (CELADE, 1988).

tants (7 out 10) lived in rural areas. Given the subsequent process of economic transformation, a substantial decrease in the contribution of agriculture to the regional GDP has occurred, and by 1990 less than 40% of the labor force was employed in agriculture. At the same time, urban areas have taken on a important economic, social, political, and cultural significance to such a degree that in 1995, 45% of the total population resided in an urban area. In reality, this 40 year period has been a stage of intense *urbanization.* Between 1950 and 1990, urban areas have more than quadrupled their population, increasing from 2.6 million to almost 13 million people, while in rural areas population decreased by a factor of 2.5 (Table 5). This discrepancy between urban and rural growth rates has resulted in an accelerated urbanization. Projections indicate that Central America will reach the year 2000 with 18 million urban inhabitants, i.e., more than 48% of its total population will live in urban areas.

While all Central American countries have experienced substantial urbanization, they have followed different trajectories (Table 6). During the period, Panama and Nicaragua exhibited the highest urban proportions. As early as 1980, it was estimated that more than half of their populations could be classified as urban. Nonetheless Panama, like Guatemala, experienced lower rates of increase in the urban proportion than the regional average. By contrast, Costa Rica and particularly Honduras, have had the most rapid increases in urbanization. However, Honduras shares with Guatemala the largest rural proportion in the region. The changes mentioned illustrate the heterogeneity of settlement patterns in Central America. Urban population growth rates have increased at mean annual rates that have systematically been greater than growth rates for the total population and have often doubled rural growth rates, as illustrated in the case of El Salvador, Honduras and Nicaragua. During the last decade of the century, the rate of urban population growth is expected to decrease to levels lower than those for 1950-1970. Despite this change, the differential between urban and rural growth rates will tend to increase.

On the other hand, urbanization in Central America has shown a certain bias toward concentration. The most visible evidence of this bias is seen in Panama, whose metropolitan area concentrated about 35% of the total population of the country in 1990 (Table 7). The concentration dynamism can also be seen in the other countries by means of the large and increasing proportion of the population living in each national capital. In turn, around these cities urban complexes have developed that incorporate formerly independent towns into a web of daily relations. One example of this trend is shown in Costa Rica: the "dispersed" metropolitan area of San José with an estimated population of 1 million people in 1990 represents an overflow of the national capital beyond its historic borders and its de facto merger with the seats of three neighboring provinces. Recent "metropolitanization" is obvious when we observe that the population of the capital cities of Central American countries represented 11.5% of the total number of inhabitants in 1950, and had increased to 20.6% in 1990.

While population is increasingly concentrated in metropolitan areas, all evidence suggests that the concentration of industrial, commercial and financial activities in metropolitan areas is even greater than that of population. For this reason, their contribution to national production is particularly important. Equally important is the fact that metropolitan expansion requires the commitment of a substantial part of national resources to provide infrastructure and basic services, sometimes to the detriment of other parts of the country. Even when poverty and unemployment frequently become more visible in these metropolitan areas, the problems are not attributed to the degree of concentration but rather to the structure and function of society and national economy. These observations suggest that although metropolitan areas as such are not real obstacles to the development process, there may be a need to introduce changes in their styles of operation. In fact, there are substantial potential advantages to spatial concentration if the role of metropolitan areas' economies is redefined and if the benefits are distributed more equitably.

SOCIAL AND SPATIAL HETEROGENEITY OF DEMOGRAPHIC DYNAMICS

Until now we have considered only average national rates. These rates are simply the weighted results of the different demographic behavior within each country. Because they are means, they reveal little of the underlying processes and are of meager use for policy formulation. The heterogeneity of social reality makes it useful to examine variations in demographic parameters among subgroups. Although in this section we will discuss only fertility and mortality data because more information is available on these processes, it is important to remember that migration also varies considerably among population subgroups. The figures in this section refer to different areas of population settlement and to broad socio-occupational groups in Guatemala, Honduras, and Panama. These estimates refer to two five year periods: one at the beginning of the 60s and the other at the end of the 70s.

In terms of variation among *geographic contexts*, the TFR reaches its lowest intensity in the metropolitan areas and in the principal cities of each country, and increases as it moves to "other urban areas" and rural areas, particularly those that are furthest from the urban environment (Table 8). Although this observation is true in both periods under consideration, the differences detected increased with time. In 1960-65, women residing in the major cities of Guatemala had an average of 1.6 more children than women in remote rural areas. In Honduras, the difference was an even larger 2.5 children. Fifteen years later the levels of the TFR in cities had decreased by 1 child in the case of Guatemala, and 1.5 children in Honduras. On the other hand, in remote rural areas there was a slight increase in fertility probably due to a decrease in maternal mortality. Because of both changes noted, the differences between the TFR in the two types of contexts reached 2.8 children in Guatemala and 4.8 in Honduras. In Panama, the urban-rural difference increased from 2.7 to 3.3 children between the two periods, an evolution that appears to derive from the nationwide diffusion of factors favorable to a decrease in fertility.

There is greater heterogeneity in reproductive behavior among *socio-occupational groups*. In the first of these five year periods, the difference between the TFR of the "medium high" occupational categories and non-salaried agricultural workers reached 3.3 children per woman both in Honduras and Panama. However, specific levels for each country were different. In the following five year period, these discrepancies increased in these two countries to 5.0 and 3.7 children respectively, while in Guatemala the difference was 3.4 children per woman. This results shows that the decrease in fertility manifested itself first in the "medium-high" group, while the group of salaried agricultural and non-agricultural workers continued to exhibit markedly higher reproductive rates at the end of the 70s. Since, in general, the greater part of the population in these countries works in lower status occupations, important decreases in fertility level will only occur when these groups have experienced significant fertility declines, as the case of Panama suggests. In any case, there is evidence of substantial decreases in the TFR of the women in the non-salaried, non-agricultural sector in Guatemala and Honduras.

Infant mortality estimates indicate that rates are also significantly lower in the metropolitan areas than in "other urban areas" and in rural areas. In 1960-65, the infant mortality rate for the Panama City metropolitan area (29 per 1000) was only about 37% of the estimate for remote rural zones (78 per thousand). In the second half of the 70s, the metropolitan infant mortality rate decreased to 27% of the rural rate (the rates were 13 and 48 per thousand, respectively). In Guatemala, if one considers the probability of dying within the first two years of life, the difference between metropolitan areas and remote rural settlements was slightly lower and tended to remain the same over time. Both differences by place of residence and among socio-occupational groups are important. These discrepancies are particularly marked when we compare "medium high" status workers and agricultural workers.

For example, in Honduras in 1960-65, the risk of death that children of non-salaried agricultural workers were exposed to was twice that faced by children of those who comprise the "medium-high" category (130 and 65 per thousand respectively). Fifteen years later, the ratio had increased to 2.4 (with rates respective to 105 and 44 per thousand). Similarly, in Guatemala the probability of death before reaching the second year of life was 2.7 times higher among salaried agricultural workers (173 per thousand) than among the "medium high" category (64 per thousand). In the case of Panama, the infant mortality rate among non-salaried rural workers (49 per thousand) practically tripled what was estimated for the "medium-high" category (17 per thousand). These figures show the high levels of mortality in the majority of the countries in the region as well as the great heterogeneity within countries.

In addition to differentials by place of residence and socio-occupational strata, there are other differentials by variables such as parent's level of education or usual language used in the home (as a rough indicator of ethnic groups). In numerous studies, the level of *maternal schooling* is inversely associated with differences in child survival. Specifically, in Honduras at about 1980, children of women with no education had infant mortality rates (112 per thousand) that were triple the rates of those children born to mothers with 7 or more years of schooling

(39 per thousand). Differences of this type do not occur exclusively in high mortality countries. They are also apparent in cases such as Costa Rica, where data from the 1984 population census showed illiterate women had a mortality rate (35 per thousand) that was also three times greater than that of children born to mothers with secondary or advanced schooling (13 per thousand). As with infant mortality, the level of maternal education is strongly associated with the average number of children ever born. The differences in fertility according to number of years of maternal schooling are apparent both in countries with high fertility rates and also in those where fertility has declined significantly, having observed that in the process of transition that the discrepancies have tended to increase at least temporarily. For example, in Honduras in 1960 women with 7 or more years of schooling had an average of close to 6 children while those with no schooling had around 8. Twenty years later the first group had 50% fewer children while fertility among the second group had increased to slightly more than 8 children per mother as an average.

Turning to *ethnic* differentials, the results of previous research indicate that the indigenous population is among the most vulnerable demographic groups. They experience the highest risk of dying and high fertility rates as well. In Guatemala, for example, the probability of dying within the first two years of life for all indigenous children combined is estimated to be as high as that of children of salaried agricultural workers of all ethnicities.

During the 1960s and 1970s, the TFRs for indigenous women in Panama and Guatemala remained relatively constant, were much higher than the national average in each country, and were similar to those estimated for rural workers. The fact that the indigenous population and the rural population have similar demographic rates should not be surprising because most indigenous residents of Guatemala and Panama live in rural areas and work in agriculture.

The recognition that most births and infant deaths occur in the most depressed geographic areas and among the poorest socioeconomic groups is an important guide for health programs and particularly for infant health programs. Several studies have indicated, in a systematic manner, that both infant mortality and fertility tend to be increase as one moves from metropolitan areas to the more remote rural areas. These findings should not be taken to mean that "remoteness" or "urbanness" is a cause of demographic behavior. Rather, urban-rural differentials are simply the external manifestation of what have been essentially inequitable development processes. This historical context must be considered if we want to trace the roots of unequal economic, social and cultural conditions which characterize urban and rural areas.

In an attempt to provide a general interpretation of the differences already described, we begin by recognizing that there has been a higher degree of economic development in urban than in rural areas. Urban areas have also undergone a greater degree of labor force differentiation than rural areas. Given these conditions, urban social structures tend to be characterized by a higher percentage of middle and upper class inhabitants as well as by a high frequency of salaried workers. At the same time, given the political importance of urban areas, the State tends to have a greater presence and higher visibility in cities. These factors affect daily reality in cities because basic social services (health, environmental drainage, education and culture, housing and social security) and labor and salary policies are both more common and more effective in densely populated areas. In addition to these economic, social and political characteristics which are more common in urban settings, certain cultural characteristics are also more common. Specifically, we refer to middle and upper class values and ideologies as well as incentives for social mobility (theoretically viable within the margins of a diversified economic and social structure).

CHALLENGES FOR THE END OF THE 20TH CENTURY

The previous sections have identified several signposts for the probable direction of socioeconomic change in the last decade of this century. Of course, a substantial proportion of the Central American population in the 21st century was already alive in 1990, but there are still uncertainties as to its future trends. Many of these unknown factors are linked to changes which are introduced in a conscious and deliberate manner.

Certainly, there is a substantial need to understand the current situation and what the future holds for the Central American population. In the previous sections, we have attempted to synthesize the available knowledge about this situation and the socio-demographic evolution of Central America. We also referred to future trends in size, structure and distribution of the population. Now we must synthesize some of the challenges that these trends entail.

We turn first to *fertility*. Even though fertility goals can be controversial, there is agreement that couple should freely decide on the number of children they have. However, the right to freedom of choice makes sense only when the family has adequate means of controlling fertility should they wish to do so. Data from demographic surveys in a number of Central American countries suggest that a significant portion of births are "unwanted"; i.e., the median number of children women have is higher than the median number they would consider "ideal." The difference is especially large among the lower classes and people residing in rural areas. Similarly, a high proportion of women of childbearing age say they prefer not to have any more children; i.e., 66% of the women in Panama, 55% in Costa Rica and 48% in Honduras (United Nations, 1989).

These empirical findings reveal that governments have to improve couples' ability to exercise their right to have the number of children they prefer. The data also suggest the existence of a social inequality in the exercise of such a right to choose desired family size. These observations become even more important when we consider that a significant amount of infant and maternal mortality and of abortion is related to insufficient spacing between pregnancies and pregnancy at an early or advanced age. Furthermore, inadequate pregnancy spacing and very early and very late age at birth are much more common among lower income women. In order for couples to be able to exercise their reproductive rights fully, they must be offered appropriate information about the subject, emphasizing the responsibility involved with being a parent. Similarly, access to existing and efficient means of contraception should be made available so that couples can carry out their decisions. Obviously, use of these means of contraception will increase as the benefits of lower fertility (including lower health risks for mothers and children, increased possibility of greater social equality, and access of greater opportunities in the distribution of the gains in material progress) are seen more clearly.

The analysis of socio-demographic situation in Central America shows that it is imperative to strengthen programs directed toward dramatically reducing *infant mortality*. The experience of Costa Rica in this regard can serve as a point of reference for the other countries in the region. Many methods which could be adopted in the health care field are relatively easy and low-cost. However, intervention of the health sector, while of the greatest need and urgency, is not sufficient. It should be accompanied by a more general social mobilization process that involves education and in grass-roots social organizations. On the other hand, rather than adopting generally-employed child mortality reduction programs, the intercountry differences suggest that these policies must be adapted to local, social and environmental conditions in order to increase their effectiveness. Lastly, all available indicators suggest the existence of a close reciprocal relation between infant mortality and fertility. The risk of death tends to increase as the number of children per woman increases. But fertility also tends to be higher in those social classes characterized by high mortality. From these results, we could infer that actions related to fertility and child mortality do not work against each other but instead mutually reinforce each other.

The nature and implications of *international migration* are more complex. Although limited information restricts our knowledge in this area, international migration is certainly heterogeneous and its study requires diverse analytical and operational perspectives. First, movement across the national borders is deeply rooted in the history of Central America. These traditional flows of people will probably continue thorough the rest of the century. In many cases, they are seasonal, cyclical or transitory trends, closely linked with cycles of agricultural production. In other cases, this migration has involved permanent changes in residence. Obviously, the intensity of migration between the countries in the region has been increased by the socio-political conflicts which have devastated Central America in the last decades. If the peace accords in several countries take permanent root, large numbers of people who were forcibly displaced are likely to demand to return home. This implies the adoption of policies to facilitate repatriation of the displaced. Repatriation poses severe problems with regard to employment, access to productive resources, and where to settle within the country. The development of a strategy which would pool the efforts of regional governments certainly could provide increased ability to solve problems of this type.

A second important issue is emigration outside of the region, primarily to North America. While this emigration may decrease as violence in Central America diminished, it is equally likely that the transfer of skilled human capital to North America will continue for many years. For this reason, regional governments as well as scientific and technical agencies should look for the ways to reduce this loss of talent. Examples include national and region-wide initiatives to establish rapid means of communication among professionals and technicians who live in Central America with colleagues that have emigrated. These links might include the establishment of exchange and cooperation programs that contribute to the transmission of innovation. Many emigrants from Central America find themselves in irregular legal situations in their destination countries ("undocumented"). Action should be taken to require the ratification of bilateral agreements that reduce the risk of a mass expulsion. Another issue that cannot be overlooked when analyzing the situation of emigrants is that of the remittances. It is, of course, a complex topic that involves microsocial dimensions at a family level as well as dimensions that affect society as a whole. Mechanisms need to be designed to contribute to the productive use of these monetary flows, without infringing on individual rights. At the same time, dependence on large remittance flows may create additional problems if the size of remittance flows eventually declines. Should this occur, countries might design procedures to bring together external resources, through bilateral or multinational agreements, for the purpose of reincorporating returning emigrants in productive activities in their home countries.

With respect to the *spatial distribution of the population*, the immediate future will see an increase in urbanization. In the 1990s, if recent trends continue, the urban population will experience a net increase of more than 5 million people, while the rural population will grow to a little over 3 million. In other words, the urban sector will absorb 60% of the population growth that population projections indicate will take place during this decade. While it is probable that the rate of mean annual growth of urban areas will tend to decrease, by the end of the century it will still be at a regional average of over 30 per thousand while the rural population will be close to 118 per thousand. Additionally, city-dwellers will continue to be disproportionately female and the proportion of young adults of working age will increase. Underlying these trends is substantial migration from rural areas. We can say tentatively that if the assumptions of the projections are correct, the net transfer of population from the countryside to the urban centers will reach approximately 1.4 million people. In the year 2000, urban dwellers will be majority in all the countries except Guatemala and Honduras, although a high rate of urbanization is also projected to occur in these countries. In some countries, like Panama and Costa Rica, the rural population will experience growth rates of close to 10 per thousand, implying a strong negative net migration.

As previously noted, implications derived from *population change* transcend the demographic sphere, encompassing social and economic repercussions, such as those affecting the labor market, and health, education, housing and pension systems. These effects occur in several ways. First, variations in the size of the total population have important effects on the need for public programs, and therefore affect the distribution of public funds. Second, changes in the age structure of the population affect the structure of demand for these public services including education, health, social security or nutrition. Labor market supply by households also differs according to age. Internal population distribution, particularly between urban and rural zones, create differences in the nature of needs for public services, and establish parameters for the location of future services. One such example is housing: more migration to urban areas will increase demand for urban housing. Fourth and finally, demographic changes can directly affect the need for public services. For example, a high fertility rate implies a greater need for, for example, maternal and child health care.

These implications of demographic trends are not solely numerical abstractions. Behind these figures are the people that comprise the societies of Central America with all of their economic, political, and cultural differences. The data offered, with all its imperfection, indicate great, and largely unpostponable, challenges that cannot be ignored in designing the future of the region. In beginning this task, we should recognize that the key to construction of a new social, economic and political reality lies in increasing human potential through a socially equitable process of productive transformation.

ACKNOWLEDGEMENTS

This chapter is an abbreviated version of the paper presented at the Conference by CELADE, which is based on an internal working document entitled "The Population of the Central American Isthmus in the Shadow of the 21st Century: Dimensions, Challenges, and Potentials," prepared by Miguel Villa with Jorge Martínez and Jorge Rodríguez. The editors of the Spanish volume edited the original paper.

REFENCES

BID. 1987. *Progreso económico y social en América Latina: Informe 1987*, Washington, D.C., Banco Interamericano de Desarrollo.

CELADE. 1989. *Tendencias, perspectivas e implicaciones de la dinámica demográfica centroamericana*, San José de Costa Rica, Centro Latinoamericano de Demografía (mimeo).

_____. 1990a. *Boletín Demográfico*, No. 45.

_____. 1990b. *Boletín Demográfico*, No. 46.

_____. 1990c. *Factores sociales de riesgo de muerte en la infancia, los casos de Costa Rica, Honduras y Paraguay*, Santiago de Chile, Centro Latinoamericano de Demografía (Serie OI, No. 41; LC/DEM.G.88)

CELADE. 1991a. *Boletín Demográfico*, No. 47.

_____. 1991b. *América Latina: proyecciones de población por área geográfica y de población económicamente activa,*

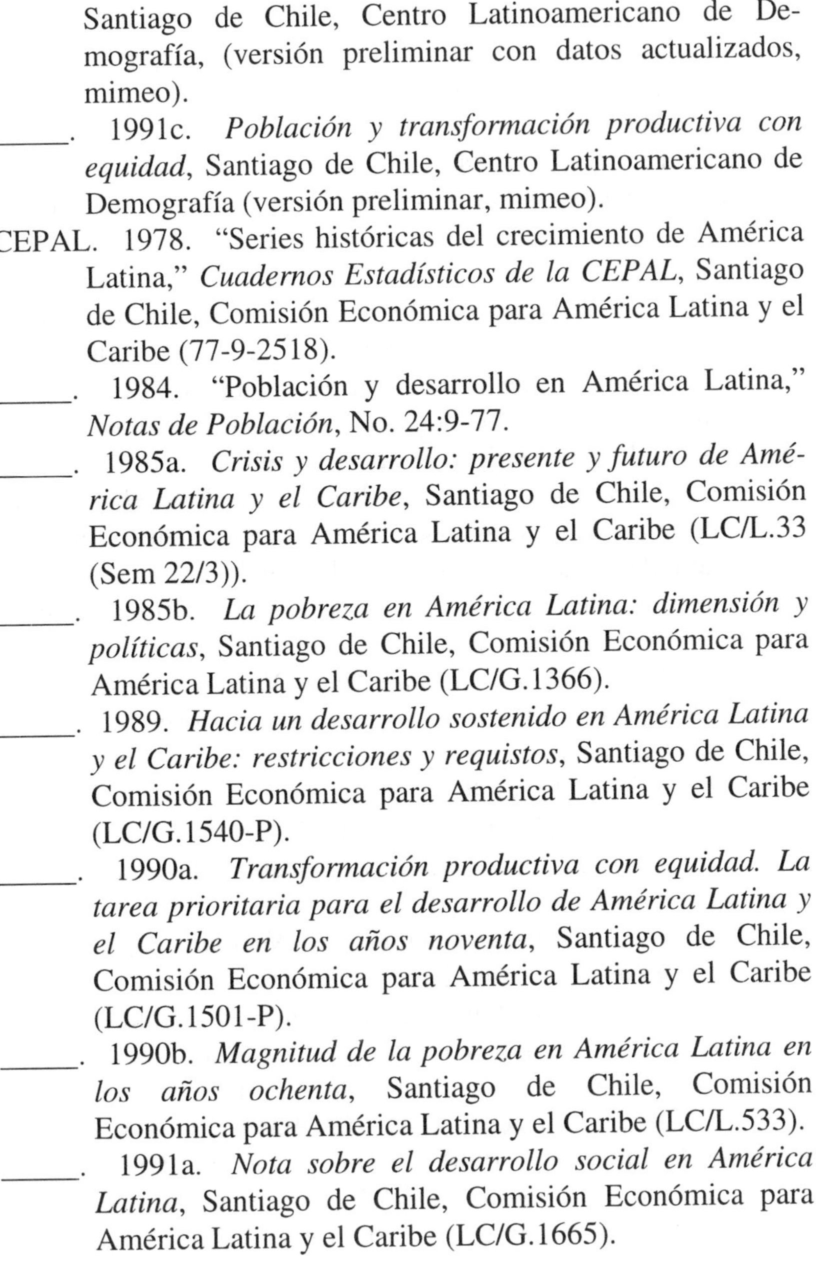

Santiago de Chile, Centro Latinoamericano de Demografía, (versión preliminar con datos actualizados, mimeo).

_____. 1991c. *Población y transformación productiva con equidad*, Santiago de Chile, Centro Latinoamericano de Demografía (versión preliminar, mimeo).

CEPAL. 1978. "Series históricas del crecimiento de América Latina," *Cuadernos Estadísticos de la CEPAL*, Santiago de Chile, Comisión Económica para América Latina y el Caribe (77-9-2518).

_____. 1984. "Población y desarrollo en América Latina," *Notas de Población*, No. 24:9-77.

_____. 1985a. *Crisis y desarrollo: presente y futuro de América Latina y el Caribe*, Santiago de Chile, Comisión Económica para América Latina y el Caribe (LC/L.33 (Sem 22/3)).

_____. 1985b. *La pobreza en América Latina: dimensión y políticas*, Santiago de Chile, Comisión Económica para América Latina y el Caribe (LC/G.1366).

_____. 1989. *Hacia un desarrollo sostenido en América Latina y el Caribe: restricciones y requistos*, Santiago de Chile, Comisión Económica para América Latina y el Caribe (LC/G.1540-P).

_____. 1990a. *Transformación productiva con equidad. La tarea prioritaria para el desarrollo de América Latina y el Caribe en los años noventa*, Santiago de Chile, Comisión Económica para América Latina y el Caribe (LC/G.1501-P).

_____. 1990b. *Magnitud de la pobreza en América Latina en los años ochenta*, Santiago de Chile, Comisión Económica para América Latina y el Caribe (LC/L.533).

_____. 1991a. *Nota sobre el desarrollo social en América Latina*, Santiago de Chile, Comisión Económica para América Latina y el Caribe (LC/G.1665).

OPS. 1990. *Las condiciones de salud en las Américas, Edición de 1990*, Washington, D.C., Organización Panamericana de la Salud (Publicación Científica No. 524).

Pellegrino, A. 1989. *Migración internacional de latinoamericanos en las Américas*, Caracas, Universidad Católica Andrés Bello/Centro Latinoamericano de Demografía/Agencia Canadiense para el Desarrollo Internacional.

PNUD. 1990. *Desarrollo humano. Informe 1990*, Bogotá, Programa de las Naciones Unidas para el Desarrollo, Tercer Mundo Editores.

PREALC. 1989. *Interrelaciones entre población y desarrollo. Bases para políticas de población en el istmo centroamericano*, Santiago de Chile, Programa Regional del Empleo en América Latina y el Caribe (PREALC, Serie Documentos de Trabajo No. 339).

Schroten, H. 1987. "La migración interna en Guatemala durante el período 1976-1981," *Notas de Población*, No. 43:47-97.

UNICEF. 1991. *Declaración mundial sobre la supervivencia, la protección y el desarrollo del niño. Plan de acción para la aplicación de la declaración mundial*, New York: UNICEF.

UNICEF, OPS and CELADE. 1988. *La mortalidad en la niñez en Centroamérica, Panamá y Belice, 1970-1985*, San José de Costa Rica, Fondo de las Naciones Unidas para la Infancia/Organización Panamericana de la Salud/Centro Latinoamericano de Demografía (CELADE, Serie OI, No. 1003; LC/DEM/CR/G.20).

United Nations. 1989. *World Population at the Turn of the Century*, New York, Department of International Economic and Social Affairs (ST/ESA/SER.A/111).

Uthoff, A. 1990. "Población y desarrollo en el istmo centroamericano," *Revista de la CEPAL*, No. 40:139-158.

Urzúa, R. 1979. *El desarrollo y la población en América Latina*, Ciudad de México, Programa de Investigaciones Sociales Relevantes para Políticas de Población en América Latina (PISPAL) y Siglo XXI Editores.

TABLE 1. CENTRAL AMERICA. TOTAL POPULATION, RELATIVE GROWTH, DENSITY AND PERCENTILE DISTRIBUTION BY COUNTRY, 1950-2000

	Total Population (1000s of People)							Relative Growth (1950=100)						
Countries	1950	1960	1970	1980	1990	1995	2000	1950	1960	1970	1980	1990	1995	2000
Central America	9109	12303	16732	22117	28891	33104	37672	100.0	135.1	183.7	242.8	317.2	363.4	413.6
Costa Rica	862	1236	1731	2285	3015	3374	3711	100.0	143.4	200.8	265.1	349.8	391.4	430.5
El Salvador	1940	2570	3588	4525	5252	5943	6739	100.0	132.5	184.9	233.2	270.7	306.3	347.4
Guatemala	2969	3964	5246	6917	9197	10621	12222	100.0	133.5	176.7	233.0	309.8	357.7	411.7
Honduras	1401	1935	2627	3662	5138	5968	6846	100.0	138.1	187.5	261.4	366.7	426.0	488.7
Nicaragua	1098	1493	2053	2771	3871	4539	5261	100.0	136.0	187.0	252.4	352.6	413.4	479.1
Panama	839	1105	1487	1957	2418	2659	2893	100.0	131.7	177.2	233.3	288.2	316.9	344.8
	Density (inhabs. per 2km)							Relative Distribution (%)						
	1950	1960	1970	1980	1990	1995	2000	1950	1960	1970	1980	1990	1995	2000
Central America	18.2	24.6	33.5	44.3	57.8	66.2	75.4	100.0	100.0	100.0	100.0	100.0	100.0	100.0
Costa Rica	17.0	24.4	34.1	45.1	59.5	66.5	73.2	9.5	10.0	10.3	10.3	10.4	10.2	9.9
El Salvador	92.2	122.1	170.5	215.1	249.6	282.4	320.3	21.3	20.9	21.4	20.5	18.2	18.0	17.9
Guatemala	27.3	36.4	48.2	63.5	84.5	97.5	112.2	32.6	32.2	31.4	31.3	31.8	32.1	32.4
Honduras	12.5	17.3	23.4	32.7	45.8	53.2	61.1	15.4	15.7	15.7	16.6	17.8	18.0	18.2
Nicaragua	8.4	11.5	15.8	21.3	29.8	34.9	40.5	12.1	12.1	12.3	12.5	13.4	13.7	14.0
Panama	10.9	14.3	19.3	25.4	31.4	34.5	37.5	9.2	9.0	8.9	8.8	8.4	8.0	7.7

Source: CELADE (1990a).

TABLE 2. CENTRAL AMERICA: ANNUAL BIRTH, DEATH, MIGRATION, AND POPULATION GROWTH RATES, IN FIVE YEAR PERIODS, 1950-2000

Countries	1950-55	1955-60	1960-65	1965-70	1970-75	1975-80	1980-85	1985-90	1990-95	1995-2000
A. Crude Birth Rates (per 1000)										
Central America	49.62	49.09	47.76	45.32	42.99	41.29	39.30	37.41	35.42	33.10
Costa Rica	47.33	48.23	45.31	38.32	31.50	31.69	30.19	28.31	25.52	23.17
El Salvador	48.30	49.11	47.80	45.46	42.81	41.37	37.96	36.32	36.04	34.81
Guatemala	51.27	49.38	47.81	45.60	44.55	44.30	42.68	40.77	38.66	36.34
Honduras	51.38	51.31	51.15	50.14	48.67	43.79	42.30	39.80	37.06	33.80
Nicaragua	54.13	52.14	50.33	48.38	46.79	45.58	44.21	41.80	38.70	35.41
Panama	40.30	41.01	40.84	39.31	35.73	30.99	28.01	26.68	24.93	22.82
B. Crude Death Rates (per 1000)										
Central America	20.09	17.94	15.66	13.47	11.46	10.34	9.09	7.71	6.69	6.07
Costa Rica	12.64	10.98	9.18	7.28	5.83	4.96	4.16	3.97	4.02	4.16
El Salvador	19.89	17.41	14.79	12.54	10.79	10.99	10.79	8.40	6.81	6.36
Guatemala	22.38	20.58	18.26	15.89	13.38	11.95	10.46	8.92	7.63	6.66
Honduras	22.31	20.30	18.13	15.85	13.62	11.17	9.08	8.07	7.16	6.40
Nicaragua	22.60	19.68	17.01	14.64	12.61	11.61	9.69	7.98	6.65	5.74
Panama	13.18	10.94	9.58	8.43	7.32	6.00	5.38	5.16	5.15	5.23
C. International Migration Rates (per 1000)										
Central America	-0.33	-0.34	-0.94	-1.64	-3.34	-3.76	-4.08	-2.48	-1.54	-1.22
Costa Rica	0.00	0.00	0.00	0.00	0.00	3.01	3.01	2.01	1.01	0.00
El Salvador	-2.03	-1.91	-1.73	2.42	-6.12	-9.93	-16.75	-8.60	-4.51	-3.34
Guatemala	0.00	0.00	-1.20	-2.08	-3.61	-4.71	-4.09	-3.09	-2.29	-1.66
Honduras	2.36	2.00	0.86	-7.19	-3.24	1.89	2.60	0.00	0.00	0.00
Nicaragua	-1.32	-1.35	-1.53	-1.95	-2.30	-5.94	-1.35	-0.29	-0.24	-0.21
Panama	-1.17	-1.02	-1.57	-1.35	-1.25	-1.09	-0.96	-0.87	-0.78	-0.72

(Continued on next page)

(Table 2 continued from previous page)

D. Medium Annual Population Growth Rates (per 1000)										
Central America	29.20	30.80	31.17	30.20	28.19	27.52	26.12	27.22	27.19	25.81
Costa Rica	34.69	37.25	36.13	31.04	25.68	29.75	29.03	26.34	22.50	19.01
El Salvador	26.37	29.79	31.28	35.34	25.90	20.45	10.42	19.33	24.71	25.11
Guatemala	28.89	28.80	28.35	27.62	27.56	27.64	28.13	28.76	28.74	28.03
Honduras	31.43	33.01	33.88	27.10	31.81	34.50	35.83	31.73	29.90	27.40
Nicaragua	30.21	31.11	31.78	31.78	31.88	28.03	33.17	33.53	31.80	29.46
Panama	25.95	29.04	29.69	29.54	27.16	27.60	21.66	20.66	19.00	16.87

Source: CELADE (1990a).

TABLE 3. CENTRAL AMERICA: TOTAL FERTILITY RATE, LIFE EXPECTANCY AT BIRTH AND INFANT MORTALITY RATE BY FIVE YEAR PERIODS, BY COUNTRY, 1950-2000.

Country	1950-55	1955-60	1960-65	1965-70	1970-75	1975-80	1980-85	1985-90	1990-95	1995-2000
A. Total Fertility Rates (number of children per woman)										
Central America	6.82	6.92	6.92	6.63	6.20	5.81	5.42	5.04	4.64	4.22
Costa Rica	6.72	7.11	6.95	5.80	4.34	3.89	3.50	3.26	3.02	2.81
El Salvador	6.46	6.81	6.85	6.62	6.10	5.70	5.21	4.86	4.51	4.16
Guatemala	7.09	6.93	6.85	6.60	6.45	6.40	6.12	5.77	5.36	4.90
Honduras	7.05	7.18	7.36	7.42	7.38	6.58	6.16	5.55	4.94	4.34
Nicaragua	7.33	7.33	7.33	7.10	6.71	6.31	5.94	5.50	5.01	4.50
Panama	5.68	5.89	5.92	5.62	4.94	4.06	3.46	3.14	2.87	2.65
B. Life Expectancy at Birth (in years)										
Central America	45.48	48.32	51.43	54.51	57.63	59.41	61.79	64.72	67.19	68.89
Costa Rica	57.26	60.15	63.02	65.64	68.08	70.80	73.53	74.67	75.19	75.60
El Salvador	45.26	48.57	52.34	55.92	58.75	57.42	57.15	62.15	66.40	68.00
Guatemala	42.09	44.19	47.03	50.12	54.00	56.39	58.98	61.99	64.81	67.19
Honduras	42.31	44.99	47.94	50.89	53.96	57.65	61.94	63.95	65.80	67.47
Nicaragua	42.28	45.40	48.51	51.61	54.70	56.26	59.81	63.26	66.22	68.50
Panama	55.26	59.34	61.99	64.27	66.34	69.19	70.98	72.08	72.79	73.30
C. Infant Mortality Rate (per 1000 live births)										
Central America	145.72	131.45	116.79	102.51	88.37	76.73	65.01	53.37	44.09	37.84
Costa Rica	93.78	87.68	81.29	67.67	52.55	36.56	23.28	19.4	16.65	14.8
El Salvador	151.06	137.03	122.67	110.31	99.01	87.28	76.98	57.4	42.76	37.28
Guatemala	140.55	131.05	118.99	107.64	95.07	82.35	70.39	58.71	48.48	40.27
Honduras	195.74	172.01	147.19	123.74	100.56	89.82	78.43	68.37	59.71	52.17
Nicaragua	167.37	148.28	130.86	114.8	99.89	92.96	76.44	61.62	49.85	41.28
Panama	93.04	74.91	62.69	51.6	42.82	31.57	25.65	22.67	20.79	19.47

Source: CELADE (1990a).

TABLE 6. CENTRAL AMERICA: BASIC INDICATORS OF URBANIZATION, BY COUNTRY, 1950-2000 (PERCENTAGES) A/.

Country	Degrees of Urbanization (%)							Tempo of Urbanization (per 1000)					
	1950	1960	1970	1980	1990	1995	2000	1950-60	1960-70	1970-80	1980-90	1990-95	1995-00
Central America	29.0	33.6	37.6	41.4	44.6	46.4	48.3	29.6	22.3	19.6	14.6	8.0	7.8
Costa Rica	33.5	34.2	38.6	43.1	46.7	48.5	50.4	2.1	12.2	10.9	8.0	7.8	7.5
El Salvador	35.7	37.0	39.4	43.0	46.8	48.8	50.8	3.5	6.3	8.8	8.5	8.4	7.8
Guatemala	24.5	32.5	34.4	37.2	38.1	38.7	39.4	28.3	5.6	8.0	2.3	3.2	3.8
Honduras	17.6	22.0	28.0	34.8	40.7	44.4	48.2	22.4	24.3	21.8	15.6	17.2	16.4
Nicaragua	35.0	39.6	47.0	51.1	55.3	57.6	59.8	12.4	17.1	8.4	7.9	8.2	7.5
Panama	35.9	41.4	47.2	49.6	52.9	54.6	56.2	14.2	13.2	4.9	6.5	6.4	5.6

Source: CELADE, (1991a).

a/ The degree of urbanization is expressed by the percent of the total population which resides in urban areas; the tempo of urbanization is the medium annual rate of population growth of the proportion urban, which is equivalent to the difference between the urban population growth rate and the population growth rate for the whole population.

TABLE 7. CENTRAL AMERICA: POPULATION OF THE PRINCIPAL METROPOLITAN AREAS, 1950, 1070, 1990 AND 2000

Countries	Primary Metropolitan Areas	Population (in 1000s)				Medium annual growth rate (per 1000)			Percentage of the National Population			
		1950	1970	1990	2000	1950-70	1970-90	1990-2000	1950	1970	1990	2000
Costa Rica	San Jose	190	425	1000	1270	40.3	42.8	23.9	22.0	24.6	33.2	34.2
El Salvador	San Salvador	185	470	1150	1500	46.6	44.7	26.6	9.53	13.1	21.9	22.3
Guatemala	Guatemala City	300	720	1400	1850	43.8	33.3	27.9	10.1	13.7	15.2	15.1
Honduras	Tegucigalpa	75	270	670	950	64.1	45.4	34.9	5.35	10.3	13.0	13.9
Nicaragua	Managua	115	410	900	1200	63.6	39.3	28.8	10.4	20.0	23.2	22.8
Panama	Panama City	180	455	835	1050	46.4	30.4	22.9	21.4	30.6	34.5	36.3

Source: CELADE based on national data.

TABLE 8. CENTRAL AMERICA: DIFFERENCES IN FERTILITY AND INFANT MORTALITY BY SPATIAL CONTEXT AND SOCIO-OCCUPATIONAL STRATA IN SELECTED COUNTRIES, 1960-1980.

Spatial Contexts and Socio-occupational Strata	Total Fertility Rates						Infant Mortality Indicator a/					
	Guatemala		Honduras		Panama		Guatemala		Honduras		Panamá	
	1960-1965	1975-1980	1960-1965	1975-1980	1960-1965	1975-1980	1960-1965	1975-1980	1960-1965	1975-1980	1960-1965	1975-1980
Country	6.9	6.4	7.5	6.5	5.3	3.9	149	118	110	82	49	29
Spatial Context												
Metropolitan Area	3.9	4.0	3.0	86	71	29	13					
Principal Cities	5.5	4.5	5.2	3.7	4.7	3.4	125	96	81	57	39	28
Other Urban Areas	5.6	7.1	5.2	5.8	4.3	143	103	99	77	48	30	
Periurban Areas	6.6	6.4	5.2	148	121	54	34					
Distant Rural Areas	7.1	7.3	7.7	8.5	7.4	6.7	159	124	119	92	78	48
Socio-Occupational Strata												
Medium High		3.8	5.5	3.8	3.8	2.9	64	55	65	44	27	17
Salaried Non-Ag	5.4	5.2	3.9	121	97	41	21					
Non-Salaried Non-Ag	6.1	4.9	6.7	5.5	5.3	4.0	151	116	105	74	42	27
Salaried Ag.	7.5	7.2	7.9	8.0	7.1	6.0	173	137	119	99	61	42
Non-Salaried Ag.	7.1	8.8	8.8	7.1	6.6	151	116	130	105	71	49	
Indigenous Population	6.7	6.7	6.0	6.3	171	128						

Source: DGEC and CELADE (1984) for Guatemala; DGEC, CONSUPLANE and CELADE (1986) for Honduras; MIPPE and CELADE (1983 and 1984) for Panamá.

a/ The indicator used for Guatemala is the probability of dying in the first two years of life.

Chapter Two

A RAPID LOOK AT THE FERTILITY TRANSITION BY ZONE OF RESIDENCE IN CENTRAL AMERICA AND PANAMA

JOSE MIGUEL GUZMAN

INTRODUCTION

The population of the Central American Isthmus is characterized by a history full of similarities, but also of differences. An analysis of the demographic transition process in the region shows on one hand countries like Costa Rica and Panama which began this process quite early, and on the other hand, countries like Guatemala, Nicaragua and Honduras, who were drawn into the process much later. El Salvador is in an intermediate position, but closer to the latter group of countries (see CELADE, 1993).

This chapter intends only, as indicated in the title, to provide a brief look at the process of fertility transition in the Central American Isthmus.[1] We focus on two issues. The first is to put this process of change into a wider temporal background. Second, we provide fertility estimates for urban and rural zones for a broader time period permitted by available data.

The emphasis on these two aspects of the transition is due to the central objective of this chapter. This study tries to replicate a similar analysis for four Latin American countries carried out by the author in collaboration with Jorge Rodríguez (Guzmán and Rodríguez, 1993). For this reason, the hypotheses presented and the analysis which follows are similar to those in the earlier study.

According to the usually accepted description, fertility is high and variable during the pre-demographic transition period (with few differences between groups) and then begins to de-

---

[1] Because of the lack of available data, Belize is not included in this analysis.

population, motivated—at least at the beginning—by the extension of education and its perception as a vehicle for social mobility. It is this "wager on the future" as indicated at the beginning of this chapter, that would explain the fertility change in social sectors which, at least at the beginning, were not experiencing the structural conditions for a decline.

The results of the study show that in general, with the sole exception of Costa Rica, significant differences remain between rural and urban fertility, even though fertility has declined in both sectors. This may be an indication of the importance of structural factors tied to the standard of living in each zone which may be affecting one or more of the proximate determinants of reproductive behavior or the effective ability of women to implement their reproductive decisions.

A complete understanding of the process of fertility change in Central America obviously requires a more in-depth study than is possible here. The hypotheses proposed here require validation with data which may be of a more qualitative than quantitative nature. At the same time, it is necessary to examine in greater detail the analysis of the simultaneity in fertility changes even in conditions that are as diverse as those observed. There is a long way yet to go.

REFERENCES

Acuña, B. 1980. "La mujer en la familia y el valor de los hijos." Heredia: Universidad Nacional de Costa Rica. Instituto de Estudios Sociales en Población.

ADS and CDC. 1993. *Encuesta Nacional de Salud Familiar. FESAL-93. Informe preliminar*. San Salvador.

ADS and DHS. 1987. *El Salvador. Encuesta Nacional de Salud Familiar FESAL-85*. San Salvador.

Behm, R. 1980. "Diferencias socioeconómicas del descenso de la fecundidad en Costa Rica." 1960-1970. San José: CELADE, 1980. Vol. 1.

Bravo, J. 1993. "Visiones teóricas de la transición de la fecundidad en América Latina: Tiene relevancia un enfoque difusionista?" *Notas de Población* XX (56):33-55.

CELADE. 1993. *La población del Istmo Centroamericano en el umbral del Siglo XXI: Dimensiones, desafíos y potencialidades.* Serie A, No. 277.

_____. 1995. *Boletín demográfico.* Año XXVIII (55). Santiago, Chile.

CCSS. 1994. *Encuesta Nacional de Salud Reproductiva. Fecundidad y formación de la familia.* Programa de Salud Reproductiva, Departamento de Medicina Preventiva. San José, Costa Rica.

DGE and CELADE. 1984). *Guatemala: Las diferencias socioeconómicas de la fecundidad, 1959-1980.* CELADE, Serie A. No.1045. San José, Costa Rica.

DGEC, CONSUPLANE and CELADE. 1986. *Fecundidad. Diferenciales geográficos de la fecundidad, 1960-1983. EDENH-II y otras fuentes.* Volumen 4, Serie A, No. 10457/IV.

Guzmán, J.M. y Rodríguez, J. 1993. "La fecundidad pretransicional en América Latina: Un capítulo olvidado." *Notas de Población*, XXI (57):217-246.

Guzmán, J. M. 1992. *Fecundidad y mortalidad infantil en Honduras. Breve análisis de la información proveniente de la Encuesta Nacional de Epidemiología y Salud Familiar ENESF-1991/92.* CELADE, Santiago, Chile (Mimeo).

INEC and CELADE. 1991. *Encuesta Socio-demográfica Nicaragüense ESDENIC'85. Informe General.* Managua, Nicaragua.

INCAP and IRD/DHS. 1989. *Encuesta Nacional de Salud Materno-Infantil 1987.* Ciudad Guatemala.

MPPE and CELADE. 1984. *Panamá. El descenso de la fecundidad según variables socio-económicas y geográficas*

(Sources for Table 1)
Source: Values estimated by backward census projection, own children method and other sources and methods (see text).
* Estimates based on population projections (CELADE, 1995).
** Encuestas Demográficas y de Salud y de Salud Familiar. Nicaragua (PROFAMILIA and CDC, 1993) and INEC and CELADE (1991); Salvador (ADS and CDC, 1993); Costa Rica (CCSS and DCD, 1994); Honduras (Guzmán, 1992); (Guatemala (DHS, 1989).

TABLE 2. COALE NUPTIALITY INDEX (IM)*, BY CENTRAL AMERICAN COUNTRY, CIRCA 1950 AND 1960

Country/Date	IM	Absolute Change
Guatemala		
1950	0.585	
1964	0.608	0.023
El Salvador		
1950	0.695	
1961	0.724	0.029
Honduras		
1950	---	
1961	0.655	---
Nicaragua		
1950	0.569	
1963	0.678	0.109
Costa Rica		
1950	0.582	
1963	0.628	0.046
Panamá		
1950	0.646	
1960	0.647	0.001

* The Coale index is obtained by weighting the proportion of women in union by the fertility rates of the Coale standard schedule (1967). These rates are as follows: 15-19: 0.300; 20-24:0.550; 25-29:0.502; 30-34:0.447; 35-39:0.406; 40-44:0.222; 45-49:0.061
Source: Costa Rica and Honduras (Guzmán y Rodríguez, 1993); El Salvador and Panamá (Rosero-Bixby, 1992); Nicaragua and Guatemala (own calculations)

ANNEX 1. TOTAL FERTILITY RATES

EL SALVADOR

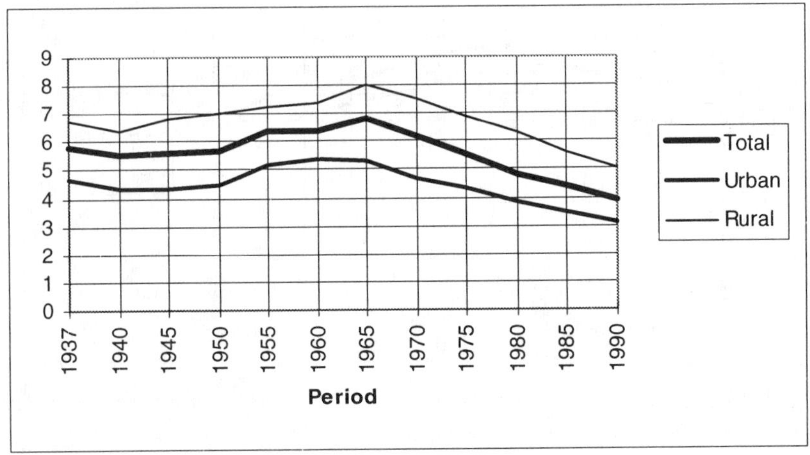

GUATEMALA

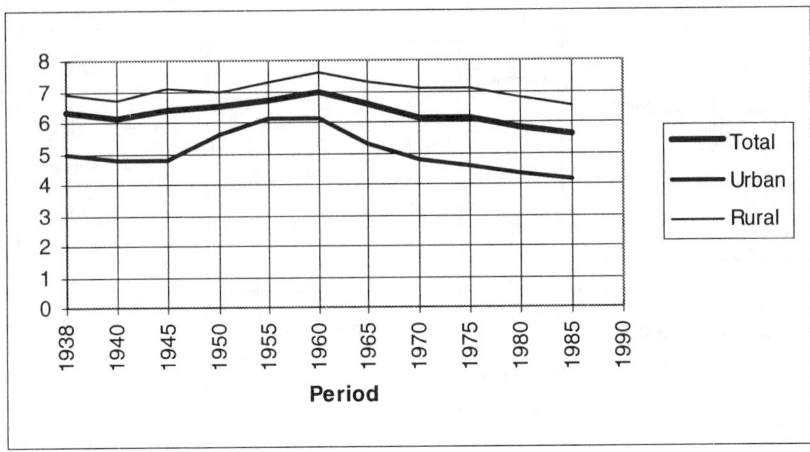

NICARAGUA

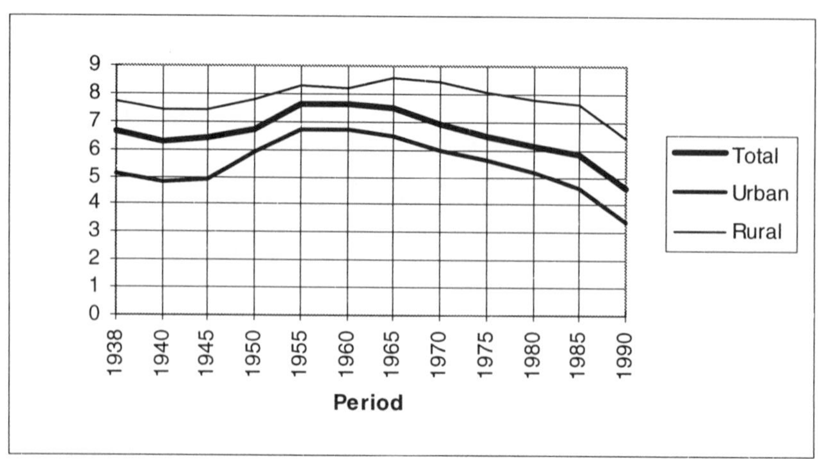

HONDURAS

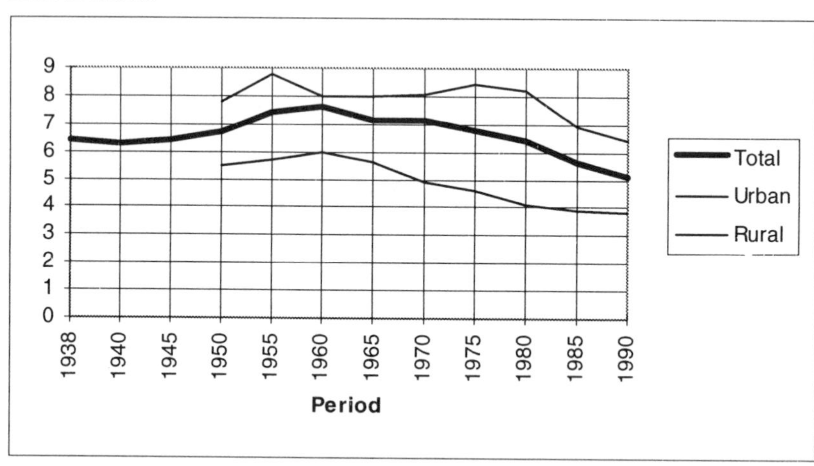

PANAMA

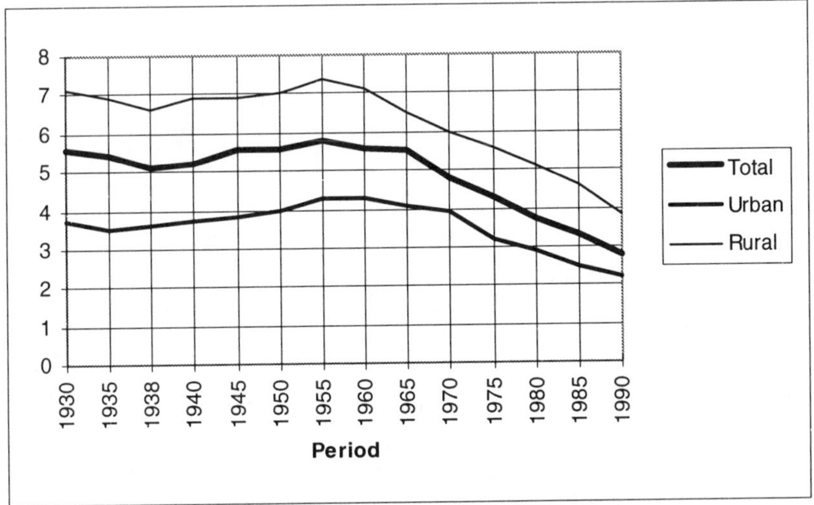

COSTA RICA

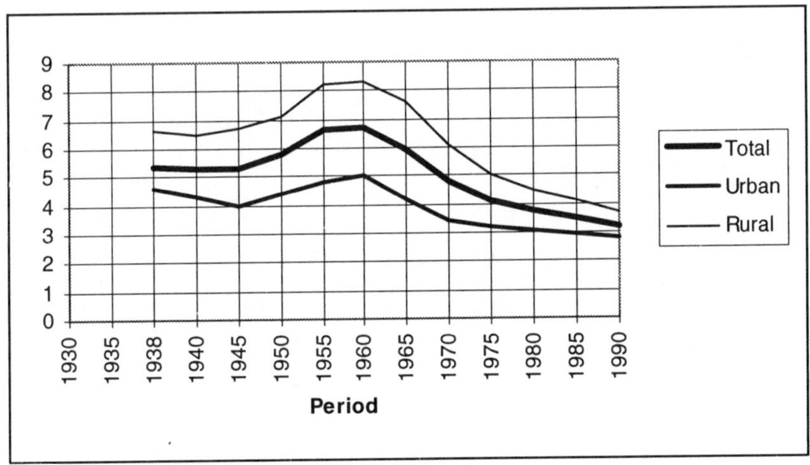

LOW INTENSITY WARFARE, HIGH INTENSITY DEATH: THE DEMOGRAPHIC IMPACT OF THE WARS IN EL SALVADOR AND NICARAGUA

MITCHELL A. SELIGSON AND VINCENT MCELHINNY

How violent were the recent civil wars in El Salvador (1980-1991) and Nicaragua (1975-1990)?[1] The summaries of estimated war related deaths are shown in Table 1 and Table 2 for both countries. The estimates are wide and varied, largely because both conflicts warranted regular news coverage and legislative debate in the U.S., often raising the same questions that were asked during the Vietnam War relating estimates of body-counts and the level of U.S. involvement. Throughout both wars, the issue of combatant and noncombatant deaths served a critical political purpose in generating or mollifying support for government and insurgent forces. As the presentation and analysis of the available data on war-related deaths will show, actual counts are highly contested from year to year, and variation in estimates hinge on controversial definitions of combatant versus noncombatant and other ambiguities within the "politics of human rights measurement."[2]

The reliability of the data is questionable for several reasons. First, they were collected under highly politicized conditions. Second, the counts are incomplete. Third, the methodologies used to collect the data are not consistent. For all of these reasons, conclusions drawn from these estimates should be

[1]For the purposes of this paper, the Nicaraguan Civil War and the subsequent Contra War will be referred to as a single conflict, although the political nature of each war had different implications for reporting war-related deaths.

[2]For a similar summary of this issue in Argentina's "Dirty War," see Alison Brysk, "The Politics of Measurement: The Contested Count of the Disappeared in Argentina," *Human Rights Quarterly*. 16 (1994) pp. 676-692; and *Human Rights and Statistics: Getting the Record Straight*. (1992) Thomas B. Jabine & Richard P. Claude eds., Philadelphia: University of Pennsylvania Press.

used only with great care. The first section of this chapter attempts to substantiate several of the competing estimates of war-related casualties that were published during both the Salvadoran and Nicaraguan conflicts. Until more reliable estimates become available, the figures summarized in Tables 1 and 2 are useful in framing the preliminary qualitative comparison of the conflict intensity based on the Salvadoran and Nicaraguan survey data that follows in the next section. They allow us to speculate on the prospects for sustained democracy in these two countries. Finally, Brysk has highlighted the social value of human rights information in the democratization process. In the discussion, some implications of the ongoing transitions will be offered.

COMPARATIVE BACKGROUND

How violent was the Salvadoran Civil War? If we accept the commonly cited estimate of 75,000 total war related deaths, for an average population during the decade 1980-91 of 4.9 million, one in every 66 Salvadorans perished in war-related violence.[3] Similarly, in Nicaragua an estimated 80,000 combatants and non-combatants perished in the Civil War and the subsequent Contra War, meaning that approximately one of every 38 Nicaraguans died. The Salvadoran and Nicaraguan conflicts were two of the more destructive conflicts in terms of loss of human life, comparable to the Iran - Iraq War, where the ratios were 1:60-100[4] for Iran, and 1:50 for Iraq. They were far more violent than was World War II for the United States, the country that has labeled the conflicts in Central America "low-intensity wars." The United States lost 362,561 soldiers during the war out of a population of 140 million, or a ratio of 1:387, compared

---

[3]The estimate of 75,000 has been cited by the United Nations - Salvadoran Truth Commission Report, *From Madness to Hope* (1992). Population is taken as an average over the course of the war.

[4]This ratio (and those that follow) take the following form: 1:60-100 means that one person out of every 60 to 100 people in the population died.

to 1:66 in El Salvador and 1:38 in Nicaragua. In terms of a broader, international perspective, however, even as destructive as the Salvadoran and Nicaraguan wars were, other recent conflicts, both past and present, have been much worse. A comparison of the magnitude of human loss in recent conflicts is shown in Table 3.

The ratio for Mozambique for the conflict of 1976-1992 was 1:13-33. The Angola conflict of 1975-1991 was worse: 1:20-25 people lost their lives. East and Southeast Asia have experienced three devastating conflicts beginning with the Korean War where one of every seven North Koreans died, compared to a 1:49 ratio for South Koreans. Vietnam suffered massive losses in the period 1960-1975, estimated to have run as high as 1:10-15. The level of human destruction in Cambodia in the 1970-1980s was astronomically high, with a ratio of 1:2.5-3. Rwanda with 1:7.5-15 (1994), is one recent case. Certainly high death wars are not exclusive to Third World countries. The U.S. loss ratio in its own Civil War (1865) was 1:55. In World War I, one of every 12 Serbs, 28 French and 30 Germans perished. Likewise in World War II, the ratios for Poland (1:5), Yugoslavia (1:10) and the Soviet Union (1:10) reflect an intensity of conflict in excess of the recent Central American wars. Moreover, if ethnicity is compared to nationality, the magnitude of the loss of Jewish life during WWII exceeds all other national estimates (1:1.5). Only the Allied bombing of Hiroshima produced a comparable civilian death ratio, at 1:1.8.[5]

Nonetheless, the Salvadoran and Nicaraguan conflicts rank as two of the costliest in recent Latin American history, comparable to the 1932 *matanza* in El Salvador where one in

---

[5]See Table 3 note a for sources. Population estimates are taken from B.R. Mitchell, *International Historical Statistics: Africa, Asia, Oceania*. New York: Stockton Press, 1992, see note b, Table 3.

every 48 Salvadorans perished, and the Mexican Revolution where one in ten died.[6]

INCOMPLETENESS OF THE HUMAN RIGHTS ESTIMATES

The first notable caveat to the data in Tables 1 and 2 is that there is missing information for several years. Of the types of deaths covered, the estimates for military-related deaths in El Salvador are clearly the most incomplete, with no data, or partial estimates for 1982, 1984, 1990-1991. Table 2 reveals that little reliable information is available on yearly estimates of civilian and military war-related deaths. Therefore only aggregate totals for both the Civil War and the Contra War are presented for Nicaragua. For El Salvador, as a result of the report of the Truth Commission, we have greater knowledge of proportionate responsibility for civilian deaths related to the conflict, than in Nicaragua where no such comprehensive study has yet been performed.

OVER-ESTIMATES AND UNDER-ESTIMATES

El Salvador

The Government of El Salvador (GOES), the Salvadoran Armed Forces (FAS), and the United States Department of State each presented estimates of Salvadoran civil war deaths and other human rights violations throughout the course of the war that were substantially lower than estimates made by Salvadoran non-governmental human rights organizations such as Tutela Legal (TL), Socorro Juridico (SJ) and the Comisión de Derechos

[6]For the purposes of this study, the absence of Guatemala is due to the absence of survey data with which to compare the "objective" estimates of deaths. In terms of conflict intensity, however, Guatemala probably surpasses both El Salvador and Nicaragua in terms of level of civilian casualties.

Humanos de El Salvador (CDHES), on which most international organization estimates were based. This divergence is particularly evident in 1981, where there was a considerable difference between the GOES and CDHES estimates of civilian deaths for the entire year: 5,328 and 17,303 respectively. Also final estimates show a range that varies by over 37,000, with FAS as the most conservative with 37,907, the U.S. State Department offering a mid-range estimate of 55,000, and various human rights organizations settling on the upper figure of 75,000.

The reasons for this divergence, which seemed to emerge most dramatically in 1981, but are ultimately reflected in the final estimates, are several. First, as Americas Watch observes in its 1983 report, "Violence shifted significantly to the countryside [in late 1980-81], making it more difficult for human rights groups (with offices in the capital city) to secure reports or verify them."[7] Major army offensives and civilian massacres in Morazán, Chalatenango and San Vicente during 1980-82 highlighted instances of casualties that were not recognized by GOES and U.S. officials until the post-war negotiations. On the one hand, the non-governmental human rights group estimates, such as those of Tutela Legal and CDHES were partly based on unverified reports, while on the other hand, GOES and U.S. Embassy reports probably underestimated the actual number of deaths and tended to conflate civilian and combatant deaths.

Secondly, as Lisa North notes, estimates of war casualties corresponded with the legislative military aid appropriation cycles in the U.S., particularly in the early part of the war. Between 1981-1983, in order to obtain Congressional approval for military aid, President Reagan, on four occasions, "certified" that the human rights situation was improving in El Salvador. Despite the fact that these certifications were contradicted by most

---

[7]Americas Watch (1983) *Second Supplement to the Report on Human Rights in El Salvador.* p. 9.

However, the FAS claim of only 5,287 total civilian deaths due to the war seems far too low, and calls into question the validity of the military components of its final estimate. While the State Department estimate of 55,000 total war related deaths approximates the cumulative minimum number of war deaths derived from the yearly totals, it is well below the cumulative maximum. There is some remaining ambiguity stemming from a lack of clear distinctions between civilian and military related deaths. FAS and GOES estimates tended to view civilians who were killed in conflictive zones as combatants. Non-governmental human rights organization estimates used different criteria to distinguish civilians from combatants, however their figures focused almost entirely on civilian deaths or relied on FMLN radio reports for FAS casualty estimates. In cases where combatant estimates were combined with civilian estimates, using two or more different sources, there is a possibility for some overlap due to this definitional problem (see yearly totals for 1982, 1983 & 1989 in Table 1).

The sum of these concerns raises the greatest reliability questions regarding the combat death estimates. The civilian death total of 50-60,000 seems to be most reliable. As noted above, the majority of these deaths have been attributed to FAS and GOES security forces.[13] Total civilian and military deaths attributed to the war can be safely estimated to be within the range of 80,000 and 94,000, omitting the lowest FAS total estimate of 37,907 based on highly questionable validity and the US Embassy estimate of 55,000. The cumulative totals in Table 1 may underestimate the actual number of deaths due to the missing information regarding combatant deaths for several years. This estimate of military and civilian deaths due to war related

---

[13] Despite certain violations by the FMLN, the Truth Commission estimated that over 90% of the civilian deaths were carried out by the Armed Forces, GOES security forces, or right wing death squads.

violence, while plausible, precludes a more concise estimate considering the caveats of the available data.

Nicaragua

Unlike El Salvador, there are few, if any, reliable estimates of yearly civilian and combatant war-related deaths—in either the Nicaraguan Civil War or the Contra War. In addition, the political motivations for organizations who reported human rights violations were reversed during the Contra War. The Comisión por la Protección y Promoción de los Derechos Humanos (CNPPDH) and the Comisión Permanente de los Derechos Humanos (CPDH) are the two primary Nicaraguan human rights organizations responsible for investigating violations during the Contra War. The state-funded CNPPDH was more critical of Contra abuses, although it performed investigations of Nicaraguan security forces that led to the convictions of many Sandinista offenders. The CPDH is a quasi-independent organization that emerged during the late 1970s, but was more critical of the Sandinista government during the 1980s. CPDH reports were compromised by its publication of allegations unsubstantiated by subsequent investigations and by accepting donations from the U.S. National Endowment for Democracy, whose efforts were sympathetic to the Contras.[14] Both Nicaraguan agencies worked with international human rights organizations such as Americas Watch and Amnesty International in documenting violations of the rights of civilians during the Contra War. A third human rights agency, the Asociación Pro Derechos Humanos (APDH) was established in

---

[14]In 1986, CPDH accepted $50,000 from the NED for report duplication in the U.S.. *Envío* editorials have criticized CPDH for soft criticism of the Contras in their reporting of human rights abuses. One noted example is CPDH's reporting of only 15 Contra kidnapping cases out of an estimated 912 during 1987. See Paul Laverty (1986*) Human Rights Report - The CPDH: Can It Be Trusted?* Glasgow, Scotland: Scottish Medical Aid For Nicaragua.

1986 to investigate alleged Contra violations. Largely funded by $3 million in U.S. "humanitarian aid" to the Contras, APDH reports were found to be consistently unreliable.[15]

The data in Table 2 show a greater consensus on the total number of war-related deaths during the Contra insurgency of the 1980s, than for the Sandinista-led insurrection. Clodfelter presents two different estimates for the Civil War, and confers greater reliability on the lower estimate of 10,000 deaths for the entire duration.[16] This low figure seems unlikely due to other references to 20,000 losses during the September 1978 campaign and the final offensive from May - July, 1979 alone. The U.S. State Department conservatively concludes that a figure of 50,000 is most likely.

For both conflicts there is general agreement that many of the war-related deaths were of civilian non-combatants.[17] No formal aggregate estimates have verified a reliable proportion of civilians to combatants. However, two factors suggest that civilian war-related deaths were high during the Civil War. During the Civil War, both armies were fairly small. The FSLN never counted more than 5,000 armed troops until late May 1979, compared to just 700 as of August 1978. The National Guard also only numbered approximately 13,000 at this time. Even though the FSLN had a relatively small fighting force, the National Guard made little attempt to distinguish between civilian and combatant, directing their energies into repression of civilians more than fighting the Sandinistas. Moreover, while the spontaneous uprisings, as in Monimbo in 1978, and the groundswell of popular support for the FSLN during the final offensive, may have increasingly confused such distinctions, the government

---

[15]Catholic Institute for International Relations (1987) *Right to Survive, Human Rights in Nicaragua*. London, p. 39-40.
[16]Op. cit. pg. 1173.
[17]Clodfelter, Sklar and Walker all concur on this point.

bombing of popular neighborhoods and indiscriminate retaliation by the National Guard left little doubt among national and international observers that civilians experienced the lion's share of the casualties.[18]

For the Contra War, the distinction between combatant and non-combatant, becomes more complicated. Both the Sandinista army (EPS) and the Contra forces were considerably larger during the 1980s, reaching levels as high as 80,000 and 15,000 respectively.[19] Fighting was limited largely to the countryside (Zelaya, Chontales, Boaca, Matagalpa, Jinotega, and Nueva Segovia) unlike the urban battles of Sandinista insurrection (Managua, Matagalpa, León, Masaya, Chinandega, Estelí), thus making verification of human rights violations difficult. Claims of consistent Contra attacks against civilians were supported by extensive interviews with witnesses by Nicaraguan and international human rights organizations.[20] Such organizations have also documented killing of civilians by EPS and Sandinista

[18]Timothy Wickham-Crowley also emphasizes the cross-class alliance that formed in an effort to depose Somoza, including members of the private sector as well as the poorest campesinos. For this reason as well as the urban context of the fighting and the indiscriminate methods of repression employed by the government, victims of the repression were spread among all social classes, not limited to the poor nor to the FSLN cadre. See *Guerrillas and Revolution in Latin America* (1992) Princeton: Princeton University Press, pp. 275-81.

[19]Ibid. p. 179. There is some doubt that Contra forces ever actually reached above 10,000 regulars. The Contras formally demobilized 19,613 combatants in July 1990, although only 16,000 weapons were turned in. The FSLN estimates that only 50% of the demobilized forces were actually combatants. *Envío*, July 1990, p. 40.

[20]The CNPPDH (Boletín, Dec. 1985) gives 1,062 investigated and confirmed killings of civilians by Contra forces for the period 1980 to June 30 1985. See Catholic Institute for International Relations (1987) *Right to Survive, Human Rights in Nicaragua*. London, p. 53. Many of the Contra victims were social service workers (teachers, health care workers, coop administrators), as part of the Contra strategy to neutralize the government's social programs in remote regions. Investigation of Contra abuses was also obstructed by kidnapping of human rights workers.

security forces.[21] The U.S. State Department has selectively employed these contesting accounts as part of a massive campaign to delegitimize the Sandinistas, often distorting available information beyond recognition for political ends.[22] However, no summary reports which distinguish civilians from combatants, and which attempt to assign proportional responsibility to either the Contras or Sandinista security forces have been issued. There is general agreement among international human rights organizations, that there existed no government policy of extra-judicial execution or murder, while the Contras were found to demonstrate a consistent pattern of violating Article 3 of the 1949 Geneva Conventions, which governs protections due non-combatants during war.[23]

---

[21] The most notable incidents include the EPS killing of 14-17 Miskito civilians in Zelaya in Dec. 1981, and the similar killing of 69 Miskito civilians in Puerta Cabezas in 1982. See Americas Watch (AW) 1982, *On Human Rights in Nicaragua*, New York, pp. 64-65; and Lawyers Committee for International Human Rights (1985) *Nicaragua Revolutionary Justice,* p. 140. Former DGSE official Alvaro Baldizón claims that the Sandinista Interior Ministry forces (DGSE), under direction of Minister Tomás Borge, directed the murder of some 2,000 people. Americas Watch has challenged this claim, and reports that the number of recorded killings outside combat and disappearances for which the Nicaraguan government is responsible is closer to 300 between 1980-86. These incidents were committed by DGSE or Army agents in remote areas of Matagalpa and Jinotega, and in some cases involved torture. Many Sandinista violators have been convicted of these offenses and imprisoned. See AW (1986) *Human Rights in Nicaragua 1985-86*, New York, pp. 127-149 and *Nicaragua, A Human Rights Chronology* July. 1979-July 1989 (1989) p. 13. Other noted Sandinista abuses involved forced relocation of Miskito and Sumu communities in 1981-83, forced recruitment, lack of due process for incarcerated Contra prisoners and the suspension of civil liberties under the declared state of emergency.

[22]For instance, in a May 9, 1984 speech, Reagan declared that "There has been an attempt to wipe out an entire culture, the Miskito Indians, thousands of whom have been slaughtered or herded into detention camps where they have been starved and abused." In Sklar (1989) p. 105. This seems to lack credibility, given that conditions at the camps had improved considerably that year, certain EPS violators had been prosecuted, and later in 1984 resettlement in the Río Coco region was permitted.

[23]See Americas Watch (1989) p. 13. this conclusion was further reinforced by U.S. Congress' periodic decisions to end funding for the Contras, forcing the Reagan administration to pursue illegal covert means of supporting the insurgency.

In sum we find general agreement on the total number of deaths due to the Contra War, approximately 30,000, with little confirmation on the distinction between civilians and combatants. The FSLN estimate of 61,826 seems an unlikely overestimate of actual casualties, perhaps inflated for political reasons. Similarly for the Civil War, if we rule out the low estimate of 10,000, there is a consensus around 50,000 war-related deaths, with no clear indication of how many of those were non-combatants. Thus an estimate for both conflicts combined of approximately 80,000 war-related deaths, with perhaps 40,000 of those being non-combatants seems plausible.

WAR DEATH ESTIMATES: SOME TENTATIVE CONCLUSIONS

This summary does not include the most recent violence in El Salvador that has been estimated by ONUSAL, the United Nations Observer team, to have reached over 9,135 homicides in 1994 and 7877 homicides in 1995. El Salvador ranked as the second most violent region in Latin America by the Pan American health Organization, with 136.5 homicides per 100,000 - second only to Medellín, Colombia.[24] It is difficult to distinguish what proportion of these killings were politically motivated, however there are considerable indications that reformed death squads are operating in a manner that may be comparable to the early war years. Similarly in Nicaragua, of the estimate 250,000 people bearing arms during the Contra War, only 16,000 weapons were collected from the Contras and the weapons buy-back

---

[24]*La Prensa Gráfica*, Mar. 24, 1995. Report by the Salvadoran Attorney General on the level of violence. In addition to homicides, there were 6,443 victims wounded in attacks, and 3,600 reported death threats. The current homicide rate remains at an average of 20 persons per day, which represents a rate of violent deaths that is higher than the average rate of violent deaths over the course of the war. If added to the war-related, the total climbs to approximately 110,000. *Estudios Centro Americanos*, Vol. 569 (March 1996) pp. 240-249. See also the Pan American Health Org. (1994), "Las Condiciones de Salud en las Americas," Vol. 1.

designs for both studies were area probability samples, relying upon the best available census and census mapping information.

THE RELEVANT QUESTIONNAIRE ITEMS

The surveys upon which we are basing our analysis were primarily designed to measure the political attitudes and behaviors of the populations of the two countries, and therefore the information on the consequences of the violence are limited. One relevant independent variable, however, was conceptualized as victimization in the wars. For that purpose, three items were included, one to measure deaths of relatives, a second to measure internal refugees and the third to measure international refugees. The items themselves are as follows:[25]

WC1. Have you lost some family member or close relative as a result of the armed conflict of the last decade? (include disappeared) 1. Yes. 2. No.

WC2. Has some member of your family had to flee or abandon his/her home because of the conflict of the last decade? 1. Yes 2. No.

WC3. And has some family member had to leave the country? 1. Yes 2. No.

FINDINGS

Overall Results

We first report upon the overall results on the three items for the two countries. (Table 4 contains the results.)

---

[25]In Nicaragua, the first item was altered in form somewhat. It read: "Diga Ud. si durante el conflict armado de la última década: ¿Algún miembro de su familia fue asesinado por esa causa?" ("Tell me if during the armed conflict in the last decade: was any member of your family killed?") The main difference in the two forms of the question is that in El Salvador, in addition to "familia," the item included reference to "pariente cercano" (close relative). We assume that the term "familia" includes both categories, but it may have been responsible for higher reporting in El Salvador than in Nicaragua.

Table 4 contains a great deal of important information. First, we see that in both countries, slightly over one-third of the population have had family members who were killed during the violence. While this seems like a very large proportion, the reader should be cautioned not to misinterpret to mean that one-third of the people of El Salvador and Nicaragua were killed. Rather, one-third of all of the people in these two countries had relatives who died during the conflict. Second, given the per capita data reported on in the first part of this paper, it is surprising that the death rate in Nicaragua reported in the survey is not higher than El Salvador. If we accept the maximum death rate figures for both countries, and percapitize them by their present populations as calculated in the 1994 census of El Salvador and the 1995 census of Nicaragua, the death rate in El Salvador would be .018%, and in Nicaragua .036%, or almost double. Third, a somewhat higher percentage of the respondents in both countries had family members who were forced to abandon their homes and migrate to some other place in order to escape the hazards of the war. Finally, international migration produced by the war occurred at a somewhat lower level in both countries, but still affected the relatives of over one quarter of all of the people in El Salvador and Nicaragua.[26] Estimates of migration suggest that somewhere between 648,871 and 1,403,642 Salvadorans became international refugees, or as much as over one-quarter of the entire 1994 population left the country during the conflict. The survey figure of 27% seems on target. The official estimates for internal refugees is up to 577,182, or only 11.5% of the 1994 population compared to our survey figure of 36.3%. In Nicaragua, sources suggest as many as 613,700 people became international refugees, or 15% of the 1995 population compared with

---

[26]For data see: Sergio Aguayo and Patricia Weiss Fagan, *Central Americans in Mexico and the United States.* Boulder: Westview; Segundo Montes, *Desplazados y Refugiados.* San Salvador: UCA, 1985; Edelberto Torres-Rivas, *Report on Condition of Central American Refugees and Migrants.* San José, Costa Rica: FLACSO, 1985.

our figure of 29%, while as many as 350,000 Nicaraguans became internal refugees, or 9% of the population, compared to our survey figure of 29%. The lack of congruence between the two sources here may be a result of confusion over the internal versus international displacement.

GEOGRAPHIC DISTRIBUTION OF VICTIMS

We now turn to the geographic distribution of the victims. Was it safer to live in the capital city, or remote areas? Figures 1 and 2 show the departmental distribution for each country. Zelaya was excluded in the Nicaragua study. In El Salvador, the departmental average varies considerably, from a high of 72.5% in Cuscatlán to a low of 17.0 in Ahuachapán. The relatively low level of casualties in Santa Ana is certainly not unexpected, for this was a portion of the country that suffered very little damage in the war. Indeed, the entire Western portion of the country, including the departments of Santa Ana, Sonsonate and La Libertad suffered little from the war, although one must hasten to add that these were the regions most affected during the Matanza of 1932.

The high death rate in Cuscatlán, however, might come as a surprise since so much of the reporting on the war concentrated on the combat in the border region with Honduras (Chalatenango, Cabañas and Morazán). It was there where the FMLN is reported to have had its strongest outposts and the army was the most aggressive in attacking the guerrillas, namely, the northern departments of Morazán and Chalatenango. In fact, Chalatenango ranks second, Cabañas fourth and Morazán fifth, indicating a high level of casualties. But it is often forgotten that the longest and most persistent fighting took place no more than 40 kilometers from San Salvador on the skirts of the Volcán Guazapa, and in and around the town of Suchitoto. These areas are in Cuscatlán (Figure 1). Consequently, our survey seems to reflect with great accuracy the geographic impact of the war: the departments that we know to have been most highly affected show up in the survey as the departments with the largest number of family members having suffered losses. These results increase considerably our confidence in the survey as an accurate source for measuring the demographic impact of the wars of Central America.

In Nicaragua, (see Figure 2), we see a similar pattern, with important differences. The highest reported deaths occurred in Nueva Segovia, Estelí and Madriz, departments that were centers of the Contra War. Managua and León have the lowest death rates. It is easier to compare the pattern found in the two countries by examining Figure 3. Overall, the patterns are similar, but the extremes in El Salvador are greater; the department of highest violence is higher than in Nicaragua, and the department of lowest violence is lower.

GENDER

In conventional warfare, soldiers are overwhelmingly male and represent the largest number of casualties. In the infamous Chaco war between Bolivia and Paraguay, it is said that a substantial portion of the male population of the country was wiped out. In Central America, the wars were not conventional, fought by guerrilla armies with many women soldiers and fought by government armies that killed many female civilians.

While the data cannot tell us about the gender of the victims, it can tell us about the gender of the survivors. As Table 5 shows, males and females were affected in nearly identical proportions in both countries, with males have a slight edge in both countries.

SOCIO-ECONOMIC STATUS OF THE VICTIMS

Our central hypothesis regarding the socio-economic status of the victims is that they were poorer than the non-victims. Our survey provides us with indirect evidence of the socio-economic status of the victims. We make the plausible assumption that the socio-economic status of the victims, on average, does not differ dramatically from that of the survivors. For example, we would not expect that the average level of education of victims to differ significantly from the average of their survivors, except to the extent that survivors are likely to be older than the victims (it is the young who fight and die in wars) and the young, on average, are more educated than their parents.

Age

It is difficult to draw conclusions about the age of the victims from the age of the survivors. But, we wish to know if those whose family members were killed in the wars were younger or older than those who did not have family members who were victims. The results shown in Table 6 show that there were in fact no significant differences among the two groups. In both countries, those with relatives killed were slightly older than those who did not have relatives who died in the war.

Education

In Table 7, we present the first clear evidence supporting the hypothesis that the victims were poorer than those who survived. The mean education level of the families of those killed in both El Salvador and Nicaragua is lower than for those who did not loose anyone during the war. In the case of El Salvador, the difference is statistically significant.

Occupation

But education alone does not tell us all we need to know about the families of those who were killed. A clearer indication is provided by examining the occupations of the survivors. Figure 4 shows the distribution of occupations in the survey and the relative impact of the war on each. It is not surprising that the soldiers in the sample were the most heavily affected by the war. Far more interesting are the remaining occupations. We see that those who worked in the public sector in clerical jobs experienced a relatively low level of loss. Even more surprising, perhaps is the low level of loss among students since it was thought that students were especially likely to be victims in the war. However, it must be remembered, we are dealing with the families of those killed, and students in the present sample were likely to have been fairly young during the war years. In contrast, the two most highly affected groups are professionals and landless peasants who rent or sharecrop land. In many ways, this finding reveals much about the war; it affected El Salvador's poorest citizens, as well as its best off. Indeed, it affected the social extremes more than it did the center.

Figure 5 shows for Nicaragua the relationship between occupation and loss of a family member. It is surprising to see how different this result is from that in El Salvador. In Nicaragua the most seriously affected group were public sector office workers, whereas in El Salvador this was the least affected group. A similar contrast appears among the renter/sharecropper population, which in El Salvador was highly affected, but in Nicaragua was among the least affected. It should be noted that in Nicaragua we did not include a code for soldier, and therefore did not have any information on the impact of the war on this group. It is possible that some of those who identified themselves as public sector office workers were in reality soldiers and therefore the deaths in this category were exaggerated.

These sharp contrasts between El Salvador and Nicaragua help suggest the fundamentally different nature of the two conflicts. In Nicaragua the deaths were spread across the board, especially if we assume that many of the deaths attributed to the public sector employees were actually military deaths. In El Salvador, however, the war affected those at the extremes, farm land renters on the one hand and professionals on the other. We will see these differences more clearly when we examine the ideology of the population.

Income

We also have information on the income of the respondents. In Figures 6 and 7 the relationship between war casualties and income is displayed. As can be seen, no overall pattern emerges for either country.

IDEOLOGY AND THE FAMILIES OF THE VICTIMS

The above analysis demonstrated few major differences among the families of the victims of the violence in both El Salvador and Nicaragua other than the lower level of education among the victims than the non-victims. The conclusion that one can draw from this analysis is that the effects of the war were widespread, cutting across class and socio-economic lines. These results make it appear as if there are no real differences between the impact of the war in the two countries, but as the following analysis reveals, nothing could be further from the truth. In fact, what we have discovered is that political ideology, far more than the socio-economic and demographic characteristics of individuals, explains the impact of the war on life and death.

We first looked at political party affiliation of the survivors to try to determine something about the political preferences of those killed. We know from a great deal of voting behavior research, that party loyalties tend to run in families. While it is abundantly clear that not all children take on the party of their parents, it is also clear that it is far more common to find children of the same party as their parents than it is to find children of different parties. Similarly, party preference tends to include the extended family as well. Important exceptions are well known, such as the Chamoro family in Nicaragua, but those are merely visible exceptions to the general rule. We feel confident, therefore, in using the party affiliation and ideological preferences of the survivors as a reasonable measure of the affiliation and preferences of those who were killed.

Figure 8 compares the impact of war losses by party affiliation of those who survived. We focus only upon the major party groupings of left and right in the two countries. It is clear from Figure 8 that there is a strikingly different pattern in the two countries. In El Salvador, those associated with the left, i.e., the FMLN, suffered war casualties at a rate far higher (sig. < .001) than those on the right, i.e., ARENA. In Nicaragua, however, while the left (FSLN) also suffered higher casualties than those on the right (UNO), the differences are small and statistically insignificant.

Further evidence of the differential impact of ideology on war deaths is revealed in Figure 9, which uses a left-right scale. Each individual who responded to the survey was asked to locate themselves on a continuum from left-to-right that had ten points on it. As can be seen in the figure, ideology had a strong impact in El Salvador and almost none in Nicaragua. In El Salvador the extreme left suffered a far higher proportion of casualties than those in the center or right, although there is a slight increase among those on the extreme right. In Nicaragua, no such pattern is uncovered, and indeed there is a slight decline among those on the extreme right.

DISCUSSION AND CONCLUSIONS

It is clear from the evidence presented that the two cases under study are very different. In both cases, the violence cut across all socio-economic sectors, but in El Salvador it largely affected those with leftist ideological sentiments. In Nicaragua, however, there were really two wars. The first was the war against Somoza, one in which nearly all sectors of Nicaraguan society participated, although the left was more heavily engaged than the right. The second was the Contra War, the war to unseat the Sandinistas, in which the right fought against the left. Therefore, in Nicaragua, all sectors suffered, whereas in El Salvador, one sector suffered far more than any other.

We can speculate about the impact of this differential suffering on the reconciliation process underway in each country since the wars came to an end. El Salvador has been far more successful than Nicaragua putting the war behind it and reconstructing a new, more peaceful society. Nicaraguans, on the other hand, have been thus far unable to agree on the basic structure of the post-war society. Perhaps because the war cut such a wide ideological swath in Nicaragua, there is less willingness to compromise, whereas in El Salvador, the left suffered disproportionately and therefore might be more willing to compromise to save themselves from further suffering.

We should also comment upon our methodology. We have combined the estimate of war deaths from various sources with two surveys of the survivors of the conflicts. In doing so we have uncovered important evidence supporting the view that the war in El Salvador was one directed largely against the left. The survey research instrument, not often used by demographers to obtain information of this sort, has proven to be surprisingly useful.

TABLE 1. SUMMARY OF ESTIMATED CIVILIAN AND MILITARY DEATHS DURING THE SALVADORAN CIVIL WAR, 1979-1991

	1980	1981	1982	1983	1984	1985	1986	1987	1988	1989	1990	1991	Total
1. Civilian Deaths	(9,825 + 1,476[a])[4] 14,343[3] 11,903[8]	16,357[3] (6,116- 13,353)[7]	12,547[3] 5,339[9] 5,962[8]	5,826[3] 5,569[8]	2,860[3]	1,832[12] 1,543[3] (335- 2,287)[20]	1,821[3] 1,091[12]	1,415[3]	1,891[3] 301[14] 261[15]	432[14] 3713[3] [193[+] (250-500)][15]	1,323[3]	1,035[3]	36,988(min) - 65,161(max)[d] 40-50,000[6] 67,390[3] 5,287[10]
2. Combat Deaths	(658f + 3,477F)[4]	(500f + 801F)[7]	1,200F[7] 953F[5]b	(12,98F[5]b (4,316f + 1,693F)[7] 774f[4]	334f[19]	749F[20] (1,034f + 426F)[7] (1,123f + 397F)[20]	(900f + 459F)[21]	(1004f + 470F)[21] (809f+ 500F)[7] (459F 900f)[13]	(1,111f + 455F)[7] 826f[14]	(401f + 600F)[15] (784f + 208F)[7] (1,902f 446F)[18]	852[18]		10,360F(max) 12,274f(max)[d] 30,000F[22] 14,000f[11] (23,840f+ 9,140F)[10]
3. Disap-pearances	979[1]	927[1]	1,177[1]	526[1]	196[1] 205[3]	185[3] 81[12]	39[12] 213[3]	213[3]	253[3]	293[3]	164[3]	157[3]	5,292[d]
4. Yrly.Total Civ.&Combat Losses (1+2+3) Min.[c] Max.[c]	9,600[16] 14,713[1] 16,415 19,457	5,328[16] 17,303[1] 8,344 18.585	8,494[c][5,8] 13,794[1] 7,469 14,924	8,167 12,361	552[16] 2,402[1] 3,399 3,399	1,980 3,992	2,663 3,393	2,937 3,102	1,795 3,725	1,628 6,354	2,339 2,339	1,192 1,192	37,907[10] 55,000[2] 75,000[7]
5. Cum. Total Min.[c] Max.[c]	16,415 19,457	24,759 38,042	42,000[7] 32,228 52,966	47,000[7] 40,395 65.361	43,794 68,726	45,774 72,718	48,437 76,111	53,374 79,213	53,169 82,938	54,797 89,292	73,000[e][7] 57,136 91,631	*58,328* *92,823*	***58,328*** ***92,823***

(continued on next page)

TABLE 4. SURVEY RESULTS OF WAR VICTIMS IN EL SALVADOR AND NICARAGUA

Respondents with family members who:	El Salvador	Nicaragua
WC1. Were Killed	34.0%	35.0%
WC2. Became Internal Refugees	36.3%	38.9%
WC3. Became International Refugees	27.2%	29.0%

TABLE 5. GENDER OF THE SURVIVORS

	El Salvador		Nicaragua	
	Male	Female	Male	Female
% With Relatives Killed	34.6	33.5	35.3	34.7

TABLE 6. MEAN AGE OF THE SURVIVORS

	El Salvador	Nicaragua
Relatives Killed	38.1	35.9
Relatives Not Killed	37.1	34.8

TABLE 7. MEAN YEARS OF EDUCATION OF THE SURVIVORS

	El Salvador	Nicaragua
Relatives Killed	5.4**	5.7
Relatives Not Killed	6.2	6.3

** sig. < .01

FIGURE 1. RESPONDENTS WITH FAMILY MEMBER KILLED DURING CONFLICT, EL SALVADOR

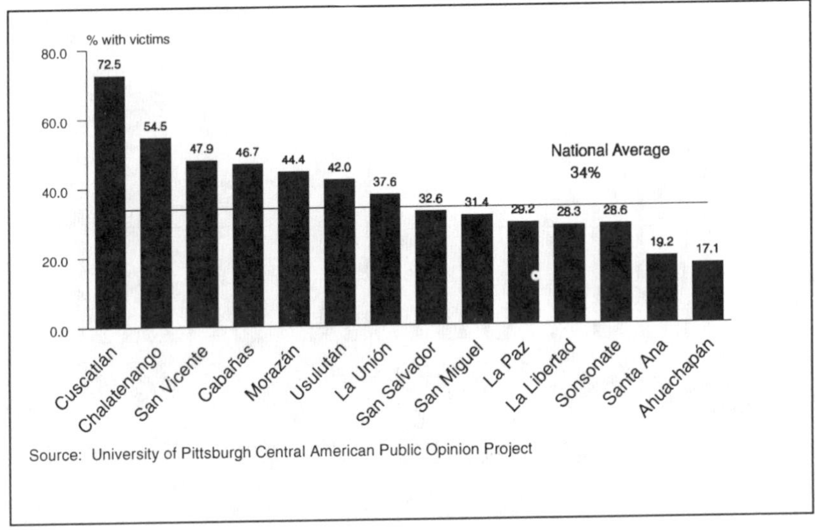

Source: University of Pittsburgh Central American Public Opinion Project

FIGURE 2. RESPONDENTS WITH FAMILY MEMBERS KILLED DURING CONFLICTS, NICARAGUA

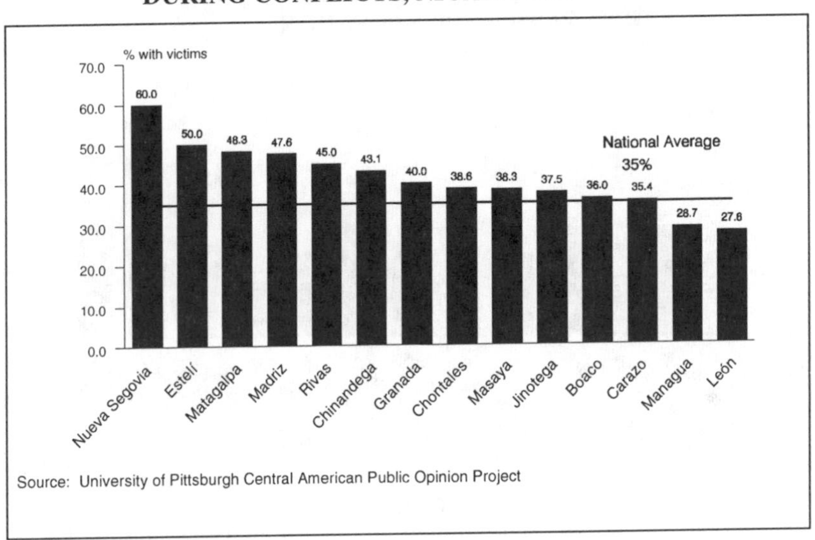

Source: University of Pittsburgh Central American Public Opinion Project

FIGURE 3. RESPONDENTS WITH FAMILY MEMBERS KILLED DURING CONFLICTS, EL SALVADOR AND NICARAGUA

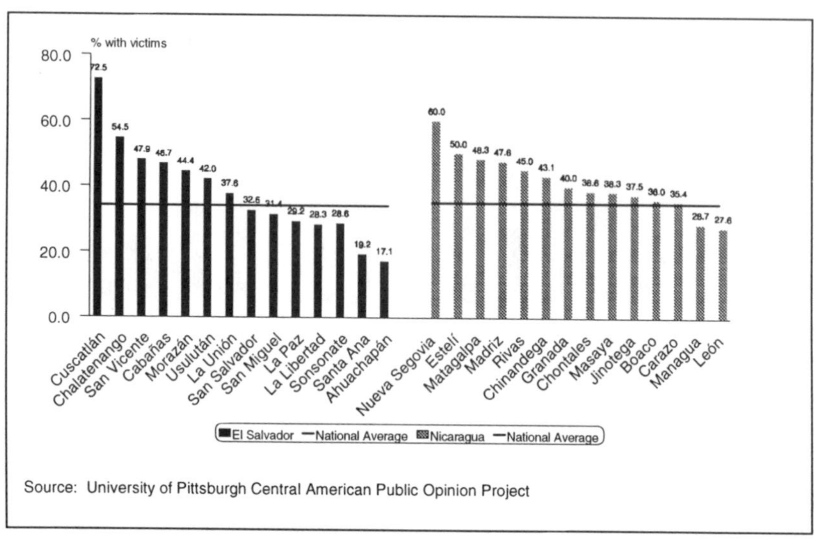

Source: University of Pittsburgh Central American Public Opinion Project

FIGURE 4. MEMBER OF FAMILY KILLED IN WAR, BY OCCUPATION, EL SALVADOR

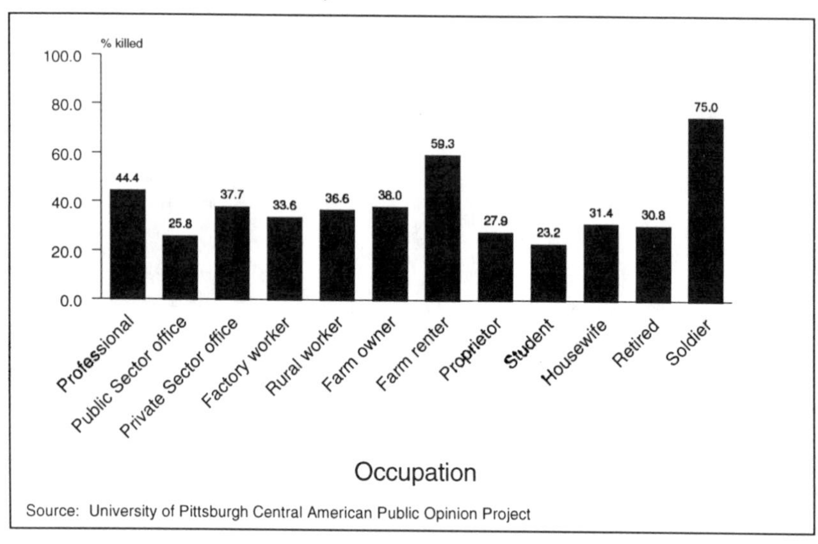

Source: University of Pittsburgh Central American Public Opinion Project

FIGURE 5. MEMBER OF FAMILY KILLED IN WAR, BY OCCUPATION, NICARAGUA

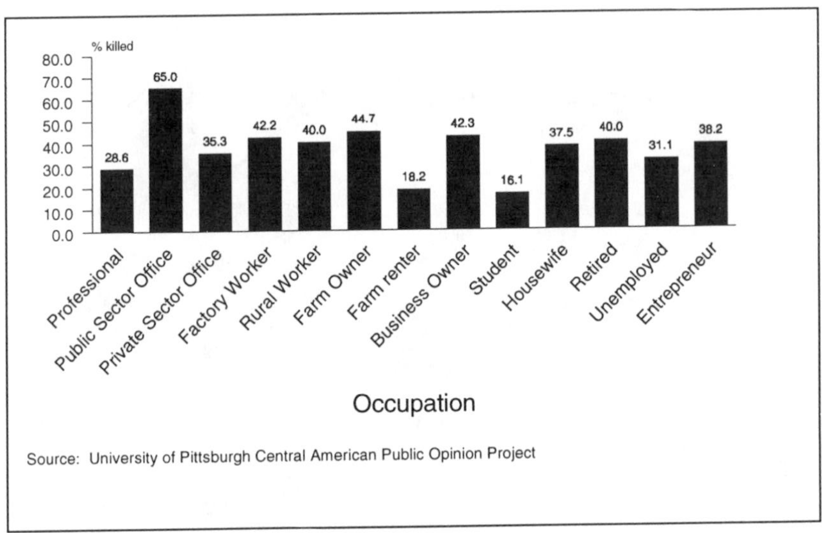

FIGURE 6. FAMILY MEMBER KILLED, BY INCOME, EL SALVADOR

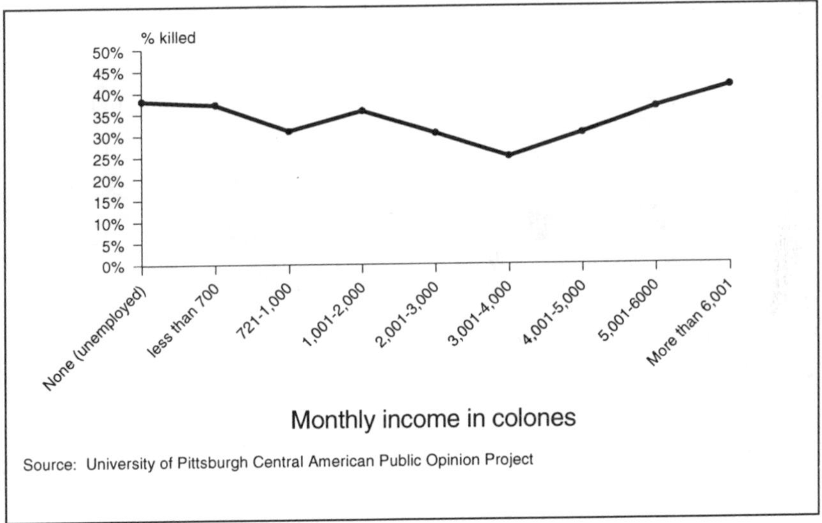

FIGURE 7. FAMILY MEMBER KILLED, BY INCOME, NICARAGUA

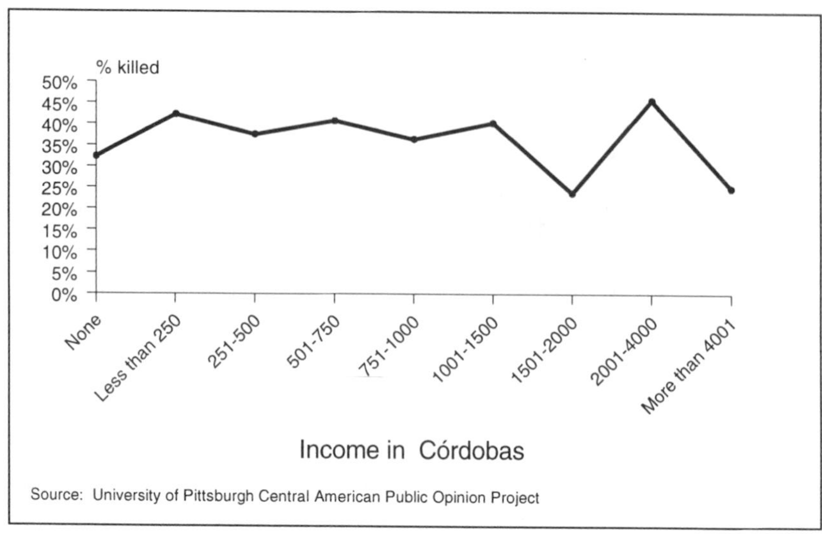

FIGURE 8. FAMILY MEMBER KILLED, BY PARTY, EL SALVADOR AND NICARAGUA

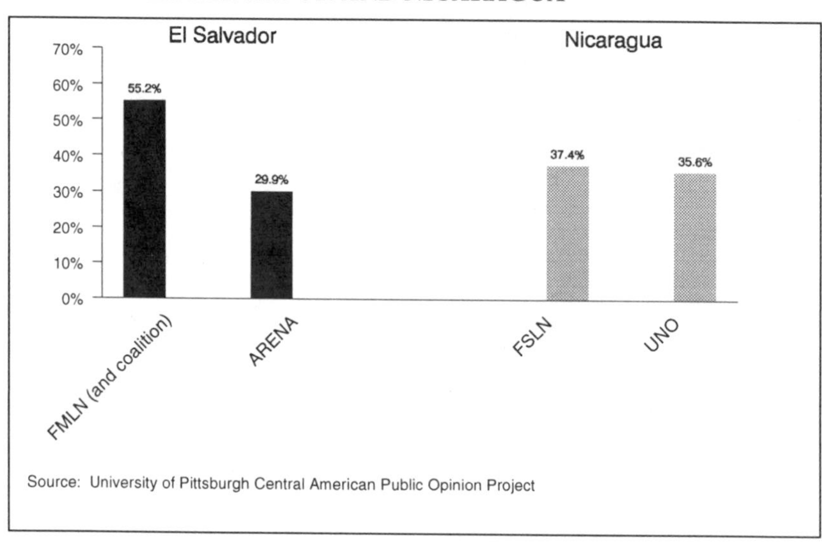

FIGURE 9. FAMILY MEMBER KILLED, BY IDEOLOGY, EL SALVADOR AND NICARAGUA

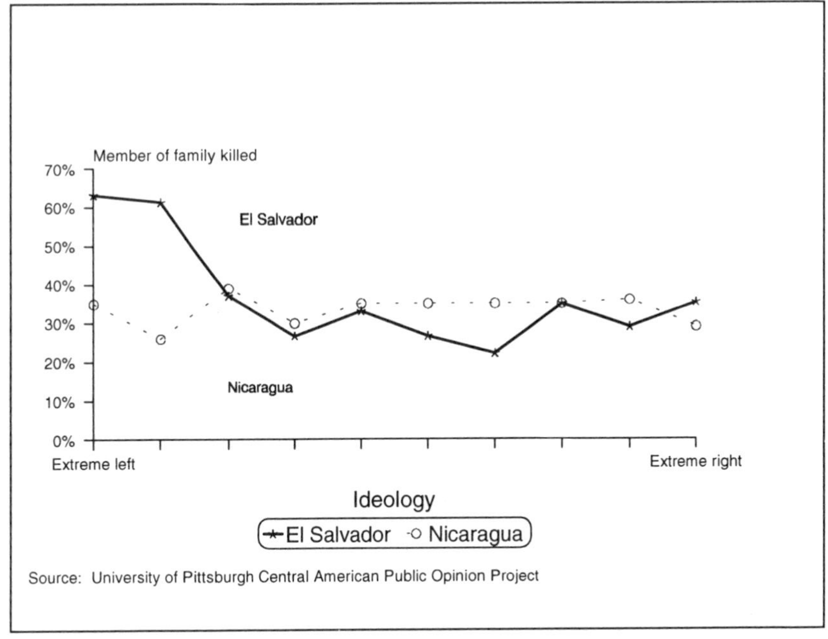

Source: University of Pittsburgh Central American Public Opinion Project

when Perefán de Rivera[12] carried out the first assessment (*repartimiento*) of indigenous peoples.

In Panama there were almost no restricted indigenous peoples. What is presented comes from different sources for the few indigenous groups that existed in the Panama and Natá area. The Darien region was emptied of indigenous people and abandoned after the first colonial settlements between 1510 and 1520. Vedragua had still not been conquered, and we do not know what the indigenous population was in this area or in the Mosquitia and Petén regions.

THE INDIGENOUS POPULATION CIRCA 1581

The figures for Chiapas and Soconusco have been interpolated based on calculations by Gerhard and Gasco, respectively.

The data for Honduras comes from tributaries estimated by Linda Newson for 1582 and then multiplied by 5.[13] Data for Nicaragua comes from a census of tributaries carried out in 1581 and analyzed and processed by Linda Newson.[14]

Calculations for Guatemala and El Salvador come from the same authors used for the 1550 estimates.

The figures for the indigenous population of Costa Rica are based on Perfán de Rivera's assessment (repartimiento) multiplied by 5. Calculations relative to Panama are derived from a report to the Judge of the High Court (*oidor de la audiencia)*, Alonso Criado de Castilla.[15] As in the previous map, there is nothing that can be said about the figures in areas that had still

---

[12]Fernández, León. *Encomiendas y reducciones. Colección de Documentos para la historia de Costa Rica.* Vol. II. San José, Editorial Costa Rica, 2da Edición, 1976, pp. 26-30.

[13]Newson, Linda. *The Cost of Conquest*, pp. 289-291.

[14]Newson, Linda. *Indian Survival...* pp. 238-239.

[15]AGI, Panama, Legajo 11. "Summary description of the kingdom of Tierra Firme..." 1575.

escaped Spanish domination: Mosquitia, Darien, Petén, Talamanca, etc.

THE INDIGENOUS POPULATION CIRCA 1684

At first we tried to carry out a calculation based on an extensive document classified in the AGI with the catalogue number: Accountancy 815 *(Contaduría 815)*. However we were unable to obtain a satisfactory calculation. The document has too many lapses and unequal information. In some cases it is overwhelmingly detailed while in others, details are extremely lacking. Moreover, the criteria used by the different officials who gathered the information do not seem to meet the minimum requirements for coherence.

The publication of a detailed document concerning the salaries of the members of the Audience of Guatemala[16] in 1684 allowed us to carry out a reasonable estimate of the total indigenous population based on the calculation of taxes. Keeping in mind the changes in tax coverage which occurred from the 16th century on, a multiplier of 3 was applied.

The information for Panama was taken from the visit by Bishop Morcillo.[17]

THE INDIGENOUS POPULATION AT CIRCA 1800

Thanks to the administration of the last Bourbon kings, we have a very detailed list of tributaries that allows us to estimate the indigenous population at the end of the colonial period. To do so we have used an interpolation between data obtained

---

[16]Enriquez Macias, Genoveva. "New documents for the historic demography of the Audience of Guatemala at the end of the 17th century." *Mesoamerica*, 1989, vol. 17, pp. 121-183.

[17]Visit of Bishop Pedro Morcillo Rubio and Auñon, 1736, published in Gasteazoro, Carlos Manuel. "An unpublished geographic relation of Panama." *Revista Loteria*, vol. III, No. 32, 2nd edition, August 1968, pp. 67-76.

for 1788[18] and 1805.[19] The total number of resulting tributaries was multiplied by 5 in order to obtain the total population.

THE INDIGENOUS POPULATION CIRCA 1900

For the end of the 19th century, it is possible to use as a baseline for calculations censuses and vital statistics records.[20] Nonetheless, not all countries included in their censuses a classification of the population by ethnic group and as such it is necessary to continue with indirect and approximate estimates. The indigenous population of Chiapas was estimated based on the Mexican census of 1900.

THE INDIGENOUS POPULATION CIRCA 1980

Figures by Davidson and Counce[21] were used which came from censuses, informants and field work. The indigenous population in Chiapas was estimated based on the Mexican census of 1980.

---

[18]ACGA a.3 Leg 246 Exp. 4912, p. 39. General map that summarizes the 23 particulars of the Kingdom and shows the number of villages in each part and the existing tributaries.

[19] "General summary that shows all the provinces, parishes, towns and tributaries of the entire Kingdom, 1806." *Boletín del Archivo General del Gobierno*, Guatemala, 1946, p.229.

[20]Ver Baires Martínez, Yolanda. "La población indígena de América Central Hacia 1900." *Anuario de Estudios Centroamericanos*. Vol. 15-2, 1989, pp. 81-89.

[21]Davidson, William V. and Counce, Melanie A. "Mapping the Distribution of Indians in Central America." *Cultural Survival*, Vol. 13(3), 1989, pp. 37-40.

TABLE 1. INDIGENOUS POPULATION AROUND 1500-1524

Region and Ethnicity	Number	Source
Southern Mexico and Belize:		
Chiapa (1511)	275000	Gerhard
Soconusco (1511)	80000	Gerhard
Belize and Petén	400000	Bolland
Guatemala (1520)		
Northwest	260000	Lovell
Verapaz	208000	MacLeod
Northeast	17500	Thompson
Southeast	33000	Feldman
Totonicapán	105000	Veblen
South-Central (Quichés) A	823000	Carmack and Veblen
South-Central (Cakchiqueles) E	250000	Lutz and Lovell
East-Central (Pokomames) G	58000	Miles
East-Central (Chortíes) B	120000	Thompson
Atitlán (Tzutujiles) E	72000	Madigan and Orellana
Southeast (Pipiles) C	100000	Fowler
El Salvador (1519)		
West Lempa	450000	Fowler
East Lempa	300000	Fowler
HONDURAS (1524)		
West and Central	600000	Newson
East	200000	Newson
Nicaragua (1524)		
West	546570	Newson
Central	178838	Newson
Mosquitia	38148	Newson
Nicoya	62692	Newson
Costa Rica (w/o Nicoya)	337308	Denevan
Panama		
West	500000	Denevan
East	500000	Denevan

TABLE 2. INDIGENOUS POPULATION AROUND 1550

	Region	Population		Region	Population
1	Chiapa	125100	15	Olancho	8000
1a	Ciudad Real		16	Tegucigalpa and Choluteca	
1b	Tuxtla		17	León	29000
2	Soconusco	7000	18	Nueva Segovia	
3	Verapaz	52000	19	Matagalpa	
4	Guatemalan Altiplano	323000	20	Granada	25000
4a	Totonicapán		21	Mosquitia	
4b	Quezaltenango		22	Nicoya	3300
4c	Sololá		23	Costa Rica	120000
5	Suchitepéquez		23a	Valle Central	
6	Valle de Guatemala	31000	23b	Térraba and Boruca	
7	Escuintla	9000	23c	Talamanca	
8	Chiquimula	12000	24	Veragua	
9	Sonsonate	14000	25	Panamá	800
10	San Salvador	45000	26n	Darién	
11	San Miguel	30000	27	Selva Lacandona	
12	Gracias	21000	28	Petén	
13	San Pedro Sula and Tencoa				
14	Comayagua	12000		Total	956200

TABLE 3. INDIGENOUS POPULATION AROUND 1580

	Region	Population		Region	Population
1	Chiapa	99800	15	Olancho	5695
1a	Ciudad Real		16	Tegucigalpa and Choluteca	3315
1b	Tuxtla		17	León	6001
2	Soconusco	6630	18	Nueva Segovia	776
3	Verapaz	15000	19	Matagalpa	1562
4	Guatemalan Altiplano	207000	20	Granada	7355
4a	Totonicapán		21	Mosquitia	
4b	Quezaltenango		22	Nicoya	1800
4c	Sololá		23	Costa Rica	54000
5	Suchitepéquez		23a	Valle Central	
6	Valle de Guatemala	11000	23b	Térraba and Boruca	
7	Escuintla	2700	23c	Talamanca	
8	Chiquimula	3300	24	Veragua	400
9	Sonsonate	7840	25	Panamá	100
10	San Salvador	25200	26n	Darién	130
11	San Miguel	16800	27	Selva Lacandona	
12	Gracias	8845	28	Petén	
13	San Pedro Sula and Tencoa	2375			
14	Comayagua	8615		Total	546079

TABLE 4. INDIGENOUS POPULATION AROUND 1680

	Region	Population		Region	Population
1	Chiapa	55823	15	Olancho	1005
1a	Ciudad Real		16	Tegucigalpa and Choluteca	2834
1b	Tuxtla		17	León	8950
2	Soconusco	3417	18	Nueva Segovia	2648
3	Verapaz	16466	19	Matagalpa	5903
4	Guatemalan Altiplano		20	Granada	9795
4a	Totonicapán	19511	21	Mosquitia	
4b	Quezaltenango	11373	22	Nicoya	532
4c	Sololá	21777	23	Costa Rica	
5	Suchitepéquez		23a	Valle Central	1545
6	Valle de Guatemala	63823	23b	Térraba and Boruca	73
7	Escuintla	13442	23c	Talamanca	
8	Chiquimula	9020	24	Veragua	1320
9	Sonsonate	62073	25	Panamá	1470
10	San Salvador	8124	26n	Darién	
11	San Miguel	2477	27	Selva Lacandona	
12	Gracias	3876	28	Petén	
13	San Pedro Sula and Tencoa	1362			
14	Comayagua	3264		Total	293646

TABLE 5. INDIGENOUS POPULATION AROUND 1800

	Region	Population		Region	Population
1	Chiapa		15	Olancho	2530
1a	Ciudad Real	50115	16	Tegucigalpa and Cholutec	6513
1b	Tuxtla	17186	17	León	876
2	Soconusco	5105	18	Nueva Segovia	3205
3	Verapaz	54192	19	Matagalpa	15612
4	Guatemalan Altiplano		20	Granada	17022
4a	Totonicapán	61670	21	Mosquitia	
4b	Quezaltenango	25162	22	Nicoya	488
4c	Sololá	28277	23	Costa Rica	
5	Suchitepéquez	13219	23a	Valle Central	1575
6	Valle de Guatemala	89096	23b	Térraba and Boruca	
7	Escuintla	14984	23c	Talamanca	
8	Chiquimula	36937	24	Veragua	11058
9	Sonsonate	22651	25	Panamá	7660
10	San Salvador	56447	26n	Darién	556
11	San Miguel	11077	27	Selva Lacandona	
12	Gracias	17330	28	Petén	
13	San Pedro Sula and Tencoa	2791			
14	Comayagua	3740		Total	587069

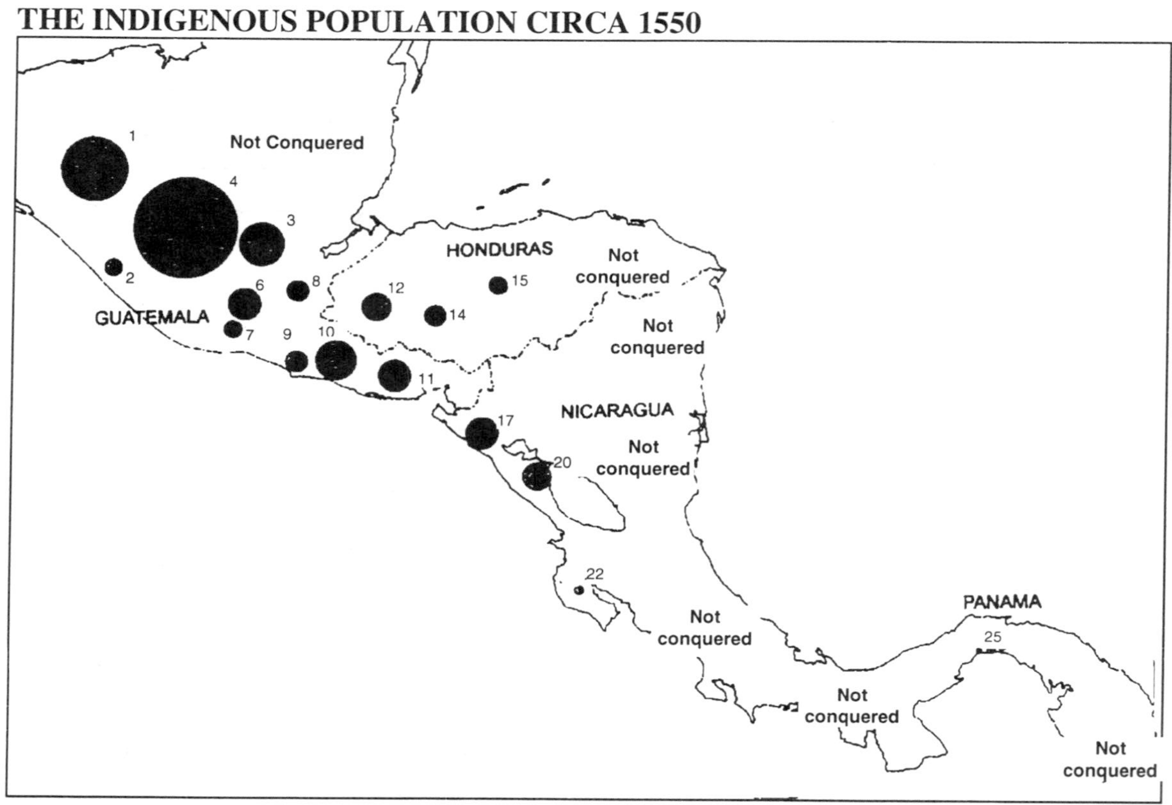
THE INDIGENOUS POPULATION CIRCA 1550
Not Conquered
1
4
3
2
6
8
GUATEMALA
7
9
10
11
HONDURAS
12
14
15
Not conquered
Not conquered
NICARAGUA
17
20
Not conquered
22
Not conquered
PANAMA
25
Not conquered
Not conquered

THE INDIGENOUS POPULATION CIRCA 1580

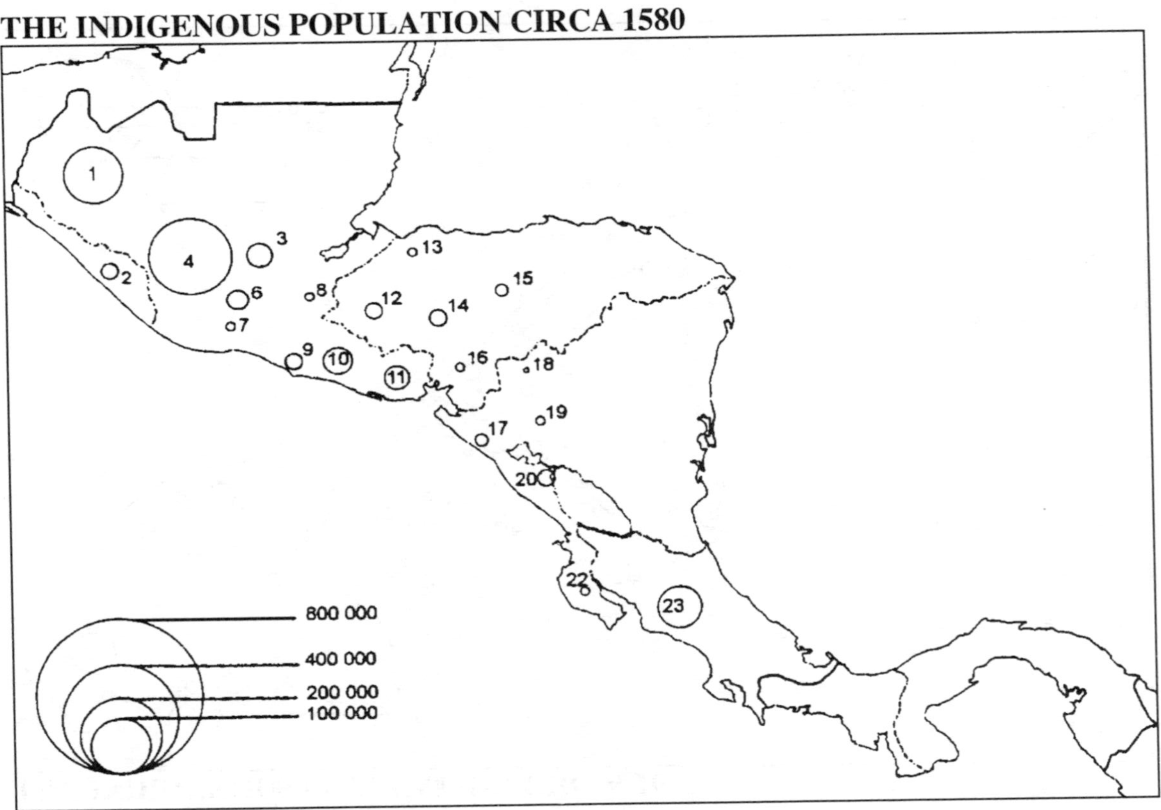

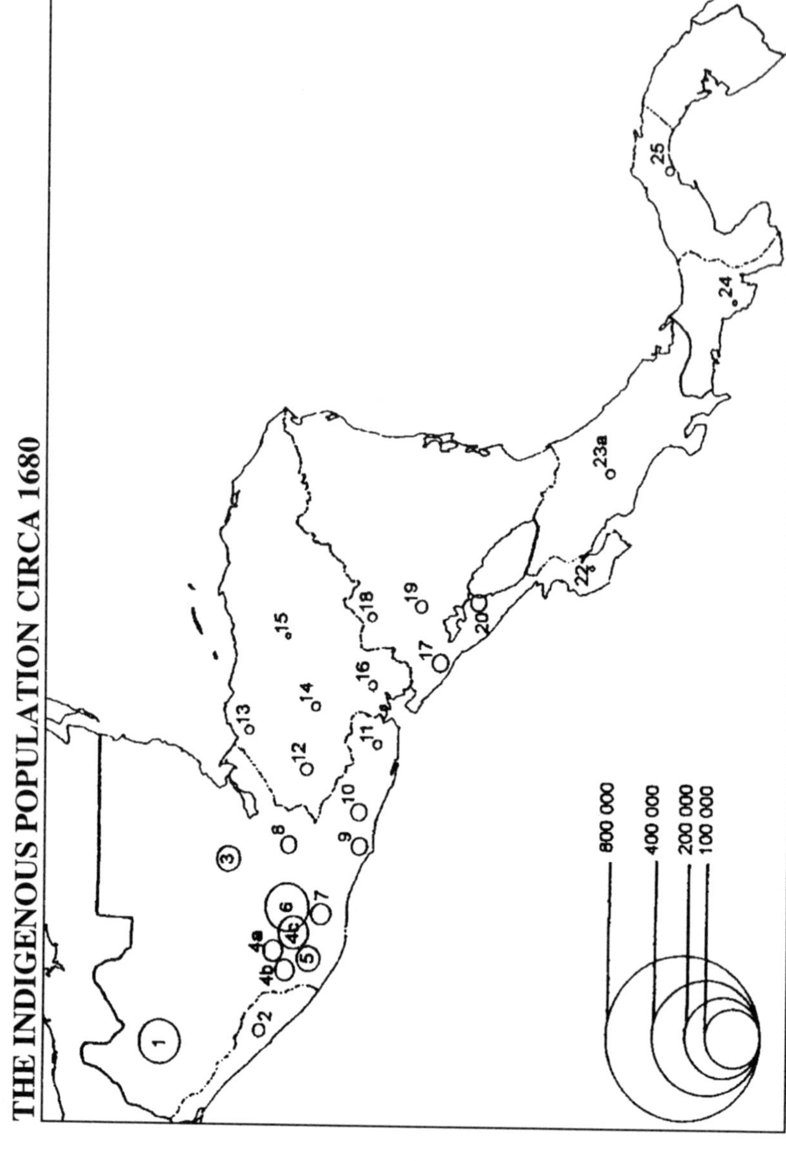
THE INDIGENOUS POPULATION CIRCA 1680
1
2
3
4a
4b
4c
5
6
7
8
9
10
11
12
13
14
15
16
17
18
19
20
22
23a
24
25
800 000
400 000
200 000
100 000

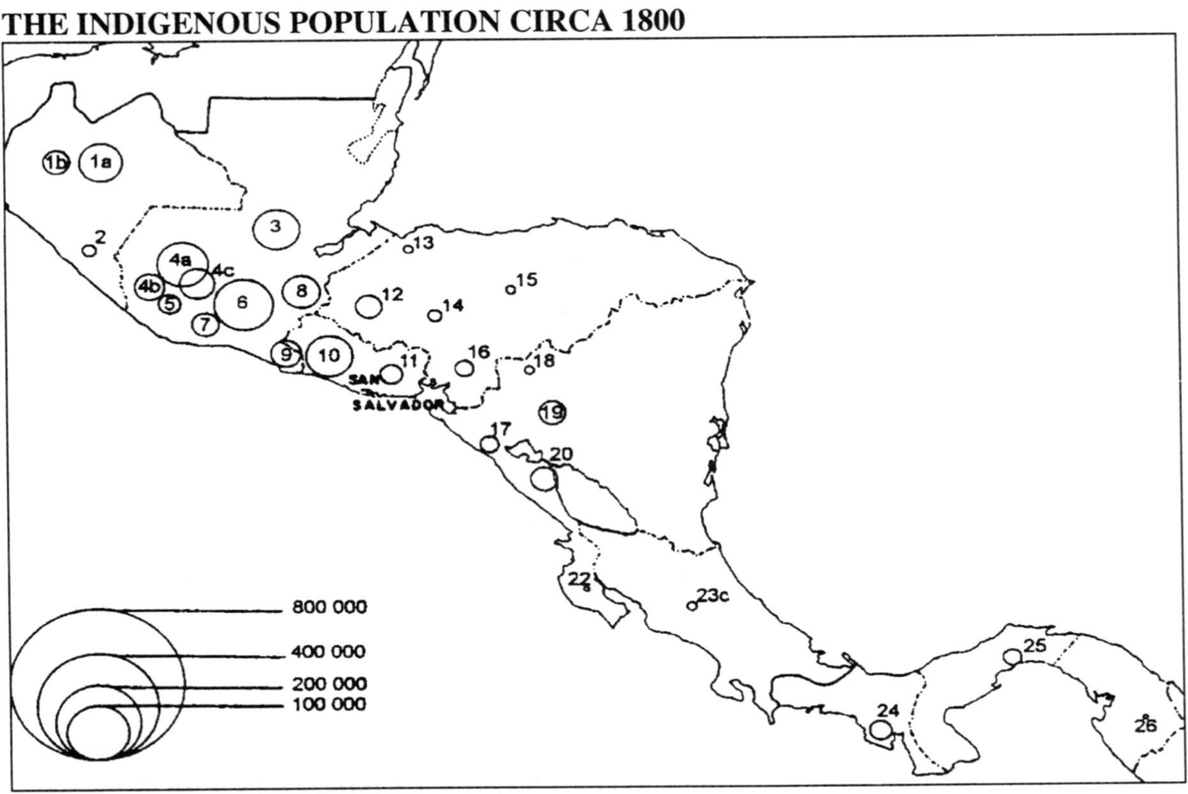
THE INDIGENOUS POPULATION CIRCA 1800
1b
1a
2
3
4a
4b
4c
5
6
7
8
9
10
11
12
13
14
15
16
17
18
19
20
22
23c
24
25
26
SAN
SALVADOR
800 000
400 000
200 000
100 000

drastic for the remainder of the sixteenth century, and may not have abated until the 1630s or 1640s. Many factors—warfare, culture shock, ruthless exploitation, slavery, forced migration and resettlement—were responsible for Maya demise, and worked together in horrific, fatal unison. Of all the agents jointly at work, however, none proved more destructive than an array of diseases introduced by Spaniards from the Old World to the New (Cook and Lovell 1992). As many as eight pandemics (smallpox, measles, typhus, plague, alone or in withering combination) lashed Guatemala between 1519 and 1632, with some twenty-five episodes relating to more localized, epidemic outbreaks recorded between 1555 and 1618 (Lovell 1992a). Maya depopulation during this period was but one downward spiral of a general, though regionally variable, pattern of New World decline. The Americas in the sixteenth and seventeenth centuries in all likelihood were the scene of the greatest destruction of lives in human history (Lovell 1992b).

At different times and in different places during the first half of the seventeenth century decline ceased and recovery began. Table 1 indicates that, by the 1680s, the Maya population of Guatemala numbered more than at any time in the preceding one hundred years. A fall in numbers between 1684 and 1710, however, suggests that the process of recovery was irregular. Disease lingered throughout the colonial period, causing reversals in the upward movement of population in certain regions of Guatemala even in the eighteenth and nineteenth centuries (Lovell 1988). By the time Archbishop Pedro Cortés y Larraz (1958) coordinated a diocese-wide survey in the late 1760s, the population he and local clergy recorded for Guatemala numbered some 315,000 inhabitants, of whom 220,000 were considered Indian (Woodward 1980; García Añoveros 1987). The actual Maya population, Cortés y Larraz makes clear, was undoubtedly higher, since his report is full of references to "infidel Indians" living as "fugitives in the mountains" well beyond the reach not just of Christian fellowship but also of effective enumeration and incorporation into what the archbishop considered "proper society". The archbishop's report, faults and all, allows us to envision the colonial period drawing to a close with Maya Indians constituting some seventy percent of the total Guatemalan population, a percentage that would remain constant well into the next century (García Añoveros 1987; Lutz 1993).

DEMOGRAPHIC TRENDS, 1778-1994

The 1770s are a watershed in terms of our sources and calculations. Prior to that period, available data are almost entirely based on counts of Indian tributaries or the taxes they paid. Until the 1770s, therefore, population is estimated essentially by multiplying surrogate categories or indices. The method works reasonably well for calculating Maya population but does not permit any confident measure to be made of total population. The more systematic treatment of Cortés y Larraz (García Añoveros 1987) does make such a calculation possible, as well as providing a reliable measure of ethnic composition: seventy percent Maya and thirty percent non-Maya (Ladinos, Mestizos, Mulattoes, Spaniards, and Blacks). A survey conducted several years after that of Cortés y Larraz calculated the total population in 1778 to be 355,000, which we reckon included a Maya component of about 248,500 (Juarros 1936; Woodward 1980, 1983). Unlike earlier colonial counts, which fluctuate through time and across space, the 1778 totals mark the beginning of a period of steady growth in the Guatemalan population as a whole.

For the early nineteenth century, available data once again facilitate straightforward calculation of both Maya and non-Maya population. In 1804, we estimate that Spaniards and Ladinos numbered approximately 125,000, which suggests an Indian total of about 292,000. By 1820 the two groups had grown, respectively, to 150,000 and 350,000 (Luján Muñoz 1976; Lutz 1994; Pinto 1989).

The estimates that span the decades between 1820 and 1870 are based on Woodward's reckoning (1983:7) that total population "increased at an average annual rate of about 1.2 percent during that period." Woodward does not provide much specific data as to differences in Indian and Ladino rates of growth. However, scattered baptismal data for 1858-1882 pertaining to the Indian "west" and the Ladino "east" of the country (MacLeod 1973; Lutz and Lovell 1990), broken down by ethnic group and identifying children born in or out of wedlock, indicate far higher legitimacy among Mayas than among Ladinos (Woodward 1983; Ortmayr 1991). Maya preference for marriage as opposed to Ladino propensity towards informal union raises an interesting question: could matrimonial stability among Mayas translate into higher rates of fertility and population growth than those found in the case of Ladinos? If we believe subsequent government censuses, apparently not.

Between 1820 and 1870 the population of Guatemala grew from 595,000 to 1,080,000, reflecting an indigenous increase from 416,000 to 756,000. By the time of the first official census, taken in 1880, the Maya had more than doubled in size since Independence (1821). According to government sources, it took closer to seventy years, not sixty, for doubling next to occur.

The 1880 census represents another watershed in the data, for it furnishes our first officially verified statement of Maya numbers, 844,000 out of a total population of 1.2 million. Total Maya numbers, however, include at least three regional estimates (Huehuetenango, Quezaltenango, and Totonicapán), as the 1880 census openly acknowledges. Mayas at that time constituted sixty-nine percent of the national population. From 1880 onward official reports and censuses show a gradual but seemingly inexorable decline in the percentage of the total Guatemalan population classified as Indian (Table 2). We find this intriguing. Is it mere coincidence that the percentage of population considered to be Maya Indian starts to diminish after the coming to power of Justo Rufino Barrios, the enactment by his Liberal government of sweeping land and labor reforms, and the emergence of the "modern" nation-state with all its Ladino priorities? To what extent does falling Maya percentage objectively reflect the "success" of Guatemalan social integration? Could it not instead be the result of statistical manipulation, a self-fulfilling prophecy advanced by non-Maya officialdom long desirous of a whiter, less-Indian Guatemala?

On the other hand, falling Maya percentage may be a result of falling Maya fertility brought about by disruptions to sedentary family life caused by strict enforcement of *mandamiento* legislation. Under the terms of *mandamiento*, authorized by President Barrios in 1876, highland Maya communities were required, by law, to send men and women to work on coffee plantations that had been established on the Pacific piedmont with a view to developing Guatemala's commercial agricultural potential. Investment by domestic and foreign capital resulted in coffee emerging three-quarters' way through the nineteenth century as Guatemala's principal export crop, a position it has maintained in the national economy from the time of President Barrios until today. By the 1880s, McCreery (1986) informs us, *mandamiento* furnished each year "at least one hundred thousand" highland Maya workers for weeks or months at a time. Over the decades, even after the demise of *mandamiento* and other forms of coercion, the numbers involved in seasonal migration grew steadily, approaching 400,000 in the 1960s (Schmid 1967). Maya fertility must surely have been affected by these massive, disruptive movements.

Table 2 shows that the total Maya population and the total Guatemalan population rise in every national census conducted between 1880 and 1973. The percentage of population considered Maya Indian, however, declines: from 68.9 percent in 1880 to 64.8 percent in 1921, 55.7 percent in 1940, 53.6 percent in 1950, 42.2 percent in 1964, and 43.8 percent in 1973. Another way of interpreting these figures is to consider that, as of 1964, in the eyes of the state, the Maya no longer constitute the majority of the Guatemalan population. They assume, instead, status as a demographic minority, one to which, socially, they have been relegated for centuries. Cultural and numeral inferiority from this point on coincide.

The 1973 census was the last "pre-violence" enumeration undertaken in Guatemala. A census was carried out in 1981, but conditions of civil war prevented any accurate count from being made, especially in the countryside. Between 1980 and 1984, the Maya suffered dreadfully from what Carmack (1988) has aptly termed a "harvest of violence." Some researchers and organizations (Le Bot 1988; NACLA 1991; Tzian 1994; Cotjí Cuxil 1995) counter the statistical and, more lately, ethnic cleansing of the Maya by insisting on higher Maya numbers and a greater Maya percentage than government reckoning indicates. Official records continue to calculate the Maya presence in declining percentage terms (see AVANCSO 1992:24; Orellana González 1992; Tzian 1994). A census conducted in April 1994, which Guatemalan demographers anticipated would reveal a national population of twelve million, for the first time ever inquired about Maya languages and ethnic identity (Ruíz 1994). The results of this census have sparked considerable controversy in the Guatemalan press and have caused no end of confusion, for the Instituto Nacional de Estadística (INE) could only account for 8.3 million inhabitants (Hernández 1995; Salvatierra 1995). To that figure INE added another 1.1 million (a margin of error of 11.8 percent) to compensate for missing information about nonrecorded inhabitants.

CONCLUSION

How many Guatemalans are there? How many of them can be considered Maya? How many Guatemalans actually live in

Guatemala? How many reside outside the country, in Mexico, in the United States, and Canada?

The 1994 census, after correction on the part of the state institution that conducted it, suggests that 9.4 million Guatemalans live in Guatemala, of whom 42.8 percent are said to identify themselves as Maya (Díaz 1995). To these calculations must be added a sizeable figure for the number of Guatemalans who live in the United States and Canada, perhaps as many as one million people, lots of whom are Maya (Burns 1993; Hagan 1994; Jonas 1995). The official count for Guatemalan refugees resident in Mexico is 45,000, the majority of them Maya; unofficial counts are considerably higher (Guatemala News Watch 1995). There are still thousands of displaced persons within Guatemala itself, which the 1994 census formally acknowledges. We think it reasonable to conclude, therefore, that Guatemalan Mayas must number between five and six million, not all of them permanently tied to the land of their ancestors.

From a historical point of view, the fact that so many Mayas survive is remarkable. They number more than twice what they did when Spaniards first invaded Guatemala almost five centuries ago, and more than ten times their population at Independence. These figures indicate a capacity for survival few Native American populations have been able to sustain. Neither past nor present iniquities can prevent Maya Indians from being a decisive force in the shaping of Guatemalan society in the coming century.

ACKNOWLEDGEMENTS

An earlier version of this paper appears in the *Latin American Research Review*, 29:2 pp. 133-140 (1994). We thank Elisabeth Sirucek and Judy Walker for secretarial assistance and Richard N. Adams for his critical commentary of earlier drafts. Our interest in historical demography is indulged at length in *Demography and Empire: A Guide to the Population History of*

García Añoveros, J.M. 1987. *Población y estado sociorreligioso de la diócesis de Guatemala en el último tercio del siglo XVIII.* Guatemala: Editorial Universitaria.

Guatemala, Dirección General de Estadística. 1881. *Censo general de la república de Guatemala, levantado [en] el año de 1880.* Guatemala: Establecimiento Tipográfico de "El Progreso".

_____. 1894. *Censo general de la república de Guatemala, levantado en 26 de febrero de 1893 por la Dirección general de estadística y con los auspicios del presidente constitucional, general Don José María Reina Barrios.* Guatemala: Tip. y encuad. "Nacional".

_____. 1924-1926. *Censo de la población de la república, levantado el 28 de agosto de 1921.* 4°. censo. 2 vols. en 3 partes. Guatemala.

_____. 1942. *Quinto censo general de población, levantado el 7 abril de 1940.* Guatemala: Tipografía nacional.

_____. 1957. *Sexto censo general de población, abril 18 de 1950.* Guatemala.

_____. 1971-1972. *Séptimo censo de población, 1964.* 3 vols. Guatemala.

_____. 1975. *Octavo censo población, 26 de marzo de 1973.* Guatemala.

_____. 1984. Instituto Nacional de Estadística. *Censos nacionales de 1981:Noveno censo de población, cifras definitivas.* 2 vols. Guatemala.

Guatemala News Watch. 1995. "Officical Census Results." In *Guatemala News Watch* 10 (6): 3.

Hagan, J.M. 1994. *Deciding to be Legal: A Maya Community in Houston.* Philadelphia: Temple University Press.

Hernández, R. 1995. "Censo no refleja la realidad del país". *La República*, 1° de mayo, pp. 2-3.

Instituto Nacional de Estadística. 1989. *Encuesta sociodemográfica*, Vol. 3.

Jonas, S. 1995. "Transnational Realities and Anti-Immigrant State Policies: Issues Raised by the Experiences in Central American Immigrants and Refugees in a Trinational Region." In *Estudios Internacionales* 6 (11): 17-29.

Juarros, D. 1936. *Compendio de la historia de la ciudad de Guatemala*. Third edition. 2 vols. Guatemala: Tipografía Nacional.

Le Bot, Y. 1988. "Guatemala: 4 millones de Indios." In *Trace* (CEMCA: Centre d'Etudes Mexicaines et Centroamericaines) 13:11.

Ligorred, F. 1992. *Lenguas indígenas de México y Centroamérica*. Madrid: Editorial MAPFRE.

Lovell, W.G. 1988. "Enfermedades del Viejo Mundo y mortandad amerindia: La viruela y el tabardillo en la Sierra de los Cuchumantanes de Guatemala, 1780-1810." In *Mesoamérica* 16: 239-85.

_____. 1992a. "Disease and Depopulation in Early Colonial Guatemala." In *"Secret Judgments of God": Old World Disease in Colonial Spanish America*. Noble David Cook and W. George Lovell, eds. Norman and London: University of Oklahoma Press, 49-83.

_____. 1992b. "Heavy Shadows and Black Night": Disease and Depopulation in Colonial Spanish America." In *Annals of the Association of American Geographers* 82 (3): 426-43.

_____. 1992c. *Conquest and Survival in Colonial Guatemala: A Historical Geography of the Cuchumatán Highlands of Guatemala, 1500-1821*. Revised edition. Montreal and Kingston: McGill-Queen's University Press.

Lovell, W.G. and CH. Lutz. 1995. *Demography and Empire: A Guide to the Population History of Spanish Central America, 1500-1821*. Boulder: Westview Press.

Lovell, W.G., C.H. Lutz, and W.R. Swezey. 1984. "The Indian Population of Southern Guatemala, 1549-1551: An groups. It is worth mentioning that the figures used in this study from the 1994 census are preliminary.

Definition of the Indigenous Population

The National Institute of Statistics has attempted to keep the concept of ethnic group separate from all racial considerations.

From the time of the first population census (1778), the terms "indigenous" and "*ladino*" (as the equivalent of non-indigenous) appear within the concept of race. The origin of these terms has not been sufficiently studied, even though the fact has been noted that in some dictionaries from the last century, that in addition to its current meaning, the word "*ladino*" was also used to mean "a person who speaks two languages" (Spanish and an indigenous language.) However, this term has been traditionally used to designate the non-indigenous group, not considering this as a racial classification, but rather as a group defined by cultural characteristics.

Acknowledging the difficulty in formulating a precise definition of the indigenous population, the instructions for the 1950 census were limited to indicating that "the census taker should consider the social status ('la estimación social') in which the person is held in the place where the census is being carried out" (1957). For the above mentioned reason, attempts were made as often as possible to utilize the services of census-takers from the locality who were perfectly familiar with the local method of categorizing a person as indigenous or non-indigenous. In the 1981 census the definition from the 1950 census was adopted, which used as a baseline the social status in which the person was held in the place where he or she was counted.

In the 1994 census, the individual right of "self-identification" with one's ethnic group was respected, and this information was obtained by a direct question.

DEMOGRAPHIC CHARACTERISTICS

Sex and Age

The indigenous population structure comprises 42.8% of the population, according to the preliminary figures from the most recent population census carried out in 1994. The indigenous population represented 41.9% of the population in the 1981 census. This indicates that the indigenous population exercises a marked influence on the demographic characteristics of the population of the country.

The composition of the population by age and sex, is primarily a result of mortality and fertility behavior. The analysis of the population by sex reveals that the proportion of males is greater in the indigenous population. It has declined from 100.9 to 99.7 in the indigenous population and from 98.1 to 94.4 in the non-indigenous population.

The age structure in the indigenous population is similar to that of the non-indigenous population. Both are young populations in which those at young ages are relatively numerous. The median age of the indigenous population decreased between 1981 and 1994, from 16.6 years old to 15.8 years old which implies that the population is getting younger. In the non-indigenous population, the median age has increased, primarily as a consequence of the decrease in fertility.

Population Distribution

The indigenous population is not evenly distributed within the territory of the Republic, as shown in Table 1 and Figure 5 which show the proportion of the population which is indigenous by region.

According to this table, the largest portion of the indigenous population is located the highlands and north of the country. These regions contain departments populated almost exclusively by indigenous people.

SOCIAL CHARACTERISTICS

The majority of the indigenous population are farmers, with a predominantly subsistence economy. They live in sedentary communities and preserve many of their cultural characteristics such as language, art, music, as well as a strict family structure.

Literacy

Literacy, defined as the ability to read and write, was considered in the population census to be one of the primary measures to estimate the cultural level of the population.

In the past two censuses, the investigation of literacy was undertaken in the population from 7 years of age and onwards, since this is considered the minimum age to enroll in school.

The results obtained provide an outline of the advances obtained in raising the cultural level of the population, particularly among females within the indigenous population. However, within the indigenous population, nearly 63% of females and 43% of males continue to be illiterate.

Marital Status

Statistics on the marital status of the population are essential to analyze the dependency relationship, consumption needs, and housing problems. They are also important in demographic studies as a factor that influences the size and structure of the household and family.

Available data on marital status demonstrates different aspects with regard to sex and age which deserve a brief mention. If the population 15 years or older in each ethnic group is taken as a baseline and distributed proportionally by marital status, the figures presented in Table 3 are obtained. Between 1981 and 1994, in both populations, the percentage of "single" persons decreased significantly. Also, the percentage of persons who declared they were "married" is higher than those who were "living together" and the percent of people in both marital statuses increased.

It is interesting to note the low percentage of divorced persons (slightly higher in the non-indigenous population) and the higher proportion of widows/widowers in the indigenous population. It is possible that this last characteristic can be attributed to persons who declared themselves to be widows/widowers when their partner disappeared.

FERTILITY

The existence of a large indigenous female population in Guatemala has considerable importance in determining the level and trends of fertility in the country.

According to the preliminary data from the last population census carried out in April of 1994, indigenous women represented 40% of the majority population in the groups with highest fertility rates: they are 49% in rural areas, and 58% of these are involved in agricultural activities. Additionally indigenous women account for 43% of the births in the country.

Given the fact that the conditions to which each of the two populations are subjected are very different (as shown in Table 6), it is assumed that there is a differential in fertility behavior. To analyze fertility, the principal source is the preliminary tabulation of the 1994 population census, carried out by the National Statistics Institute (INE) of Guatemala. This work presents a brief analysis of the fertility rates, both in the indigenous and non-indigenous populations.

Fertility Estimates

The information on fertility comes from answers to questions asked of all women between 15 and 49 years of age about the total number of live births they have had and the birth date of their last live birth. The answers to both questions allow us to estimate the cumulative or retrospective fertility rates, and the current fertility rates.

Differentials in Fertility

Preliminary results allow us to use three socioeconomic variables to measure the differentials in fertility between indigenous and non-indigenous populations, specifically: place of residence, economic activity, and level of schooling of women aged 15 to 49.

According to the estimates made, the Total Fertility Rate (TFR) for indigenous women is 5.34 children per woman. For non-indigenous women it is 3.86 children per woman, with a differential of 1.5 children between the two populations. (See Table 6.)

Place of Residence

When differentiating between the indigenous and non-indigenous population according to their place of residence in urban and rural areas, the level of fertility of the indigenous women is higher than that of the non-indigenous women. In other words, rural indigenous women have higher fertility levels than rural non-indigenous women, and the same is true for urban areas.

Type of Activity

The level of fertility that is estimated for working indigenous females is 2.54 children, while for those who do not work the median number of children per female is 5.70. This is a differential of 3.2 children per female.

These differentials in fertility reaffirm that the participation of females in economic activities are inversely related to the fertility rate.

Number of Years of Maternal Education

The educational level of the mother is considered a good indicator for the analysis of fertility differentials. As shown in table 6, according to the estimates obtained, the higher the level of schooling of the mother the fewer the number of children she has.

MORTALITY

Mortality at early ages constitutes a high proportion of the total deaths. Infant and child deaths have a close relationship with the environment, since they are higher when the sanitary, socioeconomic, and cultural conditions in which the population lives are unfavorable.

The estimates of the mortality rate for infants and children under two years of age, obtained from the 1981 census, is higher in the indigenous population than in the non-indigenous population (128 and 101 deaths per thousand live births, respectively.) This higher mortality rate in part is caused by the lower educational level, and the primarily agricultural and rural economy of this population. But even when these variables are controlled, the child of the indigenous farmer continues to have a higher risk of death. When the conditions are highly adverse (salaried agricultural worker and illiterate mother), both ethnic groups share a similar high levels of mortality.

Estimates of infant mortality obtained by data from the 1994 census indicate that the probability of dying between birth and one year of age in the period between 1992-93 was 51 deaths per thousand live births in the indigenous population. Ten years earlier it had been 85 deaths per thousand live births. In the non-indigenous population, the probability of death is estimated at 50 in 1992-93 and 70 per thousand live births ten years earlier.

The primary causes which determine the high probability of death in the first years of life is the lack of doctors and social assistance centers in rural areas where the largest proportion of

INTRODUCTION

A large gap in earnings between indigenous and nonindigenous people in the labor market exists in Guatemala. The effect of equalizing characteristics has been examined: about 50 percent of the overall earnings gap is due to differences in characteristics (Psacharopoulos and Patrinos 1994). But it is not clear whether equality in characteristics—more specifically, human capital—would lead to a 50 percent reduction in the earnings gap for all indigenous people. This is because there are many indigenous groups in Guatemala, diverse and geographically segregated, with different cultures, languages and customs. Ethnic groups in Guatemala are also segregated by occupation and industry. They have differential access to resources, power and regional centers (including Metropolitan Guatemala).

Most of the research on ethnicity in Central America looks at two groups: indigenous and nonindigenous populations. While indigenous people are disadvantaged relative to the nonindigenous group, the many groups that make up the indigenous population are often times not very similar in terms of personal and group characteristics. But the differences within these groups are important for public policy.

The 1989 Guatemalan Household Survey identifies indigenous people by self-selection and language spoken. Ethnic group affiliation is, therefore, determined on the basis of language. Dividing the indigenous sample into the main ethnic groups (Quiché, Kakchiquel, Kekchi, Mam and "other" indigenous groups) produces widely different and dramatic results in terms of schooling, earnings, the returns to schooling and estimates of the upper bound of discrimination (or unexplained portion of the earnings gap).

Each ethnic group fares differently relative to the dominant or "mainstream" population. This has been shown in the United States where, for example, Hispanics do better or worse depending on where in Latin America they come from (see, for example, Reimers 1983). Immigrant groups' experience depends on many factors besides education and skill levels. These additional factors include what Borjas (1992, 1995) refers to as "ethnic capital". That is, the socioeconomic performance of today's workers depends not only on parental skills, but also on the average skills of the ethnic group in the parent's generation. Ethnicity has an external effect on the human capital accumulation process, and strong externalities may prevent the intergenerational convergence of ethnic differentials. Borjas (1995) shows the importance of neighborhood clustering of ethnic groups in the United States, which is one means by which "ethnic capital" is transferred from generation to generation.

Social relationships develop as individuals try to make the best use of their individual resources. They are not only components of social structures, they are also resources for the individual. Loury (1977, 1987) introduced the concept of social capital into economics and defined it as the set of resources that inhere in family relations and in community social organizations useful for the cognitive or social development of a child. These resources differ and constitute an advantage for children in the development of their human capital. People begin life with endowments of nontransferable advantages of birth—social capital—which are conveyed by parental behaviors bearing on later-life productivity. In such a world, the deleterious consequences of past discrimination for a minority group are reflected in the fact that minority young people have, on average, less favorable parental influences on their skill-acquisition processes. Further, families group themselves together into communities and certain local public goods—such as public education, peer influences which shape the development of personal character, contacts which generate information about the world of work and friendship networks which evolve among persons situated in the same or closely related communities. Access to these communities

Subtracting equation (4) from (5) yields the difference between the hypothetical nondiscriminatory earnings of indigenous workers and their actual earnings. This difference reflects the different returns to the same income-generating characteristics:

$$\text{Ln}\,\overline{Y}_i^* - \text{Ln}\,\overline{Y}_i = \hat{b}_n \overline{X}_i - \hat{b}_i \overline{X}_i = \overline{X}_i(\hat{b}_n - \hat{b}_i) \qquad (7)$$

Adding equations (6) and (7) yields:

$$\text{Ln}\,\overline{Y}_n - \text{Ln}\,\overline{Y}_i = \hat{b}_n(\overline{X}_n - \overline{X}_i) + \overline{X}_i(\hat{b}_n - \hat{b}_i) \qquad (8)$$

This could be written as:

$$\text{Ln}\,\overline{Y}_n - \text{Ln}\,\overline{Y}_i = \hat{b}_i(\overline{X}_n - \overline{X}_i) + \overline{X}_n(\hat{b}_n - \hat{b}_i) \qquad (9)$$

Thus, according to equation (8), the overall earnings gap can be decomposed into two components: one is the portion attributable to differences in the endowments of income generating characteristics $(X_n\text{-}X_i)$ evaluated with the nonindigenous worker pay structure (b_n); the other portion is attributable to differences in the returns $(b_n\text{-}b_i)$ that nonindigenous and indigenous workers receive for the same endowment of income-generating characteristics (X_i). This latter component is often taken as reflecting wage discrimination. This is known as the Oaxaca (1973; see also Blinder 1973) decomposition, which allows for estimation of discrimination from earnings functions estimated at the indigenous means (or nonindigenous wage structure). Other methods are used to estimate discrimination in the literature, including a pooled regression method developed by Oaxaca and Ransom (1994). But in order to keep it simple, the original Oaxaca technique is employed here.

RESULTS

Higher levels of schooling correspond to higher returns to schooling by ethnic group. Table 1 presents data on earnings and schooling by ethnic group from the 1989 household survey. Schooling levels are lower for indigenous groups, especially for the Quiché. Indigenous people in general possess about half the schooling of Ladinos. While the average Ladino male worker possesses over six years of schooling, the Quiché have less than three years of schooling. Ladino males earn on average 264 *quetzales* per month, which is almost twice the monthly earnings of "other" indigenous groups. The Kekchi are the highest earners among indigenous people, with 194 *quetzales* per month on average.

There exist large differences within the indigenous population. While the average earnings of a Quiché male worker are higher than for "other" indigenous males, their level of schooling is low, at only 2.9 years, relative to 3.5 years for "other" indigenous groups. The most schooled indigenous groups are the Mam and the Kekchi, with 3.7 years.

Rates of return to schooling are higher for groups with high levels of schooling than for less schooled groups. Estimates of rates of return to schooling come from the semi-logarithmic equations reported in Annex Table 1. Some indigenous groups receive lower returns to schooling, while the Mam receive very high returns to schooling. The Quiché receive low returns to schooling and possess few years of schooling. The Mam experience very high returns to their schooling investments, at 10.4 percent, which is very close to the estimate for Ladinos, at 10.5 percent. The Kakchiquel and the Kekchi also experience high returns to schooling, at 8.7 and 9.5 percent. The Quiché receive very low returns, at only 5.4 percent.

While indigenous groups receive very low earnings and much less schooling, what is the reason behind this discrimination? Or is it more accurate to say that the explanation depends on the group in question? Overall, previous research has shown that much of the indigenous-nonindigenous earnings differential is unexplained. That is, even with equal productive characteristics indigenous people would earn much less than nonindigenous people. In fact, it is estimated that up to 50 percent of the overall indigenous-nonindigenous earnings differential could be due to discrimination (Psacharopoulos and Patrinos 1994).

But by disaggregating by ethnic group, the results of estimating the decomposition model outlined above show that the level of discrimination (or unexplained component of the earnings gap) varies widely. Table 2 presents summary evidence derived from estimating the Oaxaca model. More summary information is presented in Annex Table 2. On the one hand, the Kekchi appear to experience no discrimination, and the Kakchiquel and the Mam experience very little discrimination, 23 and 38 percent. On the other hand, the Quiché and "other" indigenous groups experience very high levels of discrimination, 43 and 57 percent. In the case of the Quiché it would appear that low returns to schooling are responsible. For the Kekchi (and to a lesser extent the Kakchiquel and the Mam), increasing the schooling of the nonagricultural work force would eliminate (or nearly eliminate) the earnings differential between them and the Ladino work force.

Ladino males have a particularly large earnings advantage over Quiché and "other" indigenous males. Yet equalizing characteristics between these two groups and Ladinos would reduce the overall earnings differential by only 43 percent for the Quiché and 57 percent for the "other" indigenous groups. Smaller overall differentials exist between Ladinos and the Kakchiquel and the Kekchi. But equalizing characteristics would drastically reduce earnings differentials between these two groups and Ladinos. In the case of the Kekchi, equalizing characteristics would actually reverse the earnings advantage. In fact, Ladino earnings would be 47 *quetzales* less than Kekchi earnings if both groups possessed equivalent amounts of human capital.

Estimates of discrimination in the labor market assume that no previous discrimination occurred. For example, equalizing characteristics, which would take several decades, would affect the returns to schooling. Thus it may not turn out that the Kekchi would surpass Ladinos if they had equivalent characteristics. The lower schooling levels may be due to discrimination of access. The models used here do not control for that possibility. Thus, caution is required when interpreting the results of such models.

DISCUSSION

Most of the research on ethnicity in Guatemala typically examines two groups: indigenous and nonindigenous. While indigenous people are disadvantaged relative to the nonindigenous group, the many ethnic groups that make up the indigenous population are often times not very similar in terms of personal and group characteristics. The differences within these groups are important for public policy. The indigenous-nonindigenous comparison in Guatemala may be too simple. Using Guatemala's 1989 Household Survey the indigenous population is disaggregated into the four main groups in order to examine the question of ethnicity in terms of schooling attainment, earnings and the returns to schooling reveals that higher levels of schooling correspond to higher returns to schooling by ethnic group.

The level of discrimination (or unexplained component of the earnings gap) varies widely. While the Kekchi appear to experience no discrimination, and the Kakchiquel and the Mam experience very little, the Quiché and "other" indigenous groups experience very high levels of discrimination. In the case of the Quiché it would appear that low returns to schooling are responsible. For the Quiché, it is therefore necessary to increase the returns to schooling, while also increasing the level of schooling.

Specific interventions are required to encourage the Quiché to enroll their children in school, including expansion of the National Bilingual Education Program. Bilingual education, since it also promotes increased attendance, higher levels of attainment and better command of the Spanish language (World Bank 1995a), may also help increase the productivity of (or returns to) schooling for the Quiché. Such targeted interventions may help promote convergence of ethnic differentials and allow the particularly disadvantaged ethnic groups to better convert the schooling process into earnings. But given the external effects of ethnicity (or "ethnic capital") on the human capital accumulation process, other measures may be necessary.

For the Kekchi (and to a lesser extent the Kakchiquel and the Mam), increasing the schooling of the nonagricultural work force would eliminate (or nearly eliminate) the earnings differential between them and the Ladino work force. Thus, efforts to increase the schooling level of the Kekchi (and the Kakchiquel and the Mam) may be sufficient to reduce ethnic differentials.

The research presented here suggests that different responses may be required depending on the group in question. But given the importance of "ethnic capital", efforts to increase schooling among the indigenous population, let alone efforts to increase the returns to schooling, will be limited for groups such as the Quiché if other interventions are not also tried. Such interventions may include fertility reduction efforts, the encouragement of female employment and early childhood development programs. Such efforts are part of the effort to increase investments in child quality. Lower fertility rates imply that families can devote more individual attention to their children. Female employment reduces the reliance on children to supplement family income allowing the children to attend school. Early childhood development allows for compensatory efforts to make up for deficient home environments. Policy interventions designed to make up for the deficient family structure are critical because the pre-school years are most important when it comes to family structure affecting educational attainment (Garasky 1995; Lichter, Cornwell and Eggebeen 1993; Currie and Thomas 1995).

Other efforts are also necessary in order to build up the positive aspects of "ethnic" or "social" capital. It may be necessary to substitute informal, spontaneous social capital with formal efforts aimed at improving the social structure in some settings (Coleman 1990). Interventions are especially necessary in order to improve access to education. Such measures include social marketing or awareness campaigns intended to overcome lack of knowledge, and/or changes in the location, schedule, staffing, content or beneficiary costs of services to make them more relevant to social and material conditions (World Bank 1995b). This is being attempted in Guatemala through the *Eduquemos a la Niña* program. It supports dissemination and communication campaigns geared towards increasing girls' (particularly indigenous) school enrollment.

Public policy designed to facilitate family social capital would seek to maximize parental involvement with children. The strengthening of the social capital of the communities surrounding schools involves a process of establishing and strengthening the interactions among parents of students. The more than 20 registered *Escuelas Privadas Mayas* in Guatemala attests to the fact that this is entirely possible in the indigenous communities as these schools are entirely spontaneous community initiatives (UNICEF and Universidad Rafael Landívar n.d.).

In this paper it was not possible to replicate the intergenerational models reviewed above. But if their results are generalizable, then there is a need to consider policy shocks, such as schooling for the present generation, since they will have an effect on the schooling and income of future generations of that ethnic group.

Further research on ethnic groups, especially indigenous populations marginalized by European conquest, is needed. However, better data that allows researchers to differentiate among specific ethnic groups is necessary. Questions aimed at obtaining proper identification of ethnic groups is needed. Examples include the United States Census, which asks about specific race/ethnic groups, including American Indian tribes, and ancestry. Questions about ancestry, in addition to language and self-perception, are needed in order to prevent reductions in estimates due to overreliance on the individual's language use and identity. Other questions that can be used include geographic origin, faith, traditions (the 1991 Canadian Aboriginal Peoples Survey includes detailed questions about language and traditional activities; see Statistics Canada 1991), territory and dress. In this way policy makers can better design appropriate interventions for the economic and social advancement of all groups in society.

ACKNOWLEDGEMENTS

The views expressed here are those of the author and should not be attributed to the World Bank. This paper was presented at the conference by James Cercone, to whom the author is extremely grateful. The author thanks Eduardo Velez, George Psacharopoulos and Suzanne Roddis for comments.

REFERENCES

Arends, M. 1992. "Female Labor Force Participation and Earnings in Guatemala." In G. Psacharopoulos and Z. Tzannatos, eds., *Case Studies on Women's Employment and Pay in Latin America.* Washington, DC: The World Bank.

Blinder, A. S. 1973. "Wage discrimination: Reduced form and Structural Estimates." *Journal of Human Resources* 8: 436-65.

Borjas, G. 1992. "Ethnic Capital and Intergenerational Mobility." *Quarterly Journal of Economics* 107(1):123-50.

Borjas, G. 1995. "Ethnicity, Neighborhoods and Human-Capital Externalities." *American Economic Review* 85(3): 365-90.

Castles, I. 1991. *Census of Population and Housing, 30 June 1986: Census 86—Australia's Aboriginal and Torres Strait Islander People*. Australian Bureau of Statistics.

CELADE (Latin American Demographic Center). 1992. *Demographic Bulletin* 25(50).

Chiswick, B.R. 1988. "Differences in Education and Earnings across Racial and Ethnic Groups: Tastes, Discrimination, and Investments in Child Quality." *Quarterly Journal of Economics* 103(3): 571-97.

Coleman, J.S. 1990. *Foundations of Social Theory*. Cambridge: Harvard University Press.

Currie, J. and D. Thomas. 1995. "Does Head Start Make a Difference?" *American Economic Review* 85(3): 341-64.

Farley, R. 1990. "Blacks, Hispanics, and White Ethnic Groups: Are Blacks Uniquely Disadvantaged." *American Economic Review Papers and Proceedings* 80(2): 237-41.

Garasky, S. 1995. "The Effects of Family Structure on Educational Attainment: Do The Effects Vary by the Age of the Child?" *American Journal of Economics and Sociology* 54(1): 89-105.

Goldmann, G. 1993. The Aboriginal Population and the Census 120 Years of Information - 1871 to 1991. Statistics Canada, Ottawa (mimeo.).

Lichter, D.T., G.T. Cornwell and D.J. Eggebeen. 1993. "Harvesting Human Capital: Family Structure and Education Among Rural Youth." *Rural Sociology* 58(1):53-75.

Loury, G. 1977. "A Dynamic Theory of Racial Income Differences." In P.A. Wallace and A. Le Mund, eds., *Women,*

TABLE 1. EARNINGS, SCHOOLING ATTAINMENT AND THE RETURNS TO SCHOOLING, MALES, AGES 15-64, NON-AGRICULTURAL WORKERS

Ethnic Group	Earnings (*quetzales*/ month)	Mean Years of Schooling	Returns to Schooling (%)	R^2	N
Quiché	152	2.9	5.4	0.069	354
Kakchiquel	180	3.3	8.7	0.163	306
Mam	172	3.7	10.4	0.314	27
Kekchi	194	3.7	9.5	0.191	69
"Other" Indigenous	142	3.5	6.4	0.152	88
Ladino	264	6.2	10.5	0.333	3116

Source: ENSD 1989, from earnings functions presented in Annex Table 1.
Note: $US=2.8 *quetzales*

TABLE 2. ESTIMATES OF THE UPPER BOUND OF DISCRIMINATION

Ethnic Group	Percent
Quiché	43
Kakchiquel	23
Kekchi	0
Mam	38
Other Indigenous	57

Source: ENSD 1989, computed from earnings functions presented in Annex Table 1.

ANNEX TABLE 1. EARNINGS FUNCTIONS AND MEAN CHARACTERISTICS

	Ladino		Quiché		Kakchiquel		Mam		Kekchi		Other Indigenous	
Variable	X (s.d.)	b (t-stat)	X (s.d.)	b (t-stat)	X (s.d.)	b (t-stat)	X (s.d.)	b (t-stat)	X (s.d.)	b (t-stat)	X (s.d.)	b (t-stat)
Education	6.2 (4.4)	0.105 (37.4)	2.9 (3.0)	0.054 (4.4)	3.2 (3.2)	0.087 (7.1)	3.7 (4.0)	0.104 (2.9)	3.7 (3.3)	0.095 (3.1)	3.5 (3.9)	0.064 (2.2)
Experience	22.5 (13.6)	0.056 (17.9)	25.8 (13.5)	0.024 (2.4)	25.5 (13.8)	0.049 (4.7)	26.2 (15.8)	0.052 (1.9)	26.1 (12.6)	0.071 (2.4)	26.5 (14.4)	0.042 (1.4)
$(\text{Experience})^2$	690.2 (744.1)	-0.001 (13.3)	844.9 (810.9)	0.0001 (1.9)	838.7 (815.1)	-0.001 (4.1)	928.3 (921.8)	-0.001 (1.7)	838.3 (731.1)	-0.001 (2.3)	910.2 (866.6)	-0.001 (1.2)
Loghours	3.9 (0.3)	0.262 (6.6)	3.8 (0.3)	0.273 (2.3)	3.9 0.3	0.218 (1.8)	3.9 (0.3)	0.354 (1.1)	3.9 (0.3)	0.269 (0.8)	3.7 (0.3)	0.802 (2.4)
Constant	1.0	3.171	1.0	3.450	1.0	3.407	1.0	2.674	1.0	3.018	1.0	7.163
N	3116		354		180		172		69		142	
R2	0.333		0.069		0.163		0.314		0.191		0.152	

Source: Computed from ENSD 1989.

moval, and primary education) which in turn do not take into consideration other sources of well-being."

I propose, therefore, to combine the two methods into one. In combining the two methods, the following categories were established:

a) Poor by both methods (chronic poor)

b) Poor by poverty line method but not basic unmet needs method (conjunctional poverty)

c) Poor by basic unmet needs method but not poverty line method (structural poverty)

d) Not poor by either method

In the applications that have been made using the integrated poverty method, the overlap of households between the two methods is low. The hypothesis that the poverty line method assumes, that "those who are found above the minimum food threshold are also found above the threshold for other needs" is refuted since households defined as non-poor by the poverty line method are, by definition, found above the food threshold, and a large percentage of these demonstrate unmet needs according to the basic unmet needs method. Given that the two methods start off with different definitions of poverty, and consequently, different approaches to measurement, the use of the integrated poverty method should be taken as the intersection of the two wholes and not in partial form. The integrated poverty method is an attempt, therefore, to capture the largest number of dimensions which are related to poverty.

Information Sources

In November and December of 1994, a census was undertaken in Cahuita district as part of the project entitled "The relation between poverty and the environment from a gender perspective in a long term development project in the Talamanca area of Costa Rica." This project has been carried out since 1994 as a joint effort between the Institute for Social Studies on

Population (IDESPO) of the National University, and by the Tropical Agronomy Center for Research and Training (CATIE). A total of 868 households were visited, and 3,612 persons were interviewed from whom information on the socioeconomic condition of the family members was obtained, as well as on the hygienic and sanitary conditions, and the infrastructure of the household.

The instrument used was a questionnaire similar to the one used by the Multi-Purpose Household Survey, and a module on land use and tenancy was added.

STUDY AREA: CAHUITA DISTRICT

Talamanca is a canton in the province of Limón, located on the Atlantic coast of the country. It has an area of 2,809 square kilometers, which make it the second largest canton in the country (and, approximately 6% of the total area of the country). It is divided into three districts: Bratsi, Sixaola, and Cahuita.

Talamanca is one of the most underdeveloped cantons in the Costa Rica. In a study undertaken by the Ministry of Planning (MIDEPLAN and FNUP, 1991), rural poverty at the canton level was studied using the population and household censuses of 1973 and 1984. The study showed that about 60% of the population of the rural cantons fell into one of the three levels of basic unmet needs. However, I would like to point out that within the group identified as "extremely low" were located the cantons of Talamanca, Buenos Aires, Guatuso, Los Chiles, and La Cruz.

Despite the fact that Costa Rica as a whole has indicators of the quality of life which are very high within Central America, large differences exist in the interior of the country. In Table 2, the human development index is shown for Costa Rica, the Metropolitan San José Area, the Huetar Atlantic Region, and for the Talamanca canton, and these substantial differences within Costa Rica can be observed. Talamanca stands out as one of the poorest cantons.

With regards to health conditions, Talamanca canton has the highest mortality rate due to infectious diseases, the highest percentage of underweight newborns, and an infant mortality rate that in the 1983-85 period was almost double that of other regions in the country.

Another important aspect worth mention is that in Talamanca three ethnic groups coexist: indigenous, blacks and whites. Cahuita is the third largest district within the canton, with an area of 173.4 square kilometers, and according to the study conducted in 1994, a population of 3,612 people and 868 households. Its population is practically all rural.

THE MEASUREMENT OF POVERTY BY DIFFERENT METHODS

The application of methods to measure poverty in Cahuita were: poverty line, basic unmet needs (with four variants), and the integrated poverty method. These methods showed the very interesting results which are presented below.

Using the poverty line method, the percentage of poor households is almost double than that observed for the entire country (16% versus 29%) (Table 3). This difference is due to a much higher the percentage of households in extreme poverty in Cahuita: for Costa Rica the percentage is 7.1%, while for Cahuita it is 17.1%.

Using the basic unmet needs method, large differences with the previous method were shown, given that the percentage of poor households (about 70%), is markedly higher than with the poverty line method. Four variants of this method were tried:

A. Poverty index as the sum of 16 unweighted variables.

B. Poverty index as the sum of 16 weighted variables.

C. Poverty index as the sum of 9 unweighted dimensions.

D. Poverty index as the sum of 9 weighted dimensions.

The unweighted methods had more symmetric and less variable distributions than the weighted methods.

There were also significant differences, in the results for these four variants, between methods that use the 16 variables (A and B) and methods that use 9 dimensions (C and D). For example, the percentage of non-poor households is three times greater in Method B than in C, and five times greater than D. With regards to poverty levels, important differences are also demonstrated (Figure 1).

In Method B the percentage of non-poor households increases in comparison to Method A. A cross-tabulation of the two methods showed that the difference is due to the households classified at a mild level of poverty by Method A and those classified as non-poor households by Method B.

When Methods C and D are compared, Method C ranks a greater number of households in the medium level while Method D ranks a greater number of households at a very poor or a mildly poor level. However, the two methods estimate equal percentages of extreme poverty.

Furthermore, between Methods A and B, differences are shown above all in the estimates of non-poor households.

In addition, the percentages of households in extreme poverty are doubled when the method that uses 9 dimensions is employed, and there are no differences between weighted and unweighted methods.

In the integrated poverty method, the method involved cross-tabulating the poverty line and the basic unmet needs methods. This information is presented in Table 4. In the application of this method, four categories were obtained:

a) Poor by both methods (chronic poverty)

b) Poor by poverty line method but not basic unmet needs method (conjunctional poverty)

c) Poor by basic unmet needs method but not poverty line method (structural poverty)

d) Not poor by either method

The percentage of poor households by both methods is substantial, contrary to what has been found in other applications. Additionally, there are no significant differences between the percentages in Methods A and B, and between Methods C and D.

The households in Cahuita that are not poor by the basic unmet needs method but are poor by the poverty line method are called conjunctional poor. There are relatively few of these in the district, especially if they are estimated using Methods C and D (particularly, Method D).

The households in Cahuita that are poor by the basic unmet needs method, but are not poor by the poverty line method, that is households that suffer from structural poverty, have the highest percentages poor, especially if they are estimated with Methods C and D.

With regard to households classified as not poor by either method, using Methods A and B the percentages are 20% and 25% respectively, but using methods C and D the percentage is less than 9%.

FACTORS ASSOCIATED WITH POVERTY

Once the problems related to measurement of poverty in Cahuita district were considered, we decided to use the basic unmet needs method with variant A to study several factors related to poverty. The following variables were selected: household head characteristics (sex, age, marital status, and nationality), and household characteristics (size, type, land tenancy).

Sociodemographic Characteristics of Heads of Households and Poverty Levels

In 1984, in Talamanca canton, 12% of the households were headed by females. According to the data for Cahuita in 1994 this percentage was 15%. The percentage in Cahuita is lower than the national average. However, for Costa Rica as a whole, the percentage of households headed by females is generally higher in urban than rural areas. In 1992, 16% of the households in rural areas were headed by females, while in urban areas this figure was 24.2% (FLACSO, 1993).

While studying male and female heads of households and poverty, we found that in Cahuita 76% of the households headed by males had some degree of poverty while for those households headed by females the proportion was 70%.

However, when different levels of poverty are examined, we can see that the poor households headed by males are located more in the "mild poverty" category while those headed by females are in the "extreme poverty" category.

With respect to the marital status of head of household, there are important differences observed by the level of poverty. The degree of poverty is generally higher for household heads in consensual unions than for married heads of households (Table 5).

The average age of household heads is 43.7 years old. Households in extreme poverty have, on average, older heads (47.2 years old), and households with a medium level of poverty have the youngest heads (41.5 years old) (Figure 3).

Cahuita is a community where 14% of its population is foreign-born. According to the data analyzed, poverty affects foreigners more than Costa Ricans. The majority of the foreigners residing in the district are Central American, especially Nicaraguans.

Household Characteristics and Poverty

The analysis of the relation between the household characteristics and poverty were conducted with two variables: size of home and type of home.

The typology employed was developed by Kuhlman and Soto (1994) who used the relation between relationship and

SD is considered to reflect stunting, an indicator of chronic malnutrition or illness. Low weight-for-height (<-2 SD) reflects wasting, an indicator of acute malnutrition or frequent severe infections. Low weight-for-age (<-2 SD) reflects general malnutrition. Weight-for-age is more difficult to interpret than the other two indicators, because a child may be underweight due to long-term illness, general lack of food, or recent infection. Because of this, results will only be presented for height-for-age and weight-for-height. The patterns observed with regard to weight-for-age are similar to those for height-for-age, since the problem of acute malnutrition is minimal in the four countries examined.

Typically, the anthropometric z-scores in a population are normally distributed. To illustrate this point, Figure 1 shows the distribution of height-for-age in three of the surveys analyzed here. While the distributions are shifted from each other, indicating differing levels of chronic malnutrition in the three countries, the shape of the distribution is almost identical in the three cases. Furthermore, inspection of anthropometric data from a large number of countries shows that the standard deviation of the z-scores themselves is generally quite constant across countries (Yip, 1994). As the nutritional status of a population improves, improvements are observed in the entire distribution, not just among those children in the tail of the distribution.

Because of the constancy in shape and degree of spread in the distribution of anthropometric z-scores, it is possible to use the mean z-scores as an indicator of nutritional status. Examination of the mean z-score has certain advantages over the use of percentages below a fixed cutoff (such as -2 SD). First, because each child contributes more information to the computation of the mean z-score (actual value) than to the computation of the percent in the tail (yes/no), the mean can be estimated with greater precision. Second, the mean is less affected by measurement errors than is the percent in the tail. For example, if height is measured with an error of ± 1 cm., the mean z-score will be unaffected, but the percent below -2 SD will be artificially inflated.

The disadvantage of using the mean z-score as an indicator of the nutritional status of a population is that it is not intuitive. How does one interpret a mean height-for-age z-score of -1.3? One solution is to convert the mean z-score into a predicted percent stunted, assuming that the z-scores are normally distributed with a constant standard deviation of one. Thus, a mean z-score of -1.3 translates to 24.2 percent below -2 SD. This method of computing the percent below -2 SD will be called the "indirect method". Through simulations, it can be shown that the standard error of the predicted percent below -2 SD using this indirect procedure is considerably smaller than the standard error of the direct observed percent below -2 SD (Table 2). For example, if the true prevalence of stunting were 20 percent, the standard error of the estimated prevalence is roughly two-thirds as large using the indirect method compared to the direct method. A similar improvement in the standard error would required more than a doubling of the sample size. This improvement in precision is particularly important when results are desired for small geographic areas or for subgroups of the population.

In this analysis, geographic patterns of malnutrition were examined by mapping the mean z-scores for regions of the countries. Sample sizes for departmental level analyses were generally insufficient, since the surveys were not designed with the intention of providing departmental statistics (the countries have from 14 to 22 departments each). Maps were produced using SAS/PROC GMAP. Maps were produced separately for the 1987-88 surveys (El Salvador, Guatemala, Honduras) and the 1993-94 surveys (El Salvador, Honduras, Nicaragua). To maintain comparability across the region, the 1987-88 map includes only children 3-35 months of age and the 1993-94 map includes only children 3-59 months of age.

percent) and San Salvador (16 percent). The more mountainous areas of Honduras, extending southeast into Nicaragua have elevated rates compared to the lower elevations in either country.

There is little variation in rates of wasting in 1993-94, with all regions showing rates very similar to the expected rate in the reference population. For each country, the lowest rates are found in the regions surrounding the capital cities (Tegucigalpa, Managua and San Salvador). The highest rates are found in the Western region of El Salvador and the southernmost region of Honduras, both with a rate of 3.4 percent.

Differentials

Because of the generally low rates and lack of variation in the prevalence of wasting (low weight-for-height), the analysis presented here will only focus on rates of stunting (low height-for-age). It is universally the case for these seven surveys that rates of stunting are higher in rural areas than in urban areas (Table 4). Education of the child's mother is also a strong predictor in all the countries, with the rates among children whose mothers had no education being at least two and a half times greater than the rates among those whose mothers had at least 7 years of education. There is likewise a strong socio-economic gradient, with monotonically improving rates of stunting shown in all countries as the socio-economic status improves. On the other hand, there are no statistically significant differentials by gender for any of the countries. Rates of stunting are clearly lowest in the first year of life and highest in the fifth year for all the countries examined. The largest increase occurs between the first and second years.

Trends

In El Salvador and Honduras, more than one survey has been conducted since 1987, so it is possible to examine trends in these countries. In El Salvador, the overall trend toward improved rates of stunting is clear (Table 3). Both the 1988 and the 1993 surveys are considered to be of high quality and the magnitude of the change between the two surveys is rather large. The observed stunting rate (direct method) declined from 30.7 percent to 23.0 percent and the mean z-score shifted upward from -1.42 to -1.21.

The improvement in stunting rates in El Salvador was fairly dramatic in three of the regions (Central, Metropolitana, and Oriental). The other two regions (Occidente and Para-Central) showed no change whatsoever. Improvements were observed in all of the subgroups identified above (Table 4). The overall trend for the country was further augmented by the fact that between the two surveys, the percent of the population living in urban areas and the percent with at least seven years of education increased.

In Honduras, the trends in stunting are less clear. There was virtually no change in the mean height-for-age z-score or the observed percentage stunted between 1987 and 1991 (Table 3). On the other hand, the 1994 survey showed a significant worsening of nutritional status. This increase in rates of stunting was found in all seven regions of the country and was especially pronounced in the urban areas and among children whose mothers had higher levels of education (Table 4)[2].

The increase in stunting rates may reflect a real worsening of living conditions in Honduras. Unfortunately, the large standard deviations observed in the Honduras 1994 survey for all three indicators (height-for-age, weight-for-height, and weight-for-age) draw into question the validity of the results. Examination of the mean z-score minimizes the importance of random

[2]Caution must be used in examining trends by the indicator of household amenities since the definition of this variable is not common to the two surveys.

errors, but the possibility of bias cannot be ruled out. One potential problem is the inaccurate assessment of the child's age. Although there are no obvious errors in the distribution of ages (such as heaping or a skewed age distribution), the fact that a birth history was used for assessing ages in 1991/92 but not in 1993/94 could have contributed to greater variation in the assessment of age for the latter survey. Given these problems it is impossible to make definitive conclusions about recent trends in Honduras.

With regard to wasting (low weight-for-height), there are no discernible trends in El Salvador. Honduras shows significant trends toward higher weight-for-height, with the distribution of weight-for-height z-scores shifting to the right with each survey. However, for reasons just described, these trends must be interpreted with caution.

DISCUSSION

This analysis has demonstrated that the prevalence of chronic undernutrition remains high throughout Central America, but that there is considerable variation in the levels of chronic undernutrition across the region. In general, rates of stunting decline as one moves south-eastward through the region, with the highest rates being observed in northwestern Guatemala. Rates are generally higher in the more mountainous regions. On the other hand, rates of wasting are quite low and show little geographic pattern. The only two regions where the wasting rate exceeds seven percent are in western and southern Honduras.

Stunting rates are highly correlated with type of place of residence, mother's education level and socio-economic status, but not sex of the child. Trends in nutritional status in El Salvador have clearly shown an improvement in stunting rates. Trends in Honduras appear to point toward a deterioration in stunting, but apparent data quality problems in the latest Honduras survey make it impossible to draw definitive conclusions.

The rate of childhood stunting can be viewed as an overall indicator of the health and well-being of children in a population. Because of the many casual mechanisms involved in promoting the growth of children, chronic malnutrition is less likely to be affected by specific policy changes, but more so by general improvements in the living conditions of families. The same can be said of child mortality rates. However, monitoring of nutritional status has certain advantages over monitoring of infant or child mortality. Because infant mortality is a relatively rare occurrence (approximately 4-7 percent for these countries), fairly large sample sizes are required in surveys to obtain robust estimates of the infant mortality rate. Rates of stunting on the other hand can be estimated with considerably smaller relative error with smaller sample size. As a consequence, it is possible to estimate region-level or even department-level estimates of chronic malnutrition without expanding sample sizes beyond what is commonly utilized in national surveys. This advantage is further enhanced by the use of the indirect technique of estimating the stunting rate.

Furthermore, as mortality levels reach fairly low levels in these countries, it will become increasingly difficult to detect improvements in childhood well-being using mortality measurements. As the causes of childhood mortality shift toward more "endogenous" causes, the ability of mortality measurements to reflect overall health status will diminish.

Collection of anthropometric data does require a high degree of training and supervision of field staff. The utility of the results can be severely hampered by inappropriate weighing and measuring of children or inaccurately assessing ages. Specialized software is required for the processing of anthropometric data. But similar difficulties are faced in the assessment of child mortality rates through a birth history questionnaire. Without careful training and supervision of interviewers in probing for "forgotten" neonatal deaths, direct estimates of mortality can be severely underestimated. Life table software which allows for left- and right-censoring is needed to obtain accurate estimates.

Nutritional status of children has other advantages as an indicator for monitoring. Unlike many other indicators of well-being, it is objective and does not rely on a respondent's understanding and interpretation of questions. It does not require that the respondent remember any events in the past other than the date of birth of the child. International guidelines have been set for the interpretation of anthropometric data. Finally, nutritional status is comparable across settings, thus allowing for the kind of regional analysis presented here.

APPENDIX: CREATION OF THE HOUSEHOLD AMENITIES INDEX

Because questions on the amenities available to the household were asked in different ways and about different amenities, no attempt was made to create comparable socio-economic indices across the surveys. Where indices of socio-economic status already existed for the datasets, these were used. A description of the indices used follows:

El Salvador, 1988. Count amenities among the following: 1) electricity, 2) television, 3) refrigerator, 4) vehicle, 5) cook with electricity or gas, 6) flush toilet, and 7) at least 4 rooms in the house. Index grouped as: Low=no amenities, Medium=1-2 amenities, High=3-7 amenities.

El Salvador, 1993. The following were considered: 1) electricity, 2) television, 3) refrigerator, 4) automobile, 5) cook with electricity or gas, 6) flush toilet, 7) at least 4 rooms in the house, 8) masonry or adobe walls, 9) concrete, tile or Duralite roof, 10) non-dirt floor, 11) piped water in house or patio, and 12) telephone. A weighted score was constructed of these items, where each item received a score of the inverse of the proportion of women with that amenity. The index of the weighted counts was grouped as: Low=score of 0-5.29, Medium=score of 5.3-13.99, High=score of 14.0-45.0.

Guatemala, 1987. Amenities were put into two groups: low value (radio and bicycle) and high value (television, refrigerator, motorcycle, car and tractor). The index was created as Low=no amenities, Medium=only low value amenities, High=at least one high value amenity.

Honduras, 1987. No index constructed.

Honduras, 1991/92. Amenities were put into two groups: low value (radio) and high value (television, refrigerator, and electricity). The index was created as Low=no amenities, Medium=only low value amenities, High=at least one high value amenity.

Honduras, 1993/94. Count amenities among the following: 1) electricity, 2) cook with electricity or gas, 3) flush toilet or latrine, 4) at least 2 bedrooms in the house, 5) concrete or adobe walls, 6) non-dirt floor, 7) piped water within 300 meters. Index grouped as: Low=0-2 amenities, Medium=3-4 amenities, High=5-7 amenities.

Nicaragua, 1993/94. Amenities were put into two groups: low value (radio) and high value (television, refrigerator, and electricity). The index was created as Low=no amenities, Medium=only low value amenities, High=at least one high value amenity.

ACKNOWLEDGEMENTS

I owe great thanks to the many people who willingly shared these datasets with me and helped me understand the peculiarities of each, particularly Mario Cáceres, David Hubacher, Farid Matuk, Dick Monteith, Kinnon Scott, Anne Swindale, and Stan Terrell. I also wish to thank Ray Yip and Kelley Scanlon for their helpful insights on the interpretation of anthropometric indicators.

FIGURE 2a. MEAN HEIGHT—FOR—AGE Z—SCORE CENTRAL AMERICA - 1987-1988 SURVEYS (3-35 MONTH OLDS)

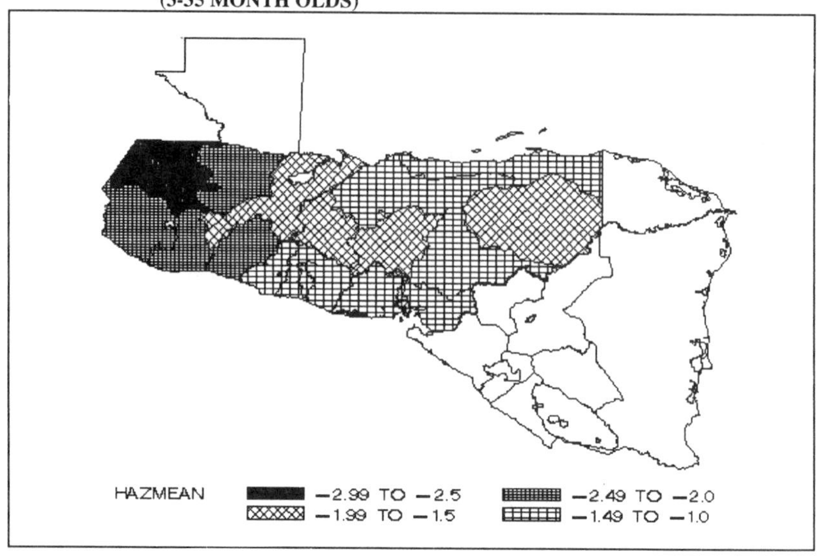

FIGURE 2b: MEAN WEIGHT—FOR—HEIGHT Z—SCORE CENTRAL AMERICA - 1987-1988 SURVEYS (3-35 MONTH OLDS)

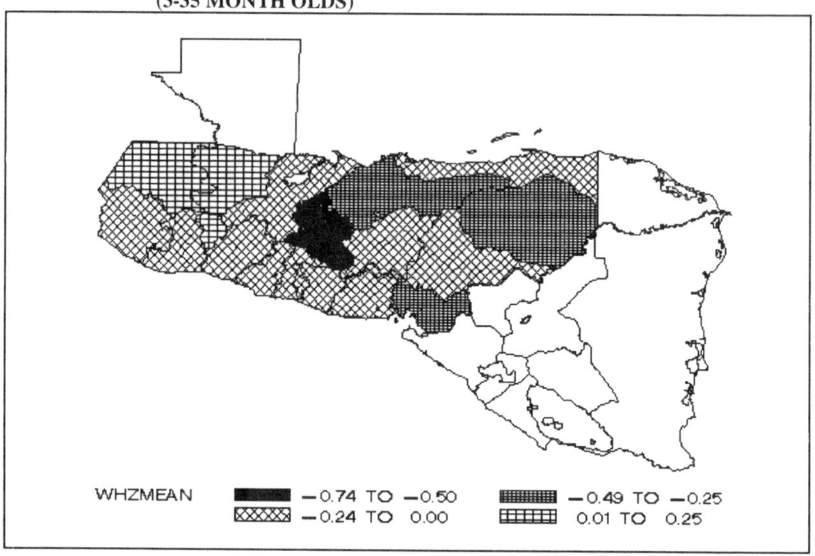

FIGURE 3a: MEAN HEIGHT—FOR—AGE Z—SCORE CENTRAL AMERICA - 1993-1994 SURVEYS
(3-59 MONTH OLDS)

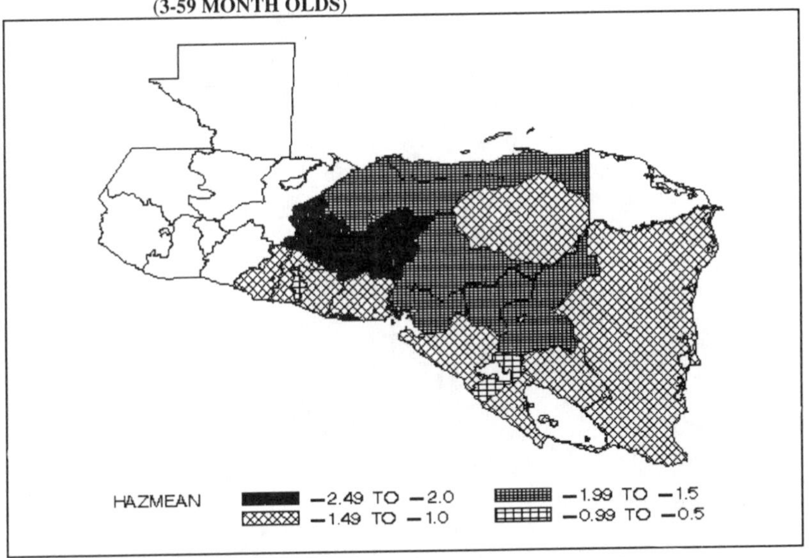

FIGURE 3b: MEAN WEIGHT—FOR—HEIGHT Z—SCORE CENTRAL AMERICA - 1993-1994 SURVEYS
(3-59 MONTH OLDS)

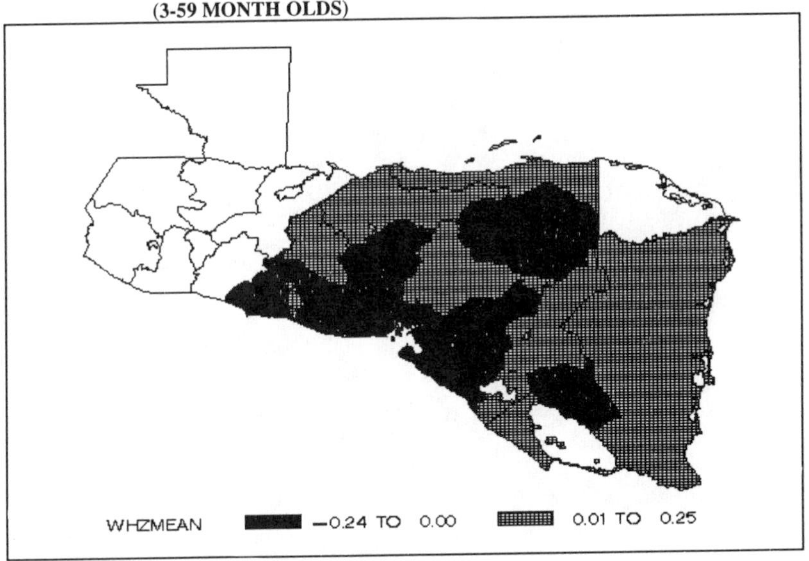

Chapter Ten

MATERNAL MORTALITY AND MORBIDITY IN EL SALVADOR

ISABELLA DANEL, LAURENCE GRUMMER-STRAWN, JOSE M. CACERES, AND PAUL STUPP

Maternal mortality, known as "the silent epidemic," is frequently underestimated in developing countries. Even less is known about maternal morbidity, and the limited information available comes from hospital studies. Since the majority of women in these countries give birth at home, hospital studies are not representative of all deliveries.

A population-based household survey was carried out in El Salvador between January and March 1993. A total of 6,207 women of reproductive age were interviewed. Maternal mortality was estimated based on the survival status of the respondent's sisters. Women who had been pregnant in the two years prior to the survey were asked about several problems during pregnancy, delivery and the post-partum period. Maternal morbidity is described using several demographic and reproductive variables.

The national maternal mortality ratio was estimated at 158 per 100,000 live births for the period 1983-1993. This figure is more than three times larger than that reported by the Ministry of Health in 1988 (47 per 100,000 live births). In general, the use of prenatal services was 68 %, the hospital delivery rate was 51% and the cesarean rate, based on the population, was 13.3 %. However, there are large differences depending on factors such as the area of residence and the level of education.

The percentage of women who reported maternal morbidity was high. The self-reported incidence of important causes of maternal morbidity during delivery include: hemorrhage (35%), fever (15%), prolonged labor (15%), loss of consciousness (11%), possible preeclampsia (8%), and convulsions (2%).

The prevalence of self-reported prenatal morbidity was higher in women who received prenatal care. This finding generates questions about the interpretation of some self-reported morbidities. On the other hand, the self-reported prevalence of morbidity during delivery was higher in women who gave birth at home compared to women who gave birth in a hospital. Studies such as this one are a first step toward understanding and prevention of maternal morbidity and its sequelae.

INTRODUCTION

The International Decade of the Women, 1975-1985, focused attention on the problems of women. Studies carried out during this period brought into the open the magnitude of maternal mortality and led to a "call for action" by the World Health Organization (WHO) during the international conference on Safe Motherhood held in Nairobi in 1987 (Mahler, 1987). The Pan-American Health Organization (PAHO) estimates that in the Americas approximately 28,000 women die during pregnancy, delivery, and the post-partum period each year. In 1990, during the XXIII Pan-American Health Conference, a Regional Plan of Action for the Reduction of Maternal Mortality in the Americas was approved (OPS,1990). The goal of this plan is to reduce maternal mortality in the Americas by 50% by the year 2000.

Documenting a reduction in maternal mortality can be difficult due to substantial underregistration of maternal deaths. This is the reason that PAHO has called maternal mortality "the silent epidemic" (PAHO, 1993). The lack of knowledge about the magnitude is derived in part from the fact that maternal deaths are frequently not reported. Even in the United States with its very well developed system of vital registration, it has been shown that maternal mortality is underregistered by 37% (Koonin et al., 1988). In Honduras, a study showed that the actual number of maternal deaths was 4.4 times higher than the number officially reported (Castellanos et al., 1990).

This degree of underregistration underscores the necessity for better methods of evaluating the true magnitude of maternal mortality. The development and use of instruments which can measure maternal mortality, in a reliable manner, are critical for evaluating whether PAHO and the member states of the region are reaching their goals. Recently the sisterhood survival method has been applied in large household surveys to measure maternal mortality. This method has permitted more reliable population-based estimation of the national maternal mortality ratio than is provided by official statistics.

Maternal mortality has been called the tip of the iceberg (Abou Zahr C., 1991). Millions of women suffer acute and chronic morbidity as a result of pregnancy and delivery. It has been estimated that there are more than 100 episodes of acute morbidity for every maternal death (Koblinsky et al., 1993). An understanding of maternal morbidity is important given its relationship with maternal mortality, maternal disability and perinatal morbidity and mortality. Most studies of maternal morbidity are based on data from hospitals. However, many women in developing countries give birth at home. For this reason, these studies are not representative of all deliveries. Given the lack of information, a WHO technical advisory group has emphasized the necessity of conducting population-based studies of maternal morbidity.

The 1993 National Survey of Family Health (FESAL-93) is the fifth in a series of surveys that the Salvadoran Demographic Association has carried out since 1973 to study fertility trends and the use of contraceptives in El Salvador (WHO, 1990). Since 1985 issues related to maternal and child health have also been included. FESAL-93 provided the opportunity to obtain population-based information on maternal mortality and morbidity and was the first survey which collected information of this type in El Salvador.

METHODS

Selection of the Sample

FESAL-93 employed a three-stage probability sampling design. In the first stage, census sectors were selected proportional to the size of the population as measured by the number of households in the sector. Two hundred twenty-five sectors were selected from a total of 12,743. The second stage involved the random selection of 40 consecutive households within each chosen sector. In the last stage, one woman of reproductive age (WRA), 15 to 48 years old, was selected from each household to be interviewed. The probability of choosing a woman was inversely proportional to the number of WRA in the household. To compensate for the unequal probability of selection, weights equal to the number of WRAs in the household were included for all observations in the data set (ADS and CDC, 1994).

Collection and Entry of the Data

Four teams, each of which included four interviewers, two anthropometrists, and a team supervisor, conducted the interviews between March 1 and July 15, 1993 using a pretested questionnaire. Survey topics included fertility, prevalence of contraceptive use, infant mortality, and maternal and child health, including maternal mortality and morbidity. Data quality was ensured by the supervisors who reviewed the questionnaires and by consistency checks in the data entry program. Since the data were entered each day immediately after the field work, the corrections were made rapidly when any inconsistencies were found in the data.

Estimation of Maternal Mortality

Maternal mortality was estimated directly using information from each respondent concerning the death or survival of her sisters. Each r[illegible] was asked the name of each of her sisters (daughters of h[illegible]). Then respondents were asked which sisters were living [illegible] [wh]ich had died. In the case of a death the respondent was [illegible] the age at death and year of death, and if the death occur[illegible]ing pregnancy, delivery or in the six weeks after the birth [illegible]tpartum period). Sisters who died during pregnancy, deli[illegible] the post-partum period were classified as maternal deaths. [illegible] methods allows the calculation of maternal mortality rates (per [illegible]00 WRA) and ratios (per 100,000 live births) by age groups [illegible] a specified period of time.

Measures of Maternal Mortality Included in T[illegible] Chapter

In this section we provide definitions of the [me]asures of maternal mortality used in this chapter.

The *maternal mortality ratio* is the number of maternal deaths per 100,000 live births. It is calculated using the maternal mortality rate and the general fertility rate. Both are adjusted for the age distribution of the FESAL-93 sample. This indicator measures the risk of dying during a given pregnancy.

Life-time reproductive risk is the risk of dying a woman faces during her reproductive years due to maternal causes. This indicator depends both on the risk of dying during a given pregnancy and on the number of pregnancies a woman has.

Proportional maternal mortality is the proportion of all deaths occurring to WRA due to maternal causes.

Sampling Frame for the Maternal Morbidity Module

Women answered questions in this module if they reported having a pregnancy between January 1991 and the date of the interview (March through July 1993). Information was obtained about events during the LAST pregnancy during this time period and not about all pregnancies. Questions were asked

ie, hemorrhage, swelling
about specific complications, f-d questions were included
of the feet and nausea. No o than those specified in the
This means that complicati that the data do not include
questions may have occu omplications.
any information on these

RESULTS

Sample

Of the 9 ouseholds selected for the sample, 73% had a WRA, 6.5% not occupied, and only 1.1% refused to participate in interview. Complete interviews were obtained from 94.7 f the households with at least one eligible woman. In 4% of e households the eligible woman was absent despite several sits. In only 0.3% of households, the eligible woman efus to participate. The completion rate for interviews did not ar appreciably by area of residence. None of the selected secrs had to be excluded for reasons of security, as had happened previous surveys in El Salvador. A total of 6,207 completed terviews were obtained. All interviews were used to estimate aternal mortality and the utilization of health services. A total 1,945 women answered questions in the maternal morbidity odule. The results presented are for 1,858 of these women hose pregnancies did not end in a pregnancy loss and reached at ast 20 months of gestation.

laternal Mortality

For the period 1983-1993 the average maternal mortality atio was 158 per 100,000 live births (Table 1). The life-time eproductive risk was 0.0066. This figure means that for each 52 women who reach reproductive age, one died during pregiancy, delivery or the postpartum period. Almost one out of ive deaths (19%) to women of reproductive age were due to naternal causes. In 1988, the mid-point for the estimation of maternal mortality, there were a total of 71 maternal deaths reported officially in the El Salvador vital statistics (Table 2). This represents a ratio of 47 per 100,000 live births. The estimate obtained from FESAL-93 is more than three times greater and suggests that the annual number of maternal deaths in El Salvador is currently around 240.

Use of Health Services

To be able to compare the results in this period with the period 1983-1988, rates were calculated only for the last live birth since the same method was used in the previous FESAL survey (ADS and CDC, 1989). Table 3 shows that that use of prenatal services increase by 4 percentage points from 67% to 71%. The hospital birth rate also increased by 4 percentage points from 52% to 56%. The prevalence of contraceptive use for women in unions increased by 6 percentage points, from 47% to 53%.

However, there are large differentials among different groups of the population. The use of health services varied considerably by characteristics such as area of residence and level of education (Figures 1 and 2). Use was higher in the metropolitan area than in rural areas and was strongly associated with women's level of education. Women with higher levels of education were more likely to use health services. The strong association with women's education occurs for all three health services studied: prenatal care, hospital delivery, and contraceptive use.

Cesarean Delivery Rates

The overall cesarean section rate for the last pregnancy in the period 1988-1993 was 13.3% (Table 4) . This represents an increase of 50% over the rate in the period 1983-1988 (8.5%). The cesarean rate increased for all population groups. However, again there are large differences by area of residence and education level of the woman. The rate was 8.1% in rural areas compared with 21.3% in the metropolitan area. It was 6.3% for women with no education compared with 26.5% for women with more than 10 years of education.

Multivariate Logistic Regression Analysis

To adjust for confounding among the explanatory variables, we used a logistic regression model to estimate the odds of receiving prenatal care, a hospital delivery, and a cesarean delivery. The variables included in the model were those available in the FESAL-93: socioeconomic status, education, age group, area of residence, parity and, for the hospital delivery model, if the woman received prenatal care.

As shown in Table 5, the results show that the odds of prenatal care are higher for nulliparous women (those having their first pregnancy) than among women at parity four and higher. The non-use of prenatal care was significantly higher among women of lower socioeconomic status compared with those of higher socioeconomic status and among women with less than seven years of school. None of the area of residence variables is significantly associated with prenatal care after adjusting for socioeconomic status, education, parity, and age group.

Hospital deliveries were much more likely among women at parities less than four and much less likely among women with low socioeconomic status and with fewer than seven years of education. However, hospital delivery was strongly associated with area of residence. Women in the metropolitan area were five times more likely to have a hospital delivery than women in rural areas and two times more likely than women in other urban areas.

Cesarean deliveries were strongly related to parity. Women in the metropolitan area had twice the probability of having a cesarean compared to women in rural areas. Residence in other urban areas was not significantly associated with cesareans compared to residence in rural areas. However, in contrast to hospital deliveries, the likelihood of a cesarean delivery is not associated with socioeconomic status. Only women with no education had a significantly lower probability of having a cesarean compared to women with 10 years or more of education.

Prenatal Maternal Morbidity

In the sample as a whole, 6.3 % of women reported prenatal hemorrhage, 8% reported hypertension (with a history previous to the pregnancy), 14.2% reported gestational hypertension (without any previous history), 18.3% reported anemia, 34.7% reported swelling of the feet, and 54.4 % reported dizziness. The report of the FESAL-93 survey reported differences related to residence, age, level of education, socioeconomic status, and parity. Figure 3 shows that women who had at least one prenatal visit had a higher probability of reporting all these morbidities. The prevalence of self-reported anemia and previous hypertension is more than double in women who had prenatal care. From the morbidities shown in this figure, those least related to prenatal care are nausea (51.9% for women with no prenatal care vs. 55.5% for those with prenatal care) and gestational hypertension (12.8% vs. 14.7%).

Morbidity During Delivery

A total of 1.8% of women report convulsions during childbirth (without having had a previous history of convulsions outside of pregnancy). 11.1% reported loss of consciousness, 15 % reported prolonged labor (more than 24 hours), 16.7 % reported hypertension, 24.1 % reported fever, and 28.6 % reported heavy bleeding. Compared with prenatal morbidity, the prevalence of self-reported morbidity during delivery is less associated with prenatal care (Figure 4). The differences in the prevalence among women receiving prenatal care and those that did not receive it are small. Convulsions and loss of consciousness were slightly more likely to be reported by women with prenatal care while fever and bleeding were slightly more likely among those without prenatal care.

However, there are larger differences in the prevalence of morbidity during delivery by place of delivery (Figure 5). With the exception of convulsions, all other morbidities had a greater self-reported prevalence among women who did not give birth in a hospital. For example, the probability of loss of consciousness is almost two times greater among women who did not give birth in the hospital than for women who had hospital deliveries.

The general prevalence of self-reported heavy bleeding during delivery was 28.6 %. The differences in reporting of this problem by residence and level of education are minimal and vary between 25.7 % for women in other urban areas and 31.4% in women in rural areas (Figure 6). However, large differences are revealed if the prevalence of bleeding and a history of loss of consciousness are combined (Figure 7), an indication that bleeding is life threatening. Women in rural areas have a probability that is more than twice that of women in the metropolitan area. Women with no education are more than four times as likely to report such bleeding as women with more than 10 years of education.

DISCUSSION

Maternal Mortality

An estimate of maternal mortality of 158 deaths per 100,000 live births was obtained from FESAL-93 using the direct sisterhood survival method. This method has been used to obtain direct and indirect estimates of maternal mortality and has been shown in several studies to produce reliable estimates.[1] Since 1989, this method has been used in several studies in Latin America including in Bolivia in 1989 and 1994 (Sommerfelt et al., 1991; Gutierres et al., 1994), Peru in 1992 (Marckwardt, 1993), and Ecuador (Olmedo et al., 1995). These studies have provided ample evidence that maternal mortality is underestimated in official statistics. In El Salvador, the data suggest that only 30% of maternal deaths are officially registered. The under-registration generally occurs for two reasons. First, some burials occur without registration of the death. Second, some maternal deaths are misclassified as non-maternal.

As part of its plan to reduce maternal mortality, PAHO recommends strengthening of maternal mortality surveillance systems so that better information can be provided on its magnitude and causes (OPS, 1990). Ideally, this means reviewing all deaths occurring to women of reproductive age and an in-depth investigation of deaths which occurred during and after pregnancy. However, until maternal mortality surveillance systems have improved and begin to provide reliable data, studies like the FESAL-93 which use the sisterhood survival method continue to be necessary to demonstrate the gap between official statistics and the true magnitude of the problem.

Use of Health Services

The use of health services improved slightly between the five year period 1983-88 and 1988-93. In the latter period 71 % of women reported having at least one prenatal visit during the last pregnancy. Of these women, 56% gave birth in a hospital, 36% were attended at delivery by a trained midwife, and 5.3% gave birth without any assistance (ADS and CDC, 1994).

---

[1]For example, Bangladesh (Shahiduuah, 1995); Bail (Wirawan and Linnan, 1994); Tanzania (Walraven et al., 1992); Bolivia (Rutenberg, 1990).

Neither prenatal care nor hospital delivery was associated with the woman's age after adjusting for other variables. Nulliparous women were much more likely to use prenatal services than women with four or more previous pregnancies. There were no significant differences in the use of prenatal services by area of residence which suggests that geographic access is not an important obstacle to the use of these services. However, significant differences were noted by socioeconomic status and level of education which suggests that there are economic and social obstacles.

Hospital delivery was more strongly associated with parity than with prenatal care. Women with fewer than four previous pregnancies were much more likely to have cesarean deliveries than women of higher parity. As in the case of prenatal care, hospital delivery was associated with higher socioeconomic status and higher levels of education. However, in contrast to prenatal care, hospital delivery was very strongly associated with area of residence. It is not very surprising that women in the metropolitan area were five times more likely to deliver in a hospital than women in rural areas.

Hospital delivery is recommended for women with certain risk characteristics and generally results in better maternal and perinatal outcomes. We found that women who had at least one prenatal visit were significantly more likely to deliver in a hospital compared with women not receiving prenatal care, even after adjusting for other variables in our model. It is not clear if this association is related to the prenatal care itself or to the fact that women who go for prenatal care are more highly motivated and more likely to go to the hospital as well. However, it seems plausible that once a woman has made contact with the health care system via prenatal care she is more likely to return to a hospital delivery, especially if the contact has been positive.

Cesarean Delivery Rates

The general cesarean delivery rate was 13.3% for the period 1988-1993. PAHO recommends that this rate should not be higher than 15% (OPS, 1991). A rate less than 5% suggests that women who need this procedure do not have access to it while a rate greater than 15% suggests that women are unnecessarily exposed to the risks of anesthesia and surgical complications. The current Salvadoran rate is acceptable and all studied population groups had rates greater than 5% suggesting that access to cesarean delivery is adequate for a large part of the population. The lowest rates were among women in rural areas (8.1%) and women with no education (6.3%).

However, the cesarean rates are extremely high for some sub-groups of women. Women in the metropolitan area have a rate of 21.2%. Women with 10 years or more of education have a rate of 26.5% which is higher than rates in some developed countries. These women tend to have a higher socioeconomic status, or better nutritional status, and are generally in better health. No biological explanation exists for such a high rate which suggests that other factors, are probably playing a role.

Using our logistic regression model we found that the odds ratio for cesarean deliveries were different compared with those for hospital deliveries. For example, after adjusting for factors such as parity and area of residence, the odds for cesarean delivery were similar for women in all socioeconomic groups, whereas the odds at a hospital delivery were twice as high for women of high socioeconomic status compared with those from a low socioeconomic status. The odds for women with no education of cesarean delivery were slightly lower than for other women, but this negative association was not as strong as for hospital deliveries. This suggests that while obstacles to hospital delivery existed for some group of women, they were nevertheless being referred to hospitals for cesarean sections when obstetrical emergencies arose.

Use of Health Services and Maternal Mortality

The use of health services is promoted as an important means of improving maternal health. Therefore it is desirable to evaluate the impact of health services on maternal outcomes. Although it is not possible to evaluate mortality outcomes using the methodology of this survey, it is theoretically possible to evaluate the impact of health services on the prevalence of maternal morbidity. However, this study shows that there are problems in the interpretation of self-reported information on morbidity with respect to the use of health services. We found, for example, that all antenatal morbidities which we measured were more prevalent among women who received prenatal care than among women who had not received prenatal care. It is unlikely that prenatal care actually increases the prevalence of prenatal morbidity. More likely, women who experience problems like bleeding have a higher probability of visiting a clinic to receive treatment. Another explanation for this finding is that prenatal care increases women's knowledge about pregnancy complications which were perhaps not apparent. The prevalence of self-reported anemia is more than double among women who had prenatal care. It is likely that during the prenatal visit, the hematocrit was checked and the patient was told she had anemia. In general, women are not aware that they have anemia until the hematocrit falls to very low levels.

Given these contradictions, it is more appropriate to use other indicators of maternal health to evaluate the efficacy of prenatal care. These include pregnancy and perinatal outcomes like stillbirths, neonatal deaths, and birthweight. Unfortunately, the results of FESAL-93 were limited by the fact that only 48.5% of women knew the birthweight of their infants. Furthermore, the small sample did not permit an evaluation of the impact of prenatal maternal morbidity on perinatal mortality.

In developing countries, morbidity during delivery is most closely linked with maternal mortality. Since it is difficult to prevent many of these complications, efforts to improve care during delivery and the treatment of obstetrical emergencies are a key part of the WHO recommendations for reducing maternal mortality (WHO, 1991). The results of FESAL-93 show that women who received prenatal care were less likely to report convulsions and the loss of consciousness during pregnancy.

In contrast to the prenatal care results, hospital births are consistently associated with a lower self-reported prevalence of morbidity during delivery. With the exception of convulsions, all of the morbidities studied are more prevalent among women who did not give birth in a hospital. This result can be interpreted in several ways. On one hand, it is likely that hospital delivery reduces the likelihood of some of these morbidities (severe bleeding with the loss of consciousness, prolonged labor, fever). On the other hand, women with complications should be referred as soon as possible to the hospital. Women can develop complications at home and give birth in a hospital. This referral process tends to increase the prevalence of complications among women who give birth in a hospital. Under ideal circumstances, all women with complications would give birth in the hospital. However, in El Salvador, the prevalence is higher among women who give birth outside of the hospital, suggesting that the referral process does not function adequately.

Complications during childbirth occurred in all groups of women. The results of the FESAL-93 show little difference, for example, in the prevalence of heavy bleeding during delivery among different areas of residence or educational levels. However, notable differences are found in the development of life-threatening bleeding, defined as *bleeding associated with loss of consciousness*. While heavy bleeding was reported by 28.1% women with 10 years or more of education and by 30.5% of women without education, a minimal difference, bleeding with loss of consciousness was reported only by 5.8% of women with 10 years or more of education compared with 27.7% of women

TABLE 1. MATERNAL MORTALITY INDICATORS, EL SALVADOR: 1989-1993

Maternal Mortality Ratio	158/ 100,000 live births
Lifetime Risk	0.0066 (1/152 WRA*)
Proportionate Maternal Mortality	19%

*Women of reproductive age

TABLE 2. MATERNAL MORTALITY INFORMATION GAP

	Maternal Mortality Ratio*	Number of Maternal Deaths Annually
1988 Official Report	47	71
1983-1993 FESAL Estimate	158	240

*Per 100,000 live births

TABLE 3. MATERNAL HEALTH SERVICE UTILIZATION, EL SALVADOR, 1983-1993*

Selected Maternal Health Services	1983-1988	1988-1993
% receiving prenatal care	67%	71%
% delivering in hospital	52%	56%
% receiving post-partum care	40%	**
Contraceptive prevalence	47%	53%

* Last live birth

** Data not available for last live birth

TABLE 4. C SECTION RATES, EL SALVADOR, 1983-1993

Characteristics	FESAL - 88	FESAL - 93
Total	8.5%	13.3%
Area		
Metropolitan	17.4%	21.3%
Other Urban	13.4%	14.8%
Rural	3.6%	8.1%
Educational Level		
None	5.1%	6.3%
1-3	3.7%	8.8%
4-6	10.5%	13.6%
7-9	9.0%	16.1%
10+	21.4%	26.5%

TABLE 5. RELATIVE ODDS RATIOS FOR PRENATAL CARE, HOSPITAL DELIVERY OR C-SECTION USING A MULTIVARIATE LOGISTIC REGRESSION MODEL

Characteristic	Prenatal Care	Hospital Delivery	Cesarean Section
Socioeconomic Status			
Low	0.35**	0.45**	0.84
Medium	0.61	0.91	1.19
High	1.0	1.0	1.0
Education			
None	.24**	0.29**	0.46*
1-3	0.32**	0.33**	0.59
4-6	0.38**	0.54*	0.92
7-9	0.65	0.75	0.68
10+	1.0	1.0	1.0
Age Group			
15-19	0.73	0.48	0.3
20-29	1.21	0.82	0.6
30-39	1.13	1.3	0.81
40-49	1.0	1.0	1.0
Area of Residence			
Metropolitan	1.47	5.53**	2.56**
Other Urban	0.97	1.47**	1.44
Rural	1.0	1.0	1.0
Parity			
0	2.74**	4.1**	6.36**
1	1.29	2.32**	4.55**
2-3	1.26	2.11**	2.59**
4+	1.0	1.0	1.0
Prenatal Care			
Yes		1.55**	
No		1.0	

* p-value < 0.05
** p-value < 0.01
*** During the last pregnancy with a live birth

FIGURE 1. UTILIZATIONOF MATERNAL HEALTH CARE SERVICES BY AREA OF RESIDENCE

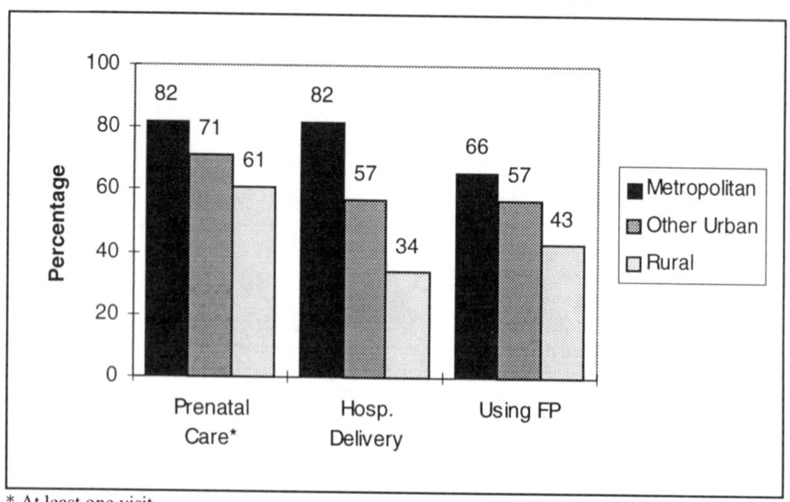

* At least one visit

FIGURE 2. UTILIZATION OF MATERNAL HEALTH CARE SERVICES BY EDUCATION LEVEL

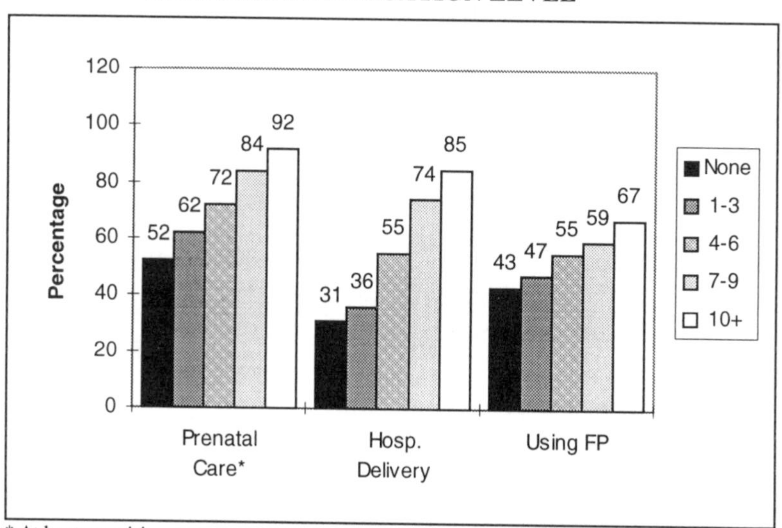

* At least one visit

FIGURE 3. PREVALENCE OF ANTENATAL MORBIDITY REPORTED BY WOMEN WITH AND WITHOUT PRENATAL CARE

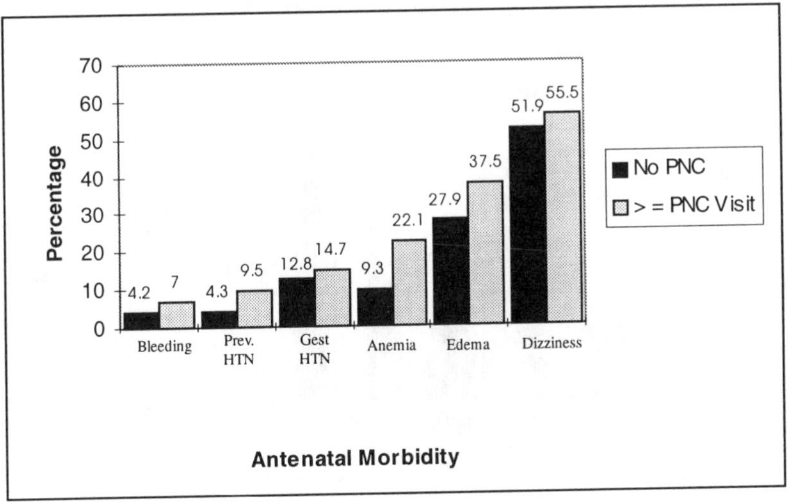

FIGURE 4. PREVALENCE OF MORBIDITY DURING CHILDBIRTH REPORT BY WOMEN WITH AND WITHOUT PRENATAL CARE

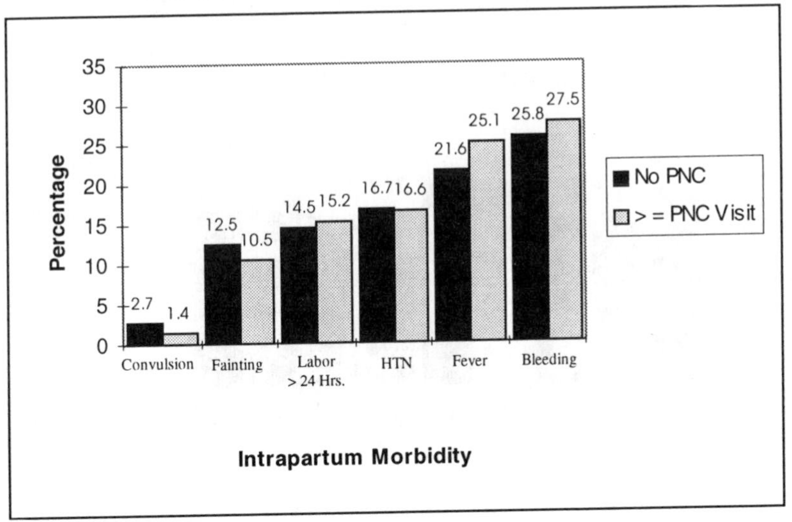

FIGURE 5. PREVALENCE OF MORBIDITY DURING CHILDBIRTH REPORTED BY WOMEN ACCORDING TO PLACE OF DELIVERY

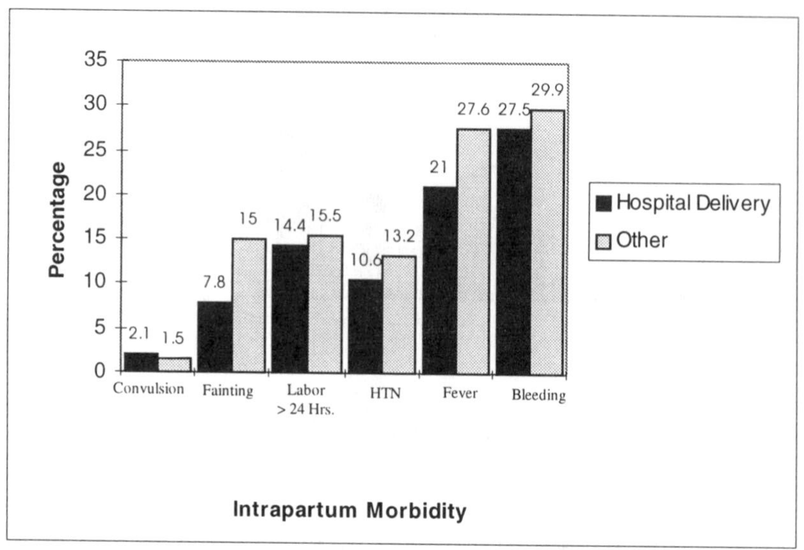

FIGURE 6. PERCENT OF WOMEN WHO REPORT INTENSE BLEEDING DURING CHILDBIRTH

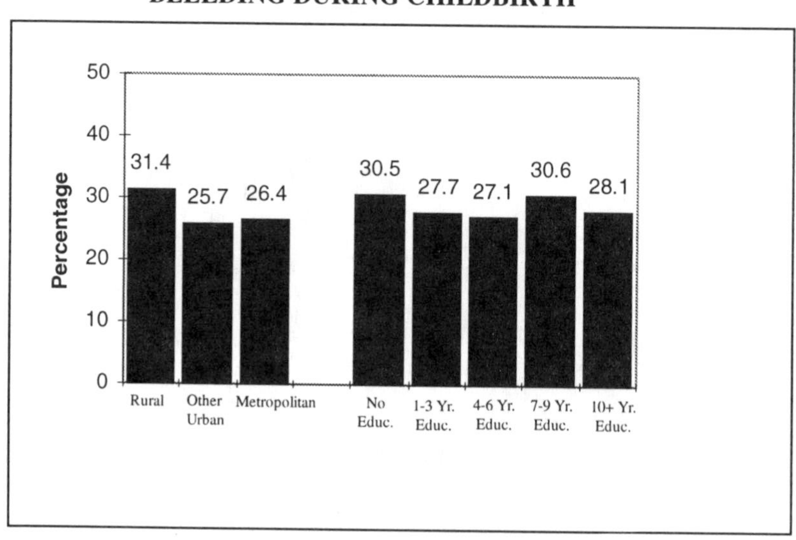

FIGURE 7. PERCENT OF WOMEN WITH INTENSE BLEEDING DURING CHILDBIRTH WHO REPORT LOSS OF CONSCIOUSNESS

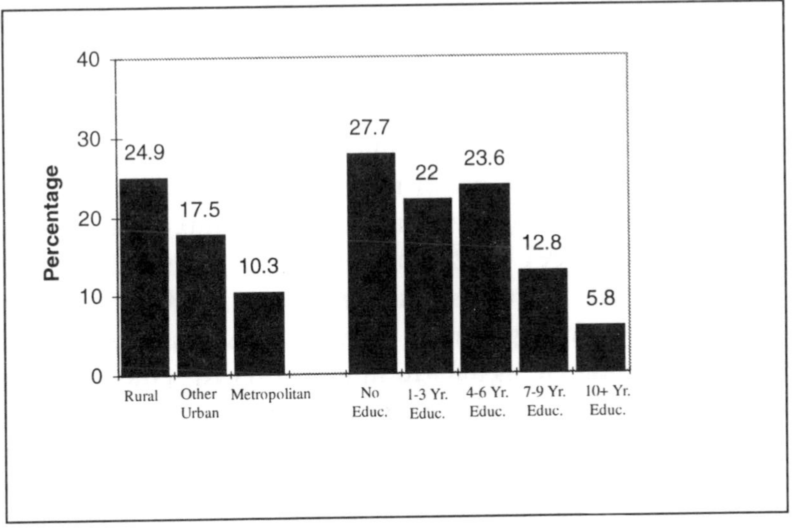

33.4 births per 1000 population, 74.6% of which occurred in hospitals and 14.4% in CCSS. This phenomenon increased further: in 1980 the birth rate declined to 30.6 per 1000, with 92.2% of births in hospitals and 86.0% in CCSS hospitals, since the transfer of hospitals from the Social Protection program which began in 1974 had already been completed by 1980. Both the reduction in birth rates and the increase in the proportion of births which occur in hospitals continued to grow until the proportion of deliveries taking place in hospitals surpassed 90%, with the consequent increment in participation in CCSS which reached 93.5% in 1992. In other words, in Costa Rica, delivery care is provided almost exclusively by Social Security hospitals, since less than 10% of deliveries occur in the private sector or outside of a medical center. This situation is clearly reflected in Table 2, which shows the total number of annual hospitalizations in CCSS. About 35% of hospitalizations are due to causes related to pregnancy, delivery or the postpartum period, a situation which is more important if one examines the hospitalization of women 15 to 44 years old, as shown in Table 3. In this table, data from 1987 are compared with those from 1992, subdividing the groups by cause to see more clearly that pregnancy and delivery complications are more frequent than normal deliveries as a cause of hospitalization among women of reproductive age in Costa Rica. The proportion with complications is around 40%.

A large part of this 40% consists of complications of delivery and among these is a high proportion of cesarean deliveries, which according to the following data have increased consistently since 1982:

Cesarean Deliveries as a Percent of all Deliveries, by Year

1980	15.89%	1984	14.74%	1988	18.25%
1981	15.43	1985	15.16	1989	19.28
1982	13.89	1986	16.27	1990	19.77
1983	14.11	1987	18.00	1991	19.70
				1992	20.88

Given that cesareans are expensive procedures from the point of view of medical care and risky not only for the mother, but also for the child, we have separated in Table 4 hospitalizations of children less than one year old from 1987 and 1992 by cause, to show more clearly the proportional increase in perinatal causes of hospitalization like newborn jaundice, maladies associated with gestational length, and respiratory problems of newborns. In Table 5, hospitalizations of children under one year old due to perinatal problems can be examined in greater detail based on data from 1990 and 1992 to simplify the analysis. From these figures, it is clear that other forms of perinatal jaundice are more frequent than isoimmunization, constituting the most frequent perinatal problems, with problems because of short gestation and low birth weight in third place.

To emphasis the importance of the topic we include Table 6 in which we tabulated the proportion of the 62,515 hospital admissions for delivery or abortion in the CCSS in 1990 who underwent surgical intervention by type of intervention and age of the patient. The figures indicate that the most frequent type of surgery in these patients was an episiotomy and that the frequency of this procedure declines with age. In second place is the cesarean, which increases with age, and third is hysterectomy which also increases with age.

Furthermore, the cesarean phenomenon varies by hospital and the figures show that in 1980 and 1981 a large proportion of cesarean deliveries took place in the four San José hospitals and in hospitals in the cities of Alajuela, Cartago, Turrialba, Golfito and Puntarenas. Ten years later six other hospitals are added to this list: Grecia, San Ramón, Heredia, San Carlos, Limón, and Ciudad Neilly. The most notorious increases are those in two hospitals: Carlos Luis Valverde Vega in San Ramón and San Vicente de Paul in Heredia, followed by San Francisco de Asís in Grecia and the San Carlos Hospital in Ciudad Quesada (Table 7). A woman giving birth in the San Ramón hospital had a 30.9%

ries of birth weight, we used the categories specified in the New Revision on the International Classification of Diseases

RESULTS

Characteristics of Medical Care

Figure 9 confirms the situation described in the Introduction and in Table 7: seventeen of the 24 hospitals of CCSS have cesarean rates of more than 14%. Seven of them have rates lower than 20.8%, the national average proportion, including: the Carit Institute, the Calderón Guardia Hospital, the William Allen Hospital in Turrialba, the la Anexión Hospital, the Dr. Tony Facio in Limón, and the Ciudad Neilly Hospital. The San Juan de Dios Hospital, which has always had a rate above the national average, shows an increase to almost 30%, while the hospitals in the Central North region not only maintain their past position, but show a general increase in 1990-91. The same is true of the San Carlos Hospital, the group which was combined into the Max Terán Hospital in Quepos, which having maintained an average below 14% for a long time, increased to 24.9% in 1993. This rate was even higher than that of the Monseñor Sanabria Hospital, the regional hospital of the Pacific Central, which always had had a rate higher than the national average. To this group should again be added the Golfito Hospital, which returned to the high rates it experienced in 1980-81. Special mention should be made of the Dr. Enrique Baltodano Hospitals in Liberia and Guápiles and the Tómas Casas and Dr. Escalante Pradilla Hospitals of Pérez Zeledón because they remain below 14%, a status which was lost by the Max Terán and la Anexión Hospitals in 1993. Figure 2 shows the position of hospitals with regard to the rate of cesareans they performed in 1993.

In the same table (Table 9), we show another, complementary indicator, the proportion of normal deliveries, which confirms the contradiction pointed out in the introduction: referral hospitals continue to provide care for high proportions of normal deliveries (more than 40%); so much so that in less technically sophisticated hospitals this indicator is less than 39%. Because of the nature of cesareans, i.e., a planned procedure (data shown below support this assertion), they are, by definition, referable.

In Table 10, we show the cesarean rate, grouped by the quarter of the calendar in which the delivery occurred. The table shows that the cesarean rate in the first two quarters and the fourth quarter is about the same, but it is higher in the third quarter (July, August, and September). The same table shows that the cesarean rate is very high in patients referred from outpatient services: it is slightly higher than 50%. It is also high in patients who died, who comprise only 1.3 patients per 100,000 deliveries. Mortality rates are 3.8 per 100,000 in patients with cesareans and less than 1 in 100,000 deliveries for patients without cesareans. In other words, mortality is 5.4 times higher in women who had a cesarean (3.8 divided by 0.7 = 5.4). The causes of death in the six patients with cesareans are concentrated in maternal-related conditions and in the effects of anesthesia. Other information shown in Table 10 is that the cesarean rate increases along with the number of prenatal visits. The mean number of prenatal visits is 3 for women who have cesareans and 2.6 for other pregnant women.

The admission diagnosis of women about to give birth along with the percent of cesareans is shown in Table 11. Disproportion, abnormalities in the reproductive organs and the soft muscles of the pelvis, and pre-delivery hemorrhage stand out because more than 90% of births in these cases are cesareans.

We should point out that of the 6,938 complicated deliveries because of abnormalities of the soft muscles of the pelvis, 91.41% consist of a uterine scar left by previous surgery, which is the justification in 96.54% of the 6,102 cesareans performed for the same group. This implies that 82.89% of cesarean births involve women who had a previous cesarean.

Since a single patient can simultaneously have up to four of these diagnoses, the totals in the columns of this table are larger than the total number of deliveries in the study. However, only 33,217 of the 76,622 (43.5%) of deliveries in the study were classified as completely normal (code 650x). High proportions of women having cesareans also present with abnormal position or presentation of the fetus and with hypertension which complicates the pregnancy and the delivery.

An important variable in the use of services statistics is the length of hospital stay, which is measured in periods of 24 hours called "*estancias.*" Given that cesareans involve surgical intervention, both total hospital stays and preoperative hospital stays are recorded. Both variables are shown in Table 12, which shows that most of women who do not have cesareans stay in the hospital for a day, while the majority of those undergoing cesareans stay for 2 or 3 days. The result is to increase the proportion of cesarean deliveries among women with longer hospital stays to the point where more than 50% of those who stay three days or more have cesareans. Given that the distribution of days in the hospital is positively asymmetric, we compare the median, several percentiles, and the mean below.

Statistic (in days)	Cesarean	Non cesarean
Arithmetic mean	3.5	1.7
Standard Deviation	3.0	1.5
25th Percentile	2.0	1.0
Median	3.0	1.0
75th Percentile	4.0	2.0

Examining these figures leaves no doubt that cesareans increase the length of stay in the hospital, which increases the cost of care not only because of the costs of the hospital space but also because the cost extends to problems in the family caused by the mother's absence added to the problems for her normal functioning caused by major surgery. Preoperative stays in the case of cesarean deliveries are also shown in Table 12 and can be explained by other surgical intervention, of which episiotomy is the most frequent (remember Table 6). Since preoperative stays comprise a part of total stays, we note that the cesarean rate behaves in the same way: it increases with the increase in the number of days of previous stay in the hospital. The cesarean rate is very low for women who have stays of one day, i.e., stays involving admission and discharge in a single day. For these women, most have preoperative stays of zero days. Special mention should be made of 12,291 cesareans with only a one day preoperative stay plus 852 with zero days, since these are patients who are likely to have been admitted knowing (from prenatal visits) that they require a cesarean. If one takes only these deliveries into account, one obtains a cesarean rate of 17%, leaving only 3.7% of cesareans performed to solve unforeseen complications. This is 25% higher than the 14% which is accepted as the maximum limit under the norms of the CCSS.

Conditions of the Newborn

It is frequently said that events which affect the mother during pregnancy and delivery also affect the fetus and the newborn. Some of these events and effects are not yet clearly established, but many of those associated with cesareans are well known. In Table 13, we have shown some characteristics of the infants produced by the 76,722 deliveries which we analyzed. The cesarean rate is 32.5% between 30 and 35 weeks of gestation, closer to 14% prior to 30 weeks, and around the current national figure of 20.8% in gestations longer than 35 weeks. The median is 39 weeks for cesarean deliveries and 40 weeks for noncesareans. Another variable related to the length of gestation is birthweight, which also appears in Table 13. As expected, the highest rate of cesareans occurs in the category of low birth weight with 28.3% of babies weighing less than 2500 grams, even though the mean birthweight is 3,123 grams for babies delivered by cesarean and 3,156 for others.

With respect to the condition of the baby at birth, from data in Table 13, we can calculate late fetal mortality of 14.3 per 1000 deliveries in CCSS hospitals. But when the groups of interest are separated, the result is that the rate is 7.3 per 1000 deliveries for cesareans, and 16.1 per 1000 non-cesareans. In other words, the rate is 2.2 times higher for non-cesareans than for cesareans. The percent of cesareans is higher among children who show signs of life after separate from the mother's body, than among those who have already died by this time. Perinatal causes of hospitalization of children less than 1 year old, which are shown in Table 14, show that while cesarean section can reduce late fetal mortality, it can increase the risk of hospitalization and of death in the hospital for perinatal causes. 42.84% of hospitalization and 52.6% of hospital deaths of those less than one year of age are attributable to perinatal causes, and most have cause-specific mortality percentages which are higher than that in all other causes combined. There were 816 hospitalizations and 8.33% mortality due to respiratory difficulty, while total hospital mortality for those less than one year of age is 1.63%. Birth trauma has the same mortality rate (8.33%) but in absolute figures it is a less frequent problem.

Personal Characteristics of Women Giving Birth

Women between 10 and 14 years old, who are less than 1% of the total (0.68%), have a cesarean rate of 20.77% which is practically equal to the national rate. Women 15 to 19 have the lowest cesarean rate (15.31%) and for women over 20, the rate increases with age until it reaches 28.38% in the group 45 to 59, which is the smallest age group (less than 0.19%). The average age of women giving birth is 27 years for patients who have cesareans and 25.7 for others. The difference is larger in the 75% percentile: 32 and 30 years, respectively. Table 15 also show differentials by marital status. Divorced and currently married women have the highest cesarean rates, and those in consensual unions and widows have the lowest. Cesarean rates vary also according to the number of pregnancies (including the delivery in the study): the rate is higher than the national figure for primiparas and those with two or three pregnancies. Then it declines consistently to a low level of 9.89% for those with 11 pregnancies, and continues with erratic variations but almost always over the 14% accepted as a maximum (Table 15).

The socioeconomic status of patients can be inferred from their insurance status and occupation (Tables 16 and 17). In Table 16, it is clear that the cesarean rate varies with insurance status, from around 40% in employees of CCSS and in patients that pay directly, to 14.88% in the group insured by the State who are indigents. It is also lower than the total of 20.8% for those in the No-Contributions Program who are also indigent. For those with direct insurance (salaried workers), the rate is around 25%. In Table 17, we have ordered occupations by the cesarean rate from high to low with the result that the highest rate, around 30%, is found among those employed in the social services like education and health, communications, entertainment and culture, finance and insurance. The lowest rates are found among those employed in agriculture, undefined categories, floriculture and cattle raising.

Variations in the cesarean rate by the woman's canton of residence are shown in Table 18, which also includes figures by region. Within each region, we ordered the cantons according to the magnitude of the cesarean rate. All cantons in the Central North region have rates about 14% and only in the cantons of Goicoechea and Coronado is the rate less than 20%. The highest rates are recorded in Flores, Heredia Centro, San Isidro and San Rafael de Heredia with more than 30%. The residents of the Pa-

ACKNOWLEDGMENTS

The data on which this chapter is based were provided by the Continuous Statistical System of the Medical Services in the Costa Rican Social Security System (CCSS), which is under the direction of our Section. Our Section is responsible for the design, supervision, management, training of personnel, and the dissemination of statistical results.

Since the data are the result of the daily work of the CCSS's Health System, we would like to acknowledge the participation of the personnel who, in Clinics and Hospitals, recorded, coded and edited the questionnaires for collecting the data.

We also acknowledge the Regional Directorates, who provide support to the Supervisors of the Records and Health Statistics, in their task of instructing, training, and supervising the health centers under their responsibility.

We would like to acknowledge all the personnel of the Biomedical Information Section who control, critique, correct and enter the data so that they can be electronically analyzed, as well as those who summarized, analyzed, typed and distributed among a large clientele the products of very hard work.

We also recognize the constant support which we received from the Information Directorate in electronically tabulating the data which, because of their volume and complexity, would have been impossible to process in any other way.

We cannot conclude without expressing gratitude for the enthusiastic collaboration and opportunity that the Department of Support Services provided us in the reproduction of the work and in the design of the covers.

To all of these people we express our sincere thanks.

REFERENCES

Moya de Madrigal, L. 1995. Algunas características de la atención de los menores de un año y sus madres. ("Characteristics of Care for Children under One Year and for Mothers") Serie Estadísticas de la Salud No. 6B. Información Biomédica, Caja Costarricense de Seguro Social.

_____. 1989. Algunas características de la atención de los menores de un año en los hospitales de la Caja Costarricense de Seguro Social. ("Characteristics of Care for Children Under One Year in the Hospitals of the Costa Rican Social Security System") Serie Estadísticas de la Salud No. 6A. Información Biomédica, Caja Costarricense de Seguro Social.

TABLE 1. BIRTHS, BIRTH RATES PER 1000, AND PERCENT RECEIVING HOSPITAL CARE IN THE CCSS, COSTA RICA, 1960-1992

	Births (1)		
Year	Costa Rica	per 1000 pop.	% C.C.S.S
1960	59,499	48.1	5.1
1961	62,131	48.4	5.5
1962	62,624	47.0	6.2
1963	63,798	46.2	6.6
1964	61,753	43.1	7.1
1965	62,909	42.5	7.2
1966	62,963	41.1	7.1
1967	61,963	39.2	7.2
1968	59,213	36.3	6.9
1969	57,984	34.5	9.3
1970	57,757	33.4	14.4
1971	58,309	32.8	16.0
1972	57,438	31.5	17.3
1973	53,505	28.6	20.6
1974	56,770	29.6	23.4
1975	58,140	29.5	41.8
1976	59,969	29.6	59.1
1977	62,178	29.8	75.3
1978	67,660	31.5	81.5
1979	69,245	31.2	83.7
1980	69,988	30.6	86.0
1981	72,260	30.7	86.0
1982	73,120	30.2	85.7
1983	72,953	29.2	87.8
1984	76,878	29.9	90.5
1985	84,337	31.9	91.9
1986	83,194	30.6	92.5
1987	80,326	28.8	92.7
1988	81,376	28.4	93.8
1989	83,460	28.4	94.9
1990	81,939	27.2	95.1
1991	81,110	26.3	93.7
1992	80,164	25.2	93.5

(1) Percentages calculated based on the total number of births registered in Costa Rica.
Source: Biomedical Information, CCSS and the DGEC.

TABLE 2. NUMBER OF HOSPITAL ADMISSIONS BY YEAR AND PERCENTAGE IN BROAD DIAGNOSTIC GROUP, CCSS HOSPITALS, 1983-1993

Chapters C I E, IX	Year of Occurrence										
	1983	1984	1985	1986	1987	1988	1989	1990	1991	1992	1993
Total	263,244	278,392	301,592	298,632	302,230	300,729	303,742	290,988	289,634	298,011	298,088
Percentage	100	100	100	100	100	100	100	100	100	100	100
Health Checkup	3.27	3.41	3.45	3.92	4.24	3.5	4.1	4.20	4.24	4.50	4.53
Infectious and Parasitic	4.41	4.31	4.74	5.21	4.99	3.9	3.9	4.14	3.59	3.18	3.06
Neoplasms	3.59	3.63	3.37	3.65	3.83	4.2	4.2	4.08	4.43	4.57	4.58
Nutritional Disease	2.26	2.24	2.19	2.18	2.25	2.2	2.3	2.22	2.23	2.15	2.17
Disease of Blood and Related	0.71	0.66	0.62	0.61	0.67	0.7	0.6	0.61	0.62	0.66	0.62
Mental Disorders	3.13	3.16	2.96	2.74	2.73	3.0	2.7	2.56	2.32	2.16	2.17
Nervous System Disease	2.98	2.99	3.02	3.22	3.19	3.1	3.1	3.04	3.26	3.58	3.54
Circulatory Disease	5.65	5.43	5.16	5.06	5.13	5.1	5.0	4.97	4.96	4.92	4.95
Respiratory Disease	7.62	7.64	8.10	6.90	7.61	6.7	6.1	6.17	6.38	6.30	6.47
Digestive Disease	6.81	6.89	6.63	6.88	7.10	7.4	7.5	7.59	8.02	8.50	8.30
Genitourinary tract Disease	7.40	7.23	6.79	6.83	7.06	7.3	7.0	6.88	6.85	6.92	6.93
Pregn., Delivery, Puerperium	32.87	34.06	34.72	34.67	33.28	34.8	35.4	35.97	35.14	34.37	34.55
Skin disease	1.81	1.68	1.77	1.89	1.77	1.7	1.5	1.47	1.51	1.52	1.50
Musculosketetal Disease	2.76	2.73	2.71	2.64	2.81	2.9	2.8	2.73	2.72	2.86	2.78
Congenital Abnormalities	1.57	1.59	1.58	1.55	1.55	1.6	1.6	1.46	1.74	1.82	1.75
Perinatal Disorders	3.68	3.22	3.05	3.06	2.97	3.3	3.5	3.52	3.67	3.75	3.76
Injury and poisoning	8.43	8.05	7.84	7.81	7.59	7.4	7.3	7.20	7.10	7.04	7.21
Symp., signs and ill-defined	1.05	1.10	1.30	1.19	1.25	1.2	1.2	1.20	1.24	1.19	1.14

Source: Biomedical Information, CCSS

TABLE 3. HOSPITAL ADMISSIONS OF WOMEN 15 TO 44 BY PRINCIPAL CAUSE, CCSS, 1987 AND 1992

Principal Cause	1987	1992
Total	141,393	143,905
Percent	100.00	100.00
Infectious and Parasitic	0.82	0.52
Neoplasms	2.47	2.81
Endocrine, nutri. and immune Disorders	1.02	0.87
Blood disorders and Related	0.08	0.12
Mental Disorders	1.71	1.25
Dis. of Nervous System and Sense Organs	1.01	1.07
Dis. of the circulatory system	1.59	1.33
Dis. of Respiratory system	1.43	1.09
Disorders of the digestive system	3.27	3.80
Disorders of the urinary tract	0.92	0.66
Disorders of the genitals	6.32	6.05
Abortion	5.92	6.21
Complications of Pregnancy and Delivery	39.45	40.17
Other Complications of Preg. and Delivery	1.14	1.40
Normal Delivery	24.03	22.77
Skin and Subcutaneous Tissue Disorders	0.72	0.61
Disorders of the musculoskeletal system	1.68	1.45
Injury and poisoning	1.87	1.67
Without pathological findings	3.77	5.32
Symp., signs and ill-defined	0.78	0.83

Source: Biomedical Information, CCSS

TABLE 4. ADMISSIONS FOR CHILDREN UNDER 1 YEAR OF AGE BY PRINCIPAL CAUSE, CCSS HOSPITALS, 1987 AND 1992

Principal Cause	1987	1992
Total Admissions	28,050	25,950
Percent by Cause	100.00	100.00
Infectious and Parasitic	18.05	9.50
Neoplasms	0.35	0.24
Endocrine Disorders	0.25	0.14
Metabolic and immune disorders	0.95	0.71
Blood disorders and Related	1.01	0.55
Mental Illness not involving Psychosis	0.07	0.10
Disorders of the Eye and Adnexa	0.24	0.29
Disorders of the Ear and Mastoid Process	0.75	0.67
Other nerve or sense disorders	0.72	0.77
Nerves and Sense disorders	1.70	1.73
Dis. of the circulatory system	0.17	0.23
Dis. of Respiratory system	19.16	15.96
Disorders of the digestive system	3.13	3.48
Disorders of the genitals	0.76	0.68
Skin and Subcutaneous Tissue Disorders	1.78	0.98
Disorders of the musculoskeletal system	0.15	0.18
Congenital Anomaly	6.01	7.06
Problems related to Length of Gestation	6.96	8.98
Respiratory Conditions of Newborns	6.12	7.92
Perinatal Infection	3.20	4.76
Neonatal Jaundice	13.09	17.33
Other perinatal	2.30	3.68
Injury and Poisoning	1.42	1.57
Examine -- no pathology	12.03	13.08
Symp., signs and ill-defined	1.32	1.16

Source: Biomedical Information, CCSS

TABLE 15. DELIVERIES AND PERCENT CESAREAN, BY CHARACTERISTICS OF THE MOTHER, CCSS, 1993

Characteristics	Deliveries			Percent Cesarean
	Total	Cesarean	Other	
Total	76,622	15,960	60,662	20.83
Age				
10-14	520	108	412	20.77
15-19	12,697	1,944	10,753	15.31
20-34	54,902	11,653	43,249	21.23
35-44	8,355	2,213	6,142	26.49
45-59	148	42	106	28.38
Marital Status				
Single	14,467	2,655	11,812	18.35
Married	44,476	10,452	34,024	23.50
Widowed	155	24	131	15.48
Divorced	662	181	481	27.34
Consens. Union	16,651	2,610	14,041	15.67
Unknown	211	38	173	18.01
No of pregnancies				
1	23,346	5,300	18,046	22.70
2	18,456	3,960	14,496	21.46
3	13,781	3,368	10,413	24.44
4	8,442	1,633	6,809	19.34
5	4,951	754	4,197	15.23
6	2,954	376	2,578	12.73
7	1,793	224	1,569	12.49
8	1,113	132	981	11.86
9	699	78	621	11.16
10	418	45	373	10.77
11	263	26	237	9.89
12	171	31	140	18.13
13	100	11	89	11.00
14	58	8	50	13.79
15	41	5	36	12.20
16	13	3	10	23.08
17	11	2	9	18.18
18 or more	12	4	8	33.33

Source: Biomedical Information, CCSS

TABLE 16. DELIVERIES AND PERCENT CESAREAN, BY TYPE OF PAYMENT, HOSPITALS OF CCSS, 1993

Type of Payment	Deliveries			Percent Cesarean
	Total	Cesarean	Other	
Total	76,622	15,960	60,662	20.83
Insured	56,881	12,431	44,450	21.85
Direct	15,576	3,876	11,700	24.88
Family	40,716	8,321	32,395	20.44
Employee of CCSS	589	234	355	39.73
I.V.M	429	91	338	21.21
Direct	135	36	99	26.67
Family	294	55	239	18.71
I.N.S.	14	5	9	35.71
Transit Accident	10	4	6	40.00
Professional Risks	4	1	3	25.00
Direct Payment	2,259	906	1,353	40.11
Total	1,655	670	985	40.48
Partial	604	236	368	39.07
No Contributions Prog.	202	33	169	16.34
State Insured	16,355	2,433	13,922	14.88
State Pensioners	80	14	66	17.50
Foreigners	366	39	327	10.66
Covered by Agreement	60	5	55	8.33
Other	306	34	272	11.11
Unknown	36	8	28	22.22

Source: Biomedical Information, CCSS

(Table 18 continued from previous page)

Huetar North Region	4,389	902	3,487	20.55
San Carlos	2,847	690	2,157	24.24
Guatuso	297	48	249	16.16
Sarapiquí	824	116	708	14.08
Los Chiles	421	48	373	11.40
Chorotega Region	6,050	898	5,152	14.84
Abangares	321	66	255	20.56
Nicoya	820	159	661	19.39
Santa Cruz	672	129	543	19.20
Hojancha	139	26	113	18.71
Nandayure	229	42	187	18.34
Bagaces	289	47	242	16.26
Tilarán	346	55	291	15.90
Cañas	506	69	437	13.64
Liberia	1,059	135	924	12.75
La Cruz	351	39	312	11.11
Carrillo	515	57	458	11.07
Upala	803	74	729	9.22
Pacific Central Region	3,995	936	3,059	23.43
Esparza	398	113	285	28.39
Montes de Oro	248	69	179	27.82
Aguirre	482	129	353	26.76
Puntarenas Central	2,170	486	1,684	22.40
Parrita	226	50	176	22.12
San Mateo	60	12	48	20.00
Orotina	263	52	211	19.77
Garabito	148	25	123	16.89
Brunca Region	7,168	994	6,174	13.87
Golfito	768	154	614	20.05
Osa	545	91	454	16.70
Corredores	865	120	745	13.87
Coto Brus	1,010	132	878	13.07
Pérez Zeledón	3,009	391	2,618	12.99
Buenos Aires	971	106	865	10.92
Huetar Atlantic Region	7,749	1,238	6,511	15.98
Limón Central	2,154	460	1,694	21.36
Siquirres	1,143	176	967	15.40
Talamanca	524	79	445	15.08
Pocosí	2,399	331	2,068	13.80
Matina	784	108	676	13.78
Guácimo	745	84	661	11.28
Others and Foreigners	352	41	311	11.65
Unknown	15	4	11	26.67
Others	337	37	300	10.98

Source: Biomedical Information, CCSS

Chapter Twelve

MIDWIVES AND FORMAL PROVIDERS IN PRENATAL, DELIVERY AND POST-PARTUM CARE IN FOUR COMMUNITIES IN RURAL GUATEMALA: COMPLEMENTARITY OR CONFLICT?

DOLORES ACEVEDO AND ELENA HURTADO

In this chapter we examine whether prenatal, delivery and post-partum care is provided by traditional as well as formal providers in rural Guatemala, and to what degree these two types of providers complement or conflict with each other. We analyze information obtained in four rural Guatemalan communities in the months of May and June 1994, from in-depth interviews and focus groups with mothers of children less than five years old, as well as from in-depth interviews with midwives and formal providers.

From women's point of view, we found that the complementarity between midwives and formal providers is different in the case of pregnancy, delivery and the post-partum period. During pregnancy, there was considerable complementarity between the two types of care, especially in ladino communities. For delivery, practically all indigenous women were attended by a midwife, while in ladino communities, half of women delivered in the hospital. In the post-partum period, family members and midwives provided care almost exclusively.

From the midwives' point of view, midwives and formal health services provide complementary services and, in general, midwives recognize that in the case of complications, biomedical services are better. There are some conflicts about certain practices which midwives are accustomed to using, but which are discouraged by the Ministry of Health's service providers, such as the use of the temascal (sweat bath) in the Mayan area of the country.

The largest conflicts occur from the point of view of the biomedical providers who have ambivalent feelings about the "incorporation" of midwives in providing care for women.

Finally, we recommend that the complementarity between midwives and formal providers be strengthened, especially by extending midwives' role in referring women with complications.

INTRODUCTION

In developing countries between half and three quarters of deliveries are attended by midwives (Laideen, 1985). In rural areas, it is common for women to use these providers at the time of delivery, as well as for advice and prenatal and post-partum care. The use of formal health services is generally restricted by problems of access, lack of economic resources, and cultural norms which make it more desirable to be attended by a midwife. However, some studies have shown that it is imprecise to talk about a dichotomy between traditional and formal health services. It is more correct to refer to "medical pluralism" (Cosminsky and Scrimshaw, 1980), that is, to the simultaneous use of traditional and formal medical resources. For example, Castañeda Camey (1992: 529) reports that in Morelos, Mexico "users are accustomed to demand (traditional and modern medical) services, coordinating and complementing resources." The coexistence of different types of providers suggests that pregnancy-related health services could be improved through closer collaboration between health providers of different types.

In Guatemala, the infant mortality rate is approximately 73 per 1000 live births. Almost a third of these deaths occur within the first 28 days of life (Schieber et al., 1994). On the other hand, approximately seven out of 10 deliveries are attended by midwives; in some rural areas the figure is nine out of 10 deliveries (Schieber et al., 1994). The coverage for formal health services is low. For example, according to Leedam (1985), in

1976 there were approximately 3 doctors and 2 nurses for each 10,000 inhabitants. By contrast, there are more than 30 midwives for each 10,000 Guatemalans. According to Putney and Smith (n.d.) there are 20 midwives for each 10,000 Guatemalans, of which 70% are trained.

In this chapter we examine whether prenatal, delivery and post-partum care is provided by traditional as well as formal providers in rural Guatemala; to what degree these two types of providers complement or conflict with each other; and how the relationship between the two groups of providers can be improved in order to provide better care during pregnancy, delivery and the post-partum period. For this purpose, we analyze information obtained in four rural Guatemalan communities in May and June 1994, from in-depth interviews and focus groups with mothers of children less than five years old, as well as from in-depth interviews with midwives and formal providers.

In the following sections we present an analytical framework which will facilitate the interpretation of the data obtained during field work. This framework does not constitute an exhaustive review of the pertinent literature, but rather a selection of ideas which allow us to understand better the coexistence of different systems of health beliefs and health practices. Later, we summarize the process of collecting the data and the techniques used to analyze them, and we briefly describe the four communities in which the study was carried out. Then we present the results in the following order: (1) women's views about the role of midwives and formal providers in pregnancy-related care, (2) midwives' views about their own role and the role of their counterparts (formal providers), and (3) formal providers' views about their role and that of their counterparts (midwives). In the last sections of the chapter, we present conclusions and a series of recommendations about how to facilitate better collaboration between midwives and the formal health services in order to improve pregnancy-related care in rural areas.

ANALYTIC FRAMEWORK

In the anthropological literature, practices related to birth (prenatal, delivery, and post-partum care) are assumed to reflect cultural forces and societal beliefs, and changes in these practices are assumed to reflect social and cultural changes. However, different belief systems can coexist, even if there are discrepancies among them. For example, in industrialized countries a tension exists between the biomedical belief system which sees birth as a medical risk for which modern obstetrical technology is enlisted, and more traditional beliefs, according to which birth is a social celebration (McClain, 1982).

In a review of the anthropological literature on childbirth which was conducted at the beginning of the 1980s, McClain (1982) found that recent anthropological studies, as well as other publications in medical and public health journals, showed the flexibility of systems of practices and beliefs related to birth. Several of these studies analyzed what happens to these systems in societies undergoing modernization, both from the point of view of pregnant women and the different options they have for care during pregnancy, as well as from the perspective of traditional providers and their way of adapting themselves to social change (McClain, 1982). Sheila Cosminsky's studies on Guatemala can be counted among this type of analysis (Cosminsky, 1982, 1987; Cosminsky and Scrimshaw, 1980). Furthermore, studies conducted in the 1990s, for example, the work on the role of midwives in Morelos, Mexico by Castañeda Camey (1992) and García Barrios et al. (1993) have provided evidence that there is an interaction, rather than a dichotomy, between traditional and formal systems.

The existence of a plurality of pregnancy-related health care systems resulted in a recognition by World Health Organization (WHO) of the importance of traditional providers. Furthermore, WHO recommended to developing countries that they incorporate traditional providers into governmental health services. Two practical considerations were crucial. First, in the majority of these countries, especially in rural areas, formal health services were inadequate. Moreover, it was widely believed that in order to introduce family planning services, it was essential to collaborate with providers who were socially and culturally closer to potential contraceptive users. Starting in 1970, WHO promoted the formal recognition of traditional pregnancy-related care providers, as well as the establishment of training programs so that midwives could serve as "extensions" of the ministries of health (Leedam, 1985). In 1978 at the Alma-Ata conference, explicit support was given to the idea that, with additional training, traditional midwives could be turned into a valuable resource for ministries of health. Later delegates at the Safe Motherhood Conference in Nairobi in 1987 declared that no maternal health program could function effectively at only one level (Roy and Anderson, 1989; Flemming, 1994). Therefore, the Conference concluded that trained midwives are a key element in reproductive health because they can provide necessary supervision and advice during pregnancy, delivery and the post-partum period, attend deliveries, and act as the link with the health care system to which they can refer women when necessary.

Since 1935, the government of Guatemala has attempted to regulate traditional midwives and to require them to be trained through a licensing program—midwives call the licenses "papers" or "carnet" (identification papers). Articles 98 and 99 of the Governmental Decree of April 16, 1935 delegates the responsibility for granting permits to midwives by means of an examination process to the Dirección General de Servicios de Salud.[1] This decree also says that any midwife who is summoned to attend the training course and does not do so is prohibited from attending deliveries (Putney and Smith, n.d.). In 1953, regulations to give licenses to traditional midwives were introduced.

[1]General Directive for Health Services.

Section F, Article 15, Decree No. 74 dated May 9, 1955 authorizes the Ministry of Health to extend authorization certificates to traditional midwives after an aptitude examination. The training programs date from early 1955.[2]

In the 1980s, the Guatemalan Ministry of Health, like other nations in the region, adopted the model recommended by WHO. That is, it formally recognized midwives, established of a system of registration for these traditional providers, granted them licenses, administered a midwife training program, and indicated that a part of midwives' job would be to promote the use of family planning methods (Leedam, 1985). To date, these continue formally to be the general characteristics of the relationship between the Ministry of Health and midwives. The duration of the current training program is 15 consecutive days, 8 hours a day, and it covers nine areas of study. This program is regulated by the Division of Maternal-Child Health of the Ministry of Health. It is organized by the personnel of each Health Area (which are equivalent to departments) of the country, and it is conducted by the District Nurse with support from auxiliary nurses (Putney and Smith, n.d.).

The formal health services' recognition of the midwives' work does not imply a relationship which is symmetric or free from conflict. In the first place, the fact that only trained midwives are recognized reflects the prevalence in the biomedical system of beliefs about the system of traditional health beliefs. Many programs consider only those who have been given biomedical training in prenatal and delivery care to be midwives. However, there are places with a long tradition of training and use of empirical midwives in providing care during pregnancy, delivery and the post-partum period. For example, in Guatemala,

---

[2]Several international organizations, for example, UNICEF, CARE, UNFPA and USAID, have supported the training of midwives in Guatemala at some time.

midwives who are not trained by the Ministry of Health are legally prohibited from attending deliveries (Putney and Smith, n.d.). However, many in the Mayan population of Guatemala believe that midwives are born to be to their profession and midwives have traditionally had a prominent place in the community as ritual specialists (Paul and Paul, 1975). Cosminksy (1982) has noted that in Guatemala during the 1970s, training for midwives involved the adoption of biomedical methods and the explicit condemnation of traditional methods. For example, she indicates that midwives were taught not to use herbs, temascal (sweat) baths, and the squatting position for giving birth, despite the lack of empirical evidence in some cases that these practices are dangerous. Cosminsky (1977) has suggested that midwives thought that they could be jailed for practicing without a license. On the other hand, the efforts to "modernize" midwives can alienate them from their clients, which can weaken their role as a link with formal health services. According to Leedam (1985) it is important to find a balance between the traditional baggage of midwives and the necessity of inculcating them with formal practices "based on scientific criteria."

The conflict between the medical profession and midwives has occurred in many societies. For example, in the United States at the beginning of the century (1910-1930), there was a heated debate in medical circles and even in the popular press about the role that midwives should have in a modern society (Litoff, 1978 and 1986). Two factors contributed to the attack on midwives. First, there was general concern about an oversupply of recent graduates from medical school and a perception that this problem could be reduced if midwives were prohibited from providing care for pregnant women. Furthermore, maternal and infant mortality rates in the U.S. were higher compared to European countries and midwives were blamed for this problem. However, paradoxically, a series of studies during that period had demonstrated that the maternal mortality rate was lower in areas where the proportion of deliveries attended by midwives was greater (Litoff, 1978 and 1986). On the other hand, there were cultural and ethnic factors which made midwives more visible. Since 1880, a wave of immigrants from southern and eastern Europe arrived in the U.S. Since the beginning of the 18th century, midwives had been gradually replaced by doctors among the middle and upper classes. However, the arrival of immigrants from countries in which midwives were socially respected figures gave a new boost to this type of provider (Litoff, 1978 and 1986).

To date, the tension between traditional and formal belief systems of care during pregnancy and delivery has not been resolved even in developed countries. In their study on birth practices in four societies, Jordan (1983) referred to the natural childbirth movement in the United States, which she says idealizes traditional practices. However, these movements are marginal. For example, at the beginning of the 1980s only 2% of deliveries in the United States were attended by midwives. Similarly, in western developed countries, conflicts between the medical profession and (trained) midwives persist. In 1994 in Ontario, Canada, the provincial government incorporated more than 50 legalized midwives into the health system. Many of these midwives previously had practiced outside the formal system. The reaction of doctors has been clearly negative because they fear the competence of midwives, as well as the potential danger of greater legal demands on the part of patients since they foresee that midwives will refer patients with complications to them (Williams, 1994).

In Guatemala, the tension between traditional and biomedical systems of health care is influenced by the coexistence of indigenous and ladino cultures. The Guatemalan population is divided, approximately in half, into two principal ethnic groups: indigenous and ladino. The indigenous consider themselves descendants of the Mayas and possessors of their cultural legacy.

The ladinos constitute the mestizo population of Guatemala. As has been noted by several authors (for example, Warren, 1992), the distinction between the two ethnic groups is not rigid, nor is it a racial distinction. Furthermore, the identity of both groups is fluid. Currently, there is a major debate both in Guatemala and among U.S. academics about the association of modernization and the replacement of the indigenous by the ladino culture (Warren, 1992). Authors like Warren (1992) have proposed that modernization is not a linear process and social change is not necessarily associated with the loss of indigenous culture in favor of ladino culture. Even though in this paper we will not attempt to make an explicit contribution to this debate, we distinguish between indigenous and ladino villages and we explore the differences between the use of traditional and formal providers in the two types of villages. A linear modernization perspective would suggest that in indigenous areas we should find a greater preference for traditional providers. However, it is difficult to arrive at this type of conclusion based on a qualitative study such as this one, since it is not possible to "control" for other factors (such as income and access to formal services), other than ethnic identity, which may influence the use of midwives.

Several previous studies have documented differences between the ladino and indigenous population in the use of formal health services during pregnancy and delivery. Pebley et al. (1996) recently analyzed the Guatemalan DHS of 1987 and concluded that, even controlling for important variables such as level of education and distance to formal services, indigenous women were less likely to use formal providers than ladino women. However, as the authors indicate, the 1987 Guatemalan DHS only recorded the health care provided used by the respondent who was "most highly trained." It is likely that ladino women used both formal providers and midwives. A qualitative study such as ours allows us to detect the way in which (indigenous and ladino) women combine traditional and formal resources. In

were translated into Spanish and transcribed by interviewers. Interviews in Spanish were transcribed by interviewers from the tapes. The transcriptions were typed and later, the interviewers reviewed and corrected the typed transcripts, using the taped interviews for reference.

Data Analysis

During the data analysis, we carefully read the transcripts from the focus groups and from interviews with mothers, midwives, personnel of the Ministry of Health (health posts and centers), and private doctors. While reading the interviews, we coded the information on several topics of interest which had been previously defined, such as "services provided by the midwife," "services offered by formal providers," "referral of complicated cases of delivery from the midwives to formal providers," etc. In a second reading of the transcripts, information was tabulated to determine the most important points in mothers', midwives', and formal providers' discussions of each topic. In addition, we used a text string-search program to confirm the regularities that we observed. Tabulations were also made to obtain descriptive statistics such as the proportion of women who were cared for by a midwife, a formal provider, or by both during their pregnancies. In a third reading of the transcripts, we extracted citations to illustrate "trends" which were revealed in the tabulation of the data.

Description of the Communities

Indigenous Communities

Indigenous Village I. This village is located 12 kilometers from the municipal capital. However, there is no public transportation from Indigenous Village I to the municipal capital. The trip by car takes approximately 1½ hours because of the poor state of the road, and the trip by foot takes two hours.

The village has approximately 550 inhabitants. The majority of the population speaks K'iche. Very few women are bilingual and only a portion of the male population speaks Spanish fluently. Almost all inhabitants were born in Indigenous Village I and very few have emigrated permanently. However, families migrate temporarily to Suchitepequez, Coatepeque and Escuintla to work on cotton plantations.

In Indigenous Village I, the dwellings are very dispersed. The distance between two contiguous dwellings varies from 15 minutes to an hour and a half. The furthest dwellings are located three hours from the center of the village. All houses have a temascal (steam) bath in the patio. The temascal is made of stone. To take a steam bath, the stones are heated and water is poured on top of them.

The most important economic activities are subsistence agriculture (corn and beans) and home production of incense or "copal." Even the poorest families have a piece of land, even though not all produce enough to be self-sufficient.

Drinking water is obtained from springs or wells which are shared by several families. The sources of water are located far from the dwellings and especially during the time of year when the wells dry up, women expend considerable effort in carrying water. Currently there is a committee to provide the community with running water. The water project was scheduled to be finished by December 1994. In addition to running water, latrines were being installed. The village does not have drainage nor do plans exist to introduce it. There is also no electricity, no telephone, and no communal mail service. In addition to the water committee, there are four other community improvement committees. We were told that the existence of these committees is one of the major changes which have taken place in Indigenous Village I in the last several years, and that this change will make the village "wake up."

In contrast to the other three study communities, there is no health post in this village. The health care resources available include three health promoters, eight injectionists, six midwives, and a curer. There is no pharmacy. Medicines are purchased in a local shop, a shop in the neighboring town, and pharmacies in the municipal capital. Outside of the village, there is a health center in the municipal capital and a private doctor who visits the village on weekends. Residents also use some providers in a town in the neighboring department of Huehuetenango.

Indigenous Village II. This village is located in the department of Chimaltenango and there is public transportation to the municipal capital. The village has about 630 inhabitants. The majority of men and approximately half of women speak Spanish as well as Kaqchikel. Very few people emigrate. The most important economic activity is agriculture. Crops include corn, wheat, beans, lima beans, vegetables (peas and broccoli), flowers and some fruit.

Water is obtained from two public taps. In addition, there is a small river from which residents take water for irrigation. All households have latrines, but some families do not use them. There is no drainage. Garbage is frequently burned and organic material is used as fertilizer. There is also electricity. There is no telephone, telegraph or mail service in the community, but residents use these services in the municipal capital.

The village has a health post, six promoters, two midwives, and two curers. The population buys medicine in three small local shops. Residents also use formal providers in the municipal capital, including the health center, a hospital, private doctors, pharmacies and services of the Catholic Children's Fund.

Ladino Communities

Ladino Village I. This village is located in the department of Jalapa, approximately 10 kilometers from the municipal capital. Public transport runs between the village and the municipal capital. The municipio in which this village is located has a population of approximately 22,250 inhabitants. However, we were unable to obtain precise information about the number of inhabitants in the village itself. All of the population is ladino.

The principal economic activity in Ladino Village I is agriculture. Residents cultivate corn, beans, tomatoes, tobacco, and broccoli. There are three "social classes" : (1) the land owners who are also the livestock owners and those that are identified as the rich of the village, (2) those who rent land from others in order to farm, and (3) those who work the land under a share-cropping system. In theory, the share-cropping system consists of the land owners and the share-croppers sharing the cost of the inputs to production, while the landowner contributes his land and the worker his labor—and the labor of day-laborers with whom he subcontracts. At harvest, the crop is theoretically divided in half. However, according to several informants, when the time for dividing the harvest arrives, the landowner typically retains all the profits, since according to his accounts, the worker still owes him money. In the opinion of one informant, in Ladino Village I, this system of labor (exploitation) has not created a social breakdown, because the land is not very concentrated: approximately 50% of families have some land. A high level of social tension associated with the share-cropping system was perceived.

According to several informants in Ladino Village I and other villages in this municipio, a large number of people have emigrated to the United States from this village. International migration began approximately 15 years ago and had accelerated in the previous five years. The primary destinations of the international migrants are Stamford, Connecticut; Trenton, New Jersey; Los Angeles, California; Boston, Massachusetts; and New York City. Several informants mentioned that one consequence of international migration has been the creation of a social distinction between families of migrants ("who can build their beautiful houses") and the rest. Other consequences mentioned by informants included the disintegration of the family as well as cases of AIDS brought back by returning migrants.

In Ladino Village I, the only services available were electric light, mechanical wells for irrigation, as well as a canal for irrigated agriculture, and mail service. The inhabitants of Ladino Village I have chain pumps in their houses, but the community lacks running water. For excreta disposal, some wealthy families have septic tanks. In general, the population has not responded well to the program promoting latrines. The proportion of households with latrines is unknown. As is true throughout the municipio, there is no garbage collection system. Therefore, garbage is generally burned by the population.

Ladino Village I is the only village in the municipio which has a health post. In this health post, between 300 and 360 people are served per month. The population also uses the health center in the municipal capital, which primarily covers the population north of the municipio, while the health post in Ladino Village I covers the villages south of the municipio. Other health resources used by the population are four health promoters, two pharmacies, six midwives (several of whom are also curers), and three curers. The inhabitants of Ladino Village I also use the hospital in Jalapa and private doctors and hospitals in that city.

Ladino Village II. The village is located in the department of Chimaltenango. Approximately 10 years ago, Ladino Village II was divided into two villages. Because of the proximity of the two communities, it is difficult to distinguish between them. For this reason, we interviewed people in both communities. The majority of the population is ladino, although a group of indigenous families have recently immigrated into the village.

The principal economic activity is agriculture, although there are many people, especially men, who leave the village to work in other places, such as Guatemala City. There had been some migration to the United States, although not as much as we observed in Ladino Village I.

In Ladino Village II water is abundant. There are several natural springs, several of them piped, and several public washing facilities. There is also electricity and the majority of the households have latrines.

The village has a health post. Among other health providers, we identified a health promoter, three midwives, two bone-setters, and several shops where medicines are sold. Furthermore, residents use health centers in the municipal capital and in Chimaltenango, and several providers, both formal and traditional, in the municipal capital, such as private doctors, a hospital administered by nuns, and several spiritual healers ("brujos").

In Ladino Village II, we observed some tension between evangelical protestants and catholics. Even though in Ladino Village I, half of the population is catholic and the other half protestant, there do not appear to exist divisions for religious reasons. In Indigenous Village I and Indigenous Village II, the majority of the population is catholic.

In the next section, we summarize the views of women interviewed in each of the villages on the role of midwives and formal providers in providing care during pregnancy, delivery and the post-partum period.

VIEWS OF WOMEN

In this section, we present the viewpoint of women expressed both in the in-depth interviews and in the focus groups. During the interviews, respondents were asked about the care they received when they had their youngest child. Underscoring the continued importance of midwives, a large proportion of women combine care given by midwives with formal provider care. Furthermore, it is clear that they rely on midwives because they offer services not offered by formal providers, that are highly valued by women, such as massage and temascal baths. It is also clear that women prefer to give birth at home, instead of the hospital, if the delivery is uncomplicated. This preference is stronger in indigenous than ladino areas.

Prenatal Care

Advice during Pregnancy

Respondents were asked who gave them advice during their last pregnancy. Both indigenous and ladino respondents frequently answered that they had not asked anyone for advice. They mentioned frequently that, except in the case of first pregnancies, it is not necessary to ask for advice, "because one already knows what to do." Even in the case of women pregnant for the first time, only a minority of women said they had asked for advice.[4] In indigenous communities, typical advice was not to lift heavy objects, not to walk or go out a lot, to take care of oneself, to eat sufficiently, not to take medicine (except for vitamins). In Indigenous Village II, one of the respondents explained:

> You have to take care of yourself. You shouldn't take any medication. You have to eat what appeals to you. You are not going to lift heavy things because it will harm you, and you should not walk too much. When you get tired, you sleep.

---

[4]However, in some cases, when the interviewer probed she found that the respondent had received some type of advice. It is possible that the method of asking the question introduced a bias in the responses. For example, women may have understood the word "advice" ("consejo") to refer to structured and formal advice and not to the recommendations that family members or friends give them as a part of daily life. In the interviews, interviewers probed carefully what advice women received. When necessary, they gave respondents examples of the type of advice that might have been received (for example, what to eat), and asked them to remember the advice they had been given during their first pregnancy.

Similarly, in the ladino villages, the most common advice is not to exert oneself and not to lift heavy things, to eat well, to take care of oneself, not to take medicines, to be calm and not to get angry. Respondents also said that pregnant women should not sleep a lot, even if they are tired, because the baby can "get stuck."

Prenatal Care Provided by Midwives

In both types of communities, the majority of women relied on midwives. In the indigenous communities, practically all respondents received care from midwives during their last pregnancy and also during previous pregnancies. In the ladino villages almost three-quarters (29 of 40) of respondents received advice or care during pregnancy from a midwife.

In indigenous communities, midwives are among the first people to know that a woman is pregnant. Women pregnant for the first time usually talk about their symptoms with their mother-in-law or mother, who in turn find a reliable midwife to visit the pregnant woman. Multiparous women generally advise midwives of their pregnancies by themselves, sometimes when the pregnancy is advanced, i.e., at 6-8 months of gestation. In ladino communities, women generally tell their husbands first about their pregnancies and then tell their mother or mother-in-law. Frequently, the husband suggests which provider the woman should consult.

Prenatal visits with a midwife take place both in the midwife's house and in the pregnant woman's house. In focus groups in Indigenous Village II, women said that pregnant women go to the midwife's house, but in interviews in the two indigenous villages women said that the midwife comes to pregnant women's houses. In Ladino Village I, respondents said that pregnant women generally visit the midwife, but in Ladino Village II respondents said that some midwives provide care in their clients' houses—making periodic rounds, for example, visiting every 15 days.

In both indigenous and ladino villages, an important task for midwives is confirming pregnancy. Even though midwives diagnose a pregnancy only by touching a woman's abdomen, women generally report having confidence in the midwife's ability to determine whether or not the woman is pregnant.

In indigenous villages, midwives provide advice during pregnancy. The advice is related to work and the amount of effort that the pregnant woman should undertake. Pregnant women should not work too much or carry bundles that are too heavy like firewood or water. In general, midwives do not give precise advice on diet, but recommend that the woman "eats well," although in Indigenous Village II respondents said midwives recommend foods considered "alimento" (nutritious) like Incaparina[5], milk, oatmeal, porridges and eggs. It appears that there are no restrictions regarding diet during pregnancy. Women reported more frequently in indigenous villages than in ladino villages that midwives give advice about not working too hard or about diet during pregnancy.

In indigenous areas, in a typical prenatal visit, the midwife sees, touches and massages the pregnant woman's abdomen. Especially in Indigenous Village I, the examination is carried out in the sweat bath or temascal (called *tuj* or *chuj* in Mayan languages). The purpose of using the sweat bath and of massaging the pregnant woman is to heat up the body and ensure that the baby is in the correct position. In Indigenous Village II, focus groups respondents said that sometimes women do not tolerate the heat of the *tuj* and then the midwife carries out the examination somewhere else, i.e., the midwife does the exam wherever the woman prefers. To massage the pregnant woman, the mid-

[5]Incaparina is a powdered high calorie, high protein beverage that is reconstituted with water or milk and eaten or drunk.

wife warms her hands over a fire, covers them with oil or with emollient, depending on what the woman provides, and touches and massages the abdomen of the woman with both hands.

In ladino villages, when asked what midwives do in their first prenatal visit, several interviewers responded that the midwife "only takes a look," "touches," or "massages." For example, they said: "she only came to massage me," "she only massaged my stomach with oil, only that," "she only looked at my stomach," "she only touches one's stomach, because midwives are not like doctors; midwives only touch, nothing more." Women explained that the purpose of these massages is to see if the baby is okay and if the baby is in a bad position, to correct it. Other functions of massage are: "development of one's body," "calming one's body," and to loosen the child because "sometimes they get stuck." An interesting distinction between Ladino Village I and Ladino Village II is that in the second village, as occurred in the two indigenous villages, women said that the midwife coats her hands with some type of oil to give the massage, while in Ladino Village I, respondents did not mention that the midwife used oil. It is worth noting that massage is without a doubt the aspect of the midwives' work during the prenatal exam that is most commonly mentioned; moreover, it was frequently the only aspect mentioned. Even when the woman in question receives prenatal care from a formal provider, massage, and to a lesser extent "seeing whether the baby is okay," is considered the almost exclusive responsibility of midwives. For example, in Ladino Village I, one woman had received all her prenatal care from a formal provider, but in the seventh month she visited a midwife, at the advice of her mother, to see whether the child was okay.

The importance of prenatal massage provided by Guatemalan midwives has been documented in a previous study by Cosminsky (1982) carried out at the end of the 1970s in two communities, one predominantly indigenous (Chuchexic in Santa

Lucia Utatlán) and the other ladinoized indigenous (the plantation San Felipe). In our own field work, we were able to verify that massage continues to be the central task in prenatal care provided by midwives. The comparison with the Cosminsky (1982) study indicates that there does not appear to have been an erosion of this aspect of traditional prenatal care between the end of the 1970s and the mid-1990s. It is clear that massage is highly valued by women and that in general they believe that only midwives can provide this service.

However, midwives do not offer only traditional care. For example, in indigenous villages, one respondent mentioned that the midwife herself gave the respondent prenatal vitamins. In the ladino communities, some midwives give or prescribe vitamins, either in pill form or as injections, in addition to advice and massage. The distinction between traditional and formal services is not always clear. For example, in Ladino Village I, one woman who received prenatal care from a doctor and from a midwife reported having visited the midwife "so that she would give me vitamins."

In indigenous areas, women take as given that a midwife will care for them during pregnancy and that the same midwife will attend them during delivery and the post-partum period. Except in unusual cases (such as that of a woman in Indigenous Village II who was living in the capital city during her last pregnancy), midwives are considered indispensable resources for prenatal care. In ladino villages, women frequently said that one reason for going to a midwife for prenatal care is to establish a relationship so that at the time of delivery, the midwife will take charge. In Ladino Village I, one of the participants in the focus group for women 35 years and older explained:

> There are many women who give birth at home, then to be sure they get the midwife involved so that at the last moment they can be sure. One also goes to the doctor to be sure that the baby is okay.

That is, in addition to checking the pregnancy, visits to the midwife are a "social ritual," in which the woman and the midwife become familiar with each other to prepare for the delivery. Jordan (1983) notes that during prenatal visits in Yucatán, Mexico, the midwife talks to the pregnant woman during the massage. She asks questions such as how the woman feels and if the woman has pain. They talk about the date of the delivery and the midwife tells the woman where she feels the head of the baby is. In addition to issues related to pregnancy, the woman and the midwife talk about other subjects. According to Cosminsky (1982), at the end of the visit, Guatemalan midwives spend time "joking" with the mother of the pregnant woman. However, in our study, the respondents did not mention chatting with the midwife as an important part of prenatal visits.

Prenatal Care Provided by Formal Providers

Although all indigenous women and most ladino women reported having been cared for by midwives, a high proportion combined care from a midwife with care from some type of formal provider, for example, the personnel of the Ministry of Health (health posts or centers) or a private doctor. In general, no conflict is perceived in receiving care from different types of providers. The respondents expressed different types of reasons for seeking care from traditional and formal providers, which indicates that complementarity exists between the two types of services. Moreover, several women mentioned having visited a health post or center at the suggestion of the midwife, in some cases because she determined that the woman had some type of problem with the pregnancy.

In indigenous villages, pregnant women who seek prenatal care from a formal provider, do so at the suggestion of the midwife. Especially in Indigenous Village II, midwives regularly counsel women to go for prenatal care to the health post in the community. One respondent said:

> Then the midwife saw me, massaged my stomach, told me that the baby was okay. You shouldn't lift heavy things, take sweat baths, don't go taking remedies, pills, because the child could come out disabled, without eyes, without feet. You should go to the health post so that they can give you vitamins and a vaccination. Because that way, the baby won't get sick.

In both Indigenous Village I and Indigenous Village II, approximately half of the respondents had been to a health post or center for prenatal care during their last pregnancy—in addition to seeing the midwife. In Indigenous Village II, women go to the health post where they receive vitamins (which they also refer to as "alimentos"), they get prescriptions for ways to stimulate the appetite, and they get an anti-tetanus vaccination. In Indigenous Village I, it is common for women to go to the health center in the municipal capital to confirm that they are pregnant, to check to see if the pregnancy is going well, and if the child is okay, and in the correct position. Most respondents had visited the health center only once during the last pregnancy. The principal reason for not going to the center more often was problems of access—as mentioned above, there is no transport and it is a two hour walk to the municipal capital from the village. However, women in the village believe that if the pregnancy appears normal during the initial visit to the center, there is no reason for additional visits.

In ladino villages, 70% of women receive prenatal care from a formal provider. Of these, 30% use only a formal provider and 70% use both a formal provider and a midwife. In Ladino Village II, during the focus group with women ages 18 to 34, in response to a question about whether most women go to the health post or to a midwife, one women said: "to both, we go both to the health post and to the midwife." In the same village, another respondent explained: " the doctor has one type of experience and the midwife has another." Several women said that the midwife advised them to go to the health center or post. Respondents said that the health center or post gives out prenatal vitamins. The functions performed by formal providers which were most commonly mentioned were: "to carry out an examination," to listen to the baby's heart beat, to take the pulse and blood pressure, and to give medications for problems of pregnancy such as nausea.

In ladino villages, women believe that when there are complications during pregnancy, it is best to go to a formal provider. Several respondents said that when there are problems, the midwife herself suggests that the woman go to a health post or center or to the hospital. During the focus groups, we discussed what the participants would do if their wives, in the case of men, or if they themselves, in the case of women, experienced bleeding during pregnancy. The uniform response was that they would go to the hospital to treat a serious problem. In Ladino Village II, in the focus group with women 18 to 34 years, participants said that in this case, one has to go to the hospital because if not, one becomes drained of blood ("desvacía"), but first one should ask for advice from the midwife and "she herself will go with you."

Delivery Care

In indigenous communities, midwives attend the great majority of deliveries. In Indigenous Village II, 19 of the 20 deliveries mentioned by respondents were attended by midwives in the woman's house. In Indigenous Village I, 16 of the 19 deliveries were attended by midwives. Among the rest, two were attended by family members and in one the woman delivered her baby alone.

When a woman begins to have pains (contractions), her husband or other relative goes to advise the midwife. At the delivery, the midwife, the husband, and female relatives are usually present. Relatives take responsibility for preparing the delivery place and the necessary materials. Very important among these

home, when the child is coming out wrong, [for example] there are children who come out feet first." In several cases, the respondent mentioned that the midwife herself accompanied the patient to the hospital.

In the ladino villages, when deliveries are attended by a midwife, on occasion, the husband and mother and/or mother-in-law are present. The role of the midwife is to "give you courage," receive the child, cut the umbilical cord, and clean the child and mother. Several women reported that the midwife gives them pills or injections to speed up the delivery—this also happens in deliveries in the hospital. As during prenatal care, midwives in these villages rely more on biomedical practices (pills/injections) during the delivery process than in indigenous areas. The fact that some ladino midwives give medications to speed up delivery shows that "modernization" or co-optation of midwives by the biomedical system does not necessarily result in the safest practices.

Post-partum Care

In indigenous communities, post-partum care falls to the midwife and the family members of the woman who has just given birth. The midwife bathes the woman and the newborn. The midwife massages the abdomen of the woman to warm her and so that her internal organs return to their places. The midwife visits the woman daily during the week following delivery. In Indigenous Village II, some women reported that this is currently the situation, but that in the past the midwife visited the woman for a longer period. During the post-partum visits the midwife examines the umbilical cord and bathes the woman in the temascal where she massages her stomach and back.

In indigenous villages, the "dieta" or post-partum period practices have been relaxed. Even though tradition dictates 20-40 days of care, women report beginning their regular work 15 days after delivery. The most important recommendation during the post-partum period is to avoid cold in the form of air, water, and food classified as cold.

In ladino communities, the midwife occasionally does the woman's housework after the delivery, such as washing clothes. One of the midwives in Ladino Village I takes care of women giving birth in her own house. The new mother remains there for two or three days during which the midwife "kills her chickens" (to make broth). According to the respondents, during the 40 days after delivery, women do not visit formal providers. Nor is it very common for the woman to visit the midwife or the midwife to visit the woman. Only three women reported contact with a formal provider (in all cases because of a complication) and five reported contact with a midwife, during the post-partum period.

In Ladino Village I and II, during the "dieta," support is provided above all by the women of the family and to a lesser degree, by friends and neighbors. In ladino communities practically all women mentioned having observed the "dieta," by not doing housework and taking it easy after the delivery. Women count on help from their mothers, mothers-in-law, other relatives, friends, and women hired to do the housework. Help with housework include grinding corn, making tortillas, cooking, washing clothes, taking care of children, etc. In some cases, the husband also helps out. Another element of the "dieta" which is frequently mentioned is to avoid eating "cold" things such as avocados and beans, so that the child does not get colic. Some women also said that during the "dieta" it is not good to get wet.

COMPLEMENTARITY OR CONFLICT?

In summary, the analysis of the interviews with mothers and focus groups indicate that, from women's point of view, the degree of complementarity between midwives and formal providers depends on whether the care is given during pregnancy (prenatal care), delivery, or the post-partum period.

Prenatal Care

A high proportion of both indigenous and ladino women visited traditional and formal providers during pregnancy. There is no evidence that this fact constitutes a conflict. On the contrary, several respondents said that midwives themselves advised their clients to go to the health post or center. The most significant aspect of this combination of providers is that women perceive that the advice and treatment offered by each type of provider are different. For example, the verbs used to describe prenatal care given by midwives are very different from those used to describe an examination at a health post or center. Midwives "look," "touch," "feel," "massage," "warm up," "straighten out" the pregnancy (that is, put the baby in the correct position). In the health post or center, they "examine," "control," "put in equipment," "vaccinate," "give vitamins or food." In Ladino Village II, during a focus group with women 18 to 34, when the moderator asked participants how the midwife examined them, one participants said "they don't examine us, they only tell us if its okay or not." On the other hand, respondents frequently said that, if there are complications during the pregnancy or if they foresee a difficult delivery, the midwife advises them to visit a formal provider.

The indigenous and ladino villages are similar in that women in both ethnic groups report combining the two types of prenatal care. However, the simultaneous use of traditional and formal providers seems to be more common in ladino communities. It is possible to interpret this finding in terms of the "modernization" process. That is, it can be argued that ladino women use formal providers (both exclusively and in combination with midwives) than indigenous women because ladino culture has greater affinity with the western biomedical system. However, it is more likely that in this study, part of the difference between the two ethnic groups is due to problems of access. In

Indigenous Village I there is no health post, while the other indigenous village and the two ladino villages all have health posts.

Delivery

In the indigenous communities there is little complementarity between traditional and formal providers in delivery care. Practically all women reported having given birth while attended by a midwife. However, one woman who gave birth in a hospital (in Indigenous Village II) perceived and expressed the conflict between traditional and hospital practices:

> What they did that was bad was bathe me with cold water; here I bathe myself with hot water and there I was bathed with cold water and I was going to die, I came back worse...I bathe myself in the temascal and there I was bathed with cold water and for that reason I was going to die.

In ladino areas, half of respondents said that they had given birth in the hospital. However, women generally felt that it is better to give birth with a midwife if the pregnancy is normal. Frequently, they decide to go to the hospital because of complications arising during prenatal care or complications which occurred during delivery. Midwives influence the women's decision to go to the hospital in cases of complications. Nevertheless, some women went or said they would have preferred to go to the hospital, even though there were no complications.

Post-partum Period

During the post-partum period there is little complementarity among traditional and formal providers, since women rely primarily on midwives. However, in ladino areas, the midwives' roles seems to be limited during this period. In indigenous areas, women mentioned that the time period during which midwives visit women who have just given birth has been shortened over time. In some interviews, women said that they consulted formal providers only if there are complications like fever, and that midwives influence the decision to seek help from formal providers.

In this section we have presented women's views about the use of traditional and formal health resources during pregnancy, delivery, and the post-partum period. We found that women combine both types of providers because they perceive them as providing different types of services. Women are aware that in high risk situations, it is better to go to a formal provider. According to the interviews, midwives collaborate with the health care system, that is they advise women to use the services of this system. In the next section, we analyze the content of interviews with midwives, focusing on how they perceive their role versus the role of formal providers.

VIEWS OF MIDWIVES

Interviewed midwives were identified through a census of providers in the community and through information provided in interviews with mothers, in focus groups, and in interviews with key informants. All of them were chosen because they are the most commonly used midwives in the community and those in which people had the most confidence. Some are older and no longer see many women, but in the recent past were very popular midwives.

In the indigenous villages, five midwives were interviewed, three in Indigenous Village I and two in Indigenous Village II. Of the midwives in Indigenous Village I, two were trained by the formal health system after being empirical midwives and one was an empirical midwife. None of the three treat children, except for newborns in the post-partum period. In Indigenous Village II, one respondent was a trained midwife and the other considered herself to be a curer/masseuse (as well as a midwife). The first one gives oral rehydration solution to children with diarrhea, but not other types of treatment. The curer had taken a course on medicinal plants given by a non-governmental organization (NGO), but in addition was a specialist in massaging pregnant women and women in the post-partum period. She did not regularly attend deliveries, although she described one case in which, because of the absence of the midwife, she had attended a delivery.

In ladino communities, seven midwives were interviewed: five in Ladino Village I and two in Ladino Village II. All of them were trained midwives, that is, they had taken a training course given by the Ministry of Health. However, all but one were midwives before taking the course. All have at least one other role as a health provider aside from being midwives. For example, in Ladino Village I, one midwife is "the lady in the pharmacy," a midwife, and a curer. Another woman in this village is a midwife, curer, and family planning promoter (for APROFAM)—this midwife was funded by APROFAM to go to the United States to train in the area of family planning. In Ladino Village II, the two women who were interviewed, in addition to being midwives, "know how to cure"—they see both adults and children as patients. These cases indicate that the distinction between traditional and biomedical providers and between trained and empirical midwives is to a certain degree artificial. For example, a trained midwife may have begun her career as an empirical midwife. Training does not guarantee that midwives will abandon their traditional practices (and we are not suggesting that this would be desirable, in any case). In addition, midwives also commonly work as curers and both roles often combine the use of traditional remedies with medicines. Similarly, in the case of Morelos, Mexico, Castañeda Camey (1992: 532) reports that: "it is often observed that a trained midwife continues to use the concepts of traditional and herbal medicine at the same time as patent medicines."

Prenatal Care

In indigenous communities, when a woman or her family "asks a favor" of the midwife (i.e., that she takes care of the pregnant women), the same midwife usually attends the delivery and provides post-partum care. Midwives describe this relationship as a "responsibility" or a "promise" that they have acquired, which obliges them to carry out the prenatal visits, to attend the delivery when they are called, whether it comes during the day, at night, or in the early morning, "rain or shine" and to provide post-partum care to women until they are "aliviadas" or "sanas," i.e., healthy.

Midwives see prenatal care as including telling the woman and her family if the pregnancy is okay or not, how far along the pregnancy is and when to expect the birth. They also believe their role includes massaging the pregnant women to warm the body and to assure that the baby is born in a good position. In Indigenous Village I, the midwife visits the woman every 15 days. In Indigenous Village II, the midwife and the curer who were interviewed said that women come to their house, but when women are very heavy and "don't want to walk" they visit them in their houses.

In prenatal visits, all midwives massage women, either in bed or inside the temascal, according to which the patient prefers. In the bed, the midwife puts emollient or oil on her hands and warms them over a fire before massaging the woman's abdomen. In the temascal, the midwife does not use emollient, because she becomes warm as does the woman; she massages the woman and hits her gently with small tree branches with leaves. The midwife in Indigenous Village II said that, if the woman does not want to go into the temascal, she gives her a little red wine to warm her up. If women have some kind of pain, the midwife also massages them in the temascal. A midwife in Indigenous Village I commented that this was the hardest part of her job, because she got heated up in the temascal and "when I return home on the road I run into breezes and sometimes I get stomach cramps."

During prenatal visits, midwives give women advice about the activities that they need to avoid. A specific piece of advice which was mentioned is that women should eat a little even if they do not have any appetite and to eat everything they want. Generally, midwives also refer them to the health center so that they can be "examined," they can "immunized," and they can be given "vitamin pills" or a prescription to buy them. Midwives do not prescribe medicines and they share with women a fear of taking any medicine during pregnancy because it might cause the child to be born with a defect. Furthermore, midwives recognize hemorrhage as a complication of pregnancy since it can be associated with a miscarriage.

In ladino villages, midwives mentioned that their work during pregnancy is to give the woman advice about diet and to check to see whether the child is in a good position. Some ladino midwives recognized that when the child is in the wrong position, they can try to change its position through massage. However, in Ladino Village II, one midwife, when asked if she tried to change the position of the baby said:

> No I don't. That's [the doctors'] job, because doctors tell us...if a child is in the lateral position and he has the cord there, pulling him to put him in the right position can strangle him.

It is likely that this midwife responded in this way because she perceived us as disapproving of a practice which may have been contraindicated by formal medicine. Another ladino midwife said that it is not advisable to give massages before the fourth month.

In interviews in ladino villages, midwives frequently mentioned that they advised women to go to the health post or center. A midwife in Ladino Village II said that during pregnancy, she not only advises her clients to go to the health center, she also goes with them herself. Among the most common reasons given by midwives for referring women to the health posts were: (1) so "that they can get a prescription for their prenatal vitamins," although some midwives mentioned that they also prescribed vitamins or give injections; (2) so that they get prenatal care "in cases in which they cannot give birth at home." If the midwife finds that the child is in a bad position, she asks the woman to go to the health post or center to see if she has to give birth in the hospital. One midwife in Ladino village I explained: "if the pregnancy is going badly, if the child is in the wrong position, I tell her 'go to the hospital...this [delivery] is not for here, go';" and (3) so that the woman gets vaccinated against tetanus. Some women said that they do not want to get immunized because it may harm the baby.

Delivery

In indigenous villages, someone from the pregnant woman's family goes to call the midwife and she comes "at any hour." Midwives massage the patient and give her some olive oil to drink "in order to loosen the body." One midwife mentioned that she lubricates the exterior of the birth canal with oil to make it easier for the child to come out. The same midwife commented that the body of primiparas is "new" and therefore their deliveries are more difficult.

In Indigenous Village I, if the woman prefers, the birth occurs in the temascal. In Indigenous Village II, the use of the temascal for the delivery appears to have declined, but the temascal continues to be used during the post-partum period. The position for delivery is generally in a squatting position—a woman in Indigenous Village II described how the midwife had hung a cord from the rafters of the room so that she could hold on to it and push. Midwives always emphasize the role of the woman during labor which consists of "exerting themselves" when the time comes. Their own role in the delivery is "receiving" the baby, "cutting the cord," and "bathing and cleaning" the child and mother. The role of the husband and the relatives is principally to hold the woman at the moment of birth.

Midwives recognize very slow delivery or failure to deliver the placenta as complications of pregnancy. Another complication, principally for primaparas, is that "they have very small bodies." The placenta in K'iche is called "flower" or "companion." Midwives and their patients use these euphemisms to talk about events in women's reproductive lives[6] — traditionally there has been a lot of reticence to speak openly about these issues. One midwife attributed difficult deliveries to the current tendency to a more liberal attitude in talking about these topics: "This is happening because our parents in the past said that one should not say anything to girls about delivery because they would talk about it." Other explanations for complications are "lack of care" ("descuido") by women, their activities ("too much weaving" in Indigenous Village II), problems with their husbands, taking medicine, becoming cold (because of washing a lot, getting wet, leaving the house), taking medicine which makes them sick, or divine will.

In the ladino villages, midwives said that, during the delivery, they did the following things: prepared the bed, cleaned the woman, cleaned the mouth and eyes of the child (so that the amniotic fluid does not blind the child); wrap, clean, and weigh the child. Midwives also give women infusions (of herbs) to help them in the delivery. However, they were reluctant to talk about pills or injections given to accelerate the delivery, probably because they know that this practice is not recommended. Several midwives mentioned that when they see complicated deliveries, that is those in which the child is in a bad position or cases of

---

[6]For example, they use expressions like asking how long its been since you have not seen "your clothes" or since you have not "washed" in order to find out about the last menstruation.

woman would not be able to carry out the indispensable work of her daily life. According to what this midwife says, binding is a "secret" among the indigenous population.

Even though few women in ladino villages mentioned that midwives visited them during the post-partum period, several midwives said that they visit women to do their cleaning (bathing) and to massage them; and that they visit them (daily) until the umbilical cord falls off. They also mentioned that they advise women to avoid eating fresh or uncooked things, because "they will give the child colic." No one cited a single case in which a midwife referred a woman to a formal provider during the post-partum period.

CONFLICT OR COMPLEMENT?

Indigenous midwives who have received training from the Ministry of Health know that they should refer women to the health services for prenatal care and in the case of any obstetrical complications. In general, they appear to accept referral to a great degree. Here is only one of many examples in the transcripts:

> They told us that if they do not give birth within 12 hours, they have to be taken to the hospital, that's what they told us at the health post. I told them [pregnant women] that they had to be taken to the hospital since they had not yet given birth.

Indigenous midwives usually do not see a conflict between the prenatal care they provide and that provided by the public health services. Sometimes midwives even say that exams in the health post are superior to their own. But in all cases, they see care from the two systems as being complementary and the midwife as indispensable. For example, a midwife in Indigenous Village I explained: "Yes and I also send them to the health center. There they give them a better, more correct, exam, but I have to visit them at home."

However, sometimes midwives perceive a contradiction between their practices and those recommended by the health services, especially regarding the use of the temascal. For example, one midwife in Indigenous Village I said:

> In the health center they tell us that we should bathe women in warm water, people around here do not want that. They only want the temascal. They say: "we are used to the heat of the temascal and if you bathe us in warm water we will get sick."

Finally, indigenous midwives feel obliged to go to the health services every month to report on births and newly pregnant women. A midwife from Indigenous Village I explained: "We go purely by force...I have to go, I have to take my lunch, I have to use my own money to get there." Midwives who have not received training from the formal system perceive that they have a problem. On one hand, even if they are regularly attending births, they deny or minimize the fact that they are not licensed. They also do not refer women or neonates to the health services because of this concern and because they worry that their patients will not be taken care of by the health services. The empirical midwife in Indigenous Village I, responding to a question about why she attends only her own family members and close neighbors, said:

> Because I'm afraid, because I don't have papers, I am not legalized. If for some reason some delivery becomes complicated, I would not know what to do and that makes me very worried...I would not be able to enter the hospital.

Midwives who have not been through any training course, usually felt that there were obstacles (real or perceived) to leaving home for a week or more to go to the municipal or departmental capital where the courses are normally held. Sometimes they are afraid of traveling alone or they doubt their ability to learn. Others could not leave their families alone or stop caring for their patients.

> Because I can't go alone to Totonicapán (departmental capital) to take the course. I also felt that I don't have the ability to pass the course nor would anyone help me. Because if my children told me they would take me to Totonicapán maybe I would do it, but I can't do it alone.

In the ladino villages the interviews with midwives revealed that traditional providers feel that they themselves and formal practitioners provide complementary services during pregnancy and delivery—during the post-partum period, the complementarity is very limited. In general, midwives feel that giving vitamins, administering tetanus vaccine, and treating women when they have complications during pregnancy and/or delivery is part of the responsibility of formal medicine. On the other hand, they believe themselves to be trained to supervise pregnancies, to give advice to women, to see if the child is okay by means of massage, to detect problems (especially malpresentation) during pregnancy or delivery, and to refer these cases to formal providers. There were practically no remarks that showed antagonism between midwives and formal providers. One of the few comments of this type was made by a midwife when referring to the way in which she monitors labor:

> And I tell her I am experienced, thank God, so I examine her and I say, if they bring her to me at night, "you are going to give birth tomorrow ... I go to see her, to see if there has been any change. Because... labor can be deceiving. That is why in hospitals they give birth in the bathroom. One has to control. This is not talked about in the hospital, but there are incidents of inadequate care. All humans are fallible.

In this section we have synthesized midwives' opinions about the role which both they and formal providers play in providing care during pregnancy, delivery and the post-partum period, as well as about the complementarity between the two. There appears to be an understanding that in cases of complications, the formal services are better. How do formal providers view midwives and about their interaction with them? The following section deals with this issue.

VIEWS OF FORMAL PROVIDERS

As in the case of midwives, formal providers who were interviewed were identified from the census of providers, the interviews with midwives and key informants, and focus groups.

In indigenous areas, five providers from the biomedical system were interviewed: three in health service coverage area in which Indigenous Village II is located, and two in the coverage area which includes Indigenous Village I. In Indigenous Village II, we interviewed the nurse in charge of the village health post, the doctor who was head of the health center in the municipal capital, and a doctor who was head of an "integrated center" in Chimaltenango (the department capital). As mentioned before, in Indigenous Village I there is no government health post. Therefore, we interviewed the personnel in the health center in the municipal capital: a graduated nurse and a rural health technician. The doctor in charge of the health center could not be interviewed since he was not present during the week of the study in the village.

Although the situation has changed for the better, in indigenous communities, many of the government health service staff do not speak the language of the area in which they work. This was true of doctors visited in Chimaltenango, and the health technician and nurse interviewed in Indigenous Village I. The latter explained the situation in the following way when asked if she spoke K'iche:

> I understand a little, although it is difficult. When necessary, we ask the janitor to help. He speaks K'iche. The secretary and the staff who have been working here longer understand [local] people. The majority of people who come in can speak Spanish. There are some people who have difficulty, like those in [Indigenous Village I].

Naturally, the existence of linguistic barriers between women and formal providers is one of the reasons that may explain the clear preference for midwives in indigenous communities.

In ladino villages, we carried out eight interviews with formal providers: staff of health posts and centers and private doctors. In Ladino Village I, we interviewed the doctor in charge of the health center in the municipal capital, the health technician assigned to the health center, and the nurse in charge of the health post in the community. In Ladino Village II, we interviewed a doctor and a nurse in the health center in Chimaltenango (departmental capital), a doctor in the health center of the municipal capital, a nurse in charge of the health post, and a private doctor with a practice in the municipal capital and in Chimaltenango.

Prenatal Care

In indigenous areas, biomedical providers recognize that midwives provide most prenatal care. The doctors in the health centers said that the majority of their patients were in urban areas and not in villages, although sometimes on market days they see patients from villages. The nurse in Indigenous Village II said that only "some" pregnant women come to the health post for prenatal care since "most go to the midwife." On average, he sees about one pregnant woman a week. This provider described prenatal visits as "examining and taking blood pressure" and said the problems for which pregnant women consult him are malnutrition, lack of appetite, and swollen legs.

In indigenous areas, formal providers report that most midwives are trained. One of the doctors calculated that in Chimaltenango only 15% of midwives had not received training. He explained that in health centers they schedule monthly meetings with the midwives, even though they do not always take place.

Formal providers in ladino areas said that during pregnancy, women consult them about as frequently as they see midwives. Among the reasons that women have for visiting midwives was "to gain confidence" that the midwife would attend them at the time of delivery. Formal providers also talked about an affinity between women and midwives:

> There are women who begin their prenatal care with a midwife, because they have a lot of confidence in them, they are in their communities, they have attended the other deliveries, so the relationship is special.

During prenatal care, the formal provider sees if the delivery can be attended by the midwife, that is, if there are likely to be any complications. Formal providers talked in a positive tone about the fact that midwives know how to identify problems during pregnancy and refer women to formal providers in the case of problems. For example, the nurse in the health post in Ladino Village I said:

> Yes, I refer patients to them. Including for their vaccinations. They have a lot of experience and just by seeing women, sometimes not even examining them, they can tell how the patient is and they refer them to me.

However, they also underscored the fact that, midwives occasionally employ practices that formal providers do not approve of. For example, on the treatment of urinary tract infections during pregnancy—identified by formal providers as a recurrent problem—one provider said:

> Sometimes there are also medicines that they take that the midwife herself prepares, saying that it is to prevent problems during pregnancy, and sometimes these same medications give us problems with urinary tract infections...They prepare a type of infusion and the truth is that only they know [what it is] and it could be this that is one of the causes.

Delivery

In indigenous villages, biomedical providers said that, regarding prenatal care, they do not do much; rather it is the midwives who attend deliveries and refer emergencies to the hospital. The doctor in the municipal capital referred to the problem that some midwives, especially in urban areas, use oxytocin during the delivery.

In ladino areas, during the interviews with formal providers, there were two principal themes concerning attention during delivery. First, formal providers expressed the belief that, in the case of normal deliveries, the midwife can take charge. The health center doctor in the municipal capital corresponding to Ladino Village I explained:

> If it is a problem of risk, let's say, a referral to the hospital ...If the woman is okay and the child in a good position, and she wants to give birth at home, we ask her who is her midwife...We have a register of midwives who have not come to [the health post for training]. Then, if [the midwife] is a woman who has attended births for a long time, who for some reason has not come here [for training] or because she does not want [to come] or because she is very old, we are not going to take away from her the benefit of attending this [pregnant] woman.

A private doctor, who practices in the capital of the municipio in which Ladino Village II is located and in Chimaltenango, told us about how he collaborates with midwives during delivery. He accompanies the midwife to the house of the woman who is going to give birth, examines the woman, sees the degree of dilation and that everything is okay, and then leaves. This doctor explained that this was a must because many women are unwilling to have a man attending their delivery. He added that if there are complications, the midwives "call immediately and they know, they are well trained, because they know when there is a problem, they have to rely on the hospital."

The other recurrent theme was that frequently midwives give medications to speed up delivery or which make women push before they should, despite the fact that this practice is not recommended and midwives have been told not to use it.

Post-partum Period

In indigenous communities, formal providers recognize that post-partum consultation with the biomedical sector is non-existent (Indigenous Village II) or very low (in department or municipal capitals). It is midwives who provide care for women in the post-partum period. Similarly, interviews with formal providers in ladino villages confirmed that women almost never go to these providers during the post-partum period. For example, the doctor in the health center in the capital of the municipio in which Ladino Village I is located and the nurse in the health post in Ladino Village I said, respectively:

> In most cases, for post-partum care, women come only in cases where there are problems, otherwise they do not come, despite what we tell them.

> Well, generally it is rare for a woman to come to us after delivery. Generally she goes to the midwife.

Complementarity and Conflict

Biomedical providers recognize that midwives are able to provide care during pregnancy, delivery and the post-partum period, and for newborns, and to refer cases of complications. However, formal providers' attitude is ambivalent. On one hand, they accept the experience of the midwives and the need for their services; on the other hand, they made clear that there is a hierarchical relationship in which they themselves "know" and midwives "don't know" and "have to change their behavior."

The doctor in the health center in the capital of the municipio in which Indigenous Village II is located identified a current conflict with midwives, especially in the urban area of the municipio, about the use of oxytocin in during labor:

> Finally we called the midwives' attention to the bad management of patients. I sued two midwives in the village in open process in court. I don't know who taught them to use sintocinin (oxytocin) which causes maternal exhaustion and uterine rupture. In two cases, the mothers and the children died. The two had twin pregnancies. The investigation established that sintocinin had been used. Now they say that [the midwives] are afraid of me. Because of the bad management of patients by midwives, perinatal deaths [of the child] have also occurred. This has happened here in the village.

The same doctor talked about an idea that he had for improving delivery care. This idea illustrates the negative attitude toward midwives and the recognition of the economic barrier to access to private doctors by the population:

> I have been talking with the hospital [run by one of the NGOs] about the idea of setting up a birthing center which would charge the same amount as midwives, but with doctors not midwives.

The nurse in the health post in Ladino Village I provided another example of a conflict. Referring to the content of the "aguas" (infusions) that midwives give to women during pregnancy and which he identified as a probably cause of urinary tract infections, he commented:

> They never say... not them, because they are under my control, the midwives. We have a monthly meeting... They have not even told me what is in the infusions they prepare. They don't say anything because I have scolded them. I believe that there are things that have to be eliminated from the community.

The health center technician in the municipal capital of Ladino Village I said, regarding midwives abandoning harmful practices:

> Little by little, changes are occurring gradually. People have been used to doing [these things] for a long time and they are not

> going to change overnight. But yes they are doing what is possible and many of them have improved their behavior...

Some formal providers said that the principal mechanisms for keeping midwives under control are: the periodic meetings in the health centers or posts; the threat of taking away their "carnet," that is, the trained midwife license; and the threat of not giving them forms to register births. In addition to these control mechanisms, a formal provider indicated that midwives accept formal health services because "they consider themselves part of the health center." He added that "if they were not involved within the same health sector, I think that we would have problems, but they consider themselves to be part of the health services."

It is worth emphasizing that midwives are the only traditional providers with whom the personnel of the Ministry of Health have contact. In the (very common) case of midwives who are also curers, their relationship with the formal health system is only in their capacity as midwives. The health technician in the municipal capital of Ladino Village I said:

> For example, Doña Lidia [who is both a midwife and a curer], we have been trying to put her in the health group in order to maintain a closer relationship with her and to be in control of some things which she does not have to give up. We try to talk to her in her role as a midwife.

CONCLUSIONS

In this paper we found that women in the four study communities combine the use of traditional and formal providers for prenatal care. However, in the indigenous villages, all women gave birth with the help of a midwife, while in ladino areas half went to the hospital. In ladino villages midwives frequently refer women who have difficult deliveries to formal providers. During the post-partum period, the complementarity among the two types of providers is almost non-existent. In general, women—

indigenous and ladino—do not go to formal providers after giving birth.

From the perspective of midwives, they can care for women during pregnancy and delivery when there are no complications. Midwives perceive little conflict with formal providers, even though in indigenous communities it appears that there is a higher degree of antagonism than in ladino communities. For example, they perceive that the use of the temascal is questioned by the Ministry of Health personnel.

On their part, the formal providers recognized the ability of midwives to provide care for normal cases, to identify risky situations, and to refer women to formal providers. This recognition does not preclude points of conflict between the two groups of providers. From the point of view of the Ministry of Health, midwives have to abandon practices that are not recommended—note that in some cases, as in the administration of oxytocin, these are not traditional practices, but rather biomedical practices. In addition, several biomedical providers were ambivalent about the role of midwives and expressed the need to "control them."

In terms of the differences between indigenous and ladino villages, we observed that indigenous midwives are seen by women and by themselves as indispensable in providing care to women from the time a woman becomes pregnant through the post-partum period. The midwives may have more status and be more valued in indigenous areas than in ladino areas. Although its use has diminished, without a doubt the most important difference in preventive and therapeutic resources consists of the use of the temascal (sweat bath) in indigenous communities. The concept of "hot" in pregnancy, delivery, and the post-partum period is very important in the indigenous area. Pregnancy is considered a hot condition that must be maintained as hot through the use of massages and hot baths in the temascal. The process of delivery is a transition to "the cold" of the post-partum period through the loss of blood/liquids and because "the stomach becomes empty." During the post-partum period, therefore, one should avoid everything which is "cold" (water and cold activities and foods). In ladino villages the concept of "cold" is central to the post-partum period, especially with regard to food. In terms of traditional providers, we found that ladino midwives tend to use more formal medical resources (for example, vitamins and oxytocin) than indigenous midwives. Finally, among biomedical providers we did not find a difference in attitude about midwives between indigenous and ladino areas. However, it is worth mentioning that linguistic problems make communication between traditional and formal providers more difficult in indigenous communities.

In summary, in the four studied rural communities, during pregnancy, delivery and the post-partum period, midwives provide services which are different that those offered by formal providers. Midwives' services are highly valued by women, especially in indigenous communities. Moreover, midwives provide contact between the community and biomedical services and are able to refer complicated cases to formal providers. Therefore, it is clear that midwives are and will continue to be a key element in whatever effort is undertaken to reduce maternal morbidity and mortality in Guatemala. We agree with Castañeda Camey (1992) and García Barrios et al. (1993) in that models of health care for rural women have to combine traditional and formal medical resources.

RECOMMENDATIONS

Based on the information presented in this paper, we present the following recommendations:

1. Pregnancy and delivery care are without a doubt areas in which the complementarity between both types of providers can be strengthened, given better training of midwives in the diagno-

sis and referral of women with complications. In a recent study, Schieber et al. (1994) analyzed the factors which contributed to neonatal mortality in a rural community in Guatemala. Among the most significant factors were premature delivery, cases in which the baby is in the wrong position, and prolonged labor. The authors conclude that midwives should be trained to diagnose complications and to refer women to health services or take them to the hospital if problems occur during delivery.[7]

2. Furthermore, midwives could be trained to extend their work providing care for normal pregnancies. For example, although midwives currently perceive that health centers or posts are supposed to immunize women against tetanus, it would be feasible to train midwives themselves to give these immunizations. This may be a way to increase the acceptability of tetanus immunization. However, we recognize that tetanus immunization, as well as vitamins, have been used as a means of bringing women into formal services and ceding these functions to midwives may reduce these incentives to go to the health post/center.

3. Since the post-partum period is an area in which complementarity is weakest, future programs for training midwives and for coordination between them and formal services should emphasize training midwives to detect signs of risk at this stage. We also found that during the post-partum period, women receive little attention from either traditional or formal providers. Future public health campaigns should emphasize the importance of postnatal care. Additionally, we found that, when women already have other children, women go to receive prenatal care later and ask for (and receive) less advice about their pregnancy

---

[7]In a study of the role of midwives in the detection of high risk pregnancies and newborns in a rural Sudanese community, Ibrahim et al. (1992) concluded that a training program for midwives reduced neonatal mortality by 25%.

than those having their first child. Therefore, the necessity of care during all pregnancies should be emphasized in the future.

4. Since, in both indigenous and ladino villages, respondents said that one of the problems for midwife training is that it is difficult and expensive for midwives to attend training courses in the health center, these courses should be given in the villages themselves.[8]

5. There appears to be potential for coordination of formal services with other traditional providers, in addition to midwives. Collaboration with midwives in their role as curers is a way in which advances in this direction could be made.

AKNOWLEDGEMENTS

The data collection for this study was part of a project conducted by Noreen Goldman (Princeton University) and Anne Pebley (RAND), supported by NICHD (Contract No. R01 HD27361 and R01 HD31327) and carried out in collaboration with INCAP directed by Dr. Hernán Delgado. This work would not have been possible without the dedication and professionalism shown by our fellow fieldworkers: Marta Amanda Barrera, Gladys Castillo, María Charuc, Nora Coj, Marty Yolanda Coroy, Marta Teresa González, Reyna del Carmen López, Catalina Lorenzo, Manuela Mejía, Idalma Mejía de Rodas, Lilian Navas, Marta Lidia Ponce, María Elena Sucuquí, Blanca Sulecio, Berta Tepaz y Juana Julia Tepaz. Finally, we gratefully acknowledge all the interviewees and the participants of the focal groups in the

[8]It is also important to provide more practical courses in which, for example, midwives would be taken to visit health centers/posts and to hospital services. Currently, courses tend to be too theoretical and to a certain degree, ignore the extensive experience that midwives have. On occasion, the instructors in these courses have no experience themselves in providing pregnancy or delivery care.

four communities who shared their experiences and opinions with us.

REFERENCES

Castañeda Camey, X. 1992. Embarazo, Parto y Puerperio: Conceptos y Práctica de las Parteras en el Estado de Morelos, 34(5): 528-532.

Cosminsky, S. 1977. Childbirth and Midwifery on a Guatemalan Finca. *Medical Anthrop.*, 1, 69.

_____. 1982. Knowledge and Body Concepts of Guatemalan Midwives. In *Anthropology of Human Birth.* Kay, M.A. (ed.). Philadelphia: Davis, 233-252.

Cosminsky, S. and M. Scrimshaw. 1980. "Medical Pluralism on a Guatemalan Plantation," *Social Science and Medicine*, 14B: 267-278.

Fleming, J.R. 1994. "What in the World is Being Done about TBAs? An Overview of International and National Attitudes to Traditional Birth Attendants," *Midwifery*, 10: 142-147.

García, B., J.J. Urrutia, and M. Behar. 1977. Creencias y conocimientos sobre la biología de la reproducción en Santa María Cauqué," *Guatemala Indígena* 12: 53-81.

García Barrios, C., et al. 1993. "Percepción de las Parteras sobre Factores de Riesgo Reproductivo," *Salud Pública de México*, 35(1): 74-84.

Gonzalez, N.S. 1963. "Some Aspects of Child-bearing Child-rearing in a Guatemalan Ladino Community," *Southwest J. Anthrop.*, 19, 411.

Hurtado, E. 1984. "Estudio de las características y prácticas de las comadronas tradicionales en una comunidad indígena de Guatemala." In E.M. Villatoro (ed.). *Etnomedicina en Guatemala.* Centro de Estudios Folklóricos. Colección Monografías, 1: 251-264.

Kay, M.A. 1982. "Writing an Ethnography of Birth." In *Anthropology of Human Birth*, M.A. Kay (ed.). Philadelphia: Davis, 1-24.

Ibrahim, S.A., et al. 1992. "The Role of the Village Midwife in Detection of High Risk Pregnancies Newborns," *International Journal of Gynaecol Obstet*, 39: 117-122.

Jordan, B. 1983. *Birth in Four Cultures*. Montreal: Eden.

Koblinsky, M., J. Timyan, and J. Gay (eds.) 1993. *The Wealth of Women*. Westview.

Leedan, E. 1985. "Traditional Birth Attendants," *International Journal of Gynaecol Obstet*, 23: 249-274.

Litoff, J.B. 1978. *American Midwives: 1860 to the Present*. Westport, Connecticut: Greenwood.

_____. 1986. *The American Midwife Debate*. Westport, Connecticut: Greenwood.

McClain, C. 1982. "Toward a Comparative Framework for the Study of Childbirth: A Review of the Literature. In *Anthropology of Human Birth*, M.A. Kay (ed.). Philadelphia: Davis, 25-59.

Paul L. 1975. "Recruitment to a Ritual Role: The Midwife in a Maya Community," *Ethos* 3: 449-467.

Paul, L. and B. Paul. 1975. "The Maya Midwife as a sacred Specialist: A Guatemalan Case," *American Ethnologist*, 2: 707-726.

Pebley, A.R., N.Goldman, and G. Rodríguez. 1996. "Prenatal and Delivery Care and Childhood Immunization in Guatemala: Do Family and Community Matter?" *Demography*, 33 (2), April. Erratum in *Demography*, 33 (2).

Putney, P. and B. Smith. (n.d.). Estudio acerca de las Prácticas de las Comadronas Tradicionales en el Altiplano de Guatemala. PRITECH Informe para la Misión AID/Guatemala (documento mimeografeado).

Royston, E. and S. Armstrong (eds.) 1989. *Preventing Maternal Deaths*. Geneva: World Health Organization.

Schieber, B., et al. 1994. "Risk Factor Analysis of Peri-neonatal Mortality in Rural Guatemala." Bulletin of PAHO, 28(3): 229-238.

Villatoro, E. 1994. "La comadrona a través de la historia en las prácticas: una experiencia en el área Ixil, Quiché." Centro de Estudios Folklóricos, USAC, La Tradición Popular, No. 97-1994, 20 p.

Warren, K. 1992. "Transforming Memories into Histories: The Meaning of Ethnic Resurgence for Mayan Indians." In *Americas.* New Interpretive Essays, Alfredo Stepano (ed.).

Williams, L.S. 1994. "Doctors' Reactions Mixed as Midwives Enter Health Care Mainstream in Ontario," *Can Med Assoc J* 150(5): 730-734.

World Health Organization (n.d.). Midwifery: its Role in Safe Motherhood and Beyond (pamphlet).

Chapter Thirteen

TRENDS AND DIFFERENCES IN FERTILITY, USE OF CONTRACEPTIVES AND MATERNAL AND CHILD HEALTH SERVICES IN EL SALVADOR: 1988-1993

JOSE MARIO CACERES HENRIQUEZ,
LAWRENCE GRUMMER-STRAWN,
PAUL STUPP,
JOSE DAVID ARAYA, AND
JUAN CARLOS SALGUERO

A comparison of the results of family health surveys conducted in El Salvador in 1988 and 1993 showed that the overall fertility rate decreased from 4.17 to 3.83 children per woman. The greatest decreases were among women in rural areas, illiterate women and women older than 25, groups in which the use of contraceptives increased the most. The greatest increase was in the use of temporary methods, and among non-using women who wanted to use contraception, two-thirds preferred these methods. Nonetheless, six out of ten users had been sterilized.

The use of prenatal check-ups and well-baby check-ups has shown improvement in the last 5 years. Hospital births have been remained at 50% but the use of postpartum check-ups decreased and continues to be under-utilized in El Salvador. In 1993, increases in all types of immunizations were found, particularly for polio and DPT. In that year, coverage varied from 87% for BCG to 82% for polio and DPT. The prevalence of diarrhea among children under 5 years of age decreased from 29% in 1993 to 24% in 1993, but continues to be higher in rural areas and for the children of illiterate women.

The infant mortality rate decreased from 54 per thousand in 1983-1988 to 41 per thousand in 1988-1993. In general, mortality among children under five years of age decreased from 68 to 52 per thousand. The interval since the previous birth was found to be the primary differential in infant mortality in El Salvador, given that the probability of death was higher when the interval was less than 24 months. This result demonstrates the positive effect of spacing pregnancies in the decrease of infant mortality, and particularly, in post-neonatal mortality.

INTRODUCTION

El Salvador, with a population estimated at 5.2 million inhabitants and an area of approximately 21 thousand square kilometers, is one of the smallest and most densely populated countries in the Americas. It is located in Central America, bordering on the north with Honduras, on the south with the Pacific Ocean, on the west with Guatemala, and on the east with Honduras and Nicaragua (with the Fonseca Gulf in between). Historically, its population dynamics have been characterized by continued high birth and death rates, and internal as well as international migration. Mortality and migration were drastically affected by the armed conflict that lasted from the end of the 70s until the beginning of the 90s. This conflict prevented the fielding of the National Population Census planned for 1981, and created obstacles to regular and complete registration and processing of vital statistics.

The Salvadoran Demographic Association (ADS) was founded in 1962. Among its objectives was to analyze population dynamics and propose alternative solutions, particularly with regard to fertility determinants. For this reason, since 1973 a series of national surveys have been undertaken to study the trends and differentials in fertility and the use of contraception in El Salvador. In 1985, other important topics related to infant and maternal health were added to the surveys, to obtain a broader panorama of the process of adoption of reproductive health services by the population. Although six surveys have been carried out, only the two most recent (1988 and 1993) contain enough information to analyze trends in reproductive health indicators with the possibility of using the same denominators.

The 1988 and 1993 surveys were carried out by the ADS with the technical assistance of the Division of Reproductive Health of the Centers for Disease Control and Prevention (CDC). In the 1993 survey, the support of an advisory committee was comprised of representatives from the Ministry of Public Health and Welfare (MSPAS), the Ministry of Planning and Coordination for Economic and Social Development (MIPLAN), The Office of the Census and Statistics (DIGESTYC), the Salvadoran Social Security Institute (ISSS), the U.S. Agency for International Development/El Salvador), and the ADS.

METHODS AND MATERIALS

In the 1988 and 1993 surveys, sample selection was conducted in three stages. The first step was to select the census sectors, within the framework provided by the DIGESTYC. The second was to select from within each census sector a segment of 30 households in 1988 and 40 in 1993. The third was to select at random an eligible woman of childbearing age (WCA) for the interview, maintaining a selection probability inversely proportional to the number of WCA in the household. To compensate for this unequal selection probability, the number of WCAs in the household was used as a weight.

The major differences between the surveys is that in 1988, the age range for women in their childbearing years was defined as 15 to 44 years old, while in 1993 the age range was extended to 49. The 1988 sample was geographically self-weighted with area probability for the following three strata or dominions: the Metropolitan San Salvador Area (AMSS), other urban areas (Rest of Urban), and rural (Rural), while the 1993 sample was geographically self-weighted at the national level, including 100% of the country's households as the sample framework. In 1988, only 90% of the national households were included, because insecurity due to the armed conflict made it impossible to visit the other 10%. For this reason, in 1988 it was also necessary to apply weights to compensate for the excluded households. Sample size increased from 5,460 households in 1988 to 9,000 in 1993, to make it possible in the latter sample to analyze possible causes of death in children under 5. The sample yielded 3,579 complete interviews in 1988, and 6,207 in 1993.

Another difference was that in 1988 all children under 5 living at the time of the interview were included in the analysis of diarrhea prevalence and immunization rates, while in 1993, one child was selected at random. This selection was also used for the analysis of post-partum check-ups. Furthermore, in the 1988 survey, the use of infant and maternal health care referred to the last living child born in the previous five years of the woman being interviewed, while in 1993, all live births in the five years preceding the interview were included.

In this paper, indicators are included for the cases where it was possible to calculate the same denominators by means of a secondary analysis, maintaining as a criteria the actual comparability of results. For this reason, the results presented in this paper may differ slightly from those published in previous reports.

RESULTS

Trends and Differences in Fertility and its Proximate Determinants

The Total Fertility Rate (TFR) in El Salvador decreased to 4.17 children per woman in the period from 1983-1988, and to 3.83 in the period from 1988-1993. This decrease basically corresponds to that observed in the country's rural areas, where the TFR was more than 5.59 in the first period, and was 4.94 in the second. In contrast, in urban areas fertility showed an increase (Table 1). By educational level, the greatest decreases were among illiterate women (0.55 children per woman) and among women with 7-9 years of schooling (0.40 children per woman). Among women with 1-6 years of schooling, the rate stayed the same, while it increased among women with 10 or more years of schooling.

In the decade 1983-1993, the fertility level did not change for women under 25, remaining at a level of 125 children per 1000 women from 15-19 years of age, and 221 children per 1000 women among those aged 20-24 years old (Figure 1). If we examine age- and place of residence-specific fertility rates, only in rural areas did a decrease occur at all ages. By contrast, in the Metropolitan San Salvador Area, there were decreases only among women aged 25-29 and 35-39, and in other urban areas, only among women aged 40-44. The decrease among illiterate women started at age 25, since in women at younger ages age-specific rates tended to increase. Among women with 1-6 years of schooling, the primary fertility decrease occurred among women aged 30-34. Among women with 7-9 years of schooling, considerable decreases were seen among women aged 20-29. Fertility among women with 10 or more years of schooling increased in all age groups, except among women aged between 35 and 39.

Age at the time of the first sexual relations or the first union (whether legal or not), are demographic variables that can have a significant role in fertility reduction, in the sense that the more the initiation of sex is delayed, the fewer years a woman spends at risk of pregnancy, and the fewer children she is likely to have. Comparing the 20-24 year old group to the 40-44 group at the time of the interview, we can confirm that in two decades, the proportion of women who had first sexual intercourse before age 18 has decreased from 53% to 43%, as has the age of the first union, from 45% to 33%. However, the proportion of women who had their first child before age 18 has only decreased from 27% to 24% (Table 2.) The average age of the first sexual intercourse or the first union increased by one year, but the age at birth of the first child has remained practically the same over the two decades at about age 20. Considering that the proportion of children breast-fed decreased in the five years under study, and that the average duration of maternal lactation remained constant (data not presented), we can infer that the decrease seen in fertility rates was the result of contraceptive use.

Differences and Trends in the Prevalence of Contraceptive Use

The prevalence of contraceptive use in El Salvador increased from 47% to 53% between 1988 and 1993. In contrast to what happened prior to 1988, 73% of the increase in prevalence during these five years was due to temporary methods. Nonetheless, female sterilization continues to be the most used method in El Salvador. In 1993, of the total number of women who reported using any method, 6 out of 10 chose sterilization. In urban areas, the increase in prevalence was minimal, and occurred only with temporary methods while permanent methods tended to decrease. On the other hand, in rural areas, contraceptive use increased from 34% to 43%. This increase occurred in temporary as well as in permanent methods (Table 3). Even with these increases in rural areas, contraceptive use continues to be significantly lower in rural than in urban areas (Figure 2).

With regard to women's educational levels, results of both surveys indicate that the increase in contraceptive use was directly related to years of schooling. In 1993, use varied between 43% among women with no formal schooling and 68% among women with ten or more years of schooling. This difference has remained constant since 1988, despite the fact that the greatest increase between 1988 and 1993 was among women without any formal education. Among this group of women, sterilization is predominant: even in 1993 of the total number of contraceptive users, three out of four had been sterilized.

Since 1988, women between 30 and 39 were the most likely to use contraception. The proportion of this group using contraceptives increased from approximately 58% in 1988 to 66% in 1993. Increases among women under 35 primarily consisted of temporary methods. However, the increase among women 35 or older primarily consisted of permanent methods. With regard to the number of living children at the time of the interview, in 1988 as well as in 1993, use increases up to the point when the woman has three children. This is the group of women who uses contraceptives the most. After parity three, it begins to decline. Use among women with three living children went from 62% in 1988 to 71% in 1993. The relative increase in this group was similar to that seen among women with only one child. Among women with three children, the increase was almost the same for temporary and permanent methods; however among those that only had one child, the increase consisted primarily of temporary methods.

The MSPAS decreased nationally as the primary supplier of contraceptives, from 57% to 49% in the five year period. This decrease was greater in urban areas other than the Metropolitan San Salvador Area. In contrast, the ADS and ISSS showed increases in all areas, with the exception of the Metropolitan San Salvador Area where the ISSS decreased by one point (Table 4). Even with the decrease in MSPAS as a supplier, its facilities are still the primary source of contraceptives, regardless of the place of residence of women. The second most important source in urban areas is the ISSS, but in rural areas it is the ADS. Commercial pharmacies also play an important role in urban areas.

Reasons given for non-use of contraception which are related to pregnancy, fertility or sexuality decreased from 73% to 60% between 1988 and 1993. This pattern was more evident in urban areas other than the Metropolitan San Salvador Area and rural areas (Table 5). The decrease was primarily among women who were in the post-partum period or breast-feeding, which are conditions consistent with a decrease in recent fertility. By contrast, there was an increase in reasons *un*related to pregnancy, fertility, or sexual activity; these reasons were primarily stated as "I don't like it", and were identified by the interview team as a hidden rejection of family planning. It is worth pointing out that of the four reasons specified, religious reasons dropped from the third place in 1988 to fourth place in 1993. In both years, the opposition of the spouse or partner had more weight. This second series of reasons constitute a challenge to information, education and communication programs in El Salvador.

Prevalence of temporary contraceptive use could increase if the service offered met the demand. Among women who reported at the time of the interview or afterwards that they wanted to use contraceptive methods, the preference for temporary methods increased from 54% in 1988 to 66% in 1993. There was a strong dominance of injection (32%) and oral (23%) methods. In contrast, the preference for female sterilization decreased (Table 6.) It is important to note that in rural areas, the percentage of women who reported they wanted to use contraceptives either currently or in the future but who at the time of the interview had not decided which method to use decreased from 22% in 1988 to 15% in 1993. This could be a result of the expansion of community-based programs that develop information, education and interpersonal communication activities about family planning.

One way to measure the effectiveness of family planning programs, is to establish the unmet need, defined as the need for services. To this end, women who need family planning services at the time of the interview are defined as women who did not report infertility, who were not pregnant or did not want to become pregnant at the time of the interview, who were sexually active, and who were not using any contraceptive method. With this definition, it can be said that in El Salvador the unmet need decreased only 0.8% between 1988 and 1993. The percentage of women who needed family planning services rose in urban areas but decreased in rural areas (Table 7). Data from both surveys allow us to infer that in El Salvador the decrease of the proportion of women at risk for an unwanted pregnancy was due to the prevalence of contraceptive methods given that the changes in other factors were minimal.

Differences and Trends in the Use of Maternal and Child Health Services

The MSPAS Integrated Norms for Maternal and Child Care state that in order for the prenatal check-up be considered early, it should occur in the first 12 weeks of pregnancy. These norms define four as the minimum acceptable number of prenatal check-ups that the pregnant woman without risks should have in order for this service to meet the requirements of being periodic or continuous. Taking the pregnancy associated with the last live birth in the two years prior to the interview as the denominator, it can be stated that nationally the prenatal check-up service that met these requirements demonstrated improvement during the five years between surveys. The percentage of women who had had a prenatal-checkup in the first three months of their pregnancy increased from 42% in 1988 to 50% in 1993. The percentage of women who had four or more check-ups increased from 49% to 59% (Table 8). It can also be said that for both requirements, improvements were seen only in the Metropolitan San Salvador Area and rural areas. In other urban areas, the percentage of women who had had a prenatal check-up in the first three months of their pregnancy decreased from 60% to 55%. In 1993, meeting both requirements was inversely related to the degree of urbanization in the place of residence of the mother.

Meeting both requirements in 1988 as well as in 1993, was directly related to educational level. However, significant improvements were seen only among women with less than four years of schooling. In 1993, the use of prenatal care in the first three months of pregnancy varied from 34% among those women who had no formal schooling to 79% among those that had ten or more years of schooling. The percentage of women who had four or more check-ups varied from 39% among the former group and 87% among the latter. With regard to the age of the mother, the greatest increases were among women under age 35. Women 35 or older were the least likely to meet the requirements.

Taking into account ownership of goods and services [1] in the home as an indicator of socio-economic level, it can be said that the use of prenatal care as established by the MSPAS norms is positively related to the possession of goods. In 1993, the use of prenatal check-ups in the first three months of pregnancy varied from 33% among those that did not have any of the selected goods to 66% among those that had three or more. The proportion that had four or more prenatal visits varied from 39% to 75%. For the first requirement, no increase was seen among women with three or more goods, but for the second requirement, the increase was similar to that observed among women who did not have any of the selected goods.

In both 1988 and 1993, those at the highest parity were least likely to use prenatal care as stipulated in the MSPAS norms. The use of a prenatal check-up in the first trimester varied from 49% in 1988 among women who were having their first birth, to 31% among those who were having their fourth or higher birth. In 1993, this variation was from 55% to 38%. Similarly, the proportion who had 4 or more prenatal visits varied from 57% for first births to 39% for those having their fourth or higher birth in 1988, and from 68% to 46%, respectively, in 1993.

---

[1]This refers to ownership in the home of a gas or electric range, toilet, electric lights, television, refrigerator, or car.

Possession of goods in the home as a socio-economic indicator is directly related to the percentage of women who had a hospital birth. It can also be stated that despite the decreases seen in urban areas and among women with four or more years of schooling, in the 1988 and 1993 survey results, hospital births are directly related to the degree of urbanization in the place of residence, and the educational level of the mother. However, the relation between the age of the mother at the time of birth and the number of births she has had is inverse to hospital care at birth (Table 9).

In the period between 1991-1993, the percentage of mothers in the Metropolitan San Salvador Area who had hospital care at birth (87%) was 2.5 times greater than those in rural areas (34%.) With regard to educational levels, differences increased and even more so when they are related to possession of goods in the home. Among women with ten or more years of schooling, the percentage who had hospital care at childbirth (87%) was 2.8 times greater than the estimate for women with no formal schooling (31%). With women with three or more goods in the home (82%) it was more than three times greater than among women with none of the goods in consideration (25%). With regard to childbirth, the relation established in the 1991-93 period is that the percentage of women who had hospital care at birth when it was the first birth (67%) was twice the estimated when it was the fourth or higher birth (33%).

Post-partum check-ups are the least used maternal and child health services in El Salvador and while other services demonstrated improvements in the five year period between surveys, the use of post-partum care decreased (Figure 3). Even though MSPAS norms recommend a check-up in the first month after birth, in this study we have expanded the time frame for the initial visit to two months post-partum. The results of the survey indicate that the percentage of women who had a check-up within the two month period ended decreased from 29% in 1988 to 24% in 1993 (Table 10). Use of post-partum checkups within the two months after birth is directly related to the degree of urbanization in the place of residence, the educational level of the mother, and the possession of goods in the home. In 1998, the proportion having a post-partum visit within 2 months varied from 43% in the Metropolitan San Salvador Area to 21% in rural areas, from 59% among women with ten or more years of schooling to 21% among those with no formal schooling, and from 46% among those that had three or more goods in the home to 16% among those that had none. In 1993, these proportions ranged from 37% in San Salvador to 17% in rural areas, from 42% to 12% in the extremes of educational level, and from 34 to 13% in possession of goods. There is no definitive trend with regard to age or number of births, but the smallest decrease in the use of post-partum check-ups was among women under age 25 and among those women that had their first birth during the years under study.

Among all the most recent births in the two years prior to the surveys, the percentage of children that were taken to well baby check-ups (within 2 months after birth) increased from 42% between 1986-88 to 59% between 1991-93. This result shows that the trend in well-baby check-ups is opposite to that for maternal post-partum check-ups. In both periods, the use of well-baby visits increased with the degree of urbanization of the place of residence, the educational level of the mother, and the possession of goods in the home (Table 11). With regard to the age of the mother at the time of birth, the results of the 1988 survey show no definite trend, but in the 1993 survey the use of well-baby visits decreases as the age of the mother increases. With regard to number of births, the use of well-baby visits was twice the estimated percentage when it was a fourth or higher order birth (33%).

In the 1986-88 period, among women with 7 or more years of schooling or with three or more goods in the home, more than 60% had taken their child to a well-baby clinic in the two months after birth which probably explains why in these groups experienced the smallest increases in the use of well-baby visits compared to 1991-93. In contrast, women aged 35 or older were least likely to take their children to well baby clinics both in 1986-88 and in 1991-93. For the other analyzed variable groups, the increases over time are significant.

Differences and Trends in Immunization Levels and Prevalence of Diarrhea in Children Under Age 5

To evaluate immunization levels in children under age five, we define a child who has completed all recommended immunizations as having received one dose of anti-tuberculosis vaccine (BCG), three doses of anti-poliomyelitis vaccine, three doses of anti-diphtheria, tetanus and pertussis vaccine (DPT) and one dose of anti-measles vaccine, independently of whether these doses were recorded on the health card or came from information directly provided by the mother.

In the 1988 survey, we found that at the national level, 81 per cent of children less than 5 had been completely immunized against measles, 77% against TB, and 61 percent against polio, diphtheria, tetanus and whooping cough. In the 1993 survey, increases were seen in the levels of all vaccinations but primarily for polio and diphtheria which had the lowest coverage in 1988 (Table 12). The increase in coverage for these vaccinations varied from 30 percentage points in the Metropolitan San Salvador Area to 15 in the remaining urban areas, and 20 percentage points in rural areas (Figure 4).

In the 1993 survey, there are clear differences between coverage in the Metropolitan San Salvador Area and in rural areas, but not between the other urban areas and rural areas, except in the case of BCG which varied from 91% in other urban areas to 83% in rural areas. The reason is probably that in rural areas there is less access to hospital care at birth even in the MSPAS sites where this vaccine is generally given at the time of birth.

To establish the prevalence of diarrhea, we asked if children under age 5 had had diarrhea in the two weeks prior to the interview, including on the day of the interview. Diarrhea was defined as one or more liquid stools per day for at least 24 hours. Following this criteria, the prevalence of diarrhea in children under age five decreased from 29% in 1988 to 24% in 1993 (Table 13). The prevalence of diarrhea decreased primarily among children under age three, residents in rural areas, and among children of illiterate mothers as well as among those with a higher level of schooling.

Despite these decreases, the prevalence of diarrhea in 1993 was 7 percentage points greater in rural areas than in the Metropolitan San Salvador Area, and 13 percentage points greater among children whose mothers had no formal schooling than among those whose mothers that had 10 or more years of formal schooling. It should be noted that the prevalence of diarrhea among children under one year of age is at least twice that estimated for children who reached their fourth birthday.

Differences and Trends in Infant and Child Mortality

The level of infant mortality decreased from 54 per thousand live births in 1983-88 to 41 per thousand live births in 1988-93. This decrease was due to the fact that post-neonatal mortality was reduced practically in half in the period under study (Table 14). Mortality in the 1-4 year old age group decreased slightly from 15 to 12 per 1000 among those that survived the first year of life. In general, mortality among children under age five decreased from 68 per thousand in 1983-88 to 52 per thousand in 1988-93. The decrease in infant mortality in El Salvador is pronounced although mortality levels remain almost three times greater than the level estimated for Costa Rica in 1990 (15 per 1000 live births).

In 1988-93, the relationship between infant mortality rates and maternal age at birth were U-shaped, as expected. The highest rates are observed for mothers under age 20 and those between 40-49 years of age (Table 15). With regard to order of birth, infant mortality is greater for the children at parity four and higher.

Differentials in infant mortality by the interval since the previous birth are substantial in El Salvador. For intervals of less than 24 months, the probability of dying (66 per 1000) was twice that for intervals between 24 and 47 months (28 per 1000). The effect of interval between births primarily affects the level of post-neonatal mortality (Figure 5). This result demonstrates the positive effect of pregnancy spacing in the decrease of infant mortality.

DISCUSSION

The decline in fertility levels in El Salvador between 1983-88 and 1988-93 was the result of an increase in the prevalence of contraceptive use. We reach this conclusion because aside from this factor, there was no significant change in other proximate determinants of fertility in ways that would account for the fertility decline. In fact in the case of breast-feeding, the number of children who were breast-fed actually decreased. Another element that reaffirms this position is that the fertility decline occurred exactly in the same groups of women (such as rural and illiterate women) where the greatest increases in prevalence of contraceptive use were shown. The findings indicate that an increase of at least 10 % in the prevalence of contraceptive use can be expected in rural areas, given the fact that the unmet need for family planning services in rural areas was at the 13% level in 1993. By contrast, in urban areas or among women with a higher educational level, improvements in fertility levels or in the prevalence of contraceptive use would not appear to be very likely.

The fact that three-quarters of the increase in the prevalence of contraceptive methods was in temporary methods and that in 1993, two-thirds of women who wanted to use contraceptives preferred temporary methods (with strong emphasis on hormonal methods), may mean that in the future increases would depend on the accessibility to temporary methods. Increases in the availability of these methods can only be made by reinforcing current community-based programs.

The Ministry of Health decreased as a source of contraceptives between 1988 and 1993 especially in urban areas other than the Metropolitan San Salvador Area. In these other urban areas, the percentage of women who had prenatal check-ups in the first trimester of pregnancy and who received hospital care at birth also decreased. The percentage of women who used post-partum check-ups in the first two months after birth in these areas also decreased by 16 percentage points. In San Salvador, the decrease was only six points and in rural areas it was four points. We can expect to see that with the decentralization of the Ministry of Health which began in 1985, and with the modernization of the State, these trends will reverse. On the other hand, any expected improvements will depend on the efforts of the Salvadoran Social Security Institute or non-governmental organizations which are developing health programs or projects.

Increases in the use of well-baby check-ups and in immunization levels among children under age five, and the decline of the prevalence of diarrhea are consistent with the decrease in infant mortality in El Salvador which went from 54 per 1000 live births in 1983-88 to 41 per 1000 in 1988-93. It can also be argued that the increase in the prevalence of contraceptive use contributed to the decrease in infant mortality and especially in post-neonatal mortality. When the inter-pregnancy interval was less than 24 months the probability of dying before reaching one year of age (66 per 1000) was more than double than that for intervals between 24 and 47 months. It is also worth noting that even though the decline in infant mortality appears to be pronounced (and higher than expected), data evaluation confirmed that the decrease was real and did not result from methodological differences. However, it must be emphasized that despite these decreases, the levels of infant mortality in El Salvador are still high compared with Costa Rica (15 per 1000 in 1990).

REFERENCES

Salvadoran Demographic Association and Centers for Disease Control, Division of Reproductive Health. 1989. *National Family Health Survey* (FESAL-88), El Salvador.

Salvadoran Demographic Association and Centers for Disease Control, Division of Reproductive Health. 1994. *National Family Health Survey* (FESAL-93), El Salvador.

Ministry of Public Health and Welfare, Office of Health. 1991. *Integrated Norms for Maternal and Child Care*, El Salvador.

Monteith, R.S., C.W. Warren, J.M. Caceres, and H.I. Goldberg. 1991. "Change in Contraceptive Use and Fertility: El Salvador, 1978-1988." *Journal Biosocial Science* 23:79-78.

TABLE 1. AGE-SPECIFIC FERTILITY RATES (PER 1000 WOMEN) AND TOTAL FERTILITY RATES (TFR) FOR THE PERIODS 1983-1988[1/] AND 1988-1993[2/], BY AREA OF RESIDENCE AND EDUCATIONAL LEVEL

	Age Groups (Years)							
Area of Residence and Educational Level	15-19	20-24	25-29	30-34	35-39	40-44	TFR	No. of cases (unweighted)
Total								
1988	125	221	183	135	98	73	4.17	(3579)
1993	124	221	168	126	86	39	3.83	(5752)
Area of Residence								
Metro San Salvador								
1988	87	164	135	77	47	9	2.59	(936)
1993	101	177	123	87	35	13	2.69	(1667)
Other Urban Areas								
1988	99	192	153	104	75	52	3.37	(1093)
1993	102	218	164	112	78	28	3.51	(1697)
Rural								
1988	164	275	230	187	146	115	5.59	(1550)
1993	158	263	210	166	126	64	4.94	(2388)
Educ. Level (Years)								
None								
1988	211	289	238	167	153	122	5.90	(772)
1993	226	296	203	169	120	55	5.35	(1092)
1 - 3								
1988	212	259	202	150	93	45	4.80	(769)
1993	197	283	197	130	98	43	4.74	(1186)
4 - 6								
1988	149	237	164	118	47	54	3.85	(880)
1993	161	232	171	105	57	27	3.76	(1313)
7 - 9								
1988	100	262	159	75	83	22	3.50	(524)
1993	100	220	133	103	53	13	3.11	(1033)
10 or more								
1988	32	106	129	93	75	0	2.18	(634)
1993	32	131	137	109	50	11	2.34	(1128)

[1/]From March 1983 to February 1988.

[2/]From March 1988 to February 1993.

TABLE 2. PERCENT WHICH HAD FIRST SEXUAL RELATIONS, A FIRST UNION AND A FIRST BIRTH BEFORE COMPLETING A GIVEN AGE, BY CURRENT AGE: WOMEN 15-49 YEARS OLD

	Age at First Sexual Relations					Ever	Has Not Had Sex	Median Age	No. of Cases (Unweighted)
Current Age In Years	<15	< 18	< 20	< 22	< 25				
15-19	10.2	(29.4)	(31.8)	NA	NA	(31.8)	68.2	NA	(1152)
20-24	9.6	43.3	62.3	(69.7)	(72.6)	(72.6)	27.4	18.7	(1159)
25-29	15.5	45.7	62.7	73.9	86.4	90.2	9.8	18.5	(1157)
30-34	14.6	50.8	68.0	80.0	88.3	96.2	3.8	17.9	(1006)
35-39	13.5	50.9	71.4	81.5	89.8	96.5	3.5	17.9	(725)
40-44	16.7	53.2	70.4	82.9	90.8	98.7	1.3	17.7	(530)
45-49	14.7	52.2	70.7	82.6	92.5	98.7	1.3	17.8	(454)
Total	(12.8)	(43.6)	(58.0)	(65.9)	(72.0)	(75.5)	24.5	18.5	(6183) *

(continued on next page)

(Table 2 Continued from previous page)

Current Age In Years	Age at First Union					Ever	Never In Union	Median Age	No. of Cases (Unweighted)
	< 15	< 18	< 20	< 22	< 25				
15-19	6.7	(24.2)	(27.1)	NA	NA	(27.1)	72.9	NA	(1157)
20-24	6.6	33.3	52.0	(62.9)	(67.1)	(67.1)	32.9	19.8	(1161)
25-29	10.9	36.9	54.1	65.8	79.5	85.6	14.4	19.5	(1160)
30-34	10.8	42.5	60.8	72.6	82.6	93.1	6.9	18.8	(1010)
35-39	8.6	40.8	62.8	73.2	83.7	94.7	5.3	18.8	(726)
40-44	10.6	44.9	61.7	75.5	84.8	97.0	3.0	18.6	(531)
45-49	10.9	43.3	62.4	74.7	86.5	97.1	2.9	18.7	(455)
Total	(8.8)	(35.4)	(50.3)	(59.1)	(66.2)	(71.7)	28.3	19.4	(6200) *

(continued on next page)

(Table 2 Continued from previous page)

Current Age In Years	Age at First Birth < 15	< 18	< 20	< 22	< 25	Ever	Never Had Birth	Median Age	No. of Cases (Unweighted)
15-19	2.2	(16.4)	(21.1)	NA	NA	(21.1)	78.9	NA	(1157)
20-24	2.9	24.2	45.7	(59.7)	(64.8)	(64.8)	35.2	20.5	(1161)
25-29	3.0	25.4	45.7	60.7	79.0	84.7	15.3	20.6	(1164)
30-34	3.3	28.4	52.3	67.3	81.2	92.7	7.3	19.8	(1009)
35-39	3.4	27.8	51.4	67.6	83.7	94.7	5.3	19.9	(724)
40-44	4.0	27.3	47.8	67.2	82.0	96.4	3.6	20.2	(533)
45-49	2.5	25.7	48.1	66.1	81.7	96.7	3.3	20.0	(453)
Total	(2.9)	(23.8)	(41.6)	(53.5)	(63.5)	(69.5)	30.5	20.3	(6201)*

( ) Exposure time partially truncated

NA Not applicable

* Excludes 24 cases which did not report the date of first sexual relations, 7 cases which did not report the date at first union, and 6 cases which did not report the date of the first birth.

TABLE 3. CONTRACEPTIVE USE, TYPE OF METHOD, YEAR, AND SELECTED CHARACTERISITICS: MARRIED WOMEN AND WOMEN IN CONSENSUAL UNIONS AGED 15-44 YEARS

Selected Characteristics	Total				Type of Method and Year: Permanent Methods		Temporary Methods	
	1988		1993		1988	1993	1988	1993
Total	47.1	(2276)	53.3	(3659)	30.2	31.9	16.9	21.4
Area of residence								
Metro San Salvador	64.4	(534)	66.4	(1005)	38.2	36.9	26.2	29.5
Other Urban Areas	56.4	(669)	56.7	(1015)	34.7	32.7	21.7	24.0
Rural	34.2	(1073)	42.8	(1639)	24.2	28.2	10.0	14.6
Level of Education (Years)								
None	33.6	(567)	43.4	(836)	27.0	32.4	6.6	11.0
1-3	43.9	(548)	47.2	(828)	33.8	34.7	10.1	12.5
4-6	50.9	(573)	54.6	(853)	33.9	34.1	17.0	20.5
7-9	54.5	(285)	59.5	(551)	29.0	30.7	25.5	28.8
10 or more	64.8	(303)	67.5	(591)	23.9	25.2	40.9	42.3
Age (Years)								
15-19	17.1	(227)	22.5	(336)	1.9	0.4	15.2	22.1
20-24	36.6	(476)	40.0	(733)	8.8	8.9	27.8	31.1
25-29	51.1	(539)	57.8	(873)	31.1	29.6	20.0	28.2
30-34	57.3	(485)	66.4	(805)	43.0	46.0	14.3	20.4
35-39	59.4	(322)	66.6	(529)	48.4	54.2	11.0	12.4
40-44	53.2	(227)	55.5	(383)	48.5	50.0	4.7	5.5
Number of Living Children								
0	10.0	(169)	10.4	(252)	0.5	2.0	9.5	8.4
1	34.1	(405)	43.0	(699)	3.0	4.7	31.1	38.3
2	54.3	(524)	59.6	(938)	28.5	30.9	25.8	28.7
3	62.1	(504)	71.4	(782)	51.9	56.7	10.2	14.7
4	60.5	(292)	66.9	(418)	51.4	55.3	9.1	11.6
5	47.4	(167)	54.7	(233)	36.8	42.8	10.6	11.9
6 or more	34.0	(215)	37.6	(337)	28.1	27.4	5.9	10.2

Note: The figures in parentheses are the unweighted number of cases.

TABLE 4. SOURCE OF CONTRACEPTIVES, BY AREA OF RESIDENCE AND YEAR OF SURVEY: MARRIED WOMEN AND WOMEN IN CONSENSUAL UNIONS AGED 15-44 WHO ARE USING CONTRACEPTION

			Area of Residence					
Source	Total		Metro San Salvador		Other Urban Areas		Rural	
	1988	1993	1988	1993	1988	1993	1988	1993
MSPAS	56.9	48.9	40.4	36.4	61.0	48.6	67.1	61.6
ADS *	12.6	15.3	8.6	12.8	9.3	12.5	18.9	20.0
ISSS	11.5	14.5	23.4	22.4	10.4	15.7	2.7	5.8
Pharmacy	8.2	9.3	9.6	13.4	10.4	10.0	5.1	4.7
Clinic/Private Doctor	4.3	4.2	9.3	7.2	2.4	4.1	1.7	1.4
Other **	6.0	7.5	8.7	7.2	6.2	8.6	3.8	6.5
Don't Know	0.3	0.3	0.0	0.7	0.2	0.3	0.7	0.0
Total	100.0	100.0	100.0	100.0	100.0	100.0	100.0	100.0
No. of cases (unweighted)	(1085)	(1978)	(338)	(673)	(377)	(589)	(370)	(716)

* Includes clinics and programs based in the community (posts).

** Includes the couple , school, friends/neighbors/family members, the church, midwife, and market.

TABLE 5. REASON FOR NOT UNSING CONTRACEPTION, BY AREA OF RESIDENCE AND YEAR OF SURVEY: MARRIED WOMEN AND WOMEN IN CONSENSUAL UNIONS WHO ARE NOT USERS, AGED 15-44

	Total		Area of Residence: Metro San Salvador		Other Urban Areas		Rural	
	1988	1993	1988	1993	1988	1993	1988	1993
Reasons related to pregnancy, fertility, and sexual activity:	*73.4*	*59.7*	*74.3*	*67.0*	*78.6*	*61.0*	*71.4*	*56.4*
Postpartum/Breastfeeding	29.5	15.7	22.4	13.5	26.4	16.1	32.4	16.4
Currently Pregnant	21.7	24.4	22.8	27.9	21.5	23.4	21.6	23.5
Menopause/subfecundity/sterilized	10.7	9.3	13.1	13.0	13.2	11.2	9.2	7.0
Trying to Get Pregnant	7.3	7.0	11.8	10.2	8.9	6.7	5.7	6.0
Not Sexually Active	4.2	3.3	4.2	2.4	8.6	3.6	2.5	3.5
Reasons not related to pregnancy, fertility, and sexual activity:	*26.5*	*39.9*	*25.6*	*32.9*	*21.5*	*38.8*	*28.5*	*43.1*
Fear/ Had Side Effects	11.3	9.1	11.8	9.0	9.7	10.1	11.7	8.8
Partner Opposes	5.0	4.3	4.2	3.1	3.2	3.9	5.8	5.0
Religious Reasons	3.4	3.1	1.7	0.7	2.3	1.5	4.3	4.7
Doesn't Like It	0.5	13.8	0.8	12.5	0.0	14.2	0.6	14.1
Other Reasons *	6.2	9.6	7.1	7.6	6.3	9.2	6.0	10.5
Don't Know/Didn't Respond	*0.1*	*0.4*	*0.0*	*0.2*	*0.0*	*0.2*	*0.1*	*0.6*
Total	100.0	100.0	100.0	100.0	100.0	100.0	100.0	100.0
No. of cases (unweighted)	(1190)	(1681)	(196)	(332)	(292)	(426)	(702)	(923)

* Includes: Lack of Knowledge of Methods, Advanced Age, Too Far and Other Unspecified Responses.

TABLE 6. PREFERRED METHOD, BY AREA OF RESIDENCE AND YEAR OF SURVEY: MARRIED WOMEN AND WOMEN IN CONSENSUAL UNIONS AGED 15 TO 44, NON-USER WHO WANT TO USE CONTRACEPTION

			Area of Residence					
Preferred Method	Total		Metro San Salvador		Other Urban Areas		Rural	
	1988	1993	1988	1993	1988	1993	1988	1993
Female Sterilization	28.5	20.2	32.2	26.2	28.1	19.0	27.3	17.9
Oral Contraceptives	20.8	23.1	20.3	17.8	19.5	25.2	21.8	24.7
Injection	18.7	32.0	18.2	33.8	19.5	31.0	18.5	31.7
Natural Methods	6.2	5.0	9.8	4.4	8.6	5.0	3.5	5.2
Other *	8.3	6.2	10.5	7.5	8.7	6.2	7.0	5.4
Don't Know	17.6	13.5	9.1	10.2	15.7	13.6	21.8	15.2
Total	100.0	100.0	100.0	100.0	100.0	100.0	100.0	100.0
No. of cases (unweighted)	(550)	(727)	(116)	(186)	(150)	(193)	(284)	(348)

* Includes IUD, Condoms, Vaginal Methods and Male Sterilization.

TABLE 7. UNMET NEED FOR FAMILY PLANNING SERVICES*, ACCORDING TO THE NEED FOR SERVICES, BY AREA OF RESIDENCE, AND YEAR OF SURVEY: WOMEN 15-44 YEARS OLD

Reported Condition	Area of Residence							
	Total		Metro San Salvador		Other Urban Areas		Rural	
	1988	1993	1988	1993	1988	1993	1988	1993
Not in Need of Service	*90.0*	*90.8*	*95.2*	*94.1*	*93.2*	*92.2*	*85.0*	*87.3*
Using Contraception	31.3	33.8	39.6	39.5	34.2	33.6	24.7	29.6
Currently Pregnant	7.2	7.1	4.6	5.8	6.0	6.2	9.4	8.7
Trying to Become Pregnant	5.8	5.9	5.2	5.0	5.6	5.4	6.2	7.1
Not Sexually Active	42.1	41.2	42.8	41.4	44.0	43.9	40.6	39.1
Menopause/ Infertility/ Sterilized	3.7	2.8	3.1	2.5	3.4	3.1	4.1	2.8
In Need of Services	*10.0*	*9.2*	*4.8*	*5.9*	*6.8*	*7.8*	*15.0*	*12.7*
Total	100.0	100.0	100.0	100.0	100.0	100.0	100.0	100.0
No. of cases (unweighted)	(3579)	(5752)	(936)	(1667)	(1093)	(1697)	(1550)	(2388)

* Women who have an unmet need for services are defined as: Not reporting infertility, not currently pregnant, not trying to get pregnant, sexually active, and not using a contraceptive method.

TABLE 8. PERCENTAGE WHO HAD THEIR FIRST PRENATAL VISIT IN THE FIRST TRIMESTER OF PREGNANCY AND THE PERCENTAGE WHO HAD 4 OR MORE PRENATAL VISITS, BY SELECTED CHARTERISTICS: LAST LIVE BIRTHS FROM 1986 ONWARD (FESAL-88) OR FROM 1991 ONWARD (FESAL-93)

Selected Characteristics	Prenatal Visit in the First Trimester		4 or More Prenatal Visits		No. of Cases (Unweighted)	
	1988	1993	1988	1993	1988	1993
Total	42.2	49.6	49.2	58.8	(1232)	(1859)
Area of residence						
Metro San Salvador	58.6	66.8	68.1	77.3	(235)	(431)
Other Urban Areas	59.9	55.0	62.5	63.4	(318)	(500)
Rural	29.6	38.3	37.7	47.3	(679)	(928)
Educational Level						
None	24.5	34.0	30.7	39.3	(315)	(429)
1-3	27.8	43.0	35.5	51.5	(310)	(436)
4-6	49.4	46.2	57.2	58.0	(305)	(421)
7-9	60.1	57.8	65.1	70.5	(160)	(300)
10 or more	77.1	79.2	85.2	87.2	(142)	(273)
Age of the Mother						
< 25	42.8	49.1	49.1	59.5	(689)	(1064)
25-34	43.9	53.8	52.2	62.0	(439)	(654)
35 or more	31.9	36.5	39.0	40.6	(104)	(141)
Ownership of Goods*						
None	23.4	33.1	33.4	38.5	(261)	(610)
1-2	33.7	46.2	41.6	59.7	(558)	(521)
3 or more	65.7	65.5	69.6	74.7	(413)	(728)
Parity						
First	49.2	55.0	57.2	67.8	(316)	(495)
2-3	46.6	53.1	52.2	60.7	(490)	(817)
4 or more	31.0	38.1	38.9	45.7	(426)	(547)

*Refers to the following goods and services: kitchen with gas or electricity, indoor toilet, electric light, television, refrigerator, and automobile.

TABLE 9. PERCENTAGE WHO DELIVERED IN A HOSPITAL, BY SELECTED CHARACTERISITICS: LAST LIVE BIRTH FROM 1986 ONWARD (FESAL-88) OR FROM 1991 ONWARD (FESAL-93)

	Hospital Delivery		Unweighted Cases	
Selected Characteristics	1988	1993	1988	1993
Total	52.0	53.7	(1232)	(1859)
Area of residence				
Metro San Salvador	89.8	87.1	(235)	(431)
Other Urban Areas	66.4	59.9	(318)	(500)
Rural	34.1	34.2	(679)	(928)
Educational Level				
None	30.1	30.7	(315)	(429)
1-3	37.6	37.0	(310)	(436)
4-6	60.9	56.5	(305)	(421)
7-9	73.5	74.1	(160)	(300)
10 or more	88.9	86.7	(142)	(273)
Age of Mother				
< 25	55.5	54.4	(689)	(1064)
25-34	49.1	57.7	(439)	(654)
35 or more	40.2	32.8	(104)	(141)
Ownership of Goods*				
None	25.9	25.4	(261)	(610)
1-2	45.6	47.0	(558)	(521)
3 or more	77.3	81.6	(413)	(728)
Parity				
First	63.6	66.9	(316)	(495)
2-3	56.6	57.6	(490)	(817)
4 or more	36.7	33.0	(426)	(547)

*Refers to the following goods and services: kitchen with gas or electricity, indoor toilet, electric light, television, refrigerator, and automobile.

TABLE 10. PERCENTAGE WHO HAD A POSTPARTUM VISIT IN THE FIRST TWO MONTHS, BY SELECTED CHARACTERISTICS: LAST LIVE BIRTH FROM 1986 ONWARD (FESAL-88) OR FROM 1991 ONWARD (FESAL-93)

	Postpartum Visit in the First 2 Months		No. of Cases (Unweighted)	
Selected Characteristics	1988	1993	1988	1993
Total	29.3	23.5	(1232)	(1253)
Area of Residence				
Metro San Salvador	43.1	37.1	(235)	(315)
Other Urban Areas	39.5	23.1	(318)	(358)
Rural	20.6	17.2	(679)	(580)
Level of Education				
None	20.9	11.8	(315)	(250)
1-3	19.7	16.0	(310)	(276)
4-6	33.3	27.4	(305)	(282)
7-9	30.3	27.8	(160)	(225)
10 or more	58.9	42.2	(142)	(220)
Age of the Mother				
< 25	26.6	22.1	(689)	(750)
25-34	34.9	28.8	(439)	(412)
35 or more	25.5	14.6	(104)	(91)
Ownership of Goods*				
None	16.3	13.1	(261)	(358)
1-2	22.8	20.3	(558)	(349)
3 or more	46.3	34.1	(413)	(546)
Parity				
First	28.7	25.5	(316)	(495)
2-3	32.2	25.0	(490)	(480)
4 or more	26.3	18.9	(426)	(278)

*Refers to the following goods and services: kitchen with gas or electricity, indoor toilet, electric light, television, refrigerator, and automobile.

TABLE 11. PERCENTAGE WHO HAD A WELL-BABY VISIT IN THE FIRST 2 MONTHS, BY SELECTED CHARACTERISTICS: LAST LIVE BIRTH FROM 1986 ONWARD (FESAL-88) OR FROM 1991 ONWARD (FESAL-93)

	Well-Baby Visit in First 2 Months		No. of Cases (Unweighted)	
Selected Characteristics	1988	1993	1988	1993
Total	42.4	58.6	(1232)	(1859)
Area of Residence				
Metro San Salvador	57.9	67.6	(235)	(431)
Other Urban Areas	51.7	65.1	(318)	(500)
Rural	33.7	50.6	(679)	(928)
Level of Education				
None	28.7	46.7	(315)	(429)
1-3	32.0	51.4	(310)	(436)
4-6	43.5	60.3	(305)	(421)
7-9	62.2	65.1	(160)	(300)
10 or more	71.0	74.2	(142)	(273)
Age of the Mother				
< 25	43.3	61.7	(689)	(1064)
25-34	44.9	58.1	(439)	(654)
35 or more	27.7	37.5	(104)	(141)
Ownership of Goods*				
None	24.2	45.4	(261)	(610)
1-2	36.0	58.8	(558)	(521)
3 or more	62.8	69.2	(413)	(728)
Parity				
First	51.5	69.1	(316)	(495)
2-3	44.9	59.3	(490)	(817)
4 or more	31.8	45.9	(426)	(547)

* Refers to the following goods and services: kitchen with gas or electricity, indoor toilet, electric light, television, refrigerator, and automobile.

TABLE 12. PERCENTAGE OF CHILDREN WITH COMPLETE IMMUNIZATION AGAINST BCG, DPT, POLIO OR MEASLES, BY AREA OF RESIDENCE AND VACCINE: CHILDREN LESS THAN 5 YEARS OF AGE

	Complete Immunization		No. of Cases (Unweighted)	
Selected Characteristics	1988	1993	1988	1993
Total				
BCG*	77.3	87.4	(2520)	(2611)
DPT **	61.4	82.0	(2228)	(2314)
Polio **	61.5	82.2	(2228)	(2314)
Measles*/***	81.0	86.3	(2061)	(2186)
Metro San Salvador				
BCG	85.7	92.4	(487)	(618)
DPT	59.2	88.9	(428)	(538)
Polio	57.7	89.0	(428)	(538)
Measles	85.6	90.8	(400)	(510)
Other Urban Areas				
BCG	84.9	90.7	(638)	(729)
DPT	64.7	79.9	(574)	(642)
Polio	65.6	80.1	(574)	(642)
Measles	81.9	84.3	(524)	(612)
Rural				
BCG	71.6	83.4	(1395)	(1264)
DPT	60.8	80.3	(1226)	(1134)
Polio	61.1	80.5	(1226)	(1134)
Measles	79.1	85.4	(1137)	(1064)

* Immunization considered complete with one dose.

** Excludes children 0-5 months of age and immunization is considered complete with three doses.

*** Excludes children age 0-8 months.

TABLE 13. PREVALENCE OF DIARRHEA IN THE TWO WEEKS PRIOR TO INTERVIEW, BY SELECTED CHARACTERISTICS, BY AREA OF RESIDENCE AND YEAR OF INTERVIEW: CHILDREN LESS THAN 5 YEARS OLD

Selected Characteristics	Prevalence		No. of cases (unweighted)	
	1988	1993	1988	1993
Total	29.1	24.4	(2520)	(2611)
Age of Child (in Completed Years)				
Less than 1	38.3	30.5	(574)	(553)
1	44.6	34.6	(517)	(547)
2	28.9	23.1	(485)	(519)
3	15.9	16.1	(475)	(492)
4	13.6	15.5	(469)	(500)
Area of residence				
Metro San Salvador	19.3	19.8	(487)	(618)
Other Urban Areas	26.6	23.5	(638)	(729)
Rural	33.2	26.9	(1395)	(1264)
Level of Education (Yrs. Completed)				
None	33.1	26.8	(693)	(596)
1 - 3	31.4	28.3	(632)	(592)
4 - 6	27.9	27.6	(616)	(589)
7 - 9	21.9	19.2	(315)	(408)
10 or more	24.0	14.3	(264)	(426)

TABLE 14. INFANT AND CHILD MORTALITY RATES, BY SOURCE AND PERIOD

Mortality	FESAL-88 1983-88*	FESAL-93 1988-93*
Infant Mortality **	54	41
Neonatal	20	23
Postneonatal	34	18
Child Mortality (1-4 years)***	15	12
Total (0-4 years)	68	52
No. of Births (unweighted)	(2640)	(4287)

* The period begins March of the first year and runs through February of the fifth year.

** Infant mortality includes deaths which occur before exact age 1 year (per 1000 live births). Neonatal mortality refers to deaths which occur before completing 29 days of live (per 1000 live births). Postneonatal mortality refers to deaths which occur after the first 28 days of life and before completing the first year of life (per 1000 live births).

*** Child mortality refers to deaths which occur after completing the first year of life and before reaching the 5th birthday (per 1000 children who survive their first birthday).

TABLE 15. INFANT AND CHILD MORTALITY RATES, BY DEMOGRAPHIC CHARACTERISTICS: MARCH 1988 TO FEBRUARY 1993

Demographic Characteristics	Age of the Child at Death* Infant			Child	Total	No. of Births
	Total	Neonatal	Postneonatal	(1-4yrs)	(0-4yrs)	(unweighted)
Total	41	23	18	12	52	(4287)
Age of the Mother at the Birth						
Less than 20	54	33	21	10	64	(961)
20-29	32	17	15	12	43	(2393)
30-39	43	19	24	14	57	(835)
40-49	(79)	(79)	(0)	(7)	(86)	(98)
Birth Order						
1	38	24	14	6	43	(1207)
2-3	37	19	18	16	52	(1719)
4-6	43	24	19	12	54	(977)
7 or more	(59)	(37)	(22)	(15)	(73)	(384)
Interval since Previous Birth**						
First Birth	38	24	14	6	43	(1207)
< 24mths	66	33	33	16	81	(933)
24-47mths	28	14	13	15	43	(1469)
48 months or more	37	26	11	7	44	(658)

( ) Indicates that the estimated rate is based on the experience of fewer than 500 births during the period.

* See definitions at the bottom of Table 14.

** It was not possible to calculate the interval for 20 births.

FIGURE 1. AGE-SPECIFIC FERTILITY RATES FOR THE PERIODS 1982-1988 AND 1988-1993

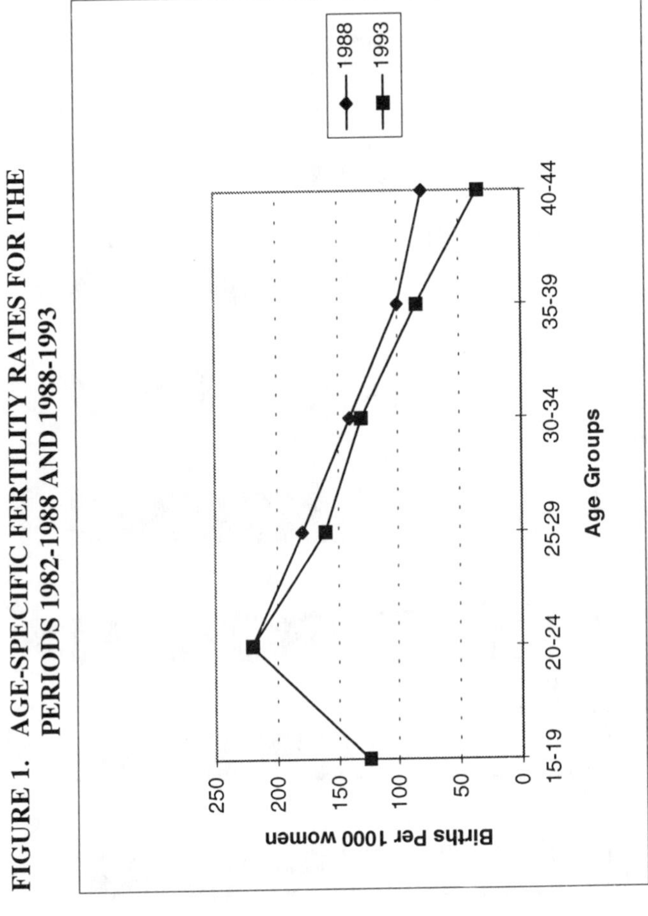

FIGURE 2. CONTRACEPTIVE USE PER YEAR, TYPE OF METHOD AND AREA OF RESIDENCE

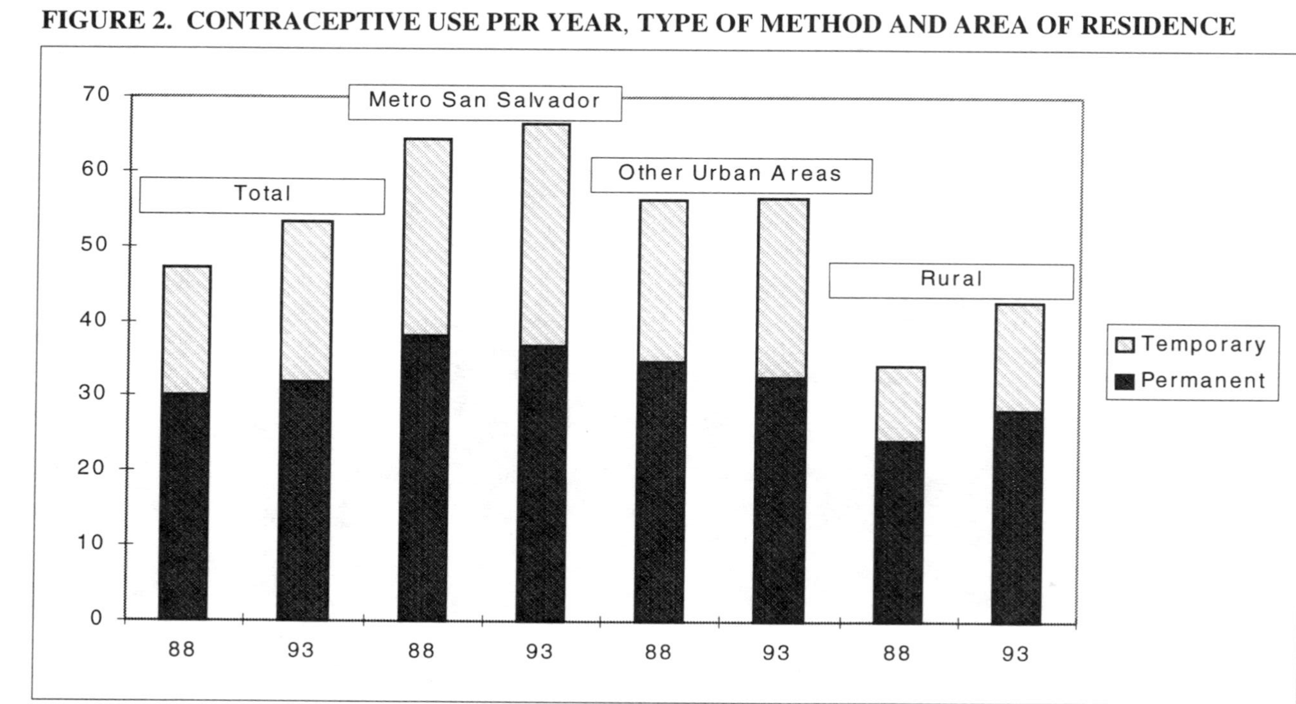

FIGURE 3. USE OF MATERNAL AND CHILD HEALTH SERVICES

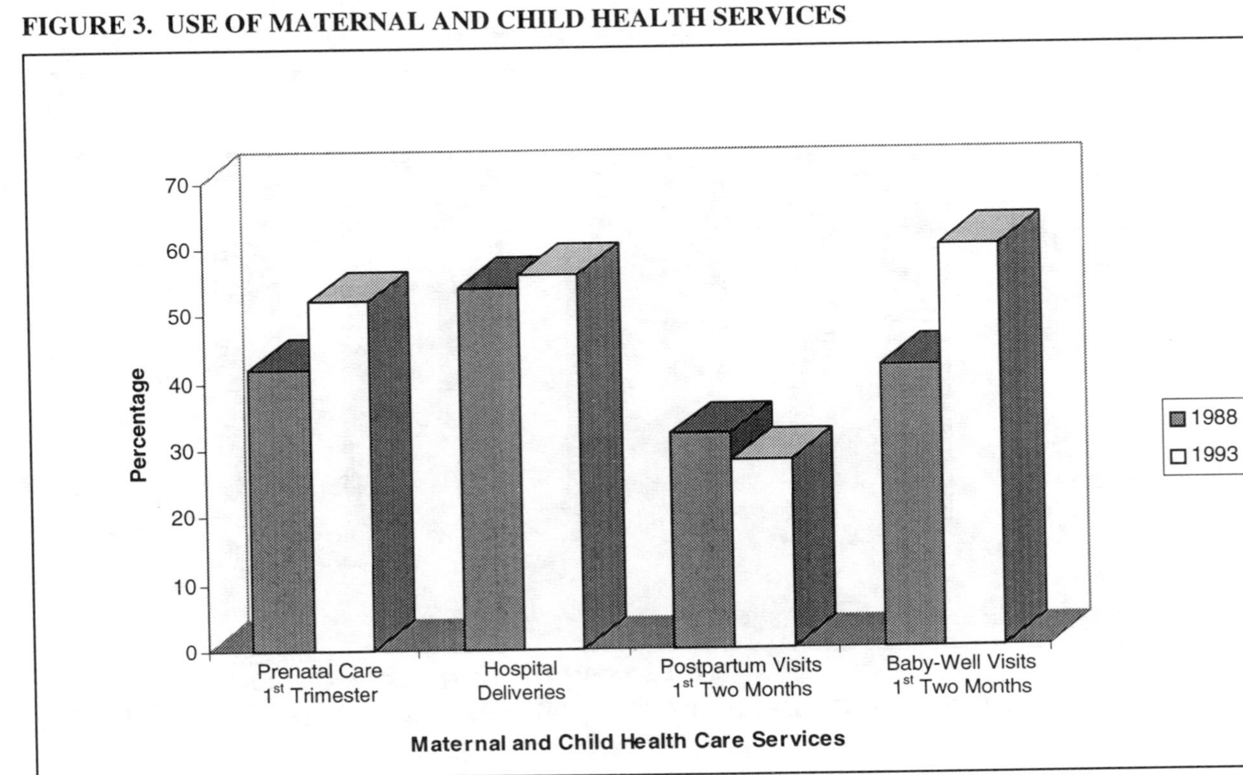

FIGURE 4. PERCENTAGE OF CHILDREN WITH COMPLETE IMMUNIZATION, CHILDREN LESS THAN 5 YEARS OF AGE

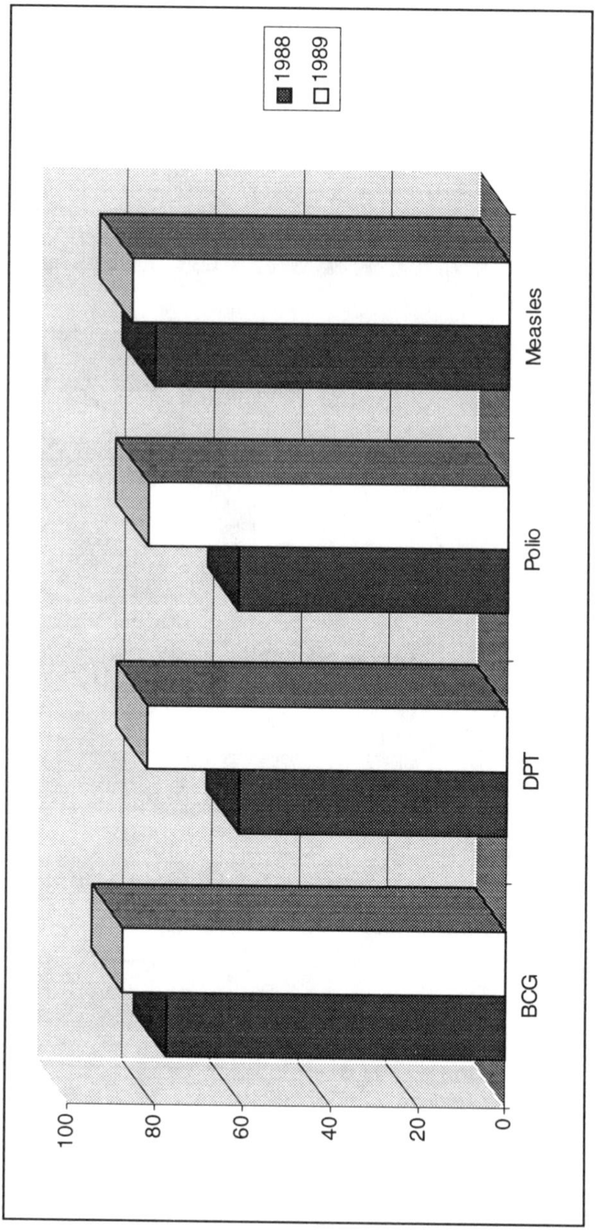

100
80
60
40
20
0

BCG
DPT
Polio
Measles

1988
1989

FIGURE 5: INFANT AND CHILD MORTALITY RATES, BY DEMOGRAPHIC CHARACTERISTICS: MARCH 1988 TO FEBRUARY 1993

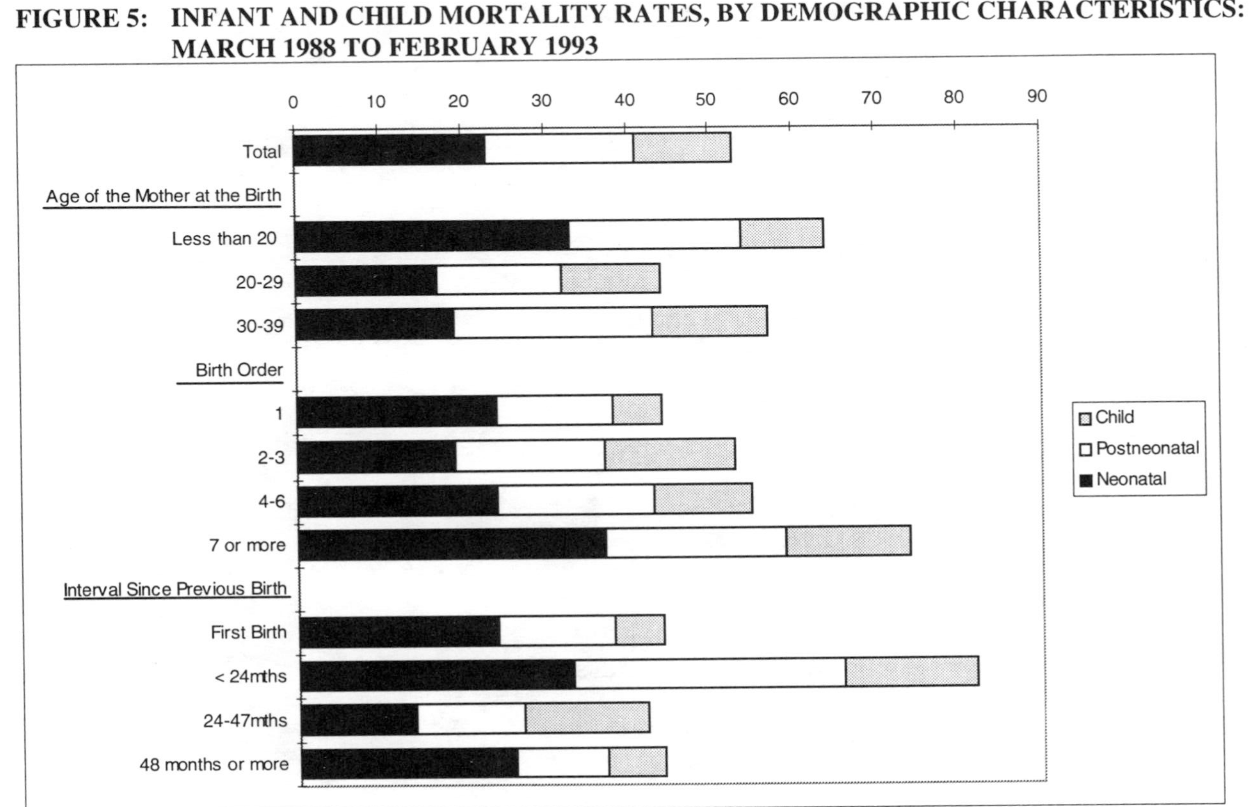

Chapter Fourteen

USE OF CONTRACEPTION AND KNOWLEDGE OF HEALTH TECHNOLOGIES

ARODYS ROBLES

INTRODUCTION

Are the behavioral aspects of use of family planning and primary health care services linked? The question addresses a key assumption in the rationale of reproductive health programs. In this paper we address the basic hypothesis underlying this assumption: that women who use contraceptives are more likely to have knowledge of health technologies to improve child survival. They would also be more amenable to use available health services or seek the necessary health technologies to treat their child. The study seeks to elucidate the relationship between knowledge and use of contraception and knowledge and use of health technologies. The analysis looks at the determinants of knowledge and the relationship between knowledge and use of health technologies.

Both, use of contraception and improvement of child health involve a behavioral change. Adoption of contraception implies a conscious decision to modify behavior in order to attain a desired pattern of family formation. Changes in behavior however are contingent upon knowledge about the effective means of controlling fertility (Coale,1973). Similarly, changes in child survival also entail a series of behavioral changes. Decline of child mortality in developed countries at the beginning of the century was associated with changes in personal health behavior (Preston and Haines, 1991; Ewbank and Preston, 1990). These changes came about when the knowledge base of disease causation enabled individuals to modify behavior in order to attain better health.

Considerable resources are spent today in the promotion of health technologies such as immunization and use of oral rehydration therapy (ORT). While vertical interventions have been adopted because of their simplicity, their impact on child survival ultimately depends on the ability of the mother to use them effectively. A mother needs to know the immunization schedule the child requires and the proper way of using oral rehydration packets. But most important, a mother first has to understand the benefits of using these technologies and be able to acquire them at the appropriate time. Consequently, an integral part of both family planning programs and primary health care programs is the dissemination of information on contraception and child care that will result in better health of mothers and children.

Efforts to examine the links between family planning and child survival have focused largely on the effect of contraceptive use on maternal child health (MCH) and stress the biological consequences of changes in reproductive patterns (Hobcraft, 1987; United Nations, 1994). It is known that the use of contraception has a positive effect on child survival through increasing the length of birth intervals and decreasing the occurrence of higher order births. For society as a whole, the decline in the number of births and of high risk pregnancies results in less pressure on the health system.

Along with the new findings on the importance of birth-spacing and prevention of high risk births, came the acknowledgment that family planning did not translate automatically into improved child survival (Bongaarts,1987; Bongaarts, et al. 1988; Potter, 1988; Allman and Rohde, 1988). Bongaarts (1987) pointed out that in spite of the known physiological consequences of maternal age, high order births, and short birth intervals, the existence of offsetting mechanisms hinder the possible reductions in infant mortality derived from adoption of contraception. In particular, Bongaarts noted the increase in the proportion of first order births, and in births occurring at an interval shorter than two years.

The exchange that followed Bongaarts assertion (Bongaarts, Trussell, and Potter, 1988) served to highlight the behavioral aspects associated with the adoption of contraception and societal factors that remained unmeasured. Concurrent with the adoption of contraception other practices such as prolonged breastfeeding and postpartum abstinence also changed. At an aggregate level, the proportion of births born to mothers with low socioeconomic status increased.

The one aspect that remained unmeasured, was the effect that the use of health services had in the outcome of births. Adequate prenatal care, for example, is higher for women of high socioeconomic status which in turn are the most likely to adopt contraception. Also, use of modern health services mediates the effects on child survival of curtailed breastfeeding and influences the adoption of contraception (Potter, 1988).

While the biological relationships between child survival and fertility control have been well documented, little has been studied in terms of the joint use of the two interventions. Integration of these programs has occurred either through addition of family planning to existent health facilities or through appending health interventions to existing family planning programs (Sirageldin and Mosley, 1988). Research that examines the linkage between use of family planning and child survival varies considerably in its different approaches. Some examine the relationship from an institutional perspective while other focus on behavioral aspects. Interestingly, results also vary among the different studies.

Warren et.al. (1987) using data for Guatemala in 1983 and for Panama in 1984 examined the use of contraception according to whether women had used MCH services such as prenatal care, postpartum check up, and well baby care. The analysis is based on information from currently married women 15-44 whose last live birth was within five years of the interview. In both countries the proportion of women who use contraception is significantly higher among women who have used more than one MCH service. Across all comparisons, contraception use was higher in Panama than in Guatemala and higher for non-indigenous women, and for urban residents. Results, as the authors acknowledge, do not permit an assessment of the influence of use of MCH services on the decision to use contraception. In both countries contraceptive use increases as parity increases while the use of MCH services remained constant.

The factors present in both the decision to use child survival interventions and contraceptive technology were examined by Wong and Agarwal (1992) for Tunisia using individual and community data collected in the 1988 Demographic Health Survey. The authors examine the socioeconomic and community characteristics associated with seeking treatment for a child with diarrhea and with using a modern contraceptive method. They conclude that different factors are associated with each of the health interventions examined. Socioeconomic and community characteristics are associated with seeking treatment for a child with diarrhea but not with using contraception. For contraception, it is the community characteristics that matter. Wong and Agarwal suggest that "using one intervention is an independent decision from the other."

Wilopo and Mosley (1993) in a study using data for West Timor island in Indonesia, test the hypothesis that decisions about practicing fertility control and using modern health interventions are made jointly. The authors argue that this decision is motivated by the desire to have a "limited number of healthy children." The hypothesis is tested using information at the individual, household, and community level. The analysis is carried out for ever use of a modern contraception and for use of all child survival interventions (maternal tetanus toxoid immunization, antenatal care, childhood immunizations and growth monitoring). Each dependent variable is included as an explanatory variable of the other. The study concludes that women living in localities covered by child survival programs are more likely to use family planning. Use of family planning is even higher for women who are knowledgeable about child survival technologies. In terms of policy Wilopo and Mosley state that "governments can promote the diffusion of new ideas and behaviors like contraceptive practice indirectly as well as directly through a variety of institutions including well organized health programs."

Another examination of the impact of programs is carried out by Juárez (1992) who examined the availability of health and family planning services and education on fertility and child mortality levels. The study used individual and community data collected in the 1987 Demographic Health Survey of Ecuador. Juárez, claims that institutions establish norms and specific actions that affect the survival and fertility strategies. The analysis shows that the presence of health services is associated with a decline in infant mortality and fertility levels. The existence of educational services is also associated with lower levels of fertility and infant mortality. Although the data is analyzed at an aggregate level, the author interprets the trends as changes in individual behavior.

Hossain (1987) asserts that government interventions in schooling and health generate price alterations such that households reduce fertility and increase child survival. Using household and community data for Bangladesh, the author estimates the effect on public programs on child survival, fertility, and schooling. Results show that for fertility and child survival the presence of a family planning clinic has the biggest impact being the only public program that has a significant cross effect.

In an influential paper, Rosenzweig, and Schultz (1982) examined the hypothesis that education lowers the cost of using health and contraception technologies. The authors argued that education and health or family planning programs may substitute for each other by reducing prices and disseminating information.

They use individual and community data to assess the effects on child health and fertility of variations in education and on cost and availability of health services. Results show that the information role of education and health programs is larger for the less educated women. In addition, the authors claim that they are partial substitutes for one another.

The programmatic linkage of health and family planning were also examined by Sirageldin and Mosley (1988). The authors propose a framework on how family planning activities influence the health system. A first linkage refers to whether programs have purely demographic objectives or are integrated into the health system. Another linkage are the sociobiological influences on health of family planning programs. This influences, the authors argue, have a cost saving effect. Third, indirect linkages exist between family planning programs and health. These operate through different factors such as nutrition, income, and education.

The views on the linkage between family planning and child survival can be summarized into two broad premises. One view would postulate that it is volitional aspects that bring about both the adoption of fertility control and behavior that results in better child health. If this is the case and the two health technologies are available jointly then women will tend to use both simultaneously. If they are not, then it is better-off women who will seek both of them. Implicit in the alternative view is that it is the existence of institutional resources that bring about the joint utilization of the two technologies. The presence of services will trigger a simultaneous change in fertility and child survival. According to this view it is schooling that has the biggest impact on the link between the two. In other words, in the absence of institutional resources one would likely find very wide differentials in the utilization of family planning services and child survival technologies. What is not clear, however, is whether knowledge of health technologies is transmitted simultaneously or whether other factors intervene to condition the transmission of specific knowledge about health technologies.

STUDY POPULATION

The way in which knowledge and use of contraception is related to knowledge and use of health technologies is examined in this paper using information from Bolivia (1989) and Guatemala (1987) collected in the Demographic and Health Surveys (DHS). In both countries contraceptive prevalence is low and infant mortality is among the highest of Latin America. Use of maternal-child health services, however, is different in the two countries.

Several characteristics of the study population make it particularly interesting. First fertility is high in both countries (TFR is 4.9 in Bolivia and 5.6 in Guatemala). While in both countries approximately 70% of the women knew at least one contraceptive method, contraceptive prevalence is below 20% in both of them. Infant mortality is also high in both countries (IMR in the five years before the survey was 96 per 1000 in Bolivia. In Guatemala it was 73.4 per 1000 for the ten years before the survey). Prenatal care, however, differs considerably in both countries. In Bolivia in 47% of the births reported the mother had received pre-natal care, in Guatemala in 72.9% of the reported births.

Ethnic differences are also an important element in studying knowledge and use of family planning and health technologies. Indigenous populations in both countries not only have different cultural traits than the rest of the population, but also speak a different language. These differences constitute an important barrier to access to knowledge about family planning and health technologies since the language in which almost all of the family planning and primary health programs are carried out is Spanish. While some indigenous people speak or understand Spanish, few read it or use it everyday.

Bolivia and Guatemala not only have the highest levels of fertility and mortality in Latin America, but also the largest differences in mortality levels between indigenous and non-indigenous populations. Differences in mortality have persisted even after a considerable decline in overall mortality rates. Mortality under 5 years of age was almost 20% higher for children of indigenous women in Guatemala (142 vs. 119.6) and more than 50% higher for children of indigenous women in Bolivia (185.8 vs. 122.3), according to results from recent DHS surveys (INE. Bolivia, IRD, 1990; MSPAS,INCAP, IRD, 1988).

In Guatemala 37.11 % of the population described themselves as indigenous in the Demographic Survey of 1989. In Bolivia, according to the Demographic Survey of 1988, 56% of the population 5 years of age or older spoke an indigenous language.

The population of Guatemala and Bolivia share other important socioeconomic characteristics. A large proportion of the population lives in rural areas (48.7% in Bolivia and 65.2% in Guatemala). In addition, in both countries a large percentage of the labor force is employed in agriculture (42.3% in Bolivia and 49.9% in Guatemala). In both countries the indigenous population is highly concentrated in the rural area. Almost 82% of the indigenous population lives in rural areas in Guatemala as does approximately two thirds of the indigenous population of Bolivia (INE. Bolivia, 1989; INE. Guatemala, 1988).

Educational levels are low in both countries. In Guatemala 42.4% of the population 7 years and older had never received any instruction and 45.8% had only completed primary school. In Bolivia 19.4% of those 5 or older had no instruction and 41.1% had attended at least one year of primary school.

THE ORGANIZATION OF HEALTH SYSTEMS AND FAMILY PLANNING PROGRAMS

In neither of the countries are child survival and family planning programs integrated. The organization of the health systems is characterized by the existence of many uncoordinated institutions. In both countries the health sector includes private sector, social security organizations, and the Ministry of Health. The latter is supposed to cover all the population not covered by the other institutions. According to WHO, in Bolivia only 34% of the population had access to health services. In Guatemala this percentage was 50%. Both are among the lowest coverage in Latin America. According to the same source, only 17% of the population of Bolivia and 27% of the population of Guatemala are covered by social security (OPS, 1990).

In both countries family planning activities have been outside the domain of the government. In Guatemala, most of the information and distribution operations are concentrated in one NGO. In Bolivia, virtually no organization has family planning as its only activity; several NGOs provide family planning services as part of their reproductive health projects.

Health Sector in Bolivia

Resources managed by the Ministry of Health are organized at three levels. A first level consists of provision of ambulatory care and community activities. The district hospitals are part of the second level. A third level is formed by regional hospitals and specialized clinics. More than half of the professional personnel employed by the Ministry of Health is concentrated in the third level. The same occurs with technical personnel and auxiliary nurses.

A wide range of community activities are carried out by health posts. Those carried out by medical personnel include visits to schools and households. Non-medical personnel such as community health workers (*responsables populares de salud*) carry out other outreach activities. Other activities include the organization of women in mother's clubs and health committees. The impact of these outreach activities, although difficult to assess accurately, seem to be rather minor. Statistics are reported at the aggregate level and include repeated activities.

Perhaps the main problem with the health sector is the uneven distribution of resources. The disparity between urban and rural areas is the largest one. The medical personnel of the Ministry of Health increased by 19% between 1981 and 1988 in the urban areas. In the rural areas it decreased by 1% during the same period of time (Ministerio de Previsión Social y Salud Pública, 1989). Table 1 illustrates this differences through a series of indicators estimated from the 1988 Population and Housing Survey.

No adequate statistics on morbidity or mortality exist in Bolivia, but infectious diseases continue to be the major public health problem. More than 20 thousand cases of malaria are reported every year. In spite of immunization efforts, cases of measles continue to be high among children. Tuberculosis rate is the highest in Latin America. The problem is aggravated by a low completion of treatment (67%).

Among children, diarrheal diseases and respiratory infections are among the highest in Latin America and the main cause of consultations and hospitalizations. Death from pneumonia among infants is the second highest reported for Latin America.

Although the government has in recent years developed a comprehensive maternal child health plan, coverage continues to be very low. In the year 1991, the births attended by the Ministry of Health and by the Social Security added up to 52,608. The estimated number of births in Bolivia is above 200 thousand a year.

Family Planning

Family planning activities began in Bolivia in 1974 when the Ministry of Health approved the inclusion of educational activities on fertility regulation. The activities were justified strictly in terms of women's health and were restricted to post-partum visits. In 1975 the Maternal-Child Health program began to operate financed by UNFPA, WHO, and USAID (Sociedad Boliviana de Salud Pública, UNICEF, OPS, 1989).

The initiation of the program was shortly followed by strong pressures from the catholic church. Actions taken by the church caused a considerable delay in the implementation of the program. It was only in 1984 that family planning education and services were institutionalized and included as part of the maternal child health programs. To this date, several projects have been carried out by the Ministry of Health with support from international agencies. Activities include the supply of family planning methods and education of the medical personnel. Coverage, however, continues to be quite low. In 1992, for example, 20,382 women attended family planning consultations out of an estimated 720,000 potential users.

Given the difficulties that the government had in launching the reproductive health program, national and international NGOs took over the provision of family planning services and education. More than 90% of IUDs, pills, condoms, and tablets are currently supplied by NGOs. Family planning consultations are also provided mainly by NGOs. Since NGOs carry out their activities in the principal cities, 95% of family planning consultations take place in urban areas.

HEALTH SECTOR IN GUATEMALA

Even more than in Bolivia, provision of health services in Guatemala is characterized by lack of coordination. A diverse array of institutions provide curative health services. Adequate legislation to organize the provision of health care does not exist. The Ministry of Health and the Social Security Institute (*Instituto Guatemalteco de Seguridad Social)* are the main institutions of the health sector. Within the government, however, several other offices carry out health activities such as provision of ambulatory care or health insurance. Of the 641 registered NGOs only 30 have signed specific agreements with the Ministry of Health. Finally, the private sector performs numerous activities that range from the provision of ambulatory care to the sale of insurance, and distribution of medicines (IGSS.Guatemala, 1986).

In spite of the wide array of medical providers, actual coverage is as low as in Bolivia. Coverage by the Social Security Institute is approximately 13%. Coverage by the Ministry of Health is estimated to be 25% of the country's population. The private sector is concentrated mainly in the capital city of the country. Of the 2926 health clinics privately operated, 2077 are in the metropolitan area.

Overall, health resources are largely concentrated in the metropolitan region of the country. Of the personnel of the Ministry of Health 51% of medical professionals and 40% of auxiliary nurses are in the metropolitan region. Of those employed by the Social Security Institute, 60% are located in hospitals in the capital city (Dirección de Salud Pública y Asistencia Social, 1989).

The resources managed by the Ministry of Health which in most areas of the country is the only institution that provides health services are organized with urban areas as the core of a network that extends towards the rural areas. Services provided by the Ministry of Health are hospital, health centers, health posts, government or municipal pharmacies. Hospitals are located in the large urban centers and function as the main referral center for the area. Health centers are either type A with beds and in most cases laboratories or type B with fewer personnel and usually attended by only one doctor. Health centers type B are responsible for supervising the health posts which are run by an auxiliary nurse and a "rural health technician" (Ministerio de Salud Pública y Asistencia Social, 1989). Given that 70% of the population of Guatemala lives in rural areas, this organization of services means that auxiliary nurses or rural health technicians are the only resource for a majority of the population, and particularly for the indigenous population 80% of whom live in rural areas.

Services are heavily concentrated in the urban areas and particularly in the Metropolitan region where the capital city is located (see Table 2). All of the hospital beds are located in the urban areas and particularly in the departmental capitals. The number of beds per one thousand persons is similar in most of the regions except for the Metropolitan region (2.2) where it is more than twice the national average and in the North-West (0.4) where it is less than half the national average. The percentage of births attended by physician or birth attendant is less than half in most regions of the country. It is higher in the Metropolitan area (91%) and very low in the North (15.7%) and South-East (28%).

As in Bolivia, infectious diseases represent the major demand in the health system, and particularly infectious diseases among children. Under 5 mortality accounts for more than one third of the total number of deaths in the country. Intestinal infections represented the major cause of mortality in 1987. More than half of deaths due to intestinal infections occurred among children under 5. The same happens with respiratory infections and malnutrition which are the second and third cause of death in the country.

Diseases preventable through immunization have been declining with the exception of measles. In spite of recent immunization campaigns, measles continues to be an important cause of death among children. Among the adult population, malaria, dengue and tuberculosis are important causes of mortality.

In spite of the lack of adequate coverage, births exert considerable pressure over the health system. Only one fourth of births that occur in Guatemala annually are attended by physician. In the rural areas the percentage is only 15%, and among indigenous women a mere 8%. Consequently, perinatal and maternal deaths are rather high. The maternal mortality rate has been estimated at 12.9 per 10,000. In addition, complications of pregnancy and birth account for 40% of hospitalizations in the country.

Family Planning

The major provider of family planning services in Guatemala is APROFAM, an NGO founded in 1964. APROFAM provides clinical services (prenatal, birth, delivery) through a network staffed by more than 121 medical professionals. Community services comprise a wide range of activities from training of health promoters in ORT, immunization and family planning, to dissemination of information and training of medical personnel.

Results from the Demographic Health Survey showed that approximately a third of contraceptive users identified APROFAM as the provider. Another source of contraceptives were the pharmacies. Overall, the population identifies family planning as a private activity.

The adoption of contraception technology in Guatemala has been very slow. There has been little change in use since 1983. A slight increase occurred from 1978 to 1983 among married women between 15-44 years of age. Virtually all of the change, however, is attributable to an increase in the number of women sterilized. Results from the 1987 DHS show that sterilization continues to be the most used method of fertility control. Among women of 30-34 years of age, half of those counted as current users of contraception are sterilized. The proportion is two thirds for women older than 35 years of age.

Overall, in both countries institutional factors and lack of resources have hindered the implementation of a maternal child health plan that integrates family planning and child survival interventions. The uneven distribution of health resources within the country is also an important deterrent to integration of fertility control and child survival. The implications for the present study are that: first, the health system did not offer women in either of the two countries the possibility of adhering to a comprehensive reproductive health strategy. Second, if women wanted to utilize both types of health technology due to a conscious decision, some women will be in a better position than others to do so.

Analytic Strategy

The relationship between history of family planning and knowledge and use of health technologies, is examined for a set of women for which the complete reproductive history since marriage is known, i.e., those that were married or in union not more than five years before the survey, have been married or in union only once, and have not had a child born more than five years before the survey. This includes 15% of all women interviewed (788 out of 5162) in Guatemala and 934 out of 7923 in Bolivia. In this way, differences between women are not largely influenced by changes over time in the availability of health services and contraceptive methods.

The information about specific knowledge refers to the time of the survey, and it is not possible to know the exact time of its acquisition. Given this fact, we constructed a series of measures that summarize each woman's experience with the use of child survival interventions and family planning (see appendix 1 for a list of variables).

In order to obtain an indicator of the timing of use of contraception we examined whether contraception was used before the first birth or not, and whether contraception was used for the purpose of spacing or stopping.

To summarize health behavior during pregnancy, we created several indicators of the care received or sought by the woman during pregnancy. Since the unit of analysis are the women and not the children a summary measure was created for each woman in order to distinguish whether attention was received for all births, for none of the births, or for at least one birth. The indicators summarize whether the woman sought or received a tetanus toxoid injection during pregnancy, whether she received any type of prenatal care, and whether she received any assistance at delivery.

A separate summary measure was created for breast-feeding in order to measure the proportion of time that each woman had breastfed her children during the first year. The measure is computed as follows:

$$BF_j = \frac{\sum_{i=1}^{CEB_j} \frac{MB_{ij}}{\sum_0^m Months_{ij}}}{CEB_j}$$

where MB_i indicates the number of months that child i was breastfed, truncated at 12 months.

$\sum_0^m Months_{ij}$ indicates the number of months that the child i of mother j has been alive during the first year.

CEB_j is the number of children born alive to woman j.

BF_j takes the value of zero for woman j if she did not breastfeed any of her children, and the value of 1 if she breastfed all her children during 12 months or whatever portion of the year they have been or were alive. Values in between indicate the average proportion of time that each woman breastfed her children during the first year.

Two indicators of knowledge of contraception were created using information on spontaneous knowledge of contraception: whether the respondent knows any modern method, and whether she knows a source where to obtain a modern method.

We begin by examining the determinants of knowledge. We examine the association of three sets of factors. First, the woman's position to receive and take advantage of information and new technology (Place of residence, educational attainment, ethnicity). Second, a set of indicators (described above) that summarize a woman's health behavior throughout her pregnancy history. And third, a set of indicators that summarize a woman's contraceptive experience.

Each of the variables representing knowledge is coded as a dichotomous variable. Accordingly, we estimate the following logit model:

$$\ln[\frac{P}{1 - P}] = a + bX$$

where:

P	is the probability that woman has knowledge about oral rehydration solutions, a modern contraceptive or a source for a modern contraceptive.
a	is a constant.
b	is a vector of parameters to be estimated and
X	is a set of covariates.

Given that childbearing is what gives the woman the opportunity to come in contact with specific knowledge or services, we compare the estimates for all women to those who have had a child. In addition we control for number of children.

We then focus on specific knowledge of oral rehydration solution (ORS). The rationale to focus on this particular health technology is that in contrast with immunization it implies a modification of the knowledge base of the population. Since for diarrheal diseases it is not possible to achieve herd immunity, as it is the case with other infectious diseases, it cannot be the target of national one-time campaigns as it occurs with immunization. In addition, while knowledge about oral rehydration therapy is spread through the health system, it does not depend on the existence of health infrastructure.

RESULTS

Tables 3 and 4 show the association between a woman's characteristics and her knowledge of oral rehydration and contraception. We include those predetermined variables that may affect the woman's ability to acquire knowledge.

In both countries residence in an urban area is an important determinant of knowledge of contraception but not of oral rehydration. This result summarizes the situation of health services outlined above. In both countries health activities—family planning and curative services—are concentrated in the urban areas. In addition, oral rehydration has been emphasized as especially suitable for the rural areas where health services are not easily accessible.

As expected, education and particularly secondary education is an important determinant of the acquisition of knowledge. The difference in knowledge between women of different educational levels is important in Guatemala but not in Bolivia. In Guatemala differences by educational level increase when controlling for children ever born. In Bolivia, in contrast, they tend to decrease.

Indigenous women are in a particular disadvantaged position. In Guatemala being indigenous has a strong negative effect on specific knowledge. The effect is consistent despite the number of children that a woman has. Interestingly, in Bolivia being indigenous is not a disadvantage to acquire knowledge of oral rehydration. Again, this is consistent with the fact that in Bolivia a large percentage of the indigenous population lives in the rural areas where ORS campaigns have been carried out.

Exposure to information, as measured by ownership of a radio and by having heard the family planning message has a different effect on both countries. In Guatemala it is important for knowledge of contraception but not for knowledge of oral rehydration. In Bolivia the opposite occurs, those with a radio are more likely to have knowledge of oral rehydration, and having heard the family planning message appears to have no impact on knowledge.

Tables 5 and 6 explore the relationship between health behavior and knowledge. Health behavior is summarized by whether a woman received prenatal care, has received a tetanus toxoid immunization, and the proportion of time that she has breastfed her children. Results show that having received prenatal care for at least one child is the single most important determinant of having specific knowledge of a health technology.

In both countries breastfeeding has a strong negative relation with knowledge. It is particularly strong for knowledge of contraception. Given that the variable summarizes the whole experience of each woman with breastfeeding it probably identifies a group of women that either due to residence or culture have different health behavior and knowledge. Furthermore, these results seem consistent with the assertion that women who adopt contraception also modify their behavior in other ways (Bongaarts, 1987; Potter, 1988).

In Bolivia, having received a tetanus toxoid immunization in any of the pregnancies does not have a definite influence on knowledge except for knowledge of a source for modern contraception. In Guatemala, it has a stronger influence on knowledge of oral rehydration than on source for modern contraception, and no relation to knowledge of modern contraception. In both countries the maternal child health guidelines call for vaccination of any pregnant woman that comes in contact with a health establishment. The difference between the two countries might be an indication that in Guatemala to learn about oral rehydration it is necessary to come in contact with a health establishment, but not in Bolivia. Such interpretation is consistent with the fact that in Bolivia at the time of the survey a strong ORT campaign was under way. In Guatemala ORT promotion has only begun in recent years.

Table 7 shows the relationship between knowledge and history of contraceptive use. In both countries ever use of contraception is positively and significantly associated to acquisition of knowledge. Curiously, spacing does not show any strong association with knowledge. Having used contraception before the first birth seems to identify a group of women who have not yet had extensive contact with the health system.

To integrate the determinants of knowledge of ORS we have estimated a set of equations using the three sets of variables discussed above (Table 8 and Table 9). In Guatemala, education and ethnicity are the most important factors influencing knowledge of ORS. Contact with the health system is positively and significantly associated with knowledge of ORS. The coefficients for these two sets of variables are rather consistent in all the equations.

The variables related to contraceptive use show different results. Having used contraception before the first birth is negatively associated to knowledge of ORS. Ever use, however, has a strong and positive effect and a strong effect when it is included with BEFORE (i.e., use of contraception before first birth) but is much weaker by itself. In particular having used contraception before the first birth seems to identify a set of women with different characteristics.

For Guatemala, when the three sets of variables are included in the analysis, their significance changes. Education and indigenous have a stronger effect than in the previous models. The importance of tetanus toxoid and prenatal care is inverted. Having used contraception before the first birth has a stronger effect than ever use of any method.

In Bolivia, education and having received prenatal care have a strong effect on knowledge of ORS. Interestingly, in the case of Bolivia, being indigenous was not significant in any of the models. The inclusion of prenatal care modifies the significance of the other variables, in particular the differences between educational levels.

The last two columns of the table show separate estimations for urban and rural areas. It is worth noting the sharp difference between the two. In the rural areas education and listening to a radio are the more important determinants of knowledge of ORS. In the urban areas the effect of the two variables is not significant. Again, this is consistent with the disparity in the distribution of services and health personnel. It highlights, however, that even in rural areas, the position of a woman is what will enable her to take advantage of health technologies.

Finally, to assess the influence that the presence of a health facility has, the percentage of women with specific knowledge or behavior was estimated. Results are presented in Table 10. Unfortunately, information on health facility is only available for Guatemala. In addition, several clusters of the Metropolitan Region do not have health center information. To be able to include all the data, we created a category to identify the missing values. The results are presented only for distance to a health service with family planning services since they are almost identical to those for distance to a health center with ORT services and to distance to a health center with MCH services.

As distance to a health center increases, the percentage of women with specific knowledge or that have had access to health technologies decreases. The decrease is sharper, however, for those variables related to use of knowledge and use of family planning.

CONCLUSION

In both countries the way in which health services are provided thwarts the possibility of acquiring knowledge about family planning and health technologies simultaneously. Provision of family planning services in Bolivia and Guatemala, have been organized separately from the main organization of health services.

Private initiatives and NGOs play an important role in the dissemination of information and distribution of contraceptive methods. In both countries there is also considerable difference in the possibility of obtaining family planning services between urban and rural areas. Given the difficulties in accessing health services, it is the relative position of women that has a strong influence on the knowledge about health technology that they have. In both countries education and ethnicity strongly influence the ability of a woman to benefit from existing knowledge. Differences between women of different educational levels are greater in Guatemala than in Bolivia.

This relative position of women, however, is not an insurmountable obstacle to dissemination of specific knowledge about health technology. There is indication that when programs have specific targets, they can overcome certain barriers. Promotion of ORT has been directed to areas with difficult access to health services and to populations that face important barriers. Accordingly, residence in a rural area had no importance for acquisition of knowledge about ORS. Furthermore, in Bolivia ethnicity was not an important determinant of knowledge of ORS.

Contact with the health establishments is also an important element in the acquisition of knowledge about health technologies. Even when contact is not systematic, as is apparently the case with tetanus toxoid immunization, it has an important influence on acquisition of knowledge.

Conclusions about the importance of contraceptive use for the acquisition of health knowledge are mixed. On the one hand there is evidence that for a group of women acquisition of knowledge is much less costly than for others. On the other hand for these women purchasing health care may be economical enough so that they do not need to acquire knowledge about health technology. This seems to be the case for those women who use contraception before the first birth. This might be particularly true in countries such as Bolivia and Guatemala with large disparities in the distribution of health resources.

An important measurement issue, however, needs to be further studied. While it is usually assumed that child survival and use of contraception are endogenous, it is not clear that it is always so. The relationship might depend on the particular setting where it is studied. In countries such as Bolivia and Guatemala where family planning and child survival provision is, not only not integrated, but rather independent of each other, the acquisition of knowledge could possibly be triggered by a different set of factors.

ACKNOWLEDGEMENTS

Part of the information on health was collected by Jaime Montaño in Bolivia and by Rafael Haeussler in Guatemala. Research on which this paper is based was carried out while at the Department of Population Dynamics, Johns Hopkins University and was supported by a grant from MACRO/IRD and by the Population Council. Comments by Henry Mosley and by Rebeca Wong to an earlier version of the paper are gratefully acknowledged.

REFERENCES

Allman, James and Rohde, Jon. 1981. "Infant Mortality in Relation to the Level of Fertility Control Practice in Developing Countries." *International Population Conference: Manila v. 2*. Liege, Belgium, International Union for the Scientific Study of Population.

Bongaarts, John. 1987. "Does Family Planning Reduce Infant Mortality Rates?" *Population and Development Review.* 13(2):323-334.

Bongaarts, John, James Trussell, and Joseph Potter. 1988. "Does Family Planning Reduce Infant Mortality: An Exchange." *Population and Development Review.* 14(1):215-236.

Coale, Ansley. 1973. "The demographic transition reconsidered." *Proceedings of the International Population Conference, Liege*, International Union for the Scientific Study of Population. p. 53-57

Dirección de Salud Pública y Asistencia Social. Dirección General de Servicios de Salud. 1989. *Red de establecimientos del Ministerio de Salud Pública y Asistencia social.* Guatemala: Unidad de Programación, D.G.S.S.

Ewbank, Douglas and Samuel H. Preston. 1990. "Personal Health Behavior and the Decline in Infant and Child Mortality: the United States, 1900-1930." Pp. 116-149 in *What We Know about Health Transition: the Cultural, Social and Behavioral Determinants of Health*, John Caldwell et al. ed. Australia: The Australia National University.

Hobcraft, J. 1987. "Does Family Planning Save Children's lives?" *International Conference on Better Health for Women and Children through Family Planning, Nairobi, Kenya*, 5-9 October, 1987.

Hosmer, D. and S. Lemeshow. 1989. *Applied Logistic Regression.* New York: John Wiley and Sons.

Hossain, Shaikh I. 1989. "Effect of Public Programs on Family Size, Child Education and Health." *Journal of Development Economics*, No. 30.

IGSS, Guatemala. 1986. *Informe Anual de Labores, 1986*. Guatemala: Instituto Guatemalteco de Seguridad Social.

INE, Bolivia. 1989. *Bolivia Encuesta Nacional de Población y Vivienda 1988. Resultados Finales.* La Paz, Bolivia: Instituto Nacional de Estadística, UNFPA.

INE, Guatemala. 1988. *Encuesta Nacional Sociodemográfica 1986- 1987. Demografía. Total República. Volumen I.* Guatemala: Instituto Nacional de Estadística.

INE. Bolivia. Institute for Resource Development. 1990. *Encuesta Nacional de Demografía y Salud 1989*. Bolivia: INE. Institute for Resource Development. DHS.

Juárez, Fátima. 1996. "Institutions, Interventions and the Reduction of Fertility and Infant Mortality." United Nations. Population Division. *Child Survival, Health and Family Planning Programmes and Fertility*. New York: United Nations.

Ministerio de Previsión Social y Salud Pública. 1989. *Bolivia: situación de salud y sus tendencias. Cuaderno de trabajo*. Bolivia.

Ministerio de Salud Pública y Asistencia Social (MSPAS) and Instituto de Nutrición de Centroamérica y Panamá (INCAP) and Demographic and Health Surveys. 1989. *Encuesta Nacional de Salud Materno Infantil 1987*.

OPS. 1990. *Las condiciones de salud en las Américas. Vol. I*. Washington: OPS.

Potter, Joseph. 1988. "Birth Spacing and Child Survival: A Cautionary Note Regarding the Evidence from the WFS." *Population Studies*.42(3):443-450.

Preston, Samuel and M. Haines. 1991. *Fatal Years Child Mortality in Late Nineteenth-Century America*. Princeton: Princeton University Press.

Rosenzweig, Mark R. and Schultz, T. Paul. 1982. "Child Mortality and Fertility in Colombia: Individual and Community Effects." *Health Policy and Education*. 1982; 2(3/4).

Sirageldin, Ismail and Mosley, Henry W. 1988. "Health Services and Population Planning Programs: A Review of Interrelations."

Sociedad Boliviana de Salud Pública. UNICEF. OPS/OMS. 1989. *Historia y perspectivas de la salud pública en Bolivia*. Bolivia.

Sommerfelt, A. Elizabeth et al. 1991. *Maternal and Child*

Health in Bolivia: Report on the In-depth DHS Survey in Bolivia 1989. Columbia, Maryland USA: Institute for Resource Development.

United Nations. 1994. *The Health Rationale for Family Planning: Timing of Births and Child Survival.* New York: United Nations Population Division.

Warren, Charles W. et. al. 1987 "Use of Maternal-Child Health Services and Contraception in Guatemala and Panama." *Journal of Biosocial Science*. 1987 Apr; 19(2):229-43

Wilopo, Siswanto A. and Mosley, Henry W. 1996. "The Relationship of Child Survival Intervention Programs to the Practice of Contraception." United Nations. Population Division. *Child Survival, Health and Family Planning Programmes and Fertility*. New York: United Nations.

Wolowyna, Oleh and Guido Pinto Aguirre. 1990. *Sobrevivencia infantil en Bolivia*. La Paz, Bolivia: Consejo Nacional de Población (CONAPO).

Wong, Rebeca and Agarwal, Kokila. 1992 "The Common Determinants of Utilization of Child-Survival and Fertility-Control Interventions." Paper presented to the *International Population Conference: Montreal, Canada.*

TABLE 1. BOLIVIA. SELECTED CHARACTERISTICS BY REGION

	Proportion					
Department	Under 5 Mortality (q)5	With Electricity	Illiterate	Indigenous	With Radio at Home	With Piped Water in the Home
(A) Urban						
Chuquisaca	0.1082	0.90	0.13	0.02	0.54	0.65
La Paz	0.1199	0.95	0.07	0.01	0.65	0.51
Cochabamba	0.1279	0.96	0.05	0.01	0.49	0.77
Oruro	0.1471	0.93	0.03	0.00	0.41	0.85
Potosa	0.1896	0.94	0.12	0.04	0.41	0.73
Tarija	0.1021	0.83	0.10	0.00	0.76	0.86
Santa Cruz	0.1012	0.88	0.04	0.00	0.53	0.71
Beni	0.1101	0.70	0.03	0.00	0.70	0.70
Pando	0.0937	0.78	0.02	0.01	0.67	0.87
(B) Rural						
Chuquisaca	0.1690	0.13	0.53	0.29	0.17	0.01
La Paz	0.1701	0.36	0.18	0.08	0.17	0.04
Cochabamba	0.2491	0.39	0.32	0.26	0.11	0.36
Oruro	0.2053	0.34	0.13	0.04	0.15	0.14
Potosa	0.2434	0.13	0.37	0.28	0.11	0.25
Tarija	0.1466	0.23	0.30	0.00	0.19	0.28
Santa Cruz	0.1300	0.31	0.13	0.08	0.14	0.15
Beni	0.1427	0.13	0.12	0.00	0.30	0.28
Pando	0.1843	0.08	0.14	0.14	0.19	0.18

Source: INE. Bolivia. Encuesta Nacional de Población y Vivienda

TABLE 2. GUATEMALA. SELECTED CHARACTERISTICS, BY REGIONS

Region	Population	Distribution by Regions	Percentage Indigenous	Percentage with No Schooling	Households: Without Toilet	Households: With Water From River
Metropolitan	1,638,828	20.1	19.3	16.2	8.7	3.9
North	607,650	7.4	90.6	51.0	47.3	44.4
North-East	792,442	9.7	2.6	33.3	40.5	19.5
South-East	784,560	9.6	3.1	29.3	51.1	18.6
Central	885,257	10.8	33.4	28.5	21.3	2.9
North-West	1,073,529	13.2	82.3	48.2	56.6	36.3
South-west	2,203,711	27.0	58.7	34.6	38.0	12.8
Peten	176,552	2.2	19.2	28.3	47.0	37.6
Total	8,162,529	100.0	41.9	32.5	34.7	16.8

Region	Hospital Beds Per 1000 Pop.	Births Attended by Physician	Percentage Below Poverty Line	Percentage Indigent
Metropolitan	2.2	91.4	64.3	30.0
North	0.8	15.7	91.7	77.8
North-East	1.0	40.3	75.7	53.6
South-East	0.7	28.0	82.2	64.6
Central	0.7	69.6	82.0	59.1
North-West	0.4	45.0	90.6	80.7
South-west	0.7	59.5	83.4	66.9
Peten	0.9	43.4	77.3	53.6
Total	1.0	51.3		

Source: INE. Guatemala, 1989; Ministry of Health, 1991. INE. Guatemala, 1991.

TABLE 3. COEFFICIENTS AND STANDARD ERRORS OF LOGISTIC REGRESSIONS OF WOMEN'S CHARACTERISTICS ON KNOWLEDGE OF HEALTH TECHNOLOGIES. GUATEMALA 1987

Variables	Knowledge of ORT		Knowledge of Modern Contraceptive		Knowledge of Source for Modern Contraceptive	
	Coefficient	Std. Error	Coefficient	Std. Error	Coefficient	Std. Error
All Women						
urban	0.3267	0.1918	1.2136	0.2323 ++	1.3177	0.2238 ++
edprim	0.6955	0.2003 ++	0.8307	0.1926 ++	0.6002	0.2042 ++
edsec	0.8963	0.2840 ++	1.9472	0.4214 ++	2.9286	0.5072 ++
radio	-0.0323	0.1762	-0.0903	0.1872	0.2024	0.1926
message	0.3015	0.1763	0.8444	0.1850 ++	0.5683	0.1910 ++
indigen	-1.6038	0.2611 ++	-1.658	0.2203 ++	-2.0822	0.2820 ++
Intercept	-1.0275	0.2038 ++	-0.6284	0.1955 ++	-1.1216	0.2117 ++
Women with at Least One Child						
urban	0.3628	0.2136	1.1874	0.2567 ++	1.3153	0.2532 ++
edprim	0.8167	0.2147 ++	0.7686	0.2155 ++	0.5068	0.2283 +
edsec	1.188	0.3255 ++	2.1114	0.5161 ++	3.4572	0.7552 ++
radio	0.15	0.1911	-0.0613	0.2064	0.3037	0.2135
message	0.0769	0.1983	0.691	0.2076 ++	0.3731	0.2163
indigen	-1.7495	0.2707 ++	-1.6887	0.2470 ++	-2.3725	0.3309 ++
Intercept	-0.6872	0.2203 ++	-0.4885	0.2201 +	-0.9003	0.2362 ++
Women with at Least One Child						
urban	0.4114	0.218	1.2021	0.2570 ++	1.3914	0.2575 ++
edprim	0.911	0.2238 ++	0.8015	0.2183 ++	0.5634	0.2360 +
edsec	1.3437	0.3349 ++	2.1788	0.5182 ++	3.5953	0.7592 ++
radio	0.1321	0.1967	-0.0808	0.2083	0.2811	0.2188
message	0.1292	0.2036	0.7213	0.2094 ++	0.4451	0.2219 +
indigen	-1.7462	0.2763 ++	-1.6805	0.2492 ++	-2.4046	0.3384 ++
CEB	0.7071	0.1362 ++	0.3598	0.1419 +	0.6527	0.1497 ++
Intercept	-1.9203	0.3331 ++	-1.0971	0.3281 ++	-2.0396	0.3626

+ significant at .05 level
++ significant at .01 level
Source: Demographic Health Survey, Guatemala 1987

TABLE 4. COEFFICIENTS AND STANDARD ERRORS OF LOGISTIC REGRESSIONS OF WOMEN'S CHARACTERISTICS ON KNOWLEDGE OF HEALTH TECHNOLOGIES. BOLIVIA 1989

Variables	Knowledge of ORT		Knowledge of Modern Contraceptive		Knowledge of Source for Modern Contraceptive	
	Coefficient	Std. Error	Coefficient	Std. Error	Coefficient	Std. Error
All Women						
urban	0.1608	0.1617	0.6013	0.1840 ++	0.3378	0.1675 +
edprim	1.2836	0.4202 ++	0.9387	0.6373	1.6864	0.4139 ++
edsec	1.8423	0.4371 ++	2.415	0.6402 ++	2.595	0.4318 ++
radio	0.4132	0.1908 +	0.0482	0.2283	0.0256	0.1905
message	0.2112	0.1555	0.3199	0.1699	0.1206	0.1708
indigen	-0.3214	0.2207	-1.174	0.3389 ++	-1.2319	0.2134 ++
Intercept	-2.4555	0.4572 ++	-2.9033	0.6660 ++	-1.6574	0.4452 ++
Women with at Least One Child						
urban	0.1767	0.1748	0.7454	0.2031 ++	0.4687	0.1830 +
edprim	1.3469	0.4249 ++	2.5702	1.4594	1.8875	0.4935 ++
edsec	2.0984	0.4468 ++	3.9661	1.4618 ++	2.7065	0.5128 ++
radio	0.4648	0.2014 +	0.1077	0.2531	-0.047	0.2138
message	0.3339	0.1723	0.2616	0.188	0.1153	0.1916
indigen	-0.2608	0.2346	-1.2575	0.4020 ++	-1.3458	0.2415 ++
Intercept	-2.339	0.4710 ++	-4.5688	1.4760 ++	-1.8065	0.5265 ++
Women with at Least One Child						
urban	0.2107	0.1775	0.7607	0.2039 ++	0.4729	0.1832 ++
edprim	1.3967	0.4304 ++	2.5719	1.4597	1.8883	0.4936 ++
edsec	2.2034	0.4541 ++	3.9845	1.4623 ++	2.7126	0.5130 ++
radio	0.5269	0.2051 ++	0.1235	0.2536	-0.0367	0.2142
message	0.3523	0.1749 +	0.2639	0.1884	0.1175	0.1917
indigen	-0.2579	0.2378	-1.2497	0.4023 ++	-1.3442	0.2415 ++
CEB	0.5532	0.1223 ++	0.1821	0.1368	0.0927	0.1286
Intercept	-3.3396	0.5334 ++	-4.884	1.4964 ++	-1.9632	0.5704 ++

+ significant at .05 level
++ significant at .01 level
Source Demographic and Health Survey Bolivia 1989

TABLE 5. COEFFICIENTS AND STANDARD ERRORS OF LOGISTIC REGRESSION OF HEALTH BEHAVIOR ON KNOWLEDGE OF HEALTH TECHNOLOGIES. GUATEMALA 1987.

Variables	Knowledge of ORT		Knowledge of Modern Contraceptive		Knowledge of Source for Modern Contraceptive	
	Coefficient	Std. Error	Coefficient	Std. Error	Coefficient	Std. Error
All Women						
ttox	1.0592	0.2200 ++	0.0668	0.2266	0.5191	0.2274 +
prenat	1.5108	0.1686 ++	2.0865	0.1804 ++	1.6127	0.1737 ++
bfeeding	0.7312	0.2300 ++	-1.0929	0.2098 ++	-0.8696	0.1971 ++
Intercept	-1.9284	0.1871 ++	-0.3470	0.1409 +	0.0712	0.1390
Women with at Least One Child						
ttox	0.8918	0.2145 ++	0.0217	0.2276	0.4933	0.2289 +
prenat	1.1295	0.1712 ++	2.0179	0.1859 ++	1.5711	0.1791 ++
bfeeding	-0.6395	0.2896 +	-1.5030	0.3216 ++	-1.1167	0.3153 ++
Intercept	-0.4988	0.2583	0.0587	0.2765	0.3120	0.2758
Women with at Least One Child						
ttox	0.8318	0.2179 ++	-0.0149	0.2296	0.4880	0.2297 +
prenat	1.1730	0.1741 ++	2.0399	0.1874 ++	1.5730	0.1792 ++
bfeeding	-0.3457	0.3051	-1.3423	0.3314 ++	-1.0883	0.3295 ++
CEB	0.4693	0.1277 ++	0.2436	0.1348	0.0373	0.1308
Intercept	-1.4828	0.3775 ++	-0.4588	0.3961	0.2307	0.3955

\+ Significant at .05 level
++ Significant at .01 level
Source: Demographic Health Survey, Guatemala 1987

TABLE 6. COEFFICIENTS AND STANDARD ERRORS OF LOGISTIC REGRESSION OF HEALTH BEHAVIOR ON KNOWLEDGE OF HEALTH TECHNOLOGIES. BOLIVIA 1989.

Variables	Knowledge of ORT		Knowledge of Modern Contraceptive		Knowledge of Source for Modern Contraceptive	
	Coefficient	Std. Error	Coefficient	Std. Error	Coefficient	Std. Error
All Women						
ttox	0.2862	0.1725	-0.3138	0.1827	0.5299	0.1827 ++
prenat	1.7351	0.1659 ++	1.8682	0.1893 ++	1.4801	0.1602 ++
bfeeding	0.7451	0.2194 ++	-1.4312	0.2199 ++	-1.3520	0.1985 ++
Intercept	-2.0867	0.1854 ++	-0.8721	0.1452 ++	0.2983	0.1361 +
Women with at Least One Child						
ttox	0.1476	0.1687	-0.2789	0.1826	0.5397	0.1827 ++
prenat	1.3237	0.1661 ++	2.0174	0.2183 ++	1.4991	0.1646 ++
bfeeding	-0.4208	0.2714	-1.1463	0.2881 ++	-1.2464	0.3088 ++
Intercept	-0.7544	0.2557 ++	-1.2472	0.2909 ++	0.1918	0.2762
Women with at Least One Child						
ttox	0.1276	0.1698	-0.2789	0.1826	0.5510	0.1833 ++
prenat	1.4471	0.1722 ++	2.0167	0.2195 ++	1.4746	0.1659 ++
bfeeding	-0.0778	0.2851	-1.1485	0.2979 ++	-1.3898	0.3421 ++
CEB	0.4985	0.1246 ++	-0.0038	0.1321	-0.1447	0.1312
Intercept	-1.8592	0.3791 ++	-1.2392	0.4017 ++	0.5409	0.4258

\+ Significant at .05 level
++ Significant at .01 level
Source Demographic and Health Survey Bolivia 1989

TABLE 7. COEFFICIENTS AND STANDARD ERRORS OF LOGISTIC REGRESSION OF CONTRACEPTIVE USE ON KNOWLEDGE OF ORT

Variable	Guatemala		Bolivia	
	Coefficient	Std. Error	Coefficient	Std. Error
before	-2.1874	0.4184 ++	-0.4784	0.2325 +
spacing	-0.8287	0.4629	-0.5240	0.2474 +
Ever Use	2.7542	0.4338 ++	1.5778	0.2384 ++
Intercept	-0.9944	0.0911 ++	-0.9424	.0920 ++
Women with at Least One Child				
before	-0.2009	1.1243	0.2977	0.2728
spacing	1.3821	0.7909	-0.4517	0.2620
Ever Use	3.0738	0.5491 ++	1.2318	0.2477 ++
Intercept	-0.8019	0.0989 ++	-0.5883	0.0966 ++
before	-1.1889	0.4801 +	0.4345	0.2774
spacing	-0.3877	0.4570	-0.3718	0.2650
Ever Use	2.0141	0.4238 ++	1.1730	0.2498 ++
CEB	0.4313	0.1231 ++	0.4147	0.1157 ++
Intercept	-1.3206	0.2200 ++	-1.2412	0.2085 ++

+ Significant at .05 level
++ Significant at .01 level
Source: Demographic Health Survey Guatemala, 1987 Demographic Health Survey Bolivia, 1989

TABLE 8. COEFFICIENTS AND STANDARD ERRORS OF LOGISTIC REGRESSION PREDICTING KNOWLEDGE OF ORT GUATEMALA, 1987

	Model 1		Model 2		Model 3		Model 4	
	Coeff.	Std. Error	Coeff.	Std. Error.	Coeff.	Std. Error	Coeff.	Std. Error
edprim	0.889	0.231 ++	0.942	0.229 ++	0.904	0.232 ++	0.871	0.233 ++
edsec	1.480	0.346 ++	1.741	0.333 ++	1.163	0.328 ++	1.451	0.346 ++
indigen	-1.229	0.243 ++	-1.344	0.240 ++	-1.249	0.244 ++	-1.129	0.251 ++
CEB	0.971	0.124 ++	1.034	0.123 ++	1.036	0.123 ++	1.000	0.124 ++
ttox	0.953	0.245 ++	0.879	0.242 ++	0.915	0.243 ++	0.922	0.246 ++
prenat	0.607	0.206 ++	0.774	0.199 ++	0.697	0.201 ++	0.648	0.205 ++
before	-1.952	0.489 ++	-1.416	0.468 ++			-1.501	0.463 ++
Ever Use	0.944	0.264 ++			0.565	0.238 +		
Intercept	-2.847	0.293 ++	-2.839	0.290 ++	-2.943	0.293 ++	-3.071	0.307 ++

+ Significant at .05 level
++ Significant at .01 level
Source: Demographic Health Survey Guatemala, 1987

TABLE 9. COEFFICIENTS AND STANDARD ERRORS OF LOGISTIC REGRESSION PREDICTING KNOWLEDGE OF ORT. BOLIVIA 1989

Variable	Model 1		Model 2		Model 3	
	Coefficient	Std. Error	Coefficient	Std. Error	Coefficient	Std. Error
edprim	1.636	0.436 ++	1.203	0.443 ++	1.207	0.442 ++
edsec	2.553	0.445 ++	1.704	0.458 ++	1.776	0.454 ++
radio	0.604	0.206 ++	0.567	0.212 ++	0.600	0.210 ++
message	0.372	0.168 +	0.235	0.176		
CEB	1.111	0.104 ++	0.975	0.113 ++	0.966	0.113 ++
prenat			1.338	0.176 ++	1.359	0.175 ++
Ever Use			0.425	0.172 +	0.431	0.172 +
Intercept	-4.635	0.487 ++	-4.717	0.502 ++	-4.685	0.500 ++

Variable	Urban Area		Rural Area	
	Coefficient	Std. Error	Coefficient	Std. Error
edprim	0.333	0.536	2.413	1.073 +
edsec	0.854	0.536	3.158	1.101 ++
radio	0.094	0.261	1.197	0.385 ++
CEB	1.069	0.145 ++	0.884	0.191 ++
prenat	1.207	0.222 ++	1.370	0.300 ++
Ever Use	0.425	0.204 +	0.421	0.327
Intercept	-3.396	0.605 ++	-6.283	1.168 ++

+ Significant at .05 level
++ Significant at .01 level
Source: Demographic Health Survey Bolivia, 1989

TABLE 10. PERCENTAGE OF WOMEN WITH SPECIFIC KNOWLEDGE AND USE OF HEALTH SERVICES BY DISTANCE TO HEALTH CENTER WITH FAMILY PLANNING SERVICE

	KNOWS ORT	KNOW MOD	KNOW SOUR	PRENAT	EVER USE	ASTDEL	TTOX
0 kms	26%	54	67	25	29	22	10
N	1619	1458	1619	1458	1619	1458	1458
1-5 kms	23%	40	57	21	19	16	11
N	1468	1285	1468	1285	1468	1285	1285
More 5 kms	21%	27	46	18	12	14	10
N	999	864	999	864	999	864	864
Missing	21%	74	81	25	40	28	7
N	1074	1001	1074	1001	1074	1001	1001

Source: Demographic and Health Survey, Guatemala 1987

APPENDIX 1

Variable	Name Definition
Urban	Place of residence is an urban area. Variable is coded 1 for urban areas and 0 for rural areas.
Education	
edprim	Woman has at least one year of primary education.
edsec	Woman has at least one year of secondary education.
	Reference category is No Education
radio	Whether the woman listens to the radio (yes=1, no=0).
message	Whether the woman has ever listened to the family planning message (yes=1, no=0).
indigen	For Guatemala, whether the woman was identified as indigenous or "Ladina" (if indigenous indigen=1). For Bolivia, indigenous women are those who said the predominant language used in the household is an indigenous one or whether she answered a questionnaire not in Spanish.
ttox	Whether the woman received a tetanus toxoid shot in any of the pregnancies (yes=1, no=0).
prenat	Whether the woman received prenatal care in any of the pregnancies (yes=1, no=0).
astdel	Whether the woman received assistance at delivery by medical personnel in any of the pregnancies (yes=1, no=0).
bfeeding	Average proportion of time that each woman breastfed her children (see text for a full explanation of this variable).
CEB	Total children ever born as coded in the DHS standard recode files.
before	Whether the woman used contraception before the first birth (yes=1, no=0).

spacing	Whether the woman used contraception for spacing purposes. These are women who used contraception between intended pregnancies.
Ever use	Ever use of any method as coded in the DHS standard recode files.
knowsors	Whether the woman knows about Oral Rehydration packets (yes=1, no=0).
knowmod	Whether the woman knows a modern contraceptive method spontaneously (yes=1, no=0).
knowsour	Whether the woman knows a source for a modern contraceptive method (yes=1, no=0).

Chapter Fifteen

REGIONAL DIFFERENCES IN FAMILY SIZE PREFERENCES IN COSTA RICA AND THEIR IMPLICATIONS FOR TRANSITION THEORY

ALBERT I. HERMALIN, ANN P. RILEY,
AND LUIS ROSERO-BIXBY

This paper examines the role of region in shaping family size preferences among rural Costa Rican women. Trends in preference by region are traced across several surveys and contrasted with trends in regional differentials in actual family size. A multilevel analysis is then carried out based on the 1981 Contraceptive Prevalence Survey in which two measures of desired family size are regressed against individual, community, and regional variables. The strong effect of region on preferences is contrasted with its role as a determinant of actual family size and of contraceptive use, and the implications of the findings for competing theories about the demographic transition are discussed in some detail.

INTRODUCTION

The fertility transition in Costa Rica shows a number of distinct stages. The total fertility rate (TFR) fell from 7.7 to 5.5 between 1960 and 1968, the year a national family planning program was launched; and then declined more rapidly to 3.7 in 1976 (United Nations, 1985). Between 1976 and 1986, however, there was little further change as the TFR fluctuated around 3.7 births, and the contraceptive prevalence rate among married women fluctuated between 65 and 70 percent (Asociación Demográfica Costarricense, 1987). Since 1986, the fertility transition appears to have resumed as TFR has declined to 3.2 births in 1993 and the contraceptive prevalence rate has increased to 75 percent (Caja Costarricense de Seguro Social, 1994).

An analysis of the desired levels of fertility over this period helps explain the fertility trends. In fertility surveys conducted from the 1960s to 1986, Costa Rican women younger than 35 years have given average desired family sizes (ADFS) ranging between 3.1 and 3.9 children in urban areas and between 4.1 and 4.6 in rural areas (Table 1). These strikingly stable figures across quite diverse surveys support the claims that the period of rapid fertility decline in Costa Rica was a process of actual family size adjusting to meet desired family size, and that a stall occurred between 1976 and 1986 (Gendell, 1985; Bongaarts, 1986). Since the change in the ADFS during the fertility transition was minimal, the force that drove the fertility decline was a rapid diffusion of contraceptive use. In rural areas, for example, the use of contraceptives dramatically increased from 24% to 64% between 1969 and 1976 (Table 1). In contrast, the absence of a continued decline between 1976 and 1986 can be largely attributed to the persistent desire of Costa Rican women to have three or four children. During this stage, access to contraceptive methods was not a critical factor (Hermalin et al., 1986).

This equilibrium state between TFR and ADFS appears to have ended after 1986 and a second fertility decline appears underway. As Table 1 indicates, between 1986 and 1993 ADFS declined from 3.5 to 3.1 in urban areas, and from 4.8 to 3.6 in rural areas, and as noted, the TFR has declined in each sector as well. A perhaps more sensitive barometer of family size preferences—the proportion of respondents who want less than three children—shows an increase from 28 percent to 34 percent between the 1986 and 1993 surveys, with 40 percent of women under age 35 expressing this preference at the latter date. (Caja Costarricense de Seguro Social, 1994, Tables 11.4 and 11.5).

Understanding the determinants of fertility preferences is thus crucial to understanding the moderately high levels of fertility prevailing in Costa Rica and to forecast the possibility of further declines.

This paper also seeks to explore some of the larger theoretical issues associated with fertility change by examining the relative importance of region on different facets of reproductive behavior. The European fertility project established the importance of language, religion, and region on marriage patterns and marital fertility levels, net of education and other indicators of development (Coale and Treadway, 1986; Sharlin, 1986; Knodel and Van de Walle, 1986). The extent to which these differentials reflected differences in fertility preferences or levels of fertility regulation is difficult to determine from the historical record. For currently developing countries, the WFS has demonstrated substantial regional differences, as well as among linguistic and religious groups, in fertility and contraceptive use in a number of countries (see summary by Cleland, 1985, pp. 242-243). Less is known about the extent of regional differences on family size preferences. Lightbourne (1985, p. 194) states that fertility preferences vary relatively little by social group compared to fertility and contraception, though he notes places with ethnic and religious differences on preferences and a rural-urban differential in sub-Saharan Africa. Cleland maintains that there is little evidence from surveys over time of a decline in fertility preferences prior to an actual decline in fertility (1985, p. 244). Pritchett (1994) on the other hand views desired family size as the driving force of fertility change and questions whether there is an independent effect from the provision of family planning services through programs or other means.

As part of the analysis of the determinants of fertility preferences, we will be examining the role of regional differences on this variable and comparing it with the role of region on measures of actual family size and contraceptive use. The differential effects across these measures, combined with over-time trends in preferences by region, help clarify the nature of the fertility transition ongoing in Costa Rica. Regional differences in preferred family size may reflect variation in cultural norms and family values, as well as predict further trends in fertility.

This paper studies desired family size in rural and semi-urban areas (towns with less than 20,000 inhabitants) only during the period from 1976 to 1986. Almost half of the Costa Rican population lives in the countryside, and the nation's economy depends heavily on export crops such as coffee and bananas. Despite economic difficulties, the living standards of campesinos in Costa Rica are remarkably high for a developing country. The infant mortality rate, for example, was 17 per one thousand births in rural areas in 1981-84, denoting a level of health superior to that existing in the capital city, where this rate was 25 (Asociación Demográfica Costarricense, 1987: Table 8.2). Perhaps the major geographical axis of differentiation is the one between the Central Valley and lowlands. The Central Valley comprises more developed areas, but at the same time, its campesinos share more traditional values inherited from Spanish colonizers. In contrast, in the coastal areas the level of socioeconomic development is lower and there are important African and Indian cultural influences due to immigration from the Caribbean islands and neighboring countries. In the Central Valley, the small family farm is an important unit of production, whereas on the coasts, larger agricultural units employing farm labor are dominant. With regard to population programs, family planning services are provided as part of health services, which have excellent coverage (Mata and Rosero-Bixby, 1988). As in most of the Latin American countries, the Costa Rican government has not strongly endorsed the idea of population control, especially after the rapid fertility decline occurred. Rather, the provision of family planning is based on health and human-rights considerations.

The remainder of the paper is organized as follows: the next section discusses the concept of preferences and its measurement and describes the model we will be using; in Section 3, we review some prior research on family size preferences and develop the measures to be used in this analysis; The fourth section presents some descriptive data on preferences and related characteristics from the various provinces of Costa Rica, while section 5 gives the multivariate results; a discussion of the results and their implications is given in section 6.

THE CONCEPT OF PREFERENCE AND ITS MEASUREMENT

The concept of fertility preferences has come to play a pivotal role in theories and analyses of reproductive behavior. In general terms, it is often viewed as playing an intervening role, translating characteristics of the couple and their environment into their demand for children and thereby exerting considerable influence (along with actual family size or supply of children) on the desire for additional childbearing and the current practice of contraception or other means of fertility regulation (Bulatao and Lee, 1983; Hermalin, 1983).

Attempts to measure fertility preferences have been a prominent element in most KAP surveys, the World Fertility Survey, the Contraceptive Prevalence Surveys and most recently the Demographic and Health Surveys. Questionnaire wording and placement have varied across surveys and sometimes across countries within a given comparative project. A useful review of the WFS experience on this topic is given by Lightbourne (1985), who sets out the questions used, discusses issues of reliability, presents comparative data, and investigates the various uses of the data. These uses range from estimating the fertility level implicated by the stated preferences, to understanding the social and economic forces that shape preferences, to studying changing preferences over time.

Our focus in this paper is primarily the second—examining the individual, community, and program characteristics that influence measures of desired family size, with an emphasis on persistent regional differences. Since we will examine these patterns by age and to a certain extent across surveys, we also provide some insights into the changing pattern of preferences.

Fertility preferences have been modeled and measured in a number of different ways. A key conceptual question is whether couples make a single decision about their desired fertility at the time of marriage and stick to it with little variation, or whether they decide on each child one by one, taking into account past childbearing experiences and current conditions. Various intermediate perspectives between the single and sequential decision-making models are also possible (see, for example, Bulatao and Fawcett, 1983, pp. 2-3).

Each conceptual model points to a different line of questions for measuring fertility preferences. A measure of demand for total number of children, often obtained by a question on total number of children preferred if one could start over, would reflect fertility intentions in the single decision framework. On the other hand, demand for the next child, often obtained by a question about whether more children are desired (or the number of additional children desired), most closely captures the sequential decision perspective. Along with these two questions, additional preference-related information is sometimes collected on whether the last birth was wanted (with the occasional distinction of whether the last birth was wanted at all, or at the time it occurred); and for those wanting more children, when the next birth is desired.

At one level, there are "algebraic" identities among the various measures. The difference between ideal and actual family size should indicate whether another child is desired, and hence coincide with the direct question on desire for more children. Likewise, a measure of total number of children desired can be constructed from the number of living children and the number of additional children desired. It is of course an empirical question whether these alternate derivations will be identical, and comparisons across countries show wide variation (see, for example, Lightbourne, 1985, Table 8.3 for a WFS cross-country comparison of proportions wanting no more children obtained from the direct question and the contrast between desired and actual family size).

Despite their interrelationships, the measures of "ideal" family size and the desire for additional children are, in Bulatao and Fawcett's (1983) phrase, "phenomenologically distinct," and are often treated separately (see also, McClelland, 1983 for a discussion of the relative merits of the two types of questions as measures of demand). The conceptual framework guiding this research maintains this distinction and is illustrated in Figure 1. The framework is an elaboration of the National Academy of Science model (see Bulatao and Lee, 1983; Hermalin, 1983) which views exogenous social structural and individual characteristics as determining the demand for children and the potential supply of children. These in turn determine the level of motivation to control fertility, which together with the costs of contraception determine whether a means of fertility regulation is currently used. Figure 1 spells out in more detail the place of preferred family size and the desire for additional children within this framework and their relationship to other factors in the reproductive process. The figure is meant to be suggestive of the process, rather than exhaustive. For example, there may be other influences on some of the dependent variables, and it is understood that there will be measurement error associated with each.

The model attempts to trace a woman's reproductive span from the age of menarche or the earliest marriageable age, distinguishing in particular the period just prior to her last birth and the subsequent period. A woman's age at marriage is viewed as determined by her and her family's socioeconomic characteristics as she approaches marriageable age, as well as the community's environment which includes the cultural setting as well as the socioeconomic and demographic structure. Typically, program characteristics do not play a strong role in determining age at marriage. In the first period, emphasis is given to the factors that shape preferred family size and the way that preference, together with other factors, affects the nature and level of the proximate variables that will determine the quantity and pace of childbearing. In this representation, preferred family size is viewed as established shortly after marriage and influenced by the characteristics of the marriage and by a set of intervening preference variables. These intervening variables which shape a woman's family size preference can take many forms and a few are suggested below the figure. They will be reflective of individual, program, or community characteristics. For example, we expect a woman's preference not only to reflect her own values about childbearing as influenced say, by her education and work experience, but also to be influenced by a community or ethnic group's norms about family size or by information about desirable family size from a family planning program.

It is also possible to view preferred family size as undergoing change as a woman ages in response to a couple's childbearing experience, their changing socioeconomic conditions, and changes in their environment. The latter would include social changes occurring in their community, as well as changes in the degree of contact with a family planning program and the advent of new outlets and services. In this case one would need to extend the figure over several segments, allowing for the influence of past childbearing as well as the changing individual and environmental factors. In either case, the centrality of preferred family size as a key intervening variable emerges clearly. It is affected by a wide range of individual and structural influences on the level of fertility, and in turn it helps determine the level and nature of the proximate variables that shape the fertility outcome. According to Figure 1, whether a woman at the time of observation desires to have additional children and the number more she desires are largely determined by her preferred family size and her actual family size. In accord with the National Academy framework, we also view the desire for more children, the timing of any additional children wanted, and the costs of contraception as determining whether the couple is currently practicing some form of fertility regulation. Costs are multidimensional, reflecting monetary, subjective, and community factors and accordingly, as Figure 1 reflects, can be influenced by many of the prior variables.

The emphasis in this paper is on exploratory analysis of preferred family size, though as we describe below we utilize information on desire for additional children to measure this concept. As noted above, and reflected in Table 1, indicators of desired family size in rural areas remained high over a long period. Correspondingly, total fertility rates ceased to fall once the spread of contraception brought actual fertility into close alignment with desired fertility. For this reason, identification of individual, program, or community factors associated with variation in preferred family size can provide important clues as to future directions of fertility in Costa Rica and may point to useful policy interventions.

Our strategy is as follows: since many of the variables listed as intervening preference variables are unmeasured in our data set, we will utilize the exogenous individual, program, and community characteristics as well as several intervening demographic variables. For the community variables, we use a measure of modernity which is scaled from 0 to 15, depending on the presence or absence in the community of schools, stores, health facilities, factories, piped water, electricity, garbage collection, telephone service, and several other indicators. In addition, we introduce a set of dummy variables to represent the seven provinces of Costa Rica to examine the potential that regional characteristics not captured by modernity and the other measured variables account for preferred family size differentials. We will also compare the level of regional differentials in preferred family size with regional differences in actual family size and contraceptive use, employing similar multilevel specifications.

To the extent that regional differences in preferred family size persist in the multivariate analysis, the next stage of research will be to identify the theoretically relevant characteristics of each province that might account for such differences and test their influences by substituting their values for the regional dummies. One advantage of the multilevel strategy is that we can assemble data for the appropriate areal level after the fact and combine it with the micro data so long as each respondent can be uniquely identified with a specific community or area (see Hermalin, 1986). In the next section we briefly review some prior research on desired family size in Costa Rica and establish the measures we will be using. Then after presenting some descriptive data about these measures and other characteristics of the provinces, we turn to the multivariate analysis.

PREVIOUS RESEARCH ON PREFERRED FAMILY SIZE AND MEASURES TO BE EMPLOYED

The meaning, reliability, and level of family size preferences in Costa Rica have received a significant amount of attention. In the 1960s, San José and rural Costa Rica were part of a comparative Latin American fertility project. Stycos (1984) summarizes the nature of attitudes toward family size from these studies as follows:

> Viewed in isolation, the degree of attitude change in Costa Rica seems unusual; but viewed in a comparative context, Costa Rica is hardly unique. In the Latin American region generally there is certainly nothing unusual about vagueness, ambivalence or inconsistency with respect to fertility attitudes.... In seven metropolitan cities studied in the early 1960s, from 28 to 55 percent of the women said they had never thought about the number of children they wanted, and Costa Rica was in the middle of the

> range. In the rural surveys conducted in four Latin American countries in the late 1960s the proportions who had not thought about preferred family size ranged from one-half to two-thirds; from 31 to 44 percent failed to give a numerical response to the questions of preferred size or additional numbers wanted; and between one-fifth and one-third were unable or unwilling to choose between a 'large' and a 'small' family. (Stycos, 1984, p. 37).

Similarly, Lightbourne's (1985) review of World Fertility Survey experience on preferences generally shows a much larger discrepancy between those reporting not wanting more children and the measure found by contrasting actual and preferred family size for Latin America than for other regions (Table 8.3).

Important insights into the reliability of family size preferences were obtained from a reinterview about 18 months later of a sizeable proportion of the women interviewed for the Costa Rican WFS in 1976. About three-quarters of the 2622 women aged 20-49 and in a marital union in 1976 were reinterviewed (Stycos, 1984). Overall, 74 percent of the women gave identical responses on wanting more children; 44 percent gave the identical response on preferred number of children, while another 29 percent differed by one child (Stycos, 1984, p. 8). Though on one hand these levels of reliability may indicate confirmation of the instability of attitude described above; on the other hand they are quite in accord with levels of reliability on these items carried out in other countries as part of the WFS project, often with much shorter intervals between test and retest (Stycos, 1984, pp. 37-38).

At the same time, the analysis provided by Stycos shows a considerable amount of slippage of attitudes. While there was generally good consistency between the preferred number and the desire for more children, it was still the case, for example, that 30 percent of the nonsterilized women under 45 who wanted no more gave a preferred number that was in excess of their actual number. Changes in attitudes were highly associated with these discrepancies. As illustration, of those who had less than their preferred number at the first interview but said they wanted no more, 50 percent switched to wanting more at the second interview. Similarly, 82 percent of the women who had more than or the same as their preferred number but said they wanted more children at the first interview, switched to wanting no more at the second interview (Stycos, 1984, Table 15).

The patterns by age revealed that of the younger women (20-29) those who had less than their preferred number rarely changed response on desire for more children. The large majority of younger women were in this category. Among the smaller proportion who had more than or the same as their preferred number, about half changed response on desire for more children, and 90 percent of those changes were to wanting no more children. Among the women over 30, the highest proportion of changed response was among those who had not reached their preferred number, and most of the change was from "wanting more" at the first interview to "wanting no more" at the second interview (Stycos, 1984, Table 28).

The reasons for the inconsistencies in preferences noted in Costa Rica and some other Latin American countries are not well understood. Some respondents may view the questions on wanting more children as referring to the near term rather than an indefinite future, and answer accordingly. Alternately, the differences may be more in respondents' understanding of the hypothetical question of "ideal" number of children if they were starting over again, and they may answer in terms of a different set of conditions than those they experienced. And, of course, both of these forces may be operating.

The measures we developed for investigating family size preference in 1980 are guided both by the prior research on reliability and by the questions utilized in the 1981 Contraceptive Prevalence Survey. In this study all non-sterilized women were asked if they wanted to have any additional children. Sterilized women were assumed to want no additional births. Both the sterilized and those who wanted no more children were asked, "If you were able to choose, how many children would you have?" (In the WFS, this question was phrased as: If you were able to choose exactly the number of children you would like to have in your entire life, how many children would you have? (Dirección General de Estadística y Census, 1978).) Women who wanted more children were asked when they wanted the next birth and the number more they wanted. All women were asked whether the last birth was wanted; and more specifically, whether unwanted pregnancies were timing failures or number failures.

The fact that women who wanted more children were not asked the hypothetical or "ideal" question about preferred size places some constraints on the measures that can be developed. It is possible of course to study who wants more and who wishes to stop at various ages or parities and these analyses will be reported separately. Given our focus here on preferred family size two measures are possible:

1) For women who want more, add the number more wanted to the number of living children; for those who want no more, use the number given in response to the hypothetical question stated above. We call this measure of preference "DFSA."

2) Women who want more are treated as in measure (l): the number more wanted is added to the number of living children. For those who want no more, we infer their preferred number by taking the number of living children and subtracting one if the last birth was not wanted. For this subgroup then, their preferred number is constrained to be equal to or one less than their actual family size. This second measure is called "DFSB."

In the analysis to follow we make use of both measures. DFSB has the general advantage of not mixing an "ideal" number for one group, which may incorporate desired changes in marital timing and social and economic constraints, with the actual experience and prospects of the group who still want more children. For the older women, however, the advantage lies with the first measure, DFSA. A high proportion will have completed their childbearing and DFSB will constrain their preferred number to lie within one of their actual, which limits it as an independent measure of preference. DFSA among the older women may be more subject to rationalization, but it is difficult to obtain preferences of older women that are not contaminated by rationalization to some degree (Pullum, 1983). An additional benefit is that DFSB provides the potential for reducing the number of non-numeric responses, since values for subjects who respond with, "up to God," "I don't know," etc., may be imputed from actual family size. We do not take advantage of this feature of DFSB since any comparison between DFSA and DFSB would be contaminated by differences in the sample populations. For this reason, and because the proportion of non-numeric responses in the survey is low (12%), we exclude them from all analyses.

In the next section we present trends in each preference measure by province, along with other regional characteristics.

PROVINCIAL TRENDS AND DIFFERENTIALS IN FAMILY SIZE PREFERENCES AND OTHER CHARACTERISTICS

We noted earlier that a primary strategy of this analysis would be to examine the degree of provincial difference in family size preferences as a first approximation to an array of intervening variables not directly measured (see Figure 1). Persistent regional differences in fertility have long been noted in demographic research, but much less is known about areal differences in family size preferences.

This section reviews regional differences from three perspectives. First we look broadly at provincial differences in demographic, socioeconomic, and family planning program characteristics. We then focus on the rural portions of each province and examine desired family size patterns in some detail and lastly we use the 1981 Contraceptive Prevalence Survey (Rosero, 1981) to describe further the characteristics of each province in terms of the covariates to be used in the multivariate analysis.

Map 1 shows that Costa Rica is divided into seven provinces. Four of them—San José, Alajuela, Cartago, and Heredia—are largely, but not exclusively, in the central plateau and radiate in pie-shape wedges from metropolitan San José. The other three—Guanacaste, Puntarenas, and Limon—are in the lowlands—Limon in the East, Puntarenas in the South and West, and Guanacaste in the Northwest. Despite the high level of cultural, social, and economic homogeneity of Costa Rica, there have been long-standing differences across regions. Stycos (1978) reviews some of the historical forces and presents data for the 1960s which show the three low-land provinces with distinctively high fertility, infant mortality, proportion of out-of-wedlock births, proportion of births at home, and much lower population density (Stycos, 1978, Table 9; data refer to both urban and rural portions of each province). In the 1960s and early 1970s these provinces were also distinctly lower than the others in literacy and availability of electricity, but by the early 1980s, the differentials had narrowed considerably (Dirección General de Estadística y Census, 1963; 1973; 1983). The provinces are also subject to considerable internal migration. In the central valley, San José and Heredia showed net in-migration between 1968 and 1973 while Alajuela and Cartago experienced net outflows; among the lowland provinces, Guanacaste experienced very high net out-migration in this period, while Limon showed strong net in-migration, and Puntarenas was very little affected by migration on balance (Universidad de Costa Rica, 1976, Tables 48, 49).

A national family planning program was initiated in 1968, and data on the professional hours allocated to family planning services each year through governmental outlets is available.

These inputs expressed as yearly hours per married women aged 15-44 are shown below for each province for two periods between 1968 and 1981:

YEARLY PROFESSIONAL HOURS ALLOCATED TO FAMILY PLANNING PER MARRIED WOMEN, 15-44, BY PROVINCE, 1968-1981

	1968-75	1975-81	Total 1968-81	% Change 1968-75 to 1975-81
San José	1.29	1.30	2.59	.5
Alajuela	1.16	1.36	2.52	16.8
Cartago	.86	.73	1.59	-14.3
Heredia	.98	.94	1.92	-4.0
Guanacaste	1.32	1.36	2.68	3.4
Puntarenas	.71	.95	1.67	34.0
Limon	.54	.87	1.41	59.7

In the first seven years of the program, Guanacaste was an early target of inputs and along with San José and Alajuela received the most services. In the period from 1975-81, the level of services was maintained in these three provinces, while they were substantially increased in Puntarenas and Limon, which had the lowest inputs in the first seven years. As a result over the whole period, 1968-81, San Juan, Alajuela, and Guanacaste emerge with the most input of services under this measure, while the other four provinces resemble each other at a lower level of inputs.

Table 2 moves from this background to present the two measures of desired family size and actual family size by age for the rural portions of each province.

The data are presented for three points in time: the 1976 World Fertility Survey, the 1981 Contraceptive Prevalence Survey, and the 1986 Contraceptive Prevalence Survey. This permits an examination both of trends and of stability in provincial differentials since sampling variation may give rise to considerable fluctuation (see the notes to Table 2 for a discussion of standard errors). In addition to presenting the provincial averages, Table 2 also presents the provincial rankings from high to low, for DFSB and actual family size. To anticipate, we present below in Table 7 the ranking of the provinces on DFSA, including a ranking after adjusting for a number of other factors. Accordingly, we emphasize here the provincial difference in actual family size and the preferences of younger women since these fluctuate less by the measure employed.

The provincial data for actual family size among older women shows a continuation of the trend reported for the 1960s, with the three coastal provinces recording the highest levels in 1976 and 1981, and Puntarenas and Limon generally showing high levels among the younger women as well. Guanacaste, however, shows a distinct change over time. By 1986, actual family size there among older women ranks fifth among the provinces; for younger women, it has moved from rank five in 1976 to the lowest level among the provinces in 1986. This movement in actual family size seems in accord with its rank on desired family size which is consistently very low for younger women and quite low, relatively, for older women. It is intriguing to conjecture whether the early attention given to this province by the family planning program played a role in this pattern of change in preferences, which is quite distinct from the other coastal provinces despite their similar socioeconomic levels. Analyzing the effect of the program on preferences however, will require more detailed data at both the micro and macro levels than is now available.

Among the younger rural women, San José, Cartago, and Limon generally display higher preferences (see DFSB), with Limon moving to a more intermediate position by 1986. Guanacaste consistently displays the lowest relative preference, while Alajuela, Heredia, and Puntarenas occupy intermediate positions that fluctuate somewhat over time. (The sharp fluctuation for Puntarenas from a low relative position in 1976 and 1981 to a high level in 1986 is hard to interpret. Desired family size among younger women in Puntarenas changed very little while most other provinces were declining.) It should be stressed that these averages are unadjusted for any other factors, and whether these differentials persist in the face of controls remains to be tested. Accordingly, we postpone further discussion of relative standings.

Table 2 also helps clarify some of the measurement issues associated with family size preference and points to increasing consistency over time. For 1976 three measures are available, the "ideal" question asked in the WFS of everyone, and the DFSA and DFSB measures defined above. The comparison of the WFS measure and DFSA indicates the extent to which those who want more gave a different "ideal" number than the total obtained by adding together the number of additional children desired and the number of living children since those who want no more are asked their "ideal" under both measures. These two measures show almost no difference across provinces for the younger women, and only small differences among the older women. Those reflect only net differences, of course, and may mask a sizable number of discrepancies among individual respondents.

Differences between DFSA and DFSB arise from respondents who want no more children who give a number of "ideal" children which differs from their number of living children (less the last birth, if unwanted). If DFSA and DFSB tapped the same attitude identically, one would expect on average a small negative difference in DFSA minus DFSB, since some women will overshoot their preference by more than one birth, and DFSB permits an adjustment for only the last "unwanted" birth. A positive difference between DFSA and DFSB indicates that a portion of the women who report wanting no more children report an "ideal" number greater than the actual. This may arise from several sources: women who became sterilized but now desire one or more additional children; a difference in time perspective wherein some women who say they want no more are thinking of specific durations which are shorter than their remaining reproductive lives; viewing the hypothetical question as implicitly allowing a change in the "ground rules" in terms of family income, husband cooperation, etc., and giving a larger number commensurate with this new life style. As the last three columns in Table 2 show, in 1976 younger women who wanted no more children tended to give an ideal number larger than their actual on average, but over time, the magnitude of this difference has decreased in absolute terms, and in several provinces has turned negative, suggesting that the adjustment for an unwanted last live birth did not fully capture the amount of unwanted fertility. The implication of a substantial amount of unwanted fertility among the older women is suggested by the number of provinces with large negative values for the difference between DFSA and DFSB. In 1981, five of the seven provinces show negative values for DFSA minus DFSB, with the most substantial differences in the three coastal provinces. By 1986, only three of the provinces are negative, and the magnitudes are generally reduced.

To conclude this section we take a more detailed look at the characteristics of the rural portions of each province as revealed by the 1981 survey, since these characteristics will serve as the covariates for the multivariate analyses to follow. Tables 3a and 3b present these data for younger and older women in a union, respectively. These tables demonstrate considerable variability in the socio-demographic and community variables across provinces. Among the younger women, for example, the proportion of women who want no more children ranges from 17.1% in Cartago to 41.0% in Limon. Less variability in the proportion of women who want no more children is observed among women aged 30-49 years, presumably because older women are at a later stage of the family building process, and most of these women want no more children.

The proportion of women in consensual unions is also highly variable. Guanacaste and Limon have the highest percentage of women in consensual unions and Cartago the lowest, for both age groups. Overall, more younger women (23.6%) are in consensual unions than older women (19.6%), perhaps because consensual unions become legal after a certain period, but this pattern varies somewhat by province.

The percentage of women who worked in the last year also varies by province, but the rank order differs somewhat for younger and older women. More women aged 30-49 reported working in the last year than women aged 15-29 years. Perhaps women with older children who can take care of younger siblings are more able to work outside the home. Additionally, the economic demands of large family size may necessitate that more women enter the labor force.

Education varies considerably across provinces, with rural women in Heredia having almost two years of education more than any other province in both age groups. Limon has the lowest average years of education. Younger women have more education than older women in every province.

There is also considerable difference across provinces in the level of modernity of the rural communities, as measured in this survey. The communities in the three lowland provinces—Guanacaste, Puntarenas, and Limon—have many fewer of the social and economic indicators of modernity (defined above) than those in the other provinces, with Heredia, Alajuela, and Cartago being the leaders in this respect.

The provinces also differ in the proportion of women who have a family planning outlet in their community, one measure of the availability of family planning. (For other measures of family planning availability for Costa Rica, see Hermalin et al., 1988). It is of interest to note that Guanacaste, which, as noted, was an early target of the program demonstrates relatively high levels of availability on this measure.

According to the framework in Figure 1, we expect many of these characteristics to affect desired family size and since they are also variable across province, we turn to multivariate analysis to explore their net effects and to examine provincial differences after taking these characteristics into account.

MULTILEVEL ANALYSIS OF FACTORS AFFECTING DESIRED FAMILY SIZE, ACTUAL FAMILY SIZE AND CONTRACEPTIVE USE

This section presents the multivariate analysis of desired family size and, for comparison, actual family size and contraceptive use. As indicated by Figure 1, our framework is conceptually multilevel in that we view family size preference as determined by individual, community, and program characteristics. In this analysis, however, we do not employ one attractive feature of the multilevel strategy, the possibility of interactions between individual characteristics and the macro program and community characteristics (Hermalin, 1986). In other words, we are assuming that while community characteristics will affect the level of desired family size, it will not affect the relationship between the individual-level variable and the dependent variable. Preliminary tests did not indicate the presence of theoretically relevant interaction terms, though further investigation of this issue may be warranted.

A cumulative logistic multiple regression model is employed (McCullagh, 1980; Winship and Mare, 1984). In this procedure, desired family size, the dependent variable, is treated as an ordinal variable which reflects different levels of response, but with no assumption that differences across categories represent an interval scale. This appears to be more realistic than treating desired family size as an interval scale since couples may not be as fixed on a specific number as on some acceptable range; and the costs of exceeding the preferred number by one child would be quite different at parity two than at parity five. The logistic regression model, in contrast with the linear least squares approach, also makes fewer assumptions about the form of the data. For example, it does not require the covariates to be multivariate normal.

The logistic procedure estimates that the probability of

$$Y \geq j = \frac{1}{1+e^{-\alpha_j - X_i \beta}} \tag{1}$$

where the range of the dependent variable is 0, 1, . . ., k, and j = 1, 2, . . ., k. α_j is the intercept, X_i is the vector of observations of the independent variable for the i'th observation and β is the vector of regression parameters. The regression produces a series of intercepts and a single regression coefficient for each independent variable. The k intercepts and the regression coefficients are sufficient to solve for the probability of being in any of the k + 1 categories.

Following Figure 1, the independent variables are characteristics of the union: age at first union, type of union (consensual or marriage), and duration of union. A quadratic term ($\text{duration}^2/100$) is included to better capture the shape of the relationship between desired and actual family size and duration of marriage. Socioeconomic characteristics are measured by women's education, measured as years of schooling, and whether she worked outside the home in the past year. The program variable included is whether there was a family planning outlet in the community; and the community itself is characterized by its level of modernity based on a checklist of whether or not 15 different items (such as schools, electrification, etc.) are present. We also indicate whether the community of residence is in the central valley or not since some provinces cover both the plateau and the lowlands. Lastly, to investigate whether there are persistent differences across provinces representing the range of intervening variables affecting family size preference, we introduce a dummy variable for each provinces with San José as the omitted area.

The results from the logistic regression model are presented in Tables 5a and 5b, for younger and older women respectively. In each table the dependent variables are the two measures of desired family size (DFSA and DFSB) and for comparison, actual family size. (Although actual family size is an interval scale, we have employed the same structure as for desired family size, mainly for comparison purposes, and to avoid the additional assumptions of multivariate normality.) The estimates of the regression coefficients are given along with their chi-square value, and the probability of achieving or exceeding the indicated value. The overall goodness of fit is given by -2 x log-likelihood and the degrees of freedom. Also shown is R^2, which is the counterpart of the multiple regression coefficient and is similarly interpreted. In using logistic regression with an ordinal scale, the number of categories and their cutting points must be defined. Table 4 presents the distribution of women according to detailed categories of the three dependent variables. After demonstrating that the use of a greater number of cutting points had little effect on the regression coefficients, a three-category division was employed as follows. For younger women, O to 2 children, 3-4, 5 or more; for older women, O to 3 children, 4-5, 6 or more. These categories were employed for all three dependent variables.

It is difficult to interpret the regression coefficients directly, given the structure of equation 1. In general, a negative coefficient means that increased values of the independent variable will produce a lower average desired or actual family size, with a higher proportion of respondents in the lowest categories. (The coding of the independent variables is shown in Tables 3a and 3b.) To make clearer the implications of the regression, we show in Figure 2 the implied distribution of desired family size in each province, but first we review some of the general features of the regressions.

Table 5a indicates that for younger women, the regressions for the two measures of desired family (DFSA and DFSB) are similar. This is to be expected since many of those women still want more children, and that group is treated equivalently under both measures. The regressions for desired family size, however, are quite different from those for actual family size. The latter as indicated in Figure 1 is driven mostly by the proximate variables insofar as they are available in the model—age at marriage, duration of marriage—and by education which probably reflects individual differences in contraceptive use (or other proximate variables) not measured directly. There is only one significant regional difference; and the program variable measuring whether there is an outlet in the community is associated with lower actual family size.

By contrast, for the desired family size measures among younger women, three to four of the regions are significantly different from San José, the omitted category, and in the direction of lower preference. Among the individual characteristics, preference does increase with duration of marriage and it is lower for those in a consensual union. Since duration of marriage is associated with age, actual family size, and stage of family building, this effect may reflect cohort differences in desired family size and/or rationalization about preferences on the basis of actual experience. Separating the effect of rationalization in response to a desired family size question from other factors poses several difficulties as noted by Pullum (1983) and McClelland (1983). The individual socioeconomic variables of education and work experience show no relation to stated preferences. If we treat provinces as proxies for unmeasured community factors, it would appear in keeping with Figure 1 that community characteristics contribute more than the individual socioeconomic characteristics to the intervening preference variables. At the same time, the individual variables appear to play a stronger role in determining the level of the proximate variables employed in actual family building.

For the older women, where a high proportion want no more children, DFSB, which constrains those who want no more to lie within one of the actual, closely resembles the regression of actual family size, as shown in Table 5b. Both are driven strongly by the demographic variables (particularly marriage duration), and education (which as noted previously probably reflects the levels of the other proximate variables). Women in the Central Valley, controlling on other characteristics, have more children (thus, higher DFSB levels). Two of the regions show significant departure from San José, the omitted category, in the direction of lower actual or DFSB fertility. The results for the DFSA measure, in which those who want no more are asked their ideal number, are again different in a number of ways. Duration and type of union remain significant, but education does not, and four of the six regional coefficients display significantly lower desired fertility than rural San José. It should be noted that for all the measures, higher community modernity is associated with lower actual or desired fertility; for actual fertility (and DFSB) having a family planning outlet in the community is associated with higher values. This probably arises because many of the outlets were rather recently located in areas of high fertility and therefore had little impact on the older women.

To further explore the effect of province, Figure 2 presents for each province the expected distribution of desired family size according to the regressions in Tables 5a and 5b. The distributions were calculated according to equation 1 by setting all the continuous independent variables at their mean; the categorical variables were set to assume that the women were: married; did not work in the last year; were not living in the Central Valley; and had an outlet in the community. Once the values of the other independent variables were set, the appropriate provincial coefficients were substituted to calculate each expected distribution.

The results are quite striking: among younger women, the three provinces with the lowest desired family size are Puntarenas, Limon, and Guanacaste, judging either by the higher proportion preferring 0 to 2 children or the lower proportion wanting 5 or more. These three are distinctively lower on both DFSA and DFSB, than the other four provinces, with Guanacaste showing substantially lower desired family size than Puntarenas or Limon. Similarly, among older women, on DFSA, the same three provinces emerge in the multivariate analysis with distinctively lower preferences. The distributions for the three provinces resemble each other closely. By contrast, the distributions for actual family size indicate that Guanacaste, Puntarenas, and Limon follow closely behind San José in being at the high end of achieved fertility. (Since DFSB for older women closely parallels actual family size, the distributions for this measure follow the pattern just described.)

For younger women, the multivariate controls for actual family size have the effect of ranking Limon and Guanacaste at the low end while Puntarenas displays an intermediate level of fertility among the provinces. In general, the distributions by desired family size (excluding DFSB for the older women) vary more across provinces than do the distributions of actual family size in keeping with the pattern of provincial coefficients found in Tables 5a and 5b.

To this point we have shown that there is considerably more influence of province on desired family size than on actual family size. (Among older women, this is less true for DFSB since it parallels actual family size.) In general, actual family size is driven more by the demographic variables and the individual socioeconomic characteristics, while desired family size is more sensitive to community and cultural values insofar as these are tapped by the measure of modernity and the provincial proxies.

Where do the determinants of contraceptive use fit along this continuum? At the provincial level, the proportion of younger women using any method of contraception in 1981 ranged from 56 percent in Limon and Puntarenas to 69 percent in Heredia; among older women, the range was wider, from 61 percent in Limon to 81 percent in San José.

Table 6 presents a logistic regression in which current contraceptive use for younger and older women is regressed against the same set of independent variables. We also introduce the desire to limit or space children since according to Figure 1 and prior analyses, this is a major determinant of fertility regulation. The results for younger women show, as expected, strong effects on contraceptive use among those who desire to limit or space future childbearing, in addition, use is significantly higher at longer marital durations, and with more education. Beyond these motivational, social, and demographic characteristics, there are no significant differences in contraceptive use among the provinces, or by level of modernity or the availability of an outlet in the community.

The situation among older women is more complex. Contraceptive use, as with the younger women, is strongly affected by the desire to limit or space; it is also influenced by the type of union. Unlike the case of the younger women, however, community variables play a role, with use higher in more modern communities, lower in the central valley, and lower in three of the provinces: Guanacaste, Puntarenas, and Limon.

DISCUSSION

In this section we first give attention to the differences among provinces in desired family size vis-a-vis actual family size, with special emphasis, given the long-standing historical patterns, on the three lowland provinces—Guanacaste, Puntarenas, and Limon—versus the others. As an aid to our discussion, Table 7 presents the rank order of the provinces from high to low on DFSA and AFS, for 1976, 1981, and 1986 based on the data in Table 2. Also included for 1981 is the adjusted rank order after controlling for the other variables shown in Table 5 via the cumulative logit. (See Figure 2 for the resulting distributions.)

For the older women, the unadjusted actual family size rankings indicate higher fertility among the three lowland provinces in 1976 and 1981 with a shift (for Guanacaste) in 1986. Adjusting the actual family size for the other variables does mitigate the apparent high fertility profile, especially for Limon. By contrast, for DFSA the reported data for 1976, 1981, and 1986 show the lowland provinces markedly decreasing their desired family size relative to the other provinces so that by 1986 they occupy three of the four lowest ranks. The multivariate regression in 1981 confirms this trend since on the adjusted distributions Guanacaste, Puntarenas, and Limon are the lowest of the seven provinces. If one attempts to paint a dynamic picture from these cross-sections, it appears that the three lowland provinces were characterized by relatively high desired and actual fertility into the early 1970s. Preferences in these provinces started to change quite rapidly in the late 1970s and early 1980s, but actual fertility responded more slowly. The gap between actual and desired fertility for the older women is confirmed by Table 2 which shows negative values for DFSA-DFSB, which means that many women who wanted no more children gave ideal preferred family sizes lower than their actual. It is also supported by Table 6 which shows that contraceptive use was lower in these three provinces in 1981 after controlling for the other variables shown. Whether the lower contraceptive use was due to lower accessibility or the lack of knowledge and normative support, given limited previous experience, is difficult to determine. The one measure of availability used in Table 6 was not a significant factor in contraceptive use. At face value this points to more deeply seated "cost factors" hindering contraceptive use, but the measure of availability employed reflects current availability and may not adequately capture recent history. Whatever the source, it does appear that there were constraints for couples in the lowland provinces in converting their relatively lower fertility desires into practice. Some of the differential may also be caused by post-hoc rationalization by women who have exceeded their desires.

A comparison among older women of the adjusted actual fertility size ranking for 1981 with the adjusted preference ranking for that year reveals the extent of the discrepancy in standing across all the provinces. As noted, the three lowland provinces all have adjusted desired fertility ranks lower than their ranks on actual fertility, with Guanacaste and Puntarenas showing the largest discrepancies. Heredia occupies the same intermediate ranking on both actual and desired fertility, and San José appears at the high end of both actual and desired. The largest discrepancy occurs for Cartago and Alajuela. In both cases, they are at the low end of actual fertility but at the high end of desired fertility. In the case of Cartago, the discrepancy in rankings is also apparent from the unadjusted rankings in 1976 and 1981, and confirmed by its position in 1986. For Alajuela, the unadjusted data for 1976 and 1981 show high concordance between actual and desired fertility at low relative standings. It is only after adjustment that the discrepancy appears, and the data for 1986 are in accord with the pattern revealed by the adjustment.

The pattern for younger women appears to confirm the emerging trends for the older women. For the lowland provinces, the unadjusted as well as adjusted data identify them as among the lowest in desired family size. In Guanacaste, the low relative standing on both actual and desired fertility at every time point is clear; for Puntarenas, the low relative standing in desired family size in 1976 and 1981 (adjusted and unadjusted) seems contradicted by its number one ranking in 1986. We have no explanation. (For this change and determining whether this is simply a chance fluctuation will have to await additional data.) In addition, Puntarenas tends to show a major discrepancy in its relative standing on actual family size, versus desired family size in 1976 and 1981. Limon shows a trend toward lower relative desired family size and a comparison of the adjusted rankings for DFSA and AFS in 1981 shows concordance in the two rankings. In general, the comparison of the adjusted rankings of actual and desired fertility for 1981 reveals that in the lowland provinces, which have been characterized traditionally by high fertility, younger women desire the lowest fertility and are achieving these levels relative to those in the other provinces. These patterns among the younger women tend to confirm the emerging trends among the older women and it is instructive to note that the 1981 adjusted rankings of provinces on desired family size are very similar for the younger and older women. In this connection it should be noted that Table 6 reveals no provincial effects on contraceptive use for younger women once the other variables are taken into account. It thus appears that the younger women in each province have the knowledge and accessibility to achieve their desired family size goals and that differentials across provinces will be driven largely by differences in these goals rather than by the availability of family planning methods. Understanding how family size intentions come about becomes all the more important therefore for predicting the future course of fertility in Costa Rica.

CONCLUSION

The previous section focused on the implications of the findings for Costa Rica. To conclude, we address some of the broader issues for fertility research that emerge from this analysis. First we address some measurement issues and then more general questions of studying fertility differentials.

Care must be exercised in choosing a measure of family size preference. The results achieved with the two measures employed in this analysis, DFSA and DFSB, differ substantially for the older women. DFSB, which restricts desired family size to lie within one of actual, naturally produces results close to those for actual family size. The very different pattern attained with DFSA indicates that a substantial number of older women in Costa Rica in 1981 who did not want more children reported ideal family sizes that differed markedly both positively and negatively from their actual, adjusted for the wantedness of the last birth. (Note the positive and negative differences in DFSA-DFSB in Table 2.) The reasons for the differences are no doubt numerous, including substantial unwanted fertility, regret among women who became sterilized, post-hoc rationalization about changed conditions, etc. Although DFSB per se is not a measure usually employed in studying desired family size, the measures employed to study demand for children do tend to vary and it is important to be sensitive to the effect of this variation on the results achieved. The results in Table 2 also demonstrate the potential insights that can be gained from having more than one measure, particularly over time. The reduction of the discrepancies between DFSA and DFSB across provinces between 1976 and 1986 suggest that families were coming closer to achieving their preferences. The close concordance between the measures employed by the WFS and DFSA for younger women indicates that the ideal number reported by those who want more children will be close to that obtained by adding their current size to the number of additional children wanted. More analyses that examine both gross and net differences across different measures should produce useful insights into understanding each of these measures.

The results of this analysis indicate that there may be a benefit from studying different portions of the fertility process with the same set of indicators, as long as these are meaningful from a modeling standpoint. Family size preferences, achieved family size, and contraceptive use are clearly different aspects of reproductive behavior, and it is important to develop explicit models of how these relate to one another and to the factors affecting fertility, as we have attempted to do in Figure 1. At the same time, looking at the "reduced form" of these outcomes may be instructive in identifying the locus of effects, the relative importance of individual, family, or community variables on reproductive outcomes [what Cleland (1985: 238) refers to as establishing the proper unit of analysis]. Together with the type of trend data presented, these comparisons also provide some insight into the role of motivation to reduce fertility vis a vis the availability of the means to do so.

A major finding is that unlike the reported inferences from the WFS (Lightbourne, 1985: 194) it appears that family size preference does vary by social characteristics if by social we include characteristics of the community—measures of modernity and the provincial proxies. In this sense, community seems to be operating like religion or ethnic group, where Lightbourne (1985: 194) does indicate differentials in preference in some instances. We do confirm that the individual social and economic characteristics have little apparent effect on preference. Rather, it appears that these characteristics have more effect on actual family size, which we interpret as representing their influence on the proximate determinants which regulate the pace and number of children. Contraceptive use seems to occupy an intermediate position in that it is influenced both by community and individual characteristics.

Our findings are also at some variance from Cleland's assertion (1985: 244) about the minor role of preference in fertility decline. Although there was little change in desired family size for Costa Rica as a whole, the data show that there were provincial differences in desired family size and that these changed over time, particularly in the areas with high initial values. In addition, changes in fertility followed in predictable ways from these shifts in preference. Whether these changes in preference were responding to structural factors or the diffusion of new ideas, including the idea of regulation, or some mixture of the two is difficult to determine from the data on hand. There were sharp structural changes in the lowland provinces in education and in some developmental indicators. At the same time, the period in question also witnessed substantial expansion of the family planning program.

Of course, these findings are based on an analysis of a particular time and place and must be confirmed by other analyses. In general, the community data collected in the WFS and DHS have not been employed to study differentials in preferences, and the potential for additional replications is thus considerable.

Future research must also go behind the provincial proxies to determine what aspects of community and culture account for the differences in preference. The provincial effects per se are merely another name for ignorance since they do not illuminate the specific mechanisms that account for the differentials. The fact that these effects persist even when a measure of modernity is included suggests that factors such as differences in the value of children and the normative environment play a large role, though these are not easily measured (see, however, Bulatao and Fawcett, 1983 for an analysis incorporating value of children). To our mind these are more likely candidates than the more standard sociological and socioeconomic factors, and indeed preliminary research with this model originally included variables such as distance to the nearest urban center, occupation of head of household, and levels of infant mortality. These were dropped from the final model in the interests of parsimony because they showed almost no effect on preferences. Given the multilevel framework, it is possible to substitute for each province measures more directly reflective of cultural factors, and of socioeconomic structural characteristics, and examine which ones are most influential on family size preferences. This should be a high priority for future research.

ACKNOWLEDGEMENTS

An earlier version of this research was presented at the 1989 annual meeting of the Population Association of America, and supported in part by the U.S. National Institutes of Child Health and Human Development, Contract No. 1 HD-62902. The authors gratefully acknowledge research and manuscript assistance from Karen Glaser, Lora Myers, Judy Mullin, Ingrid Naaman, Mary Scott, and Shiauping Shih.

REFERENCES

Asociación Demográfica Costarricense. 1987. *Resultados de la Encuesta Nacional de Fecundidad y Salud.* San José: ADC.

Bongaarts, J. 1986. The Transition in Reproductive Behavior in The Third World. In J. Menken (ed.), *World Population and U.S. Policy.* Pp. 105-132. New York: W.W. Norton.

Bulatao, R.A. and J.T. Fawcett. 1983. Influence on Childbearing Intentions Across the Fertility Career: Demographic and Socioeconomic Factors and the Value of Children. Papers of the East-West Population Institute, No. 60-F. Honolulu, Hawaii: East-West Center.

Bulatao, R.A. and R.D. Lee, with P.E. Hollerbach and J. Bongaarts, (eds.). 1983. *Determinants of Fertility in Developing Countries: A Summary of Knowledge.* New York: Academic Press.

Caja Costarricense de Seguro Social. 1994. *Fecundidad y Formación de la Familia. Encuesta Nacional de Salud Reproductiva 1993.* San José, Costa Rica: Reprinted by the US Department of Health and Human Services, CDC.

Cleland, J. 1985. "Marital Fertility Decline in Developing Countries: Theories and Evidence." In J. Cleland et al. (eds.), *Reproductive Change in Developing Countries.* New York: Oxford University Press.

Coale, A.J., and R. Treadway. 1986. "A Summary of the Changing Distribution of Overall Fertility, Marital Fertility, and the Proportion Married in the Provinces of Europe." In Ansley J. Coale and Susan Cotts Watkins (eds.), *The Decline of Fertility in Europe*. Pp. 31-181. Princeton, NJ: Princeton University Press.

Direccion General de Estadística y Census. 1963. *Census Población, 1963*. San José, Costa Rica.

_____. 1973. *Census Población, 1973*. San José, Costa Rica.

_____. 1978. *Encuesta Nacional de Fecundidad 1976: Costa Rica*. San José, Costa Rica.

_____. 1983. *Census Población, 1983*. San José, Costa Rica.

Gendell M. 1985. "Stalls in the Fertility Decline in Costa Rica, Korea, and Sri Lanka." World Bank Staff Working Papers, No. 693.

Hermalin, A.I. 1983. "Fertility Regulations and Its Costs: A Critical Essay." In R.A. Bulatao et al. (eds.), *Determinants of Fertility in Developing Countries: A Summary of Knowledge*. National Research Council, Panel on Fertility Determinants, New York: Academic Press.

_____. 1986. "The Multilevel Approach To Family Planning Program Evaluation." Chapter III in *Addendum to Manual IX: The Methodology of Measuring the Impact of Family Planning Programmes on Fertility. Population Studies*, No. 66:15-24. New York: United Nations.

Hermalin, A.I., A P. Riley, and L. Rosero-Bixby. 1988. "A Multi-Level Analysis of Contraceptive Use and Method Choice in Costa Rica." In A.I. Hermalin, B. Entwisle, and J. Casterline, Principal Investigators, *Effects of Contextual Factors on Fertility Regulation in Costa Rica and Egypt*. Final Report, NICHD Contract No. 1 HD-62902. Ann Arbor, MI: Population Studies Center of the University of Michigan.

Jensen, E. 1985. "Desired Fertility, the 'Up to God' Response, and Sample Selection to Sias." *Demography* 22(3):445-54.

Knodel, J. and E. Van de Walle. 1986. "Lessons From the Past: Policy Implications of Historical Fertility Studies." In Ansley J. Coale and Susan Cotts Watkins (eds.), *The Decline of Fertility in Europe*. Pp. 390-419. Princeton, NJ: Princeton University Press.

Lightbourne, R.E. 1985. "Individual Preferences and Fertility Behaviour." In J. Cleland et al. (eds.), *Reproductive Change in Developing Countries*. New York: Oxford University Press.

Mata, L. and L. Rosero-Bixby. 1988. "National Health and Social Development in Costa Rica: A Case Study of Intersectorial Action." Washington, D.C.: Pan American Health Organization, Technical Paper No. 13.

McLelland, Gary H. 1983. "Family-Size Desires as Measures of Demand." In R. A. Bulatao et al. (eds.), *Determinants of Fertility in Developing Countries: A Summary of Knowledge*. National Research Council, Panel on Fertility Determinants. New York: Academic Press, 1: 288-343.

McCullagh, P. 1980. Regression Models for Ordinal Data (with discussion). *Journal of the Royal Statistical Society* 42, Series B:109-142.

Oberle, M.W., D. Sosa, S. Becker, L. Morris, and L. Rosero-Bixby. 1988. "Contraceptive Use and Fertility in Costa Rica, 1986." *International Family Planning Perspectives* 14(3):103-108.

Pritchett, L.H. 1994. "Desired Fertility and the Impact of Population Policies." *Population and Development Review* 20(1):1-55.

Pullum, T.W. 1983. "Correlates of Family-Size Desires." In R.A. Bulatao et al. (eds.), *Determinants of Fertility in Developing Countries: A Summary of Knowledge*. National Research Council, Panel on Fertility Determinants. New York: Academic Press.

Rosero, L. 1981. *Fecundidad y Anticoncepción en Costa Rica 1981*. San José: Asociación Demográfica Costarricense.

Rosero, L., M. Gomez, and V. Rodriguez (n.d.). Determinantes de la Fecundidad en Costa Rica. Costa Rica: Dirección General de Estadística y Censos.

SAS Institute. 1987. *SAS/STAT Guide for Personal Computers*. Version 6 Ed., SAS Institute, Inc., Cary, NC, U.S.A.

Sharlin, A. 1986. Urban-rural Differences in Fertility in Europe During the Demographic Transition. In Ansley J. Coale and Susan Cotts Watkins (eds.), *The Decline of Fertility in Europe*. Pp. 234-260. Princeton, NJ: Princeton University Press.

Stycos, J.M. 1978. Patterns of Fertility Decline in Costa Rica. International Population Program. New York: Cornell University, Ithaca.

_____. 1984. "Putting Back the K and A in KAP: A Study of the Implications of Knowledge and Attitudes for Fertility in Costa Rica." *WFS Scientific Reports* No. 48. Voorburg, Netherlands: International Statistical Institute.

United Nations. 1985. *Socio-economic Development and Fertility Decline in Costa Rica*. New York: United Nations, Department of Economic and Social Affairs.

Universidad de Costa Rica, Instituto de Investigaciones Sociales. 1976. *La Población de Costa Rica*. San José, C.R.: Ciudad Universitaria Rodrigo Facio.

Winship, C. and R. Mare. 1984. "Regression Models With Ordinal Variables." *Annual Sociological Review* 49: 512-25.

TABLE 1. THE EVOLUTION OF FERTILITY, DESIRED FAMILY SIZE AND CONTRACEPTIVE USE BY AREA, COSTA RICA, 1964-1993

Area	Year	Total Fertility Rate	Contraceptive Prevalence Rate	Desired Family Size	
				All Ages	Ages <35
Urban/ San José	1964	5.2	49%	4.1	3.9
	1976	2.8	73%	3.9	3.5
	1981	3.2	70%	4.0	3.5
	1986	3.0[a]	74%	3.5	3.1
	1993	2.8[b]	77%	3.1	--
Rural	1969	7.2	24%	4.9	4.6
	1976	3.9	64%	4.7	4.1
	1981	3.9	60%	5.1	4.3
	1986	4.1	64%	4.8	4.1
	1993	3.7[b]	72%	3.6	--

Note: For 1964, urban refers to San José except for the total fertility rate. The contraceptive prevalence rates and desired family sizes for 1964, 1969 and 1976 are for women in union aged 20-49 years. Before 1993, the average desired family size was computed including non-numeric responses (about 10% of the samples) as eight desired children; for 1993, the non-numeric (about 2% of the sample) were excluded.

[a]Data for 1984.

[b]Data based on births from 1988-1993.

Sources:

- Asociacion Demografica Costarricense, 1987: Table 5.9 (fertility rates before 1993), Table 4.6 (contraception in 1981 and 1986), and Table 6.5 (desired family size in 1981 and 1986).
- Rosero et al., n.d.: Table 6.5 (contraception in 1964, 1969, and 1976), Table 5.4 (desired family size in 1964, 1969, and 1976).
- Caja Costarricense de Seguro Social, 1994: Table 7.10 (total fertility rate, 1993); Table 9.14 (contraception, 1993); Table 11.7 (desired family size, 1993).

TABLE 2. MEASURES OF DESIRED FAMILY SIZE AND ACTUAL FAMILY SIZE BY AGE AND PROVINCE OF RURAL COSTA RICA, FOR 1976, 1981, AND 1986

	DFSB[a]			Rank DFSB[b]			WFS[c]	DFSA[d]			DFSA-DFSB		
Province	1976	1981	1986	1976	1981	1986	1976	1976	1981	1986	1976	1981	1986
DESIRED FAMILY SIZE, AGES 15-29													
San José	3.72	3.72	3.20	2	1	3	4.01	4.06	3.86	3.32	.23	.14	.12
Alajuela	3.05	3.19	3.12	6	4	4	3.54	3.32	3.17	3.19	.17	-.02	.07
Cartago	3.98	3.71	3.24	1	2	2	4.16	4.15	3.75	3.28	.17	.04	.04
Heredia	3.34	3.13	2.68	4	5	7	3.62	3.57	3.18	2.80	.32	.05	.12
Guanacaste	2.92	2.82	2.73	7	7	6	3.45	3.29	2.99	2.84	.53	.17	.11
Puntarenas	3.33	3.12	3.26	5	6	1	3.82	3.86	2.95	3.41	.49	-.17	.15
Limon	3.47	3.20	3.05	3	3	5	3.87	3.79	3.03	2.85	.40	-.17	-.20
DESIRED FAMILY SIZE, AGES 30-49													
San José	6.41	5.31	4.94	2	3	3	6.66	6.17	5.42	5.18	-.24	.11	.24
Alajuela	5.94	4.97	4.53	6	6	5	5.89	5.68	4.30	4.62	-.26	-.67	.09
Cartago	6.14	5.12	4.93	4	5	4	7.35	6.88	5.60	5.30	.74	.48	.37
Heredia	5.51	4.59	4.10	7	7	7	5.85	5.69	4.24	4.20	.18	-.35	.10
Guanacaste	6.01	5.26	4.20	5	4	6	5.74	5.95	4.25	4.04	-.06	-1.01	-.16
Puntarenas	6.70	5.81	5.00	1	1	2	6.25	6.31	4.96	4.22	-.39	-.85	-.78
Limon	6.37	5.57	5.33	3	2	1	6.29	6.59	4.79	4.36	.22	-.78	-.97

(continued on next page)

(Table 2 continued from previous page)

	Ages 15-29						Ages 30-49					
	AFS			Rank AFS			AFS			Rank AFS		
	1976	1981	1986	1976	1981	1986	1976	1981	1986	1976	1981	1986
San José	2.28	2.18	2.10	4	2	3	6.11	4.96	4.50	4	4	2
Alajuela	2.06	1.69	2.04	7	7	4	5.51	4.53	3.71	6	5	7
Cartago	2.51	2.05	2.01	2	3	5	6.04	4.49	4.11	5	6	4
Heredia	2.10	1.92	1.78	6	4	6	5.49	4.26	3.78	7	7	6
Guanacaste	2.24	1.76	1.72	5	6	7	6.12	5.10	3.91	3	3	5
Puntarenas	2.56	1.91	2.25	1	5	1	6.74	5.78	4.42	1	1	3
Limon	2.41	2.44	2.21	3	1	2	6.53	5.24	5.14	2	2	1

[a] DFSB is measured by adding the additional children wanted to the number of living children for those who want more, and using the number of living children (less one of the last birth was unwanted) for those who want no more.

[b] Provinces are ranked from high to low.

[c] Represents the report from all women on the "ideal" number, the number they would have in their whole life if they were able to choose exactly.

[d] DFSA is measured by adding the additional children wanted to the number of living children for those who want more, and using the "ideal" number-the number they would have if they could choose-for those who want no more.

Note on Standard Error: For 1981, the number of interviews per province range from 39 to 126 for the younger age group, with standard errors ranging from .26 to .10. For the older women, the interviews per province range from 33 to 138, with standard errors from .47 to .20. Details are provided in Tables 3a and 3b. Sample sizes by age and province for the other years are similar to those in 1981.

TABLE 3a. COVARIATES BY PROVINCE, WOMEN AGED 15-29 YEARS

	San José	Alajuela	Cartago	Heredia	Guanacaste	Puntarenas	Limon	Total
Percent Limiting[1]	28.8	20.6	17.1	21.0	32.9	29.1	41.0	25.9
Percent Spacing[2]	45.5	49.2	54.0	56.5	48.8	44.3	43.6	49.1
Percent in Central Valley (1 = Central Valley ; 0 Otherwise)	37.9	74.6	90.8	100	0	0	0	46.6
Percent in Consensual Unions 1 = Married; 2 = Consensual	19.7	15.1	2.6	4.8	57.3	27.9	48.7	23.6
Percent Women Worked in Last Year 1 = Full or part time 0 = Not worked	15.2	22.2	15.8	27.4	14.6	22.8	18.0	19.6
Percent Have Outlet in Community[3] 1 = Yes; 0 = No	22.7	53.2	14.5	19.4	40.2	27.9	33.3	32.6
Mean DFSA[4]	3.86	3.17	3.75	3.18	2.99	2.95	3.03	32.7
	(0.21)*	(0.10)	(0.15)	(0.13)	(0.13)	(0.14)	(0.26)	(0.06)
Mean DFSB[5]	3.74	3.18	3.73	3.13	2.77	3.13	3.18	3.25
	(0.20)	(0.10)	(0.15)	(0.14)	(0.13)	(0.14)	(0.19)	(0.06)
Mean AFS[6]	2.18	1.69	2.05	1.92	1.76	1.91	2.44	1.93
	(0.15)	(0.11)	(0.16)	(0.12)	(0.12)	(0.15)	(0.22)	(0.05)
Mean Years of Education (Last Completed Year)	5.69	6.34	6.75	8.35	6.82	6.24	3.95	6.44
	(0.34)	(0.25)	(0.30)	(0.43)	(0.36)	(0.36)	(0.39)	(0.14)
Level of Modernity[7] (0-15)	6.77	8.75	7.32	9.52	5.35	5.41	2.69	6.93
	(0.51)	(0.33)	(0.38)	(0.23)	(0.48)	(0.45)	(0.55)	(0.18)
Duration of Union (in years)	5.39	4.73	5.09	4.92	5.50	4.85	6.44	5.15
	(0.43)	(0.35)	(0.39)	(0.41)	(0.34)	(0.35)	(0.61)	(0.15)
Age at First Union (in years)	18.62	18.62	18.41	19.10	17.27	17.65	17.10	18.18
	(0.43)	(0.29)	(0.30)	(0.42)	(0.31)	(0.35)	(0.37)	(0.14)
N	66	126	76	62	82	79	39	530

(continued on next page)

(Table 3a continued from previous page)

Note: Includes fecund women in union.

* Standard error in parentheses.

[1]Women who state that they desire no more children or are sterilized; 1 = wants no more; 0 = otherwise.

[2]Women who want more births, but want to delay the next child by 2 years or more. 1 = wants a birth after two years or more; 0 = otherwise.

[3]Outlet refers to a health facility that provides some family planning services.

[4]For women who want more children: number of living children plus desired additional children; women who want no more or are sterilized are asked how many children they would choose if they could select the number.

[5]For women who want more: same as DFSA. For women who want no more, number of living children, or number of living minus 1 if last birth was not wanted.

[6]Number of living children at the time of interview.

[7]A scale which counts the presence of schools, electrification, piped water, etc., ranging from 0-15.

TABLE 3b. COVARIATES BY PROVINCE, WOMEN AGED 30-49 YEARS

	San José	Alajuela	Cartago	Heredia	Guanacaste	Puntarenas	Limon	Total
Percent Limiting[1]	67.6	68.8	73.7	74.7	78.0	74.7	72.3	72.6
Percent Spacing[2]	12.7	12.3	15.8	3.7	9.9	11.4	6.1	11.2
Percent in Central Valley	35.2	79.7	94.7	100	0	0	0	49.7
Percent in Consensual Unions	12.7	10.9	8.4	14.8	33.0	30.4	48.5	19.6
Percent Women Worked in Last Year	21.1	20.3	29.5	31.5	25.3	13.9	33.3	23.7
Percent Have Outlet in Community[3]	26.8	55.0	13.7	24.1	51.7	34.2	45.5	37.4
Mean DFSA[4]	5.21 (0.32)*	4.30 (0.20)	5.29 (0.28)	4.24 (0.35)	4.25 (0.23)	4.96 (0.33)	4.79 (0.47)	4.69 (0.11)
Mean DFSB[5]	5.27 (0.30)	4.80 (0.23)	4.76 (0.23)	4.42 (0.28)	5.12 (0.28)	5.75 (0.31)	5.27 (0.40)	5.03 (0.11)
Mean AFS[6]	4.96 (0.29)	4.53 (0.24)	4.49 (0.24)	4.26 (0.28)	5.10 (0.31)	5.78 (0.33)	5.24 (0.45)	4.86 (0.12)
Mean Years of Education	4.69 (0.37)	4.96 (0.28)	4.32 (0.32)	6.83 (0.49)	4.89 (0.38)	3.19 (0.26)	3.12 (0.42)	4.64 (0.14)
Level of Modernity[7]	6.59 (0.56)	8.64 (0.29)	7.86 (0.31)	9.72 (0.31)	5.26 (0.47)	4.94 (0.39)	4.66 (0.80)	7.05 (0.17)
Duration of Union	16.21 (0.75)	17.57 (0.65)	15.87 (0.70)	16.52 (0.95)	16.53 (0.72)	18.72 (0.65)	17.79 (0.95)	16.79 (0.29)
Age at First Union	20.00 (0.51)	20.98 (0.41)	21.06 (0.53)	20.61 (0.69)	20.89 (0.52)	17.89 (0.40)	19.00 (0.74)	20.25 (0.20)
N	71	138	95	54	91	79	33	561

(continued on next page)

(Table 3b continued from previous page)

Note: Includes fecund women in union.
* Standard error in parentheses.
[1]Women who state that they desire no more children or are sterilized; 1 = wants no more; 0 = otherwise.
[2]Women who want more births, but want to delay the next child by 2 years or more. 1 = wants a birth after two years or more; 0 = otherwise.
[3]Outlet refers to a health facility that provides some family planning services.
[4]For women who want more children: number of living children plus desired additional children; women who want no more or are sterilized are asked how many children they would choose if they could select the number.
[5]For women who want more: same as DFSA. For women who want no more, number of living children, or number of living minus 1 if last birth was not wanted.
[6]Number of living children at the time of interview.
[7]A scale which counts the presence of schools, electrification, piped water, etc., ranging from 0-15.

TABLE 4. DISTRIBUTIONS OF DESIRED AND ACTUAL FAMILY SIZE BY AGE

Age	DFSA[a]	DBSB[b]	AFS[c]
	AGES 15-29 (N = 560)		
0-1	2.5%	3.6%	41.7%
2	27.4	24.7	31.3
3	34.9	37.0	16.4
4	21.3	20.4	6.4
5	7.4	8.3	3.2
6	3.8	3.8	0.6
7+	2.7	2.2	0.4
Total	100.0	100.0	100.0
	AGES 30-49 (N = 530)		
0-1	1.4%	1.8%	6.3%
2	15.9	12.7	15.2
3	21.3	17.7	14.8
4	20.9	17.2	14.1
5	12.3	14.7	14.1
6	11.3	11.3	10.4
7	3.6	7.3	9.5
8+	13.3	17.3	15.6
Total	100.0	100.0	100.0

[a]DFSA is equal to the number of living children plus the number of additional children desired for women who want more births, and is the number of children a woman would choose to have in her lifetime for women who want no more births.
[b]DFSB is equal to DFSA for women who want more births. For women who want no more births, it is the number of living children minus the last birth if it was unwanted.
[c]AFS is the number of currently living children.
Note: In the regression models, DFSA, DFSB, and AFS are categorized as follows. For women aged 15-29 years, 0-2, 3-4, and 5+; and for women aged 30-49 years, 0-3, 4-5, and 6+.

TABLE 5a: MULTIPLE LOGISTIC REGRESSION ESTIMATES OF THE LIKELIHOOD OF BEING IN A SPECIFIC CATEGORY OF DESIRED AND ACTUAL FAMILY SIZE, WOMEN AGE 15-29

	DFSA			DFSB			AFS		
	β	χ^2	P	β	χ^2	P	β	χ^2	P
a_1	2.631	9.89	.002	2.449	8.44	.004	-6.426	24.72	.000
a_2	-0.355	0.81	.667	-0.675	0.65	.419	-9.139	47.51	.000
Age at First Union	-0.018	0.31	.581	-0.023	0.48	.487	0.133	7.59	.006
Duration of Union	0.149	3.67	.055	0.169	4.54	.033	0.807	33.09	.000
$\text{Duration}^2/100$	-0.222	0.13	.723	-0.051	0.01	.937	-2.592	8.24	.004
Type of Union	-0.562	5.41	.020	-0.405	2.77	.096	0.478	2.38	.123
Education	-0.032	0.94	.332	-0.029	0.77	.382	-0.141	8.52	.004
Worked in Last Year	-0.107	0.23	.632	-0.101	0.20	.656	-0.264	0.68	.410
Scale of Modernity	-0.032	1.12	.291	-0.035	1.33	.249	0.017	0.19	.664
Alajuela	-0.759	5.00	.025	-0.514	2.32	.128	-0.246	0.32	.575
Cartago	-0.109	0.08	.771	0.107	0.08	.778	0.411	0.70	.402
Heredia	-0.624	2.40	.121	-0.515	1.63	.202	-0.171	0.10	.754
Guanacaste	-1.471	14.41	.000	-1.787	21.17	.000	-0.989	4.20	.040
Puntarenas	-1.569	17.52	.000	-1.251	11.37	.001	-0.056	0.02	.897
Limon	-1.658	14.12	.000	-1.370	9.61	.002	-0.280	0.30	.585
Central Valley	-0.239	0.54	.463	-0.398	1.46	.227	-0.185	0.17	.681
Outlet in Community	0.287	6.67	.197	0.210	0.89	.347	-0.509	2.79	.095
-2 x Log Likelihood		942.64			920.79			554.02	
Degrees of Freedom		15			15			15	
$*R^2$		0.279			0.425			0.496	

$*R^2$ is the proportion of log-likelihood explained by the model.

TABLE 5b: MULTIPLE LOGISTIC REGRESSION ESTIMATES OF THE LIKELIHOOD OF BEING IN A SPECIFIC CATEGORY OF DESIRED AND ACTUAL FAMILY SIZE, WOMEN AGE 30-49

	DFSA			DFSB			AFS		
	β	χ^2	P	β	χ^2	P	β	χ^2	P
a_1	-0.077	0.01	.943	-0.262	0.05	.818	-2.871	5.42	.019
a_2	-1.737	2.66	.103	-2.152	3.55	.059	-4.743	14.49	.000
Age at First Union	0.009	0.15	.700	0.026	0.98	.323	0.042	2.16	.142
Duration of Union	0.277	17.66	.000	0.218	9.36	.002	0.425	24.69	.000
$Duration^2/100$	-0.543	9.70	.002	-0.152	0.62	.430	-0.582	6.71	.009
Type of Union	-0.795	11.95	.001	-0.443	3.46	.063	-0.364	2.69	.101
Education	-0.035	1.42	.233	-0.183	31.33	.000	-0.211	34.87	.000
Worked in Last Year	-0.307	2.23	.135	-0.019	0.01	.929	0.019	0.01	.931
Scale of Modernity	-0.086	10.71	.001	-0.145	26.04	.000	-0.155	25.64	.000
Alajuela	-0.811	6.96	.008	-0.920	7.61	.006	-0.856	6.04	.014
Cartago	0.265	0.59	.443	-0.831	5.15	.023	-0.869	4.96	.026
Heredia	-0.329	0.71	.399	-0.454	1.19	.275	-0.472	1.14	.285
Guanacaste	-0.999	8.98	.003	-0.421	1.53	.217	-0.309	0.76	.382
Puntarenas	-0.929	7.21	.007	-0.117	0.11	.744	-0.031	0.01	.932
Limon	-1.034	5.51	.019	-0.441	0.90	.342	-0.511	1.10	.295
Central Valley	-0.377	1.54	.215	0.832	6.54	.011	0.857	6.50	.011
Outlet in Community	0.283	2.07	.151	0.390	3.37	.066	0.487	4.67	.031
-2 x Log Likelihood		1096.65			975.49			892.61	
Degrees of Freedom		15			15			15	
$*R^2$		0.279			0.425			0.496	

$*R^2$ is the proportion of log-likelihood explained by the model.

TABLE 6. LOGISTIC REGRESSION MODELS FOR USE OF ANY METHODS VS. NON-USE

	15-29 Years			30-49 Years		
	β	χ^2	P	β	χ^2	P
Intercept	-2.81	6.52	0.011	1.83	1.38	0.239
Age at Union	0.06	1.87	0.172	-0.02	0.44	0.508
Duration	0.14	4.17	0.040	0.01	0.01	0.910
$Duration^2/100$	-0.01	2.66	0.103	-.00	0.80	0.370
Limit	1.77	29.77	0.000	2.62	55.3	0.000
Space	1.76	44.59	0.000	1.97	16.86	0.000
Type of Union	0.11	0.13	0.714	-0.61	5.83	0.015
Education	0.07	1.76	0.185	0.09	4.89	0.027
Women's Work	-0.19	0.45	0.504	0.50	2.35	0.125
Modernity	0.05	1.56	0.212	0.07	2.78	0.096
Outlet in Community	0.80	0.09	0.770	-0.22	0.58	0.450
Alajuela	-0.01	0.00	0.984	-0.02	0.00	0.968
Cartago	-0.22	0.21	0.643	-0.11	0.04	0.850
Heredia	0.43	0.59	0.443	-0.29	0.23	0.628
Guanacaste	0.15	0.11	0.739	-0.98	3.12	0.077
Puntarenas	0.31	0.49	0.482	-1.29	5.58	0.018
Limon	0.17	0.11	0.742	-1.43	5.12	0.024
Central Valley	0.29	0.51	0.474	-1.11	4.05	0.044

TABLE 7. RANKINGS OF PROVINCES BY DESIRED AND ACTUAL FAMILY SIZE, ADJUSTED AND UNADJUSTED FOR 1976, 1981, AND 1986, BY AGE GROUP

Province	Desired Family Size[a]				Actual Family Size			
	1976 Unadj.	1981 Unadj.	1981 Adj.	1986 Unadj	1976 Unadj.	1981 Unadj.	1981 Adj.	1986 Unadj.
				AGES 15-29				
San José	2	1	2	2	4	2	2	3
Alajuela	6	4	3*	4	7	7	5	4
Cartago	1	2	1	3	2	3	1	5
Heredia	5	3	4*	7	6	4	4	6
Guanacaste	7	6	7	6	5	6	7	7
Puntarenas	4	7	5	1	1	5	3	1
Limon	3	5	6	5	3	1	6	2
				AGES 30-49				
San José	4	2	3	2	4	4	1	2
Alajuela	7	5	1	3	6	5	6	7
Cartago	1	1	2	1	5	6	7	4
Heredia	6	7	4	6	7	7	4	6
Guanacaste	5	6	6	7	3	3	3	5
Puntarenas	3	3	5	5	1	1	2	3
Limon	2	4	7	4	2	2	5	1

*Represents a tie in rankings.

[a]As measured by DFSA, which is equal to the number of living children plus the number of additional children desired for women who want more births, and is the number of children a woman would choose to have in her lifetime for women who want no more births.

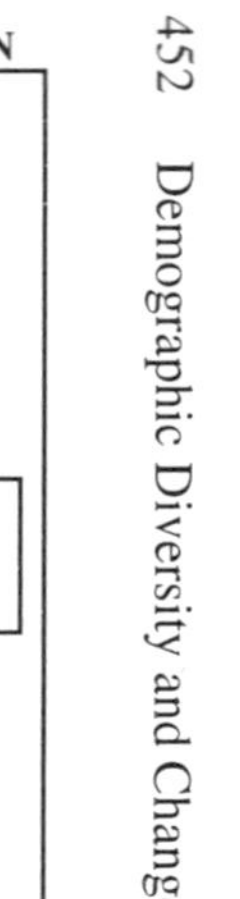

FIGURE 1. MODEL OF DETERMINANTS OF DESIRED FAMILY SIZE, ACTUAL FAMILY SIZE, AND FERTILITY REGULATION

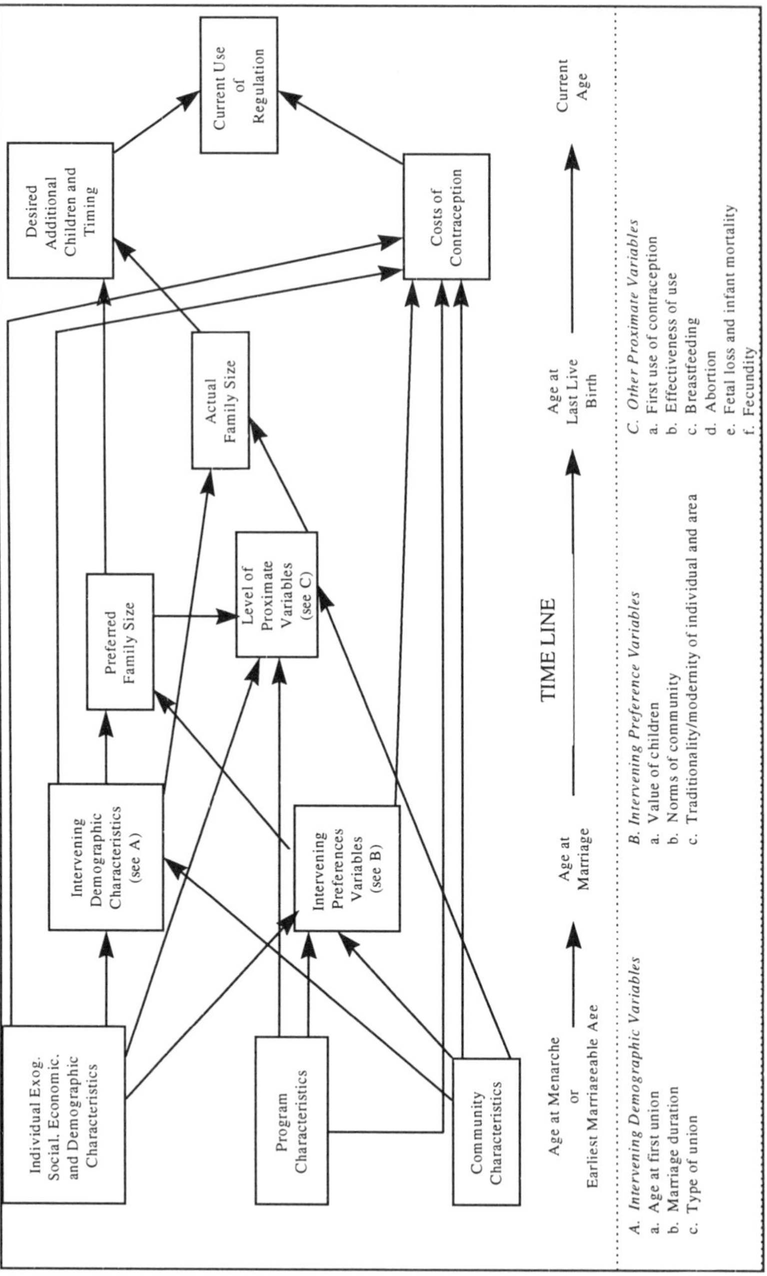

Individual Exog. Social, Economic, and Demographic Characteristics
Program Characteristics
Community Characteristics
Intervening Demographic Characteristics (see A)
Intervening Preferences Variables (see B)
Preferred Family Size
Level of Proximate Variables (see C)
Actual Family Size
Desired Additional Children and Timing
Costs of Contraception
Current Use of Regulation
TIME LINE
Age at Menarche or Earliest Marriageable Age
Age at Marriage
Age at Last Live Birth
Current Age
A. Intervening Demographic Variables
a. Age at first union
b. Marriage duration
c. Type of union
B. Intervening Preference Variables
a. Value of children
b. Norms of community
c. Traditionality/modernity of individual and area
C. Other Proximate Variables
a. First use of contraception
b. Effectiveness of use
c. Breastfeeding
d. Abortion
e. Fetal loss and infant mortality
f. Fecundity

FIGURE 2. PREDICTED DISTRIBUTION OF DESIRED (DFSA) AND ACTUAL FAMILY SIZE BY AGE AND PROVINCE FROM LOGISTIC REGRESSION*

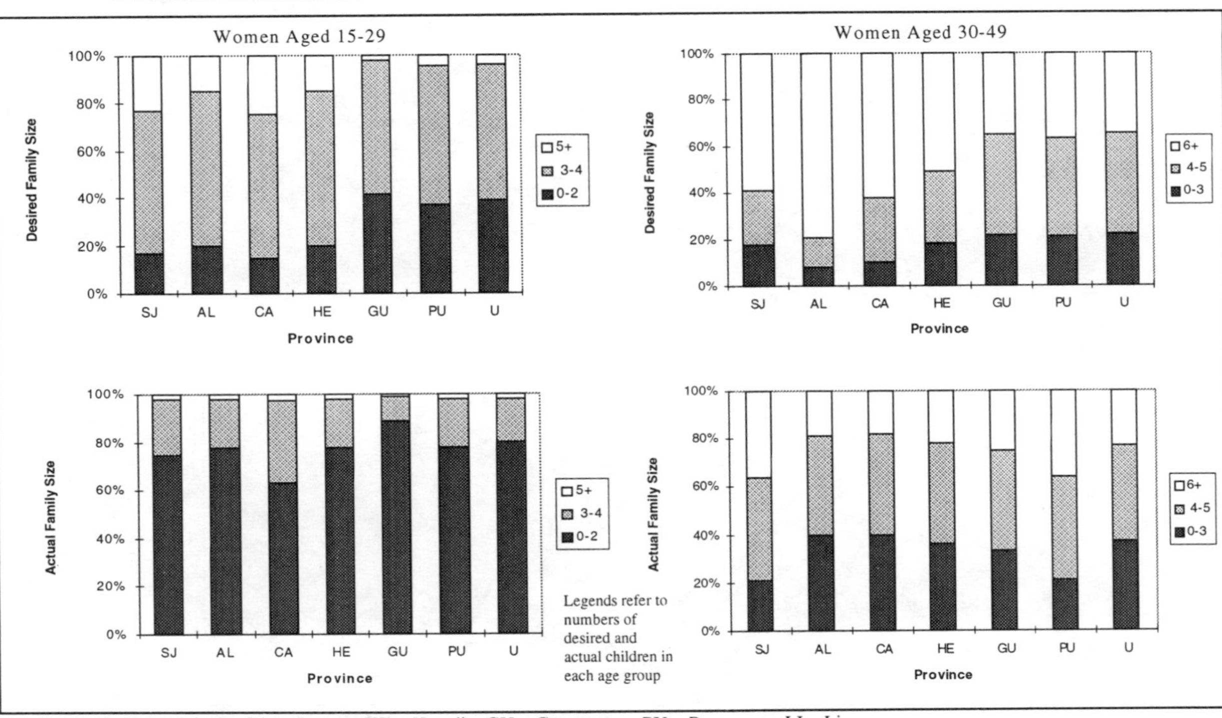

SJ = San José; AL = Alajuela; CA = Cartago; HE = Heredia; GU = Guanacaste; PU = Puntarenas; LI = Limon

*Based on regression coefficients for each region, with all other variables set at values indicated in text.

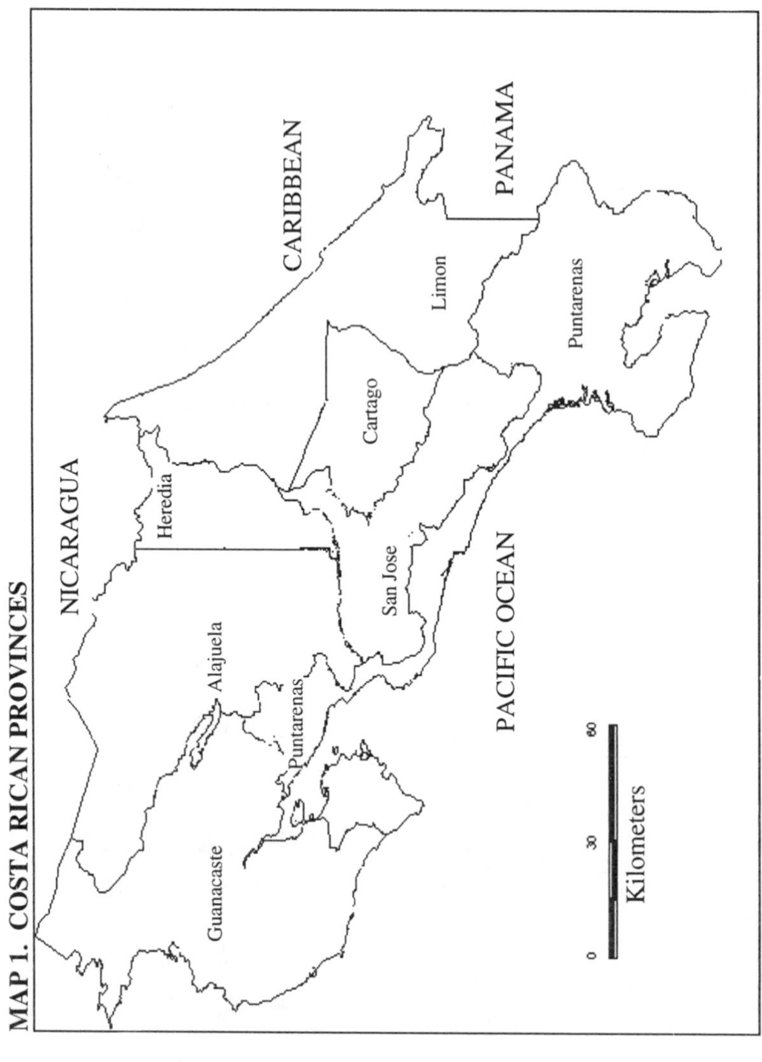

MAP 1. COSTA RICAN PROVINCES

Chapter Sixteen

THE DIFFUSION OF INFORMATION AND ADOPTION OF CONTRACEPTION IN COSTA RICA

RODNEY KNIGHT

Adoption of an innovative behavior such as the use of contraception potentially places individuals in conflict with social norms opposed to such behavior. However, programs promoting this behavior and individuals that have adopted this behavior provide information and normative influences which can offset norms opposed to such behavior. This paper studies the dynamics of diffusion of information and adoption of contraception related to the fertility decline during the 1960's and 1970's in Costa Rica. Hazard analyses find that women living in areas with more access to mass media, greater family planning program activity and higher proportions of others using contraception learn about family planning sooner. Women living in areas with higher proportions of users of contraception also adopt contraception sooner. Family planning program activity increases the rate women adopt contraception more in areas with lower use of contraception than in areas of higher use.

INTRODUCTION

The standard approach to the study of the adoption of contraception involves the examination of the effects of socioeconomic variables on the demand for and the cost of contraception (see Bulatao and Lee 1983a; Easterlin 1975). Usually the difference between the supply and demand for children determines the motivation to use contraception in such studies. This paper not only studies adoption of contraception in this way, but also examines the influence of individuals and groups on a woman's choice to adopt contraception (see Cleland and Wilson

1987; Retherford 1985; Retherford and Palmore 1983; Rogers 1973; Rogers and Kincaid 1981). Those with whom a woman interacts, including her spouse, other relatives, friends, neighbors, and family planning clinic workers, diffuse information and attitudes related to contraception to the woman, which may influence whether and when she adopts. The mass media can also diffuse information and attitudes influential in a woman's decision to adopt. In turn, the adoption of contraception would increase the diffusion of information and attitudes.

Studies of diffusion of fertility behavior have been around since the late 1950's (see Bogue 1967; Carlsson 1966; Freedman and Takeshita 1969; Hill, Stycos, and Back 1959, Palmore 1967). Since then many more studies have ensued, but few performed individual-level analyses at the national level. Two sets of national-level studies provide the basis for this study: Montgomery and Casterline's aggregate and individual-level studies of Taiwan (Montgomery and Casterline 1991; Montgomery 1993) and Rosero-Bixby's 1991 aggregate-level study of Costa Rica.

Before proceeding further, the concept of "diffusion" needs clarification. Diffusion is the process by which a source transfers an innovation to a receiver.[1] Innovations consist of new or different information, attitudes, behavior or objects. The word "different" implies that the receiver may know about the innovation, but has not adopted the innovation or fully incorporated the innovation into his or her thinking or behavior. Sources include the mass media, change agents, and individuals who know about the innovation: primarily those who have adopted the innova-

---

[1]Rogers (1983: 5) defines diffusion in a similar manner as "the process by which an innovation is communicated through certain channels over time among the members of a social system." In this definition, an innovation refers to "an idea, practice, or object that is perceived as new by the individual or other unit of adoption" (Rogers 1983: 11).

tion. Change agents include professionals or volunteers that attempt to diffuse an innovation to people they know only as clients. In terms of family planning, workers in community-based distribution programs, workers in family planning clinics and medical professionals that provide family planning services to their clients act as change agents.

This paper uses Costa Rica as the setting for a case study to examine the relative contributions of diffusion and socio-economic factors on the adoption of contraception. Costa Rica provides a good setting for a case study for various reasons. The rapid fertility decline in the 1960's and 1970's occurred primarily due to the adoption of contraception. Other possible contributors to the decline, including delayed marriage, postpartum abstinence, breastfeeding and abortion, had little influence on the decline (Rosero-Bixby 1991: 64-74). This implies that a study of the adoption of contraception provides the key to understanding the fertility decline. It also minimizes the effect on the analysis of women selectively responding to a desire for delaying births through mechanisms other than the adoption of contraception. Not only did the adoption of contraception drive the decline in Costa Rica, adoption occurred for spacing as well as stopping (Rosero-Bixby 1991: 63-64). Adoption for spacing suggests that women may have learned from others about the benefits of spacing. It seems less likely that women would have figured out on their own that spacing could have positive health benefits. Other studies of fertility in Costa Rica indicate that diffusion processes as well as socio-economic factors had an influence on the adoption of contraception and the fertility decline (Fridman 1984; Rosero-Bixby 1991). Although developing economically, Costa Rica did not have a pace of economic development that could explain the rapid increase in adoption of contraception.

DATA AND METHODS

The analyses for this study use data from: 1) the 1976 World Fertility Survey (WFS) for Costa Rica, 2) a resurvey of the WFS in 1978, 3) censuses, and 4) aggregate data compiled by Rosero-Bixby (1991). The WFS consists of interviews of 3,935 women aged 20 to 49 (World Fertility Survey 1980: 2). The resurvey was able to reach about 77 percent of the 2,626 married women (including those in consensual unions) in the WFS, which makes the number of women interviewed 2,009 (Fridman 1984: 171). The census data consist of two ten-percent samples of the 1973 census and the entire 1984 census including household information. Only one of the two samples from the 1973 census has household information. The data from Rosero-Bixby consists of aggregate information at the county level. Counties do not represent actual administrative units, rather they have been created by combining districts in order to provide areas similar in size to cantons, but with constant boundaries.

The WFS and the resurvey of the WFS provide all of the individual-level variables. The resurvey contains data for the dependent variable for the analysis of diffusion of information: the age when a woman learned that pregnancy can be prevented.[2] The original survey contains the primary source of data for the dependent variable for the analysis of adoption of contraception: a question about the number of children a woman had when she first began to use contraception (Dirección General de Estadística y Censos 1978). This question, combined with birth history data and other questions on use of contraception, provides a range of years when adoption of contraception could have occurred. The beginning of the range is used in the analyses shown. Analyses run for events based on the beginning, middle

---

[2]Learning that a pregnancy can be prevented will be treated synonymously with learning about family planning in the text that follows.

and end of this range generally only produced minor differences in coefficients. The independent variables drawn from the original survey and the resurvey include age, time, educational level, region of residence, fertility above desired number, and marital status. Fertility above desired number is found by subtracting the desired family size from the current number of living children.

In prior work, Rosero-Bixby created the bulk of the county-level variables needed for the analysis from census and registration data (1991: 97-132). Socio-economic indicators used from this data include educational attainment, female labor force participation, an index of income, and child mortality. All of these indicators, except for child mortality, have data from the censuses years of 1963 and 1973. Child mortality data for 1964 and 1973 comes from retrospective estimates based on children surviving for women age 15 to 39 in the 1973 and 1984 censuses. The measure of family planning access created from these data incorporates information from surrounding counties as well as the county of interest. Rosero-Bixby used a gravity model to give farther away counties and counties with smaller population less weight. The measure of fertility from these data is the general marital fertility rate in the counties for the years from 1958 to 1988.[3] Data for the numerator came from vital registration data, and census data was used to correct for inconsistencies. Data for the denominator came from the 1963, 1973 and 1984 censuses. The measure for surrounding county fertility created with these data weights fertility in surrounding counties with the number of marriages between the surrounding counties and the county of interest.

In the analyses, fertility serves as a proxy for the level of contraceptive use in a country or, in terms of diffusion, the de-

---

[3]Although this is technically is the general marital fertility rate (Shryock, et. al. 1976: 281), the discussion that follows will refer to it as the marital fertility rate for simplicity.

gree that users of contraception influence non-users to adopt. As a proxy this measure has problems since it can serve as a proxy for many things. Care has been taken in the analyses to include variables correlated with fertility which would confound the effect of this proxy if left out of the analyses. An estimate of the unmeasured county effects, generated with a fixed effects model, appears in all the analyses to control for such effects (see the Appendix).

The methods for the analyses indirectly study diffusion effects. Although approaches to diffusion research that qualitatively or quantitatively examine the effects of the actual content of social interaction on behavior are important to the study of diffusion, much of the data available does not lend itself to direct analysis of such social relations. Without direct data on the content of social interaction, research on diffusion uses methods that infer the diffusion of ideas and behavior based on the presence of conditions favorable to such diffusion; specifically, whether sources of information and attitudes that may influence behavior are present. Areas where many people have adopted a behavior are favorable to diffusion of the behavior because those who have adopted can act as sources of information and attitudes that reinforce the behavior. The presence of change agents who promote the adoption of behavior increases the diffusion of the behavior as well. Family planning workers operate as change agents by providing information and advice that help women to change their fertility behavior. If sources of mass media messages about the behavior are present, then the behavior would be expected to have a greater probability of diffusing. Restrictions on the advertisement of contraception, such as those found in Costa Rica at the time of the study, hinder the effectiveness of the mass media, but the mass media can still have an effect through discussions about family planning on radio or television programs, or articles about family planning in the print media.

Such discussions did occur in Costa Rica during the time period of the study.

Because this study considers the diffusion of information about contraception as well as the adoption of contraception, models need to be created for both. The hazard for the diffusion of information can be modeled in a similar fashion to the adoption of contraception. Because the diffusion of information about the innovation is part of the process of adoption of the innovation, a connection needs to be made between the models. This study makes this connection by modeling the hazard of learning about the existence of family planning and then modeling the hazard of adoption from that time on. In terms of event history spells, the first spell runs from the time when a woman first might become sexually active (age 13 for Costa Rica) to when she first learns about the existence of family planning, while the second spell runs from the time when a woman learns about family planning to when she adopts contraception.

The total discrete-time model of learning about family planning and adoption of contraception used in this study is:

$$\ln\left(\frac{\Pr_{L,t}}{1-\Pr_{L,t}}\right) = \alpha_L + \beta_L F_{t-l} + \gamma_L \sum_{j=1}^{n} \omega_j F_{j(t-l)} + \varphi_{L,I} Y_I + \varphi_{L,A} Y_{A(t-l)} + \eta_{L,I} X_I + \eta_{L,A} X_{A(t-l)} + \upsilon_L + \varepsilon_{L,t} \tag{1}$$

$$\ln\left(\frac{\Pr_{C,t}}{1-\Pr_{C,t}}\right) = \alpha_C + \beta_C F_{t-l} + \gamma_C \sum_{j=1}^{n} \omega_j F_{j(t-l)} + \phi_C K + \varphi_{C,I} Y_I + \varphi_{C,A} Y_{A(t-l)} + \eta_{C,I} X_I + \eta_{C,A} X_{A(t-l)} + \upsilon_C + \varepsilon_{C,t}$$

where $\ln(\Pr_{L,t}/1-\Pr_{L,t})$ represents the discrete-time equivalent of the hazard of learning about family planning at time t. Technically this is the log odds of the probability of learning about family planning in time t, (the subscript L implies leaving). The term $\ln(\Pr_{C,t}/1-\Pr_{C,t})$ represents the discrete-time hazard of adopting contraception, (the subscript C implies adoption of contraception); F_{t-l}, fertility in the area where the individual lives lagged l years; $F_{j(t-l)}$, fertility in the jth of n surrounding areas; K, the age when the woman learned about family planning; Y_I, a vector of individual-level diffusion covariates; $Y_{A(t-l)}$, a vector of aggregate-level diffusion covariates lagged l years; X_I, a vector of other individual-level covariates and, $X_{A(t-l)}$, a vector of other aggregate-level covariates lagged l years. Since F_{t-l} and $F_{j(t-l)}$ only represent diffusion related to social interaction between users and the woman, Y_I and $Y_{A(t-l)}$ include diffusion related to the other two sources: mass media and family planning service providers. The factor ω_j weights the lagged number of adopters in the jth surrounding area. The error term has two parts: 1) υ, the fixed unmeasured area effect, and 2) ε_t, the usual random error that varies by area and time.

RESULTS

Diffusion Information

Since the analyses can not directly measure how information diffuses from a source to a woman, the analyses focus on indirect measures of the availability of sources of information. The analyses examine four hypotheses for how sources of diffusion affect learning about family planning.

1. Women living in counties with higher levels of mass media access learn about family planning faster than women living in counties with lower levels of access.

2. Women living in counties with higher levels of use of family planning services learn about family planning faster than women living in counties with lower levels of use of services.

3. Women living in counties with higher levels of use of contraception learn about family planning faster than women living in counties with lower levels of use.

4. Women living in counties surrounded by counties with higher levels use of contraception learn about family planning faster than women living in counties surrounded by counties with lower levels of use.

The various forms of the marital fertility rate used in the analyses serve as proxies for the how much social interaction a non-user will have with users of contraception either from the county of residence or from surrounding counties (hypotheses three and four). These proxies have a negative effect on the hazard of a woman learning about family planning, but the corresponding hypotheses (three and four) have a positive effect. This apparent discrepancy occurs because the marital fertility rate has a negative correlation with the level of use of family planning.

As the diffusion hypotheses indicate, this study attempts to assess how different sources of information diffuse the knowledge that methods of family planning exist. Two models that test these hypotheses appear in Table 1. The two models are nearly identical, except that one includes the interaction between the level of fertility in surrounding counties and access to family planning. The reason for the addition of this interaction variable will become more apparent in the discussion that follows. The similarity of the results for the two models is not surprising given that the models have all the same variables in common except for one.

In addition to the coefficients for each model, Table 1 displays an estimate of the effect of the variables on the probability of a woman learning about family planning. The addition of this estimate in Table 1 helps in the comparison of the effects of variables relative to one another, since logistic regression coefficients do not give much of an indication of this. The estimates of the effects of variables on the probability of learning can be compared, because these estimates represent changes based on reasonable values for the variables. However, providing a single method for the estimate of this probability gets complicated by the presence of both continuous and categorical variables in the analyses, because each of these two types of variables requires a different measure. Although not perfect, roughly comparable measures can be created for continuous and categorical variables. In the case of a continuous variable, the measure subtracts the probability of learning due to a value of the variable one standard deviation below the mean from the probability for a value one standard deviation above the mean. The calculations use mean or typical values for all other variables. This measure provides a rough gauge of the breath of change that the variable might produce in the probability.[4] The measure for an indicator variable consists of the probability of learning about family planning for a woman in the category for the indicator variable minus the probability for a woman in the reference category. For example, for Model 1 a married women has a 16 percent higher probability of learning about family planning than a single women and a widowed women has a 31 percent higher probability than a single woman.

Both models give the expected results for the diffusion information sources variables based on the hypotheses given above. The mass media, family planning access, and the level of use of family planning in and around the area where a women lives all increase the probability that a woman learns about family planning. Although statistically significant and of substantial size (greater than ten percent effect on the probability), the effect of

---

[4]The variable could drop below one standard deviation below the mean or rise to levels above one standard deviation above the mean, but such rises or drops are much less likely. Thus, this range of one standard deviation above and below the mean represents the extent of change that appears possible to produce in a reasonable time.

the mass media should not be overplayed since the variable only measures access to the mass media and not the level of messages about family planning on the media. Presumably, women who have greater access to the mass media would receive more messages through this source, but this cannot be known for certain without some indication of the number of family planning messages sent out via the mass media.

In an opposite way, the small, non-significant effect of family planning access could be an underestimate due to problems with the measure of family planning access. The measure used is the number of visits of women to public family planning clinics. This does not adequately measure the indirect effect of family planning on diffusion of information about family planning. An indirect effect occurs when women who learn about family planning from a clinic tell others. Simply knowing the number of visits women make to clinics does not indicate whether they will tell others. A more important problem for this variable is that it does not include private providers. Because the fertility decline started in the early 1960's (see Figure 1) and the national family planning program started in 1968, the private sector must have played an important role in the early decline and perhaps an important role even after the public program started.

The number of visits to public clinics has a few other problems as a measure of family planning access which may reduce its effect in the analyses. Number of visits is not the same as the number of women visiting a clinic. In some areas fewer women could be making more visits and give the impression of greater access when the clinics are not easily accessible to many women.

The problem of geographic attribution also exists with this variable. The gravity model increases the level of access to adjust for clinics in nearby counties. It does not, however, appropriately lower the access for women in counties where women from the outside heavily use services in that county. For example, women from the outside counties visit clinics in San José giving the impression of higher access for women living in San José. Not only does this raise the number associated with access for women in San José, but it also masks the problem of longer waiting times for services (lower access) for women living in San José due to women from the outside. As a result, many women in such areas would seek out private providers for services, which the measure of access does not include.

Another problem with this variable is multicollinearity with the marital fertility in a county. Family planning access and fertility mutually reinforce one another. The level of family planning clinic activity in and around a county affects the fertility levels in and around the county. Conversely, fertility levels partially determine the provision of family planning services. Muticollinearity is the natural result of this link between these variables, which could create a downward bias in the effects of either or both variables.

The results for the marital fertility variables imply greater learning in counties with higher interaction between non-users and users of contraception. Interestingly, the level of use of contraception in surrounding counties has a much greater effect than within a county. Moreover, the level of contraceptive use in surrounding counties has statistically significant coefficients while the level of use within a county does not. When compared with the mass media and family planning access, the level of use in surrounding counties far exceeds the effect of family planning or the mass media.

Could users of contraception in surrounding counties have a stronger effect than either users within a county, family planning clinics or the mass media? Users from outside the county may have a greater effect on the diffusion of information than users within the county because by the time the women within a county become users most others in the county have already been informed by users from outside the county. In other words, information flowing from outside a county preempts much further flow of new information from within. This links in well with the social network theories of the strength of weak social ties on diffusion (see Granovetter 1973; Liu and Duff 1972). The mass media would be expected to have the greatest effect of the various sources, but since no targeted media campaigns occurred during the period the full potential of the mass media can not be assessed from this analysis. The full effect of family planning access is probably underestimated as well, for the reasons given previously. Nonetheless, these analyses point to a potentially strong effect of users of contraception on diffusion of information which needs to be taken into account in future analyses.

Given the strong effect of users of contraception from surrounding counties, the mass media and family planning access may have a greater effect in areas with fewer users in surrounding counties. These other sources may substitute for the effect of social interaction of non-users with users. The way to model this substitution effect is to include a variable with the interaction between the marital fertility in surrounding counties and the other source. Because the variable for the mass media does not include any direct information about family planning messages, the interaction of level of use and the mass media would not seen very useful. Thus, only the interaction between marital fertility in surrounding counties and family planning access has been included in the analysis.

The analysis in Model 2 does not show the expected substitution effect. Although not significant, the effect is the opposite of the expectations: low levels of use of contraception (high fertility) in surrounding counties decreases the effect of family planning access on learning about contraception. The magnitude of the effect of family planning on learning appears in Table 2.

The expected substitution effect does appear in analyses (not shown) that include an interaction of marital fertility within a county with family planning access. In an analysis with both types of interactions, the interaction between marital fertility within a county and family planning access shows the substitution effect, while the interaction between marital fertility in surrounding counties and family planning access does not. None of these tests of the interaction variable produce statistically significant effects, so neither the substitution effect nor the opposite of this effect can be substantiated from these results.

The other variables in the analyses, while not the focus of these analyses, produce some interesting results. Generally these variables produce coefficients of the expected sign and many have statistically significant coefficients. The few places where the sign of the coefficients differ from expectations are worth examining. The variable for rural central valley has a negative coefficient, which implies that women in the most rural area (non-central valley rural) learn faster than women in this region. However, in neither model are the coefficients for the region variables significant.

Female labor force participation also has seemingly unexpected negative results.[5] Women who work would seem to want to learn about and adopt contraception sooner in order to avoid breaks in work to have children. On the other hand, having many children is an inducement to earn more income, so some women, especially poorer women with larger families, may work in order to help support their family. Such women already would have delayed adoption of contraception in order to have larger family, and probably would be less likely to want to learn about and adopt contraception in the future. This second case may result in the negative effect of female labor force participation on learning about family planning.

---

[5]The variable for female labor force participation is at the county level, but the discussion will focus on individual-level behavior with the caveat that the translation of effects from county to individual level is far from perfect.

The marital status indicator variables perform as expected given that all women who are or have been in some sort of union have a greater chance of learning about family planning than single women. The ordering of the coefficients says something interesting. The order from lowest to highest probability of learning about family planning generally goes as follows: single, separated, consensual union, divorced, married, and widowed. The dynamics underlying this cannot be fully ascertained from the data available, but some possibilities can be mentioned. Although the results are significant relative to the omitted category (single) the differences between coefficients may not be significant. In addition, it could be argued that a selection bias occurs because women in certain categories have already learned about family planning by the time they reach a marital state, such as widowed women. It must be remembered that in order to reach a marital status in the analyses the woman must not already know about family planning, so the results are not due to this type of bias.

Some explanations can be given for the results. Widowed women may learn about family planning because of a demand for family planning, either related to a desire not to get pregnant due to social sanctions or because these women already have the number of children they want. Divorced women may learn about family planning faster than women in consensual unions because divorced women feel less certain about being able to care for a child. This does not hold true when comparing divorced with married women, because married women learn at about the same or faster rate than divorced women. Perhaps married women learn as fast or faster than divorced women, and faster than single women and women in consensual unions because other people expect married women to be the most interested in family planning and therefore tend to talk more with married women about family planning. The place of separated women in the order may appear surprising at first, but if separated women have a low level of sexual activity relative to the other categories, then they would have a lower demand for family planning information.

The variable for unmeasured county effects deserves special consideration. The analyses include this estimate of time-invariant unmeasured county-level variables in order to make sure that the county-level proxies for social interaction actually measure the effect of social interaction and not some unmeasured variables. Neither model produces a significant effect for this variable, which implies that these analyses do not omit relevant county-level variables.

When considering the magnitude of effects of the control variables on the probability of learning, none produce substantially larger effects than the largest effect of the diffusion variables; that for social interaction between counties. Fertility above the desired level, child mortality (dead child not replaced), region, female labor force participation, and unmeasured county effects all have modest influence on the probability of learning about family planning. Age and period (years since 1956) have more substantial effects. The largest effects occur for the education and marital status indicator variables. Overall the diffusion variables fare quite well compared to the control variables, suggesting the potential importance of sources of diffusion. Only having a college education or being a widow have a similar effect on the probability as social interaction between counties. The mass media in a county has a moderate effect, but still equal to many of the controls. For example the mass media has a similar effect to secondary education. From the standpoint of programs to promote learning about family planning, it would be easier to reach women through the mass media than to ensure they all received a secondary education. Family planning programs have a rather modest effect on the time when women first learn about family planning. However, this effect is encouraging since it would not be expected that many women would first learn about family planning by going to a clinic. Rather they would go to a clinic after learning about family planning. Therefore, most of this effect must be indirect; women who go to family planning clinics tell others about family planning. Perhaps some women who do not know about family planning see signs for family planning services (within health clinics) and then ask others about family planning.

Adoption of Contraception

Once a woman knows about family planning, how long does it take for her to adopt a method of family planning? This section tries to answer this question through analyses of the adoption of contraception. First, this section discusses hypotheses about how sources of diffusion affect adoption of contraception. Then it describes the analyses of the adoption of contraception. Five hypotheses appear below for how the diffusion variables affect the probability that a woman adopts contraception after learning about family planning.

1. Women who learn about family planning at older ages adopt contraception faster than women who learn at younger ages.

2. Women living in counties with higher levels of mass media access adopt contraception sooner than women living in counties with lower levels of access.

3. Women living in counties with higher levels of use of family planning services adopt contraception sooner than women living in counties with lower levels of use of services.

4. Women living in counties with higher levels of use of contraception adopt contraception sooner than women living in counties with lower levels of use.

5. Women living in counties surrounded by counties with higher levels use of contraception adopt contraception sooner than women living in counties surrounded by counties with lower levels of use.

As in the analyses for learning about family planning, in the analyses for adoption of contraception the various forms of the marital fertility rate serve as proxies for the how much social interaction a non-user will have with users of contraception either in the county of residence or in surrounding counties. These proxies have a negative effect on the hazard of a woman adopting contraception, but this does not present a problem for the hypotheses, since the marital fertility rate has a negative correlation with the level of use of family planning.

The diffusion hypotheses indicate that this study examines both how different sources of information aid in the diffusion (adoption) of contraception and how the timing of first learning about family planning (another diffusion process) aids in the diffusion of contraception. The results from the analyses of the hazard that a woman adopts contraception appear in Table 3. The structure of this table follows that for the analyses of learning about contraception. As mentioned in the section on data, the exact year when a woman adopted contraception is not known; only a range of years when adoption occurred can be determined from the data. The analyses presented use the beginning of the range. Other analyses, not shown, for the middle and end of the range yield similar results.

Diffusion variables produce similar results in the two models. These variables generally generate results of the expected sign, but only some of the variables produce statistically significant coefficients. The one variable that has a sign opposite from expectations is family planning access. When included by itself, as in Model 1, family planning access produces this negative result, but when the interaction between marital fertility and family planning access is included, then family planning access has a positive effect for certain levels of marital fertility. More will be said about this later.

Only a couple of the diffusion variables always have statistically significant coefficients: the age when a woman learned about family planning and marital fertility within the county. The variable for family planning access has a significant coefficient in the model with the interaction between marital fertility and family planning access. This interaction term is significant in that model. In the model without the interaction term, family planning does not produce a significant coefficient. The remaining two diffusion variables, mass media access in the county and marital fertility in surrounding counties do not yield significant coefficients.

The variable for marital fertility in the county has the largest effect, which implies a strong effect on adoption of social interaction between a woman and users of contraception in her county of residence. Although marital fertility in surrounding counties does not produce a significant coefficient, it does have a substantial effect compared to the other diffusion variables.

The results for marital fertility imply that social interaction between users and non-users of contraception within a county has a significant effect on adoption of contraception while social interaction between counties does not. Multicollinearity may weaken this result, but it is interesting that inter-county social interaction significantly affects the diffusion of information, while within-county social interaction significantly affects adoption of contraception. Such results are theoretically appealing. Diffusion of information coming from outside a county can be explained as follows: counties with lower fertility supply information to counties with higher fertility, so that by the time the fertility drops in a county much of the information diffusion has already occurred and within county diffusion has little effect. The explanation of within-county social interaction having a stronger effect on adoption than inter-county social interaction relates to the nature of influence of close versus distant social interactions. People living closer to a woman have a greater influence on her behavior than individuals both physically and perhaps socially farther away.

The age when a woman learns about family planning has the next largest effect on adoption among the diffusion variables according to Table 3. Women who learn about family planning at older ages adopt faster than women who learn at younger ages. The delay in learning about family planning results in a higher motivation to adopt for the older women because many would have adopted at a younger age if they only knew about family planning. Thus, when they do learn about family planning older women tend to have a greater conviction to adopt and as a result adopt faster.

In determining the overall effect of age, however, older women do not adopt faster than younger women. The magnitude of the coefficients for age always exceeds that for the age of learning, which implies an overall negative effect of age since the coefficients for age always are negative. Even this oversimplifies the picture a bit. Table 4 gives a better idea how age of learning and age of the woman affect adoption. Moving down the columns gives an indication of the effect of age, while moving across the rows give an indication of the effect of age at learning. For a given age, women who learn about family planning later adopt faster. A woman of age 20-29 will adopt 21 percentage points faster if she learns at age 20-29 rather than age 13-19. Such a increase in rate of adoption implies that in some cases the effect of the age when a woman learns about family planning exceeds that for the other diffusion variables, but as can be seen from the table in other cases the effect of this variable is less than other diffusion variables. Although women of a given age who learn at older ages adopt faster, moving diagonally across the table shows that younger women who have learned the same number of years in the past will adopt faster than older women. A woman of age 20-29 who learned at age 13-19 will adopt 11 percentage points faster than a woman of age 30-39 who learned at age 20-29.

As a result of the family planning variable generating coefficients with an opposite sign relative to expectations, the second model adds the interaction between marital fertility and family planning availability. Inclusion of such an interaction can help to sort out whether the effect of family planning depends on level of fertility. The interaction term has a positive and statistically significant coefficient, which implies family planning has more of a positive effect in counties with high fertility. Table 5 shows how for a medium or high value of marital fertility,[6] higher levels of family planning availability correspond to higher probabilities of adoption. In the case of low fertility, higher levels of family planning have the opposite effect. Thus, even though family planning has a negative coefficient, the negative effect on adoption of contraception only shows up at low levels of fertility.

Family planning might appear to reduce the rate of adoption in low fertility areas because of a selection bias related to these areas. Counties that reach low fertility with limited family planning services might do so because the woman have a higher motivation to adopt contraception not picked up by the other variables, whereas counties that reach lower fertility with the help of more family planning services may have less motivated women who adopt at a slower rate. The counterfactual question that cannot fully be answered with the data is what would have happened if more family planning services had been available in counties which reached reduced fertility with limited family planning services? Would women in such counties have adopted family planning faster if the level of family planning were higher? In addition, counties that reach low fertility with limited family planning services may actually have higher levels of services than indicated by the variable for family planning services, because this

---

[6]Low refers to one standard deviation below the mean, medium is at the mean, and high is one standard deviation above the mean.

variable does not include private medical practitioners that provide family planning services.

While not the focus of these analyses, the other variables in the analyses produce some notable results. In most cases these variables produce coefficients of the expected sign and have statistically significant coefficients. Some of the variables have effects of similar or greater magnitude than the diffusion variables. Marriage has a much larger effect than the diffusion variables. The ordering of the marital status categories mirrors that for the analyses of learning. Widowed women adopt much faster than other categories of women. Education, fertility above the desired level, and dead child not replaced all have effects of similar or greater magnitude than many of the diffusion variables. Female labor force participation has notably weak effects.

As in the analyses for learning, the variable for unmeasured county effects deserves special consideration because of its importance as a control for other factors. The analyses include this estimate of time-invariant unmeasured county-level variables in order to make sure that the county-level proxies for social interaction actually measure the effect of social interaction and not some unmeasured variables. Since this variable does not produce statistically significant coefficients and the effect on the probability of adoption ranges from five to six percent, the problem of omitted variables appears somewhat minor for these analyses.

The analyses of learning and adoption do not directly indicate the contribution of the various variables to the overall time to adoption from age 13 onward because the time to adoption gets divided between the time to learning and the time from learning to adoption. Although various means can be devised to combine the results of the two analyses, a simple way to show the effect of the diffusion variables on the time from start of risk (age 13) to adoption is to run analyses using this as the spell. The two models in Table 6 do just this. The results for the marital fertility in surrounding counties imply social interaction of a woman with users of contraception in other counties has the greatest effect on the adoption of contraception among the diffusion variables. Although statistically significant, social interaction within the county has little effect. Mass media neither has a statistically significant coefficient nor much effect on the probability of adoption.

Family planning has effects similar to those found in the analyses of time from learning to adoption. In the model without the interaction between marital fertility and family planning, the effect of family planning is negative and non-significant, while in the analysis with this interaction term, family planning has a moderate positive effect. Closer examination of the effect of family planning by level of marital fertility shows that, in counties with high to moderate fertility, family planning has a positive effect (see Table 7). At a high level of fertility in a county (low contraceptive use), family planning has a ten percent effect. This is relatively high compared with the other variables in the analyses, but still much smaller than the 17 percent effect of marital fertility in surrounding counties. In counties with low marital fertility (high contraceptive use) family planning has a small negative effect.

In general, most of the variables in these analyses, whether diffusion or controls, have much smaller effects on the probability of adoption than the variables have in the analyses of learning or the analyses from the time of learning to adoption. For example, in these analyses a woman with a college education only has at most a 16 percentage point higher chance of adopting contraception than a woman with no education, while in the other analyses a woman with a college education has a 26 percentage point higher chance of learning and up to 30 percentage point higher chance of adoption. The results for marriage are much different. Instead of having by far the greatest effect, being a widow has less of an effect than two of the other categories of marital status: married and consensual union. Divorced, not separated, has the lowest effect relative to being single. These results call into question the strength of the differences between and the ordering of the marital statuses in the other analyses. If the ordering of marital statuses in terms of adoption were known, then special programs might be appropriate for different categories. For instance, if widows do actually adopt faster because of a higher perceived need for family planning, special attention might be given to their needs in the design of programs.

DISCUSSION

The results of this study reveal some interesting aspects of the processes of learning about family planning and adoption of contraception which not only add to the understanding of these processes, but also suggest areas for program policy and research. Each of the diffusion variables contribute to either learning or adoption or both, but certain variables contribute more than others. Some of the results can directly contribute to policy formation, while others show the need for more and different kinds of research.

The strongest results in terms of the diffusion variables come from the marital fertility proxies for social interaction between women and users of contraception. The differing results for social interaction within and between counties raises interesting possibilities for the theory of diffusion. Social interaction between counties has a much stronger effect on learning than social interaction within counties, which suggests that information flows from outside inward, such that by the time individuals in an area can become sources to others in the area, most of the people within the area already have gotten the information. The movement of information from outside areas supports the idea that weak social links play an important role in the diffusion of information between groups (see Granovetter 1973; Liu and Duff 1972). Once a woman knows about family planning, then the social interaction within a county dominates, which indicates that individuals close to a woman, both physically and socially, have the greatest influence on her behavior.

Although this theory does not point to specific interventions to put into place, it does suggest some areas for policy emphasis. Because individuals learn from people farther away, information programs need not always cover the entire area of interest. Care must be taken to supply information to multiple areas to bridge gaps where these natural links are inoperative or weak (see Lesthaeghe 1977). Since this study only looks at the supply of basic information, the quality of the information diffused was not examined. When it comes to more detailed information about family planning, such as side effects of contraceptive methods, the quality of the information becomes important because incorrect information will have detrimental effects on program success. It may be necessary to cover more areas with the information campaign to ensure the quality of the information. The basic message is that simple information can be diffused by targeting a limited number of areas with the information, since it will diffuse to others, while more detailed information may need a more widespread and costly approach to ensure the integrity of the information.

In terms of adoption of contraception, the results of this study imply that individuals closer to the woman have a greater effect than individuals farther away. This is an interesting contrast to the theory for learning. When considering programs, this implies that programs focus on individuals close to the woman. Other studies have shown for selected villages the importance of socially connected individuals and small social groups (women's clubs) in the diffusion of information about family planning and the adoption of contraception (Kincaid, et. al. 1993; Rogers and Kincaid 1981). This study has shown in an indirect way how such social interaction can be important at the national level. As a result, this study suggests that the community-level interventions found in studies by Kincaid and others may have an impact on adoption at the national level. Certainly if social interaction has an effect with no program in place, then it may have an even stronger effect with a program in place.

The results for the mass media are less conclusive. The mass media does have an effect on the diffusion of information, but no effect on adoption. This study cannot ascertain the full effect of the mass media because the variable used for the mass media measures access and not the number of messages about family planning. Moreover, since no national information education and communication (IEC) program occurred during the period of this study, the mass media messages vary in quality and emphasis. Not all of the messages were positive; some were negative (Stycos 1971). Future research needs information about the number and content of mass media messages. Such research would also benefit from being in a country with an IEC program in some areas.

Family planning access gives mixed results in this study. The strongest effects of family planning access occur in areas with the highest fertility. In low fertility areas, family planning access even appears to reduce adoption. Based on these results, family program managers might place more emphasis on providing public services in areas of high fertility with the idea that areas of lower fertility already have some form of access from the private sector. Since the private sector was not included in the measure of access or as a separate indicator of access, the role of the private sector is unknown. However, couples using modern methods must have gotten contraceptives from somewhere, so the private sector must have been active in some areas even before the institution of the national family planning program. The omission of the private sector from the measure of access may be one of the reasons that family planning access appears to have the slightly negative effect in low fertility areas.

Among the control variables, education is one that often gets cited as a means to lower fertility. A quick glance at the results seems to confirm this given that a woman with a college education has a probability of learning about family planning 26 percentage points higher and a probability of adoption (once she has learned) from 29 to 30 percentage points higher than a woman with no education. Such a comparison does not make sense when it comes to the reality of the situation. First, most women in Costa Rica have at least primary education and second, providing college education to most women would be an expensive way to reduce fertility and beyond the means of most developing countries. It makes more sense to look at increasing educational levels from primary to secondary levels. Increasing the education of women from primary to secondary level would increase the probability of learning by eight to nine percentage points and increase adoption (from time of learning) by eight percentage points. Based on the analyses from age 13 to time of adoption, raising the education of women from primary to secondary level would increase the probability of adoption by five to seven percentage points. Clearly the programmatic effect of education does not exceed the potential effect of all the different diffusion sources. Perhaps a less expensive way to utilize education to affect fertility behavior would be to improve the sex education programs in the schools, rather than attempting to raise the overall educational level (see Stycos 1989 for a view of the effect of sex education in schools in Costa Rica).

In the end, the results of this study suggest that a combined program which takes advantage of patterns of social interaction, the mass media and family planning service providers should have the greatest effect on both the diffusion of information about family planning and the adoption of contraception. Raising the educational levels of women, or better yet enhancing the sex education programs in schools, could further supplement such a program.

Appendix: Estimating Unmeasured County Effects

This appendix describes the process to obtain an estimate of unmeasured county effects. The work of Montgomery and Casterline (1991) on aggregate fertility in Taiwan, and the later study of Montgomery (1993) on the adoption of contraception provide the bases for this method. Unmeasured county effects can be estimated with the assumption that these effects do not vary with time. Such a "fixed-effects" assumption implies that unmeasured county effects do not bias the parameters from a county-level deviations from means model of fertility. Thus, the parameters from the deviations from means model can be used to estimate the unmeasured county effect.

The method to estimate the unmeasured county effect starts with the county-level model of fertility:

$$F_{i,t} = \alpha LF_{i,t-l} + \beta_V X_{Vi,t-l} + \beta_C X_{Ci} + \upsilon_i + \varepsilon_{i,t} \tag{A1}$$

where $F_{i,t}$ represents fertility, $LF_{i,t-l}$, fertility lagged l years, $X_{Vi,t-l}$, a vector of time-varying covariates lagged l years, and X_{Ci}, a vector of time-constant covariates including the intercept or constant term. The subscript i refers to the county and t to the time. Parameters for the covariates are α, β_V, and β_C. The error term has two parts: 1) υ_i, the fixed unmeasured county effect, and 2) $\varepsilon_{i,t}$, the usual random error that varies by county and time. Taking the mean of $F_{i,t}$ over the time period for the study, T:

$$\frac{1}{T}\sum_{t=l}^{T} F_{i,t} = \frac{1}{T}\sum_{t=l}^{T}\left[\alpha LF_{i,t-l} + \beta_V X_{Vi,t-l} + \beta_C X_{Ci} + \upsilon_i + \varepsilon_{i,t}\right]$$

or $\overline{F}_i = \alpha\,\overline{LF}_i + \beta_V \overline{X}_{Vi} + \beta_C X_{Ci} + \upsilon_i$.[7] (A2)

---

[7]The bar over the variables represent the average over time. The constant covariates and the constant part of the error do not appear as averages in the equations, since the average of a constant is the constant itself. The term $\overline{\varepsilon}_i$ drops out because for regression models this is zero.

Equation A2 can be rearranged to produce an estimate of υ_i when none of the covariates, other than lagged fertility, are correlated with υ_i. In such a case, an instrumental variable approach analogous to two-stage least squares can be used to remove the correlation between $LF_{i,t-l}$ and υ_i. The case where one or more of the other covariates, such as availability of family planning clinics, are correlated with υ_i requires another approach to eliminate the bias due to this correlation. Subtracting Equation A2 from A1 gives a differences from means equation which does not include υ_i:

$$F_{i,t} - \overline{F}_i = \alpha LF_{i,t-l} - \alpha \overline{LF}_i + \beta_V X_{Vi,(t-l)} - \beta_V \overline{X}_{Vi} + \beta_C X_{Ci} - \beta_C X_{Ci} + \upsilon_i - \upsilon_i + \varepsilon_{i,t}$$

or $$F_{i,t} - \overline{F}_i = \alpha \left(LF_{t-l} - \overline{LF}_{t-l}\right) + \beta_V \left(X_{Vi,t-l} - \overline{X}_{Vi}\right) + \varepsilon_{i,t} \qquad \text{(A3)}$$

Now Equation A3 can be used to estimate the parameters for the covariates. Serial correlation between $LF_{t-l} - \overline{LF}_{t-l}$ and $\varepsilon_{i,t}$ can be removed by the use of instruments (further lagged covariates) for $LF_{t-l} - \overline{LF}_{t-l}$ in the manner analogous to two-stage least squares described earlier. This assumes the other covariates are uncorrelated with the random error term, $\varepsilon_{i,t}$. The estimates of the parameters $\hat{\alpha}$, $\hat{\mathrm{b}}_V$, $\hat{\mathrm{b}}_C$ will be used in a rearranged version of Equation A2 to estimate υ_i:

$$\upsilon_i + \hat{\mathrm{b}}_C \mathbf{X}_{Ci} \approx \overline{F}_i - \hat{\alpha}\overline{LF}_i + \hat{\mathrm{b}}_V \overline{\mathbf{X}}_{Vi} \qquad \text{(A4)}$$

Since all of the county-level covariates vary with time in this analysis, this equation reduces to:

$$\upsilon_i \approx \overline{F}_i - \hat{\alpha}\overline{LF}_i + \hat{\mathrm{b}}_V \overline{\mathbf{X}}_{Vi} \qquad \text{(A5)}$$

REFERENCES

Bogue, D.J. 1967. (Ed.) *Mass Communication and Motivation for Birth Control.* Chicago: Community and Family Study Center, University of Chicago.

Bulatao, R.A., and R.D. Lee. 1983. "A Framework for the Study of Fertility Determinants. *Determinants of Fertility in Developing Countries.*" Volume 1. Ed. Rodolfo A. Bulatao and Ronald D. Lee New York: Academic Press. 1-26.

Carlsson, G. 1966. "The Decline of Fertility: Innovation or Adjustment Process." *Population Studies* 20(2): 149-174.

Cleland, J. and C. Wilson. 1987. "Demand theories of the fertility transition: an iconoclastic view." *Population Studies* 41(1): 5-30.

Dirección General de Estadística y Censos. 1978. *Encuesta Nacional de Fecundidad 1976 Costa Rica.* San José, Costa Rica: DGEC.

Easterlin, R.A. 1975. "An Economic Framework for Fertility Analysis." *Studies in Family Planning* 6(3): 54-63.

Freedman, R. and J.Y. Takeshita. 1969. *Family Planning in Taiwan: An Experiment in Social Change.* Princeton, New Jersey: Princeton University Press.

Fridman, S. 1984. *Spatial and Temporal Aspects of Contraceptive Adoption: An Analysis of Contemporary Fertility Behavior in Costa Rica.* Diss. Cornell University.

Granovetter, M.S. 1973. "The Strength of Weak Ties." *American Journal of Sociology* 78(6): 1360-1380.

Hill, R., J.M. Stycos, and K.W. Back. 1959. *The Family and Population Control: A Puerto Rican Experiment in Social Change.* Chapel Hill: The University of North Carolina Press.

Kincaid, D. L., et. al. 1993. "Communication Networks, Ideation, and Family Planning in Trishal, Bangladesh." Revision of a paper presented at the annual meetings of the Population Association of America, Cincinnati, Ohio.

Lesthaeghe, Ron J. 1977. *The Decline of Belgian Fertility, 1800-1970*. Princeton, New Jersey: Princeton University Press.

Liu, W.T., and R.W. Duff. 1972. "The Strength in Weak Ties." *Public Opinion Quarterly* 36(3): 361-366.

Montgomery, M.R. 1993. "The Diffusion of Fertility Control in Taiwan: A Multi-level Analysis." Paper presented at the annual meetings of the Population Association of America, Cincinnati, Ohio.

Montgomery, M.R., and J.B. Casterline. 1991. "The Diffusion of Fertility Control in Taiwan: Evidence from Pooled Cross-section, Time-series Models." September revision of a paper presented at the annual meetings of the Population Association of America, Washington, D.C.

Palmore, J. 1967. "The Chicago Snowball: A Study of the Flow and Diffusion of Family Planning Information." *Sociological Contributions to Family Planning Research*. Ed. Donald J. Bogue. Chicago: Community and Family Study Center, University of Chicago. 272-363.

Retherford, R. D. 1985. "A Theory of Marital Fertility Transition." *Population Studies* 39(2): 249-268.

Retherford, R.D., and J.A. Palmore. 1983. Diffusion Processes Affecting Fertility Regulation. *Determinants of Fertility in Developing Countries*. Volume 2. Ed. Rodolfo A. Bulatao and Ronald D. Lee New York: Academic Press. 295-339.

Rogers, E.M. 1973. *Communication Strategies for Family Planning*. New York: The Free Press.

Rogers, E.M. 1983. *Diffusion of Innovations*. (3rd ed.) New York: The Free Press.

Rogers, E.M., and D.L. Kincaid. 1981. *Communication Networks: Toward a New Paradigm for Research.* New York: The Free Press.

Rosero-Bixby, L. 1981. *Fecundidad y Anticoncepción en Costa Rica 1981: Resultados de las Segunda Encuesta de Prevalencia Anticonceptiva.* San José, Costa Rica: Asociación Demográfica Costarricense, and Maryland: Westinghouse Health Systems.

Rosero-Bixby, L. 1991. *Interaction Diffusion and Fertility Transition in Costa Rica.* Diss. University of Michigan.

Shryock, H.S., et al. 1976. *The Methods and Materials of Demography*, condensed ed. New York: Academic Press.

Stycos, J.M. 1989. "Does Sex Education Corrupt? The Case of Costa Rica." Working Paper 1.19, Population and Development Program, Cornell University.

Stycos, J.M. 1971. *Ideology, Faith, and Family Planning in Latin America: Studies in Public and Private Opinion on Fertility Control.* New York: McGraw-Hill Book Company.

Universidad de Costa Rica. 1976. *La Población de Costa Rica.* San Jose, Costa Rica: UCR, Instituto de Investigaciones Sociales.

World Fertility Survey. 1980. The 1976 Costa Rica fertility survey: a summary of findings. *WFS Reports* 19.

TABLE 1. LOGIT ESTIMATES OF HAZARD OF WOMEN LEARNING ABOUT FAMILY PLANNING

(Huber Method Used to Correct for Design Effects)

	Model 1		Model 2	
	Coefficients	Effect on Probability of Learning[1]	Coefficients	Effect on Probability of Learning
Diffusion Variables				
Mass media access in county	0.002***	11	0.001**	9
Family planning availability	0.0003	3	0.001	0
Marital Fertility (MFR) in county	-0.0002	-1	-0.0002	-1
MFR surrounding counties	-0.010***	-30	-0.010***	-32
MFR surrounding * FP availability			-0.000003	
Woman's Characteristics				
Age				
(13-19)[2]				
20-29	0.514***	9	0.513***	9
30-39	0.530***	9	0.529***	9
40-49	0.669***	12	0.672***	12
Education				
(no education)				
primary	0.289*	4	0.288*	4
secondary	0.801***	13	0.803***	12
college	1.431***	26	1.432***	26
Fertility above desired	0.010	1	0.011	1
Dead child not replaced	-0.104	-1	-0.106	-1
Marital status				
(single)				
married	1.089***	16	1.090***	15
consensual union	0.950***	13	0.949***	13
widow	1.787***	31	1.796***	31
separated	0.829***	11	0.827***	11
divorced	1.066**	15	1.065**	15
County Characteristics				
Region				
(rest of country-rural)[2]				
central valley-rural	-0.175	-3	-0.175	-3
rest of country-urban	0.134	3	0.130	2
central valley-urban	0.135	3	0.142	3
San José metro	0.069	1	0.071	1

(continued on next page)

(Table 1 continued from previous page)

	Model 1		Model 2	
	Coefficients	Effect on Probability of Learning[1]	Coefficients	Effect on Probability of Learning
Female labor force participation	-0.002*	-6	-0.002	-5
Unmeasured county effects	0.0008	3	0.0007	3
Other				
Years since 1956				
(0-4)[2]				
5-9	0.276**	4	0.274*	4
10-14	0.556***	9	0.565***	9
15-20	0.546*	9	0.535*	9
Constant	-1.241		-1.147	
	Model Characteristics			
Log-likelihood	-4938.64		-4938.11	
Pseudo r-squared	0.212		0.212	
n	22686		22686	

* Significant at 0.05 level, ** 0.01 level, *** 0.001 level

[1] Continuous variable - effect of change of value of variable from one standard deviation below the mean to one standard deviation above the mean; categorical variable - effect of change from omitted category to category represented by variable; all other continuous variables set to mean value; other than when being changed, the following categorical variables are set to one: age 20-29, secondary education, married, central valley - urban, and 10-14 years since 1956

[2] Omitted categories in parentheses

TABLE 2. PROBABILITY OF LEARNING ABOUT FAMILY PLANNING FOR DIFFERENT LEVELS OF FAMILY PLANNING AVAILABILITY[1]

(Calculations based on model 2)

	Family Planning Availability			
MFR	Low	Medium	High	Change from Low to High
Low	42	45	48	6
Medium	26	26	26	0
High	14	13	11	-3

[1] Low - one standard deviation below the mean; medium - mean value; high - one standard deviation above the mean; all other continuous variables set to mean value; the following categorical variables are set to one: age 20-29, secondary education, married, central valley - urban, and 10-14 years since 1956

TABLE 3. LOGIT ESTIMATES OF HAZARD OF WOMEN ADOPTING CONTRACEPTION

(Starting when woman knows about family planning)
(Huber method used to correct for design effects)

	Model 1		Model 2	
	Coefficients	Effect on Probability of Adoption[1]	Coefficients	Effect on Probability of Adoption
Diffusion Variables				
Age learned about fp[2]				
(13-19)[3]				
20-29	1.094***	0	1.080***	0
30-39	2.773***	0	2.765***	1
40-49	5.832***	9	5.834***	10
Mass media access in county	-0.0003	-2	0.00006	0
Family planning availability	-0.0002	-3	-0.001*	5
Marital fertility (MFR) in county	-0.003***	-17	-0.004***	-12
MFR surrounding counties	-0.003	-12	-0.002	-9
MFR * fp availability[4]			0.000004*	
Woman's Characteristics				
Age[5]				
(13-19)				
20-29	-1.235***	-23	-1.219***	-24
30-39	-3.294***	-36	-3.277***	-39
40-49	-7.687***	-38	-7.666***	-42
Education				
(no education)				
primary	0.751***	12	0.751***	13
secondary	1.089***	20	1.099***	21
college	1.467***	29	1.472***	30
Fertility above desired	0.093***	14	0.093***	14
Dead child not replaced	-0.996***	-9	-0.997***	-9
Marital status				
(single)				
married	1.478***	24	1.484***	26
consensual union	1.255***	19	1.272***	21
widow	2.669***	53	2.668***	55
separated	0.668*	8	0.696*	10
divorced	1.310*	20	1.308*	22

* Significant at 0.05 level, ** 0.01 level, *** 0.001 level.

[1] Continuous variable - effect of change of value of variable from one standard deviation below the mean to one standard deviation above the mean; categorical variable - effect of change from omitted category to category represented by variable; all other continuous variables set to mean value; other than when being changed, the following categorical variables are set to one: age 20-29, secondary education, married, central valley - urban, and 10-14 years since 1956.

[2] Age held to 40-49 years.

[3] Omitted categories in parentheses.

[4] Effect on probability for this variable is included in effects for MFR and family planning availability.

[5] Age learned about fp held to 13-19 years.

(continued on next page)

(Table 3 continued from previous page)

	Model 1		Model 2	
	Coefficients	Effect on Probability of Adoption[1]	Coefficients	Effect on Probability of Adoption
County Characteristics				
Region				
(rest of country-rural)[2]				
central valley-rural	0.037	1	0.029	1
rest of country-urban	0.042	1	0.042	1
central valley-urban	0.043	1	0.031	1
San José metro	0.394	9	0.383	9
Female labor force participation	0.0006	2	0.0003	1
Unmeasured county effects	0.001	6	0.0009	5
Other				
Years since 1956				
(0-4)				
5-9	0.249	5	0.273	6
10-14	0.303	7	0.321	7
15-20	0.335	7	0.377	9
Constant	-1.396		-1.441	
	Model Characteristics			
Log-likelihood	-3034.76		-3031.24	
Pseudo r-squared	0.192		0.193	
n	7539		7539	

* Significant at 0.05 level, ** 0.01 level, *** 0.001 level

[1]Continuous variable - effect of change of value of variable from one standard deviation below the mean to one standard deviation above the mean; categorical variable - effect of change from omitted category to category represented by variable; all other continuous variables set to mean value; other than when being changed, the following categorical variables are set to one: age 20-29, secondary education, married, central valley - urban, and 10-14 years since 1956

[2]Omitted categories in parentheses

TABLE 4. PROBABILITY OF ADOPTION OF CONTRACEPTION FOR DIFFERENT AGES WHEN A WOMAN LEARNED ABOUT FAMILY PLANNING AND DIFFERENT AGES FOR THE WOMAN

(Starting when woman knows about family planning)
(Calculations based on model 2)[1]

	Age Learned About Family Planning			
Age	13-19	20-29	30-39	40-49
13-19	42	n/a	n/a	n/a
20-29	18	39	n/a	n/a
30-39	3	7	30	n/a
40-49	0	0	1	10

n/a - not applicable - outside range, because ages before when a woman learned about family planning were not included in analysis

[1]Low - one standard deviation below the mean; medium - mean value; high - one standard deviation above the mean; all other continuous variables set to mean value; the following categorical variables are set to one: age 20-29, secondary education, married, central valley - urban, and 10-14 years since 1956

TABLE 5. PROBABILITY OF ADOPTION OF CONTRACEPTION FOR DIFFERENT LEVELS OF FAMILY PLANNING AVAILABILITY AND FERTILITY WITHIN THE COUNTY

(Starting when woman knows about family planning)
(Calculations based on model 2)[1]

	Family Planning Availability			
MFR	Low	Medium	High	Change from Low to High
Low	46	45	43	-3
Medium	36	39	41	5
High	27	33	39	12

[1]Low - one standard deviation below the mean; medium - mean value; high - one standard deviation above the mean; all other continuous variables set to mean value; the following categorical variables are set to one: age 20-29, secondary education, married, central valley - urban, and 10-14 years since 1956

TABLE 6. LOGIT ESTIMATES OF HAZARD OF WOMEN ADOPTING CONTRACEPTION

(Starting at age 13)
(Huber method used to correct for design effects)

	Model 1		Model 2	
	Coefficients	Effect on Probability of Adoption[1]	Coefficients	Effect on Probability of Adoption
Diffusion Variables				
Mass media access in county	-0.00004	0	0.0004	2
Family planning availability	-0.0003	-2	-0.002***	5
Marital fertility (MFR) in county	-0.002***	-5	-0.002***	-1
MFR surrounding counties	-0.008***	-17	-0.007***	-17
MFR * fp availability[2]			0.000006***	
Woman's Characteristics				
Age				
(13-19)[3]				
20-29	0.072	1	0.077	1
30-39	-0.668***	-6	-0.662***	-7
40-49	-2.360***	-12	-2.340***	-15
Education				
(no education)				
primary	0.376***	3	0.372***	3
secondary	0.945***	8	0.948***	10
college	1.323***	13	1.319***	16
Fertility above desired	0.090***	7	0.089***	8
Dead child not replaced	-1.263***	-6	-1.255***	-7
Marital status				
(single)				
married	1.875***	12	1.882***	14
consensual union	1.550***	8	1.562***	10
widow	1.170***	5	1.163***	6
separated	0.762***	3	0.775***	3
divorced	0.153	0	0.215	1

* Significant at 0.05 level, ** 0.01 level, *** 0.001 level..

[1] Continuous variable - effect of change of value of variable from one standard deviation below the mean to one standard deviation above the mean; categorical variable - effect of change from omitted category to category represented by variable; all other continuous variables set to mean value; other than when being changed, the following categorical variables are set to one: age 20-29, secondary education, married, central valley - urban, and 10-14 years since 1956.

[2] Effect on probability for this variable is included in effects for MFR and family planning availability.

[3] Omitted categories in parentheses.

(continued on next page)

(Table 6 continued from previous page)

	Model 1		Model 2	
	Coefficients	Effect on Probability of Adoption[1]	Coefficients	Effect on Probability of Adoption
County Characteristics				
Region				
(rest of country-rural)[2]				
central valley-rural	-0.140	-2	-0.161	-2
rest of country-urban	-0.031	0	-0.033	-1
central valley-urban	-0.053	-1	-0.074	-1
San José metro	0.140	2	0.116	2
Female labor force participation	0.0005	1	0.0001	0
Unmeasured county effects	0.0004	1	0.0002	1
Other				
Years since 1956				
(0-4)				
5-9	0.417***	4	0.440***	5
10-14	0.578***	6	0.593***	7
15-20	0.714***	7	0.750***	9
Constant	-1.383		-1.436	
	Model Characteristics			
Log-likelihood	-6762.53		-6750.89	
Pseudo r-squared	0.199		0.200	
n	40719		40719	

* Significant at 0.05 level, ** 0.01 level, *** 0.001 level.

[1]Continuous variable - effect of change of value of variable from one standard deviation below the mean to one standard deviation above the mean; categorical variable - effect of change from omitted category to category represented by variable; all other continuous variables set to mean value; other than when being changed, the following categorical variables are set to one: age 20-29, secondary education, married, central valley - urban, and 10-14 years since 1956.

[2]Omitted categories in parentheses.

TABLE 7. PROBABILITY OF ADOPTION OF CONTRACEPTION FOR DIFFERENT LEVELS OF FAMILY PLANNING AVAILABILITY AND FERTILITY WITHIN THE COUNTY

(Starting at age 13)
(Calculations based on model 2)[1]

MFR	Family Planning Availability			Change from Low to High
	Low	Medium	High	
Low	19	18	17	-2
Medium	15	18	20	5
High	13	17	23	10

[1]Low - one standard deviation below the mean; medium - mean value; high - one standard deviation above the mean; all other continuous variables set to mean value; the following categorical variables are set to one: age 20-29, secondary education, married, central valley - urban, and 10-14 years since 1956.

FIGURE 1. DEMOGRAPHIC TRENDS IN COSTA RICA

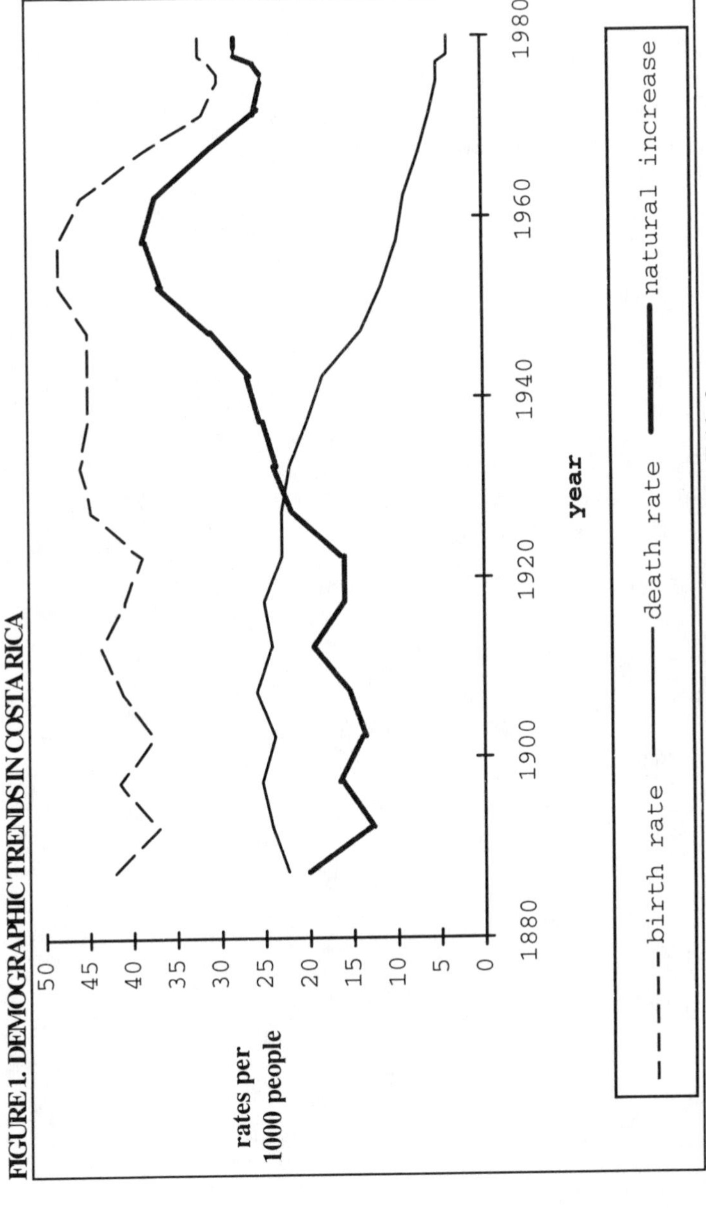

Sources: Universidad de Costa Rica 1976, Table 4; Rosero-Bixby 1981, Table 2

SPATIAL DIMENSIONS OF FAMILY PLANNING IN COSTA RICA: THE VALUE OF GEOCODING DEMOGRAPHIC SURVEYS

LUIS ROSERO-BIXBY

The article illustrates the value of geocoding demographic surveys and conducting spatial analyses to understand the service supply environment and contraceptive behavior. Three Costa Rican data sets are geocoded and pooled in a Geographic Information System (GIS): a demographic survey, an inventory of family planning facilities, and a census. Displaying survey's results on maps enhances the understanding of the spatial configuration of family planning services and users' behavior. Trend surface analyses improves survey's estimates for small areas and pin-points spatial differences. Cartographic-based measures of accessibility and of contextual characteristics have an edge in objectivity, comparability and flexibility. Multilevel models on contraceptive use and method choice suggest mixed effects of density of services and diffusion effects from neighbors. A model for the choice of family planning outlet arrives at a classic gravity formulation in which larger and closer clinics are more likely to be chosen. Demographic surveys should consider geocoding their sampling units as a routine procedure.

INTRODUCTION

This chapter uses Costa Rican data to illustrate the value of geocoding a demographic survey and conducting spatial analyses to understand the service supply environment and contraceptive behavior. The article first delineates alternative procedures for geocoding a survey and then illustrates five uses of this information, namely: (1) visual display of spatial relations; (2) spatial trends and small area estimates; (3) measuring the family planning service supply environment; (4) studying contextual and neighborhood effects; and (5) analyzing service utilization.

The last two decades have seen a substantial increase in the data available on population and family planning in developing countries. The massive World Fertility Survey (WFS) and Demographic and Health Surveys (DHS) projects are examples of this data explosion. Data sets, however, are usually used in isolation from each other under-utilizing their potential. This article addresses the issue of linking data sets in connection with: (1) demand of family planning usually from DHS-type surveys; (2) supply of services, including inventories of facilities, administrative records and Situation Analysis-type surveys (Fisher et al. 1992), and (3) the socioeconomic and physical environment as described by censuses and digital cartography. The article posits that geocoding is a cost-effective strategy to relate these data sets to each other, especially when these are pooled in a Geographic Information System (GIS) (Scholten et al 1991). Beyond data managing issues, geocoded information facilitates a multi-level strategy for studying contraceptive and other behaviors, i.e. a strategy that combines information about individuals or households (micro data) with contextual information (macro data) about the community or other aggregates (Hermalin 1986).

SETTING

Costa Rica has one of the highest Contraceptive Prevalence Rates (CPR) in the developing world: 76% according to the 1992-93 Reproductive Health Survey (ESR Spanish acronym). Its Total Fertility Rate of 3.1 births in 1991-93 is not, however, low. This combination of very high contraceptive practice and somewhat high fertility has puzzled demographers for decades. Contraceptive practice is high across all regions and social strata. The lowest CPR, which occurs among illiterate women and in rural areas outside the Central Valley, is about

70%: a figure that is not substantially different from the national average. The major provider of family planning in Costa Rica is, by far, the government, through its clinics of the Social Security Office and the Ministry of Health. Public health facilities provide for more than three-fourths of all modern contraception in the country. Although there is a substantial overlap in the population served by the Social Security and the Ministry of Health, the later tends to be more important in rural areas and among the poor than the former. The four most popular contraceptive methods are the pill (26%), sterilization (22%), condom (22%) and IUD (12%) (Caja Costarricense de Seguro Social 1994: Table 9.12).

To put things in perspective, it is important to note that a lack of geographic variation in contraceptive practice in Costa Rica reduces the pertinence of some spatial analyses in this article. Costa Rica is a country with a high degree of spatial integration and a good communications network. In addition, public health services, which include family planning, have high coverage, reaching even the most remote areas. For example, 98% of deliveries occur in hospitals. Physical accessibility, therefore, does not seem critical for practicing family planning in this country, which is well-documented in earlier studies (Rodríguez 1978; Hermalin et al. 1988). Moreover, the recent ESR showed that the median reported travel time to public family planning outlets is only 28 minutes, which is very short compared to the median of two hours and 21 minutes reported as spent in the waiting room of public clinics (Caja Costarricense de Seguro Social 1994: Table 10.6. The figures are self reported times by users of resupply methods for the most recent visit to a family planning clinic).

DATA

The chapter uses mostly three geocoded data sets:

1) The Costa Rican Reproductive Health Survey (ESR), conducted in 1992-93 by the Social Security Office with assis-

tance from the US Centers for Disease Control and Prevention (CDC). The ESR's sample is nationally representative of females aged 15 to 49. It includes 3,618 respondents in 188 clusters (Caja Costarricense de Seguro Social 1994). These clusters are a sample of the 1984 census tracts.

2) An inventory of about 300 delivery points of public family planning services. Private facilities—private physicians' offices and pharmacies—are not considered. The only information available for each clinic in this inventory is its size, as measured by an estimate of the number of consultation hours (all purposes and for family planning) provided in 1992. This estimate is based on unpublished data on outpatient consultations from the Department of Biostatistics of the Social Security Office and from the Statistics Department of the Ministry of Health.

3) About 11,000 "segmentos" (census tracts) of the 1984 census. A census tract comprises 50 households on the average, and an area of one or two city blocks or one to ten square kilometers in rural areas. This data set was used to estimate the population densities for survey clusters and the catchment populations for service facilities. The Costa Rican Statistic and Census Directorate provided the original census files.

Geocoding Procedure

The ideal situation for spatial analyses would be to have X, Y earth coordinates for every household and health facility in the country. For practical purposes, however, it is sufficient to take sampling clusters and census tracts as single points and to geocode their centroid. This means obtaining the coordinates for about 100 to 300 points in a typical survey: hardly a daunting task. Geocoding all census tracts is more demanding, but it is not essential for most of the analyses in this article. Given the purpose for which a census tract is defined (convenience of enumeration), its demographic centroid is clearly a more accurate representation of the location of the tract's population than a polygon of its entire area (Bracken 1989).

Three geocoding procedures may be considered:

1) The least expensive procedure consists of matching the survey or census to a data set which already contains X, Y coordinates. For example, in the US one could record the zip code of each sample unit and merge the survey to many commercially available geocoded data sets containing zip codes. In developing countries, however, geocoded data bases with an appropriate geographic detail are rare.

2) An alternative procedure is to locate the sampling points and tracts on appropriate maps and to read the coordinates there. These maps must be accurate, geo-referenced and of a large scale. If, for example, the typical error involved in placing the points on the map and reading the coordinates were of the order of one centimeter, working on maps with a large scale of 1:10,000 would result in a typical error of 100 meters, but on a small scale of 1:1,000,000 the error would be a disappointing 10 km. The costs involved in geocoding from maps are small, but the potential for error is large.

3) A probably more accurate, but also more expensive, alternative is to use "global positioning system" (GPS) devices to obtain the coordinates in the field from satellite signals. The accuracy of these measurements is usually of the order of 30 meters. The costs involved in this procedure come mostly from purchasing GPS devices and visiting every site on the field. The 11,000 census tracts (which include the 188 ESR clusters) were geocoded for this study by reading their centroid's coordinates from maps. Since Costa Rican census maps do not have earth coordinates, a two-stage procedure was devised. College students implemented this procedure. First, we took the earth coordinates of a series of reference points from geo-referenced maps of the National Geographic Institute. The scale of these maps is 1:10,000 in the Central Valley and 1:50,000 in other areas. We

identified one reference point (typically the church, a school, a cemetery, or the "plaza") for each census map. Usually there was one or two census maps per administrative "distrito." Second, we graphically measured X, Y plane coordinates for every tract's demographic centroid on census charts, taking the aforementioned reference point as the cartesian origin of the system. The scale of census charts ranged from 1:800 to 1:20,000. A computer merged the two sets of coordinates and maps' scales to compute projected earth coordinates, using the Lambert Conformal projection (Inter-American Geodetic Survey 1950).

Given that data errors are critical in assembling geographic information systems (GIS), these measures were validated in the field for a sample of 40 tracts, which are also ESR clusters. Field measures were taken from satellite signals with a GPS device. Figure 1 shows the discrepancy between the two estimates, as measured by the Euclidean distance between the two pairs of coordinates. The median discrepancy is about 60 meters. Discrepancies larger than 300 meters occurred in less than one-forth of observations. Considering that GPS-based measurements do have some error margin, one may say that the error in the great majority of our map-based measurements is lower than 200 meters. The probability of having errors larger than 500 meters is nil. Figure 1 also shows that errors tend to increase at smaller map's scales, especially at scales smaller than 1:3,000 (less than 33 cm. per km. in Figure 1).

The data set of health delivery points was geocoded on the aforementioned maps of the National Geographic Institute at scales 1:10,000 and 1:50,000. These data were also GPS validated for a sample of 40 points. No discrepancies larger than 300 meters occurred.

An important characteristic of the ESR is that it recorded the identification of the specific facilities used by women for family planning and other purposes. This information enhances substantially the possibilities of analysis, especially regarding consumer behavior in choosing a family planning outlet. It also permits one to have cartographic measures of the distance to the clinics which respondents use that can be compared to reported travel times.

Visual Display

An obvious use of geocoded data is for survey characteristics and results displaying on maps. Maps are an important, although under-utilized, means for conveying information, especially to statistically unsophisticated audiences. Maps are also a unique means for detecting spatial relations. More than a century ago, John Snow, the father of epidemiology, used maps to understand the spatial dynamics of a cholera epidemic in London (Haggett et al. 1977).

Map 1 displays the location of the 188 ESR sampling clusters in Costa Rica in relation to the distribution of the population. The clusters are heavily concentrated in the Central Valley around the capital city, following the pattern of the general population. But the clusters also appear reasonably spread all over the national territory. This map assures that there is a fair representation of Costa Rican geography in the ESR sample.

Map 2 illustrates for the Valley of "San Isidro del General" (window marked in Map 1) the service availability environment and the use of resupply family planning outlets by women in the sample. Outlets are connected to sampling units by black lines with thickness proportional to the number of users in the survey. The number labeling each line is the average travel time in minutes as reported by the respondents. The map also contains national roads and provincial borders. The map confirms a well known fact: the Health Posts of the Ministry of Health do not provide family planning. For example, women in cluster E conveniently have a health post nearby but they must travel several miles to obtain family planning from Health Centers in Buenos Aires or San Isidro. A Health Post is a tiny, rural facility (often built by the community) staffed with one or two "health workers" who are not allowed to prescribe contraceptives. Once a month or so, a physician may come to the Post to provide outpatient consultations, but he or she is too busy during these visits to take family planning consultations.

Health posts aside, the map shows that, as it is usually assumed, most women go to the nearest outlet. There are, however, important deviations from this norm. Women in cluster C, for example, skip the neighboring Clinic of Palmares and go further away to the health center in the city of San Isidro. Three explanations for this behavior may be (1) the clinic of Palmares (also known as Daniel Flores) was established too recently (1988) and some users don't know about its services while others are not ready to switch to this new facility; (2) that services provided in this small clinic do not fulfill users' needs; and (3) users do multipurpose shopping trips to the city of San Isidro, which is the most important urban center in the zone. Models of consumer spatial behavior (and the contemporary success of massive shopping malls) show that for single-purpose shopping trips (one good one trip) consumers indeed go to the nearest store supplying the good; however, for multiple-purpose trips consumers go to a center supplying the whole range of goods (Bacon 1984).

Map 2 also suggests a reasonable correspondence between the Euclidean distance to the outlet and reported travel times. Moreover, some travel times that appear excessive for the distance involved, become reasonable when one considers the lack of connecting roads. This is the case for the times between G and Buenos Aires (148 minutes for 10 miles) and between D and Pejibaye (90 minutes for 3 miles).

A different pattern of outlet use was observed on a map for sterilized women (not shown). Long distance trips, especially to hospitals in the capital city, are more frequent among these women –a behavior that makes sense for a method that requires somewhat sophisticated surgery facilities.

Spatial Trends and Small-Area Estimates

Sample surveys do not give stable estimates for small or medium-size geographic areas, in spite of the high demand for this information among managers. At the most, a typical survey can provide estimates for a few large regions. However, if one is prepared to accept that the variable in question (say, the CPR) varies smoothly across the space (or, at least, in a geographic neighborhood), geocoded surveys can provide improved estimates for any specific location as defined by its coordinates X and Y. These estimates are based on trend surfaces implicit in the data.

There are several techniques for identifying trend surfaces, which are broadly used in disciplines such as geology, topography, and meteorology. Those ubiquitous weather maps are an example of trend-surface estimates derived from a handful of sampling points. Trend surface analyses aims at isolating the underlying "signal" or systematic component in spatial data from the "noise" or random component. A simple technique for estimating trend surfaces (which was used in this article) is by fitting a polynomial on the X and Y coordinates with a degree to be chosen according to statistical criteria. An alternative to polynomials are nonparametric local regression models—a kind of two dimensional spline that assumes a smooth surface in the neighborhood of each observation. In a GIS framework, it is also possible to spatially smooth the data using such techniques as a roving window to compute weighted averages with neighboring observations.

This article estimates trend surface polynomials for: (1) the contraceptive prevalence rate and (2) the choice of IUD among contraceptive users. Maps 3 and 3b show the resulting surfaces. These maps do not show the estimates as shaded areas or contour lines deliberately, to avoid extrapolations to uninhabited lands. The maps show results only for meaningful human settlements.

The surface for the contraceptive prevalence rate confirms that this rate is high all over the territory. The few centers with less than 60% of couples practicing contraception are located in a northern region bordering Nicaragua and in a south-eastern region (Sixaola) bordering Panama, which also is the region with the largest concentration of indigenous population. This figure is strikingly similar to a map about the fertility transition in Costa Rica published elsewhere (Rosero-Bixby and Casterline 1994).

In contrast with the diminishing gradient out from the center observed for contraceptive prevalence, the surface for IUD choice (proportion of contraceptive users who chose this method) shows a diminishing gradient from east to west. IUD is less popular in north-western regions. Since this pattern probably mirrors the preferences and skills of providers, program managers may consider whether retraining practitioners in IUD insertion in north-western regions may be needed.

Are the patterns unveiled by these surfaces statistically significant? Do these surfaces improve significantly conventional survey estimates? Table 1 shows the improvement in the Log-Likelihood ratio for the logistic models involved in these estimates. As it is customary, the improvement is measured with reference to the null model, which is equivalent to assume that all clusters are identical to the national average. Table 1 also shows, as a contrast, the fitness of a logistic model on the probability of being in a consensual union, a behavior that is known for being strongly differentiated across spatial boundaries in Costa Rica (Glaser 1994). Note that third degree polynomials best fitted the surfaces for contraceptive use and consensual unions and a second degree polynomial fitted IUD choice. Of course, second-degree polynomials imply 5 parameters (X, Y, XY, X^2, and Y^2) and third degree polynomials imply 9 parameters. All the Chi-square statistics in the table are significant at 1%. The Chi-square values of comparing the estimated surface with the null model suggest that there is, indeed, a significant improvement over simply applying national estimates to every location. The surfaces are also a significant improvement over specific estimates for the 6 health regions of Costa Rica. The improvements in the estimates for contraceptive use and IUD choice are not, however, as large as those for the prevalence of consensual unions.

Measuring the Service Supply Environment

In measuring physical accessibility to family planning services, there are several issues poorly addressed by the literature (Chayovan et al. 1984; Hermalin et al. 1988). Some of these issues may be better addressed with geocoded data. An important concern is the internal validity of subjective assessments about distances or travel times to family planning outlets made by survey respondents or "knowledgeable" informants. A DHS comparative study of the availability of family planning and health services points out several limitations derived from the subjective nature of the data (Wilkinson et al. 1993). Accessibility indicators based on objective cartographic measures may represent an improvement in internal validity over subjective assessments. Moreover, cartographic based indicators may allow to validate the information on reported travel time to facilities and to cast some light on the issues of whether to use actual vs. perceived access indicators or micro- vs. macro-level measurements (Entwisle et al. 1984).

Figure 2 plots the reported travel time against the Euclidean distance between a respondent's residence and the family planning outlet reported as used by this respondent. A "heaping" tendency in reported travel times is evident; i. e. responses clearly cluster at 5, 10, 15, 10, 30, 45 and 60 minutes. Correspondence between the two measures is moderately high in the logarithms (correlation coefficient of 0.67). A "power" model, estimated with Poisson Regression on the logarithm of the explanatory variable (McCullagh and Nedler 1989), indicates an expected travel time of about 15 minutes for the first kilometer and time increments of 0.5% for each one-percent increase in distance. For example, the expected travel time is 36 minutes for 5 km. and it is 52 minutes for 10 km. The estimated parameters seem to be a reasonable estimate of a conversion factor from distance to travel time and a fair representation of what people usually do, which is to take a faster means of transportation for traveling longer distances.

The lack of a perfect correspondence between cartographic distances and travel times may arise from errors in the perceptions of travel times, from the use of different means of transportation, and, as noted in Map 2, from the lack of direct roads connecting two points. This article did not refine the cartographic measure based on straight lines, although such improvement is feasible in a GIS that includes roads and transportation networks. However, to take into account this shortcoming in further analyses, an indicator of the relative travel time was computed for each cluster, as the ratio of the observed times to the model-estimated (the expected) times.

A preliminary analysis of the scatterplot in Figure 2 showed a handful of outliers with reported travel times of five or ten minutes and cartographic distances in the order of 100 kilometers. These outliers came from errors made in the field and in the office identifying the outlet actually used by respondents. The cartographic information thus served to isolate and clean up this error.

There has been some debate about whether to use aggregated or individual measures of access to family planning outlets (Tsui et al.1981; Chen et al. 1983; Entwisle et al. 1984). A limitation of individual-level indicators is that information is often not available (or it is unreliable) for respondents who do not use family planning outlets (Chayovan et al. 1984). To overcome this limitation, this article computed an aggregated indicator (the average) of reported travel time for each sampling cluster, which later may be applied to every individual in the cluster. The comparison of these cluster averages with cartographic distances resulted in a nicer looking plot (non shown) than that in Figure 2. However, the estimated parameters of the corresponding model were essentially the same as in Figure 2.

It is important to note that the mean travel time to family planning outlets is not a pure supply measure. It is in part determined by consumer behavior, since not everybody in a cluster chooses the same or the closest outlet. Moreover, the perception of travel times may be biased as a function of family planning behavior (those who are more inclined to use contraception may perceive shorter travel times to the outlets), which would result in a spurious association between these two variables. Given these caveats, other accessibility indicators must be explored, for which geocoded information is especially useful.

Traditional access measures are usually based on the distance to the nearest outlet or the presence of outlets in the community or within the boundaries of administrative areas. Using services in other communities, skipping the nearest outlet, overlapping catchment areas, redundant services in a community, and competition with other potential users are issues not properly addressed by these traditional accessibility measures. Having geocoded data permitted us to compute two more refined indicators of the service supply environment: total and per capita density of services within a radius. Density indicators are not new (DaVanzo 1988). The novelty is in the flexibility for defining these indicators with geocoded data. First, there is not the constraint of using arbitrary geographic units (Makuk et al. 1991). Second, there is the freedom for defining areas of any shape and size and addressing the "modifiable areal unit problem" (Wrigley 1995). Third, it is possible to introduce distance-decay effects. Fourth, there is the flexibility for incorporating in access measures qualitative and quantitative characteristics of outlets and considering the presence of competing users (Rosero Bixby 1993).

This article relies on distance-dependent calculations of potential access and potential population—concepts widely used by geographers—to determine the density of services as an indicator of accessibility. The concept of potential is as follows: the potential number of elements (clinics, people, and so forth) at a point i is the sum of the elements existing in all locations j weighted by the inverse of the distance between i and j. The calculation is usually limited to locations within radius r from i.

The formula used for computing the <u>total density</u> of family planning services A_i is:

$$A_i = \sum_j^r \frac{H_j}{d_{ji}^b}$$

A_i	=	density of services (hours provided) for location i;
H_j	=	family planning hours provided by clinic j;
d_{ji}	=	distance between locations j and i;
b	=	distance decay exponent,
r	=	radius from i for the maximum distance to consider in the sum.

This formula has been used to measure accessibility to workplaces (Duncan 1964) and to health practitioners (Thouez et al. 1988). It has, however, the limitation that it does not consider the size of the population served, i.e. the competition among clients for a service. To correct this deficiency, Joseph and Bantock (1982) propose to compute <u>per capita density</u> considering the size of served populations C_j in clinics' catchment areas:

$$B_i = \sum_j^r \frac{H_j / C_j}{d_{ji}^b} \qquad C_j = \sum_h^r \frac{P_h}{d_{jh}^b}$$

B_i	=	per capita density of services (yearly hours per women) for location i;

Cj = population (women in reproductive age) served in the catchment area of radius r by clinic j; as estimated by the population potential for location j,

Ph = population (women in reproductive age) in all places h within the catchment area of clinic j.

This article experimented with combinations of radii ranging from 5 to 20 km. and distance-decay exponents of 0 and 1. For radii larger than about 10 km, results were not sensitive to changes in the radius nor in the decay exponent. The second panel in Table 2 shows correlation coefficients larger than 95% between total densities computed for radii of 10 and 15 km. and distance-decay exponents of 0 and 1. Similar correlation's occurred (not shown) for per capita densities. Thus, the calibration or selection of these parameters (radius and distance-decay) does not seem critical for computing the density measures introduced here.

The first panel in Table 2 compares the two density measures and two traditional measures of accessibility: the mean travel time reported by women in each cluster (a datum from the survey questionnaire) and the straight line distance between the cluster and its nearest family planning outlet (a cartographic measure that requires geocoded data). Correlation coefficients between the three cartographic measures are moderately high (65% to 70%) and with the right sign, indicating that there are both some degree of overlapping and some degree of orthogonality. In contrast, there are only modest correlation coefficients between the reported travel time and the three cartographic measures. Reported travel time and service density thus appear as two distinct dimensions of accessibility in this data set. Since substantially different pictures may correspond to different indicators, careful attention must be given to the choice of indicators of service environment. An earlier study comparing several accessibility measures in Thailand also found that results are sensitive to the choice of indicator (Chayovan et al. 1984).

An important use of accessibility indicators is for guiding decision makers in the selection of sites for new clinics and in the expansion of services in exiting clinics. Map 4 depicts the service supply environment on the Costa Rican territory as measured by the per capita service density. Note that this density measure was not computed just for the survey clusters but for every meaningful population center in the country, using the geocoded data from the inventory of facilities and census tracts. Note also the metrics of the density indicator. For example, a figure of 0.05 indicates the availability of about one service-hour per year for every 20 women in reproductive age. Managers need to understand these metrics for setting minimum standards or goals for the provision of services. Taking, for example, a minimum acceptable density of 0.05 hour-women, Map 4 shows that no town in the Central Valley is below this minimum. It also shows that priority for expanding services should be given to Southern and North-Western regions, where there are about 40 towns below the minimum.

Contextual Indicators in Multilevel Models

Multilevel models on adoption of family planning, fertility preferences and other behaviors often include as contextual factors aggregate indicators for the community or the administrative unit where the individual lives. These levels of aggregation, however, may be inappropriate if contamination across communities occur, or if the administrative boundaries are arbitrary, or if the aggregate area is too small or too large (Makuk et al. 1991). Moreover, the concept of "community" or "locality" has proved to be troublesome, especially in comparative studies (Wilkinson et al. 1993: 6). Geocoded data give flexibility in the choice of aggregate units and permit one to define units that are comparable across countries. It is, for example, possible to define a circle with a determined radius, which will be free of the constraints of arbitrary borders and will be internationally comparable.

Models of spatial diffusion and social interaction also deal with aggregate indicators for both the index community and for neighboring communities. For example, in explaining adoption of family planning, diffusion models may include as contextual explanatory factors the level of contraceptive use in the community in question and in other relevant areas for capturing the influence of neighbors (Rosero-Bixby and Casterline 1994). Once again, geocoded data give flexibility for constructing indicators about the influence of neighbors.

To illustrate these uses of geocoded data, Table 3 shows the results from two multilevel logistic regression models, on the probability of using contraceptives (conditional on being in a union) and of choosing the IUD (conditional on using contraceptives). The estimates in Table 3 are in no way intended as a full scale analysis. Both model specification and its statistical estimation may improve in a full scale analysis. The two models include as contextual regressors three indicators computed with geocoded data: (1) the percent use of contraceptives/IUD by women in a 10 km. radius computed as population potential with a distance decay correction (the index woman was excluded when computing these proportions), (2) the cluster's relative difficulty for traveling, and (3) the per woman density of family planning services in a 10 km. radius as defined before.

The propensity of other women in the area to use contraceptives or to choose the IUD shows significant effects on the adoption odds of individuals. The odds of using contraceptives increase 11% with a 10-point increase in the contextual contraceptive prevalence rate. The odds of choosing the IUD increase by 26% with a 10-point increase in the contextual percentage of IUD users. These associations may be genuine manifestations of person-to-person diffusion, but may also be just a reflection of omitted variables in the models, the effects of which have been picked up by areal prevalence. Purging the possibility of spurious effects with, for example, instrumental variables is beyond the scope of this article.

The cluster's relative travel time does not show any significant relation with adoption of contraception or IUD choice. This result suggests that using travel distances instead of Euclidean distances for computing access indicators will have little consequence for impact analyses.

Service density does not show a significant effect on contraceptive use. Although the effect of service density on IUD choice also is not significant, it is so by just a narrow margin (the z value of 1.5 is significant at 13% level). An increase in one hour per woman density of family planning services (which is a huge increase) would double the odds of choosing the IUD according to the model.

The lower panel in Table 3 shows a sensitivity analysis of using alternative access indicators in the logistic equation. For the model on contraceptive use, all cartography-based indicators do not show significant effects. The reported travel time (averaged for the cluster), in contrast, shows a significant effect: one extra hour of travel reduces by 38% the odds of using contraception. Given that there may be some endogeneity in reported travel times, this result is inconclusive.

For the model on IUD choice, no indicator outperforms the effect of per capita density of family planning services.

Clinic's Choice

Contrasting with the rich literature on health service utilization, consumer behavior in choosing a family planning outlet in developing countries has seldom been studied. Geocoded survey data make such study possible, specially if the survey recorded the identification of the outlet used by respondents and if it was complemented with a geocoded inventory of facilities.

Visual analyses such as that for Map 2 are a first step for understanding service utilization.

Statistical models are a more rigorous approach. As an illustration, this article estimated a model on the odds (O_{ij}) that a user i of resupply methods chooses the family planning outlet j. The ESR contains information for about 550 users of resupply methods from public outlets, who combined with about 300 relevant outlets result in a data set with about 165,000 observations, one for each user-outlet pair. To avoid such a big file, a matched case-control design was adopted instead. Nine "controls" (non used outlets) were randomly selected for each user, which resulted in about 5,500 observations. As required in matched case-control designs (or in discrete-choice econometric models) conditional logistic regression was used to estimate the model (Breslow and Day 1980; Greene 1990). Table 4 shows the results.

Only five explanatory variables were available for this analysis: the size of the clinic as measured by the number of weekly hours of family planning (h_j), the Euclidean distance between user's residence and clinic (d_{ij}), the clinics' catchment population potential (c_j), the proportion of outpatient consultations for family planning purposes (f_j), and whether the clinic pertains to the Social Security Office. Natural logarithms of the first three variables were entered in the model. The regression coefficients of these three variables thus measure elasticities on the odds of choosing an outlet. Moreover, the regression coefficient for the log-distance variable is an estimate of the aforementioned distance-decay effect. The model also tested selected statistical interactions of these five variables with individual and contextual characteristics. Only one interaction (between the contraceptive method adopted and clinic's size) deserved some further consideration. The estimated model in Table 4 implies the following relations:

IUD users: $$O_{ij} = k\frac{h_j^{1.3} c_j^{0.1}}{d_{ij}^3}(4.1)^{f_j}(1.9)^{S_j}$$

Other users: $$O_{ij} = k\frac{h_j^{0.4} c_j^{0.1}}{d_{ij}^3}(4.1)^{f_j}(1.9)^{S_j}$$

where k is an unknown constant and all other symbols stand for the previously defined variables.

The size of the clinic and the distance to it emerged as strong predictors of clinic's choice in this model. A one-percent increase in the weekly hours of family planning of a given clinic increases in 1.3% the odds of choosing it among IUD users and 0.4% among users of other methods. In turn, a one-percent increase in the inverse of the distance to a clinic increases by 3% the odds of choosing that clinic. The distance decay exponent for spatial analyses of accessibility and use of family planning in Costa Rica is thus 3. The size of the population served by the clinic does not appear as an influential factor in the decision of using the clinic. The relative importance of family planning in a clinic, as measured by the proportion of consultations with this purpose, is positively related to the decision of using the clinic. Going from zero to 100% family planning consultations would increase the odds of adopting the clinic four times, correspondingly, increasing that proportion by 20 percentage points will increase the odds of choosing the clinic by 33% ($[4.1]^{0.2} = 1.33$). Social security clinics are preferred over those of the Ministry of Health. The odds of choosing the former are 87% higher. This effect, as well as that of the proportion of family planning consultations, is not, however, significant at the customary 5%, but being significant at 10% justifies some attention to them.

Overall results of the choice model resemble the classic gravity formula of Newtonian physics (Haynes and Fotheringham 1984) in which the attraction between two bodies (two planets, earth and the apocryphal apple) is proportional to their masses and the distance between them. Perhaps if data on a clinic's characteristics (such as those available from situation analyses) were available in Costa Rica, elements of quality of care would explain in part the choice of a clinic beyond this simple gravity model.

CONCLUSION

This article has illustrated the feasibility of geocoding a DHS-type survey and has shown some of the payoffs of this data collection strategy. The cost of adding geo-references to a survey in Costa Rica was nil in comparison to its benefits, particularly for better understanding the family planning service supply environment. The gains from geocoding a survey increase when it is accompanied by an inventory of geo-referenced facilities and when the survey keeps track of the specific facilities used by respondents. DHS-type surveys should consider geocoding their sampling units as a routine procedure. A geocoded survey, in combination with an inventory of facilities that includes some qualitative information about clinics, seems an attractive alternative to the "Service Availability Module" currently used in the DHS program.

The article has also shown that displaying survey results on maps is an effective way for conveying information on the spatial dimensions of family planning and for understanding the service supply environment. Trend surface analyses of some results of the Reproductive Health Survey conducted in Costa Rica in 1992-93 improved survey's estimates for small areas and pinpointed important spatial differences in contraceptive prevalence and IUD choice. Measuring the service supply environment, i.e. the accessibility to family planning services, was sensitive to the indicator used. Different measures give substantially different pictures of family planning availability. Cartographic based measures, however, have an edge in objectivity and comparability. A concrete result that can contribute to improve accessibility measures in Costa Rica was the calibration of a distance decay exponent of 3 per kilometer and an elasticity of distance to travel time of 0.53. Improved measures of contextual variables were used in multilevel models on contraceptive use and IUD choice. The results regarding the impact of service density were mixed in these multilevel models. In turn, diffusion from neighbors appeared as a significant factor for the use of contraceptives and IUD choice. A model for the choice of family planning outlet arrived at a classic gravity formulation in which larger and closer clinics are more likely to be chosen. These results did not come from full scale analyses but from quick exercises devised to illustrate the use of geocoded information.

The spatial analyses in this article confirmed that accessibility to family planning services is not a likely factor in the use of contraception currently in Costa Rica. It may, however, influence the contraceptive method mix. In turn, accessibility to a clinic seems crucial in the decision to use its services. This is a somewhat trivial result. It is very unlikely that a user will travel 100 km. for a family planning consultation if she can get it from a neighboring clinic. What is not trivial is the calibration of this distance decay effect.

Understanding consumer behavior for choosing a family planning outlet seems an important and promising study field, especially in countries like Costa Rica with a high contraceptive prevalence rate. It will help in fine tuning service supply, to improve the indicators of accessibility, and to assess the impacts of quality of care. Spatial analyses are essential in such studies, as is geocoded information about users and clinics.

ACKNOWLEDGEMENTS

The research was supported by grants from the Mellon Foundation to the Office of Population Research of Princeton University, and the Swedish Agency for Research Cooperation with Developing Countries (SAREC) to the University of Costa Rica.

REFERENCES

Bacon, R.W. 1984. *Consumer Spatial Behaviour.* Oxford: Clarendon Press.

Bracken, I. 1989. The Generation of Socioeconomic Surfaces for Public Policy Making. *Environment and Planning B*, 16(4): 307-316.

Breslow, N.E., and N.E. Day. 1980. *Statistical Methods in Cancer Research, Vol. 1*. Lyon: International Agency for Research on Cancer.

Caja Costarricense de Seguro Social. 1994. *Fecundidad y Formación de* la *Familia. Encuesta Nacional de Salud Reproductiva 1993.* San Jose, Costa Rica: Reprinted by the US Department of Health and Human Services, CDC.

Chayovan, N., A. Hermalin, and J. Knodel. 1984. Measuring Accessibility to Family Planning Services in Rural Thailand. *Studies* in *Family Planning,* 15(5): 201-211.

Chen, C.H.C., R. Santiso, and L. Morris. 1983. Impact of Accessibility of Contraceptives on Contraceptive Prevalence in Guatemala. *Studies in Family Planning,* 14(11): 275-283.

DaVanzo, J., C. Peterson, J. Peterson, D. Reboussin, and Starbird, E. 1988. "What Accounts for the Increase in Contraceptive Use in Peninsular Malaysia, 1956-75?– Development vs. Family Planning Effort." Paper presented at the Annual Meeting of the Population Association of America, New Orleans.

Duncan, B. 1964. Variables in Urban Morphology. In E. W. Burguess, & D. J. Bogue (Editors.), *Contribution to Urban Sociology.* (pp. 17-30). Chicago: University of Chicago Press.

Entwisle, B., A. Hermalin, P. Kamnuansilpa, and A. Chamratrithirong. 1984. A Multilevel Model of Family Planning Availability and Contraceptive Use in Rural Thailand. *Demography*, *21*(4): 559-574.

Fisher, A., Mensch, B., Miller, R.A., I. Askew, A.K. Jain, C. Ndeti, L. Ndhlovu, and P. Tapsoba. 1992. *Guidelines and Instruments for* a *Family planning Situation Analysis Study.* New York: The Population Council.

Giggs, J.A. 1983. Health. In M. Pacione (Ed.), *Progress in Urban Geography.* London: Croom Helm.

Glaser, K. 1994. Determinants and Fertility Consequences of Consensual Unions in Costa Rica. Ph.D. dissertation, University of Michigan, Ann Arbor.

Greene, W.H. 1990. *Econometric Analysis.* New York: Macmillan.

Haggett, P., A. Cliff, and A. Frey. 1977. *Locational Analysis in Human Geography.* New York: John Wiley.

Haynes, K.E. and A.S. Fotheringham. 1984. *Gravity and Spatial Interaction Models.* Beverly Hills: Sage Publications (scientific geography series).

Hermalin, A.I. 1986. Chapter III. The Multilevel Approach to Family Planning Program Evaluation. In Addendum to Manual IX: The Methodology of Measuring the Impact of Family Planning Programmes on Fertility, *Population Studies.* No. 66 (pp. 15-24). New York: United Nations.

Hermalin, A.I., A.P. Riley, and L. Rosero Bixby. 1988. A Multi-level Analysis of Contraceptive Use and Method Choice in Costa Rica. In A.I. Hermalin, & J. Casterline (Principal Investigators.), *Effects of Contextual Factors on Fertility Regulation* in *Costa Rica and Egypt.* (NICHD Contract N01 HD-62902). Ann Arbor, MI: Population Studies Center of the University of Michigan.

Inter-American Geodetic Survey. 1950. *Proyección Lambert para Costa Rica.* Washington D.C.: Army Map Service.

Joseph, A. E. and P. Bantock. 1982. Measuring Potential Physical Accessibility to General Practitioners in Rural Areas: A Method and Case Study. *Social Science and Medicine,* 16(1): 85-90.

Makuk, D. M., B. Haglund, D.D. Ingram, J.C. Kleinman, and J.J. Feldman. 1991. The Use of Health Service Areas for Measuring Provider Availability. *The Journal of Rural Health,* 7(4): 347-356.

McCullagh, P. and J.A. Nelder. 1989. *Generalized Linear Models.* 2d ed. London: Chapman and Hall.

Rodríguez, G. 1978. Family Planning Availability and Contraceptive Practice. *International Family Planning Perspectives,* 4(4): 100-115.

Rosero Bixby, L. 1993. Physical Accessibility to Health Facilities in Costa Rica. *International Population Conference Montreal 1993.* Vol. 3 (pp. 185-190). International Union for the Scientific Study of Population.

Rosero Bixby, L., and J. Casterline. 1994. Interaction diffusion and fertility transition in Costa Rica. *Social Forces,* 73(2): 435-462.

Scholten, H. J., and M.J.C. de Lepper. 1991. The benefits of the application of Geographic Information Systems in public an environmental health. *World Health Statistics Quarterly,* 44(3): 160-170.

Thouez, J. M., P. Bodson, and A.E. Joseph. 1988. Some Methods for Measuring the Geographic Accessibility of Medical Services in Rural Regions. *Medical Care,* 26(1): 34-44.

Tsui, A. O., D.P. Hogan, J.D. Teachman, and C. Welti-Chanes. 1981. Community Availability of Contraceptives and Family Limitation. *Demography,* 18(4): 615-626.

Wilkinson, M. I., W. Njogu, and N. Abderrahim. 1993. The Availability of Family Planning and Maternal and Child Health Services. *Demographic and Health Surveys. Comparative Studies No. 7.* Columbia, Maryland: Macro International Inc.

Wrigley, N. 1995. Revisiting the Modifiable Areal Unit Problem and the Ecological Fallacy. In A. D. Cliff, P. R. Gould, A. G. Hoare, & N. J. Thrift (Ed.), *Diffusing Geography Essays for Peter Haggett*. Oxford UK: Blackwell.

TABLE 1. LOGISTIC MODELS FOR TREND SURFACES ON THE CONDITIONAL PROBABILITIES OF USING CONTRACEPTIVES, CHOOSING THE IUD, AND UNMARRIED COHABITATION

Indicators	Using Contraceptives	IUD Choice	Unmarried Cohabitation
Conditional to be:	In a union	Using contraceptives	In a union
N women/clusters	1957/185	1484/185	1957/185
Polynomial degree/parameters	3/9	2/5	3/9
LL null model	-1082.3	-528.2	-973.2
LL polynomial surface	-1068.3	-519.3	-895.5
Chi2 of surface	28.0	17.8	155.4
LL 6-region model	-1077.7	-522.8	-920.5
LL region & surface	-1064.8	-512.5	-887.1
Chi2 of surface	25.8	20.6	66.8

LL = Log Likelihood ratio

TABLE 2. CORRELATION COEFFICIENTS AMONG SELECTED MEASURES OF FAMILY PLANNING SUPPLY

Measures	Travel time	Distance to nearest	Density 10 km Total	Density 10 km Per woman
Mean reported travel time	100	43	-28	-28
Distance to nearest		100	-65	-70
Density 10 km. radius:				
Total			100	66
Per woman				100
For total density, distance decay and radius	Decay = 0, 10 km	Decay = 1, 10 km	Decay = 1, 15 km	
Decay = 0, 10 km	100	96	95	
Decay = 1, 10 km		100	98	
Decay = 1, 15 km			100	

N = 185 sampling clusters.

All measures are cartographic, except the mean reported travel time

TABLE 3. MULTIPLE LOGISTIC REGRESSIONS ON THE CONDITIONAL PROBABILITIES OF CONTRACEPTIVE USE AND IUD CHOICE

	Contraceptive Use		IUD Choice	
Explanatory variables	Odds Ratio	(z)	Odds Ratio	(z)
Individual level				
Age in 5-year groups	1.13	(3.03)	0.86	(-2.34)
Reproductive goals				
Want child now	1.00	Reference	–	
Want no more children	5.80	(11.70)	1.00	Reference
Want to defer	6.84	(10.98)	1.19	(0.93)
Education in 5-year levels	1.38	(4.03)	1.43	(3.20)
Secularization index (1 to 4)	1.07	(1.38)	1.14	(1.88)
Contextual level				
Users* within 10 km.	1.11	(1.91)	1.26	(2.41)
Relative travel time	1.00	(0.01)	0.96	(-0.18)
FP hour-year/woman, 10 km	1.08	(0.20)	2.02	(1.50)
Pseudo R2 (Chi2)	0.09	(191.14)	0.04	(38.21)
N observations	1,927		1,460	
Sensitivity, access indicator				
FP hour-year/woman, 10 km	1.08	(0.20)	2.02	(1.50)
Same, no distance decay	1.30	(0.79)	1.20	(0.37)
Same, *total* FP hour-week	1.00	(0.07)	1.05	(1.47)
Distance nearest outlet (5 km)	0.89	(-1.12)	0.88	(-0.74)
Hours reported travel time	0.62	(-2.46)	0.75	(-0.84)

*OR for 10-point increase in the contextual percentage of users.

TABLE 4. CONDITIONAL LOGISTIC REGRESSION ON THE CHOICE OF CLINIC BY WOMEN USING RESUPPLY METHODS IN PUBLIC FACILITIES

Explanatory Variable	Coefficient	Odds Ratio	z value	P>|z|
Log distance in km.:	-3.02	...	-13.90	0.00
Log weekly FP hours				
IUD users	1.27	...	3.16	0.00
Other users	0.44	...	3.94	0.00
Log catchment population	0.13	...	1.11	0.27
Proportion FP consultations	1.41	4.09	1.69	0.09
Social Security's clinic	0.63	1.87	1.67	0.09

N = 5,510. Pseudo R2 = 0.90.
Matched case-control design (9 controls per case)

FIGURE 1. DISTANCE BETWEEN MAP AND FIELD MEASUREMENTS OF TRACTS CENTROIDS BY THE SCALE OF CENSUS MAPS

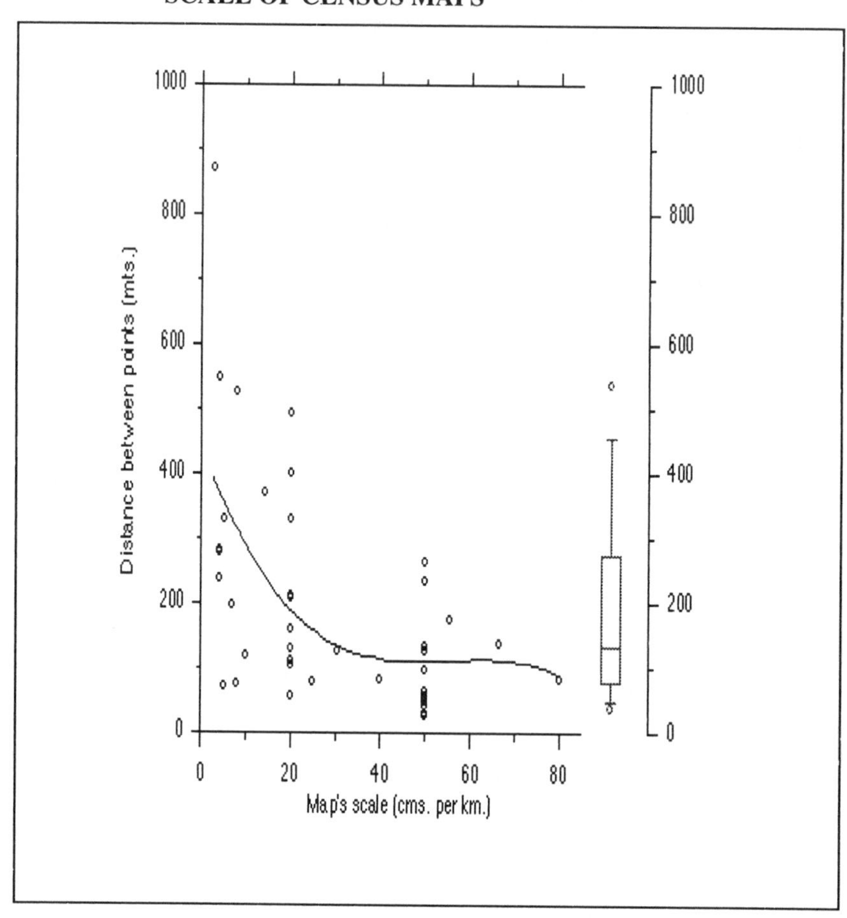

FIGURE 2. REPORTED TRAVEL TIME AGAINST CARTOGRAPHIC DISTANCE OF FAMILY PLANNING OUTLETS

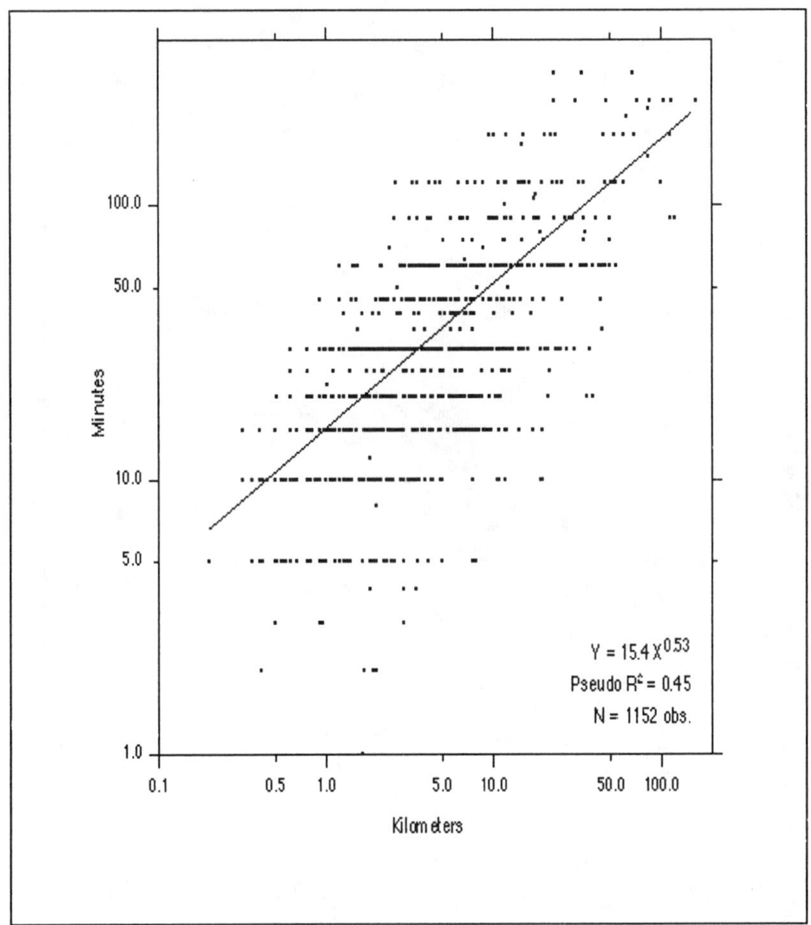

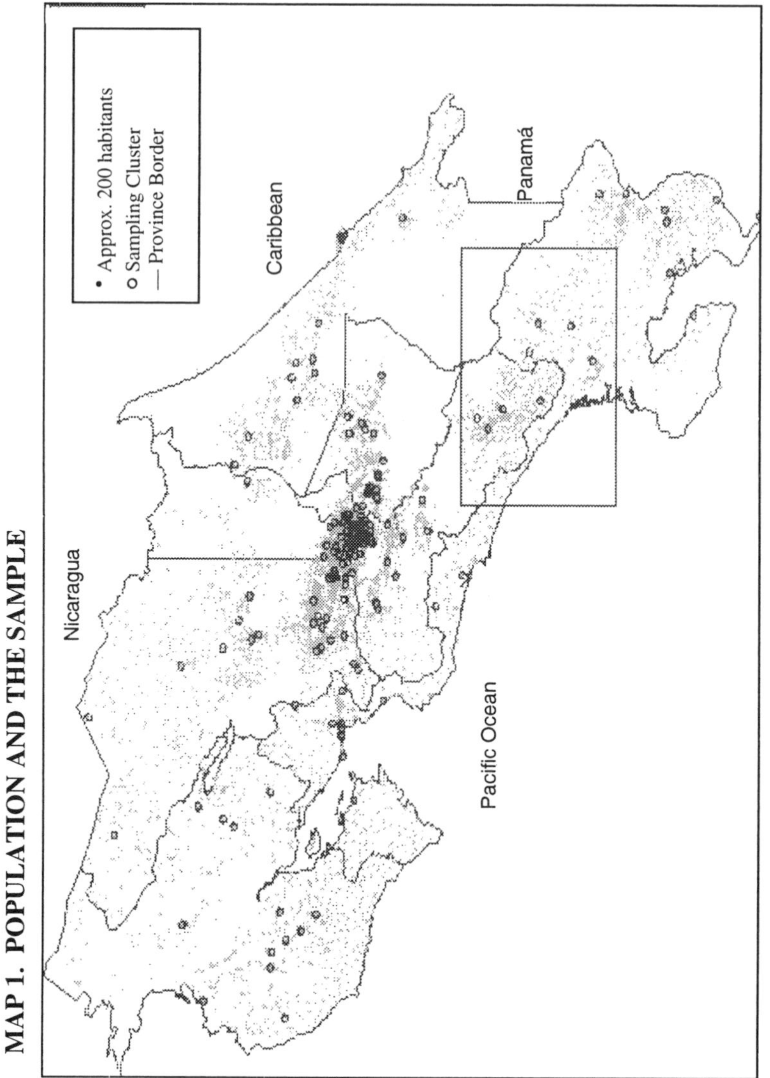

MAP 1. POPULATION AND THE SAMPLE

MAP 2. FP SERVICES USE

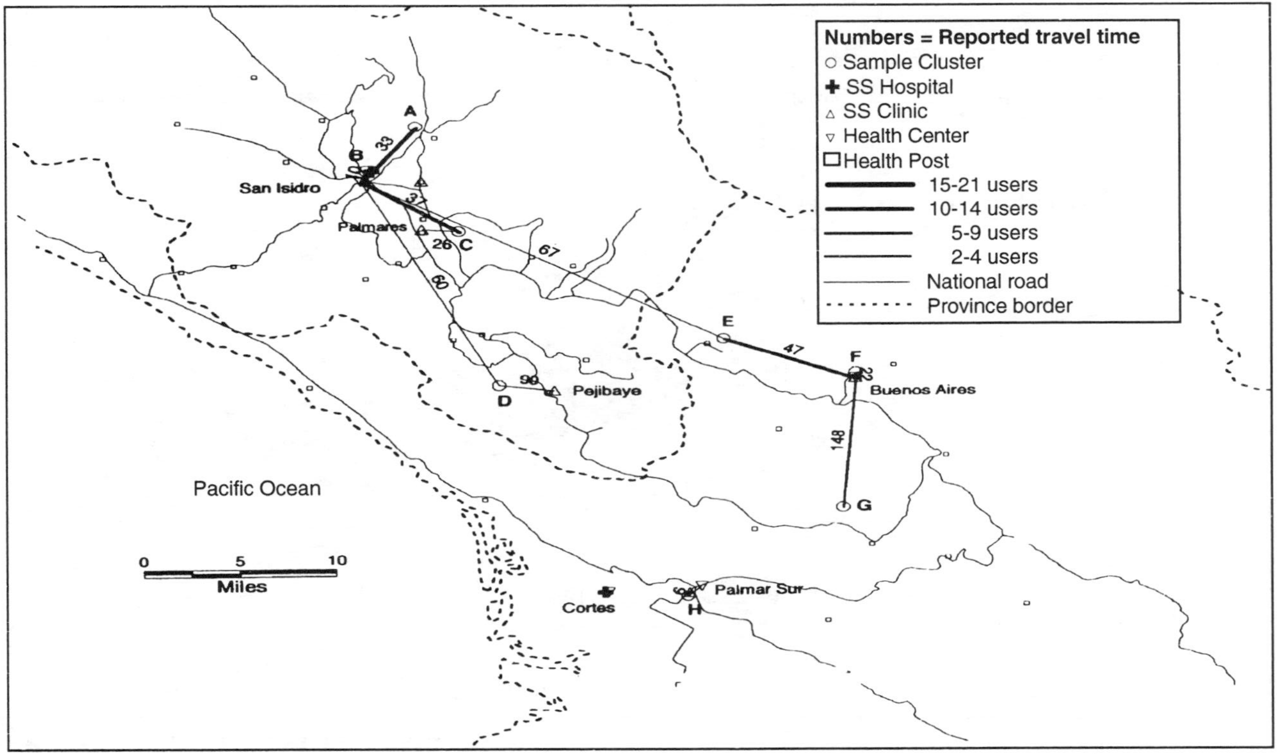

Numbers = Reported travel time
○ Sample Cluster
✚ SS Hospital
△ SS Clinic
▽ Health Center
□ Health Post
15-21 users
10-14 users
5-9 users
2-4 users
National road
Province border

Pacific Ocean

0 5 10
Miles

MAP 3. CONTRACEPTIVE PREVALENCE

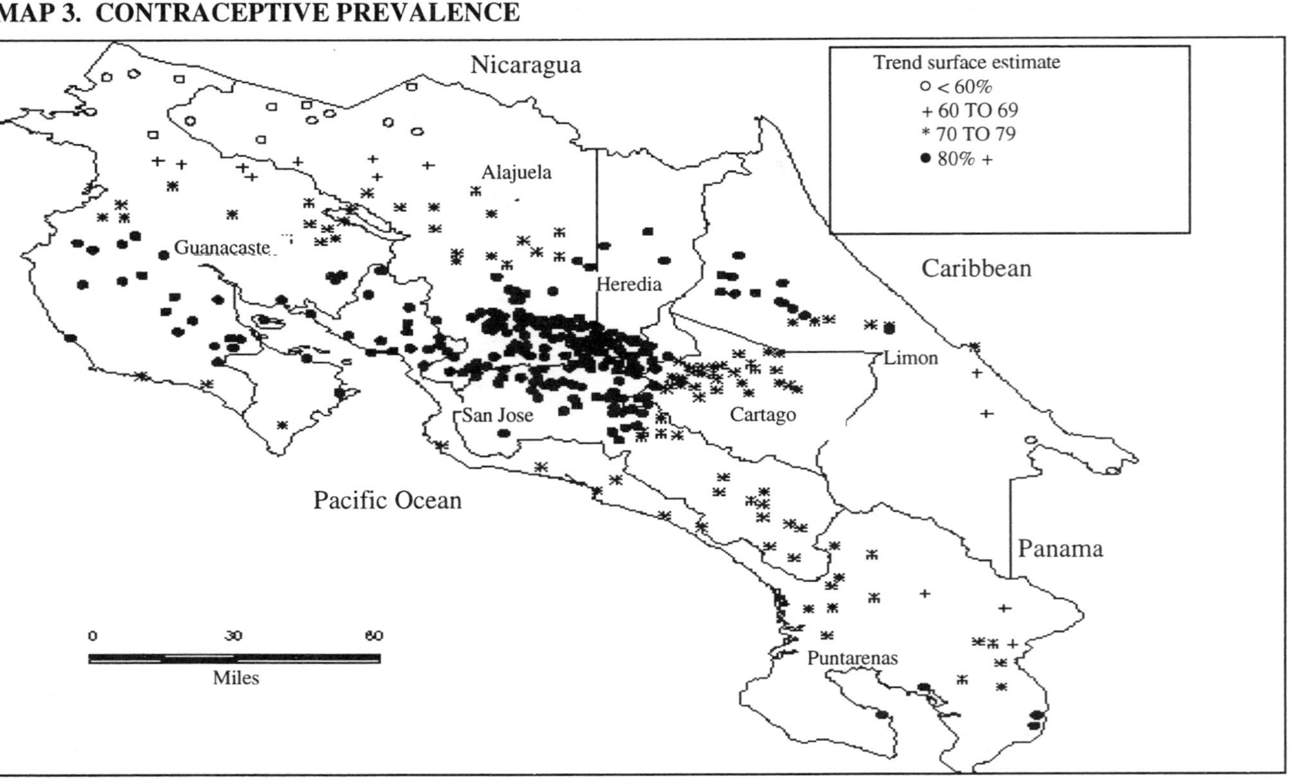

MAP 3b. IUD METHOD CHOICE

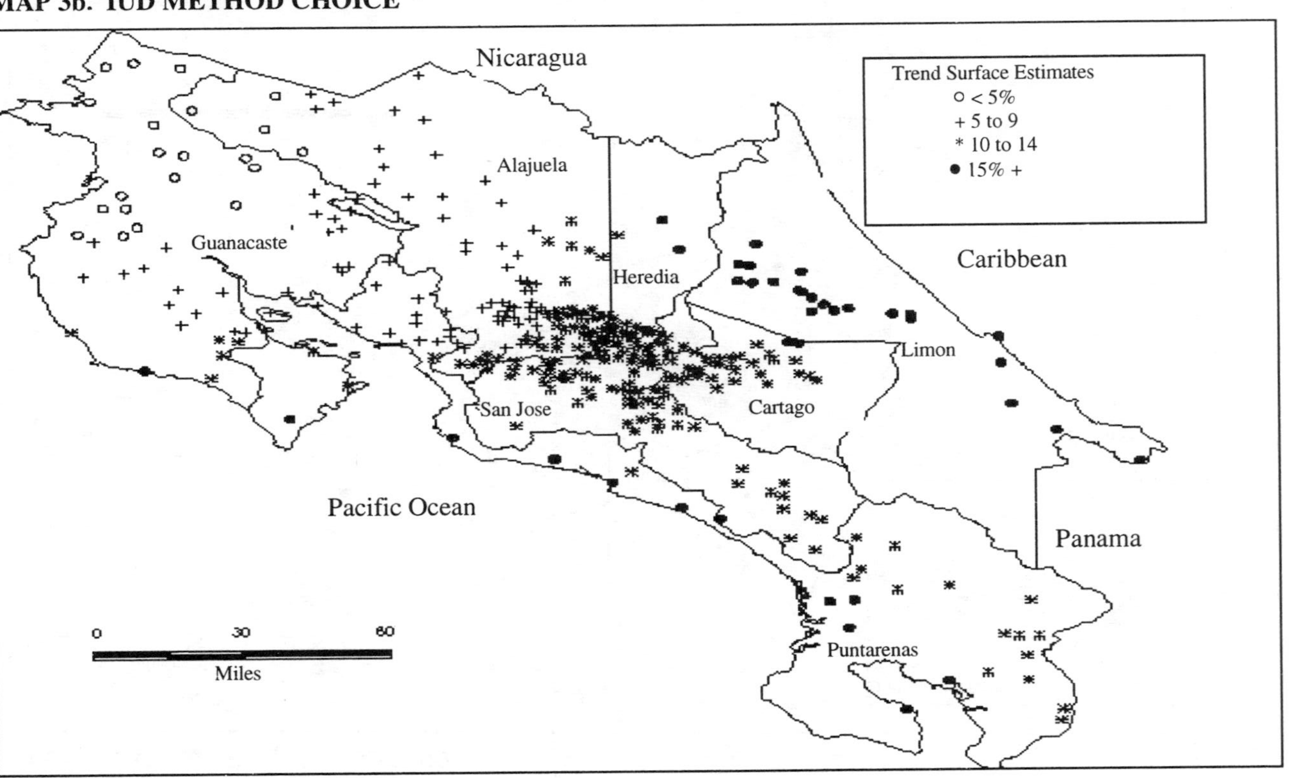

MAP 4. FAMILY PLANNING SUPPLY

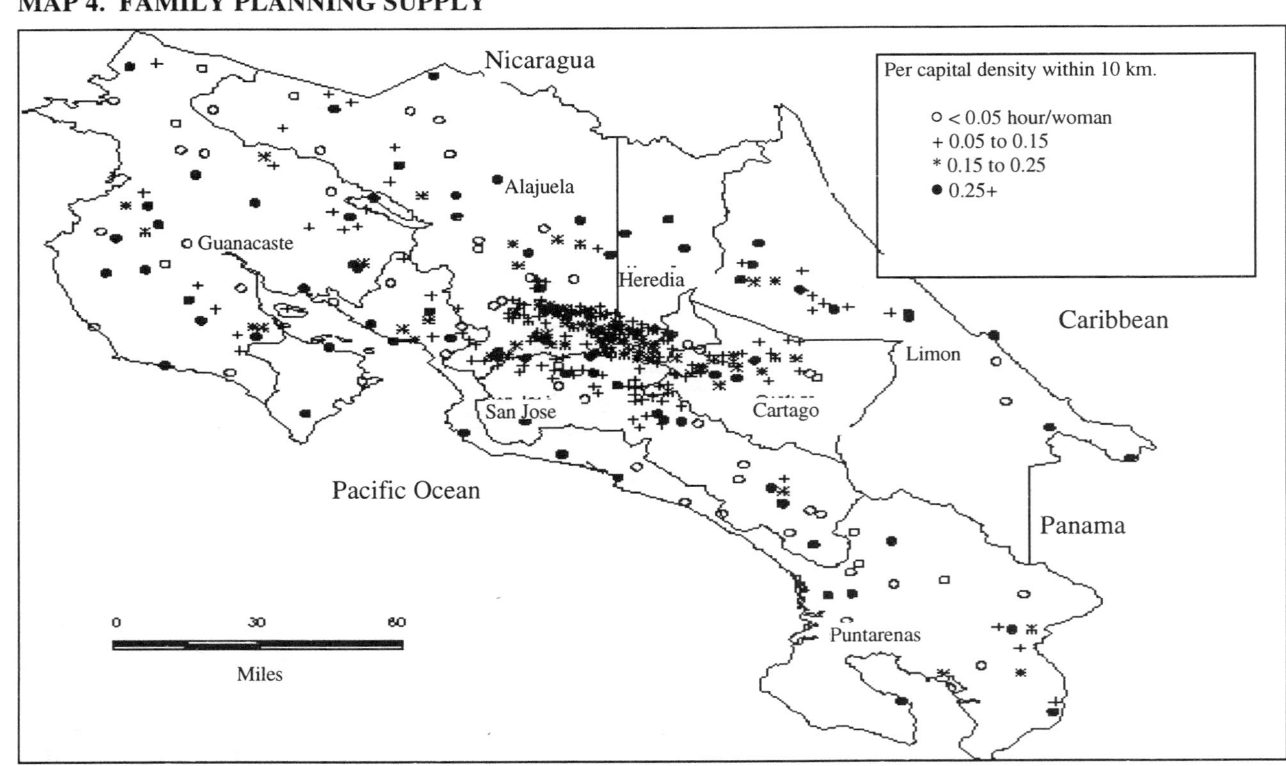

EXAMINING THE INCREASING POPULARITY OF TRADITIONAL CONTRACEPTIVE METHODS IN HONDURAS

DAVID HUBACHER, MARGARITA SUAZO,
STANLEY TERRELL, AND MARCO PINEL

In recent years, the increase in the contraceptive prevalence rate in Honduras has been dominated by a sharp rise in the use of traditional methods, while modern method use has grown very little. This paper analyzes data from two national probability sample surveys (1987 and 1991/92) and employs a new approach to explore the factors associated with this pattern. Multivariable techniques show that women interviewed in the 1991/92 survey were significantly more likely to use rhythm compared to those in the earlier period. The use of rhythm was also associated with various sociodemographic characteristics. For withdrawal, the pattern of use was distinct from that of rhythm; primarily, the time period between 1987 and 1991/92 did not have an effect on use. Also, users of withdrawal were significantly different from users of rhythm. The increase in the use of traditional methods and the slow growth of modern method use are also examined in relationship to other developments in Honduras over the same time period. This research focuses attention on these recent changes in the method mix and on the challenges confronting the family planning program.

INTRODUCTION

The use of both modern and traditional[1] methods contributes to the contraceptive prevalence rate, yet because family

---

[1]For purposes of this paper, traditional methods include rhythm and withdrawal (unless noted otherwise).

planning programs typically concern themselves with promoting and increasing the use of only modern methods, traditional methods are usually ignored. When modern method use is rising, program managers can afford to be indifferent toward traditional method use. However, when modern method use remains stagnant (or worse, decreases) and traditional method use increases, a family planning program should investigate promptly reasons for such changes. Did the gains in traditional method use come at the expense of modern methods, or is the relationship between prevalence rates of traditional and modern methods completely independent? Program managers might also want to know why traditional methods have increased in popularity, who uses them, and whether the national family planning program should take new steps to address the changes in contraceptive use patterns.

The broad goal of a family planning program is to help couples prevent unwanted births. Since traditional methods are, on average, less reliable and thus produce more unwanted births than modern methods (although traditional methods do prevent pregnancies better than using no method at all), programs tend to promote modern methods. Twelve-month failure rates for withdrawal and rhythm have been estimated at 19 and 20%, respectively, while the diaphragm (the least reliable modern method) has a failure rate of 18% (Hatcher, et al., 1994). While efficacy rates are important, method choice is often a function of personal preference and circumstance. The specific reasons why couples rely on traditional methods, instead of modern methods, are numerous: lack of knowledge about modern methods, convenience, fear of actual or perceived side effects, cultural constraints, and lack of accessibility (including cost). Programs should be aware of these reasons in order to understand better the factors influencing the contraceptive method mix.

Some previous research addressing traditional method use has been limited to describing only the characteristics of users at a given point in time. For example, a survey in Turkey found that traditional method use was associated with certain geographic regions, lower educational levels, and specific age groups (Goldberg and Toros, 1994). A study in Uganda revealed that employment status and religion were important factors influencing traditional method use (Ntozi and Kabera, 1991). These research efforts used data from single cross-sectional surveys to describe patterns associated with traditional method use.

In contrast, other research has benefited from multiple surveys conducted in the same geographic regions to examine how and if sociodemographic characteristics of specific method users varied over time. Goldscheider and Mosher (1991), used results from four iterations of the National Survey of Family Growth (conducted in the United States in 1973, 1976, 1982, and 1988) to show that the relationships between contraceptive use and religious affiliation were stable over a fifteen year period. Zablan, et al. (1989), used data from three surveys in the Philippines (1973, 1978, and 1983) to show that the strength of factors such as age, education, number of living children, and residence on the decision to use rhythm changed over time. Similar analyses on data from Sri Lanka (1975 and 1982) found traditional method use to be associated with marital duration for both survey years; whereas, the impact of variables such as ethnicity and education changed over the two surveys (Kahn, Thapa, and Gaminiratne, 1989). Though these last examples use multiple surveys to incorporate a time dimension in the analyses, they essentially compare cross-sectional results and simply describe how the profiles of specific method users have changed (or remained the same).

Honduras has experienced changes in contraceptive use patterns that challenge the family planning program to reassess their efforts; specifically, traditional method use has risen markedly while modern method use has not. These recent developments provide an interesting backdrop for studying the use of traditional methods in a new way. In contrast to the static context in which previous research has been reported, this effort attempts to analyze simultaneously the interplay of user characteristics and different time periods on method choice. The investigation draws attention to the changes confronting the Honduran family planning program and identifies the characteristics of women who are the root of such changes.

DATA AND METHODS

The four-year period in Honduras from 1987 to 1991/92 is the focus of this paper. Data used in this analysis are from two independent national probability sample surveys conducted in Honduras in 1987 and 1991/92; they are known as the Epidemiology and Family Health Surveys (EFHS). Both surveys were multistage, cross-sectional and self-weighting at the national level (excluding two departments accounting for about 2% of the Honduran population). The 1987 EFHS interviewed 10,143 women aged 15-44, while the 1991/92 EFHS included 8,082 women aged 15-49. The survey instruments were very similar in content and identical in some key areas related to fertility and contraceptive use. More details on all aspects of both surveys have been reported elsewhere (EFHS, 1987; ENESF, 1991/92).

As a basis for analysis, only women in union (consensual union or married) aged 15-44 were used. Current contraceptive use status was ascertained by asking women if they had used any one of a list of methods in the last 30 days. This list included the following: male and female sterilization, IUDs, injectables, OCs, condoms, vaginal methods, rhythm, withdrawal, and other. For women reporting more than one method in the given time period, the most efficacious was chosen to represent current use. All modern methods were deemed more efficacious than any traditional method, and the order of the latter was defined as rhythm, withdrawal, and other "folk" techniques (most to least efficacious). Rhythm and withdrawal were defined in exactly the same way in both surveys, and field teams were similarly trained.

Rhythm was described as the "calendar" method where "couples avoid sexual relations during the period a woman can get pregnant." Withdrawal was defined as "when the man is careful and withdraws before he is finished."

The new approach used in this research creates one analysis dataset by combining respondents from the 1987 and 1991/92 surveys and by adding a new variable denoting year. Since the research focuses on specific user characteristics associated with method choice, the primary analysis dataset includes only contracepting women. The important question driving this strategy is this: what distinguishes women who use traditional methods from those who use modern methods? By including only women demonstrating a clear desire to avoid pregnancy, those with the following characteristics are excluded: pregnant, amenorrheic, subfecund, currently attempting pregnancy, and sexually inactive. This decision to restrict the dataset enables us to examine more efficiently the characteristics associated with opting to use traditional methods over modern methods.

Chi-square tests of independence (with p-values of <.05 to determine significance) were used to compare users of withdrawal, rhythm, and modern methods on numerous sociodemographic variables. Then, separate logistic regression procedures were used to model the use of withdrawal and rhythm separately (women using modern methods were the basis for comparison in each of the regressions). SUDAAN software was used to incorporate the two surveys' sample designs into the estimation techniques, and "year of survey" was designated as the first stratification variable, followed by the survey-specific design variables (Shah, et al., 1991). Year of survey also serves as the primary "exposure" variable in the regression procedures to measure its effect on the decision to adopt a traditional method. The use of this variable in the context of other explanatory factors tests the hypothesis that 1991/92 served as an "independent risk factor" for adopting traditional methods.

Prior to the regression analysis, collinearity among the independent variables was checked and all continuous variables were tested for linearity on the logit. The only continuous variable which met the requirements for remaining in its original form was education. The variables "age" and "number of living children" were not linear on the logit and were made categorical using dummy variables because they showed a U-shaped relationship to the outcome of interest. Based on the curve, appropriate divisions were made to separate one group from the next, and the category with the lowest risk for the outcome was designated as the reference group. The majority of the remaining variables were dichotomous and for ease of interpretation of the coefficients, the category with the lowest prevalence of traditional method use was selected as the reference group. The modeling exercises were pursued for scientific inference about factors explaining the rise in the use of traditional methods. Given this purpose, all explanatory variables were used in the final models, though some were not significantly associated with the outcome. Retaining such variables in the models is recommended when controlling for confounding is important and when the data can support the additional variables (Rothman, 1986). Beta coefficients, adjusted odds ratios, 95% confidence intervals, and p-values will be reported in the tables.

RESULTS

The first half of the results section will describe the change in contraceptive use patterns between 1987 and 1991/92 and the second half will explore user characteristics associated with adopting traditional methods and estimate the impact of the variable "year of survey."

Changes in Contraceptive Use Patterns

Over a ten year period in Honduras (1981-1991), traditional method use has steadily increased, while modern method use appears to be leveling off. Figure 1 plots this trend and shows the most recent point estimates from the Demographic and Health Surveys and surveys conducted by the Centers for Disease Control (CDC) for thirteen other Latin American countries. Traditional methods are defined as rhythm (periodic abstinence), withdrawal, and other "folk" techniques. The eight countries in the upper left corner of the figure are those with the highest ratio of modern to traditional method use. This group includes the following: Belize, Nicaragua, Mexico, El Salvador, the Dominican Republic, Brazil (NE), Colombia, and Costa Rica. The most recent point estimate for Honduras (1991/92) places it in a small cluster with Ecuador and Paraguay. The concern which motivated the writing of this paper is that since 1984, Honduras has failed to move in the direction occupied by the first group of countries and instead, has shifted along the horizontal axis.

The largest gain in the use of traditional methods occurred between 1987 and 1991/92; the prevalence rose over four percentage points from 7.6% to 12.0% (Table 1). Modern method use showed its greatest increase in the early period (1981-1984), yet since 1984, has risen only 4.4 percentage points. Since 1987, modern methods rose less than two points.

The main components of traditional methods, rhythm and withdrawal, were at about the same level in 1987 (Table 2). Though the percent of women using each of these techniques increased over the subsequent four-year period, rhythm showed more growth than withdrawal. The prevalence of specific modern methods also changed over the two periods. Only oral contraceptives decreased in popularity since 1987, by dropping over three percentage points. The only modern method to show a sizable increase was female sterilization; it increased by three percentage points. It is important to note that the percent of women using rhythm increased more than any modern method, including that of female sterilization.

The previous table reported the contraceptive status of all women in union from both surveys. When the data from only contracepting women are reported, the importance of traditional methods is even more apparent. As a percentage of the total method mix, traditional methods rose from 18.8% in 1987 to 25.7% in 1991/92.

Examining User Characteristics

The previous section described the broad changes in contraceptive use patterns in Honduras over the last decade. This portion of the analysis will assess the user characteristics associated with method choice. Data from the 1987 and 1991/92 surveys are combined in the remaining analyses and contain only contracepting women in union.

The first section will report the findings of bivariable analyses, and the second section will report the multivariable regression results, including the contribution of the variable "year of survey."

Bivariable Analyses

Women using rhythm, withdrawal, and modern methods are very different on many important sociodemographic characteristics (Table 3). Users of withdrawal have a younger age distribution than modern method users and they have less education and fewer living children than modern method users. There is a clear difference with regard to residence as well; withdrawal users are predominately rural while the majority of modern method users are urban. Other distributions of variables that are significantly different include the following: time to a health facility, employment, functioning television, opinion about last pregnancy, desire for additional children, and whether a family planning message was heard on the radio in the last month.

The second comparison is between users of rhythm and modern methods. In general, the patterns of differences described between withdrawal and modern users are similar to those found between rhythm and modern. However, the differences are not as profound and women using rhythm appear to bridge the gap between the two groups. For instance, the age distribution for rhythm users is still younger than that of modern method users, however, it is not as young as the distribution among withdrawal users. Similarly, rhythm users are not as rural in character as withdrawal users, yet are not quite as urban as modern method users. A similar pattern is seen for time to a health facility and employment. The only variable where rhythm users (and not withdrawal users) are significantly different from modern method users is marital status; rhythm users are more likely to be married compared to modern method users.

The final comparison is between withdrawal and rhythm. Many of the differences have already been alluded to in the previous analysis that compared rhythm to modern. The variables with significantly different distributions include the following: age, education, number of living children, residence, time to a health facility, employment, and opinion about last pregnancy.

Multivariable Analyses

Results of the bivariable analyses guide some important decisions necessary to proceed with the multivariable analyses. First, because rhythm users were found to be different from withdrawal users, they cannot be combined and treated as one group labeled "traditional" method users. Second, women using modern methods were very different from both rhythm and withdrawal users; this finding provides the justification for modeling contraceptive choice. All the variables with the exception of religion and opinion about last pregnancy will be considered in the multivariable regressions. Religion will be excluded because it was only available in the 1991/92 survey. The decision to exclude opinion about last pregnancy is based on the fact that many women in the database had never been pregnant. Thus, any regressions involving this variable would exclude all such observations from the estimation procedures. Many younger women in particular would be eliminated from the analysis since they are less likely than their older counterparts to be gravid.

Also in this analysis, year of survey appears as an independent variable in the regression procedures. The inclusion of this variable returns the analysis to the original motive of this paper: to determine whether women interviewed in 1991/92 were subject to an increased likelihood of using traditional methods after controlling for other sociodemographic factors simultaneously. A corollary to this goal is to measure the strength of this factor in relation to other variables.

The regression results for rhythm and modern method users (Table 4) show that women interviewed in 1991/92 were about twice as likely to use rhythm compared to women interviewed in 1987 (adjusted odds ratio=1.98). In terms of age, only the 40-44 group was at a significantly higher risk of using rhythm compared to the reference group aged 25-39. Women with two or fewer living children were 80% more likely to use rhythm compared to women with 3-7 children. Married women and rural women were also at an increased likelihood of using rhythm in comparison to their respective reference groups. The variable denoting accessibility to health services shows that as the time it takes to reach a health facility increases, so does the probability of using rhythm; those living three or more hours from a facility are nearly two times more likely to use rhythm compared to women within one hour of services. Women who want more children were nearly 30% more likely to use traditional methods. Finally, hearing a radio message on family planning in the previous month was also associated with an increased likelihood of using rhythm over modern methods.

The findings for users of withdrawal and modern methods (Table 5) are different from the previous regression in several important ways. First, the variable "year of survey" is not a significant determinant of the decision to use withdrawal over modern methods; women interviewed in 1991/92 were no more or less likely to use withdrawal compared to women interviewed in 1987. Second, the variable for education emerged as an important factor in the model. Every additional year of education decreases the likelihood of using withdrawal by about 10%. In other words, the higher the level of education, the higher the probability of using modern methods. Two age groups (15-19 and 20-24) and the highest parity group (8+ living children) became significant in this regression of withdrawal users. As was the case for users of rhythm, married women, rural women, and women further away from a health facility were more likely to use withdrawal compared to their respective counterparts.

DISCUSSION

The four-year period between 1987 and 1991/92 had a significant impact on the decision to use rhythm but not withdrawal. This finding may reflect the fact that rhythm was promoted actively by numerous organizations in Honduras over this time period. Withdrawal, however, remains a method whose vitality survives primarily through word-of-mouth.

Women who stated their desire to have additional children (or to have a child in the case of nulliparous women) were more likely to use rhythm compared to those who did not want more children. This finding can have several possible explanations. First, it might suggest that modern methods are avoided because of concerns that such methods may have on future fertility. Second, it may indicate a general lack of concern over the consequence of method failure (while using rhythm). In the regression involving rhythm and modern method users, hearing family planning messages on the radio was seen to have a positive effect on the decision to adopt rhythm. (This variable apparently has no effect on the decision to adopt withdrawal.) Unfortunately, women were never asked about the content of the family planning radio messages they heard, thus it is impossible to know whether they were messages promoting rhythm or modern methods (or even dissuading listeners from using modern methods); all three types of messages are broadcast on Honduran radio. If radio influences contraceptive choice, the results of this analysis would suggest that messages promoting the use of rhythm were having the most impact.

Education levels were only important in the decision to adopt withdrawal; those with lower levels were more likely to forego modern methods. The profile of rhythm and modern method users was too similar in terms of education to be a significant predictor of rhythm use. In the bivariable analysis, religious affiliation (available only in the 1991/92 survey) was not found to be associated with using either withdrawal or rhythm, thus weakening some theories about the role of the Catholic church on contraceptive use patterns in Honduras.

The contraceptive prevalence trend in Honduras over the period 1981 to 1991/92 should also be viewed in relationship to fertility rates from the same time periods. The total fertility rates (TFRs) for 1981, 1984, 1987 and 1991/92, as estimated from previously mentioned sample surveys, were 6.5, 5.5, 5.6, and 5.2, respectively (Encuesta Nacional de Epidemiología y Salud Familiar, Honduras 1991/92). Though there was a sharp decline in the TFR between 1981 and 1984, the decrease in the subsequent eight year period was very slight at best.

Though this paper has used survey data as a basis for analyzing the changes in family planning use in Honduras, the remainder of the discussion section will draw upon other sources of information necessary for placing these changes in a broader context. Program information from the Ministry of Health and ASHONPLAFA (Family Planning Association of Honduras) will be the first topic to review. One of the key questions to address is whether access to health facilities deteriorated over the four year period such that it became more difficult to obtain modern family planning methods (thus leaving women to default for traditional methods). In the period 1987 to 1991, ASHONPLAFA increased the number of family planning posts from 1,303 to 1,728 (ASHONPLAFA, internal documents). The Ministry of Health also increased the number of rural health centers and physician-staffed health centers by about 12% (from 651 to 729) over the period 1987 to 1991 (Honduran Ministry of Health, internal documents). Thus it would seem that in terms of access to facilities providing family planning methods, the situation in Honduras improved between 1987 and 1991. Admittedly, the concept of "access" is more complex than simply counting the number of existing health facilities; however, it does accurately reflect at least the availability of services.

A second area to examine is the state of contraceptive supplies over the period 1987 to 1992, when the prevalence of oral contraceptive use in Honduras dropped noticeably. Though causes for this drop have been explored using survey data, the possibility of shortages of supplies of oral contraceptives needs to be addressed. The only source for this type of information is from USAID/Honduras; they conduct monitoring visits to health districts on a periodic basis to check on the availability of medications, staffing, etc. Every year they visit around 100 Ministry of Health facilities all across the nation and report their findings.

With the exception of 1987 and 1990, the percent of facilities having Oral Contraceptives (OCs) in stock has been consistently over 90% (Table 6). In 1987 the figure was only 80%, however, this does not appear to have affected the prevalence of OCs use at the time it was at its highest level (13%) in that very year (see Table 2). The drop in availability of OCs in 1990 could have possibly led to decreases in use in later years, however, lack of supplies at health facilities has never been an important reason for discontinuation according to the EFHS surveys.

Another factor that could have contributed to a decrease in the use of oral contraceptives is the increase in prices at pharmacies and ASHONPLAFA (Ministry of Health clients receive the product free of charge). At ASHONPLAFA, prices for their two brands of oral contraceptives doubled between 1987 and 1991 (ASHONPLAFA, 1987-1992); this price increase affected the product sold through the Social Marketing Program as well. The largest percentage increase in prices occurred in the period 1989 to 1990. In a related matter, Honduras experienced a severe economic crisis between 1986 and 1990 that required formal devaluation of the lempira in 1990 (Primer Informe de Seguimiento y Evaluación del Plan de Acción Nacional. 1994. SECPLAN-Secretaría de Planificación, Coordinación y Presupuesto). Unfortunately, data on the price changes at pharmacies is not available.

Finally, the last topic to discuss is the political side of family planning in Honduras. Since 1986, modern methods have been the target of attack from several different groups in Honduras. The history behind these developments is too complex to describe here, however, these matters are mentioned in various documents written by ASHONPLAFA (1994). The debate over the role of family planning peaked in Honduras in 1989 when the government voted down a proposal to create a population law to address the problems associated with high fertility and low prevalence of contraceptive use. After the measure was defeated, an opposing bill was introduced in the legislature that would have limited family planning services; this proposal was also defeated. The controversies ignited much public debate and filled the local newspapers with editorials on the issue. In 1993, new damage was inflicted on the family planning program over the use of progestin-only oral contraceptives among lactating women. ASHONPLAFA, the Ministry of Health, the Honduran Social Security Institute, and USAID/Honduras were accused by various medical and non-medical groups of promoting unsafe use of an approved contraceptive method (El Heraldo, 1993). Though this most recent example of the volatile family planning environment in Honduras occurred after the 1991/92 survey, the seeds for this type of controversy were planted in the mid-1980s.

CONCLUSIONS

Despite enormous efforts over the past decade on the part of health providers and donor agencies to increase modern contraceptive use in Honduras, the family planning program appears to have stalled in recent years. The leveling in modern method use has been countered by a rapid increase in the use of traditional methods over the same period; unfortunately, it is impossible to determine whether that increase came at the expense of modern methods. If method choice is inter-related, then the trend in Honduras would suggest that women were adopting rhythm in lieu of oral contraceptives, since the latter experienced a rapid descent over the time period.

The unusual method mix changes in Honduras provided the impetus to investigate this situation using a new approach. Combining data from two periods (different national probability sample surveys) and using multivariable analytic techniques enabled the direct measurement of the impact of "time" on contraceptive choice. Furthermore, the decision to analyze only contraceptors from the two surveys improved greatly the efficiency of the modeling to better match the primary research question.

Some important differences emerged between users of withdrawal and users of rhythm. Primarily, the four-year period between 1987 and 1991 had a significant impact on the decision to use rhythm, whereas, it did not increase the probability of using withdrawal. A number of key sociodemographic characteristics were also associated with the decision to use traditional methods instead of modern methods.

This research represents a first step toward understanding the factors influencing the decision to adopt traditional contraceptive methods. Complementary studies using qualitative techniques can also be used to shed light on this important issue confronting the Honduran family planning program.

ACKNOWLEDGEMENTS

The authors would like to thank Barbara Janowitz, Patricia Bailey, and Ward Cates of Family Health International (FHI) for their helpful comments on earlier drafts of this manuscript, as well as various staff members at USAID/Honduras. Technical input and review was provided by Emelita De Leon-Wong and Lucinda Glover, also of FHI. The statements in this document do not necessarily reflect the opinion of the authors' institutions.

REFERENCES

ASHONPLAFA. 1987-1992. "Informes Bi-Mensuales de la Sección de Ventas Comunitarias."

_____. 1994. "Pasos Hacia el Próximo Siglo. Plan Estratégico 1995-2000."

ENESF - *Encuesta Nacional de Epidemiología y Salud Familiar. Borrador del Informe Final.* 1991/92. Ministerio de Salud Pública.

EFHS - Epidemiology and Family Health Survey. Final Report. 1987. Honduran Ministry of Public Health.

Goldberg H.I. and A. Toros. 1994. "The Use of Traditional Methods of Contraception Among Turkish Couples." *Studies in Family Planning* 25(2),122-128.

Goldscheider C. and W.D. Mosher. 1991. "Patterns of Contraceptive Use in the United States: the Importance of Religious Factors." *Studies in Family Planning* 22(2),102-115.

Hatcher, R.A., et al. 1994. *Contraceptive Technology: Sixteenth Revised Edition* Irvington Publishers, Inc., New York.

El Heraldo. 1993. "Graves daños en el lactante produce minipíldora Ovrette." July 11, 1993, page 54.

Kahn J.R., S. Thapa and H.W. Gaminiratne. 1989. Socio-demographic Determinants of Contraceptive Method Choice in Sri Lanka: 1975-82." *Journal of Biosocial Science* Supplement No. 11. 41-60.

Ntozi J.P.M. and J. Kabera. 1991. "Family Planning in Rural Uganda: Knowledge and Use of Modern and Traditional Methods in Ankole." *Studies in Family Planning* 22(2),116-123.

Rothman K. 1986. *Modern Epidemiology*. Boston/Toronto: Little, Brown and Company, Inc.

Shah B.V., et al. 1991. *SUDAAN User's Manual*. Research Triangle Institute.

Zablan Z., et al. 1989. "Contraceptive Method Choice in the Philippines, 1973-83." *Journal of Biosocial Science*, Supplement No. 11. 61-74.

TABLE 1. TRENDS IN CONTRACEPTIVE USE, HONDURAS 1981-1991/92

Year	% Traditional	% Modern	% Total
1981[1]	3.2	23.6	26.8
1984[2]	4.6	30.3	34.9
1987[3]	7.6	33.0	40.6
1991/92[4]	12.0	34.7	46.7

[1]Encuesta Nacional de Prevalencia del Uso de Anticonceptivos. Resultados Generales. 1981.
[2]Maternal-Child Health and Family Planning Survey. Final Report. 1984.
[3]Epidemiology and Family Health Survey. Final Report. 1987.
[4]Encuesta Nacional de Epidemiología y Salud Familiar. Borrador del Informe Final. 1991/92.

TABLE 2. PERCENTAGE DISTRIBUTION OF WOMEN IN UNION AGED 15-44 ACCORDING TO CURRENT CONTRACEPTIVE METHOD, BY YEAR OF SURVEY

	Survey	
Method	1987	1991/92
Traditional	7.6	12.0
Rhythm	3.5	6.7
Withdrawal	4.0	5.0
Other Traditional	0.2	0.3
Modern	33.0	34.7
Orals	13.4	10.1
IUD	4.3	5.1
Female Sterilization	12.6	15.6
Male Sterilization	0.2	0.2
Condom	1.8	2.9
Injectable	0.3	0.5
Vaginal Methods	0.3	0.3
Not Contracepting	59.4	53.3
Total	100.0	100.0
Number of Women	6093	4322

TABLE 3. PERCENTAGE DISTRIBUTION OF WOMEN ACCORDING TO VARIOUS CHARACTERISTICS BY METHOD

Characteristics	Method			
	Withdrawal	Rhythm	Modern	Total
Age*†‡				
15-19	8.1	6.4	3.5	4.3
20-24	26.6	16.5	15.2	16.5
25-29	22.6	23.4	23.5	23.4
30-34	15.2	20.7	23.7	22.5
35-39	14.5	17.1	20.4	19.4
40-44	13.0	15.9	13.6	13.8
Education*†‡				
None	20.4	9.0	10.4	11.2
1-3 Years	31.6	30.2	22.4	24.2
4-6 Years	34.1	28.0	36.8	35.5
7+ Years	13.8	32.8	30.4	29.0
Number of Living Children*†‡				
0-1	21.3	20.7	13.8	15.3
2-4	46.2	53.5	57.3	55.7
5+	32.5	25.8	29.0	29.0
Marital Status†				
Consensual	49.4	38.4	48.7	47.6
Union	50.6	61.6	51.3	52.4
Married				
Residence*†‡				
Rural	69.2	53.9	41.2	45.5
Urban	30.8	46.1	58.8	54.5
Time to Health				
Facility*†‡	57.6	65.7	76.6	73.4
< 1 Hour	34.7	27.2	20.4	22.6
1-3 Hours	7.8	7.0	3.0	3.9
3+ Hours				
Total	100.0	100.0	100.0	100.0
Number of Women**	455	503	3505	4463

(continued on next page)

(Table 3 continued from previous page)

Characteristics	Method			
	Withdrawal	Rhythm	Modern	Total
Work *‡				
No	73.4	66.4	61.3	63.1
Yes	26.6	33.6	38.7	36.9
Work Outside of House				
No	86.4	87.5	85.5	85.8
Yes	13.6	12.5	14.5	14.2
Religion§				
Catholic	66.8	66.2	62.9	63.8
Other/None	33.2	33.8	37.1	36.2
Radio Functioning				
No	38.9	38.8	36.1	36.7
Yes	61.1	61.2	63.9	63.3
TV Functioning*†				
No	72.0	70.2	64.3	65.7
Yes	28.0	29.8	35.7	34.3
Wanted Last Pregnancy*‡				
No	43.4	33.5	34.4	35.2
Yes	56.6	66.5	65.6	64.8
Want More Children*†				
No	59.3	54.7	66.0	64.1
Yes	40.7	45.3	34.0	35.9
Hear a Family Planning Message on the Radio in the Last Month*				
No	69.7	64.0	62.0	63.0
Yes	30.3	36.0	38.0	37.0
Total	100.0	100.0	100.0	100.0
Number of Women**	455	503	3505	4463

* Withdrawal versus modern, $p<.05$

† Rhythm versus modern, $p<.05$

‡ Withdrawal versus rhythm, $p<.05$

§ Only available for the 1991/92 survey (n=2004 in this table)

** Some distributions are based on fewer women because of missing data and skip patterns.

TABLE 4. LOGISTIC REGRESSION MODEL FOR RHYTHM USERS SHOWING BETA COEFFICIENTS, ADJUSTED ODDS RATIOS, CONFIDENCE INTERVALS AND P-VALUES FOR 3973 HONDURAN WOMEN

Variable	Beta	Adjusted Odds Ratio	95% Confidence Interval	p-value
Year of Survey				
1987	-	1.00	-	
1991/92	0.68	1.98	(1.53,2.58)	0.00
Age of Respondent				
15-19	0.20	1.22	(0.78,1.89)	0.39
20-24	-0.21	0.81	(0.59,1.11)	0.19
25-39	-	1.00	-	-
40-44	0.32	1.37	(1.03,1.84)	0.03
Number of Children				
0-2	0.60	1.82	(1.37,2.40)	0.00
3-7	-	1.00	-	-
8+	0.32	1.38	(0.92,2.07)	0.12
Marital Status				
Consensual Union	-	1.00	-	
Married	0.46	1.58	(1.28,1.95)	0.00
Place of Residence				
Urban	-	1.00	-	
Rural	0.48	1.62	(1.26,2.07)	0.00
Time to Health Facility				
Less than 1 hour	-	1.00	-	-
1-3 hours	0.33	1.39	(1.08,1.79)	0.01
3+ hours	0.67	1.95	(1.27,3.01)	0.00
Want More Children				
No	-	1.00	-	-
Yes	0.24	1.28	(1.00,1.62)	0.05
Hear a Family Planning Message on the Radio in the Last Month				
No	-	1.00	-	-
Yes	0.23	1.26	(1.01,1.57)	0.04

Adjusting for the following variables: education, employment, functioning radio, and functioning TV.

TABLE 5. LOGISTIC REGRESSION MODEL FOR WITHDRAWAL USERS SHOWING BETA COEFFICIENTS, ADJUSTED ODDS RATIOS, CONFIDENCE INTERVALS AND P-VALUES FOR 3923 HONDURAN WOMEN

Variable	Beta	Adjusted Odds Ratio	95% Confidence Interval	p-value
Year of Survey				
1987	-	1.00	-	
1991/92	0.13	1.14	(0.87,1.51)	0.35
Age of Respondent				
15-19	0.74	2.10	(1.31,3.35)	0.00
20-24	0.66	1.94	(1.44,2.60)	0.00
25-39	-	1.00	-	-
40-44	-0.10	0.91	(0.66,1.24)	0.54
Years of Education	-0.12	0.89	(0.85,0.92)	0.00
Number of Children				
0-2	0.62	1.87	(1.37,2.53)	0.00
3-7	-	1.00	-	-
8+	0.64	1.89	(1.31,2.74)	0.00
Marital Status				
Consensual Union	-	1.00	-	
Married	0.34	1.41	(1.11,1.78)	0.00
Place of Residence				
Urban	-	1.00	-	
Rural	0.68	1.98	(1.51,2.61)	0.00
Time to Health Facility				
Less than 1 hour	-	1.00	-	-
1-3 hours	0.38	1.46	(1.12,1.90)	0.00
3+ hours	0.65	1.92	(1.24,2.96)	0.00

Adjusting for the following variables: employment, functioning radio, functioning TV, desire for more children, hearing a family planning message on the radio in the previous month.

TABLE 6. RESULTS OF USAID/HONDURAS SITE VISITS TO MINISTRY OF HEALTH FACILITIES

Year	Percent of Health Facilities with OC Supplies
1987	80%
1988	94%
1989	92%
1990	75%
1991	95%
1992	90%

Source: Ernesto A. Pinto. Informe Final de las Manitorías a las Regiones Sanitarias, USAID/Honduras, 1987-1992.

FIGURE 1. TRADITIONAL AND MODERN METHOD USE IN LATIN AMERICA

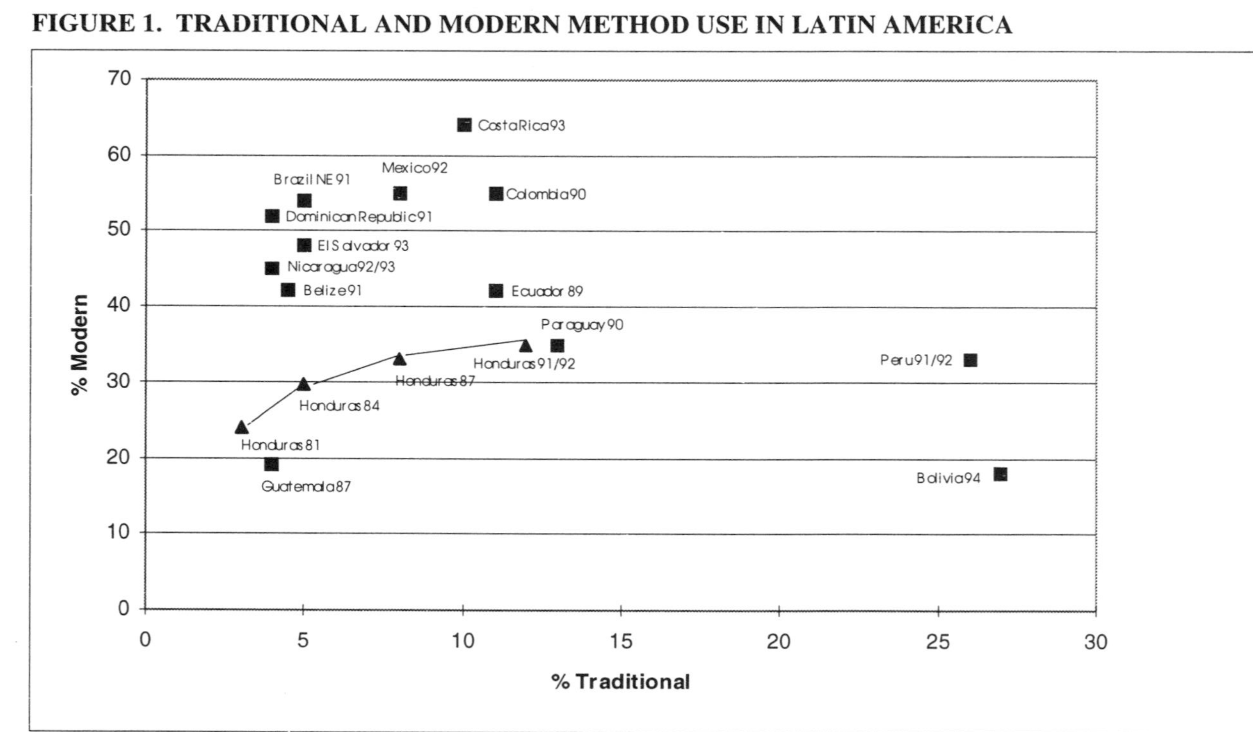

Chapter Nineteen

ADOLESCENT MOTHERHOOD IN GUATEMALA: A COMPARATIVE PERSPECTIVE

RENEE SAMARA

In Guatemala, around 28 percent of young women become mothers before their eighteenth birthday. In other Latin American countries for which we have comparable data, the percentages range from 26 percent in El Salvador to 14 percent in Brazil. Combining these data with what we know about age-specific fertility rates—Guatemala trails closely behind El Salvador and Honduras with the third highest age-specific fertility rate for 15- to 19-year-olds in Latin America—we may infer that Guatemalan females are among the most likely in both Central America, and in the entire Latin America region, to make an adolescent transition to motherhood.

Drawing on data from nine Demographic and Health Surveys, this paper offers two complementary explanations for Guatemala's relatively high level of adolescent motherhood. First, Guatemalan females are more likely than women in the comparison countries to be exposed to the risk of motherhood during adolescence. This is because of their earlier initiation of sexual activity combined with their lower levels of contraceptive use. Second, these adolescents tend to engage in sexual activity within the confines of marriage or a consensual union. This close coupling of sexual activity and union involvement means that Guatemalan women lack a major motivation to delay making an adolescent transition to motherhood: risk of out-of-wedlock childbearing. The coalescence of these factors is responsible for the situation in Guatemala where the proportion of young women having had sex within marriage by age 18 has remained virtually unchanged over the past 20 years. Until this group, which is responsible for the largest proportion of first births to adolescents, shrinks in number, the country is unlikely to witness a significant decrease in adolescent childbearing.

INTRODUCTION

In all societies, motherhood is an important life course event; in addition to replenishing a society's members, women who become mothers satisfy social expectations about women's role. Many Latin Americans regard the childless women as an aberration (Thomson 1986:30)—a socially and psychologically marginal individual (Bourque and Warren 1981:88). In this respect one cannot ignore the Catholic Church's profound influence on Latin American society: according to the Vatican, one of the chief purposes of marriage is the formation of children to be citizens of the Kingdom of God (J.E. Smith 1986). Yet throughout the region, the timing of motherhood and the sequence of events associated with becoming a mother vary both within and between countries.

This paper adopts a cross-national, comparative perspective in order to investigate the phenomenon of adolescent childbearing in Guatemala. Around 28 percent of young Guatemalan women become mothers before their eighteenth birthday [Figure 1]. In other Latin American countries for which we have comparable data, the percentages range from 26 percent in El Salvador to 14 percent in Brazil. Combining these data with what we know about age-specific fertility rates—Guatemala trails closely behind El Salvador and Honduras with the third highest age-specific fertility rate for 15- to 19-year-olds in Latin America (PAHO 1994)—we may infer that Guatemalan females are among the most likely in both Central America, and in the entire Latin American region, to make an adolescent transition to motherhood[1]. Because of its implications for individual and so-

---

[1]Reflecting these age-specific fertility rates, Guatemala's Total Fertility Rate (5.36) is the highest in Latin America (PAHO 1994:68).

cietal well-being, the relatively high level of adolescent childbearing in Guatemala deserves attention. This paper addresses three questions concerning the reproduction-related behavior of young women in Guatemala. First, which factors underlie Guatemala's high levels of adolescent childbearing? Are young Guatemalan women more likely to become sexually active during adolescence than young women in other Latin American countries? Are they less likely to use contraception? Are they more reliant upon less-effective, traditional contraceptive methods? Second, what is the union context in which young women's sexual activity and childbearing occur in Guatemala? Third, are today's young women at greater risk of becoming adolescent mothers than young women two decades ago? In the concluding section, I discuss the implications of the answers to these questions for strategic intervention to reduce the number of pregnancies and births to adolescent women in Guatemala.

Risky Transition

Both empirical research and anecdotal accounts document numerous risks associated with adolescent pregnancy and childbearing; these range in severity from role conflict and forgone opportunities to death. Role conflict may result when young women attempt to combine school attendance with motherhood. Most Latin American countries, including Guatemala, define the upper age boundary associated with secondary school to be at least 17 (UNESCO 1990). Hence, assuming no grade-level failure and year-by-year progression through the school system, motherhood before age 18 conflicts with nationally delimited ages of formal education. Aside from dropping out of school, young women may respond to this predicament more covertly by seeking an abortion. Although abortion is illegal except for strict medical reasons in all Latin American countries but Cuba, a significant number of young women, motivated by their desires to remain in school and to postpone motherhood until reaching a certain level of personal achievement, undergo illegal abortions (The Alan Guttmacher Institute 1994). Unfortunately, the illegality surrounding such abortions can produce adverse consequences including death as a result of unsafe procedures (Scribner 1994) and long-term health effects such as gynecologic problems and infertility (The Alan Guttmacher Institute 1994).

In addition to the consequences of a poorly performed abortion, the literature on health risks associated with adolescent childbearing emphasizes two findings. First, teenage women are more likely to experience obstetric complications (Bledsoe and Cohen 1993; Senderowitz and Paxman 1985). Some of these complications may result from physiological immaturity; young women do not achieve adult pelvic dimensions ideal for childbearing until ages 17 to 18 (Moermann 1982). Second, complicated deliveries increase a woman's risk of sepsis—severe infection following childbirth—and hemorrhage, one of the most common causes of maternal death (Bledsoe and Cohen 1993).

Adolescent mothers may also experience psychological trauma and socioeconomic hardship. Psychological trauma is most common among young mothers who bear children out of wedlock. In extreme cases, young unwed mothers may be rejected by their families and, without adequate income to support a child, forced into prostitution (PRB 1992:15). The young mother is also likely to find herself living in more precarious socioeconomic circumstances due to the relationship between motherhood timing and union stability. In a common sequence of events, women follow their premarital conception with a prebirth marriage in order to ensure their child's legitimacy (CEPAR 1990; Morris 1988). Because the probability of marital dissolution is especially high among women with young ages at first union (Goldman 1981), the prospective timing of an adolescent birth may indirectly increase the likelihood of becoming a single parent. Most thoroughly documented in the United States, such circumstances tend to adversely affect the economic condition of mother and child (Bruce et al. 1995).

Because of the physiological and socioeconomic links between mother and child, children born to adolescent women may also may suffer impaired life chances. Cross-nationally and within individual countries, infants born to young mothers experience a greater risk of mortality during infancy than babies born to women in their twenties (Hobcraft et al. 1985; Preston 1985). In Latin America, children born to adolescent mothers also run higher risks of abandonment, of becoming street children (PRB 1992:2), and of being pulled into a cycle of poverty, particularly in cases where the father is absent (Buvinif et al. 1992).

Finally, early childbearing affects entire societies. Regardless of whether adolescent childbearing occurs within a sanctioned union, high levels of adolescent childbearing exacerbate population growth, intensify resource shortages, and perpetuate the low status of women. The timing of motherhood affects population growth through its relation to generational length. Early initiation of motherhood shortens the time between generations, thereby producing a higher rate of population growth. Unless current rates of population growth are lowered, many countries in the Latin American region will face the onerous responsibility of nearly doubling (Viel 1989) their present levels of food production and the number of spaces in employment, education, housing and health care to prevent socioeconomic decline.

Regarding women's status, literacy and information obtained through school attendance empower women to play a full and active role in society. Moreover, formal education may constitute a pathway to employment benefiting both women and their families (Rodda 1991). Consequently, insofar as improvements in women's status vis-a-vis men depend largely upon increasing women's educational attainment and expanding jobs for women in non-marginalized occupations, high aggregate levels of adolescent fertility reinforce women's inferior social status by restricting their educational and occupational opportunities.

In summary, the numerous risks associated with adolescent childbearing for mothers, their children, and society at large justify devoting attention to this topic. In response, this paper examines the phenomenon of adolescent childbearing in Guatemala—a Latin American country with relatively high levels of adolescent childbearing—while simultaneously locating the experiences of young Guatemalan women within a broader, regional context.

DATA AND METHODS

Informed by Bongaarts' (1978) proximate-determinants paradigm, I investigate the ways in which the behavior of young Guatemalan women is similar to, and different from, their peers. I focus specifically on their union involvement, age at first sexual intercourse, coupling of sexual activity and union involvement, and contraceptive use, all before age 18[2]. Because I wish to analyze recent experience, but avoid censoring, I examine the pre-age 18 reproductive behavior of women ages 18 to 24. However, because DHS collected data about union status and contraceptive use only for a woman's current union and (in most countries) for her most recently used contraceptive method, we are forced to generalize about the adolescent union and contraceptive experiences of our cohort of interest (18- to 24-year-olds) from the behavior of women ages 15 to 17 at the time of the survey. In section two, I analyze trends over two decades by comparing the timing and sequence of adolescent reproduction-

---

[2]I base this decision to use "under 18" instead of "under 20" on the substantive rationale that childbearing before age 18 is both socially and physiologically more risky than motherhood at ages 18 and 19.

related transitions (i.e., their experiences before age 18) among two cohorts: 18 to 24 year-olds and 38 to 44 year-olds.

I use data from the 1987 Guatemalan Demographic and Health Survey (DHS) and from eight additional Phase-I DHS surveys each conducted in a different Latin American countries. Hereafter, I will refer to the eight countries—Bolivia, Brazil, Colombia, the Dominican Republic, Ecuador, El Salvador[3], Mexico, and Peru—as the "comparison group" (see Table 1).[4] The DHS offer several advantages over other reproduction-related surveys. First, they were conducted during roughly the same time period—1986 to 1991—using standard questionnaires, thereby facilitating cross-national, comparative analyses.[5] Second, because women beyond their young adult years were interviewed, the data permit analyses of trends in reproduction-related behavior over time. Both cross-national comparisons and comparisons across time contribute to our understanding of adolescent childbearing in Guatemala.

FINDINGS

I divide the discussion of findings into three sections, each corresponding to one of the research questions that motivated the analysis. The first section reviews cross-national differences in exposure to the risk of conception. The second segment presents research findings about the familial context of

---

[3] El Salvador does not appear among the comparison group during the analysis of trends over time because the El Salvadoran DHS did not collect complete birth histories.

[4] It is important to note that the countries which comprise the comparison group are Latin American countries that have not completed the demographic transition. Regrettably, the group excludes Argentina, Uruguay, and Chile, the only three Latin American countries to have reached a very advanced stage of the demographic transition (Chackiel and Schkolnik 1990).

[5] To this list, we might add that the widespread availability of these data to the international research community facilitates dialogue and cumulative research.

adolescent sexual activity and childbearing. Finally, the third section reports on trends in adolescent reproduction-related behavior over time.

Exposure to Risk: Sexual Activity and Contraceptive Use

In contrast to their Latin American peers in the comparison group, Guatemala women exhibit a greater propensity to become sexually active during adolescence and are less likely to report having used contraception. As a result, Guatemalan females face a higher risk of making an adolescent transition to motherhood.

Figure 2 displays the cumulative percent of Latin American women experiencing their first sexual intercourse by a given age. Although we find similar age patterns of transition to sexual activity (i.e., each country exhibits a relatively uniform increase in the percent sexually active by age), levels vary across countries. Higher than any of the countries in the comparison group, forty-five percent of Guatemalan women become sexually active before age 18. Interestingly, the ranking of countries in Figure 2 suggests a negative relationship between economic development and sexual activity in Latin America. Guatemala, the least economically developed of the nine Latin American countries under study, manifests the highest percentage having made the transition to sexual activity by every age, while Colombia, Brazil, and Mexico—among the most economically developed Latin American countries in the analysis—display relatively low percentages sexually active by each age.

Early transitions to sexual activity do not necessarily result in an adolescent transition to motherhood. In the United States, 56 percent of female adolescents become sexually active before their eighteenth birthday; however, their risk is mitigated by their comparatively high levels of contraceptive use and what appears to be a greater reliance on abortion to terminate unintended pregnancies (Alan Guttmacher Institute 1994). In Guatemala, the risk of pregnancy among sexually active young women is exacerbated by low levels of contraceptive use. Among sexually experienced adolescent females ages 15 to 17, fewer than four percent reported having *ever* used a contraceptive method and over half of these "ever users" relied on periodic abstinence or withdrawal [Figure 3].

The Context of Sexual Activity and Childbearing

Hinted at above, variation in exposure to the risk of conception underlies differences in pregnancy, but pregnancy does not equal a live birth. Both exposure to the risk of conception and the decision to carry a pregnancy to term are influenced by the social context of sexual activity and pregnancy. Here I focus on the context of union involvement.

Comparing the contexts of sexual activity across countries reveals that young Guatemalan females are more likely than their peers in the other Latin American countries under investigation to engage in sexual activity within the confines of a marriage or a consensual union. Shown in Figure 4, at least part of this has to do with the fact that Guatemalan women ages 15 to 17 report higher levels of involvement in consensual and legal unions than young women in any of the comparison countries except El Salvador. Over 16 percent of 15 to 17 year-olds reported having ever been in a union. Still, this does not tell us about how closely linked sexual experience is to union involvement.

If we define sexual experience as having ever had sexual intercourse, the proportion of sexually experienced young women exceeds the proportion ever-in-union in every country under investigation. It would be surprising if this were not true. Yet Figure 5 portrays country-level differences in the association between sexual experience and union involvement—the "sex-union gap." I operationalize the gap as the proportion of sexually active 15 to 17 year-old females who report having *never* been in a heterosexual union. A country's score of zero indicates no sex-union gap (i.e., no sexually active females who report being single), whereas a large positive score signifies a decoupling of sexual activity from union involvement. In Guatemala, we find a narrow gap between sexual experience and union involvement: Fewer than 15 percent of sexually active adolescent females report having never been in a union. As a result, a sizable number of young Guatemalan women lack a key motivation to delay making an adolescent transition to motherhood: risk of out-of-wedlock childbearing.

Fitting these pieces together provides a clearer picture of the configuration of proximate determinants underlying the comparatively high level of adolescent childbearing in Guatemala. They include early union involvement, a close coupling of sexual activity with union involvement, and perhaps in part because of fewer pressures to avoid out-of-wedlock childbearing, low use of effective forms of contraception among sexually active adolescent females. As a result, over 90 percent of Guatemalan women who become mothers during adolescence report having their first birth shortly after entering into their first consensual or legal union (see Figure 6). In other words, adolescent motherhood in Guatemala is largely an in-wedlock phenomenon.

Trends over Two Decades

A common theme in the literature on adolescent sexual behavior in Latin America stresses that modernization produces a loosening of social controls over young women's sexual behavior (Rosoff 1990; Senderowitz and Paxman 1985). Insofar as this is true, we would expect to find young women today more likely to make an early transition to sexual activity, thereby spending more of their adolescent years at risk of an unplanned pregnancy. Do we find evidence of this shift toward earlier initiation of sexual activity among adolescent females in Guatemala?

Table 2 presents the percentage of women in two cohorts—18 to 24 year-olds and 38 to 44 year-olds—who made the transition to sexual activity during adolescence (i.e., before age 18) in Guatemala and in the comparison countries. Close inspection reveals several interesting trends. First, the percentage of Guatemalan women who become sexually active within marriage by age 18 has remained virtually unchanged—about 33 percent—over the past 20 years.[6] This continuity is an important trend given that 90 percent of adolescent first births in Guatemala today occur to adolescent women in union.

Second, and also contrary to what we might anticipate under conditions of social disruption, the data presented in Table 2 suggest a shift away from sexual activity among young women who remain single during adolescence. More Guatemalan women appear to be either consciously or unconsciously removing themselves from the risk of adolescent motherhood by postponing their transition to sexual activity. Among the older cohort, 48 percent indicated that they had not engaged in sexual intercourse before age 18 whereas 55 percent of the younger cohort reported still being virgins at their eighteenth birthday. Of course, there is another possible explanation for this pattern: underreporting of premarital sexual activity. Fearing social disapproval, young unmarried respondents may be more reluctant to admit to being sexually active. However, there are at least two reasons to believe that the trend cannot be due solely to underreporting. First, the inter-cohort increase in the proportion remaining virgins during adolescence is consistent with the positive cross-national association among the countries under investigation between the proportions of young women who have not made the transition to sexual activity by age 18 and national-level socioeconomic de-

[6] This finding is consistent with reports of only marginal decline in the proportion of women marrying before age 20 in Guatemala during the past two decades (Alan Guttmacher Institute 1995:19).

velopment. Second, cross-cohort comparisons of the transition to sexual activity in Africa reveal similar increases in the proportions remaining virgins during adolescence in several countries (Samara 1995).

In summary, trends in the timing and sequence of sexual activity over time reveal little evidence of social disruption. Moreover, these trends emphasize two features, an unwavering commitment to early initiation of sexual activity within a consensual or legal union, and an apparent increase in the proportion of young women who remain single and sexually inexperienced throughout their adolescence.

SUMMARY AND DISCUSSION

Comparative analysis suggests that the relatively high level of adolescent childbearing in Guatemala derives from a combination of early transitions to sexual activity and low levels of contraceptive use. Moreover, because sexual activity typically takes place within a legal or a consensual union, many young women not only lack motivation to avoid early childbearing, but may actually experience pressure to have children as married adolescents. Religious and sociocultural institutions provide a favorable, and even encouraging climate for young married women to become mothers. Moreover, lingering "machismo," a cultural trait that stresses male pride and virility, plays directly into early childbearing. The coalescence of these factors is responsible for the situation in Guatemala where the proportion of young women reporting having had sex within marriage by age 18 has remained virtually unchanged over the past 20 years. And until this group, which is responsible for the largest proportion of first births to adolescents, shrinks in number, the country is unlikely to witness a significant decrease in adolescent childbearing.

Efforts to raise the age at first union, most notably through improving women's access to formal education (cf. Westoff et al. 1994), would be a logical starting point. Nonetheless, we cannot assume that increasing age at first union will be accompanied by a decrease in women's exposure to the risk of pregnancy. Prolonging the period between puberty and marriage, without accompanying changes, would simply mean an increased likelihood that a young women will become sexually active before marriage (Singh and Wulf 1990). Hence, more far-reaching changes will be necessary.

Returning to a demographic classic, in 1973 Ansley Coale outlined three preconditions for sustained decline in marital fertility: 1) fertility must be within the calculus of conscious choice; 2) reduced fertility must be advantageous; and 3) effective techniques of fertility reduction must be available. Translated into terms relevant to adolescent childbearing, we can only expect sexually active adolescent females to delay motherhood when: 1) their sexual activity and childbearing is within their calculus of conscious choice; 2) they view postponement of motherhood past adolescence as advantageous; and 3) they have access to effective means of contraception and/or abortion.

Is adolescent childbearing in Latin America within adolescents' "calculus of conscious choice"? Affirmative responses to contraceptive use suggest that at least some 15 to 17 year-old women in Guatemala view their fertility within the calculus of conscious choice. And this, of course, represents a conservative estimate since it includes only those women who satisfy all three preconditions. Devout Catholics may fail to satisfy the first precondition because they regard as inappropriate human intervention in reproductive matters. But for many teens, discussions with peers and sex education programs in school have ushered sex and reproduction into the realm of conscious choice (see PRB 1992). Still, action is predicated on meeting a second precondition.

The second precondition maintains that young women and their partners must view postponing motherhood past adolescence as advantageous. Research concerning the contextual factors influencing adolescent motherhood indicates that in the absence of alternatives to early motherhood, reductions in gender inequality, and a reduction in urban-rural inequality (for rural residents), many young women may not meet this second precondition (Samara 1994).

The third precondition for delayed motherhood asserts that effective birth control techniques—either in the form of effective contraception or abortion—be available to sexually active adolescents. Barriers standing in the way of their use of effective contraceptive methods include lack of access, lack of information, and psychological barriers. Young women who seek contraceptives are not always greeted with enthusiasm. Policies and procedures often restrict young women's access to contraceptives and other family planning services, particularly when they are not married (UNFPA 1991:3). Moreover, lack of knowledge about where to obtain contraceptives deters use. Finally, psychological discomfort sometimes plays a contributing role in nonuse. Some young women worry about their anonymity if they visit a public clinic, while others avoid a clinic visit because it requires having to confront their own sexuality. As one Latin American educator remarked: "It is as though they feel guiltier asking for contraception than they do about getting pregnant" (PRB 1994). Most likely, all of the aforementioned factors contribute in varying degrees to the rather low levels of modern contraceptive use among young, sexually active Guatemalan women.

The three preconditions represent both hurdles to motherhood postponement and primary points of entry for interventions to promote a lower incidence of adolescent motherhood. At the most fundamental level, young women must be made aware that they are at risk of becoming pregnant if they become sexually active. To this end, sex education may be useful in teaching youth before they become sexually active that sex carries serious responsibilities and requires responsible choices (PRB 1992:17).

The second point of intervention involves major social change. Opportunities for women and social inequality both influence whether a young woman becomes an adolescent mother (Samara 1994). If unable to change these social contexts, interventionists must at least be aware of these structural constraints that place limits on behavioral interventions.

At the third point of intervention, many have noted the need for family planning programs geared specifically toward youth. Such programs would necessarily provide accessible and affordable services, and assure young women's confidentiality. Ultimately, however, only a well-designed family planning program combined with socioeconomic development benefiting women will foster all three preconditions to delayed motherhood in Guatemala.

ACKNOWLEDGEMENTS

The conclusions and opinions expressed in this paper are the author's and do not necessarily represent the views of the Alan Guttmacher Institute. This research was sponsored in part by the National Science Foundation (SES-9200814) and by the Andrew W. Mellon Foundation grant to the Population Studies Center, University of Pennsylvania, "Training and Research Programs in the Demography of Less Developed Countries."

REFERENCES

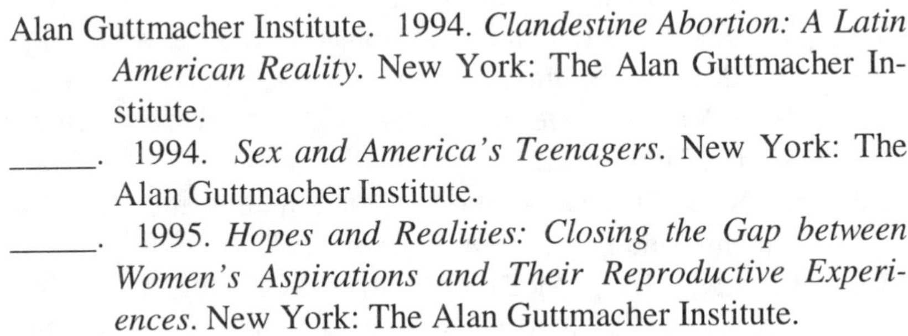

Alan Guttmacher Institute. 1994. *Clandestine Abortion: A Latin American Reality*. New York: The Alan Guttmacher Institute.

_____. 1994. *Sex and America's Teenagers*. New York: The Alan Guttmacher Institute.

_____. 1995. *Hopes and Realities: Closing the Gap between Women's Aspirations and Their Reproductive Experiences*. New York: The Alan Guttmacher Institute.

Bledsoe, C. and B. Cohen. 1993. *Social Dynamics of Adolescent Fertility in Sub-Saharan Africa.* Washington, D.C.: National Academy Press.

Bongaarts, J. 1978. "A Framework for Analyzing the Proximate Determinants of Fertility," *Population and Development Review* (41): 105-132.

Bourque, S.C. and K.B. Warren. 1981. *Women of the Andes: Patriarchy and Social Change in Two Peruvian Towns.* Ann Arbor: University of Michigan Press.

Bruce, J., C.B. Lloyd, A. Leonard with P.L. Engle and N. Duffy. 1995. *Families in Focus: new Perspectives on Mothers, Fathers, and Children.* New York: The Population Council.

Buvinif, M., J.P. Vanenzuela, T. Molina, and E. Gonzalez. 1992. "The fortunes of adolescent mothers and their children: The transmission of poverty in Santiago, Chile." *Population and Development Review* (182): 269-297.

Centro de Estudios de Población y Paternidad Responsable [CEPAR]. 1990. "Ecuador: Reproductive information and experience among young Ecuadorians in Quito and Guayaquil, 1988." Summary Report.

Chackiel, J. and S. Schkolnik. 1990. "America Latina: transición de la fecundidad en el periodo 1950-1990." Paper presented at the International Union for the Scientific Study of Population Seminar on Fertility Transition in Latin America, Buenos Aires, April 3-6, 1990.

Coale, A. 1973. "The demographic transition reconsidered." Pp. 53-72 in *International Population Conference, Liege, 1973.* Vol. 1. Liege: International Union for the Scientific Study of Population.

Goldman, N. 1981. "Dissolution of first unions in Colombia, Panama, and Peru." *Demography* (184): 659-79.

Hobcraft, J.N., J.W. McDonald and S.O. Rutstein. 1985. "Demographic determinants of infant and early child mortality: a comparative analysis." *Population Studies* (393): 363-85.

Moermann, M.L. 1982. "Growth of the birth canal in adolescent girls." *American Journal of Obstetrics and Gynecology* 143(5): 528-32.

Morris, L. 1988. "Young adults in Latin America and the Caribbean: their sexual experience and contraceptive use." *International Family Planning Perspectives* 14(4),153-8.

Pan American Health Organization [PAHO]. 1994. *Health Conditions in the Americas* (Vol. 1). Washington, D.C.: World Health Organization.

Population Reference Bureau [PRB]. 1992. *Adolescent Sexual Activity and Childbearing in Latin America and the Caribbean: Risks and Consequences.* Washington, D.C.: Population Reference Bureau.

_____. 1994. The World's Youth 1994: A Special Focus on Reproductive Health. Washington, D.C.: Population Reference Bureau.

Preston, S.H. 1985. "Mortality in childhood: lessons from WFS." Pp. 253-72 in J. Cleland and J. Hobcraft (eds.) *Reproductive Change in Developing Countries: Insights from the World Fertility Survey.* London, England: Oxford University Press.

Rodda, A. 1991. *Women and the Environment.* Atlantic Highlands, NJ: Zed.

Rosoff, J.I. 1990. "Forward." Pp. 4-5 in S. Singh and D. Wulf, *Today's Adolescents, Tomorrow's Parents: A Portrait of the Americas.* New York: The Alan Guttmacher Institute.

Samara, R. 1994. "Risky Transitions: Young Women's Sexual and Reproductive Transitions in Latin America and Sub-Saharan Africa." Doctoral dissertation, Department of Sociology, University of North Carolina at Chapel Hill.

_____. 1995. "Pathways to adolescent sexual activity and motherhood in Latin America and sub-Saharan Africa." Paper presented at the Annual Meetings of the Population Association of America, San Francisco, CA, April 6-8, 1995.

Scribner, S. 1994. "Policies affecting fertility and contraceptive use: an assessment of twelve sub-Saharan countries." Paper presented at a workshop on "The Determinants of Fertility in sub-Saharan Africa: The Policy Implications of Recent Research." Washington, D.C., May 10, 1994.

Senderowitz, J. and J.M. Paxman. 1985. "Adolescent fertility: worldwide concerns." *Population Bulletin* (4) 2.

Singh, S. And D.Wulf. 1990. *Today's Adolescents, Tomorrow's Parents: A Portrait of the Americas*. New York: The Alan Guttmacher Institute.

Smith, J.E. 1986. "Pope John Paul II and *Humanae Vitae*." *International Review of Natural Family Planning* 10(2): 95-112.

Thomson, M. 1986. *Women of El Salvador: The Price of Freedom*. London: Zed.

United Nations Educational, Scientific and Cultural Organization [UNESCO]. 1990. *Statistical Yearbook 1990.* Paris: UNESCO.

United Nations Population Fund [UNFPA]. 1991. *Population* 17(11): 3.

Viel, B. 1989. "Keynote address." The International Conference on Adolescent Fertility in Latin America and the Caribbean, Oaxaca, Mexico, Nov. 6-10, 1989 as cited in L. Remez. (1989). "Adolescent fertility in Latin America and the Caribbean: examining the problem and the solutions." *International Family Planning Perspectives* 15(4),144-8.

Westoff, C.F., A.K. Blanc, and L. Nyblade. 1994. "Marriage and Entry into Parenthood." DHS Comparative Studies No. 10. Calverton, MD: Macro International.

TABLE 1. DATA, SAMPLE SIZE, AND PERCENTAGE OF ADOLESCENT MOTHERS

Country	Survey Year	Sample Size (18-24 year-olds)	Percentage with birth before age 18
Guatemala	1987	1,417	27.4
Bolivia	1989	1,978	18.0
Brazil	1986	1,679	13.5
Colombia	1990	1,543	14.5
Dominican Rep.	1991	2,357	18.3
Ecuador	1987	1,318	15.9
El Salvador	1985	1,541	25.6
Mexico	1987	2,567	18.6
Peru	1991/92	1,373	13.8

TABLE 2. INTER-COHORT VARIATION IN ADOLESCENT FEMALES' TRANSTITIONS TO FIRST INTERCOURSE, GUATEMALA AND SELECTED LATIN AMERICAN DHS SURVEY COUNTRIES

	No Transitions by Age 18 (1)		Premarital Sex by Age 18 (2)		Sex Within Marriage by Age 18* (3)	
	18-24	38-44	18-24	38-44	18-24	38-44
Bolivia	62.7	59.2	22.7	23.7	14.6	17.1
Brazil	71.4	70.6	13.8	11.7	14.8	17.8
Colombia	70.0	58.4	14.7	20.0	15.3	21.6
Dom. Rep.	64.1	42.0	6.7	12.2	29.2	45.8
Ecuador	69.3	61.0	11.5	14.1	19.2	24.9
Guatemala	55.1	47.8	11.1	17.9	33.8	34.4
Mexico	70.4	63.0	7.5	9.1	22.1	27.9
Peru	72.4	57.9	15.1	22.2	12.5	19.9

*Or, more accurately, women in union by age 18 who reported not having engaged in premarital sex.

FIGURE 1. ADOLESCENT MOTHERHOOD: PERCENTAGES OF FEMALES AGES 18-24 WITH A FIRST BIRTH BEFORE AGE 18, GUATEMALA AND OTHER LATIN AMERICAN DHS COUNTRIES

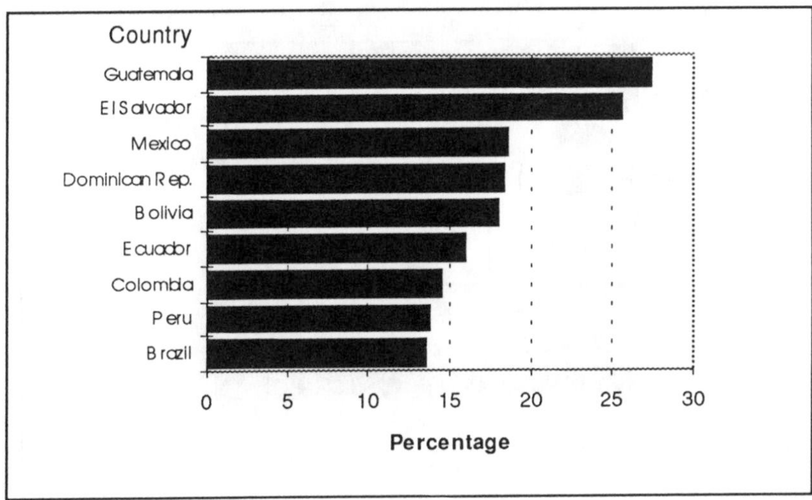

FIGURE 2. TIMING OF FIRST SEXUAL INTERCOUSE, FEMALES AGES 18-24, GUATEMALA AND OTHER LATIN AMERICAN DHS COUNTRIES

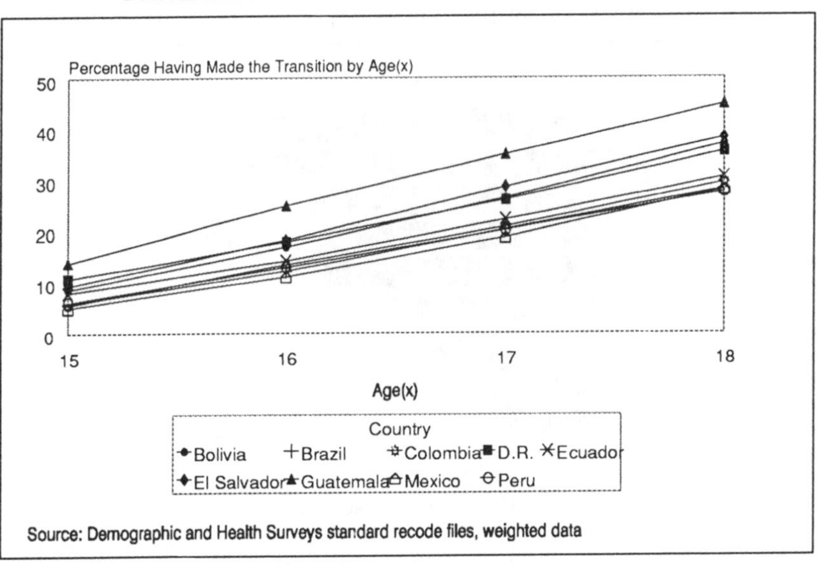

Source: Demographic and Health Surveys standard recode files, weighted data

FIGURE 3. MIX OF CONTRACEPTIVE METHODS AMONG SEXUALLY EXPERIENCED FEMALES AGES 15-17, GUATEMALA AND OTHER LATIN AMRICAN DHS COUNTRIES

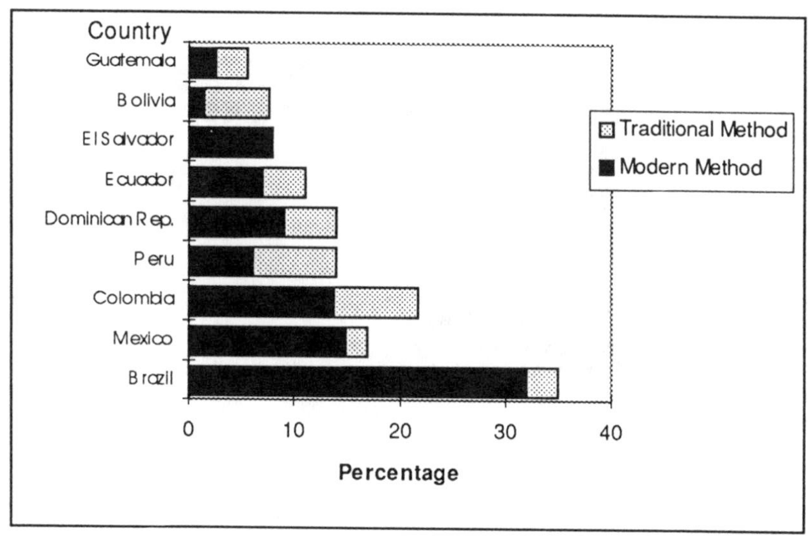

FIGURE 4. WOMEN AGES 15-17 EVEN IN UNION, GUATEMALA AND OTHER LATIN AMERICAN DHS COUNTRIES, PERCENTAGE OF GROUP.

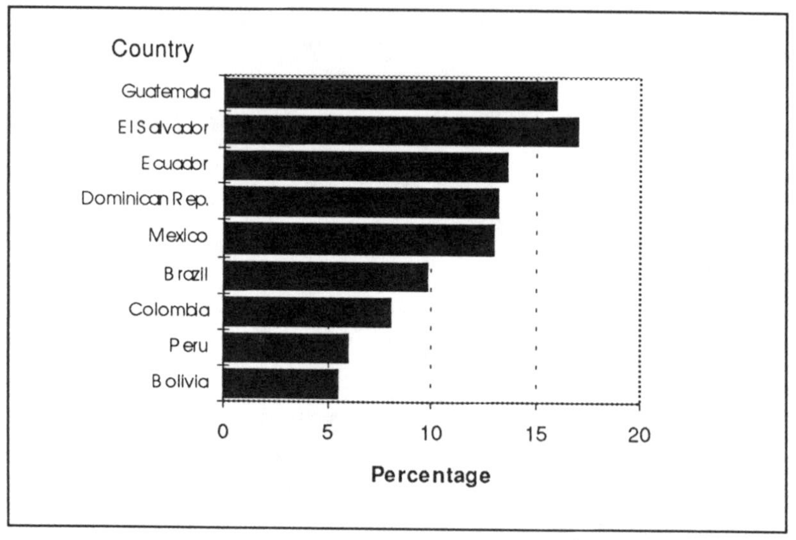

FIGURE 5. THE SEX-UNION GAP: FEMALES AGES 15-17 NEVER IN UNION AS PROPORTION SEXUALLY ACTIVE, GUATEMALA AND OTHER LATIN AMERICAN DHS COUNTRIES

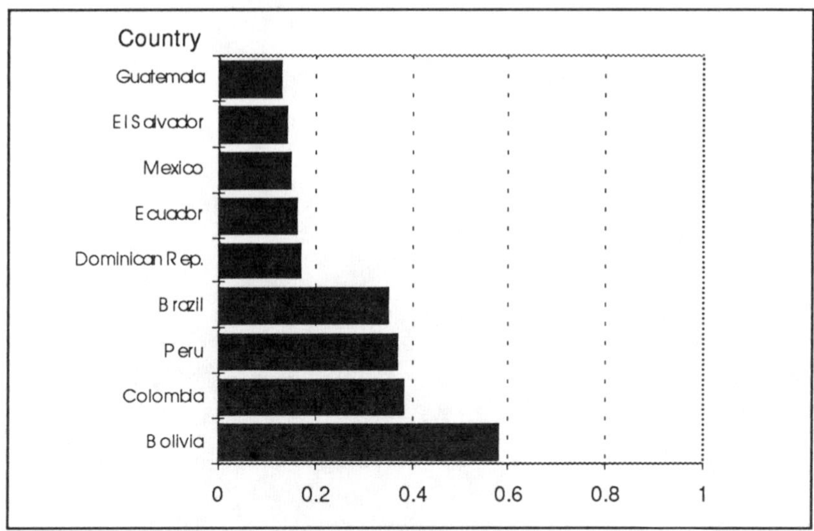

FIGURE 6. PATHWAYS TO ADOLESCENT MOTHERHOOD, GUATEMALA AND OTHER LATIN AMERICAN DHS COUNTRIES

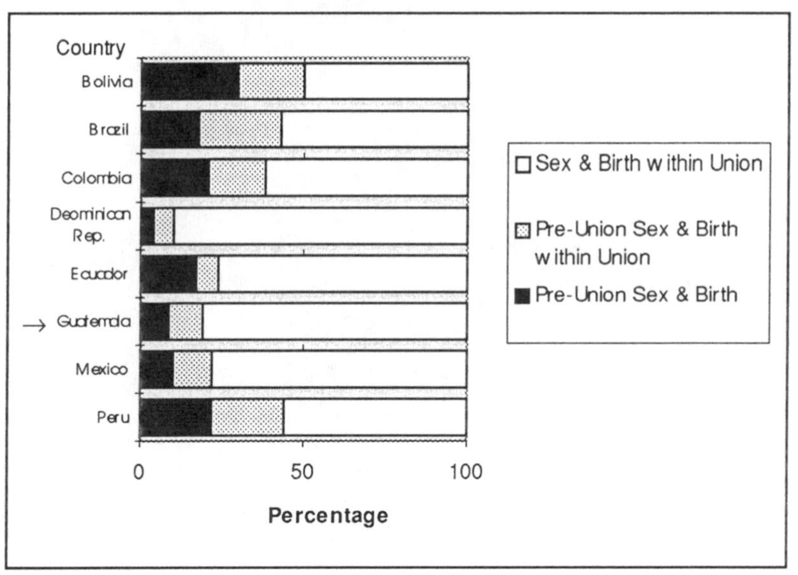

Chapter Twenty

DEMOGRAPHIC PROCESSES, LAND, AND THE ENVIRONMENT IN GUATEMALA

RICHARD E. BILSBORROW AND PAUL STUPP

This paper seeks to identify the mechanisms through which population growth and redistribution affect agriculture and land use and thereby internal migration patterns and environmental degradation. The focus is on Guatemala but the issues are also relevant for Central America as a whole. We first use population and agricultural census data to look at historical trends in population and land use in Guatemala since 1950, and to provide a guide for preparing two alternative future population growth scenarios to the year 2030. The former, retrospective view of demographic trends shows past trends in population to be directly related to trends in the total area of land used as well as fragmentation of landholdings. Future population growth scenarios are shown to lead to worsening rural employment situations. Land fragmentation and rural employment deficiencies are then related to past and expected future out-migration from rural areas. Much of this out-migration has been to other rural areas and has caused extensive deforestation in the main remaining forests of Guatemala, in the northern province of El Peten. We conclude with recommendations for further data acquisition to overcome certain limitations of the analysis, provide a list of key research questions begging for further analysis, and proffer some preliminary policy recommendations.

INTRODUCTION

The purpose of this paper is to explore the mechanisms by which population growth and the characteristics of the agricultural sector in Guatemala combine to induce migration movements which in turn cause deforestation in Guatemala. These processes also are important in other countries in the region and hence have broader relevance for Central America. We address, inter alia, the following questions: What are the key potential linkages between demographic processes and environmental degradation, especially deforestation? What are the effects of institutional factors such as land tenure and government policies on this process? How reliable is our knowledge of the interrelationships, and what are the key types of data and research analyses needed to clarify the relationships, in Guatemala and in other countries of the region? How intractible are the problems of rural Guatemala, and what policy recommendations can be proferred while we wait for more complete analyses?

In most of Latin America, population sizes have grown rapidly since the 1950s, to two to three times their size at the beginning of the period. This population growth, along with considerable economic growth and accompanying population redistribution, has vastly changed the continent's landscape, including the use of, and depredation of, its natural resources. At the same time, these changes have occurred in a context of institutions inherited from the days of the Mayas and the Spanish *conquistadores*, institutions characterized by vast economic inequality, particularly in access to productive resources such as land. In Guatemala the areas most favorable to human habitation are the highlands, which have been subjected to increasing stress as a result of these demographic and economic changes, as we shall see. This in turn has apparently induced out-migration that has shifted some of the pressures on resources to new areas of the country, causing considerable environmental degradation. This paper is concerned with the human threat to the environment, especially to the northern lowland forests of Guatemala.

Central America figures prominently in the popular media these days, but the focus on political problems and the search for political solutions obscures the underlying difficulties of achieving development for the majority of the population which continues to live in rural areas. To place the analysis of Guatemala in larger context, we first consider some of the key theoretical arguments, then briefly review the recent past experience and anticipated future changes in population growth and agricultural performance for the six principal countries of Central America (Costa Rica, El Salvador, Guatemala, Honduras, Nicaragua and Panama), and then consider the situation in Guatemala in some detail—the main focus of this paper.

THEORETICAL PERSPECTIVES ON POPULATION, LAND USE, MIGRATION AND THE ENVIRONMENT

There are two bodies of theory that are relevant to the present paper: (1) concerning the effects of population growth on agricultural families, and (2) concerning the determinants of migration, or more specifically, the determinants of out-migration from rural areas. We consider these in order.

As population growth occurs in settled agricultural areas (which at the micro level may be simply the result of more children surviving than before), families have to adjust to maintain or improve living standards. The demographer Kingsley Davis (1963) hypothesized that families respond by altering their demographic behavior, mainly by postponing marriage and/or reducing their fertility within marriage, but possibly also by out-migration. He developed his theory based on his observations of trends in northern and western Europe and Japan in the late nineteenth century. Moreover, he coined the term the "multiphasis response" to refer to the fact that all responses could occur at once, albeit to varying degrees. But Davis' approach left out the possibility of economic responses, and did not recognize the fundamental role of land use. The possibility of economic, or technological, responses was recognized in entirely independent work on the other side of the Atlantic by the Danish economist, Ester Boserup (1965). She hypothesized that increasing population pressures on the land could induce, or stimulate, households to adopt new forms of technology, forms which would both increase total output and utilize more of the increasing factor of production, labor. Thus she developed her five stages or systems of increasingly land-intensive technology, from forest- or long-fallow agriculture to annual cropping to multiple-cropping, in which the same plot of land is planted and harvested more than once in a calendar year. She further discussed how increasing amounts of the growing factor, labor, could be applied on a given area of land through a process of "land intensification."[1] Modern forms of such intensification include increasing use of chemical fertilizers and irrigation to the extent they imply a higher labor-land ratio, a higher intensity of labor use on land (Bilsborrow and Geores, 1992).

As Bilsborrow and colleagues have noted elsewhere, the above responses curiously omit the one that has been dominant throughout most of human history, and which continues to be important to the present day. This is the process of "land extensification," or the expansion of agriculture through increasing the agricultural land area (Bilsborrow, 1987; Bilsborrow and Geores, op. cit.). Thus throughout most of human history, people have moved in search of new land as their land became "tired" (or depleted of animals in the hunter-gatherer periods). And as the number of people increased, some moved to new areas, as there were always new areas to move to in the past. Note that this

---

[1]It is important to note that Boserup never wrote, nor said, that increasing population density would automatically or necessarily induce compensating changes in technology that would allow the family to at least maintain its standard of living in the face of population growth. Rather, she wrote that population growth could lead to and in a number of historical cases she examined had led to, such a positive economic response. A recent study on six African countries found Boserupian responses occurred in half of the countries but not in the other half, due to differences in the institutional and policy environments (Lele and Stone, 1992).

process of land extensification involved either appropriating nearby unused lands or migration to new lands, which would then need to be cleared for farming.

Given that in the modern industrial or post-industrial era there is also the possiblity of rural-urban migration to nearby or distant towns or cities for non-agricultural work, the possible responses to the increase in population density faced by the farm family include not only Davis' fertility response and Boserup's changes in agricultural technology but also land extensification in situ, land extensification through rural-rural migration, and out-migration to urban areas, or what might be called "throwing in the towel" from agriculture. But, proceeding full circle, Davis also invented a term that is most useful in considering these various responses, the "theory of the multiphasic response." According to this theory, the greater the response of one type, the less pressure there is for the other responses to occur. Hence, the more land that exists in a country that people *think* can be usefully expropriated for agriculture, the more land extensification will occur, and the less land intensification. This explains the tendency for agricultural production in Latin America—and Central America—to have increased mainly due to land extensification over the period 1950-80 while in Asia the increase was primarily due to land intensification (Bilsborrow and Geores, op. cit.). Similarly, the greater the agricultural responses, the less pressure or need there is for a demographic response.

Which response occurs, or which is the dominant response, during a given period of time in a particular country depends on the context, specifically the institutional and policy context. This point has been made clearly by Blaikie and Brookfield (1987), and is further elaborated in terms of the roles of particular social or economic instititions and government policies in Bilsborrow (1987). In the case of Guatemala, the combination of the existence of large areas of "untapped" land and various institutional factors, described below, led to significant land extensification and associated environmental damage.

Migration is thus the key link between population pressure in one area of a country and the opening up of new areas for agriculture in another. There are various ways in which migration decisions can be envisaged in the present context, which will only be cited briefly here since the body of literature is extensive and fairly well-developed. One is as a manifestation of the "peasant survival strategy" whereby families choose a variety of mechanisms, mainly labor allocation over time and space and across family members, to maximize their chances of survival in the context of economic pressures and uncertainty (see, e.g., Arguello, 1981). Thus out-migration is one such common response. The more traditional migration theories see migration as a response to deteriorating economic conditions in the place of origin, or to better opportunities in some other place of destination, whether through the human capital framework of Sjastaad (1962) and others or via the "push-pull" theory of Lee (1966). In any case, internal migration processes are directly linked to environmental deterioration in Guatemala, as will be seen below.[2]

BACKGROUND ON THE CENTRAL AMERICAN CONTEXT

Using United Nations "medium-variant" assumptions, the population of the region as a whole is projected to almost triple in 40 years, from 22.4 million in 1980 to 63.3 million in 2020, and the urban population to increase from 43 percent to 68 per-

---

[2]In a country which has suffered as much from political strife and violence as Guatemala has this century, such factors may also have significant effects on internal migration (and international migration) movements. A recent study has examined the roles of political violence along with the more customary economic factors on migration movements between departamentos (Morrison, 1993). Although political violence was found to affect migration flows, economic factors continued to be dominant.

cent of the total. The three northernmost countries, Guatemala, El Salvador and Honduras—the poorest three—will increase their share from 60 to 65 percent of the regional total over the period. In the period from 1961 to 1983, there was a significant increase in the density of the agricultural population (agricultural population per hectare of agricultural land) in all countries except Costa Rica and Nicaragua.

Comparing annual rates of growth in agricultural production for the 1970s and the early 1980s, it is evident that, with the exception of Costa Rica, the food production sector stagnated. This is true for agricultural production as a whole, which was affected by lower world market prices for the key agricultural exports (coffee, bananas, cacao, and cotton), as well as for basic food production, which is largely unaffected by world markets. Agricultural production depends on employment in agriculture times productivity per worker (i.e., the level of technology). Data on value added per agricultural worker for each country in 1970 and 1985 show that (a) the level of technology is highest in Costa Rica and lowest in Honduras (but two to three times as high in Costa Rica as in any of the other countries, based on FAO data on value added per agricultural worker), and (b) except for Costa Rica and Panama, there was little improvement between 1970 and 1985. While on the one hand this suggests stagnation in agricultural technology, the sizable differences between Costa Rica and the other countries can also be interpreted more positively as indicating ample potential for improving agricultural technology in the other countries of the region.[3]

An obstacle to improving agricultural production in Central America is the high proportion of the population living in poverty. With poverty defined as having insufficient income to

---

[3]For further details and additional bibliography, see Stupp and Bilsborrow (1988).

satisfy minimum needs for food, clothing and shelter, Peek (1986) estimated there to be 10 million rural Central Americans living in poverty in 1980, with Guatemala, Honduras and El Salvador accounting for some 80 percent of the total and Guatemala alone for 40 percent. In all countries of the region, except Costa Rica (34 percent), the proportion in rural areas who are poor is between 66 and 84 percent (the highest being Guatemala).

Rural poverty is associated with historical patterns of land distribution and ownership originating in the feudal systems of the Spanish colonies. Table 1 shows the distribution of land by size of farm (in three categories) and gives the number of farms in each size category. It illustrates (a) the concentration of cultivable land on relatively few large farms, and (b) the concentration of farms in the smallest size category, which is particularly extreme in Guatemala, El Salvador and Honduras—precisely the countries in which rural population density and rural poverty are highest.

In the remaining sections of this paper, we consider the possible linkages between population growth and agricultural-sector problems in Guatemala. In order to appreciate the significance of high population growth over an extended period of time, we consider two population projection scenarios, based on high and low future growth rates, in order to contrast the possible results. Neither scenario is intended as a prediction, or is even likely, but the scenarios almost certainly provide upper and lower bounds on the future population of Guatemala. The major potential effects of population growth on rural areas that we consider are: land fragmentation and poverty, rural employment and migration, and natural resources.

POPULATION PROJECTION SCENARIOS FOR GUATEMALA

Two population projections were prepared based upon two alternative assumptions about future fertility. In the high-fertility scenario, TFR declines from 6.0 in 1980 (CELADE, 1985) to 4.8 in the year 2030 (many Latin American countries, including Costa Rica and Panama, already have TFRs below 4.8).[4] In the low-fertility scenario, TFR declines to 2.0 in 2030, or roughly replacement fertility. For both fertility scenarios, mortality is assumed to gradually decline, with life expectancies at birth for males and females rising gradually from 57 and 61, respectively, in 1980, to 70 and 75 in 2030. Urbanization is assumed invariant with respect to fertility with the percentage urban in both scenarios rising from 33 in 1980 to 45 in the year 2000 and 68 in 2030.

Starting from a 1980 base year population of 6.9 million, the high fertility scenario yields a total population of 37 million in 2030, or more than five times its 1980 size (Table 2). Even under the low-fertility scenario, total population reaches 24 million in 2030, over triple its size in 1980. The projected urban populations in 2030 under the high- and low-fertility scenarios are 25.5 and 16.7 million.[5]

The rural population grows from 4.6 million in 1980 to 7.2 million by 2030 under the low growth scenario and 11.8 million under the high scenario. The agricultural labor force is projected (following SEGEPLAN, the National Planning Agency) by assuming constant age-sex-specific participation rates for the rural population (from the 1981 population census). Under the low-fertility scenario, the agricultural labor force grows from 1.1

---

[4]In the 1987 national fertility survey, total fertility rates were estimated as 6.5 in rural areas, 4.1 in urban, and 5.6 in Guatemala as a whole. Levels of contraceptive use and fertility decline both remain quite modest in Guatemala (INCAP, 1977).

[5]The only large city is the capital, Guatemala, which grew from 406 thousand in 1950 to one million in 1980 and is projected to exceed two million by the year 2000. As elsewhere in the Third World, much of its growth is due to high rates of urban fertility relative to urban mortality: Two-thirds of its growth between 1964 and 1973 was due to natural population growth (United Nations, 1980) and one third to net migration.

million in 1980 to 2.2 million in 2030, while with high fertility, it grows to 2.9 million. Under the low scenario, it levels off at a maximum in the last decade of the projection, but it continues to grow in the high-fertility scenario (c.f. Table 4).

EFFECTS OF RURAL POPULATION GROWTH IN GUATEMALA

In this section we investigate the effects of the past and future trends in population described above on agriculture and land use and on rural employment in Guatemala. These changes in rural areas will then be shown in turn to have significant probable implications for rural out-migration and the environment.

Land Fragmentation and Poverty

We first examine the issue of increasing fragmentation of plots in rural Guatemala, specifically the rapid growth in the number of <2 manzana farms, which are considered (by the National Economic Planning Agency of Guatemala, SEGEPLAN) too small to provide sufficient production and income to support an average rural family.[6] A closely related problem is landlessness, for which there are unfortunately no reliable data in Guatemala.

Out of a total national territory of 10.8 million hectares, only some 5.2 million hectares, or about 48 percent, is classified as suitable for agriculture. Of this, some 4.4 million (85 percent) was already in farms at the time of the last agricultural census (1979), but only about half of that was actually *in use* (includes pasture as well as land in crops).

Table 3 shows the highly skewed distribution of land in farms by size of farm in both 1964 and 1979, the years of the last two agricultural censuses. It also shows the regional breakdown.

---

[6]One manzana equals .7 hectares or .7(2.5) = 1.7 acres.

Land distribution in Guatemala is among the most inegalitarian in the world. In 1964, 44 percent of the farmers—the small farmers, with <2 manzanas, or *minifundia*—possessed together only 3.4 percent of the agricultural land, while at the other extreme, the 2 percent of the farmers with the largest farms, which may be called *latifundia*, had exactly two-thirds of all the land. The corresponding figures for 1979 were as follows: the *minifundia* increased to comprise 60 percent of all farms but still had only 3.7 percent of the total farm area, while the *latifundia* numbers both remained the same. Between 1964 and 1979 the total *number* of farms grew from 419,000 to 606,000, or by 45 percent, under the pressures of high rural population growth. There was clearly a substantial increase in—indeed a doubling—of very small farms, while the numbers of farms in the other categories hardly changed. We return to this later.

The total land area in farms grew by over a million manzanas, or 13.5 percent, which we will see was probably mostly at the expense of forested areas [see below]. Such an expansion of the agricultural land area is a usual response to increasing population (density) pressures whenever land is available (the process referred to as the "extensification of agriculture" in the section above), and as noted tends to precede intensification of agriculture. Nevertheless, there is some evidence of increasing intensification of agriculture as well in Guatemala, with increases in labor per land area, increased use of so-called modern inputs (fertilizers, insecticides, and other chemicals), and increased irrigation. However, these technological changes have been modest compared to those in many other developing countries, including, in the region, Costa Rica.

Comparing the data for 1964 and 1979, we see that in all regions most of the new *farmland* was in the largest (64+ manzana) size category and that it was located mainly in the northern region (the Petén), which accounted for 76 percent of the new farmland but continued to have low overall population density.

The above situation contrasted sharply with that of the very densely populated northwestern highlands region called the *altiplano*. In 1979 it contained 40 percent of the farms in the <2 mz. category and 37 percent of those in the 2-5 mz. category. Between 1964 and 1979, the number of farms in the 5-64 mz. category actually *declined* in both the northwest and central regions. Meanwhile, the number of small farms in Guatemala virtually doubled between 1964 and 1979, mainly due to the increase in the altiplano (Table 4, lower left columns). From the data on the declining number of farms in the 5-64 manzana category and the increase in the numbers of farms in the two smaller categories, especially in the altiplano, it would appear that farms in the former group were being broken up into smaller farms. Although not conclusive evidence, this, combined with prevailing land inheritance practices of partiable inheritance[7], suggests that land is being increasingly fragmented by subdivision among heirs. Indeed, the average size of the small, sub-subsistence plots under 2 mz. actually declined from 1.0 to 0.7 mz. between 1964 and 1979, which provides further evidence of fragmentation.

It appears likely that, in lieu of substantial land redistribution, future growth in the *number* of farms will continue to be predominantly in the smallest size class, and that landlessness, which is reported to be significant but for which there is no data, will also grow as long as the rural population continues to grow. The process of subdivision of land leads to greater impoverishment of the rural population, which probably contributes as a push factor (following Lee, 1966) to out-migration flows from the altiplano (see end of next subsection, 2).

---

[7]While land inheritance practices differ across ethnic groups in the altiplano, in most cases the land is divided among the sons.

Rural Employment and Out-migration

In this section we consider the potential for increasing rural employment by increasing land in use and the intensity of land use (higher labor-land ratio). This is crucial for this paper because of the linkage between employment and wage conditions and migration flows found virtually everywhere in studies of internal migration flows (for surveys, see Shaw, 1974; DeJong and Gardiner, 1981; Todaro, 1976; Bilsborrow et al. 1984, etc.). Hypothetical numbers of persons employed under various assumptions are then compared with plausible projections of the agricultural labor force, described earlier.

But before considering population factors, we must recognize the large amount of idle agricultural land in Guatemala (and many other countries). Thus, of the land in farms in 1979, a considerable proportion was actually not in use, mainly land in the two larger farm size categories: For the country as a whole, roughly *half* of all farmland was idle in 1979 (48 percent), with the percentages for the four land size strata being, respectively, 8, 23, 54 and 57 (the latter for the 64+ mz. size stratum). In addition, studies of SEGEPLAN and the Banco Central of Guatemala show that the *intensity of labor use* per unit of land is much greater on the smaller farms. On the smallest (<2 manzanas), 0.69 full-time equivalent persons are employed per year per manzana, where "full-time" is defined as working 150 days/year. In the 2-5 mz. category, intensity of labor use is .37 full-time persons per manzana. The 5-64 and 64+ mz. farms employed only .18 and .15 full-time equivalent persons/mz./yr., or considerably less labor per unit of land in actual use. These differences are, of course, partly explained by the more predominant role of raising cattle on these larger landholdings, which requires only .033 persons/mz./yr. on average).

The number of employees whose labor is fully absorbed on the land in use at prevailing intensities of labor use, given the distribution of land that prevailed in 1979, was 690,000 full-time workers. Given that the estimated agricultural labor force in 1980 was 1,115,000, it is evident that there was already considerable underemployment in agriculture. Thus, there are *two* separate static causes of the "rural employment problem" in Guatemala (and other places)—idle land and low intensity of land use on the land which *is* used. Both are closely linked to the prevailing land tenure system. Policy implications of this agrarian institutional system are addressed in the conclusions.

Let us now compare the projected sizes of the agricultural labor force under the two population growth scenarios, with employment implications also based on two alternative scenarios (Table 4). In the first employment scenario, employment is projected based on the assumption that land in use increases at a rate of 1.2 percent per year over the entire projection period, 1980-2030. (This is the rate of increase in land area in use in the most recent period observable, between 1964 and 1979.) At the same time the average intensity of labor use per unit of land is kept constant at the 1979 national average of 0.22 persons/mz. The initial discrepancy between labor demand and supply is indicated by the ratio 690/1115 = .63, which may be dubbed the measure of "employment adequacy" or EA. The EA ratio under high fertility and constant labor intensity falls to a disastrous .41 by 2030, and even with low fertility and constant intensity, it declines to .53.

In the second scenario, land in use continues to grow at 1.2 percent/year, but we also assume that the average intensity of use grows over time to a level of 0.37 persons per manzana in 2030 (the actual labor intensity on 2-5 mz. farms in 1979). It is worthy of note that under this scenario the gap between employment needs and labor force size under the *low* fertility assumption narrows after 2010, the EA ratio rising to .86. Under the assumption of high fertility with increasing intensity of land use, the employment adequacy ratio remains at roughly .66, the current level, while the absolute number of equivalent unemployed workers nearly triples as the rural population grows. It is worth restating here that the agricultural labor force projections are made under the assumption that the urban population grows from one-third to over two-thirds of the total over the 50 year projection horizon, so that we are *already* taking into account high levels of rural-urban migration.

But the issue of the total land supply in Guatemala also needs to be addressed in this context. There are two issues, one concerning the existence of a large area of land which is already in farms but is idle, the other concerning what land could be converted into farm land from other "non-uses." With respect to both of these, there is a widespread misperception in Guatemala that there is plenty of untapped land. In fact, the increase of 1.2 percent/yr. in land in use over 50 years essentially uses up *all* currently idle land (including any other land, including forest land, that has any agricultural potential but is not currently in farms—see above). Thus, the projections of employment in Table 4 *already embody* such a process of doubling land in use.[8] Another inference from this is that bringing idle land into production could significantly help ameliorate the rural employment problem for some time, but that eventually high fertility will have to be brought down to avoid further serious immiserization of the rural population of Guatemala.

Unfortunately, the situation painted above is probably more positive than warranted. Existing agricultural research in the world has been strongly oriented towards developing technologies that increase yields with *less* labor per unit of land, not more. The ongoing pace of tractorization in Guatemala and

---

[8]There still remains in Guatemala an additional 15 percent of potentially arable land which did not (in 1979) belong to farms and which could therefore be brought into production. However, this provides at most a decade to absorb population growth, and most is on lower-quality and/or inaccessible land in the Peten whose incorporation into agriculture is likely to add to environmental stress (see subsection 3 below).

elsewhere in Latin America, for example, suggests that rural employment absorption will become a significantly increasing problem in the future and will continue to contribute massively to high rates of rural-urban migration.[9] Hence, it is absolutely necessary to (a) reduce rural population growth, meaning rural fertility, (b) develop and apply more labor-intensive methods of agricultural production, to the extent possible, and (c) bring idle land which already belongs to farms into productive use. To the extent any one of these is blocked in Guatemala—such as (a) by the very active though very small religious right or (c) by the powerful landed oligarachy, which has effectively opposed land reform for four decades—this puts extreme pressure on the other one or two to change. Or else.

The existence of so much underemployment, landlessness, and rural poverty in rural Guatema!a undoubtedly has contributed to significant out-migration from rural areas. This process has been going on since the 1950s but apparently has accelerated in recent decades. The main flows have been from the densely populated altiplano or highlands to Guatemala City, the lowlands to the immediate east of the highlands, and to the Pacific Coast (in connection with the expansion of cotton production on large plantations). Migration to the northern department of El Peten, virtually completely covered by forests up to 1960, accelerated from the late 1960s up to at least 1980 (no data are available since 1981 because of the lack of a population census).[10] Thus

---

[9]Although there have been some successes on a small scale in highlands agriculture in converting small plots from corn to intensive fruit and vegetable farming (for export)—for example, the Cuatro Pinos project supported by USAID in the highlands—the feasibility of doing this on a national scale seems remote. Questions have also been raised about the broader effects of such export-led policies of promotion of non-traditional agricultural exports on poverty and equity, as well as on food security and the environment (Stonich, 1989; DeWalt, 1985; DeWalt and Stonich, 1992; Tucker, 1992).

[10]Apparently a population census was just carried out in 1994, but the results were not available at this writing.

the proportion of the population of the Peten born outside the province more than doubled between 1950 and 1973 to more than half. The annual number of (lifetime) in-migrants was seven times as high in 1973 as in 1964, and doubled again by 1981, the date of the last available population census. The net intercensal migration rate to the Peten was only 17 percent over the 14-year intercensal period 1950-64, but rose to 47 percent in 1964-73 and 49 percent in 1973-81 (SEGEPLAN, 1987: 36). The annual rate of population growth, including natural growth, fluctuated wildly over the 1973-81 intercensal period, and has probably continued to be high and unstable since.

It seems likely that the relationship between farm size and labor needs is a major mechanism by which increasing land fragmentation contributes to rural out-migration. Nevertheless, there has been no statistical examination of this key relationship in Guatemala, nor are appropriate data available on a national level. What is needed is a specialized household migration survey,[11] undertaken in both areas of origin and areas of destination, to collect data on land ownership and use and labor activity and earnings prior to the migration for both migrants and nonmigrants. With appropriate data, the effects of land size (and fragmentation) on out-migration could be statistically separated from the effects of other factors.

---

[11]A migration module could be added to an existing household economic or demographic survey, but it is almost impossible to impose on such a survey questions on the situation of a small subgroup of the population (migrants) prior to their migration. For example, the national household demographic survey of 1987 in Guatemala, carried out by the National Statistical Office (INE), and the national demographic (viz., fertility) survey of INCAP (1987), carried out as part of the DHS program, did not even collect information to identify migrants. See Bilsborrow et al. (1984) on the appropriate design of migration surveys.

Natural Resources

Major forms of environmental deterioration in Guatemala associated with population growth and its effects on rural areas and out-migration appear to include: deforestation, soil degradation, watershed destruction and flooding, and urban encroachment on agricultural land. Others include excessive pesticide use (a severe problem in most of the Pacific river basins because of its heavy use on cotton and other crops), fisheries' destruction and groundwater depletion (see Leonard, 1987; ICATA, 1984). We consider the four major forms briefly in order, before focussing on deforestation in more detail.

Figure 1 shows areas of Guatemala with heavy forest coverage in 1950 and 1985 (based on Leonard, 1987). Roughly half of the area that remained covered by dense forests in 1950 was depleted by the mid-1980s. Practically no forests existed in Guatemala by the late 1980s except in the Peten in the north, where the forest frontier recedes each year. Actual deforestation is greater than that implied by areal statistics alone as those forests that remain are often being thinned and reduced to a lower quality by extractions for fuelwood and commercial exploitation of larger, mature trees.

Although there does exist a small timber industry in Guatemala, including in the Peten where logs are illegally felled and shipped downriver westward into Mexico, the main causes of deforestation in Guatemala are the clearing of land for agriculture, the expansion of the cattle ranching, and use of forests for fuelwood.[12]

As can be seen from Figure 2, the country has experienced a number of serious environmental problems besides deforestation. Soil erosion is a widespread phenomena, directly linked to deforestation, which leads to lack of moisture retention,

[12]The potential for the timber industry is considerable in Guatemala under proper management.

especially in upland areas. The thirst for land has led families to increasingly exploit lower-quality areas, characterized by shallow, lateritic soils that can sustain agriculture for only a few years, beyond which soil degradation occurs: After a few crops, the land is often abandoned (documented in the Brazilian Amazon) as the settlers move further into the rainforest, or converted into pasture for cattle grazing—a form of extensive agriculture providing little employment per unit of land. The erosion problem is greatest on the Pacific slopes because the soil is thin, the land sloping, and there are periods of heavy rainfall. Nevertheless, there is also extensive erosion in the altiplano, with topsoil losses of 5 to 35 tons per hectare per year in some places (Leonard, 1987), most evident around Lake Atitlan. Another cause of soil loss is the abandonment of ancient Indian practices of terracing and contour planting.

Watershed destruction and consequent flooding is another form of increasing environmental deterioration. It occurs widely on the Pacific slopes, in large areas towards the Caribbean basin (along the Motagua River) and just to the south of the Petén (rivers flowing west into Mexico), where colonization has occurred only recently. In fact, every major watershed on the Pacific side has been denuded of vegetation and suffers from erosion, flooding and sedimentation of rivers (Leonard, op. cit., Ch. 4). Another consequence of soil erosion has been sedimentation in major rivers and dams supplying water for Guatemala City, and rapid river runoff has also reduced the replenishment of groundwater for the capital.

Finally, loss of agricultural land to urban areas is an issue primarily around the one large urban area, Guatemala City. While the amount of land affected is not great, it is deep, volcanic soil and readily accessible to the major urban market.

Important manifestations of environmental damage in Guatemala and elsewhere in Central America are soil degradation and watershed destruction, both caused primarily by deforestation, itself resulting from the resort to increasingly marginal lands by land-starved farmers and settlers seeking a means to eke out an existence. Land scarcity results, on the supply side, from the combination of rapid rural population growth and concentration of landholdings in large farms, where, as we have noted above, half of the land is idle. On the demand side, pressures to increase agricultural production result from the growth of urban areas and urban incomes. Population growth affects both the supply side and demand side of this equation and therefore appears to contribute to deforestation and environmental deterioration. This reduces the future productive capacity of the land, or its capacity for what has come to be called "sustainable development" (a term in vogue since the Bruntland report: see WCED, 1987). This concept refers to the capacity of the natural resource base to supply the needs of the population on a long-term basis, so that the activities of the present generation do not significantly damage the natural resource base of the country needed to satisfy the needs of future generations. It appears that the current *modus vivendi* of development in Guatemala (and many other Third World countries) is in the sense not sustainable.[13]

---

[13]The US Department of Agriculture has developed a system for determining the "land use potential" of different areas according to their soil characteristics, topography and rainfall. A study of USAID (1987) identified regions of Guatemala where marginally productive land is being used for agriculture, with resulting environmental damage. In the departments in the eastern region, along the Pacific coast, and in the densely populated altiplano, there was already more land in farms in 1979 than was classified as appropriate for agriculture. A comparison of the (excessive) land use map in the USAID study with Figure 2 above indicates that areas experiencing environmental problems tend to correspond to regions where marginal lands are being used for agriculture, or where lands may be being used too intensively.

A RETURN LOOK AT POPULATION GROWTH AS AN INITIATING FACTOR

Up to this point we have simply asserted that population growth probably contributed to the land fragmentation process described above. Others have made similar assertions in other contexts, but as far as we know, this has never been convincingly demonstrated on a national level for any country. Figure 3 below, superimposing relationships extracted directly from the latest (and almost coterminous) population and agricultural censuses of Guatemala, helps us do this.

The top line in Figure 3 is simply the number of males living in rural areas of Guatemala according to the 1981 population census, by five-year age group. Thus the number in the age group 0-4 was 413,400, the number aged 15-19 was 208,500, the number 25-29 was 133,700, etc. The middle line is also taken from the population census, and shows the number of rural males in the labor force by five-year age group. The ratio of the latter, "poblacion economicamente activa" or PEA in Spanish, to the former is the labor force participation rate for rural males. This is .21 for age group 10-14, rising quickly to .71 for 15-19, and over .9 for most older ages. This is straight-forward. A relationship derived from the third line in the figure, however, takes us a quantum leap further, and is the key to the argument that follows. It shows the number of rural males who were heads of households in Guatemala in 1979, according to the (last, alas) census of agriculture.[14] Thus headship rates were extremely low for age 15-19 (.046), then rise rapidly to .24 for 20-24, .47 for 25-29, .58 for 30-34, and above .7 for all the older age groups.

---

[14]Note that no adjustment was made for the two year difference in the times of data collection, nor was it possible to adjust for differences in coverage rates of the two censuses. Neither of these is likely to have any effect on the results. The former, in fact, means that the headship rates from Figure 3 are slightly lower than the correct figures.

What does this mean regarding the demographic effects on land use and hence (ultimately, as we have traced through in the text above) on the environment? To answer this, recall studies by Eduardo Arriaga and others on the demographic transition in Latin America (see Arriaga and Davis, 1969). In most countries in the region, including Guatemala, the transition is generally considered to have begun with a decline in mortality that commenced in the 1930s and 1940s. This resulted in an increase in the number of surviving children, including sons as well as daughters. Given the headship rates by age inferred from Figure 3, the time lapse between the decline in mortality and the fragmentation in landholdings due to the existence of more sons to divide the land among should be about 30 years. It is therefore most intriguing that the process of land fragmentation did *not* occur in the 1950-64 intercensal interval, when the number of small farms increased by less than 5 percent, but *did occur* in the 1964-79 intercensal interval when the number of small farms virtually doubled. Given the customary inheritance practice of partiable inheritance in Guatemala—division of the plot among the sons (and in some ethnic groups among all children)—the decline in mortality is likely to have been an important factor in the land fragmentation process that occurred in the late 1960s and 1970s. Similarly, the decline in mortality could not have been a factor earlier, and indeed land fragmentation was evidently trivial prior to 1964. Moreover, we would be very surprised if the fragmentation process observed in 1964-79 has not continued since, further worsening rural poverty and inequality and continuing to push out-migration. This, of course, can be checked once a new agricultural census has been undertaken.

To tie the argument together, a significant decline in mortality occurred in Guatemala, which, with fertility remaining high and constant, led to an acceleration in population growth in rural areas of Guatemala, which appears to be associated with a dramatic fragmentation of agricultural plots. This in turn is likely to have contributed to both an increase in the intensity of use on existing plots, as well as localized land clearing/deforestation and land degradation, especially in the densely populated highlands. In the absence of significant increases in agricultural productivity and effective counteracting government policies, this is also likely to have led to worsening poverty and thereby increased pressures to migrate from rural areas. Some of this migration has been to urban areas, but some has also been to other rural areas, where land is available, which primarily meant to the northern forests of the Peten.

This process is illustrated in Figure 4. Note that *two* distinct demographic phenomena are directly involved in the environmental degradation process: population growth, as an initiating factor, and internal migration, more specifically, rural-rural migration as a response to increasing pressures on the land due to rising population density and fragmentation of plots. In fact, the out-migration essentially smoothes these pressures, or transfers them physically, from one part of the country to another. Note also that it is *rural-rural migration*, as an economic or survival stragegy decision at the household level, that is closely linked to environmental deterioration in rural areas. This type of migration merits much more careful attention in the scholarly literature on linkages between population and the environment. Indeed, even migration specialists have been missing the boat: The vast majority of the research on migration in developing countries is on rural-urban migration—maybe as high as 80 percent—with less than 10 percent on rural-rural migration. This contrasts with the reality: Among the 14 developing countries with the necessary data available (on the 1960s or 1970s) from censuses on the four mathematically possible types of migration—rural-urban, rural-rural, urban-rural, and urban-urban—rural-urban migration was the largest in only three (see Bilsborrow, 1992, Table 1). Moreover, in the four Latin American countries available, both rural-rural and urban-urban migration were larger than rural-urban migration flows (in Brazil, Ecuador, Honduras and Peru). It will be interesting to see what the data show once the 1990 census data are available for most countries.

CONCLUSIONS AND RESEARCH NEEDS

The purpose of this paper has been to stimulate recognition of some plausible key linkages between population growth, agricultural land use and distribution, migration and the environment, based on an overview of trends over time in Guatemala. The goal is equally to proffer a method for elucidating these relationships that can be easily replicated. The approach uses commonly existing data from population and agricultural censuses, and thereby provides a methodology that can be used in other developing countries, in Central America and elsewhere.

To examine plausible future effects of population growth on the agricultural population, we have used a simple framework, looking at population growth both retrospectively and prospectively, and looking at the implications for headship rates, fragmentation of plots in rural areas, and rural out-migration, including to ecologically fragile environments. Knowledge of key relationships/parameters is scant in most countries because of the lack of adequate data, but there is often much already available if one looks with persistence. But at the present time, in 1995, the largest deficiency we face is *the lack of any population or agricultural census* in Guatemala since 1981, which would allow us to bring the macro-regional analysis here up to the present.

Nevertheless, to permit a more intensive investigation of issues raised in this paper, complementary *micro-level* data are also highly desirable, especially direct data on migrants. In the absence of a specialized migration survey, it would be most helpful if an existing demographic survey (e.g., fertility/mortality survey, such as the DHS/CDC surveys, which are carried out every few years in Guatemala) could acquire certain basic economic data (viz., work by household members, land ownership, land use, inheritance plans) and migration information about people (date of last move, work status before and after the last move, reason for move). Similarly, economic surveys such as labor force and expenditure surveys should include basic migration and fertility questions (date of migration, births in recent years and survival status, timing of births relative to migration, women's work, etc.). For details, see Bilsborrow and Geores (1992). Pooling resources from single-purpose surveys into a multiple-purpose survey is another auspicious approach to gather data since it is more cost-effective than a number of separate surveys and permits a much wider range of analyses. Returning to the same point regarding census data, even traditional population and agricultural censuses could be usefully exploited together if the same household identification codes were used in each.

Areas where specific research is needed, and could be carried out if appropriate datasets were available, include the following:

(a) How (and when) does rural population growth lead to increased fragmentation of landholdings, and what are its consequences under various cultural and ecological circumstances in terms of increasing intensification of land use (excessive or not?), soil degradation, and out-migration?

(b) How much landlessness is there in rural Guatemala, how do the landless survive, and with what ecological consequences, or do they tend to migrate away more than those with small plots?

(c) What is the relationship between size of holding, family labor use (and hiring in labor), and production per worker and per hectare? How can more idle land be brought into cultivation?

(d) How does increasing use of tractors affect production and the demand for labor in different regions (or crop regimes), and what are the induced effects on migration?

(e) Exactly who are the migrants arriving in the Peten—where are they coming from, what are their characteristics (previously landless, minifundistas, latifundistas, Ladino or Indian?), why did they leave their places of origin? Was it because of environmental stress? How can we measure or ascertain this stress at the farm or household level?

(f) What are the factors that affect choice of destination of migrants in Guatemala, especially out-migrants from rural areas? Why do some choose urban destinations and others the Peten?

(g) How can farmers, especially very small farmers, increase production and productivity through more intensification of agricultural methods? What factors restrict the adoption of better technology—lack of land titles, credit, agricultural extension services?

(h) How can forest assets, especially those already compromised, be managed more sustainably?

(i) What are the factors sustaining high rural fertility in families with tiny-size land plots in Guatemala? How can these be altered?

(j) What are the relative roles of clearing land for crops and clearing it for pasture in the deforestation of the Peten?

We return to the particular case of the valuable biological endowment of the forests of the Peten of Guatemala, which has a total area of 36,210 square km. As recently as the mid-1970s the Peten was covered 80 percent by forests. But during the period from 1977 to 1987 it lost a total of 300,000 hectares (3,000 sq. km.). In the most recent period available of 1987-93 the annual rate of deforestation increased to 42,000 ha./year. There have been many factors responsible for this continuing and recent increase—including continued road building by the government (and announcement of plans to build future roads, which has fueled speculative land squatting and clearing), sales of large plots at far below market prices to absentee landlords (often military cronies) for cattle ranching, announcements that some land would be set aside in the Peten for repatriation of refugees, and complete failure to rescind land titles of hundreds if not thousands of small and large plotholders who have never worked the land and only hold it illegally for future appreciation. Some claim that so much of the recent clearing is associated with cattle ranching on large plots that the process of land fragmentation and out-migration from other areas of the country is not a major contributor to deforestation, that it is therefore mainly due to political factors rather than demographic factors. Nevertheless, data on land use changes in the Peten during the period 1987-93 estimate the total lost of forests at 423,000 ha., of which only 46,000 ha., or 11 percent, was due to an increase in the pasture area (computed from data in Table 1 of Kaimowitz, 1995). Thus the process of in-migration of small farmers squatting, homesteading in the region, appears to continue to be the main proximate cause of loss of forest cover.

It is distressing that so much of the Peten has already been conquered if not devastated by the plow and cattle. So little of the region has even mediocre agricultural potential. Thus studies of "land use potential" using USDA methods find only 500,000 ha. or 16 percent of the Peten useful for agriculture (Kaimowitz, p. 4). By 1993 twice this area had already been cleared, with another 42,000 ha. being added each year. Instead, further clearing should be severely restricted and oriented to the few areas remaining with adequate soils, while reforestation should commence on other areas which will never be agriculturally productive, some of which are already abandoned.

In the course of the paper, we have tried to indicate: (a) what are some of the key interrelationships between demographic processes and rural development problems in Guatemala (about which far too little is known for other countries as well), and (b) how are the problems interrelated. Thus policies designed to ameliorate one problem may in fact exacerbate others (e.g., policies to accelerate out-migration from densely populated rural areas may worsen food security and urban congestion; bringing more land into production to increase food production and provide more employment or increase land ownership may exacerbate damage to the environment). Even policies to redistribute land, or fiscal policies (such as a presumptive land tax) to stimulate the productive use of the huge amount of idle land on large estates in Guatemala, may have damaging effects on the environment if increasing the area of land used or the intensity of use is not accompanied by improvements in land use practice. The same is true of other policies to ameliorate rural unemployment by increasing the demand for labor through raising the *intensity* of land use, such as via shifts from one crop to another or from pasture to crops, or by changes in technology (e.g., increased use of hybrid seeds, fertilizer and chemicals, and irrigation).

Despite the gaps in knowledge noted, and therefore the provisional nature of the relationships inferred in the present paper, certain policies can be recommended without waiting for more research findings. These include strengthening policies to reduce population growth through reducing unwanted fertility, which is still quite high in Guatemala, especially in comparison with other countries in Latin America; altering policies related to rural areas and rural development, including land redistribution or at least a presumptive land tax; adopting policies to stimulate higher value-added on farmland, particularly higher labor intensity, through more agricultural extension services and credit for small farmers (despite past policy recommedations intended to achieve this credit redistribution from large farmers, how much has really occurred?), and more use of natural and chemical fertilizer where the soil is becoming "cansado" from intensive use; stimuli to expand non-agricultural enterprises in small cities and towns to thereby improve off-farm income-earning opportunities; and a reduction in the urban bias in the development policies in Guatemala in general (see Lipton, 1977). Such policy changes are needed *as quickly as possible*, to buy time to implement the much broader institutional changes necessary to put Guatemala on the path towards sustainable development in the twenty-first century. The end of violence and less inequality is crucial for the Guatemalan people to be able to function in an *ambiente* in which the future is something to look forward to, to strive for a use of resources which is sustainable in the long run in the WCED sense, rather than only for short-run survival.

ACKNOWLEDGEMENTS

Earlier versions of this paper were presented at the Southern Demographic Association Meetings, Durham, NC, October 18-20, 1989; and at the Conferencia sobre Politicas de Población en Centroamérica, el Caribe y México, Antigua, Guatemala, April, 1991. The paper evolved out of work by the authors in Guatemala in 1987-88, and benefitted substantially from discussions with officials at the Ministry of Agriculture and the National Planning Agency (SEGEPLAN) in Guatemala and USAID/Guatemala, especially Harry Wing. We are grateful to USAID for financial support in 1986-87.

REFERENCES

Arguello, O. 1981. "Estrategias de supervivencia: un concepto en busca de su contenido." *Demografía y Economía* 15(2).

Arriaga, E.E., and K. Davis. 1969. *The Pattern of Mortality Change in Latin America*. Berkeley: University of California Department of Demography (Institute of International Studies, International Population and Urban Research).

Bilsborrow, R. 1992. *Rural Poverty, Migration, and the Environment in Developing Countries: Three Case Studies.* Background paper for World Development Report 1992. Policy Research Working Paper, World Development Report,

Office of the Vice President, Development Economics, World Bank. Washington, DC: The World Bank.

_____. 1987. "Population Pressures and Agricultural Development in Developing Countries: A Conceptual Framework and Recent Evidence." *World Development* 15(2):1-18.

Bilsborrow, R and P.F. DeLargy. 1990. "Land Use, Migration, and Natural Resource Deterioration: The Experience of Guatemala and the Sudan." *Population and Development Review* 16 (Supp.) 125-147.

Bilsborrow, R., and M. Geores. 1992. *Rural Population Dynamics and Agricultural Development: Issues and Consequences Observed in Latin America.* Ithaca, NY: Cornell International Institute for Food, Agriculture and Development.

Bilsborrow, R., A. Oberai, and G. Standing. 1984. *Migration Surveys in Low-income Countries: Guidelines for Survey and Questionnaire Design.* London and Dover, NH: Croom-Helm.

Blaikie, P., and H. Brookfield. 1987. *Land Degradation and Society.* London: Methuen.

Boserup, E. 1965. *The Conditions of Agricultural Growth.* Allen and Unwin.

Centro Latinoamericano de Demografía. 1985. *Guatemala: Estimaciones y Proyecciones de Población 1950-2025.* Guatemala: Dirección General de Estadística y Centro Latinoamericano de Demografía.

Collins, J.L. 1987. "Labor Scarcity and Ecological Change." Pp. 19-37 in Little, P.D., and M.M. Horowitz (Eds.), *Lands at Risk in the Third World: Local-Level Perspectives.* Institute for Development Anthropology: IDA Monographs in Development Anthropology. Boulder, CO, and London: Westview Press.

Consejo Regional de Cooperación Agricola de Centroamerica, México, Panamá y República Dominicana. 1986. *Estudios de Politicas Agricolas Globales, Guatemala*, Secretaría de Coordinación, CORECA, Guatemala.

Davis, K. 1963. "The Theory of Change and Response in Modern Demographic History." *Population Index* (294):345-66.

DeJong, G.F., and R.W. Gardner, eds. 1981. *Migration Decision Making: Multidisciplinary Approaches to Microlevel Studies in Developed and Developing Countries.* Pergamon Policy Studies on International Development. New York: Pergamon Press.

DeWalt, B. 1985. "Microcosmic and Macrocosmic Processes of Agrarian Change in Southern Honduras: The Cattle Are Eating the Forest." Pp. 165-186 in DeWalt, B., and P. Pelto (Eds.), *Micro and Macro Levels of Analysis in Anthropology: Issues in Theory and Research.* Boulder: Westview Press.

DeWalt, B, and S. Stonich. 1992. "Inequality, Population, and Forest Destruction in Honduras." Paper presented at the Seminar on Population and Deforestation in the Humid Tropics, Campinas, Brazil, 30 November - 3 December 1992, organized by the Committee on Population of the International Union for the Scientific Study of Population (IUSSP) and the Associacão Brasileira de Estudos Populacionais (ABEP).

Dirección General de Estadística, Ministerio de Economía. 1979. *III Censo Nacional Agropecuario 1979*, Vol. I, II, Tomo I, II, Guatemala.

Emling, S. 1992. "Growing Need for Farmland Erodes Guatemala Forest." *Christian Science Monitor* Jul 8:9, 16.

FAO 1985. *CAPPA: Technical Description of the CAPPA System.* Unpublished manuscript No. R7273, Rome.

_____ 1986a. *Report on Natural Resources for Food and Agriculture in Latin America and the Caribbean*, FAO Environment and Energy Paper No. 8. Rome: Food and Agriculture Organization.

____ 1986b. *1986 Country Tables: Basic Data on the Agricultural Sector.* Economic and Social Policy Department, Rome.

Gardner, F., Y. Garb, and M. Williams. 1990. "Guatemala: A Political Ecology." Environmental Project on Central America, Green Paper No. 5. San Francisco: Earth Island Institute.

Harrison, S. 1990. "Population, Land Use and Deforestation in Costa Rica, 1950-1983." Working Paper of the Morrison Institute for Population and Resource Studies, vol. 24. Stanford.

Heckadon, M.S., and A. McKay (Eds.). 1984. *Colonización y Destrucción de Bosques en Pánama: Ensayos Sobre un Grave Problema Ecológico.* Panama City: Asociación Panameña de Antropología.

Higgins, G.; A. Kassam, and L. Naiken. 1982. *Potential Population Supporting Capacities of Lands in the Developing World*, Technical Report of the Project INT/75/P13, Land resources for populations of the future, Food and Agriculture Organization of the United Nations, Rome; International Institute for Applied Systems Analysis, Vienna; United Nations Fund for Population Activities, New York.

Hotchkiss, D. and J. von Braun. 1988. "The Effects of the Increased Commercialization of Traditional Smallholder Agriculture on Health and Nutrition in Guatemala." Paper presented at the Annual Meeting of the Population Association of America, New Orleans, Louisiana, April 21-23.

Hough, R., J. Kelley, and S. Miller. 1982. *Tierra y Trabajo en Guatemala: Una Evaluación.* Washington, DC: Agency for International Development.

Instituto de Ciencias Ambientales y Tecnología Agricola. 1984. *Perfil Ambiental de la República de Guatemala*, Tomo I, Sumario Ejecutivo, Universidad Rafael Landivar, Guatemala.

Instituto de Nutrición de Centro América y Panamá. 1987. *Guatemala Encuesta Nacional de Salud Materna Infantil, Informe Preliminar.* Ministerio de Salud Publica y Asistencia Social.

Kaimowitz, D. 1995. "Land Tenure, Land Markets, and Natural Resource Management by Large Landowners in the Peten and the Northern Transversal of Guatemala." Paper presented at 1995 Meeting of the Latin American Studies Association, Washington, DC, September 28-30.

Lee, E.S. 1966. "A Theory of Migration." *Demography* 3(1):47-57.

Lele, U. and S.W. Stone. 1989. "Population Pressure, the Environment and Agricultural Intensification: Variations on the Boserup Hypothesis." Managing Agricultural Development in Africa: MADIA Discussion Paper 4, World Bank. Washington, DC: The World Bank.

Leonard, H.J. 1987. *Natural Resources and Economic Development in Central America: A Regional Environmental Profile.* New Brunswick, NJ, and Oxford: Transaction Books.

Lipton, M. 1987. *Why Poor People Stay Poor: A Study of Urban Bias in World Development.* London: Temple Smith.

Little, P.D. and M.M. Horowitz (Eds.). 1987. *Lands at Risk in the Third World: Local-Level Perspectives.* Institute for Development Anthropology: IDA Monographs in Development Anthropology. Boulder, CO, and London: Westview Press.

Marquette, C., and R.E. Bilsborrow. 1994. *Population and the Environment in Developing Countries: Literature Survey and Research Bibliography.* New York: United Nations (Population Division of the Department for Economic and Social Information and Policy Analysis).

Mendez, A. 1988. *Population Growth, Land Scarcity and Environmental Deterioration in Rural Guatemala.* Unpublished Manuscript, Universidad del Valle, Guatemala.

Micklin, M. 1989. "Guatemala." In Nam, C., W. Serow, and D. Sly (Eds.), *International Handbook on Internal Migration.* Westport, CT, and London: Greenwood Press.

Morrison, A.R. 1993. "Violence or Economics: What Drives Internal Migration in Guatemala?" *Economic Development and Cultural Change* Jul 41(4):817-31.

Peek, P., ed. 1986. *Rural Poverty in Central America: Causes and Policy Alternatives.* Unpublished, Geneva: International Labor Office.

Schmink, M. and C.H. Wood. 1987. "The 'Political Ecology' of Amazonia." Pp. 38-57 in Little, Peter D., and Michael M. Horowitz (Eds.), *Lands at Risk in the Third World: Local-Level Perspectives.* Institute for Development Anthropology: IDA Monographs in Development Anthropology. Boulder, CO, and London: Westview Press.

Secretaria General del Consejo Nacional de Planificación Económica (SEGEPLAN). 1987. *Agricultura, Población y Empleo en Guatemala*, Serie Resultados No. 5, 1984, SEGEPLAN, Guatemala.

Sjaastad, L.A. 1962. "The Costs and Returns of Human Migration." *Journal of Political Economy* 70(5):80-93.

Stonich, S. 1989. "The Dynamics of Social Processes and Environmental Destruction: A Central American Case Study." *Population and Development Review* 15(2):269-297.

Stupp, P. and R. Bilsborrow. 1988. *Población y Agricultura en América Central: Enfoque Guatemala.* Unpublished, Chapel Hill, NC: Carolina Population Center.

Tucker, S.K. 1992. "Equity and the Environment in the Promotion of Nontraditional Agricultural Exports." Pp. 109-41 in Annis, S. (Ed.), *Poverty, Natural Resources, and Public Policy in Central America.* U.S.-Third World Policy Perspectives No. 17. New Brunswick, New Jersey: Transaction Publishers.

United Nations. 1980. "Patterns of Urban and Rural Population Growth." *Population Studies* No. 68, New York, NY.

_____ 1985. *World Population Prospects: Estimates and Projections as Assessed in 1982,* Population Studies No. 86, New York, NY.

USAID/Guatemala. 1987. *Guatemala: Agriculture Sector Review*, Guatemala.

World Bank. 1985. *World Development Report, 1984.* Washington, DC.

World Commission on Environment and Development. 1987. *Our Common Future.* Oxford University Press.

TABLE 1. POPULATION AND AGRICULTURE IN CENTRAL AMERICA

	Population[a] (millions)		Percent Urban[a]		Agr. Pop.Per Ha. of Agr. Land[b]		Annual Rates of Growth (%) in Agriculture Product[c]		Annual Rates of Growth (%) in Food Product[c]		Value Added Per Agri. Worker[c] (Thousand of U.S. 1985 $)		No. of Farms (in 1,000s) and % of Land by Farm Size[d] (1975-80)		
Country	1980	2020	1980	2020	1961	1983	1971-80	1981-84	1971-80	1981-84	1970	1985	>10 ha	10-99 ha	100+ ha
Costa Rica	2.2	4.8	43	69	1.3	1.3	3.0	3.1	3.1	1.6	3.0	3.3	153(4)	43(29)	48(67)
El Salvador	4.8	13.8	41	66	2.5	3.6	3.6	1.5	4.8	1.7	1.2	1.0	251(27)	18(34)	2(39)
Guatemala	6.9	19.8	38	65	1.8	2.3	4.6	-2.6	4.4	-0.2	1.2	1.2	548(16)	49(19)	14(65)
Honduras	3.7	12.0	36	65	0.9	1.4	2.6	0.8	1.7	0.6	0.9	0.9	153(17)	39(28)	3(55)
Nicaragua	2.8	9.2	56	80	0.8	0.9	2.7	-0.3	3.1	2.1	1.3	1.4	-	-	-
Panama	2.0	3.7	50	71	1.0	1.2	3.2	0.8	3.1	0.7	1.3	1.6	55(8)	34(46)	3(46)
Total	22.4	63.3	43	68	-	-	-	-	-	-	-	-	-	-	-

Sources:
[a]United Nations, *World Population Prospects, 1982*, 1985.
[b]FAO, *FAO Producing Yearbook* 1977, 1984.
[c]World Bank, 1985; IDB, 1983; FAO, 1986b.
[d]Peek, 1986.

TABLE 2. POPULATION PROJECTIONS[a] FOR GUATEMALA: 1980-2030

	(millions)		
	1980	2030 (Low Fertility)	2030 (High Fertility)
Total	6.92	23.86	37.37
Urban	2.26	16.68	25.51
Rural	4.65	7.18	11.86

[a]For sources and assumptions, see text.

TABLE 3. GUATEMALA: LAND IN FARMS AND NUMBER OF FARMS BY FARM SIZE AND REGION, 1964-79

	Land Area (thousands of manzanas)							
Farm Size	< 2 manzanas		2-5 manzanas		5-64 manzanas		64+ manzanas	
	1964	1979	1964	1979	1964	1979	1964	1979
Central	30.8	39.6	58.5	55.8	193.9	193.5	833.5	837.4
Oriental Sur	26.3	30.3	68.1	70.9	225.0	244.1	684.0	699.7
Costera	5.4	25.2	23.9	27.0	111.0	110.9	649.6	740.7
Altiplano	73.2	112.6	147.6	158.2	480.2	479.2	399.5	365.9
Oriental Nor.	11.5	16.0	34.1	36.5	121.2	199.6	454.0	471.0
Norte	5.3	25.1	61.8	64.3	171.3	331.9	744.2	1406.5
Total	192.5	248.7	394.0	412.7	1302.7	1559.2	3764.8	4521.3
	Number of Farms (thousands)							
Farm Size	< 2 manzanas		2-5 manzanas		5-64 manzanas		64+ manzanas	
	1964	1979	1964	1979	1964	1979	1964	1979
Central	28.8	66.0	20.2	15.6	12.9	10.3	1.6	1.8
Oriental Sur	21.0	41.1	21.6	24.1	14.4	16.6	2.3	2.2
Costera	30.3	46.9	7.8	8.7	6.1	6.9	1.5	1.5
Altiplano	76.1	144.3	47.1	47.4	39.7	32.8	1.3	0.9
Oriental Nor.	10.4	27.1	11.9	12.0	8.3	11.9	1.0	1.4
Norte	7.1	36.2	20.5	20.9	14.3	22.7	1.1	5.9
Total	183.7	361.5	129.7	128.6	95.7	101.3	8.8	13.7

Source: SEGEPLAN, 1987.

TABLE 4. GUATEMALA: PROJECTIONS OF THE AGRICULTURAL LABOR FORCE AND NUMBERS OF FULL-TIME EQUIVALENT EMPLOYEES IN AGRICULTURE

(thousands)	1980	1990	2000	2010	2020	2030
Agricultural Labor Force						
Low Fertility	1115.5	1425.0	1767.6	2061.9	2247.0	2246.6
High Fertility	1115.5	1424.2	1781.3	2163.6	2552.7	2909.9
Full-Time Equivalent Employees[a]						
Persons/Manzana w/ Constant Intensity[b]	690.6	776.6	862.2	957.4	1062.8	1180.1
Persons/Manzana Rising Intensity[c]	690.6	875.4	1081.6	1323.0	1603.9	1931.0

[a]Land in use assumed to grow at 1.2 percent per year.
[b]Intensity of labor use constant at .22 full-time employees per mz.
[c]Intensity of labor use grows to .37 full-time employees per mz. in 2030.
Source: See text.

FIGURE 1. DEFORESTATION 1950 -1985

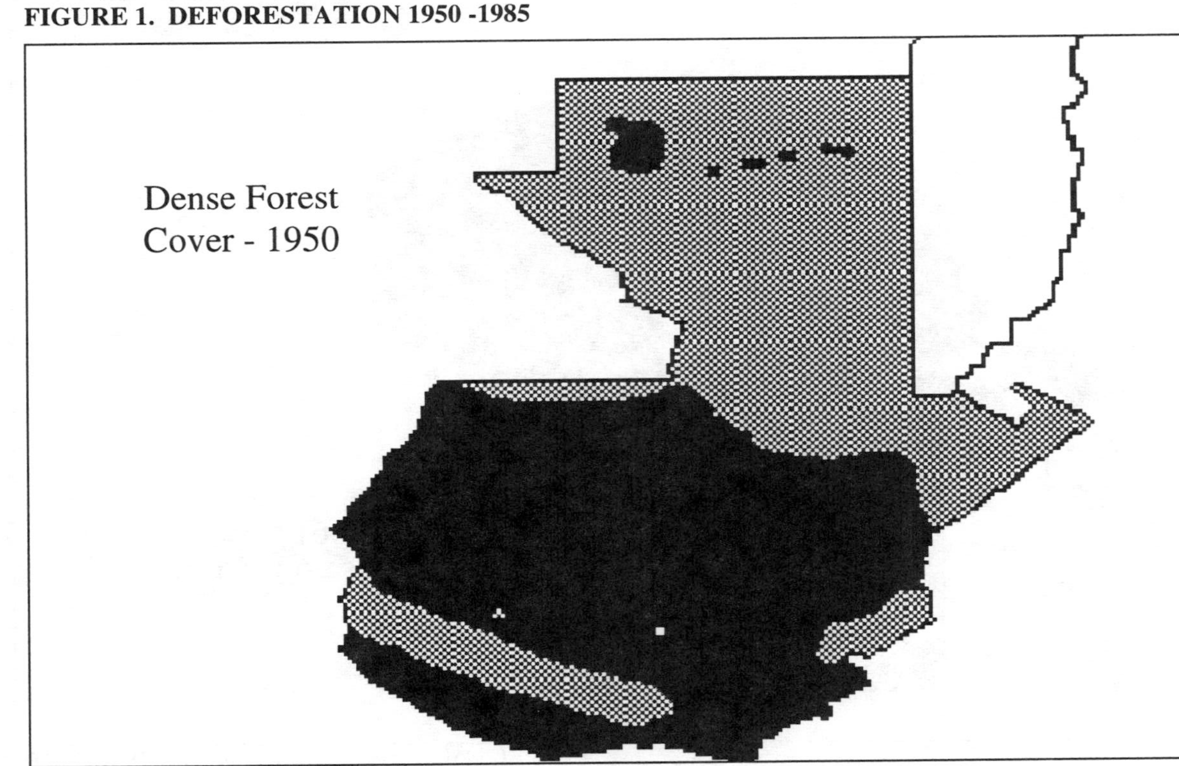

FIGURE 1. *(Continued from previous page)*

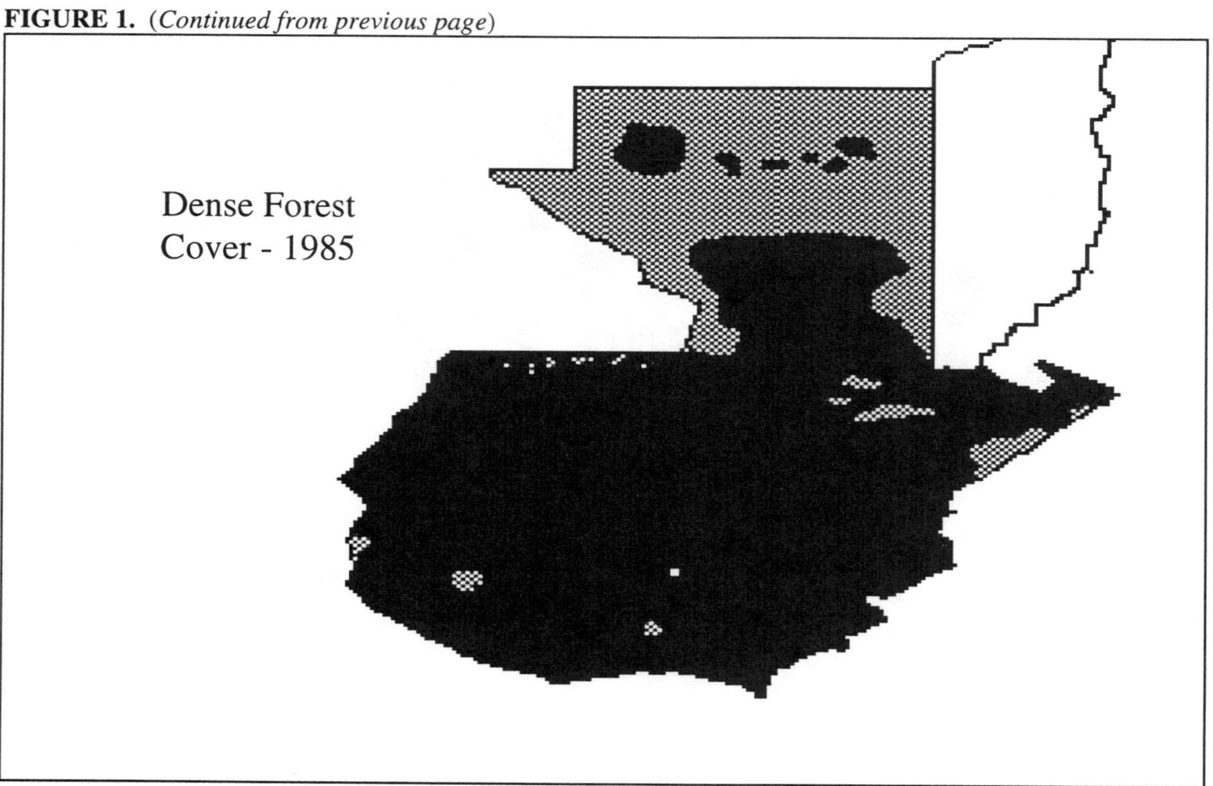

FIGURE 2. ENVIRONMENTAL DESTRUCTION

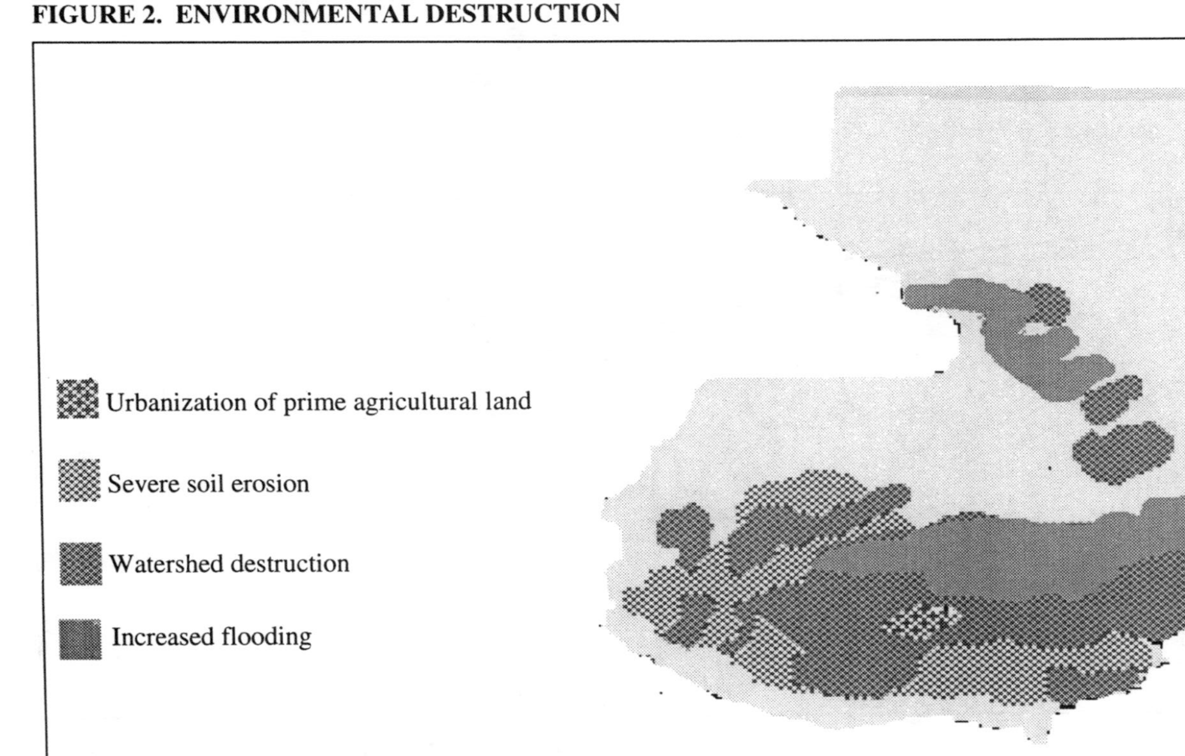

FIGURE 3. GUATEMALAN RURAL MALES BY AGE

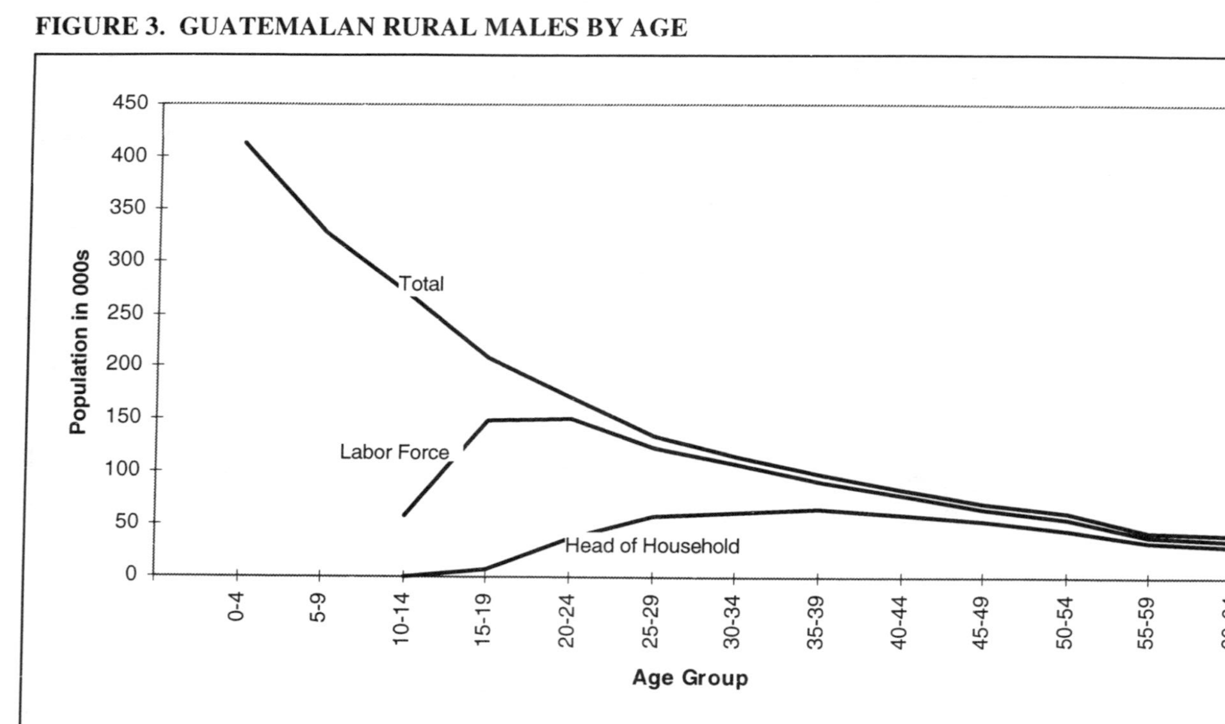

FIGURE 4. POPULATION, LAND, AND MIGRATION LINKAGES TO THE ENVIRONMENT IN GUATEMALA

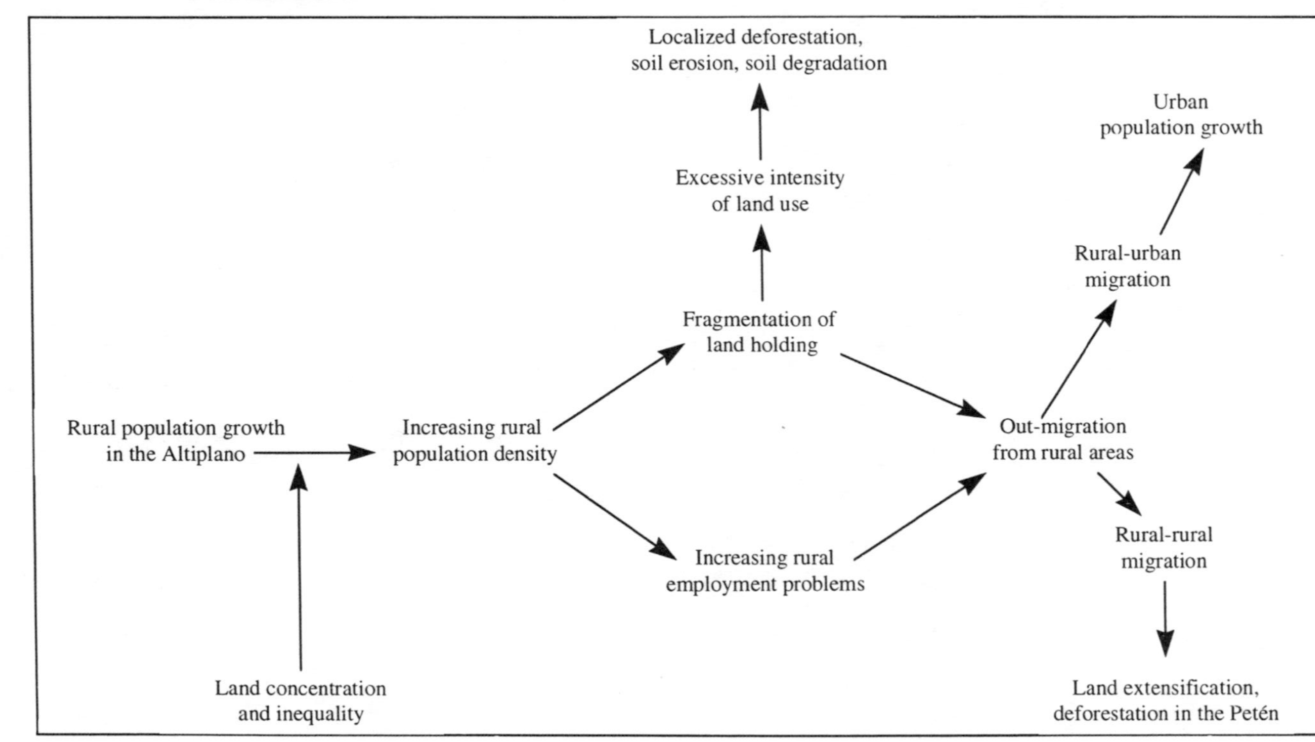

PERCEPTION AND ADJUSTMENT TO ENVIRONMENTAL HAZARDS: A CROSS-CULTURAL COMPARISON FROM HONDURAS

CATHERINE HOOVER-CASTAÑEDA

In many regions of the world growing numbers of people are inhabiting environments known to be physically hazardous. With greater access to marginal, hazard-prone environments but little capacity to manage the risks, the poor are disproportionately vulnerable to disaster. Social theory suggests people occupy hazardous environments because they consider the benefits perceived from doing so to outweigh the risks. However, hazards are not always perceived in a uniform manner because access and response to environmental information is variable. Questions remain about how socioecological variability affects risk assessment and the range of coping strategies available to a population, particularly in a multi-cultural context. This issue challenges Centralamerican municipal governments facing political, economic and conflict-prone environmental transformations as they experience rapid growth of their populations, which are often culturally diverse. Just as change may contribute to the mitigation of some environmental hazards for one sector of the population, they can potentiate a hazard threat for others.

After reviewing relevant ideas from current hazard theory, this paper examines the context of socioecological variability in environmental hazard perception and adjustment among residents of four villages from two distinct cultural realms encountered in one coastal municipality of Honduras. The arrays of environmental hazards perceived and adjustment strategies employed by informants from each village are compared in a qualitative analysis of the ethnographic data obtained. While different cultural perceptions of hazards are markedly apparent, some adjustment strategies employed present curious similarities. The environmental and cultural history of each village strongly determines the social significance of particular hazards, but the economic and political context limits the range of coping strategies available.

INTRODUCTION

Community development specialists working in less privileged regions of the world are plagued by the growing numbers of people inhabiting environments known to be physically hazardous. Moreover, in regions historically prone to floods and droughts, human induced environmental changes leading to resource degradation are being implicated in the increased incidence, magnitude, pervasiveness and variety of the less severe category of disasters plaguing poor communities (Glickman, Gilding and Silverman 1992, 28; Lavell 1993, 135). This has called attention to the links between poverty, environmental degradation and disaster, and points to a strategic need to enhance the poor's capacity to assess and manage the risks associated with their changing environment.

Managing the risks associated with changes requires a better understanding of how environmental transformations generate and modify hazardous conditions. Environmental transformations are variously attributed to the *social driving forces* of population change, patterns of resource consumption and distribution, technological change, economic structures, and political cultures (Grossman 1992; Butzer 1990; Ellen 1992; NRC 1992; Ness 1993). Population changes, for example, are widely recognized as forcing environmental transformations by altering the integrity and availability of natural resources, particularly where technology is employed to enhance carrying capacity (Whitmore, Turner, Johnson, et al, 1990; Goudie 1994). The high degree of geographic variability displayed by these forces over time has made understanding how hazards arise from their interactions with the natural world a complex chore.

Theoretically, hazards are understood as highly interactive phenomena occurring within a socioecological context. Empirical evidence for this view was developed and discussed during the 1980's (Kates 1980; Watts 1983a, 1983b; Hewitt 1983; Blaikie 1985; Johnson, Olson and Manandhar 1982; Cuny 1983; Susman, O'Keefe and Wisner 1983; Lees and Bates 1984; and Wijkman and Timberlake 1984). The debate centered on the importance of spatial, economic and cultural distributions of hazards, particularly by examining the role disasters play in the underdevelopment process (Burton, Kates and White 1993). Recently, the sociopolitical context of disasters has been the focus of research in Latin America (Wilches-Chaux 1989; Oliver-Smith 1990; Lavell 1992; Maskrey 1993; and Mansilla 1993).

This cultural/human ecology perspective on hazards and the occurrence of disasters suggests that natural phenomena like hurricanes, forest fires, landslides or droughts are not likely to be considered hazardous unless human interests are at risk of undergoing a costly change. It views disasters as occurring where and when a society is unable to adjust to the overwhelming burden of a sudden, hazardous event, and reveals how the poor are disproportionately vulnerable. It provides a valuable framework for the study of how human-environment interactions induce ecological change and therefore, insight into the social processes leading to either hazardous or sustainable conditions (Little, Horowitz and Nyerges 1987; Anderson and Woodrow 1989; Browder 1989).

This framework, developed in both geography and anthropology, is important to consider when studying the environmental consequences of population change. It is the conceptual basis of the research reported on in this paper, which examines the nature of human-environment interactions generating hazards in four rural villages from the municipality of Tela, on the Caribbean coast of Honduras (Figure 1). This municipality is home to there is little social impetus to prevent or mitigate its potential impacts (Burton, Kates and White 1993). It is experience with a hazard that provides opportunities to assess risks and test adjustment strategies. Environmental risk assessment based on experience can be enhanced with access to knowledge about the experience of others, but such access is commonly skewed (Lees and Bates 1984; Cashdan 1990).

Evidence from anthropology suggests that in relatively homogenous environments, where the cultural characteristics of its human inhabitants are also homogenous, a high degree of shared understanding about the probable causes and consequences of recurrent hazards should be apparent (Low 1990). This has been documented for environments where hazards are often considered to be extreme, as in the case of high mountains, the arctic tundra and deserts, yet where effective adaptive strategies have evolved (Johnson, Olson and Manandhar 1982; Moran 1982). However, environmentally hazardous areas are increasingly inhabited by culturally heterogeneous populations because of economic and mobility factors. Modern theory of cultural evolution suggests that as environments become more unpredictable and hazard-prone, their inhabitants are less likely to be successful at risk assessment and reduction. Cultural heterogeneity would further hamper the development of shared perceptions about hazard. Could these conditions promote resource degradation or hinder socio-political attempts to reduce vulnerability in a region? What natural resource management challenges could these conditions present to the municipal organization in Honduras or Central America as their culturally diverse populations expand?

FIELD RESEARCH METHODOLOGY

In order to help enhance the capacity of the poor to reduce the risk and uncertainties of environmental change, it is essential to understand their perception of the context for ecological change and hazards in their cultural realm. The behavioral context surrounding environmental events experienced by villagers in rural Tela was elucidated for this study through ethnographic techniques. The analysis focuses on the household and the principal village organizations. This approach recognizes the household as more the women's "private" realm and the village organization as more the male's "public" realm in rural communities (Jelin 1984; Brydon and Chant 1989). Both deserve exploration in order to reveal gender related differences in environmental assessment and adjustment processes.

A cross-cultural comparison of gender related roles and perceptions is important where men and women of distinct cultures display significantly different productive and reproductive strategies. In Tela, the Garifuna and Mestizo cultural realms have been compared by selecting two rural communities from each. From the Garifuna realm, Triunfo de la Cruz and Miami were selected. Triunfo de la Cruz was settled permanently in the 1880's, while Miami was established in 1973. From the Mestizo realm, Toloa Adentro (established circa 1930) and Cangeliquita Arriba (originally established in 1970) were selected. A socio-demographic profile of these villages was developed from the 1988 Population and Housing Census (SECPLAN 1989).

The socio-ecological data enabling the assessment of human -environment interactions in each village was obtained from several social elements accessed through two kinds of primary informants, who serve as field guides. First, the Municipal Mayor of Tela assigned a Mestizo male guide (native to a rural Tela) to assist in the research project. In representing the municipal cadastre authority, he was recognized and well received by the typically all male authorities in each community studied. With these informants, recent and historical information on land use, tenure arrangements, and fishing sites was obtained. This information is highly qualitative in nature but was field checked using 1992 air photographs (1:20,000 scale), and by referring to the ronmental information traditionally shared in the rural communities of two different, yet adjacent cultural realms? Under what circumstances is environmental transformation perceived as hazardous? How is risk manifested with environmental transformation? How are the social driving forces of environmental transformation forces manifested in the culturally different coastal communities of this municipality? How are residents of these rural communities now acquiring cultural information about environmental hazards, and how significant is the personal hazardous experience to this process? Who are the sources of information? Is the information subject to manipulation? What disasters have occurred in each community? When disaster strikes, where is help sought from? Who provides the most timely assistance? What constitutes assistance for disaster victims?

BRIEF ENVIRONMENTAL AND DEMOGRAPHIC HISTORY OF THE STUDY SITE

Among the social driving forces of environmental change, demographic factors are certainly significant. Rapid increases or decreases in population growth rates are known to promote land use transformations through changes in productivity and energy consumption (Ness 1993, 33; Butzer 1990; Ellen 1991, 268). Population growth has been an important factor in the more recent stages of environmental transformation of Tela, whose total population nears 80,000 but is 61% rural. Between 1930 and 1988, the rural population density of Tela rose from 8.5 to 34.6 persons per square kilometer. Census records indicate that immigration from throughout Honduras, other Centralamerican nations, Europe, the United States and the Middle East was very important to this demographic growth. Bringing new land into production to support this population growth is evident throughout our study area, but particularly so in the Mestizo realm. This strategy is widely recognized as the most common population increase adjustment across cultures (Ruttan and Hayami 1987).

Immigration and emigration are also recognized as important responses to extreme environmental conditions. Emigration from a region can reduce the success rate of traditional productive opportunities (de Freitas 1989, 110), but can also change land use by reducing the pressure for land. Tela is one of several north coast municipalities attracting Mestizo migrants from economically depressed rural regions of Honduras where population density is high (SECPLAN 1989).

The birth origin of residents from the four villages selected for study was obtained from the 1988 population census. At that time it is interesting to note the percentage of the total resident population from Toloa Adentro and Cangeliquita who were actually born in municipalities from southern Honduras, where the climate is significantly different from that encountered in Tela. The number of adolescent and adult immigrants to Tela from southern Honduras, as indicated in Table 1 with reference to Figure 3, likely impact adaptive strategies, especially when the importance of hazard experience on hazard perception is considered. Their environmental hazard experience has been dominated by diminishing access to productive agricultural land, water resources, educational and employment opportunities.

The Caribbean coastal zone of Honduras has historically been impacted by hurricanes and heavy rains accompanying tropical storms. The region's biologically diverse humid tropical lowland and upland ecosystems evolved in response to these climatic conditions. Annual precipitation in Tela exceeds 3000 mm per year and evapotranspiration rates are low. While annual precipitation can be heavy and exceed 2000 mm per year in much of southern Honduras, evapotranspiration often surpasses this in places, creating a negative water budget (Zuniga Andrade 1990). Conversations with several male immigrants from dry municipalities in the south, now resident in Toloa Adentro and Cangeliquita Arriba, suggest they sought settlement where water scarcity would not be a hazard. For lack of their experience with sell fresh fish at markets in neighboring villages or the town of Tela, about a 45 minute bus ride away.

There are approximately 70 rural communities inhabited largely by people of *Mestizo* origen, 62 of which have been founded since the 1960's. Only 5 of these communities had populations exceeding 1,000 in 1988 and none are located along the shoreline. The economy of these villages is largely based on agricultural and cattle production.

Toloa Adentro had a population of 808 residents in 1988, while Cangeliquita Arriba had only 319 residents. Toloa Adentro has a gradually diversifying agricultural base. In addition to subsistence production of basic grains (rice, beans, corn), African Palm is widely produced for sale to nearby palm oil factories by agricultural cooperatives and independent farmers. Cattle are extensively grazed in the Toloa Adentro area for milk products which are sold commercially. Cattle are also raised extensively in the Cangeliquita Arriba area and milk products are gaining commercial importance here. The uplands are cleared of forest primarily to cultivate basic grains for subsistence and petty commerce.

A preliminary exploration of ethnicity among residents in the four villages was possible from a 1988 census question on language spoken. From this it was ascertained that 76.5% of Triunfo de la Cruz's residents over the age of five speak Garifuna. Only 32.1% of Miami's residents over the age of five speak Garifuna because since the mid-1980's, Mestizo settlers became more common. Garifuna residents also blame adolescent disinterest in learning and practicing their language because it is not always encouraged by school teachers, who are often Mestizos.

The geographic origin of residents in all four villages was assessed from village census data from 1988. A total of 93.8% of the residents of Triunfo de la Cruz, and 87.1% of those from Miami were born in communities along the north coast of Honduras. However, only 63.4% of Toloa Adentro's population and

60.5% of Cangelica Arriba's population were born in communities of coastal municipalities, a good proportion of which are under five years of age (Table 1). Rather, many of the residents in the two Mestizo villages were born in municipalities of southernmost Honduras. The implications of this phenomena are apparent in the ethnographic material garnered from conversations with male residents in Toloa Adentro and Cangeliquita Arriba. Many of them immigrated to the area as young adults, occasionally with spouses but mostly without children. Their explanations of the move reflect a perceived lack of opportunities in their places of origin and, in retrospect, a definite satisfaction with the agricultural conditions encountered in the Tela area.

> la tierra daba tan poquito"; "Aqui [en Tela], esta verde todo el año, y siempre hay agua"; "no habia nada alla en mi pueblo"; "nos dijeron que aqui habia trabajo para los hombres"; "en esta zona [Cangeliquita Arriba], se sobra la tierra para los muchachos"; "ay pues, cuando Dios quiere, aqui [Toloa Adentro] se saca hasta tres cosechas al año, pero apenas conseguiamos una allí"

HAZARD EVENTS AND HAZARD PERCEPTIONS

In all four communities, there is an interesting contrast between hazards perceived and hazards not perceived. The following, condensed review of relevant ethnographic data obtained thusfar reveals how and why the causes and consequences of environmental change are often not fully recognized.

Toloa Adentro

In Toloa Adentro (Table 2), the current environmental hazard most widely perceived is the river rising in association with heavy rains, which are common from May to October. Elderly residents recognize this hazard as an old one. Crop losses were a typical consequence of heavy rains in the early years following settlement. As railway lines, bridges and roads improved there are families situated across the river and streams that keep their children home from school during rainy periods, for fear of the river rising and impeding any passage.

The elderly male informants from Cangeliquita Arriba also lament the disappearance of wildlife from the area. This is not directly attributed to deforestation, but to the increased population in the area, and the youth's general lack of respect for forest animals, which are hunted both for food and sport. Dogs have occasionally been used for hunting.

Both male and female informants of all adult ages in this village are primarily concerned with one particular danger: "the Armageddon brought on by communism and the pollution of young people's minds" through formal education and outsiders (Table 3). Influenced by this cosmovision promoted by evangelists and members of Jehovah's Witness, this is a community afraid of any changes imposed on them or uninitiated by them. Their relative geographic isolation makes this possible, but the consequences mean great difficulty and expense can be incurred if a serious health emergency arises. To offset this condition the community has mobilized around efforts to get potable water piped into most homes, get a health clinic built and staffed with an auxiliary nurse. They had to negotiate funding assistance for these efforts from central government and municipal authorities.

Miami

The origin of Miami appears a direct consequence of human induced environmental transformations in the area. Miami is a somewhat remote fishing village, located in the buffer zone of the recently established for ecotourism, Punta Sal National Park. It consists of about 45 small houses on a long sand bar-peninsula between the Los Micos Lagoon and the Bay of Tela. This site, adjacent to an estuarine channel, first attracted Garifuna fishermen from Tornabé (11 kilometers east of Miami) in 1972, as the productivity of their local efforts in another channel from the Lagoon decreased. All the Garifuna residents of Miami have kin and homes in Tornabé, where they usually spend weekends.

Established early in the 19th century, Tornabé is situated adjacent to a natural channel allowing the exchange of salt and fresh water between the Los Micos Lagoon and the sea. When open at its mouth, this estuarine channel has long provided enough fish for subsistence and commercial activities. Circa 1971-1972, natural sand movements along the shoreline combined with increased deposition of sediments likely contributed to a narrowing and shallowing of the channel mouth that led to its complete closure during periods of reduced rainfall. This encouraged human efforts to artificially maintain the mouth of the channel filled as much as possible, allowing passage of vehicles for the development of commerce and tourism. With this modification, fresh and saltwater exchange in the channel affects the success of fishing efforts in the channel.

In 1972, heavy tropical rains combined with the decreased drainage capacity of the Tornabé channel to flood the inland shore of the Los Micos Lagoon, particularly threatening mestizo rice growers. After the grower's request to dredge the channel mouth was rejected by the Tornabé Patronato, they employed several men from Tornabé to help dredge the mouth of the channel now adjacent to the site of the Miami settlement. These men and other young Garifuna couples moved from Tornabé to settle at the site because the fishing became so remarkably lucrative. In 1973, the first Patronato was established. The fishing activity here became a critical source of stable income to families following Hurricane Fifi, which destroyed many for a long time they have seen no concrete economic benefits to date.

Triunfo de la Cruz

In Triunfo de la Cruz, environmental change has taken a slightly different direction, but is also related to speculation about tourism and continuing encroachment by Mestizos. The village is located along the beach between two points of land. On the west is Punto de Triunfo de la Cruz, currently private property of one long standing Garifuna family, but an important source of wild food, medicinal plants and firewood for many village residents. To the northeast is the Platano River and Punto Izopo, which was declared a Biological Reserve in 1993. The Refuge extends inland from the coast and encompasses a forested area. The village realm once extended as far as 5 kilometers inland where wood, food and medicinal plants as well as small game were procured. By the late 1930's, the Garifuna were more confined to the shoreline area because of Mestizo landgrabbing for cattle grazing and settlement along the railroad line.

Fishing has always been an important activity for men from this village. Until recently, there was always someone in the extended family who could provide fish for nearly all meals. While once abundant, the local fish catch has dropped since the 1970's despite increases in effort. Consequently, the purchase price of fish for local consumption is considered skyhigh ("por las nubes"). Despite the sale price of fish, fishing income from local sites has dropped enough to push fishermen to employment in the fishing industry based in the offshore Bay Islands, which takes them away from their families for months at a time.

Other young people seek employment in nearby cities, Belize and the United States. This ensures some supply of money in the village through remittance, which has definitely improved the economic position of those families benefitted. This particular economic adjustment strategy was observed in all households with many children. It is their logical response to the limited productive opportunities in the villages studied. Families without this kind of income in Triunfo de la Cruz confront a reduced status in the community. This appears to have fueled speculation over land long considered communal in ownership.

An approximately 129 hectare patch of land, long considered communal property for a rotating system of subsistence production of manioc, was usurped in a deal between Garifuna men elected to the Patronato in 1993 and some wealthy Mestizo investors from the city of San Pedro Sula, looking to develop beachfront property into an elite resort community. The land deal was sealed in February of 1994 and manioc became scarce rapidly. More than 50 women stopped making casabe almost entirely. This reduced the demand for charcoal which was used for cooking casabe. Our elderly male informant's income was based on the elaboration and sale of charcoal to these women. Some individual women have adjusted by increasing their production of coconut bread. With the scarcity and high cost of fuelwood or charcoal, they use discarded coconut shells for baking on an outdoor fire.

Some men and women of the community were less complacent in the face of this environmental change, forming a Committee for the Defense of Communal Lands. The Committee denounced the land deal in a face off with Patronato members that led to its political restructuring. With historical evidence of communal land rights, the Committee also denounced the affair to the Prosector in charge of Ethnic Affairs within the Public Defense Ministry of Honduras in September, 1994. One and a half years later, this conflict is still awaiting an official resolution of the matter, and the developers must prepare an environmental impact statement prior to permitting.

Mestizo encroachment is widely considered the greatest threat to the Garifuna in Triunfo de la Cruz, directly impacting their cultural identity. Mestizo city residents have already purchased beachfront property and built luxurious weekend escapes, while poorer Mestizos graze cattle or settle along other borders of the village to grow corn and beans in an environment unsuitable for such activities. This physical encroachment is confounded by a more pervasive cultural encroachment of Mestizo values. Mestizo teachers are assigned to teach in the local school, and erode the youngsters pride about speaking the Garifuna language. There is a continuing impact of "outside" cultural values as seen in fancy bikes, fluorescent lighted tennis shoes, and boom boxes acquired among families with relatives in the United States. Many teenagers cannot or simply do not want to speak Garifuna anymore and leave the village when an opportunity arises. The elderly of Triunfo de la Cruz best recognize it as a loss of community values and consider this social change dangerous ("peligroso").

Hurricanes are definitely recognized as hazardous by all informants. An area just south of the village has been flooded with hurricanes and settlement was never considered there until quite recently. Concern was expressed by several residents over the impact of storms on the gradual erosion of beachfront, which has not yet threatened Garifuna homes. Both Hurricane Francelia in 1969, and Hurricane Fifi damaged houses, crops and the access road in Triunfo de la Cruz. As in the Tornabé area, there is no recall of official disaster assistance, but aid was sent from friends and family in the United States.

Most adults expressed extreme concern about the condition of the community cemetery, which has no more room for "decent" burial plots and is adjacent to the eroding beach (Table 5). This is seen as a serious hazard to community values, and new land for a cemetery must be located. One elderly female informant has expressed her despair over not being able to be buried decently or beside her deceased family members. She and others fear an unhappy afterlife that could provoke problems for descendants. Research supporting this perception comes from other coastal Garifuna communities in Honduras on the psychosocial illness called GUBIDA by Bianchi (1986). This phenomenon was earlier recognized by Coelho (1981) as anxiety resulting from a perception of inadequate reverence and support of ancestors, a central element of the Garifuna cosmovision.

The cemetery issue seems to be a very important cultural problem that the community has not been able to solve because of the scarcity of communal land. No private individual has come forth to donate land, partly because the general perception is that the Municipality of Tela should provide land for the communal cemetery. In fact, the Municipal Law of 1991 does place the responsibility of cemetery management directly in the hands of the Municipal authorities. However, several formal requests from the Patronato and another civic organization for assistance in this matter from the Mayor of Tela have been ignored since 1994.

Very apparent in Triunfo de la Cruz was the strong influence of gender on the historical perspective of the elderly. Men tend to remember when a school was constructed, when a neighbor assumed community leadership, or when communal property rights were established. Women rather focus on changes affecting interpersonal relationships over time, such as the drinking habits of conjugal partners, or the health deterioration of a child. All elderly remember hurricane devastation, but with different attention to details. Men remembered organizing to dig a ditch to drain floodwaters after Hurricane Fifi, while women remembered what household items were lost and that the school was closed for five months afterwards.

An environmental change, which is no longer recognized as important to village residents, is the depletion of one species of tree, the Yagua, which has been used for constructing the traditional Garifuna house. It is endemic to the lowland coastal forest which has been widely deforested in Tela since the 1920's. Partly in response, these houses are being replaced widely by the higher status concrete structures whenever money is available.

Despite the scarcity of Yagua, deforestation is hardly mentioned as a problem for the community.

TRADITIONAL VERSUS NON-TRADITIONAL HAZARDS

Overall, the many environmental hazards arising out of human-environment interactions are simply not equally perceived or responded to by all the residents studied in Tela. While all informants in the study recognize the existence of the traditional hurricane hazard in the area, the degree of perception varies according to experience. Another traditional but more commonly experienced environmental hazard for all Teleños is the venomous and deadly snake referred to as "barba amarilla," which can be encountered in any land based agricultural, hunting or forest activity. However, cultural adjustments to the threat reflect the gendered division of labor. As an adjustment, Mestizo mothers of boys think it critical their sons learn early how to handle a machete for protection from such hazards. Among the Garifuna, this would be a desired cultural trait for women who work more often than men in the manioc fields.

The beach flies are a traditional pest particular to the Garifuna realm in Tela. However, it is much less of a problem in homes with tile or cement flooring, like those found in Triunfo de la Cruz. The instability of the beach at Miami, which is relatively much more exposed to wind and waves, make such investments in floors less feasible. The Garifuna of Miami send their young children to live with relatives in Tornabé, in part to reduce their level of discomfort, but also because there is a school there. The Mestizo families are much less inclined to this option because they don't have relatives in nearby communities and are not comfortable sending their children on the bus to a Garifuna school in Tornabé. Rather, the Mestizo boys are taught to hunt for fishbait and fish at an early age.

Territorial encroachment is a relatively non-traditional hazard, currently most clearly perceived by the Garifuna. They perceive it as being caused by Mestizo interests to either expand agricultural and fishing activities, or to exploit beaches and parks for tourism. The lands affected are considered traditional Garifuna space, making this an issue of cultural identity. While limitations on access to land are perceived by the Mestizo, they explain it with reference to their economic condition or identity: they are poor so cannot purchase the land they need.

The non-traditional hazard of deforestation, with diverse environmental consequences, was hardly mentioned as a problem by the villagers studied. However, some of this phenomena's consequences are perceived as hazards, such as the flooding of access roads because of sediment filled drainage ditches, the deep cutting of stream embankments because runoff is so heavy, and the depletion of a tree species or wildgame.

Another non-traditional hazard that appears poorly perceived by all informants is environmental contamination and litter or poor solid waste management. The inadequate disposal of trash was only related to the proliferation of malaria or dengue bearing mosquitoes. Pesticide poisoning was never mentioned as a danger, despite its widespread use in the African Palm plantations near Toloa Adentro or in the cultivated fields of Cangelica. The use of detergents and gasoline was never related to water quality, although salinity was (a traditional drinking water hazard in Miami).

CONCLUDING COMMENTS

All the social driving forces of environmental transformation are evident in Tela, and reflect sets of cultural adjustment strategies interacting to force environmental changes and resource degradation in complex ways. Similarities and differences in the political and economic structures of these rural villages in Tela influence the cultural assessment of risks associated with

America, (Ed.) M. Helms and F. Loveland. Philadelphia: Institute for the Study of Human Issues.

de Freitas, C.R. 1989. "The Hazard Potential of Drought for the Population of the Sahel," in *Population and Disaster*, Eds. J. Clarke, P. Curson, S. Kayastha and P. Nag. Oxford: Basil Blackwell.

Ellen, R. 1991. *Environment, Subsistence and System: The Ecology of Small-Scale Social Formations*. Cambridge: Cambridge University Press.

Emel, J. and R. Peet. 1989. "Resource Management and Natural Hazards," in *New Models in Geography: the Political Economy Perspective*, Eds. R. Peet and N. Thrift. Boston: Allen and Unwin.

Galvez, E. and D. Garcia. 1993. "Participación comunitaria y turismo ecosocial en Bahía de Tela." Proyecto de Desarrollo Turistico de Bahía de Tela. United Nations Development Program, Tegucigalpa, Honduras.

Glickman, T., D. Golding, and E. Silverman. 1992. "Acts of God and Acts of Man: Recent Trends in Natural Disasters and Major Industrial Accidents," Discussion Paper. Center for Risk Management 92-02. Washington: Resources for the Future.

Goudie, A. 1994. *The Human Impact on the Natural Environment*. Cambridge: MIT Press.

Grossman, L. 1992. "Pesticides, Caution and Experimentation in St. Vincent, Eastern Caribbean," *Human Ecology*, 20 (3): 315-36.

Hewitt, K. (Ed.) 1983. *Interpretations of Calamity From the Viewpoint of Human Ecology*. Boston: Allen and Unwin.

Hohenemser, C., R. Kates, and P. Slovic. 1985. "A Causal Taxonomy," in *Perilous Progress: Managing the Hazards of Technology*, (Eds.) R. Kates, C. Hohenemser and J. Kasperson. Boulder: Westview Press. pp. 67-90.

Kates, R. 1980. "Disaster Reduction: Links Between Disaster and Development," in *Making the Most of the Least: Alternative Ways to Development*, (Eds.) L. Berry and R. Kates. New York: Holmes and Meier.

Lees, S. and D. Bates. 1984. "Environmental Events and the Ecology of Cumulative Change: The Ecosystem Concept," in *Anthropology*, (Ed.) E. Moran. Boulder: Westview.

Little, P., M. Horowitz, and A. Nyerges. (Eds.) 1987. *Lands at Risk in the Third World: Local Level Perspectives*. Boulder: Westview.

Low, B. 1990. "Human Responses to Environmental Extremeness and Uncertainty: A Cross-Cultural Perspective, Risk and Uncertainty," in *Tribal and Peasant Economies*, Ed. E. Cashdan. Boulder: Westview.

Jelin, E. 1984. "Familia y Unidad Domestica: Mundo Privado y Vida Privada. Buenos Aires." Centro de Estudios de Estado y Sociedad (CEDES).

Johnson, K., E. Olson, and S. Manandhar. 1982. "Environmental Knowledge and Response to Natural Hazards in Mountainous Nepal," *Mountain Research and Development*, 2(2): 175-88.

Lavell, A. 1991. "Desastres naturales y zonas de riesgo: condicionantes y opciones para su prevención y mitigación." San José, Costa Rica: Confederación Universitaria Centroamericana.

_____. 1993. "Ciencias sociales y desastres naturales en America Latina: un encuentro inconcluso," *Los Desastres No Son Naturales*, (Ed.) A. Maskrey. Colombia: LA RED.

Mansilla, E. 1993. "Desastres y desarrollo en México," *Desastres y Sociedad*, 1 (1).

Mitchell, J. 1989. *Hazards Research, Geography in America*, (Eds.) G. Gaile and C. Willmott. Columbus: Merrill.

Moran, E. 1982. *Human Adaptability: An Introduction to Ecological Anthropology*. Boulder: Westview.

Ness, G. 1993. "The Long View: Population-Environment Dynamics in Historical Perspective," in *Population-Environment Dynamics: Ideas and Observations*. Eds. G. Ness, W. Drake and S. Brechin. Ann Arbor: University of Michigan.

NRC, 1992. *Global Environmental Change: Understanding the Human Dimension*, (Eds.) P. Stern, O. Young and D. Druckman, National Research Council. Washington, D.C.: National Academy Press.

Oliver-Smith, A. 1990. *The Martyred City: Death and Rebirth in the Andes. Prospect Heights*, Waveland Press.

Richerson, P. and R. Boyd. 1992. "Cultural Inheritance and Evolutionary Ecology," in *Evolutionary Ecology and Human Behavior*. Eds. E. Smith, B. Winterhalder. New York: Aldine de Gruyter.

Ruttan, V. and Y. Hayami. 1987. "Population Growth and Agricultural Productivity," in *Population Growth and Economic Development: Issues and Evidence*, Eds. D. Johnson, R. Lee. Madison: University of Wisconsin.

SECPLAN. 1989. *El Censo de Población y Vivienda*, 1988, Sctría. de Plan., Coordinación y Presupuesto, Tegucigalpa.

Stephens, D. 1990. *Risk and Incomplete Information in Behavioral Eecology, Risk and Uncertainty in Tribal and Peasant Economies*, Boulder: Westview.

Susman, P., P. O'Keefe, and B. Wisner. 1983. *Global Disasters, a Radical Interpretation, Interpretations of Calamity*

From the Viewpoint of Human Ecology, (Ed.) K. Hewitt, Allen and Unwin, London.

Watts, M. 1983a. *Silent Violence: Food, Famine and Peasantry in Northern Nigeria.* Berkeley: University of California.

_____ 1983b. *On the Poverty of Theory: Natural Hazards Research in Context, Interpretations of Calamity From the Viewpoint of Human Ecology*, Ed. K. Hewitt. Boston: Allen and Unwin.

Whitmore, T., B.L. Turner, D. Hohnson, R. Kates, and T. Gottschang. 1990. *Long-term Population Change, The Earth as Transformed by Human Action*, (Eds.) B.L. Turner, W. Clark, R. Kates., J. Richards, J. Matthews and W. Meyer. Cambridge: Cambridge University Press.

Wijkman, A. and L. Timberlake. 1984. *Natural Disasters: Acts of God or Acts of Man?* Washington, D.C.: International Institute of Environment and Development.

Wilches-Chaux, G. 1989. *La Vulnerabilidad Global, Desastres, Ecologismo y Formación Profesional.* Popoyan: Servicio Nacional de Aprendizaje.

Zuñiga Andrade, E. 1990. *Las Modalidades de la Lluvia en Honduras*. Tegucigalpa: Guaymuras.

TABLE 1. BIRTHPLACE OF RESIDENTS FROM FOUR VILLAGES IN TELA, 1988 ACCORDING TO MAJOR CLIMATIC ZONES IN HONDURAS

	Cangeliquita Arriba n = 319		Toloa Adentro n = 808		Triunfo de la Cruz n = 1968		Miami n = 93	
	#	%	#	%	#	%	#	%
Population < age 5*	60	18.8	158	19.6	365	18.5	18	19.4
Caribbean Coastal Zone[1]	193	60.5	512	63.4	1846	93.8	81	87.1
Central Zone[2]	48	15.0	172	21.3	122	6.2	12	12.9
Southern Zone[3]	78	24.5	124	15.3	0	0	0	0

[1]Includes municipalities primarily within the Caribbean Coastal Climate Zone (see accompanying map), having a very wet to wet climate year-round.

[2]Includes municipalities primarily within the Central Zone of Climatic Transition, having wet climates but dry summers, where rainfall often depends on altitude and aptitude.

[3]Includes municipalities primarily within the Southern Zone, having a rainy season but dry to very dry and occasionally long summers, and high evapotranspiration.

*Included in the analysis.

Sources: 1988 Population and House in Census, SECPLAN, Tegucigalpa, Honduras, Zuniga Andrade, Edgardo, 1990. Las Modalidades de la Lluvia en Honduras, Guaymuras, Tegucigalpa, Honduras.

TABLE 2. PERCEIVED HAZARD MATRIX MEXTIZO WOMEN INFORMANTS - TOLOA ADENTRO

Hazard	Risks	Responses
Heavy rains	crops ruined	seek food donations; co-ops make case to condone any bank debts
River rises out of channel	loss of land, loss of homes, personal injury, crops ruined, loss of animals, less fish in river to catch, roads close	seek temporary refuge on high ground; seek political support to channel river, stabilize banks, maintain bridges and roads
Illness	cost of medicines, not receiving health care, prolonged illness, death	seek establishment of health center nearby; seek donations of medicine
Diminished hunting	less income, less dietary diversity	get another dog for hunter, increase hunting effort
Lack of opportunities for youth because of land shortage	youth depend on parents for support, youth are unproductive	send sons and daughters to the U.S.A. to seek jobs and send money, etc. home; send to city to learn a trade
Shortage of land to purchase or rent	getting evicted from private property, having to settle in the floodplain (riverbed), not enough land to cultivate crops for subsistence and sale	settle on private but unused land; settle in floodplain, join an agricultural cooperative; move to another village

TABLE 3. PERCEIVED HAZARD MATRIX - MESTIZO WOMEN INFORMANTS - CANGELIQUITA ARRIBA

Hazard	Risks	Responses
Armageddon	chaos, death	prayer
Communism	loss of freedom	avoid strangers, don't trust politicians
Heavy rains, river rises out of banks, roads flood	loss of crops, loss of cattle, children drowning, transportation difficult	don't send children to school; Patronato seeks assistance from municipal authorities to maintain drainage ditches and bridges on access roads
Lack of local options for girls	get married or pregnant too young	send to school or job in town with relatives or friends; send to U.S.A. to seek jobs
Snakes	bites and death	massage and suck venom, prayer
Lack of medicines in health center	costly travel to purchase medicines	some use the common medicinals from plants; borrow money, barter, seek help from Patronato
Agricultural pests	loss of crops for sale and subsistence	apply pesticides

TABLE 4. PERCEIVED HAZARD MATRIX GARIFUNA WOMEN INFORMANTS - MIAMI

Hazard	Risks	Responses
Beach flies	bites, itching, scars, infections	stay in breezy or smoky areas; send children to live in Tornabé
Beach erosion	loss of territory	move when necessary
Low fish catch	less fish for consumption, less fish to sell, less time for other activities	increase level of fishing effort, find other sources of income, complain about illegal nets to park authorities
Low dietary diversity	boring meals	buy or trade fish for fruits and vegetables, maintain access to yuca fields in Tornabé
Few economic options (especially for youth)	underoccupation in non-productive activities, involvement in bad activities (crime, prostitution), and for young women getting pregnant too young	raise pigs, encourage education when economically possible, find options in cities with relatives, friends, have babies to get support from fathers.
Conjugal competition for resources	unhappy family members, loss of resources	maintain good relations with spouse
Lack of potable water	getting sick	bring water from Tornabé
Access to firewood	dependency on others, high cost of effort	good relations with spouse, sons and brothers with boats
Hurricanes and/or heavy rain	house damage, personal injury or loss of life	repair damage after; refuge in Tornabé
Territorial incursion by non-Garifuna	loss of access to resources (fish, fishing sites, fuel-wood)	stay neighborly; make them feel welcomed, move

TABLE 5. PERCEIVED HAZARD MATRIX - GARIFUNA WOMEN INFORMANTS - TRIUNFO DE LA CRUZ

Hazard	Risks	Responses
Low fish catch	less fish for consumption, less fish to sell, less time for other activities	increase level of fishing effort, seek fishing opportunities on big boats, or other economic options
Drought	fruit trees and chickens die, wells dry up	depend on relatives or neighbors for water
No space in cemetery	can't be buried in village, won't be properly remembered after death, burial in white cemetery, unhappy afterlife	complain to Patronato, request land from municipal authority, bury on top of others or on the beach
Snakes	deadly bites	go to fields with machete and shoes
Few opportunities for youth	underoccupation in non-productive activities; involvement in crime, drugs, promiscuity, prostitution and contracting AIDS; leaving home; getting pregnant too young (women)	send teens to school in Tela on bus; seek job in city; make and sell items for tourists; organize projects and seek support from institutions; send teens to U.S.A. to find jobs
Bad influence of tourists on youth	children learn bad habits (nude swimming, drug use, begging)	keep children away from beach, restaurants; organize to control tourism

(continued on next page)

Chapter Twenty Two

MIGRATION AND ENVIRONMENTAL CHANGE IN COSTA RICA SINCE 1950

ULI LOCHER

SOME THEORETICAL CONSIDERATIONS

If migration is a response to economic opportunity, then the economic development which has taken place in Costa Rica since World War II must have sparked some significant movement of population. Under a World Systems perspective the process can be summarized as follows. The economic growth in core nations creates both demand and political pressures in a peripheral economy struggling to profit from the expansion and globalization of markets. This penetration of the core into the periphery disrupts existing patterns of social and economic organization, displaces labor and creates a highly mobile population willing to accept the risks inherent in new economic opportunities. All three major models of migration analysis—World Systems, neoclassical and new economics of migration—would agree up to this point.[1]

The impact of these changes upon the physical environment happens in various forms and stages. The frontier phase probably has the most visible impact because the removal of tree coverage dramatically transforms the landscape. It is sometimes

[1]World systems theory focuses on migration as displacement of workers by globalization and the penetration of capitalist markets into less developed regions (Portes and Walton, 1981). Neoclassical economics emphasizes regional differences in income and opportunity as triggers of a migration aimed at establishing equilibrium between demand for and supply of workers (Todaro, 1969). The "new economics of migration" looks at imperfect markets and migration as an adaptive strategy reducing risks to individuals and families without, however, effecting structural change (Stark, 1991). Douglas Massey and his collaborators have conveniently summarized these and other models of migration analysis (Massey et al., 1993; 1994).

followed by a phase of peasant agriculture which may or may not give way to the establishment of large cattle ranches or plantations. These may then either preserve a certain permanency or go into decline, leaving behind eroded, depleted or chemically damaged land. Depending on which stage of the change we focus on, we may find attraction or expulsion of migrants and expanding or stagnating populations. Similarly, the stage of the change may determine the selection of migrants: landless peasants from nearby locations during the frontier phase and plantation workers from remote areas during the plantation phase.

The installation of highly capitalized plantations falls under the heading of agricultural modernization. One would expect this process to be instrumental in initiating migratory flows which subsequently can have cumulative effects: the closer the integration of displaced and newly attracted persons with the national economic, institutional and social networks, the higher their probability of searching for higher incomes in the emerging urban centers. As the earliest migration research already postulated that every migratory stream has its counterstream, so we can postulate today that migratory streams necessarily lead to other, parallel or subsequent, migrations.

As national integration advances we can expect cityward migration to accelerate, and with it urban primacy. Since export-oriented plantations free potential migrants without stimulating much secondary city growth, we face the apparent paradox that agricultural modernization can be a powerful cause of urbanization and increasing urban primacy. This argument has a correlate proposition for regional planners: promoting agricultural development as a means to reduce migration and urbanization is a mistake unless such promotion is explicitly aimed at small farmers and labor-intensive crops.

A number of empirical questions flowing out of these theoretical considerations will be addressed in this paper, such as:

- Has agricultural modernization created the strains and conditions precipitating new migratory flows? If so, has there been a simple cause-to-effect relationship or have there been conditions limiting its occurrence?

- Has the State played its role of mediating and channeling foreign penetration in such a way that national interests are best served? If so, is there evidence which links the State's role to particular economic and socio-demographic outcomes?

- Are there cycles of migration associated with cycles of foreign penetration? If so, are they best understood as neutral links between economic development and migration or as neo-colonial exploitation of national resources?

- Has migration played its traditional role of allocating manpower where it is needed and re-establishing a balance disturbed by the advent of foreign penetration and investment? If so, is the balance so established and adjusted sustainable?

These questions will guide the presentation of data and the verification of some aspects of World Systems theory.. They will not, however, change the character of the paper which will remain illustrative rather than analytical. There will be no systematic testing of propositions against those produced by competing theories, for two reasons. First, space limitations preclude such an ambitious enterprise. Second, the differences between various theories of migration are much more questions of historical perspective and level of analysis rather than evidence of truly competing visions of the world. It is thus only fitting that analysts presently try to find ways of integrating various theoretical approaches, following the lead of Massey and his collaborators (1993; 1994).

FACTORS IN MIGRATION AND ENVIRONMENTAL CHANGE: THE FRONTIER, BANANAS AND THE CITY

The Frontier

Migratory movements hardly ever have a single cause but in the Costa Rican case the major factors can easily be seen. The first one, the frontier, refers "to the division between settled and unsettled regions of the state," it implies "a transition zone which stretches inward from the boundary and merges imperceptibly with the state core."[2] The state has been active in the clearing and settlement of frontier land. It passed laws in 1909, 1924 and 1934 allowing all citizens to claim public lands. Even better, in 1942 it passed the *Ley de poseedores en precario* which de facto legalized all squatting, giving squatters title to even privately owned land and allowing landowners compensation out of land held in the public domain. All three parties involved loved these arrangements. The state viewed them as expedient and politically less controversial than land reform measures. The large landowners saw them as a means to avert effective land reforms and an opportunity to expand and round off their holdings. Peasants and landless squatters were offered safe and peaceful access to land. Later, two institutions were founded to regulate frontier settlement: the Instituto de Tierras y Colonización (ITCO, 1962) and the Instituto de Desarrollo Agrario (IDA, 19**).[3]

Whatever the political merits of these generous policies, their effects were disastrous for the environment. Great expanses of public land were lost, and since the proof of occupation was always defined as the removal of trees, large parts of the coun-

---

[2]Prescott (1965) as quoted in Shrestna et al. (1993: 788).

[3]Porras and Villareal (1986) put much emphasis on the legal and institutional causes of deforestation without, however, establishing links with agricultural practices.

try's forest cover were destroyed.[4] Much of the land opened up this way was not put into crop production but was either abandoned or used for cattle grazing. The resulting soil erosion, especially in the hillsides, is now visible everywhere, especially in parts of San Carlos and Guanacaste (Figure 1).

A much more positive picture emerges in those frontier lands which were converted to coffee cultivation. The combination of coffee, a labor-intensive perennial crop, and shade trees —and the frequent use of sugar cane to cover the hilltops at least in some areas of the Meseta Central—had the effect of simultaneously protecting the soil from physical erosion and providing work for many times more people than did the cattle farms. Consequently, deforestation can have quite drastically different demographic impacts according to the auspices under which it happened and the land use eventually resulting from it.[5]

---

[4]Two financial incentives appear to have played a major role in the disaster that befell the forest: Forested state land was considered as waiting for the "improvement" of tree removal and was therefore priced at two colones per hectare while good land an absentee owner had lost to squatters could be priced at up to 1000 colones (ITCO, n.d.: 7). No wonder there are stories going around of landowners having invited squatters to occupy a small plot in order to exchange it for a plot up to five hundred times its size. The second incentive consisted in payments made by the public purse for "improvement" of land, either in cash or in tax write-offs. Both of these incentives make it clear that the cash value of tropical hardwood timber was a negligible factor in the destruction of the forests; most trees were simply burned.

[5]This summary is meant to contrast coffee cultivation with simple destruction of the forest cover: conventional coffee production is much less physically damaging than the combination of cattle farming and annual burning of hillsides. However, conventional coffee production does cause significant damage because chemical inputs poison soils and rivers. Organic coffee farming is both more sustainable and - surprise! - financially more rewarding (see the excellent study by Boyce et al., 1994).

Bananas[6]

Bananas will grow almost anywhere in Costa Rica but the great plantations producing for export need good soils, flat land, much water, good drainage and hot temperatures. The coastal plains along the Atlantic offer these conditions. They were taken over, starting 1899, by the United Fruit company and a few minor competitors. By 1913, UFCO already held large portions of a stretch 220 km long and 30 km wide along the Atlantic coast, over 100,000 hectares in the district of Limón alone. Within a few decades, however, soils were depleted and plant disease, the inevitable companion of monoculture, made production unprofitable. Starting in 1938 the company moved its operations to the Pacific coast, leaving behind bad land and most of its Jamaican workforce.[7]

While the demographic effects of banana cultivation were more sudden and spectacular, the environmental effects appear to have been less marked than those of the frontier. The frontier is by definition not sustainable; it has left much of the country denuded of forest cover and exposed to highly visible physical erosion. Banana cultivation is, at least theoretically, sustainable.[8] But such appearances are hard to substantiate. The fact that visible scars of soil erosion are largely absent in banana regions is attributable to the topography alone. To my knowledge there have been no complete, quantitative evaluations yet of the financial and environmental cost of chemical use in banana cultivation.

---

[6]Araya (1982) contains a useful summary of the economic history of Costa Rica; his sections on bananas are an important source here. See also: Bourgeois (1994), Acuna and Molina (1991) and, Howard and Hoadley (1990).

[7]The highly visible minority population was legally restricted to Limón province for many decades.

[8]Excessive and careless use of pesticides has caused damage both among the workforce and on some soils. However, today's operations are more careful and apparently no less profitable.

In addition, indirect environmental effects derived from the rapid increase in population and hillside farming around the plantations also should not be overlooked entirely.

Urbanization

All Central American countries have urbanized rapidly since 1950 and the proportion of the population in urban areas has reached levels between roughly 40% and 60% in 1990. Costa Rica ranks third with a population which is 47% urban. The role of migration in such urban development is well known but sometimes exaggerated. Rural-urban migration directly explains only 15% of the increase in Costa Rican urbanization 1960-1980, only 17% of the increase 1965-1990.[9] Nevertheless, the absolute numbers are impressive, especially when combined with the evidence on interregional migration. A very significant shift in the distribution of population is taking place, favoring the urban center of the country and increasing its dominance ever more.

Urban pull factors have certainly played a major role in stimulating migration since the 60s. Import substitution industries, Free Trade Zones, the rapidly expanding state apparatus and public payroll, the urban concentration of governmental, economic and educational institutions and other factors have created a disproportionate number of urban jobs. However, rural push factors have been significant, even dominant according to some authors (Brown and Lawson, 1985; Schneider-Sliva and Brown, 1985). These rural push factors are a lack of non-agricultural employment, the low labor demand of cattle farms, soil depletion and erosion and the drastic fluctuation in labor demand according to the boom and bust cycles of coffee and ba-

[9]Kingsley Davis (1965) first proposed a simple method for disaggregating the relative contribution of migration and natural increase to urbanization by alternatively holding each factor constant. This method is used here without arbitrarily attributing the unexplained residual portion to either side.

nanas which create periodic misery among large numbers of landless rural workers.

One could be tempted to exclude urban bias (in Lipton's terms) from the list of causes of rural misery and cityward migration in Costa Rica. This is, after all, a country which can pride itself on having more rural services, distributive justice and transfer payments than any of its neighbors, as well as frontier policies and plantation employment stimulating rural-directed migration. All of these points may be true but they are hardly convincing upon closer inspection. The banana enclaves have produced good incomes for the major companies but they have not caused much rural development. Even the agricultural modernization which they represent is quite irrelevant outside the enclaves. The frontier has self-destruction built-in and the coverage of rural areas by government services and institutions is far from what cities have received. The classic urban bias argument still applies: the cumulation of urban advantages leaves the hinterland ever farther behind. The urban primacy score is there to prove it: at 71.4 it is more than double the Central American median and its increase correlates closely with the urban industrial development of the past decades.[10]

Rapid urban growth has severe environmental consequences in the city itself, its immediate surroundings and the downstream parts of its watershed. However, its principle environmental effects are indirect. Urban dominance feeds to some extent on rural poverty, and rural poverty causes indiscriminate deforestation, farming on steep slopes and other survival strategies buying short-term individual gain at a long-term cost to the collectivity. This link between rural disadvantage, poverty, un-

[10]Primacy in this context refers to the percentage of the total urban population residing in the largest city according to World Bank (1992). The next-scoring country is Nicaragua at 43.2. Primacy growth since 1970 has been positive in Costa Rica, Nicaragua and El Salvador, negative in Guatemala, Honduras and Panama.

sustainable resource use, soil erosion and migration is all too obvious even in the Costa Rican case; it is the basis of much recent thinking on sustainable development (Brenes Castillo, 1989; Bilsborow and DeLargy, 1991; Leonard, 1989; Hedstrom, 1993).[11]

THE MAJOR MIGRATION STREAMS IN COSTA RICA SINCE 1900

Compared to many other Latin American countries, Costa Rica had a relatively quiet 19th century, as it moved from colonial to independent status, built up a coffee economy and expanded its population. The fateful event happened at the turn of the century with the merger of the two rival banana producers into the United Fruit Company which established a banana monopoly throughout Central America - but nowhere more complete than in Costa Rica. Many major migration streams over the next six decades were related to the production of bananas in what may have been the first country referred to, in derogatory terms, as "banana republic."

The 1927 census is the first to document lifetime migration of the Costa Rican population. At this time, the major migration streams[12] mostly involve the Meseta Central, the high valley where population has been concentrated since colonial days; this is where the centripetal migration to the frontier originated. However, there are three exceptions: Guanacaste province received significant in-migration from neighboring Alajuela, as did Puntarenas province. Most importantly, the thinly populated *Limón* province (with a population of less than 10,000) counted only 28% natives. This provides Limón with the spec-

---

[11]Section 5.4 of this paper will demonstrate empirically the relations between rural poverty, non-sustainable resource use (in the form of rapid deforestation), and migration.

[12]Only interprovincial migration can be calculated for 1927 since the birthplace question referred to province rather than canton.

tacular in-migration rate of 71.7% and a net rate of 65.1%. Where did these individuals originate? The census shows that they were drawn from all other provinces and even from abroad (Censo 1950: 66). Impressive as they are, these figures still represent conservative estimates since most plantationworkers are likely to have been temporary residents excluded from the census[13] (Figure 2).

By the time of the 1950 census Costa Rica had grown to over 800,000 inhabitants. The numerically strongest interprovincial migration streams still involved the Meseta Central where San José province received major in-migration from neighboring provinces Alajuela, Cartago and Heredia. Limón again stands out with 55% in-migrants many of whom by now must have been long-term residents of the province. The most remarkable new element in the 1950 census, however, is the emergence of *Puntarenas* province as a most attractive destination just as Limón had been a generation earlier[14] (Figure 3).

The 1963 census is the first to suggest a more precise definition of recent migration streams (as opposed to the lifetime migration given for 1927 and 1950).[15] It allows us to distinguish two very different types of rural-destined migration. The first one is directed at Golfito canton and contains migrants from many distant locations reacting to the demand for manpower on

---

[13]The 1927 census data used here are included in Tables I, XVIII and XIX of the 1950 census publication. The first of these contains the corrected figures while the later tables present the original figures, before correction. Overall the table I figures correct for undercounting in the order of 10.3% but in the case of Limón province, the correction involved 123.8% or 22,308 individuals; most of them presumably were plantation workers and their dependents.

[14]Undercounting of plantation workers appears to be less of a problem in 1950. The correction for the Limón and Puntarenas populations is only 18% and 9%, respectively.

[15]The CSUCA study does this by using two questions from the census: previous residence and length of residence at present location.

the newly established plantations. Some of these workers actually come from Aguirre where banana plantations had gone into decline. The second type of migration is directed at the expanding frontier in Pérez Zeledón, Bagaces, San Carlos and Grecia;[16] such frontier migration consists of short-distance moves from neighboring cantons.

In 1973 the census makes Costa Rica most closely resemble other Latin American countries. Urbanization is advancing at a fast pace[17] and it is the urban centers of the Meseta Central, and their emerging suburbs, which attract most migrants. The San José Metropolitan Area (SJMA) is draining surrounding cantons of their human capital. As far as rural-destined migration is concerned, banana plantations again are the major attractions, drawing migrants from distant locations to the Atlantic regions. Although numerically inferior to cityward migration, the pull of the newly expanding plantations is spectacular: the Huetar Norte and Huetar Atlántica regions have (five year) immigration rates of 32.4% and 19.1%, respectively.

The 1984 census, like its predecessor, uses a methodology more responsive to recent migratory changes.[18] It shows a proportional decline of migration;[19] even the absolute numbers of migrants involved are smaller than in 1973. Urbanization is still the dominant trend but the SJMA has changed from a net winner to a net loser while the wider Metropolitan Agglomeration is making the most significant progress. Rural-destined migration is still important but the spectacular migration rates of the 60s and 70s are now a thing of the past (Figures 4).

---

[16]Within Grecia, the migration goes mainly to the areas near the Nicaraguan border, causing population increases which later lead to the foundation of three cantons there: Upala, Los Chiles and Guatuso.

[17]Urbanization increased from 34% in 1963 to 41% in 1973.

[18]These two censuses are the first to use the "residence five years previously" question.

[19]The proportion of intercantonal movers decreased from 10.3% in 1973 to 7.1% in 1984.

The major migration streams of this century can be summarized in the following way. For many decades there has been a significant amount of frontier migration, which has gradually pushed back the forests in virtually all cantons. This migration has been steady and appears to finally have reached a plateau. Secondly, there have been great spurts of migration to the plantations. This form of labor migration has been so sudden that it has led to spectacular immigration rates in the three regions affected. Only the recent diversification of agricultural production has reduced the importance of the country's banana-driven demography. Finally, there has been an accelerating rural-urban migration which has increased the dominance of the Meseta Central and its Metropolitan Agglomeration. Generally speaking, the significant migrations of the past have been to peripheral regions while those of the present are directed towards the country's center, but the following section will show just how hazardous such generalizations can be (Table 1).

THE CRISIS OF 1981

After two decades of strong growth since 1960, the Costa Rican economy went into a deep recession in 1981 and 1982. Real wages fell by 26%, unemployment more than doubled and the number of families living below the poverty line increased by 50% to almost one million (in 1983).[20] As it became evident that the preceding boom years had been financed to a large extent by government borrowing, the Monge administration did not have much choice but to apply the IMF prescribed remedy. Government was reduced by 25%, the foreign debt was re-

[20]Data on the various indicators are presented by Tardanico (1993), Cruz et al. (1992), Portes et al. (1994); see also Fallas, 1993. While there are some questions of comparability, there can be no doubt about the severity of the crisis.

financed and the economy was "structurally adjusted" by, among other things, a 80% devaluation of the currency.[21]

The crisis brought about a dramatic change in migration patterns. As buying power and employment in the cities declined, urban destinations became much less attractive to migrants. As rural poverty[22] spread rapidly, the Frontier became again a place where the landless could eke out a living as long as there was forest to be harvested. Invadable lands became prime targets once again. Aggregate analysis does not provide sufficient detail but even at the cantonal level we observe a connection between rapid loss of tree cover and strong immigration (e.g., in Guatuso and Los Chiles; see Table A-1 in the annex).

Cantonal level analysis[23] points to the rapidity of some of the recent changes. The net migration rates given in Table A-2 show that the frontier reached Grecia some time before 1963, then collapsed during the following decade, with the cantonal net rate going from +4.5 to -67.4. The cattle farms expanded in San Carlos before 1963, in La Cruz and Hojancha before 1973, with net migration rates in the latter cases exceeding 60. Banana plantations followed the frontier in Aguirre before 1950 and in Sarapiqui just before 1973. In 1984 the evidence is that the frontier is strongly advancing in Barva, Santa Bárbara, San Pablo

---

[21]The 1960 to 1980 period had seen strong industrial growth (from 14.6% to 18.3% of GDP) but also even stronger growth of the public sector (from 9.0% to 15.0%). The principal agricultural exports (bananas, coffee, pineapples and beef) were all vulnerable as the western economies went into recession. Nevertheless, Costa Rica came out of the crisis faster and stronger than most of its neighbors.

[22]Only much later did rural poverty become a dominant political issue (Government of Costa Rica, 1991; Ministerio de Planificación, 1991; Fallas, 1993).

[23]The fact that newly created cantons in 1973 show spectacularly high net migration rates is no doubt partly due to the way in which the census handled migration. Nevertheless, the need to create new cantons in itself is an expression of a rapid influx of new populations.

and Buenos Aires and on the Nicaraguan border. The immigration to Limón province is connected with a recovery in banana production and does not necessarily imply clearing new lands.

District-level analysis allows more precise observations. As the following table shows, virtually all of the squatters who received land settlements 1979-1984 had moved into areas which in 1966 still had more than 50% tree cover. Even among the IDA-sponsored settlements we find that over three quarters of the settlers moved into those formerly forested areas. As far as the environment is concerned, this represents a great deterioration compared with the situation at the previous census.

Table 2 shows that during the years of crisis, the forest increased its role as the target of frontier settlement. Over the 1968-73 period only 3113 settlers (33.7%) ended up in districts with more than 50% forest cover but 11 years later the numbers increased to over 25000 (58.7%).[24] All this excludes the thousands of squatters whose position has not been regularized by an IDA settlement. The table also shows the rapid deterioration of forest cover in Costa Rica over the 18 year period: the number of settlers in the highest category of forest cover is cut in half—not because they moved but because, with their help, so much of the forest was cleared.

The great increase in IDA settlements—to the point that in 1979-1984 they amounted to over 40% of all rural-destined migration—is not a surprise in Costa Rican political history. It fits well with the various colonization and squatting laws which have been so effective during this century. What is unusual, however, is that all these laws, as well as the recent IDA spon-

---

[24]These numbers are necessarily approximations since the forest cover maps were not drawn in 1968 and 1979, but in 1966 and 1984. Also, the numbers of settlers had to be made comparable to the census migration tables which contain only individuals five years and older. Since the zero to four year age group makes up close to 10% of the population, these numbers are conservative estimates.

sored settlements, have put the emphasis on clearing trees rather than on true settlement and conversion to agriculture. Squatters can be legally recognized after occupying land for as little as six months and having cut only a part of the trees. They are then free to sell not so much the land as the "mejora," i.e. the improvement they have made on it by cutting trees. The buyer of this mejora can then receive legal title. There have been professional squatters who have treated parcel after parcel in this way, providing ever more land for land-hungry—and subsidized—cattle farmers. "In Costa Rica migrants have degraded marginal lands not so much by farming them, as by clearing them, selling their 'improvements', and moving on to repeat the process" (Cruz et al., 1992: 67).

If we generalize from the situation around the crisis years of 1981-1982, we can state that the central region (region codes 1, 2 and 3 in Table A-1) is shifting the weight of its population from the Metropolitan Area to more rural districts; that the Chorotega region (essentially Guanacaste province) is showing some recovery but still losing migrants; that the banana cantons are still acting as magnets and, that there are a number of rural cantons, mainly those close to the Nicaraguan border, which show evidence of increasing frontier settlement. Much of the crisis-driven settlement is directed at forested land. The country pays a heavy price in land and forest resources for the ill-advised policies preceding the crisis and those supposed to alleviate it.

THE PRESENT SITUATION

The Frontier

There are no new data comparable to the 1984 census. However, since the renewal of frontier settlement was so obviously crisis-driven, it is safe to assume that it has somewhat abated. Such episodes may well occur again. Continued population increase, illegal immigration and non-application of laws protecting the environment make it unlikely that the frontier will come to halt soon.

Public land has not been available for homesteading since 1968; the pattern of squatters' taking over good virgin land and becoming owners simply by staking it out is no longer a problem. Both the IDA-sponsored land reform and the movements of squatters are now almost exclusively directed at poor land.[25] This is, however, precisely how most of the damage is done: poor land is by definition located on steep, easily erodable slopes. In environmental terms, the official land reform policy, even after the changes made in 1968, is still counter-productive.

Population density in rural Costa Rica is still low which means that much forest land is waiting to be conquered. The technique of this conquest has not changed. The professional squatters continue to advance one or two steps a year, selling their "land improvement" to finance their meager survival, and "relatively few people are required to cause a great deal of deforestation."[26]

Bananas

Costa Rica continues to be one of the world's top banana producers.[27] In 1994, 1.9 million metric tons were sold, up by 2.2% of 1993. Rapid changes in the geographic location of the production centers remains typical, e.g., production in Osa canton almost tripled over that one year, which represented the en-

---

[25]The World Resources Institute study shows that while the proportion of settlers directed to poor and very poor soil areas has decreased from 1968-73 to 1979-84 (from 93% to 71%), their number has actually increased (from 8,844 to 30,988); see Cruz et al., 1992:11.

[26]Harrison (1991: 91), as quoted by Cruz et al. (1992: 48).

[27]Banana production is volatile. In 1913 Costa Rica already drew even with Jamaica, the then number one producer, but by 1929 Honduras exported five times more than Costa Rica. In 1965 Costa Rica ranked eleventh among the world's producers, but only five years later it ranked second (Araya Pochet, 1982).

tire increase of national production over that period.[28] If new census data were available, Table A-1 would probably show Osa to have strongly positive net migration on the order of 10%-15%.

Recent data in a different banana canton is now available thanks to a survey[29] carried out in 1994 in Puerto Viejo de Sarapiqui. It shows an astonishing level of migratory activity. Carried out among a sample of the local CCSS clinic's clientele, the survey found that only 16% of the respondents had been born in the canton, and more than half had arrived less than five years ago. Large-scale in-migration appears to continue: 26% of the sample arrived over the last two years. Three out of every ten respondents were Nicaraguan by origin (see Table 3).

All of the available evidence points to the probability that banana plantations will continue to be one of the key determinants of migration in Costa Rica. Much of that particular migration appears to consist of immigrants from Nicaragua, a neighboring country with much lower standards of living. Inequality does not explain everything but it is truly the mother of migration.

Urbanization

There is every indication that urbanization continues to advance rapidly, despite the official under-estimates published

---

[28]Statistics taken from the 1994 export statistics of the Corporación Bananera Nacional (CORBANA), as reported by *La Nación*, 5 April 1995.

[29]Special thanks to Andrew Scyner for his help in collecting this data. Size of the primary sample: n=758. A secondary sample containing all members of the households of the primary sample respondents comprised 3,352 individuals. In the absence of census information since 1984, some agencies are now resorting to local health clinics' clientele statistics in order to estimate local population sizes.

twice per year.[30] The example of the district of Pavas is illustrative. In 1984 this district had 18,068 inhabitants which the census bureau extrapolated to 43,341 in 1993. According to a census carried out by the local clinic, the population stands at over 79,000 in 1995. Similar increases have been documented in many parts of the Metropolitan Area and have given rise to a score of publications on urban subsistence (Pérez Sainz, 1990), the informal sector (Trejos, 1989), social housing (Mora and Solano, 1994) and class segregation (Lungo et al., 1992).

One of the effects of the increasing urban dominance is that the fragility of economic development typical of export-specialized rural regions is now felt increasingly in the national capital. Economic downturns are translated into urban unemployment since the Free Trade Zones react almost instantly to international fluctuations, e.g., in the volatile textile and electronics sectors. It would be premature to claim that the country derided as a banana republic has now matured into a *maquiladora* republic, but it is no doubt engaged in this direction. Whether this will result in higher levels of unemployment, increased stratification and rapid growth of *tugurios* is anyone's guess. Portes and Lungo have launched a major research initiative around this hypothesis but so far the quantitative proof of such a development has not been given.

As the urban proportion of the population exceeds the benchmark of 50% we can expect urban push and pull factors to be increasingly dominant among the determinants of internal migration. The environmental consequences of this development are not clear. Should the urban political elite succeed in furthering globalization strategies, agricultural producers may end up as losers which could accelerate migration both to the expanding frontier and to the city. However, all regimes here since 1947

---

[30]The bulletins published by the Dirección General de Estadística y Censos consist of simple projection of 1984 census data taking into account only vital data while ignoring migration.

have been populist and it is quite likely that farmers will continue to benefit from governmental largesse. "Sin finqueros no hay comida"[31] is a powerful slogan, especially at election time.

Poverty, Migration, and Deforestation

Few studies have demonstrated more than intuitively the relationship between rural poverty, migration and the loss of natural resources. In Costa Rica, this relationship can be shown to exist by combining census population data with data on deforestation.

Table 4 demonstrates the relationship between poverty level and forest cover. The poorest cantons are those which in 1960 had the most complete forest cover (73%) while the cantons with the lowest level of poverty are those with the lowest level of forest cover (28%). What is really surprising in the table is the link between this result and the net migration rates. It is precisely the most forested and poorest cantons which proved to be most attractive to migrants. This seems to contradict prevailing migration theory which can be stated simply as predicting migration streams from poorer to more prosperous areas. Our findings suggest that such theory should be reformulated. What functions as magnet for migrants is not so much prosperity as such as economic opportunity. The frontier of tropical forest offers opportunities which can be compared to those found in the cities of the Meseta Central or in the banana plantations for the coastal plains. However, the character of the opportunities changes over time; once a population of recent migrants is established it will face a rapidly changing opportunity structure. Urban industry and the agro-industry of plantations continue to produce added value and can maintain viable regional economies. The frontier is different: it resembles a short-lived mining opera-

[31]"Without plantation owners there is no food"

tion in that its resources (wood and top soil) will inevitably become exhausted over time.

CONCLUSION

Costa Rica has undergone an amount of agricultural modernization unprecedented and unmatched anywhere else in the region. The bulk of this modernization has occurred in a small number of export crops, bananas and coffee prominently among them. It has been foreign-planned, foreign financed and successful. It has created a concentrated demand for labor in selected areas of the country, and the response has been so strong that its reflection in the national censuses has been of a rare clarity. Migration to the banana plantations has been as strong and visible in 1994 as it had been before 1927. What has been equally obvious at both periods is that national boundaries are quite irrelevant once the economic conditions are right and that, therefore, the distinction of internal and international migration is an arbitrary one. Jamaican immigrants made up the majority of the population of Limón province in 1927 just as Nicaraguans form a strong minority in some banana districts of the Huetar Norte today. If the high levels of agricultural productivity are truly impressive, it should not be overlooked that they are the result not only of installing mechanized and "chemical agriculture" but also of the prevalence of child labor in coffee and foreign labor in bananas. With such limitations in mind we can accept the existence of a strong and direct causal link between foreign penetration, agricultural development and migration.

The Costa Rican State has been a strong promoter of foreign penetration in agriculture and its demographic side-effect, migration. From the concessions made to the United Fruit Company in 1899 to the negotiations of the most recent banana accords with the European Union, there has been an uninterrupted stream of measures taken to assure continued banana exports. Since 1947, the State's actions were two-pronged. On the one hand, foreign companies could act with near-complete freedom. On the other hand, a number of populist policies assured the military and social peace essential to the continued presence of the multinationals. One of these policies is embodied in a series of squatters' laws and agrarian reform measures designed to conquer the forests and push ahead the agricultural frontier. These laws have proven fateful for the country as development tools and as socio-political safety valves. Numerically speaking, frontier migration may well have been the dominant form of migration in this century, and the State's role and complicity in its promotion is beyond doubt.

Poverty and population growth are linked in a cycle of cumulative causation.[32] The evidence presented here strongly suggests that the cycle should be enlarged to comprise the environmental degradation we are witnessing in many countries today. However, other elements should be included as conditions, such as income inequality, land concentration and central government policies. Peasant squatters will not usually destroy their own land but land which is not, and most likely will never be, theirs. Secure tenure is the best protection of agricultural land, but it must be established in a context which allows smallholders to keep their land.[33]

The association of migratory cycles and cycles of foreign penetration is an intuitive one at best. With the exception of some instances of expansion and relocation in the banana sector, it is impossible to prove a close correlation of foreign investment and internal migration because the necessary data does not exist. The one instance where we can do more than just speculate is the adaptation to the crisis of 1981-82 but even there the renewed

---

[32]Keyfitz, 1990, as quoted by Cruz (1992:2).

[33]In theory, the Costa Rican government's IDA has clearly recognized this condition and has long offered a combination of legalization of titles and agricultural credit to make peasants less likely victims of price fluctuations and natural catastrophe.

migration to the internal frontier is related to poverty, and conditional upon a particular policy, rather than being the direct result of falling foreign investment. What is certain is that in either of the two examples - bananas and the frontier - it would be quite inappropriate to speak simply of neo-colonial exploitation of national human resources. The problems are largely homegrown.

Costa Rica's open economy and integration into international markets have made it easy for migration to play the adaptive role it so often does. As long as the population was predominantly rural and much uninhabited land was available, the mechanism could function as smoothly as anywhere else. It is not by accident that. Costa Rica has long held the world record in forest clearing.[34] A combination of pro-frontier legislation and non-enforcement of environmental protection laws have made the government into the principal accomplice in the environmental destruction we are currently witnessing. Costa Rica has thus become a model of the process deplored by World Systems analysts: the combination of foreign investment, soft state and free migration results in short-term advantages for all. The longer-term cost, presently born by the environment, is now starting to become apparent in productivity declines of hillside agriculture. Migration again is bound to be the mechanism by which the country will adjust to an increasing scarcity of good land. In the end, the net transfer will be one of rural resources to the city, with large long-term costs born by rural areas and large profits being made by cities, directly or as extensions of foreign interests.

ACKNOWLEDGEMENTS

I am grateful for the support received from the Social

[34]Seven percent of total forested area were cleared every year since the 1960s, according to the World Resources Institute. The quality of this information is somewhat uncertain although the magnitude of the deforestation cannot be doubted.

Sciences and Humanities Council of Canada, as well as the help of Andrew Scyner who conducted the survey in Puerto Viejo de Sarapiqué.,.

REFERENCES

Ortega, A., V. Hugo, and I. Molina Jiménez. 1991. *Historia Económica y Social de Costa Rica (1750 - 1950)*. San José: Editorial Porvenir.

Araya Pochet, C. 1982. *Historia económica de Costa Rica*. San José: Editorial Fernández Arce.

Banco Mundial. 1992. *Informe sobre el Desarrollo Mundial*. Washington, D.C.: World Bank.

Bilsborrow, R.E. and P.F. DeLargy. 1991. "Land Use, Migration and Natural Resource Deterioration: the Experience of Guatemala and the Sudan," in: Davis, Kingsley and Mikhail S. Bernstam (eds.), *Resources, Environment and Population: Present Knowledge, Future Options*. New York: Oxford University Press.

Bourgois, P. 1994. *Banano, Etnia y Lucha Social en Centroamérica*. San José: DEI.

Boyce, J.K. et al. 1994. *Café y Desarrollo Sostenible: del cultivo agroquímico a la producción orgánica en Costa Rica*. San José: Editorial Fundación UNA.

Brenes Castillo, C. 1989. "Desarrollo forestal campesino?" In: Hedstrom, Ingemar (ed.) *La situación ambientál en Centroamerica y el Caribe*, San José: DEI, Pp. 163-174.

Brown, L.A. and V.A. Lawson. 1985. Rural-destined migration in Third World settings: a neglected phenomenon? *Regional Studies*, 19(5): 415-432.

Censo de población de Costa Rica 1950 n.d. San José: Dirección General de Estadística y Censos

Censo de población 1963. 1966 San José: Dirección General de Estadística y Censos

Censos Nacionales de 1973: Población. n.d. San José: Dirección General de Estadística y Censos

Censo de población 1984. 1986 San José: Ministerio de Gobernación y Policía.

Centro de Ciencias Tropicales. 1995. Archivo de datos sobre la cobertura boscosa de Costa Rica.

CSUCA: Programa Centroamericano de Ciencias Sociales. 1978. *Estructura Demográfica y Migraciones Internas en Centroamérica.* Editorial Universitaria Centroamérica

Cruz, M.C. et al. 1992. *Population Growth, Poverty, and Environmental Stress. Frontier Migration in the Philippines and Costa Rica.* New York: World Resources Institute.

Davis, K. 1965. "The Urbanization of the Human Population." In: Geral Breese (ed.), *The City in Newly Developing Countries. Englewood Cliffs: Prentice Hall*, 1969: 5-20.

Fallas, H. 1993. *Centroamérica: Pobreza y Desarrollo Rural ante la Liberalización Económica.* San José: Instituto Interamericano de Cooperación para la Agricultura (IICA).

Flores, E. 1992. *Geografía de Costa Rica.* San José: Editorial Universidad Estatal a Distancia.

Fundación Guilombé. 1993. *Ambiente: Legalidad o violación en Costa Rica.* San José: Fundación Guilombé.

Gobierno de Costa Rica. 1991. *Costa Rica: Zonas de Mayor y Menor Desarrollo Relativo.*

Gomez, V. and U. Locher. 1995. "Evolución global de la mortalidad, la fecundidad y la migración" en: Gomez, Victor (ed.), *Actualidad Demografica de Costa Rica 1994.* San José: Universidad de Costa Rica, Programa Centroamericano de Población.

Harrison, S. 1991. Population Growth, Land Use and Deforestation in Costa Rica, 1950-1984. *InterCiencia* 16.2: 83-93.

Hedstrom, I. 1993. *Somos parte de un gran equilibrio*. San José: DEI.

Howard, A. and K. Hoadley. 1990. "Estudio de caso: La industria bananera en Costa Rica," en Artavia L., Roberto y Edward L. Felton, Jr., *Agroindustria en Centroamérica: Respuesta al Cambio*. San José: Libro Libre, 35-58.

Instituto de Tierras y Colonización (ITCO) 1988 Información General.

Keyfitz, N. 1990. "Population Growth Can Prevent the Development That Would Slow Population Growth." Laxenburg, Austria: Population Programme, International Institute for Applied Systems.

La Nación. 1995. (19 de marzo) Emergencia ... zona urbana.

_____. 1995. (5 de abril) $560 millones dejó exportación bananera.

Leonard, J. and Contributors. 1989. *Environment and the Poor: Development Strategies for a Common Agenda*. New Brunswick (USA): Transaction Books.

Locher, U. 1995. Puerto Viejo de Sarapiquí Survey: Unpublished Data.

Lungo, M. et al. 1992. "La Urbanización en Costa Rica en los 80," en: Portes, Alejandro y Mario Lungo, *Urbanizatión en Centroamérica*. San José: FLACSO, pp. 37-188.

Massey, D. S. et al. 1993. "Theories of International Migration: A Review and Appraisal." *Population and Development Review*, 19(3): 431-466.

_____. 1994. "An Evaluation of International Migration Theory: the North American Case." *Population and Development Review*, 20(4): 659-751.

Ministerio de Planificación Nacional y Política Económica. 1991. *Pobreza Rural en Costa Rica: Análisis Comparativo a Nivel Cantonal*, 1973-1984

Mora, M. and F. Solano. 1994. *Nuevas Tendencias del Desarrollo Urbano en Costa Rica*. San José: Ed. Alma Mater.

Pérez Sáinz, J.P. 1990. *Ciudad, subsistencia e informalidad. (Tres estudios sobre el Area Metropolitana de Guatemala)*. Guatemala: FLACSO.

Porras, A. and B. Villareal. 1993. *Desforestación en Costa Rica. Implicaciones sociales, económicas y legales*. San José: Editorial Costa Rica.

Portes, A. and J. Walton. 1981. *Labor, Class and the International System*. New York: Academic Press.

Portes, A., et al. 1994. "Urbanization in the Caribbean Basin: Social Change during the Years of the Crisis." *Latin American Research Review*, 29(2): 3-37.

Prescott, J. R. V. 1965. *The Geography of Frontiers and Boundaries*. Chicago: Aldine.

Schneider-Sliva, R. and L.A. Brown. 1986. "Rural-nonfarm Employment and Migration: Evidence from Costa Rica." *Socio-economic Planning Science*, 20(2): 79-93.

Shrestha, N.R., R.P. Velu and D. Conway. 1993. Frontier Migration and Upward Mobility: the Case of Nepal. *Economic Development and Cultural Change*, pp. 787-817.

Sojo, A. 1987. "Actual dinámica socioeconómica costarricense y las opciones de desarrollo sociales en el ocaso del siglo XX." *Revista Documental de Ciencias Sociales Centroamericanas*, 8: 362.

Stark, O. 1991. *The Migration of Labor*. Cambridge: Basil Blackwell.

Tardanico, R. 1993. "Dimensions of Structural Adjustment: Gender and Age in the Costa Rican Labour Market." *Development and Change*, 24: 511-539.

Todaro, M. 1969. “A model of labor migration and urban unemployment in less-developed countries.” *The American Economic Review* 59: 138-148.

Trejos, J.D. 1989. “El sector informal urbano en Costa Rica.” In: Menjívar Larín, R. y J. P. PJrez Sáinz, *Informalidad Urbana en Centroamérica*. Guatemala: FLACSO.

Varela Jara, J. 1989. *Migraciones Internas: Analysis Censal*. Heredia, Costa Rica: Universidad Nacional, IDESPO.

World Bank. 1992. *World Development Report*. Washington, D.C.: World Bank.

TABLE 1. MIGRATION RATES BY REGION, 1973 AND 1984

	1973			1984		
	In-mig.	Out-mig.	Net rate	In-mig	Out-mig	Net rate
Región Central						
Area Metropolitano	12.7	4.7	8.6	9.5	5.4	3.1
Resto Aglom. Metrop.	8.9	6.3	2.6	9.4	5.2	4.3
Resto Rural	5.1	20.6	-15.4	6.4	8	-1.6
Región Chorotega	11.7	13.3	-2.1	5.4	9.3	-3.9
Región Pacifico Central	8.2	15.8	-7.6	7.7	9.7	-1.9
Región Brunca	9.9	11.1	-1.2	6.6	6.7	-0.2
Región Huetar Atlantico	19.1	9.9	9.2	14.1	7.5	6.6
Región Huetar Norte	32.4	14.3	18	12.4	10.2	2.1

Note: The base of these estimates includes international immigration but excludes emigration
Sources: Censos de población, 1973 and 1984; Gómez and Locher, 1995.

TABLE 2. AGRARIAN DEVELOPMENT INSTITUTE (IDA) SETTLEMENTS - INITIATED BY SQUATTERS OR OFFICIALLY, BY FOREST COVER (INDIVIDUALS 5 YEARS AND OLDER)

	1968-73				1979-84			
	Squatters	IDA	Total	Total %	Squatters	IDA	Total	Total %
Metropolitan Area	0	0	0		0	0	0	
San José Periphery	0	262	262		19	319	338	
by 1966 Forest Cover								
Rural <50% Forest	3637	2494	6131	66.3	371	5622	5993	13.9
Rural 50-80% Forest	757	724	1480	16	4879	10239	15118	35.1
Rural >80% Forest	1533	100	1633	17.7	10758	11153	21910	50.9
Total	5927	3318	9244	100.0	16008	27014	43021	100.0
by 1984 Forest Cover								
Rural <50% Forest					5493	12252	17745	41.2
Rural 50-80% Forest					4151	10710	14861	34.5
Rural >80% Forest					6364	4051	10415	24.2
Total					16008	27013	43021	100.0

Source: IDA, unpublished data, 1991; adapted from: Cruz et al, 1992:66.

TABLE 3. CLIENTS AT THE PURTO VIEJO DE SARAPIQUI MEDICAL POST, ACCORDING TO YEARS OF RESIDNECE AND CITIZENSHIP

Years of Residence in the Cantón	Citizenship Nicaragua	Costa Rica	
Less than 2 years	90	195	195 (25.8%)
2 to 5 years	97	126	223 (29.5%)
Over 5 years (non-natives)	38	169	207 (27.3%)
Natives of the Cantón	0	132	132 (17.4%)
Total	225	532	757 (100.0%)

Source: Locher, 1995.

TABLE 4. RURAL POVERTY, FOREST COVER AND NET MIGRATION RATES IN COSTA RICA

Rural Poverty Level	Cantons	Mean Forest Cover in 1960 (%)	Mean Change in Forest Cover from 1960 to 1984 (%)	Mean of Cantonal Net Migration Rates
High	Talamanca, Buenos Aires, Upala, Guatuso, Los Chiles, La Cruz	73	-25	+6.7
Medium	Guácimo, Corredores, León Cortez, Jiménes, Pérez Zeledón (Alvarado is excluded because of its extremely low forest cover in 1960).	51	-28	+0.0
Low	Tilarán, Grecia, Naranjo, Atenas, Alfaro Ruiz, San Ramón	28	-19	-1.9

Notes:

The sample is based on 48 rural cantons included in the MIDEPLAN (1991) study of poverty. It includes 3 groups of 6 cantons each, located at the maximum, median and minimum levels of rural poverty.

The poverty scale contains 15 variables pertaining to public health, education and housing, as measured around the time of the 1984 census.

TABLE A-1. CHANGE IN DENSE FOREST COVER 1960 TO 1984, BY CANTON

		Dense Forest Cover in Percent of Surface			
Proportional Canton	Code	1960 Cover	1984 Cover	Change 60 - 84	Change
San José	101	0	0	0	
Escazú	102				
Desamparados	103	6	2	-4	-67
Puriscal	104	29	24	-5	-17
Tarrazú	105				
Aserrí	106	15	17	2	13
Mora	107	10	13	2	20
Goicoechea	108	18	16	-2	-11
Santa Ana	109	25	14	-10	-40
Alajuelita	110				
Vázquez de Coronado	111				
Acosta	112	30	13	-17	-57
Tibás	113	0	0	0	
Moravia	114	15	8	-6	-40
Montes de Oca	115	0	0	0	
Turrubares	116	28	37	8	29
Dota	117	40	27	-14	-35
Curridabat	118	0	0	0	
Pérez Zeledón	119	42	31	-11	-26
León Cortés	120	22	12	-11	-50
Alajuela	201				
San Ramón	202	59	56	-3	-5
Grecia	203	41	25	-16	-39
San Mateo	204	13	10	-3	-23
Atenas	205	9	3	-6	-67
Naranjo	206	4	4	0	0
Palmares	207	4	0	-4	-100
Poás	208	21	13	-8	-38
Orotina	209	16	10	-6	-38
San Carlos	210	71	46	-24	-34
Alfaro Ruíz	211	19	25	5	26
Valverde Vega	212	51	56	5	10
Upala	213	75	51	-24	-32

(continued on next page)

(Table A-1 continued from previous page)

Proportional Canton	Code	Dense Forest Cover in Percent of Surface			
		1960 Cover	1984 Cover	Change 60 - 84	Change
Los Chiles	214	72	61	-11	-15
Guatuso	215	78	58	-21	-27
Cartago	301	33	32	-1	-3
Paraíso	302	73	65	-7	-10
La Unión	303	21	13	-8	-38
Jiménez	304	64	67	3	5
Turrialba	305	76	74	-2	-3
Alvarado	306	7	19	12	171
Oreamuno	307	56	64	8	14
El Guarco	308	46	33	-14	-30
Heredia	401	87	87	-1	-1
Barva	402	28	12	-16	-57
Santo Domingo	403				
Santa Bárbara	404	22	10	-13	-59
San Rafael	405	25	6	-19	-76
San Isidro	406	18	5	-14	-78
Belén	407				
Flores	408	0	4	4	
San Pablo	409	0	0	0	
Sarapiquí	410	83	62	-22	-27
Liberia	501	52	25	-27	-52
Nicoya	502	31	12	-19	-61
Santa Cruz	503	42	26	-16	-38
Bagaces	504	36	24	-12	-33
Carrillo	505	39	34	-6	-15
Cañas	506	21	16	-5	-24
Abangares	507	18	12	-5	-28
Tilarán	508	36	25	-11	-31
Nandayure	509	21	14	-7	-33
La Cruz	510	54	36	-17	-31
Hojancha	511	15	6	-9	-60
Puntarenas	601	49	32	-17	-35
Esparza	602	17	14	-3	-18
Buenos Aires	603	71	41	-30	-42

(continued on next page)

(Table A-1 continued from previous page)

		Dense Forest Cover in Percent of Surface			
Proportional Canton	Code	1960 Cover	1984 Cover	Change 60 - 84	Change
Montes de Oro	604				
Osa	605	59	54	-5	-8
Aguirre	606	66	35	-31	-47
Golfito	607	79	65	-13	-16
Coto Brus	608	88	51	-37	-42
Parrita	609				
Corredores	610	62	43	-19	-31
Garabito	611	50	28	-22	-44
Limón	701	88	79	-9	-10
Pococí	702	62	39	-23	-37
Siquirres	703	54	48	-6	-11
Talamanca	704	88	84	-3	-3
Matina	705				
Guácimo	706	67	43	-24	-36

Notes:

1. Five cantons were excluded due to incomplete coverage of their area: Tarrazu, Alajuela, Santo Domingo, Belen and Parrita.
2. Five cantons were excluded due to classification errors in some segments of the GIS coverage: Escazu, Alajuelita, Vasquez de Coronado, Montes de Oro, Matina.

Source: Tropical Science Center, 1995.

TABLE A-2. NET MIGRATION RATES FOR COSTA RICAN CANTON, 1950 TO 1984

			Net Migration Rates			
Canton	Code	Region	1950	1963	1973	1984
San José	101	1	9.5	0.8	-0.4	-4.5
Escazú	102	1	9	7.4	5.3	3.1
Desamparados	103	1	-12.8	26.9	17.9	4.7
Puriscal	104	3	-34	-32	-19	-9.7
Tarrazú	105	3	-54.7	-31.5	-11.9	-3.1
AserrR	106	1	-13.7	-17	5.3	2.9
Mora	107	2	-28.6	-28.8	-7.4	2.4
Goicoechea	108	1	46.6	31.8	2.9	11.7
Santa Ana	109	2	-19.5	-6.8	5.3	5.7
Alajuelita	110	1	-5	28.8	17.8	-0.5
Vázquez de Coronado	111	1	-15.7	0.7	7.1	9.7
Acosta	112	3	-28.5	-38.1	-14.5	-8.6
Tibás	113	1	40.6	25.4	10.1	6
Moravia	114	1	15.4	17.2	11.4	10.3
Montes de Oca	115	1	31.8	31.3	8.2	5.8
Turrubares	116	3	30.4	-30.7	-25.6	-3.5
Dota	117	3	-31.1	-43.3	-12.9	2.6
Curridabat	118	1	33.5	23.3	14.9	21.8
Pérez Zeledón	119	6	24.7	26.8	-8.6	-2.5
León Cortés	120	3			-7.8	-0.2
Alajuela	201	2	-18.5	-2.7	6.1	3.2
San Ramón	202	3	-33.5	-22.2	-5.2	1.1
Grecia	203	3	-23.8	4.5	-67.4	-0.4
San Mateo	204	5	-28.9	-66.3	-19.5	3.4
Atenas	205	3	-48.4	-40	-9.4	-0.4
Naranjo	206	3	-40.4	-28.1	-6.5	-2.7
Palmares	207	3	-44.8	-17	-8.2	-1.9
Poás	208	3	15.2	-5.3	-3.4	5.1
Orotina	209	5	-16.1	-32	-9.6	1.9
San Carlos	210	8	36.1	18.2	-4.3	-1.3
Alfaro Ruíz	211	3	-55.6	-65.4	-5.6	-1.5
Valverde Vega	212	3	22	0.9	-2.4	0.8
Upala	213	4			72.3	4.3

(continued on next page)

(Table A-2 continued from previous page)

Canton	Code	Region	Net Migration Rates 1950	1963	1973	1984
Los Chiles	214	8			74.8	13.7
Guatuso	215	8			78.7	8.1
Cartago	301	2	-37.1	-17.1	-0.6	2.6
Paraíso	302	2	-20.4	-7.9	-3.8	2
La Unión	303	2	-21.2	2.5	8.4	15.1
Jiménez	304	3	-6.1	-12.4	-10.6	-4.7
Turrialba	305	3	6.6	-9.2	-12.1	-1.2
Alvarado	306	3	-23	-15.8	-2.4	-2.2
Oreamuno	307	2	-21.8	-2	-0.9	0.2
El Guarco	308	2	-5.3	-16.7	-2.5	3.8
Heredia	401	2	-23.5	-5.8	-8	4.3
Barva	402	2	-13.8	-8.8	2.6	7
Santo Domingo	403	2	-26.8	-2.9	2.8	4.6
Santa Bárbara	404	2	-23.1	-6.6	-3.2	9.4
San Rafael	405	2	22.4	8.9	13.1	6.1
San Isidro	406	2	-40.5	-17.7	-0.7	3.3
Belén	407	2	-34.4	-12.9	6.7	3.7
Flores	408	2	-39.9	-14.8	3.7	3.8
San Pablo	409	2			12.3	10.1
Sarapiquí	410	8			60.5	8.2
Liberia	501	4	-43.4	-34	-31.7	-5
Nicoya	502	4	20.6	-2.1	-29.2	-8.7
Santa Cruz	503	4	-25.3	-5.5	-7	-6
Bagaces	504	4	19.1	25.3	-15	-0.1
Carrillo	505	4	-21.4	0.2	-7.8	-0.5
Cañas	506	4	-9.1	-14.8	-0.5	-2.2
Abangares	507	4	4.5	-19.1	-11.8	-2.5
Tilarán	508	4	6.6	-26.4	-19	-7.2
Nandayure	509	4			-12.1	-11
La Cruz	510	4			66.4	-7.6
Hojancha	511	4			68.5	-6
Puntarenas	601	5	19	-1.6	-4.7	-1.1
Esparza	602	5	-26.2	-26.3	-6.5	0.3

(continued on next page)

(Table A-2 continued from prvious page)

Canton	Code	Region	Net Migration Rates 1950	1963	1973	1984
Buenos Aires	603	6	45.2	23.8	9.5	7.8
Montes de Oro	604	5	-6.4	-28.8	-16.6	-5.4
Osa	605	6	40.5	-6.7	0.1	1.2
Aguirre	606	5	84.7	14.1	-76.1	-13.6
Golfito	607	6	87.4	41.8	0	0.1
Coto Brus	608	6			4.5	1.6
Parrita	609	5			66.3	-5.1
Corredores	610	6				-4.5
Garabito	611	5				6.7
Limón	701	7	22.4	5.1	-22.6	-1.2
Pococí	702	7	53.2	20.1	1.8	7.6
Siquirres	703	7	42.7	14	9.1	15.4
Talamanca	704	7			40.4	14.3
Matina	705	7			61.7	6.5
Guácimo	706	7			64.1	13.9

Región Codes
1 Area Metropolitana (Región Central)
2 Resto Aglomeración Central (Región Central)
3 Resto Región Central (Región Central)
4 Región Chorotega
5 Región Pacifico Central
6 Región Brunca
7 Región Huetar Atlántica
8 Región Huetar Norte

Notes:

1. Intercantonal migration is determined by "residence five years ago" in the 1973 and 1984 censuses while the 1963 census just asked about "previous residence." The 1950 lacks a direct question concerning migration. Instead, it uses birthplace in the calculation of lifetime migration rates.
2. The following new cantons were created since 1963 (with dates of creation and original canton in parentheses): Upala, Los Chiles and Guatuso (1970, Grecia); La Cruz (1969, Liberia); Hojancha (1971, Nicoya); Parrita (1971, Aguirre); Coto Brus (1965, Golfito); Corredores (1973, Golfito); Garabito (1980, Puntarenas), Talamanca (1969, Limón); Matina (1969, Limón); Guacimo (1971, Pococi).
3. Changes in cantonal borders between 1950 and 1963 were handled by the adjustments made in the CSUCA (1978) study.
4. The underenumeration in the 1950 and 1963 censuses was estimated at 7% and 3%, respectively. Using the CSUCA corrections, this leads to some discrepancies between the original 1950 census rates and those presented here, especially in the cases of San JosJ, PJrez Zeledón, San RafaJl and Liberia.

Sources: CSUCA, 1978: 218-219, presents the corrected 1950 and 1963 rates. Varela, 1989: 104-105, contains the 1973 and 1984 rates taken from the respective census volumes.

FIGURE 1. DENSE FOREST COVER (>80%) IN COSTA RICA, 1940-1987

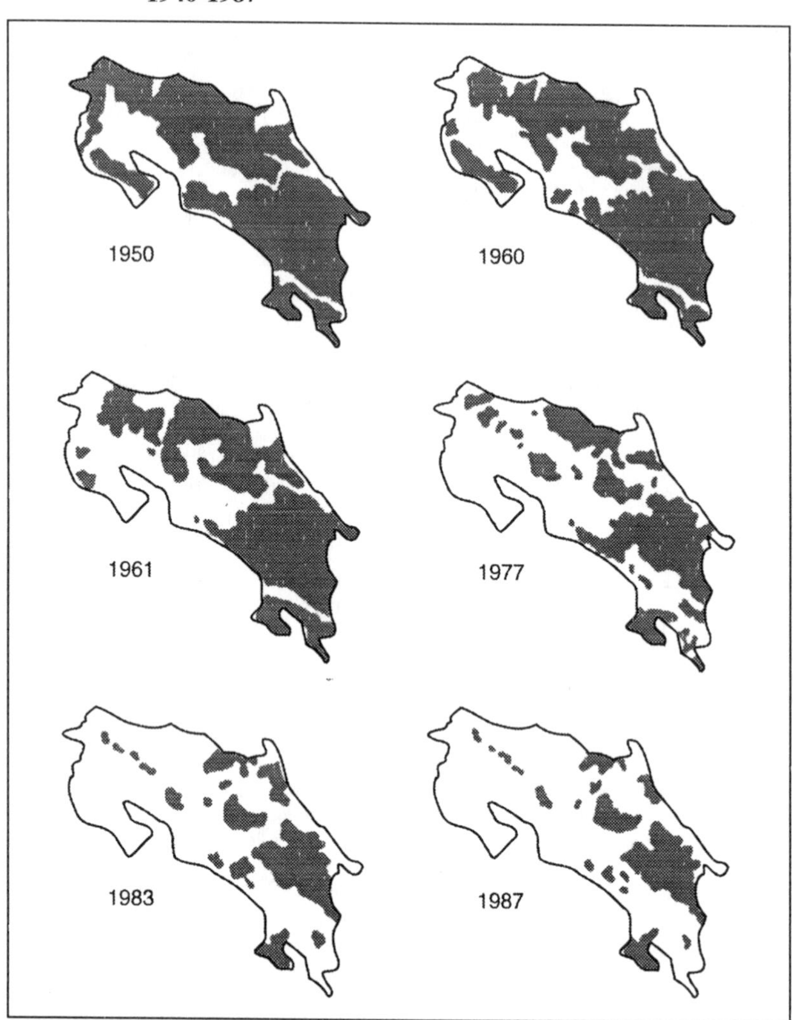

Source: Flores, 1992:178

FIGURE 2. INTERPROVINCIAL MIGRATION IN COSTA RICA, 1927

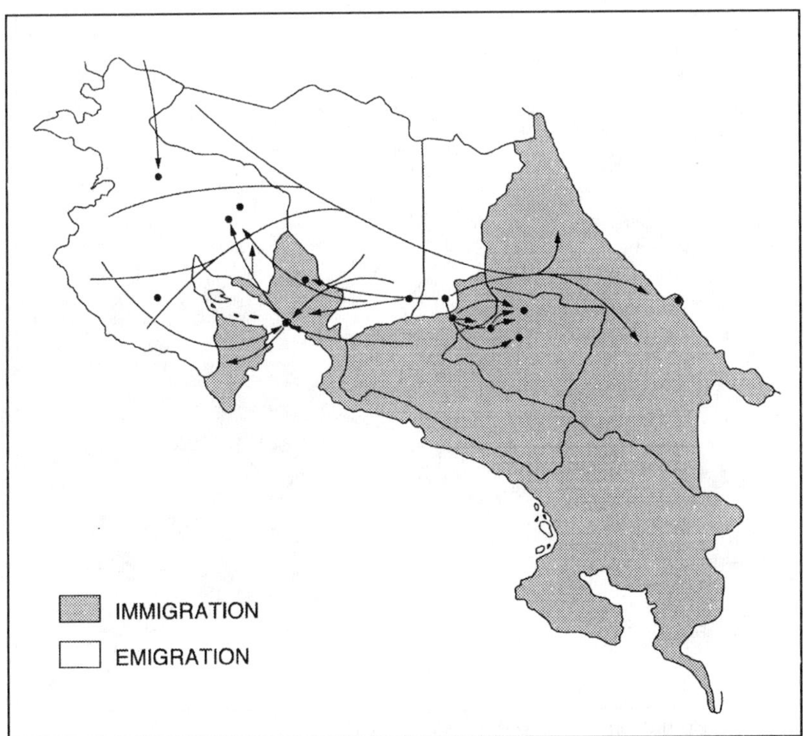

Source: Population Census 1927, figure published in Censo 1950

FIGURE 3. INTERCANTONAL MIGRATION IN COSTA RICA, 1950

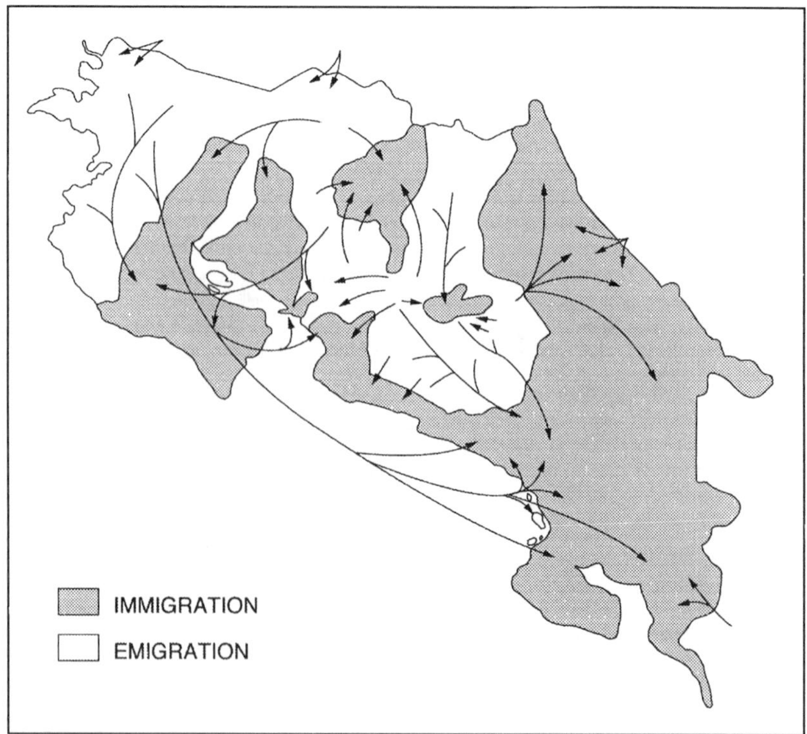

Source: Population Census of Costa Rica 1950: 78

FIGURE 4. INTERREGIONAL MIGRATION IN COSTA RICA

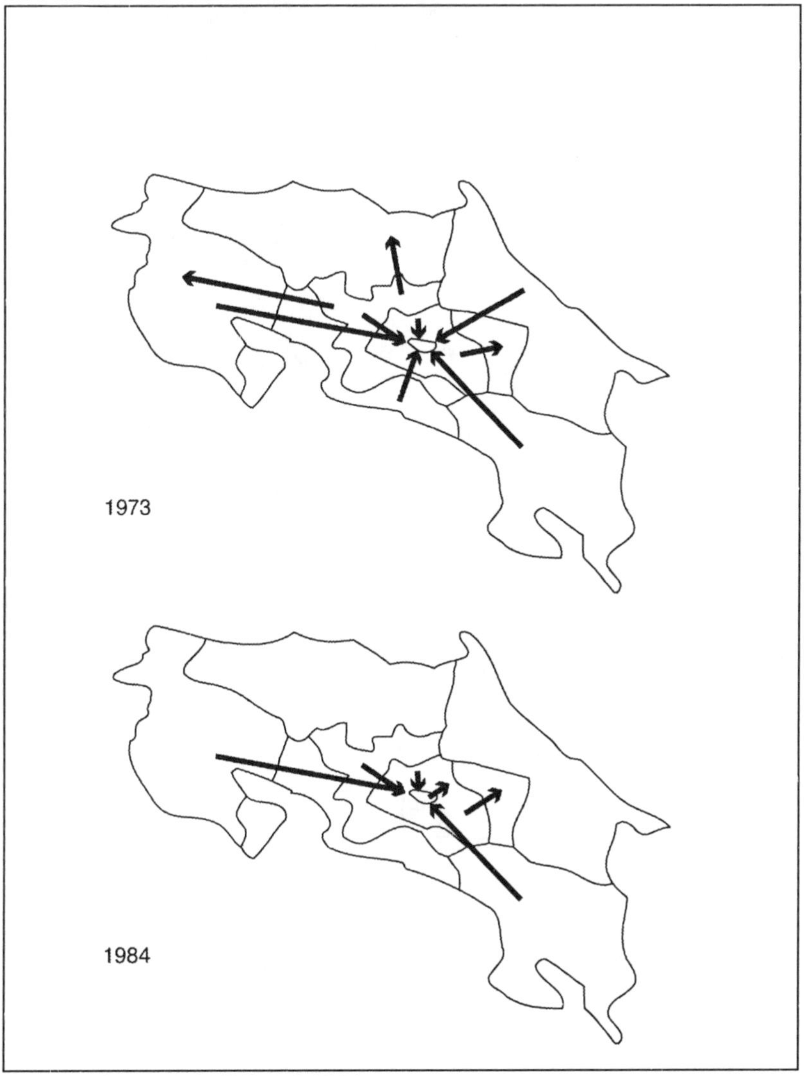

1973

1984

Source: Censos of 1973 and 1984

Chapter Twenty Three

PARTICIPATORY RESEARCH MAPPING OF INDIGENOUS LANDS IN THE HONDURAN MOSQUITIA

PETER H. HERLIHY AND ANDREW P. LEAKE

INTRODUCTION

This article outlines the design and methodology employed in a participatory mapping process undertaken to document the subsistence lands used by the indigenous Miskito, Pech, Tawahka, and Garífuna populations of the Honduran Mosquitia.[1] The project, which lasted three months, concluded with the presentation of the resulting map at the "First Congress on Indigenous Lands of La Mosquitia," held in Tegucigalpa, Honduras during 1992.

The aim of the project was to empower the indigenous population in their quest to legalize their historic rights to lands. This was to be achieved by using a participatory research approach[2] that enabled the target group to record and articulate their own knowledge of their lands and interpret it in the form of a map of the lands used for subsistence. This map now represents a powerful tool with which to justify and argue their demands for land rights. In order to distinguish this process from

[1]We use the term "indigenous" or "native" to refer to all the ethnic groups of the Mosquitia region, including the indigenous Tawahka, Pech, and Miskito peoples who have lived in the region since pre-Hispanic times, as well as the Garífuna (Black Caribs) and the descendants of ladinos ("native ladinos") who have maintained historic presence in the region.

[2]Our understanding of the concept reflects to a certain degree that of Fals-Borda (1979, 1987). The fundamental focus of participatory research, for us, is the legitimization of "popular knowledge" and its conversion to "scientific knowledge," with the objective of contributing to the development of a "science of the proletariate" through which the masses are able to conduct their own fight for social transformation.

other participatory research methods, we have called it Participatory Research Mapping, or PRM.

The project involved many people and organizations: It included the local indigenous population of La Mosquitia; staff from Mosquitia Pawisa (MOPAWI)[3]; Peter Herlihy, a university-based geographer; Andrew Leake, environmentalist and then coordinator of MOPAWI's Land Legalization Program (LLP) for indigenous lands; leaders of the indigenous organizations MASTA (Mosquitia Asla Takanka or "Unity of the Mosquitia"), FITH (Federación Indigena Tawahka de Honduras or the "Tawahka Indigenous Federation of Honduras"), and OFRANEH (Organización Fraternal Negra de Honduras or "Fraternal Negro Organization of Honduras"); and draftsmen from the National Geographic Institute (Instituto Geografico Nacional or ING). The project was financed by Cultural Survival Inc.[4] with funding from the Caribbean Conservation Corporation, the Inter American Foundation, Pew Charitable Trusts, and Wildlife Conservation International.

The structure of this document reflects the steps in the planning and implementation of the PRM project in the Honduran Mosquitia. A brief description is given on the background factors leading up to the project's inception, followed by a de-

---

[3]MOPAWI—acronym derived from the Miskito words "Moskitia Pawisa" or "Development of Mosquitia"—is a nonprofit, non-governmental organization, based on Christian principles, that has worked with the indigenous population of Mosquitia since 1985. Its mission is: "To facilitate the participation of the population of Mosquitia in its own integral development (economic, social, cultural, spiritual, and ecological) so that they can confront with pride and competitive ability the process of integration to the national context, helping in the sustainable management and understanding of their natural resources and natural environment" (MOPAWI 1992).

[4]Cultural Survival, Inc. is an international non-governmental human rights organization that supports programs and projects oriented at legalizing land rights, supporting indigenous organizations, and developing sustainable resource management programs.

scription of how the methodology was developed and put into practice. The project had two components: (i) the mapping of indigenous land use patterns and (ii) the planning, preparation, and coordination of the Congress. The procedures and methods employed in each component occurred simultaneously, but are described in two separate sections for the purpose of clarity. The Congress format, presentation styles, and impact are summarized and the document concludes with a preliminary analysis of the project.

BACKGROUND

Indigenous Lands: Current Situation

Representatives of the ethnic groups of Mosquitia signed a declaration in 1988 asking the Honduran government to legalize their lands, proclaiming that: "The indigenous people of Honduras and especially those of the Honduran Mosquitia are deprived of one of their most basic rights: legal title to their lands. A process of legalization of land tenure in favor of the indigenous peoples of Mosquitia is necessary" (*Declaración sobre Tierras Indígenas*, July 1988). The document asks the government to recognize the fact that indigenous land use includes areas of forest not used for agricultural purposes.

Reacting to these demands, at a time when armed peasants were invading indigenous lands, the National Agrarian Institute (INA) signed a 1989 agreement with indigenous leaders and local government officials concerning indigenous land tenure in Mosquitia (INA 1989; Anónimo 1989). The agreement outlined a regional process through which individual villages could obtain guarantees to "community lands." Although in retrospect this document amounted to no more than window-dressing, it was significant in that it broke with de facto government policy that awarded plots only to individual land-holders.

To implement this agreement, each native community needed to conduct a census and draft a sketch map indicating the limits of their lands. Based on this information, INA would issue each community a provisional guarantee of occupation. Three communities completed the requisites and obtained provisional rights of occupation covering a total of 19,000 hectares.

One of these communities, Krausirpe, was later included in a study of land use among the Tawahka (Herlihy 1991). This study demonstrated that the population, composed of six communities and about 650 people in 1990, used approximately 770 square kilometers of land. The zone used by the village of Krausirpe was shown to be far larger than that contemplated by INA, and it overlapped with the zones used by other neighboring communities. Only agricultural lands, which comprise 5% of the total land use area, could be considered as being used exclusively by any one community.

The research demonstrated the inadequacy of the "community-based" approach showing that it did not satisfy the land requirements of the indigenous populations of Mosquitia. The land use area used by any given community overlaped with that of other villages, and what this agreement was in effect doing was breaking this system up by assigning each village its own specific territory. Taken to its logical conclusion, the community-based approach to land titling would potentially leave the natives sitting on small islands of land surrounded by a sea of invading colonists. Traditional indigenous territories would be broken up into a checkerboard of forest and pasture (Herlihy and Leake 1990; Herlihy 1993). For this reason the indigenous people stopped submitting any further applications to INA.

As it happened, INA never issued definitive legal titles to the villages which received only provisional guarantees, and Honduras still does not as yet have a defined "política indigenista," or indigenous policy. No law deals specifically with indigenous land-tenure, although various articles of law and historic treaties infer that the indigenous peoples have historical rights to lands they have always occupied (Davidson and Cruz 1991; Leake 1992:7).

A Map of Indigenous Lands

The lack of an appropriate legal framework for the legalization of indigenous lands, together with the experiences gained from the agreement with INA and the insights from the Tawahka study, demonstrated the urgent need for a clear regional understanding of land use among the overall indigenous population of La Mosquitia. Without this knowledge, it would not be possible for either the indigenous people, let alone the government, to define a coherent and appropriate approach and policy to legalize land rights for indigenous peoples. It was within this context that the idea to map indigenous land use for the whole of La Mosquitia was born.

The idea of holding a congress on indigenous land and natural resources resulted from dialogue between representatives of Cultural Survival and MOPAWI. Cultural Survival's Central American Program Director, Anthropologist Mac Chapin, thought the quincentenary celebration of Columbus' discovery of the New World would provide a propitious occasion to hold a national-level congress concerning indigenous lands.[5] Chapin had discussions with MOPAWI Director Osvaldo Munguia, LLP[6] Coordinator Leake, and Geographer Herlihy. All agreed on the importance of holding such an event.

---

[5]Dr. Chapin was involved in a similar event, the "First Interamerican Indigenous Congress on the Conservation of Natural Resources and Environment," organized by the Project on the Management of the Wildlands of Kuna Yala (PEMASKY) in Panama during November 1989.

[6]MOPAWI began its Land Legalization Program in 1987 with the objective of providing technical and logistical support to the indigenous population in question oriented towards legalizing their land rights (MOPAWI 1990:14).

Initially, the focus was on holding what was billed as the "First Honduran Indigenous Congress on Lands and Natural Resources," similar in format to the "First Interamerican Indigenous Congress on the conservation of Natural Resources and the Environment," held in Panama during 1989. The intention was to provide a forum within which representatives from each indigenous group in Honduras could discuss issues of land tenure and conservation of natural resources within their respective regions. An important part of the exercise would be the elaboration of a map showing the approximate delimitation of each group and a census of their populations.

The project proposal was written by Herlihy and Leake (1991) who, upon evaluating the logistical and financial requirements of a national-level event, decided to reduce the geographic coverage of the project to the Mosquitia region. At the same time, they expanded the project's methods and established concrete research objectives. Their planning in this regard was facilitated by the fact that they both already knew the region and its people. Leake lived in Mosquitia as MOPAWI's LLP director while Herlihy had recently completed field research among the Tawahka Sumu in 1990 and indigenous populations of the Río Plátano Biosphere Reserve in 1991. Their previous experience in working with indigenous organizations on issues concerning lands and conservation predisposed them to taking on the role of coordinating this particular participatory research project. They played the roles of principle researchers, or so-called "participatory researchers" (referred to as "researchers" below for clarity).

PROJECT OBJECTIVES

The overall objective of the project was to enable and assist representatives of the indigenous population of the Mosquitia to construct a map of the region, showing all their settlements and their respective areas of land use or "subsistence zones."

The proposed Congress would provide a forum within which the final map could be presented by the indigenous participants to the public.

The value of this type of map had been demonstrated in discussions between MOPAWI and the government concerning indigenous land tenure policies (Herlihy & Leake 1990). One of the maps, "The Coexistence of Indigenous Peoples and the Natural Environment in Central America" (Chapin 1992),[7] was used by MOPAWI to promote the concept and development of the Tawahka Reserve and the proposed ecological corridor of protected areas in Mosquitia (Herlihy and Leake 1991, 1992; Leake 1992).

Three specific objectives were established for the project:

(a) To facilitate a process through which the indigenous population of Mosquitia could cartographically document their subsistence zones;

(b) To present reliable and useful information about the reality of indigenous land and natural resource use;

(c) To disseminate documentation about indigenous lands to all those organizations and institutions involved in the definition of strategies or politics that affect in one way or another the population of Mosquitia.

These objectives reflect the two components of the project: one technical and focused on mapping indigenous subsistence zones, the other political and oriented towards the presentation and dissemination of the information. Because of the potential political implications of the project, the researchers sought to maintain a high level of objectivity in both components. Emphasis was placed on avoiding the antagonism that the map and its data might cause between government officials and the indige-

---

[7]This map was produced by a group of Central Americanist researchers for a joint National Geographic Society/Cultural Survival project, directed by Dr. Mac Chapin.

nous peoples—that frequently characterizes similar events dealing with native lands.

METHODOLOGY

To obtain a complete panorama of indigenous land use in the Mosquitia, the whole region was selected as the study area, including all the Department of Gracias a Dios and parts of the adjacent lands in the Departments of Colón and Olancho (Map 1). The information needed for the mapping project had to be obtained from the indigenous population of over 35,000 people, spread out over the 17,000 square kilometers of the Mosquitia's tropical forests, savannas, and swamps. This was a considerable undertaking given the region's limited transportation and communications infrastructure.

The methodology used was an adaptation from that used in previous work by Herlihy (1989, 1991), which was based on obtaining land use data through participant observation, interviews, questionnaires, and formal village meetings. In this case, the data would be generated by the target population themselves and recorded by indigenous "surveyors."

Herlihy's results showed that like many other indigenous peoples, the people of Mosquitia have a high intuitive capacity to interpret spatial relationships of their respective territories. By making reference to geographical features, distances, and descriptions of the spatial relationship between various places, people are able to describe the location of a given site. When describing areas used for hunting, fishing, gathering, or cultivating, frequent use is made of place-names, or toponyms.[8] Furthermore, indigenous people tend to have detailed cognitive images or "mental maps" of the lands and natural resources that they use for subsistence.

---

[8]A toponym is the place-name of a geographic locality.

This was the type of information which the surveyors were required to record in each village throughout Mosquitia. With technical assistance and training, they would then interpret this information onto cartographic sheets and produce a detailed map of the lands used by the population in general.

Survey "Zones"

The researchers divided the study area into sectors or "zones" to facilitate the logistics of collecting the information. These study zones reflected the geographic distribution of village clusters which possess a high degree of related kin and between which there are important social and economic relations. This would include, for example, the villages along a particular stretch of a river or sea coast. Initially, 15 zones were identified, later this number increased to 22 in order to accommodate logistical peculiarities or to even out the number of communities in a particular sector.[9]

Two professional Miskito men were designated as "zone supervisors," Lic. Aurelio Ramos, of MOPAWI's LLP, and Sr. Nathan Pravia Lacayo, a freelance journalist and linguist. They were responsible for overseeing the selection and subsequent supervision of the "surveyors" in each zone. One covered the western half of Mosquitia, the other the eastern.

Selection of Surveyors

A set of criteria was established for the selection of surveyors in order to ensure that appropriate persons were chosen for the task. They were to be native-born and resident of their respective zone, well-known and respected community members, literate, and preferably with some professional skills. Most sur-

---

[9]The definition of a community includes the household in the nearby areas surrounding the principal village.

veyors were selected by their local communities, with some being nominated directly by MASTA.

All those selected were men, although this was not stipulated as a criterion. It is likely that the exclusion of women was due to cultural reasons, but may also in part be due to the fact that knowledge of extensive subsistence activities is more the dominion of men. The majority occupied or had once occupied political or religious posts, or were teachers. Many of them already knew the project researchers and had experience in working with MOPAWI.[10]

The process of working with the surveyors was based on three workshops, interspaced with two periods of field work during which they gathered data in their respective zones. Operations were based at MOPAWI headquarters in Puerto Lempira in Mosquitia, and carried out between August and September, 1992.

Workshop One

The first workshop began with the surveyors making an analysis of their culture, history, and traditional land use systems. This was done through a series of guided discussions, aimed at

---

[10]The group of surveyors included five teachers, two nurses, two agronomists, one preacher, and eleven farmers. Only three of them had not completed primary education. Each received an honorarium of 950 Lempiras for the two month field study period. At the time when they were elected by their respective communities, the surveyors did not know that they would be paid. MOPAWI, who administered the project funds, did this to avoid having payment be a motivating factor for a candidate's involvement.
The surveyors and their zones are: Olegario López - A, Ricardo Ramírez - B, Quintín Castro - B, Máximo Chow - B, Elmer Waldemar - C, Hernán Martínez - D, Moisés Alemán - E, Edimor Wood M. - F, Tomás Rivas - G, Dionisio Cruz - H, Gilberto Maibeth - I, Daniel Castellón - I, Simón Greham P. - J, Javier Rimundo G. - K, Duval Haylock - L, Eduardo Padilla - M, Electerio Pineda K. - M, Daniel Kiath - N, Cecilio Tatallón - O, Paulino Bossen - O, Sinito Waylan - P, Manuel Martínez - Q.

enabling them to identify key relationships themselves between their people, lands, and natural resources at the local and regional levels. An important exercise in this regard was the participatory drawing of a map of an imaginary community, along with the natural resources required for subsistence of its population. It is important to note that, while the material discussed formed part of the daily lives of the surveyors, very few previously had the opportunity to sit and reflect on it in such a manner.

The next step was the evaluation of the situation of lands used by the indigenous groups in relation to the advance of the agricultural-cattle front into the forests of Mosquitia. Videos and maps were shown in order to give the surveyors a panorama of the regional threat. This introductory phase of the workshop concluded with an evaluation of the potential social, cultural, and economic impact of colonization and deforestation on Mosquitia.

Following a formal description of the project and its objectives, the researchers presented a draft questionnaire, which was to be used by the surveyors for gathering their field data. The draft version served to promote discussion by the surveyors on the content and style of the questions, a process which then led to the editing of a final version. Questions were aimed at eliciting data on community subsistence zones through the collection of toponyms of the places used for agriculture, fishing, hunting, collecting, lumbering, and gold panning. A further set of questions also sought information on perceptions the people had regarding what lands "belonged" to their respective communities.

The surveyors translated the questions from Spanish into their own languages,[11] testing the relation of the structure and terminology with their own concepts of land use and geographical descriptions. Many lengthy discussions focused on each question in order to ensure their clarity. Additional adjustments

[11]Miskito, Tawahka, Pech, and Garífuna.

were made when the questionnaire was used in mock interviews with villagers in Puerto Lempira. The final version of the questionnaire was typed up in both Spanish and Miskito, and included a Miskito-Spanish glossary of specific geographical terms. Space was given under each question for the annotation of answers.

The surveyors were trained to record the information generated by the questionnaire. They learned to note the name of the places used by the community for the different activities mentioned in each question. They were encouraged to ask additional questions in order to be able to locate each site on a map. They were asked to draw sketch maps of the data they collected, though no training was given in this regard. It was thought that training might stop the surveyors from developing the cognitive maps together with local informants. Surveyors were also asked to conduct a census of each community, but this did not provide good results.[12]

The researchers considered providing surveyors with official topographic sheets (1:50,000), but decided not to. As with the idea of training people in drawing maps, these sheets could inhibit the independent drawing of the sketch maps by the surveyors. They would also require the surveyors to be trained in map-reading, and for them in turn to explain them to their respective communities before they could locate the information on them. It was also thought that individuals with political motives might use the topographic sheets to present a distorted image of the territory used by their community.

Training was given on how to conduct interviews with villagers. Cartoon drawings were used to demonstrate a surveyor at different stages of an interview. This served to generate

---

[12]The questionnaire included questions about the number of houses and residents in each community. Nevertheless, without providing the surveyors with detailed training in the rules and mechanism of the contents, the collected information was not standardized and contained many errors resulting in it not being used.

discussion among the workshop participants on the positive and negative aspects that they should consider while administering their questionnaires.

Role playing was used to introduce the surveyors to the practical aspects of administering the questionnaire. This was followed by practice sessions with a groups of villagers within Puerto Lempira, which were video-taped for subsequent analysis by the group. The often humorous setting created by these exercises made it possible to identify and correct many procedural problems in the surveyors' interview styles in a manner that would have been more difficult in a formal setting.

The first workshop ended with the surveyors planning their trips within their respective zones, a task done with the assistance of the zone supervisors. They calculated their costs and were each given the necessary funds for them to complete their work. They were also instructed in the recording of their costs and keeping receipts to document the expenses incurred.

First Field Survey

The surveyors left project headquarters in Puerto Lempira with a briefcase containing the blank questionnaires, paper, notebooks, pencils, sharpeners, liquid paper, and a clip board. They traveled by plane, truck, bicycle, and horse, but mostly by dugout and on foot.

MOPAWI and MASTA produced a series of informative news bulletins which were broadcast by the local radio station, SANI Radio. These provided information on the mapping project, its objectives, and the work of the surveyors. Written announcements were also distributed through churches, schools, and local government offices in the region. Although some people expressed their suspicion and fear of the intentions of the project, most surveyors met little resistance to their efforts. Most of them managed to notify communities of their arrival beforehand, a fact which helped enormously in this regard.

From the accounts given by the surveyors of their field work, it later became clear that information on land use was obtained in several ways. Most met first with the leaders of each community, requesting permission to hold a meeting. Some had problems organizing a communal meeting, often because of political reasons. These situations were resolved through interventions of the part of the zone supervisors. The majority met with an assembly of the entire community while others decided to meet with smaller groups or even on an individual basis. One of the most detailed data sets was obtained by a surveyor who met with a small group of villagers recognized by the community as skillful hunters.

Most surveyors used the Miskito language version of the questionnaire to collect field data. The answers were then transferred in neater writing onto the Spanish language version. Those who had problems collecting the information received assistance from the zone supervisors, who traveled continually through the study area for the duration of the questionnaire period.

Workshop Two

Having completed the first session of data gathering, all 22 surveyors met again for the second workshop with the objective of interpreting the gathered information onto maps. Although there were differences in the quality of the information obtained by each surveyor, the detail and volume of their recordings was phenomenal and reflected their commitment and interest in the project. Most of them had managed to draw sketch maps of all their zone, while others drew each community separately. Here again the quality and detail varied from person to person, with some sketches containing huge amounts of data and others very little.

During the week-long workshop, each surveyor worked with the researchers explaining, discussing, and evaluating his information. When needed, the surveyors from adjoining zones were incorporated into these discussions in order to obtain additional information, especially in overlapping areas.

The official cartographic sheets at 1:50,000 scale, produced by the National Geographic Institute (IGN),[13] were used to draw base maps of the study zones. Although these provided good physical information, they had little cultural information, based as they were on limited field classification done over 20 years ago.

With questionnaires, sketch maps, and base maps spread out on the drafting table, each surveyor worked with the researchers locating their recorded data onto the cartographic sheets. The positioning of each toponym or location of sites of particular land use was determined through dialogue between the researchers and surveyors, based on their respective empirical knowledge of a given place. Reference was made to sketch maps, which was cross referenced with the data gathered by surveyors in adjacent zones. In some cases, several hours of work were required for the location of one site, although most were relatively easier to position.[14] As the field data was plotted meticulously, point by point, onto the cartographic sheets, the surveyors became aware of the fact that their geographical knowledge of their respective zones was often far more detailed that contained on the official government maps. This in itself was an important element in the empowerment process alluded to in the general aim of the project.

---

[13]There exists complete coverage of Mosquitia at 1:50,000 scale, based on air photography. The study area of the project covered about 50 of these sheets in the series, each covering 10 degrees latitude by 15 degrees longitude, or 500 square kilometers.

[14]On one occasion the information presented by one surveyor did not conform to that contained on the base maps and it took eight hours to identify the problem. This resulted of from an error in the location of an important river on the official cartographic sheets.

Each point was assigned an alpha-numeric code, with a letter to designate the survey zone and a number to identify each community (e.g., B-7). Adjacent to these, the use of the area was noted, for example "agriculture" or "hunting." A line was drawn around all the land use points of each community, indicating the overall area used by each settlement for subsistence purposes. Another line was then drawn around the overall area, or "subsistence zone," used by the various communities within each given zone.[15]

The delimited subsistence zones reflect the extension of land subject to frequent use by the communities in the zone (Map 1). They exclude certain distant sites and those of only occasional use such as gold-panning or timber extraction sites.[16] This was done in an attempt to avoid the exaggeration of the area of land used. With the exception of those names in Spanish or English that were in common usage, local indigenous toponyms were used. The orthography was carefully reviewed by the Miskito linguist, Nathan Pravia Lacayo.

The information interpreted onto the base maps was redrawn by draftsmen from the IGN.[17] Contour lines and other unnecessary details were excluded, while the delimitations and details of the subsistence zones were emphasized. To facilitate the presentation of the information, colors were used for the delimitation of subsistence zone at the community and broader

---

[15]The researchers used relief features on the cartographic sheet to determine those cases where the topography would constitute a natural limit of a land use zone, such as a river, hills, or water divides.

[16]Details concerning the location of gold panning and the cutting of hardwoods is contained on the original questionnaires and zonal maps, deposited in the archives of MOPAWI in Tegucigalpa, Honduras.

[17]The National Geographic Institute (IGN) generously loaned the project the services of two technicians, Mr. José Ramiro Andino and Héctor Ramirez. Both played important roles in solving many technical and logistical problems that occurred during the project.

zonal level. Toponyms and land use locations to be re-checked were listed in a column on each zonal map. Once completed, the sketch maps, some measuring 3 X 1.5 meters, were enclosed in plastic tubes to facilitate transport and protection during the second field survey.

Second Field Survey

The surveyors returned to their respective zones to present and discuss the draft land use maps with the constituent communities. Just the fact that they had returned caused certain amazement in the communities, accustomed as they were to never seeing the results of surveys made on other topics such as health and education. Surveyors recount how upon seeing the draft map, community members became notably more interested. As a result, some volunteered more information during the second visit than during the first. This, in turn, motivated the surveyors to try to do the best work possible, making corrections to the draft maps. In some cases, they had meetings with persons that were no where to be found during the first survey.

Workshop Three

Having obtained the comments and revisions of their respective zonal maps, the surveyors again reconvened in Puerto Lempira for the third workshop. There were big differences in the amount of correction required for each zonal map. In one case, villagers realized that an important area of hunting had not been identified, in others only minor alterations were required. The linguist reviewed the orthography again, identifying a number of errors made when the draftsmen transcribed Miskito names from the base maps. The corrected maps of each zone were then redrawn by the IGN draftsmen.

The researchers then drafted a smaller-scale composite map, transferring the subsistence zone delimitations from the 22 new zonal maps (at 1:50,000-scale) onto a regional map at 1:250,000 scale.[18] To make the map more legible, some closely overlapping sectors were grouped together. This reduced the number of zones depicted on the final map from 22 to 17 (Map 1). Obviously, it was impossible to include the thousands of toponyms and other details shown on the new zonal maps at 1:50,000 scale. Only communities with five or more houses were shown. This map was critically reviewed by the surveyors to assure the accuracy of community locations and the delimitation of the subsistence zones in relation to the original maps. The linguist reviewed the map toponomy one last time.

The researchers next moved to Tegucigalpa for the final production of the map. IGN draftsmen redrew the final version (1:250,000 scale) in ink, while the researchers worked with a graphic designer on the format for the final map production. A master copy of the 1:250,000 scale was produced at the IGN, which was then reduced photographically to 1:500,000 scale, and also to page size (11"x 17") to be photocopied and distributed as a handout at the Congress. The IGN later published a final color version at 1:500,000 scale that includes vegetation cover for Mosquitia (MOPAWI y MASTA 1993).

Congress Preparations

MOPAWI began the process of coordinating the "First Congress on Indigenous Lands of the Mosquitia" by presenting the idea to the Director of the National Commission for the Natural Environment and Development (CONAMA), Dr. Carlos Medina. His interest and support for the event was instrumental in getting the support and participation of other government departments, including the military.

---

[18]Map published by the Joint Operations Graphics of the U. S. Defense Mapping Agency.

MOPAWI then began a publicity campaign in national newspapers presenting objective information on the aims and methods of the project, both for public interest and to preempt any possible distortion or misrepresentation that might occur. MOPAWI's Tegucigalpa-based staff[19] coordinated the logistical arrangements in consultation with the researchers and surveyors. One important aspect in this sense was the elaboration of a list of invitees in that it permitted the surveyors to have an idea of the audience at which they should focus their presentation of the map. Posters, folders, and "T" shirts with logos of the Congress were produced to give visibility and publicity of the event.

Within the context of the surveyors' field work in Mosquitia, the Congress represented a concrete goal toward which everyone worked. The discipline necessary to complete the cartographic work on time put pressures on the entire team given the time constraint imposed by the Congress date. There were days when the deadlines became nearly unbearable, demanding continuous round-the-clock work.

During the second and third workshops, surveyors began working on what they would say in the Congress. This process began with them working in small groups to "brainstorm" ideas, which were then presented in a plenary session. As expected, the list of topics included a series of politically sensitive themes related to indigenous demands for recognition of land rights and their need for economic support from the government. Without discarding these themes, the surveyors were also encouraged to consider what themes would be of interest to the audience in the Congress and press. It was thought that if the surveyors could first get and then retain their listeners' attention, they would then

---

[19]This work included the coordination of transportation and housing accommodations for national and international delegates. The Natural Resources Ministry loaned a mini-bus to transport delegates around Tegucigalpa.

be in a better position to argue for their own interests and demands.

Through discussions with the researchers, the surveyors came to a consensus that the audience would know very little about indigenous life in Mosquitia. They concluded for themselves that without this understanding, it would be difficult for the audience to understand the logic of their demands. Accordingly, the first part of the Congress would include themes related to the ecology, culture, and economy of Mosquitia. These would be followed by descriptions of indigenous land use which would then lead to the logical introduction of the land use map. Next would come the description of the threats of deforestation and ladino colonization, paving the way for the demands for legalization of indigenous land rights, presented in this case as a potential solution to protect and conserve the region.

Having identified the themes for the Congress agenda, discussion turned to how to make the presentations. To stimulate the group's thinking on the matter, video footage from an indigenous congress in another country was viewed, in which the presentations were frequently long and boring monologues. Based on the criticisms they made of the video, they suggested the characteristics of what might be a more dynamic and entertaining style of presentation. A consensus was reached that the most appropriate approach would be to make a series of short presentations of 5 to 10 minutes in length, interspaced with audio-visual materials.

With the themes and presentation styles identified, they began to select the presenters. One problem the researcher had to overcome was the fact that the surveyors would most likely select those people whom they already knew as able public speakers. To avoid this problem, an exercise was carried out, in which the well known speakers, together with a number randomly selected surveyors, were given "surprise" topics and asked to speak extemporaneously for three minutes. Their presentations were videotaped, using the camera to focus on the different facets of each person's body language. Evaluating the footage, with a good dose of humor, enabled the surveyors to make a list of criteria with which they could both select speakers and improve their own style.

The video exercise also served to highlight the fact that some of the elder surveyors, speaking in their own language, made very effective presenters. It was decided that these individuals would make their presentation in their native language, which would be translated to Spanish. Ideally, all presentations would be done in the indigenous language of each presenter, but in order to make the most of the available time during the Congress, those able to, would make their presentation in Spanish. The more complicated themes were assigned to the more experienced speakers. Certain topics, such as the historical and cultural background of each ethnic group, were presented by representatives of each ethnic group. Other topics, such as environmental patterns of a particular area, were assigned to surveyors from these particular regions.

Each presenter was responsible for developing the content of his speech. For many, the Congress would be the first time they would make a public presentation of this nature, which for some caused considerable anxiety. Most had never met, much less addressed, government officials, while for others it would also be their first visit to the capital. Each presenter wrote his speech in long hand. These texts were discussed with the researchers in groups, then reviewed and re-written again and again. This review process helped focus each presentation and allowed the incorporation of additional data.

The Congress

The "First Congress on Indigenous Lands of Mosquitia" was held on September 22-23, 1992 in Tegucigalpa. In attendance were the Honduran Vice-President (standing in for the

President), the Minister of Defense, and other high-ranking authorities from government and nongovernmental organizations. The event was attended by more than 400 invitees.

Every effort was made to create a comfortable, smart, informative, and entertaining format for the audience. Presentations were interwoven with slide shows and video clips of the indigenous culture and environments of Mosquitia. Miskito musicians played during coffee breaks, adding a festive air to the event. Regional handicrafts, published literature, and maps were displayed and put on sale. Much attention was paid to the quality of the documentation handed out to the Congress participants. Each person received a folder containing the agenda, the new regional "Indigenous Lands" map, demographic data on the Mosquitia, and maps of the deforestation and proposed protected areas in the region. The methodological process of the participatory research mapping was presented in an exhibit with photographs, maps, diagrams, and original cartographic materials. The researchers also produced a five minute video describing this same process.

The Congress was well received by the public, and the press gave it good coverage (Anónimo 1992, 1992 a, 1992b; Guzmán 1992; Schwimmer 1992; Swenarski de Herrera 1992). Two national newspapers published copies of the "Indigenous Lands" map and several of the surveyors were interviewed on radio and television. Despite concerns about the sensitivity of some of the presentation themes, these were well received by government officials. To some degree this was facilitated by the moderator of the event, an indigenous leader with a good sense of humor and diplomatic tact. Members of the government commented after the event on their positive impressions of the quality of the speeches and materials presented (Swenarski de Hererra 1992). The most impressive thing for many was that the speakers were indigenous.

OBSERVATIONS AND CONCLUSIONS

The PRM-congress process might be considered a simple series of well-defined steps, that might be repeated in other similar situations. While this is true, the successful implementation of the process in this case depended on many less-tangible factors. This section gives an account of some of these factors, but the list is by no means exhaustive.

The project involved the participation of many people, both indigenous and non-indigenous, and the success of the event reflects the sum of their individual contributions. The project could not have happened without the administrative structure of MOPAWI in both Mosquitia and in Tegucigalpa. The Director of MOPAWI, himself a Miskito, recognized the strategic value of the project and gave it top priority within the other activities of the agency. This included the designation of staff to carry out procedures that were not covered by the project's budget.

The researchers previous experience in the Mosquitia and familiarity with the idiosyncrasies of local indigenous organizations and government agencies played a significant part in facilitating the coordination of the whole event. Even so, on a number of occasions there were problems in the maintenance of public relations. A particularly difficult challenge was the avoidance of inter-institutional jealousy which often threatened the working relationship between all organizations involved. A fundamental role in this regard was played by MOPAWI's Head of Community Development, Lic. Adalberto Padilla. The cooperation of personnel from the National Geographic Institute was another critical factor assuring the project's success. The fact that their staff agreed to work long hours ensured that the cartographic work always met the tight deadlines.

The data generated through this project might be criticized given that the methodology relied on a group of native informants with limited training in relation to the scope of the research undertaken. Indeed, some surveyors had problems with the collection of information and were unable to draw the sketch maps. In spite of the care taken in the selection of the surveyors, some had limited knowledge of the geography of their zones and were not familiar with some of the subsistence practice of the villagers. Beyond the established requisites for the selection of the surveyors, a requisite should be added that they have a woodsman's knowledge of their respective zones.

The project, nevertheless, met its three primary objectives. First, it enabled the native Mosquitia population to document and map the distribution and limits of their subsistence zones. Next, it produced reliable information about the reality of indigenous land and natural resource use in Mosquitia. Finally, it provided a high-profile forum within which indigenous representatives themselves publicly presented and distributed their own data on land use.

The participatory methodology, facilitated by the institutional support of MOPAWI and Cultural Survival, inspired a high level of interest and commitment for the project among the participants. It allowed the empirical knowledge of the surveyors to interact freely and constructively with the technical and academic knowledge of the project researchers. It was a process which served to augment and legitimize the popular knowledge of the indigenous people by providing a method through which it could be effectively articulated and communicated to outsiders. The effectiveness and value of the PRM in empowering the target population was reflected in the sophisticated understanding that the surveyors were able to develop concerning the matters affecting their lands. It provided them with a foundation upon which they could base future actions towards the legalization of their land rights and self determination.

Journalist Lisa Swenarski de Herrera (1992:11) captured the significance of the process when she interviewed one surveyor, Tomás Rivas, of the Río Patuca, who said:

"The map caused a sensation.... All the people are very enthusiastic. Now I notice that the people are starting to become more aware of their natural resources, and they feel the need to unite and protect their lands."

At the end of the Congress, the indigenous people presented their own resolutions concerning land tenure, environmental conservation, and the exploitation of natural resources (Table 1).

REFERENCES

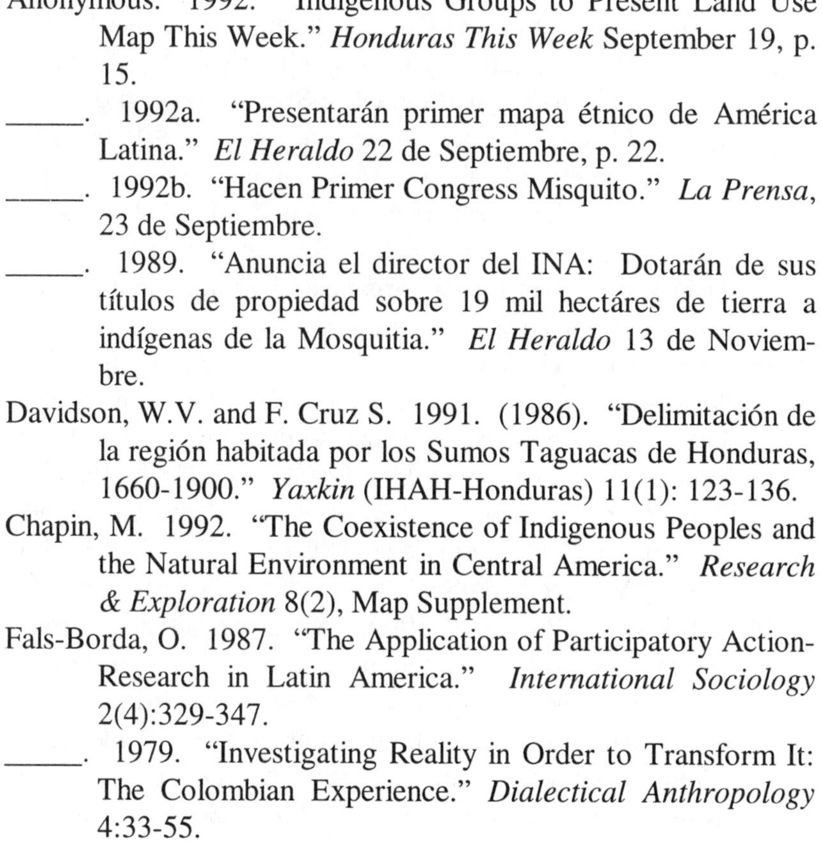

Anonymous. 1992. "Indigenous Groups to Present Land Use Map This Week." *Honduras This Week* September 19, p. 15.

_____. 1992a. "Presentarán primer mapa étnico de América Latina." *El Heraldo* 22 de Septiembre, p. 22.

_____. 1992b. "Hacen Primer Congress Misquito." *La Prensa*, 23 de Septiembre.

_____. 1989. "Anuncia el director del INA: Dotarán de sus títulos de propiedad sobre 19 mil hectáres de tierra a indígenas de la Mosquitia." *El Heraldo* 13 de Noviembre.

Davidson, W.V. and F. Cruz S. 1991. (1986). "Delimitación de la región habitada por los Sumos Taguacas de Honduras, 1660-1900." *Yaxkin* (IHAH-Honduras) 11(1): 123-136.

Chapin, M. 1992. "The Coexistence of Indigenous Peoples and the Natural Environment in Central America." *Research & Exploration* 8(2), Map Supplement.

Fals-Borda, O. 1987. "The Application of Participatory Action-Research in Latin America." *International Sociology* 2(4):329-347.

_____. 1979. "Investigating Reality in Order to Transform It: The Colombian Experience." *Dialectical Anthropology* 4:33-55.

Guzmán, D. 1992. "Al presidente Callejas: Devolución de Tierras Exigen 5 Etnias de La Mosquitia." *La Tribuna* Miércoles, 23 de Septiembre, p. 12.

Herlihy, P.H. 1993. "Securing a Homeland: The Tawahka Sumu of Mosquitia's Rain Forest." Pp. 54-62 in *State of the Peoples: A Global Human Rights Report on Societies in Danger*. Boston, Beacon Press.

_____. 1991. "Estudio de uso de tierras y delimitación propuesta para La Reserva Forestal Indígena Tawahka Sumu en La Mosquitia, Honduras." Informe, Instituto Hondureño de Antropología e Historia/MOPAWI. Pp. 1-6.

_____. 1989. "Mapping the Cultural Landscape of a Lowland Rain Forest Indian Population: The Comarca Emberá Example." Invited participant in Special Session on "The Cultural Map of Spanish America: Data and Methods" at the XV International Congress, Latin American Studies Association, San Juan, Puerto Rico, Sept. 21-23 (Due to hurricane, presented in a Special Symposium on "Mapping Indian Lands" organized by Greg Knapp at the University of Texas, Austin).

Herlihy, P.H. and L.H. Herlihy. 1991. "La herencia cultural de la Reserva de la Biosfera del Río Plátano: Un area de confluencias etnicas en La Mosquitia." Pp. 9-15 in *Herencia de nuestro pasado: La Reserva de la Biosfera Río Plátano*. Tegucigalpa, ROCAP (USAID), Fundo Mucdial para La Naturaleza (WWF), COHDEFOR. Edited by Vicente Murphy.

Herlihy, P.H. and A.P. Leake. 1992. "Situación actual del frente de colonización/deforestación en la region propuesta para el Parque Nacional Patuca." Informe, Comisionado por El Ministerio de Defensa, en su caracter de Presidente del Comite Inter-Institucional para la Delimitación del Sistema de Areas Protegidas *PLAPAWANS*. Tegucigalpa, Honduras. Pp. 1-22.

_____. 1991. *Propuesta: Reserva Forestal Tawahka Sumu.* Folleto. Tegucigalpa, Honduras: Mosquitia Pawisa (MOPAWI), Federación Indígena Tawahka de Honduras (FITH), Instituto Hondureño de Antropología e Historia (IHAH). Pp. 1-18.

_____. 1990. "The Tawahka Sumu: A Delicate Balance in Mosquitia." *Cultural Survival Quarterly* 14(4):13-16. (Spanish translation in *Yaxkin* XI(1):109-121).

Instituto Nacional Agrario (INA). 1989. "Advierte el INA: Tierras y bosques donde estan asentadas comunidades indígenas deben respetarse: Podría recurrirse a Fuerza Armadas para establecer sus derechos." Tegucigalpa, Honduras: Instituto Nacional Agraria (*Presencia del INA en La Mosquitia*) 4:2-3, 20 de Avril.

Leake, A.P. 1992. Reserva Tawahka y Parque Nacional Patuca: Estrategia de conservación y desarrollo. Propuesta, Plan de Accion Forestal Tropical Centroamericano (PAFT-CA). Tegucigalpa, Honduras: Mosquitia Pawisa (MOPAWI).

Mosquitia P. (MOPAWI). 1992. *Informe bi-anual 90-91*. Pp. 1-20. Tegucigalpa, Honduras: Mosquitia Pawisa (MOPAWI)/CADERH..

_____. 1990. *Informe Anual 1989*. Pp. 1-24. Tegucigalpa, Honduras: Mosquitia Pawisa (MOPAWI).

Mosquitia Pawisa (MOPAWI) y Mosquitia Asla Takanka (MASTA). 1993. "Tierras Indígenas de La Mosquitia Hondureña - 1992: Zonas de Subsistencia (Mapa)." Researchers Peter H. Herlihy and Andrew P. Leake. Information obtained through 22 indigenous surveyors in collaboration with other professionals. Tegucigalpa, Instituto Geográfico Nacional (1:500,000, en color).

Schwimmer, E. 1992. "Land use map presented in congress seeks to affirm Indian rights in the Mosquitia." *Honduras This Week* Vol. 5(37):1, 4, & 19.

Swenarski de Herrera, L. 1992. "Indian Land Uses Are Put on the Map: Project in Honduras Works to Protect Ancient Rights." *The Christian Science Monitor* Thursday, December 3, Pp. 10-11.

TABLE 1. RESOLUTIONS OF THE FIRST CONGRESS ON INDIGENOUS LANDS OF MOSQUITIA

Land Tenure	1. To recognize that legalization of the ancestral (historic) property rights of the lands occupied by the indigenous ethnic groups of Mosquitia is needed urgently and cannot be delayed and to demand that the Government of the Republic take immediate actions to resolve this situation which has persisted for 500 years. 2. To propose to the Government of the Republic that the legalization of land rights of indigenous peoples in Mosquitia be based on models of communal ownership at regional levels. 3. To spell out to the Government, in particular to the National Congress, that the legislative initiatives regarding policy on indigenous peoples be revised, modified, and implemented in consultation with the indigenous ethnic populations of Honduras. Also, to propose the governmental ratification of Article 169 of the I.L.O. Convention, regarding the rights of indigenous and tribal peoples.
Environmental Conservation	1. To request that the Government of the Republic take urgent measures to stop the advance of the colonization front, which advances from the headwaters of the Paulaya, Plátano, Tinto Negro, Patuca, and Segovia rivers into the tropical forests of Mosquitia, threatening the cultural and ecological integrity of this region. 2. Based on the map of indigenous lands published at this Congress, to propose that the Government define a conservation policy for the ecosystems of the Mosquitia, which are the patrimony of the indigenous and native populations that inhabit them.

(continued on next page)

(Table 1 continued from previous page)

	3. To propose that the indigenous and native populations of the Mosquitia, together with government and non-government organizations, carry out an inventory of existing natural resources in the biological corridor formed by the Río Plátano and proposed Tawahka reserves, in order to evaluate the biodiversity of the flora, fauna, and other resources that compose these ecosystems. 4. To demand that the Government of the Republic implement legislation to protect the flora, fauna, archaeology, and minerals located within this biological corridor from the contraband trade. 5. To establish a ban on the disposal of toxic wastes by any person, national or international, on the shores or in any part of Mosquitia.
Use of Natural Resources	1. To ensure that the legalization of land rights among the indigenous and native populations of the Mosquitia be defined prior to any intensive commercial exploitation of the region's pine forests. 2. To propose that, in regards to the exploitation of natural resources, priority be given to initiatives of local ethnic populations, empowering them in their capacity to make sustainable commercial use of the forests, fisheries, fauna, etc. 3. To demand that all activities related to the exploration and extracion of oil and minerals in the Mosquitia be done in consultation with the indigenous and native populations of the region, ensuring that their views are taken into account, and that the environmental impact be assessed together with the costs and benefits for the local population.

(Authors' translation: "Resoluciones" del Primer Congreso Sobre Tierras Indígenas de La Mosquitia, Tegucigalpa, 22-23 Septiembre 1992, reproduced in *Agenda 94* of MOPAWI).

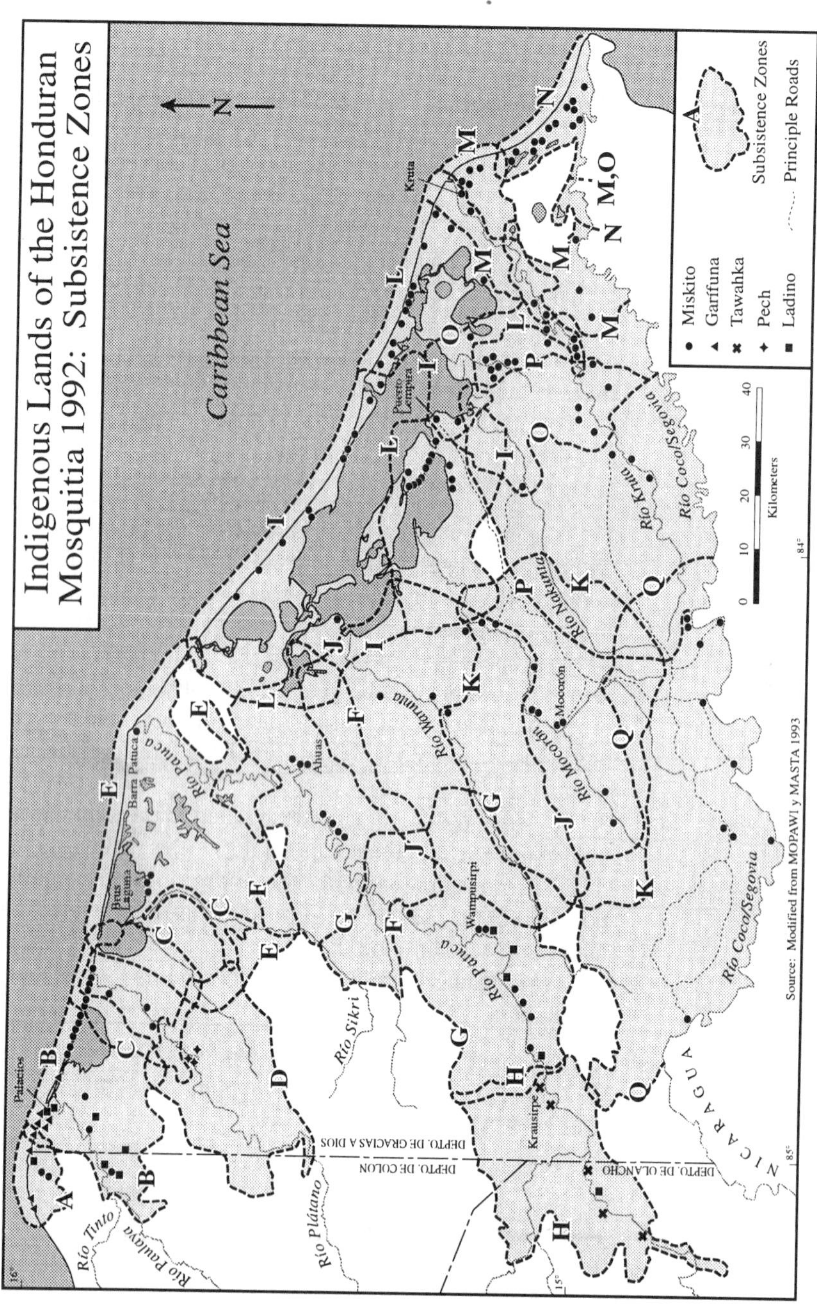
Indigenous Lands of the Honduran Mosquitia 1992: Subsistence Zones
N
Caribbean Sea
Miskito
Garífuna
Tawahka
Pech
Ladino
Subsistence Zones
Principle Roads
0 10 20 30 40
Kilometers
Source: Modified from MOPAWI y MASTA 1993
Palacios
Brus Laguna
Barra Patuca
Ahuas
Wampusirpi
Krausirpi
Mocorón
Puerto Lempira
Kruta
Río Tinto
Río Paulaya
Río Plátano
Río Sikri
Río Patuca
Río Warunta
Río Mocorón
Río Nakunta
Río Kruta
Río Coco/Segovia
DEPTO. DE GRACIAS A DIOS
DEPTO. DE COLON
DEPTO. DE OLANCHO
NICARAGUA
16°
15°
85°
84°